JIM O'BRIEN

IMMACULATE REFLECTIONS

Insights on sports from a Pittsburgh viewpoint

George Gajkovich

Replay of "The Immaculate Reception"

"You talk about Christmas miracles. Here's the miracle of all miracles. Watch this one. Bradshaw is lucky even to get rid of the ball! He shoots it out. Jack Tatum deflects it right into the hands of Harris. And he sets off. And the big 230-pound rookie slipped away from (Jimmy) Warren and scored."
—Curt Gowdy doing an instant replay on NBC television

Books By Jim O'Brien

COMPLETE HANDBOOK OF PRO BASKETBALL 1970–71

COMPLETE HANDBOOK OF PRO BASKETBALL 1971–72

ABA ALL-STARS

PITTSBURGH: THE STORY OF THE CITY OF CHAMPIONS

HAIL TO PITT: A SPORTS HISTORY OF
THE UNIVERSITY OF PITTSBURGH

DOING IT RIGHT

WHATEVER IT TAKES

MAZ AND THE '60 BUCS

REMEMBER ROBERTO

PENGUIN PROFILES

DARE TO DREAM

KEEP THE FAITH

WE HAD 'EM ALL THE WAY

HOMETOWN HEROES

GLORY YEARS

THE CHIEF

STEELERS FOREVER

ALWAYS A STEELER

WITH LOVE AND PRIDE

LAMBERT

FANTASY CAMP

STEELER STUFF

PITTSBURGH PROUD

IMMACULATE REFLECTIONS

To order copies of these titles directly from the publisher, send $26.95 for hardcover edition. Please send additional $3.50 to cover shipping and handling charges per book. Pennsylvania residents add 6% sales tax to price of book only. Allegheny County residents add an additional 1% sales tax for a total of 7% sales tax. Copies will be signed by author at your request. Discounts available for large orders. Contact publisher regarding availability and prices of all books in Pittsburgh Proud series, or to request an order form. Some books are sold out and are no longer available. You can still order the following: Doing It Right, Hometown Heroes, Glory Years, The Chief, Lambert, With Love and Pride, Fantasy Camp, Steeler Stuff, Pittsburgh Proud and Immaculate Reflections.

Art Rooney Sr. and Frank Sinatra watch the Steelers at practice in Palm Springs, California before their final regular season game of the 1972 season. This was in mid-December and the Steelers were preparing to play the Chargers in San Diego. Myron Cope spotted Sinatra in a restaurant and invited him to attend a practice, where Sinatra was inducted as an honorary general in Franco's Italian Army. The Steelers beat the Chargers 24–2 to finish with an 11–3 record. The following week the Steelers beat the Oakland Raiders, 13–7, when Franco Harris made his heroic catch-and-run for a TD in the closing seconds of the first playoff victory in team history.

This book is dedicated to Kathleen Churchman O'Brien to observe the 45th anniversary of our marriage on August 12, 1967.
She has always understood what needed to be done.
– Jim O'Brien

Copyright © 2012 by Jim O'Brien

All rights reserved

Published by James P. O'Brien — Publishing
P.O. Box 12580
Pittsburgh PA 15241
Phone (412) 221-3580
E-mail: jimmyo64@gmail.com
Website: www.jimobriensportsauthor.com
First printing, October 2012

Printed by Geyer Printing Company, Inc.
Typography by Cold-Comp

ISBN 1-886348-15-8

All autographs in this book are reproductions.

Contents

*"Inspiration is the act of drawing
up a chair to the writing desk."*
—**Anonymous**

"Jim O'Brien writes with the experience and credentials of authenticity. He has covered some of the biggest sporting events of our times from the front row seat of the press box, and he knows inner workings of the locker room. One of the extraordinary things about him is that he's a Pittsburgh guy who is immersed in the local scene, yet he has worked for papers in other cities. Few writers enjoy such a perspective. The thing that sets him apart, however, is that he has never forgotten that the heart of a story is the human side of the sports drama. His contacts serve him well. We have come to look forward to his books just as we look forward to the start of the new seasons. Every time I look up at a news event involving big moments in Pittsburgh sports history, I see Jim and his table of works. Dynasties, stadiums, and even newspapers come and go, but Jim is always on the scene with his unique take on the stories that have made a difference in our lives. He knows what it takes to be a true professional."

—Robert Dvorchak
A journalist for 44 years and co-author of
Game Over: Jerry Sandusky, Penn State and the Culture of Silence

"The history of sports in Pittsburgh is comprised of so many great stories and there's no better person to tell them than Jim O'Brien. He's as much a part of the fabric of local sports as the teams and personalities he writes about, and this latest installment of his Pittsburgh Proud series is a treasure for the city and its ardent fans."
—Howard Burns, Editor,
The Pittsburgh Business Times

Acknowledgments

This is my first book in four years. A weakened economy and problems in the book store industry kept me on the sidelines. Borders, Inc. went bankrupt and nearly all the bookstores in shopping malls that had been the key to my success are gone.

The author in me wants to write and publish more books, but the businessman in me says hold on. Let's look at the financial picture. So I had to figure out a way to continue to do this, and I would not have been able to pull it off without the continued support of so many loyal patrons, and the addition of new sources of support. To them, and to you, I say "Thank you."

My list of patrons, fortunately, is a long one:

LD Astorino/Horizon Architects, Greg Babe, Lee Baierl, Sue Baierl and Carol Baierl of Baierl Automotive Group, Rich Barcelona of Bailey-PVS Oxides LLC, Suzy and Jim Broadhurst, Jeff Broadhurst and Brooks Broadhurst of Eat'n Park Restaurants and Parkhurst Dining Corp., Bob Buzzelli and Dan Koller of Allegheny Valley Bank, William Campbell of Intuit, Inc., Don Carlucci of Carlucci Construction, Ken Codeluppi of Wall Firma Inc., Armand Dellovade of A.C. Dellovade, Don DeBlasio and DeBlasio's Restaurant, Mike Fabio of Prader-Willi Syndrome Association of Pennsylvania, Steve Fedell of Ikon Office Solutions, Jim, Barbara and Ted Frantz of TEDCO, Inc. Frank B. Fuhrer Wholesale Company, Wayne Fusaro Pancreatic Cancer Research Fund, Thomas B. Grealish of Henderson Brothers, Lou Grippo of The Original Oyster House, James S. Hamilton, Hoddy Hanna of Hanna Real Estate Services, Timothy M. Heim of HIIM Insurors, Elsie Hillman, Sy Holzer of PNC Bank, Huntington Bank, Dave Jancisin of Merrill Lynch, Bill Johnson of H.J. Heinz, William Kammerer, Tom Keane, Dave King of Nicklas King McConahy, Dan R. Lackner of Paper Products Company., Domenic Laudato of Pittsburgh Asphalt Company, Mike Lee of Lee Construction Inc., David J. Malone of Gateway Financial, Jack Mascaro of Mascaro Construction, Joseph A. Massaro Jr. of The Massaro Company, Robert F. McClurg, Nancy and Pat McDonnell of Atria's Restaurant & Tavern, John R. McGinley Jr. of Eckert Seamans, Moet Hennessy, Clark Nicklas of Vista Resources, Inc., John Paul of Highmark, Pittsburgh Section of Society of Mining Engineers, Glenn Porter and Richard Gresh of PPG Public Parking Inc., Steve Previs of Knight Capital European Ltd. in London, Clifford Rowe of P.J. Dick Corporation, Andy Russell of Laurel Mountain Partners, Robert Santillo and Dan Rains of McCarl's, Bohdan W. Stone, Rich Dietrick and Rob Meredith of Morgan Stanley, Tom Sweeney of Compucom, Robert J. Taylor of Taylor & Alsko Law Offices, Thomas J. Usher and John Surma of U.S. Steel Corp., Western Pennsylvania Caring Foundation, Sam Zacharias of Gateway Financial, John Zanardelli of Asbury Heights.

Others who have worked with me: Dr. Edwin Assid, Chuck Belliotti, Joan and Tom Bigley, Dale Blaha of Altany, Lloynd & Lindquist, Inc., Richard S. Bontz of Bontz Chevrolet, Jon C. Botula, Tom Ceponis, Dr.

Philip Dahar, Dan Bartow of Legends of the North Shore, Ann and Art Cipriani, Dave and Frank Clements, Ralph Cindrich, Todd Cover, Dr. Patrick J. DeMeo, Herb Douglas Jr., Kevin Joyce of The Carlton, Gregory L. Manesiotas, Dennis Meteny, Linda and Frank Meyer, George Morris, Jerry Morrow, Andy Ondrey, Jim Render, Jim Roddey, Linda and Frank Sam, George Schoeppner, Len Stidle, Barbara Stull and Don Yannessa.

I want to thank the following individuals for their loyal support: Tony Accamando, Dennis Astorino, Louis Astorino, Linda Barnicott, Aldo Bartolotta, R. Everett Burns, Susie Campbell, Renny Clark, Ray Conaway, Gayland Cook, Jay Dabat, Greg Dearolf, Tony Ferraro, Jeff Flicko, Gary Forcey, Bob Friend, Dr. Freddie Fu, Marshall Goldstein, Bob and Frank W. Gustine, Jr., Mike Hagan, F. Edwin Harmon, Donald J. Hastings, Dee and Wayne Herrod, Karen Horvath, Jeff James, George Jordan, Bob Keaney, Andy Komer, Robert Lovett, Jim McCarl, Mac McIlrath, Carl R. Moulton, Pitt Chancellor Mark Nordenberg, Jim Droney of Mt. Lebanon Office Equipment, Ron Parfitt, Joseph Piccirilli, Pittsburgh Tribune-Review Multimedia, Matt Polk, Rob Pratte of KDKA Radio, Charlie and Steve Previs, Michelle Hunt of Pro Football Hall of Fame, Joe Reljac, Arthur J. Rooney Jr., John Rooney, Patrick J. Rooney, Patrick J. Santelli, Fred Sargent, Vince R. Scorsone, Rich Snebold, Tom Snyder, Stanley M. Stein, Steve Stepanian, Joyce Stump, Dick Swanson of Swanson Group, Ltd., John C. Williams of FNB Bank, WQED Multimedia, Jay Yard..

Special assistance has been given to me by: David Arrigo, official photographer for Pittsburgh Pirates, Debbie Brookfield of Intuit, Debbie Keener of Reed, Smith Shaw & McClay, Joe Gordon, Beano Cook, Sally O'Leary, Dan Hart, Jim Trdinich, Burt Lauten, E.J. Borghetti, Sam Sciullo, Walt Becker, Sean Duffy, Samuel H. Foreman, Kelly Bird, Rocky Bleier, Rich Corson, Jim Duratz, George Gojkovich, Ted Harhai, Russell M. Livingston, Dr. Haywood A. Haser, Heinz History Center and Western Pennsylvania Sports Museum, Gene Musial, Harvey and Darrell Hess, Samuel M. Hillard, Joe Landolina, Patrick T. Lanigan Funeral Home, Dick LeBeau, Joseph Lohman of New York Food Company, Pete Mervosh, John Pelusi, Anthony J. Plastino II, Sharon and Alex Pociask, Joe Pohl, Bill Priatko, Rudy Celigoi, Bob Shearer, Al Tarquinio, Ron Temple, and Teddy Thompson.

This book is also dedicated to the many patrons who have passed on, and without whose support in the early stages this series would not have been possible. So this is in memory of Bill Baierl, Mel Bassi, Ed Prebor, Steve Previs Sr., Art Rooney Sr. and Bill Tillotson,

Editorial assistance and proofreading was provided by Frank Haller. Gerry Hamilton had assisted me in this manner for many years.

Bruce McGough of Geyer Printing steered this project through at the printers I have used from Day One. Bob Goodrick and Fred Wyler were of great help at Geyer as well. Denise Maiden, Rebecca Fatalsky, Cathy Pawlowski and Adam Zundell of Cold Comp Typographers came through with their "whatever it takes" attitude they learned from working for Ed Lutz for so many years. They helped me meet all deadlines. They're a winning team.

Preface

Autograph party for 'City of Champions'
sets sales records at Kaufmann's

By Roy McHugh
Pittsburgh Press Columnist at Large

August 21, 1980

For the guest of honor, an autograph party in the book section of a department store can be something very much like cruel and unusual punishment.

I've attended autograph parties where the author sits formerly at a table piled with copies of his latest tome while people hurry by as though in headlong flight from a krypton venting at Three Mile Island.

Ted Morgan's biography of Somerset Maugham is regarded by the critics as a masterpiece. On the day of his appearance at Kaufmann's there was one request for it. Jerry Kozinski came here to hustle a book called "Passion Play"—and he hustled three copies.

"You can never tell who's going to do well and who isn't," says a publicist for Kaufmann's. "We had some cooks signing autographs for that 'Dining in Pittsburgh' book and sold 150 copies in three days."

It's the all-time three-day record. The all-time one-day record of 86 copies—established yesterday—belongs to *"Pittsburgh: The Story of the City of Champions."*

Prodded slightly, Jim O'Brien, who edited the book with Marty Wolfson, called it a team effort. This was no autograph party at which the authors sat around like wallflowers. This was a production worthy of Pete Rozelle or Barnum & Bailey.

And it just happened to be Jim O'Brien's 38th birthday.

In the space it occupied on Kaufmann's ninth floor, a football field could have been laid out. From a podium, using a microphone, O'Brien, as master of ceremonies, addressed the 86 customers and many others who were there for the festivities alone. He introduced the mayor, Richard Caliguiri. He introduced real live champions whose exploits are recorded in the book. He introduced his mother, his wife and his daughter. They all helped with the proof-reading.

He and Mayor Caliguiri have a history. As a young man, Caliguiri looked after his father's bowling alley on Second Avenue in Hazelwood, and O'Brien used to stop by, as a 14-to-19-year old sports editor for *The Hazelwood Envoy* and pick up bowling scores for the local tabloid. Caliguiri gave him the latest bowling news.

"*City of Champions*" is a celebration of the 1970s in Pittsburgh. Its original title, "City of Champions of the 1970s," made that clear. But Mayor Caliguiri, who provided a preface for the coffee-table book, objected. Pittsburgh, he informed O'Brien and Wolfson, would continue to be a city of champions in the 1980s. Besides, it would date the book quickly. Chastened, the editors re-designed the cover.

I am happy to report that Caliguiri is now satisfied. The advice he gave to every loyal Pittsburgher yesterday was: "Buy this book." Not to, he implied, would be like refusing to stand for the national anthem.

Art Rooney then spoke some words that were reminiscent of his only political speech. You've heard about it, but try and stop me.

A candidate 50 years ago for recorder of deeds, Rooney told a gathering in the Syria Mosque that while he had no idea what a recorder of deeds was supposed to do, he would hire somebody who did know and stay out of the way. With that, Rooney sat down.

Yesterday, all he said was, "It's certainly good to be here and it's nice to be here as a champion. It's certainly better that getting first choice in the draft. Thank you very much."

Jackie Sherril, Frankie Gustine, Bruno Sammartino, Myron Cope, Kathy Stetler, Jerry Conboy, Bob Smizik and Norm Vargo followed Rooney to the podium. Afterward, joined by Ray Mansfield, Paul Martha, Larry O'Brien and John Garry, but not by Caliguiri and Rooney, they sat behind tables, with nameplates on them, autographed books and answered questions. It was something like Super Bowl week. Sammartino, wearing a high starched white collar and a gray pinstripe suit with a vest, signed more autographs than anyone else.

I'm assuming that all of those names are instantly recognizable to the reader. Bob Smizik and Norm Vargo were present because they helped with the writing of the book. As for Larry O'Brien and John Garry—the O'Brien and Garry who conduct WTAE-Radio's morning wake-up show—I suppose it was just an event they wouldn't have missed.

Dick Groat and Dave Giusti of the Pirates were late arrivals but not even Jim O'Brien could not say why the national marbles champions from Lawrenceville failed to show up. The Seemiller Brothers of Carrick, who are national ping-pong or table tennis champions, were also no-shows, along with some Penguins.

A two-day record is sure to be set and perhaps the three-day record will be surpassed—no mean achievement. O'Brien has sold 23,000 of these books to various corporations in town—"They'd make great Christmas gifts," he convinced them, no doubt—and that by comparison with the 86 disposed of at the autograph party, was a laugher, he said.

"*City of Champions*" is a handsome volume conceived and illustrated by Mary Wolfson, but largely put together by O'Brien, who also handled the marketing and the hoopla. He can do it all.

CITY OF CHAMPIONS—There was a star-studded lineup on hand to sign copies of the book "City Of Champions" at Kaufmann's downtown department store in August of 1980. They included, left to right front row, Art Rooney Sr., Jim O'Brien, Mayor Richard Caliguiri, Myron Cope and Jerry Conboy. The second row: Frankie Gustine Sr., Bruno Sammartino, Jackie Sherrill and Marty Wolfson.

Photos by Marlene Karas

PITT ALL-AMERICANS —Pitt's two-time All American swimmers Jan Ujevich and Kathy Stetler signed copies of "Hail To Pitt: A Sports History of the University of Pittsburgh" at Kaufmann's in August of 1982 along with illustrator Marty Wolfson and editor Jim O'Brien. That's Pitt football coach Foge Fazio in the upper left corner.

11

STEELERS

FOOTBALL

Frenchy Fuqua reveals his secret
insight into Immaculate Reflection

John "Frenchy" Fuqua is a legendary figure in Steelers' football history. He was also known as "The Count" for wearing fancy capes with his eye-catching clothing ensembles, for having gold fish in his clear plastic high heels, and for high stepping on the football field, in the locker room and at the infamous Aurora Club, an after-hours joint in The Hill District that was frequented by Ernie Holmes, L.C. Greenwood, Glen "Pine" Edwards and visited on occasion by Moon Mullins and Ray Mansfield.

Fuqua had some fashion face-offs with Greenwood to the merriment of all in the locker room from time to time to determine who was "the best-dressed" Steelers' player.

Fuqua was the Steelers' leading rusher for two seasons, 1970 and 1971, and held the record for most yards rushing in one game, with 218 at Philadelphia on December 20, 1970, until it was broken by Willie Parker with 223 against the Browns at Heinz Field on December 7, 2006. Fuqua went 85 yards for a touchdown against the Eagles, the third longest run in Steelers' history.

He rushed for nearly 3,000 yards in his seven seasons (1970–76) with the Steelers. He worked in the circulation department of *The Detroit News* in his latter days with the Steelers and on a full-time basis when his ball-playing career came to an end.

Fuqua also gained fame as the middle man in "The Immaculate Reception," which was voted the No. 1 play in pro football history even though it was a broken play and then some.

Terry Bradshaw was throwing a pass down the middle of the field to Fuqua, one of the team's most sure-handed receivers, when Jack Tatum of the Oakland Raiders collided with Fuqua, knocking the ball back upfield where Franco Harris found it and grasped it at his shoe tops and raced for a touchdown in the AFC playoffs on December 23, 1972.

Tatum was one of the fiercest, hard-hitting cornerbacks in the NFL at the time. He was responsible for dealing the blow that crippled Patriots' receiver Darryl Stingley, and he hit Lynn Swann and John Stallworth a few hard shots when they ran crossing patterns against the Raiders.

Chuck Noll once blasted the likes of Tatum and some of his teammates as being members of "a criminal element" in the NFL.

The Steelers beat the Raiders 13–7. It was the Steelers' first victory in a playoff in the team's history.

Jack Tatum of Oakland Raiders was fierce foe.

It was a fourth and ten call at the Steelers' 40-yard line with 22 seconds left to play, and the Steelers trailing, 7-6. Bradshaw ducked a strong rush, but was flattened as he let the ball go and had no idea what happened afterward. A lot of people who were at Three Rivers Stadium that day still don't know exactly what happened. Many fans were staring disconsolately at their shoe tops, believing the game was lost.

The game was not shown on Pittsburgh television because it was not a sellout.

Art Rooney Sr., the owner of the Steelers, did not see "The Immaculate Reception." He was on the elevator heading for the team locker room to console his players after a valiant effort.

"Frenchy likes to be coy about it," said Terry Bradshaw in his book, *Looking Deep*, in writing about what he termed the pivotal play in the team's history. "The glory days for the Steelers were still two years ahead, but we buried our past that day.

"If Frenchy did touch the ball first, then the play was voided. In those days, it was illegal for a ball to be touched first by another offensive player. John Madden and the Raiders felt they got shafted, and Madden is still mad as hell about it.

"Frenchy doesn't want to say and is either going to take his secret to the grave, or write a book about it himself some day."

It's one of the most famous and frequently aired sequences in sports history, yet Fuqua is often a forgotten figure in it. He teases people about whether he or Tatum touched the ball first. If he alone had touched it the ensuing catch and run by Harris would have been nullified by NFL rules in use at the time. Back then, the ball could not be touched simultaneously by two teammates on the receiving end. Today it can be.

Fred Swearingen didn't signal a touchdown right away. He checked a sideline video to help him make the call. There wasn't any official review of plays at that time. Thus instant reply was born. All TDs are now reviewed by the officials upstairs in the stadiums.

"I always have to tell that story," said Fuqua when he was in attendance at a gala dinner on the eve of Andy Russell's annual celebrity golf outing in mid-May of 2012. "I tell them everything that happened, except who touched the ball and how. Jack Tatum had to hit for it to have been a legitimate reception by Franco. But let's not beat around the bush. Jack didn't touch it. It's the only *secret* I have left in my life.

"That pass was coming to me from the get-go. Ron Shanklin and I had led the team in receiving (with 49 catches apiece) the previous season, and I was considered one of our most sure-handed receivers."

According to game reports, post-game commentary and Bradshaw's book, however, rookie receiver Barry Pearson was the primary receiver on that final play. But that was other people's version of the story, not Fuqua's.

"When Bradshaw went to the sideline to confer with the coaches before that play, I watched those blue eyes from the sideline to the huddle, and I knew he was going to throw the ball to me. Bradshaw eyed me all the way back to the huddle," offered Fuqua.

"If the timing had worked out, and the pass protection hadn't broken down—Otis Sistrunk nearly got Terry—I was wide open. I'd have gotten to the end zone or to the sideline, and Roy Gerela would have had an easy kick for a field goal to win it. I could have been the hero.

"But Bradshaw had to duck under and away from the rush—he ran to the right—and in the meantime Tatum left one of our wide receivers, Barry Pearson, and came up to cover me. The ball came my way. The ball was tipped (ricocheted really) and Franco caught it and ran away with hundreds of thousands of dollars I'd have made on that play. It took 1.8 seconds for the ball to go from my hands to Franco's hands.

"I've watched that play a hundred times. I have it on tape at home. Tatum wasn't near me, at first, when I went into my hook. I was around their 30-yard line, and I'd have taken an angle, and we'd have been, at the least, in a position where Roy couldn't miss it (a field goal try).

"Franco should have been nowhere around that ball. But some players just have a nose for it. A guy like him is always at the right place at the right time. I'm glad he was."

Head coach Chuck Noll had said, "Franco made that play because he never quit on the play. He kept running; he kept hustling. Good things happen to those who hustle." That's something Joe Paterno preached to Harris and his teammates at Penn State.

John Madden, the Raiders' coach, was protesting on the other sideline. Madden claimed that Fuqua, not Tatum, had touched the ball and the pass should have been ruled incomplete, having bounced from one offensive player to another. "It's so disappointing," Madden said, "to come down to a whole season and have it end like this."

Fuqua begs to differ, of course. "That play is shown on TV at least three times a year," he said, "and my boss at the newspaper always gave me a nod at the office the next day to acknowledge it. But what would have happened if Frenchy Fuqua caught the ball? But I was always a team player, and always thought in the team concept. If I had scored, though, I'd have given the reporters a better story than Franco. The controversy is what made that play."

* * *

Franco Harris was at the head of the table at a quarterly meeting of the Champions Committee that oversees the Western Pennsylvania Sports Museum at the Heinz History Center in July of 2012 when "the Immaculate Reception" was being screened to be part of an introductory film of highlights in Pittsburgh sports.

He asked if it could be shown again, with the accompanying music up louder. He watched it with his chin resting on his hand as if he had never seen it before. "Make sure you catch the ball this time," I warned him.

Franco Harris is focused on a screen showing him make "the Immaculate Reception."

He smiled. "It's more dramatic with the sound up," he told everyone at the table.

Later, I asked him how many times he has watched that sequence. "Jim, I can't tell you that," he said. I swear he was blushing.

"What would have happened if you had dropped the ball?" I asked.

"I'd have been famous one way or another," he said.

Photos by Jim O'Brien

Frenchy Fuqua can still picture the pass coming his way from Terry Bradshaw as the man in the middle of The Immaculate Reception.

Franco Harris is on a mural with Rocky Bleier blocking for him behind a goal post on the sidewalk at the front of the Heinz History Center. He and General George Washington are celebrated throughout the building on many similar murals or posters. There are statues of Harris with Washington at the Pittsburgh International Airport to greet incoming passengers.

Frenchy flanked by Cliff Stoudt, left, and Mel Blount, on right at the Ray Mansfield Annual Alumni Golf Outing at Diamond Run Golf Club.

Frenchy Fuqua is reunited with Franco Harris in mid-May 2012 at Andy Russell's celebrity golf tournament dinner at Heinz Field.

Les Banos:
"Immaculate Reception" was a lifesaver for Pittsburgh video photographer

The Immaculate Reception was a lifesaver for the Steelers in the 1972 AFC playoffs, but it was really a lifesaver for video photographer Les Banos.

The 2012 season marks the 40th anniversary of the amazing catch and run by Franco Harris of a pass from Terry Bradshaw that caromed off the colliding bodies of both Steelers' running back Frenchy Fuqua and Oakland Raiders' defensive back Jack Tatum.

In Pittsburgh and Puerto Rico, this year is also the 40th anniversary of the death of Roberto Clemente. He was killed in an air crash on New Year's Eve, 1972, as he was accompanying a cargo of relief goods from his native Puerto Rico to earthquake-ravaged Nicaragua.

Les Banos was supposed to be on that airplane. He had promised his good friend Roberto Clemente that he would accompany him on the flight to photograph the event.

Banos was a video photographer for both WQED and WTAE in his long professional career, and he did stints as a photographer for the Pirates, Steelers, Penguins and the University of Pittsburgh department of athletics.

He also filmed games of the Pittsburgh Valley Ironmen of the Atlantic Coast Pro Football League, a minor league team that played its home games in Duquesne, Pennsylvania.

I know the latter first-hand because I was the publicity director of the Ironmen during my senior year at the University of Pittsburgh, in 1963, and again the following season before I was drafted into the U.S. Army.

Banos and I used to get together on Sunday afternoons, the day after the Ironmen games, to edit some highlights that would be used on Pittsburgh TV on Sunday evenings. We both liked to talk, so it took us longer than it should have to do that task.

Later, in the mid-80s, I worked again with Banos at Pitt. He and I and Pat Hanlon, my assistant, joined with Banos and others at WTAE to put together a highlight film on Pitt football. Banos went to pre-season camp with the Panthers at Edinboro University. Hanlon, by the way, is now the vice-president for communications for the New York Giants Football Team, and a real success story.

Hanlon worked with Joe Gordon and Dan Edwards with the Steelers' publicity office. Hanlon had a great time exchanging barbs with Les Banos.

Banos loved to tell stories, and he had some good ones. He told us, of course, how the Immaculate Reception saved his life. He told us about his days in his native Hungary when he was a spy who infiltrated the Nazi regime, and managed to save many Jews from the death camps in Poland.

Pat Hanlon and I used to tell people in jest that Banos had been Adolph Eichmann's chauffeur. Eichmann, of course, was the Nazi general who oversaw the concentration camps and was brought to justice as one of the central figures and criminals by the Nuremberg Trials. It wasn't politically-correct humor, no doubt.

Banos was born in Hungary, but he had some Jewish bloodlines, and he was always an enterprising fellow. He was short in stature, about the same size as Myron Cope, maybe 5–5 at best. Like Cope, he puffed up his chest and came at you like a bantam rooster. He talked with a heavy accent.

Cope, by the way, was the one who popularized the phrase "The Immaculate Reception." A woman named Sharon Levesky called Cope on the radio that night and suggested the name that had been coined by her friend Michael Ord. Cope checked with his Catholic friends to make sure no one would be offended by the phrase, and went with it.

Cope's other creation, of course, was "The Terrible Towel."

Like Cope, Banos was fun to be around. I recall being in Montreal with him at a sidewalk café, enjoying some wine and food when we were there in 1967 to chronicle the entry of the Pittsburgh Penguins into the National Hockey League. Banos picked up a check, unusual for any member of the media, and did a double take when he saw the high tariff on the bill. Banos was the only one in our party who could speak and understand some French, which is always good in the bilingual community of Montreal. It didn't help him to get out of paying the steep bill. His brown eyes bulged at the numbers on that bill.

Banos befriended many of the athletes he covered in his duties as a TV cameraman. Franco Harris was one of them. Roberto Clemente was another.

When Banos died at the age of 86 on April 22, 2012 it brought back memories of this little man with the big heart and such wonderful stories.

"It is significant that he passed our way," said Harris at the Heinz History Center, where Banos had appeared the previous holiday season with a collection of his photos of Clemente. There are 50 of these photos on display in the Roberto Clemente Museum in lower Lawrenceville.

"It is amazing what Les accomplished when you look at his history and have seen his photos," added Harris. "He was a great guy, always enjoyable, a kind and gentle man. You never would have expected what he went through by how kind and gentle he was."

Banos addressed everybody as "Mister," and he liked to get up under your chin like an undersized boxer, again like Myron Cope, and tell you his stories. Banos was a dapper dresser.

Banos was busy filming the Steelers' game against the Oakland Raiders at Three Rivers Stadium on December 23, 1972. When the Steelers won that game, 13–7, on Franco's frantic catch-and-run with a deflected ball he picked off his shoe-tops for the game-winning touchdown.

It meant the Steelers would be playing another game the following weekend, on December 31, 1972, a day that will live in infamy in

Pittsburgh and Puerto Rico. The Steelers lost that one, by 21–17, to the Miami Dolphins, victimized by a fake punt by Larry Seiple of the Dolphins that was a game-changer. The Dolphins went on to win the Super Bowl and are still the only team in NFL history to do so with a perfect 17–0 record.

So Banos had to stay back in Pittsburgh to work that game for WTAE-TV instead of accompanying Clemente on his mercy mission to Nicaragua. It ended the life of Clemente, all too early, and gave Banos a bonus 40 years.

Pittsburgh sports fans were disappointed, of course, by the defeat suffered at the hands of the Dolphins, but they were far more shocked by Clemente's death. Fans over 50, and some as young as 45 or 46, can tell you where they were that New Year's Day when they were the news. What a way to start a year.

If you go to a Pirates' game at PNC Park these days you might be surprised to see how many fans still wear Clemente's name and number (21) on their backs to the ballgames. Andrew McCutcheon and Neil Walker are the two most favorite uniforms, with Clemente a close third. There's a statue and bridge outside PNC Park to memorialize the man from San Juan who came to our city and set new standards for a baseball player, on the field and off the field. Young fans are fascinated by his story and the way he died, trying to help his fellow Latin Americans when they were in trouble.

It's a shame more of them didn't hear those stories as told by Les Banos.

Jim O'Brien

Les Banos shows off some of the vintage work in his collection of Roberto Clemente photos during a show at the Heinz History Center in December of 2011.

Behind Steel Curtain
Big Ben wasn't first Steelers' quarterback to misbehave

They were the Steelers, not the Saints. A proprietor of a popular Pittsburgh bar/restaurant was boasting to me about what a great fan he is of the Pittsburgh Steelers. Yet, I learned in an ensuing discussion, that he knew absolutely nothing about Bobby Layne, Ed Brown and Bill Nelsen, all former starting quarterbacks for the Black & Gold in the '60s, or Ernie Stautner, a defensive star of the '50s and '60s and still the only Steelers player to have his jersey number (70) officially retired.

"I don't need to know that to be a Steelers' fan," protested Greg Dearolf, an owner of Atria's Restaurant & Tavern in Mt. Lebanon.

Yes, you do. Otherwise, you're an imposter, a fan of being a fan.

Dearolf has pictures on display in his establishment to prove that he hosted Hollywood's No. 1 box office draw Will Smith and Pro Football Hall of Fame quarterback Joe Montana of Monongahela on consecutive days a year or so ago. Those marquee stars and their sons were attending a top-notch quarterback camp for kids at Keystone Oaks High School's football field in neighboring Dormont. Even so, Dearolf needs to study up on his Steelers' history if he's to be a real fan, that is, a knowledgeable fan. I don't want to give Greg a hard time about this, but a history lesson follows.

To truly understand the Steelers of today, and what's gone wrong with the likes of Ben Roethlisberger, Santonio Holmes, James Harrison, Jeff Reed and Plaxico Burress, to name a few who now have a rap sheet to their credit, it helps to know that there were Steelers of the past who kept late hours, bad company, exercised bad judgment, misbehaved at times, and had scrapes with the law. They were the Steelers, not the Saints. The Steelers still have their reputation intact, and I trust the team will bounce back from its recent bouts with bad news.

To put things in their proper perspective, it also helps to talk about the so-called good old days with the likes of Steelers' alumni such as Andy Russell, Rocky Bleier, Joe Greene, Mike Wagner, L.C. Greenwood, Randy Grossman, Franco Harris and Jerry "Moon" Mullins, among others, and to hear what Craig Wolfley, Jerome Bettis, Hines Ward and Troy Polamalu have to say about what's expected of the Steelers and the proper standard that has been established for them by the Steelers organization and the team founder Art Rooney and his descendants.

"Maybe I shouldn't say this," remarked Russell, who will turn 70 next month and is also familiar with the Steelers of the last 50 years, "but there were Steelers on our team in the '60s who would make Tiger Woods look like an altar boy."

"Anybody who thinks the Steelers behaved better in those days than they do now is losing it," said Grossman, a stalwart tight end during the glory days of the '70s who turns 58 next month. "People make the good old days out to be better than they really were."

In her farewell column in a May issue of *Newsweek*, the gifted wordsmith Anna Quindlen wrote: "There is nothing quite as tedious, or as useless, as ritual recitations of the good old days, which most often weren't."

That's exactly what we're saying here. I know some things, and have been some places and shared stories through the years, that no other writer in town can offer you. I think this reflection will hold your attention. It's more than a peek behind the Steel Curtain.

Layne was succeeded at quarterback for the 1963 season by Ed Brown, who had been a great college quarterback on the last football team fielded by the University of San Francisco, and a mostly fair field general for the Chicago Bears. Brown had a mental meltdown in the season finale against the New York Giants that cost the Steelers the divisional crown.

Brown was infamous to insiders because he was an exhibitionist and was caught a few times exposing himself in hotel windows.

Nelsen succeeded him. He came to the Steelers from Southern California and never met favor with the fans in Pittsburgh. He was traded to the Cleveland Browns and promptly became a Pro Bowl performer. He and teammate Jim Bradshaw, a defensive back from UT-Chattanooga, spent a lot of time at Pittsburgh's suburban bars and after-hours clubs. I played pool with both of them late into the night. Nelsen was a handsome man. So was Jim Bradshaw. I've heard stories about Nelsen making improper advances with women at bars in Pittsburgh and Cleveland.

Terry Bradshaw was the best quarterback the Steelers ever had play for them, and a real character. He still makes me laugh. He had his difficulties finding the right woman in his life. He liked high profile beauties, beauty queens and ice skating stars for starters, but none worked out. Bradshaw still holds most of the team's passing records as well as its divorce record, failing in three marriages. Art Rooney used to advise him to find a country girl who knew how to milk cows and he'd be better off.

Joe Gilliam had two problems that kept him from succeeding in the NFL. Bradshaw was the better quarterback and kept Gilliam glued to the bench, and Gilliam developed a taste for cocaine. It undid him as a pro and later, in a relapse, led to his death.

Bubby Brister had some of Bradshaw's southern charm and strong arm, but he rankled the Rooneys when they'd hear reports of his misbehavior with women, for instance, fooling around with female fans in the parking lot at Station Square. He mistook the hoods of automobiles for Murphy beds. Brister wasn't the brightest bulb in the room, and mistook a lot of things. He once stood in Three Rivers Stadium and said, "It can get tricky in here when the wind blows in off them lakes."

Kordell Stewart had some personal issues, and stirred up interesting stories. He only spoke to the press on Wednesdays. On one of those Wednesdays he told the world that someday he would be in the Pro Football Hall of Fame. He's still waiting. He drew more comparisons, justifiably or not, to Rock Hudson rather than Rocky Bleier or Rocky Balboa. Stewart refuted the reported rumors about why he was often seen cruising in Schenley Park. His coach, Bill Cowher, always came to his defense and that annoyed some Steelers' fans.

Mike Tomczak is another former Steelers' quarterback whose name pops up in the papers and sports reports now and then because of domestic disturbance calls to police for his behavior with two different wives. Talk to Tomczak and you'd think you were talking to one of the most mature, stable individuals on the planet, yet he gets into trouble because of the way he deals with difficulties on the home front.

So Big Ben hasn't been breaking new ground as field generals for the Steelers go. Roethlisberger has a long road to haul to rehabilitate himself and his reputation, and nobody here is glossing over what he's done. He was behaving like a jerk on the Pittsburgh restaurant and club scene—"Do you know who I am?"—even before he gained national notoriety for his aggressive advances on women in Nevada and Georgia. But he is not the first sinner among the Steelers, and that goes back to the early North Side days of team owner Art Rooney.

Russell, Bleier, Wagner and Grossman all agree that the biggest difference from their playing days and now is that today there is more money, more free time and more media, and the mix is often as volatile as a Molotov cocktail or the kind of martinis they served up at Dante's, and later Froggy's in downtown Pittsburgh when the city's saloon scene shifted in the '80s. There are no secrets these days. There is no Steel Curtain to keep anyone from finding out what's going on behind the scenes.

"Hey, thirty-five years ago, somebody (Ernie Holmes) on our team was shooting a rifle at state troopers hovering over him in a helicopter on the Ohio Turnpike," said Grossman. "Imagine how that story might play today. They'd be on it round the clock."

Or how about the incident on the city's North Side back in 1983 when the team's No. 1 draft choice, defensive tackle Gabe Rivera, was left paralyzed by an auto accident in which he was driving a new car while impaired by alcohol and was jettisoned out the back window by the impact of the crash? There were other Steelers injured and even killed in late night driving accidents near the team's training camp in Latrobe, or in Bridgeville or Knoxville, in other cases that drew some media attention, but nowhere near what Big Ben's misbehavior attracted.

The Steelers had drafted Rivera when they had a chance to pick Pitt's Danny Marino in the college draft. Art Rooney told the Steelers' officials "we have to keep that kid in Pittsburgh." But they ignored him, and Marino joined the list of quarterbacks the Steelers had let get away or had given away such as Sid Luckman, Johnny Unitas, Lenny Dawson, Jack Kemp, Earl Morrall and Bill Nelsen.

"Teams should talk to us about quarterbacks," said Art Rooney in his office one day at Three Rivers Stadium. "If anybody knows anything about quarterbacks, it should be us. We're the experts on quarterbacks. We've had the best come through here. We've had some of the greatest quarterbacks slip through our hands." Luckman, Unitas and Dawson are all in the Pro Football Hall of Fame, along with other western Pennsylvania born and bred quarterbacks such as Marino, George Blanda, Jim Kelly and Joe Namath.

Dan Rooney knows the Steelers' history better than anyone. He lived it and he's written a solid book about his first 75 years with the Steelers. Maybe that's why the Steelers, despite a public clamor for Roethlisberger's head, were hesitant to get rid of another terrific quarterback. Hey, Big Ben has passed the Steelers to two Super Bowl championships.

Not many can do that. Bobby Layne was that kind of quarterback.

Bobby Layne loved the night life. Nobody in the NFL was as good at bar-hopping as Layne. His Paul Newman-like blue eyes lit up at the suggestion of checking out a late-night jazz joint. He hated it when his wife read a story that got back to Texas about his moonlight activity, but it never slowed him down. He wasn't about to move into a monastery. Layne would just get mad at the messengers, the damn media. Myron Cope, who shared a few cocktails or "hot toddies" in the company of the blond bomber, once asked Layne how he managed to keep such late hours, even on Saturday night, yet perform in a championship manner most Sundays. "I sleep fast," allowed Layne.

Bob Drum wrote a book about Bobby Layne that was called *Always on Sunday*, because Layne did perform well on Sunday, despite his drinking and carousing ways all week long. I learned that Layne drank Dewar's scotch and soda, so that became my drink during my formative years. I didn't care for Layne's manner—he could be brassy, brusque and disarming—but Cope told me I was lucky to be around him. "He's the Leif Erickson of pro football," said Cope, scolding me for my reluctance to join him, Layne and Stautner at a round table in the darkened back room. Sometimes Layne would give Cope a hard time, too, and Cope would scurry in retreat to the bar where friendlier companions could be found. Layne and Cope could be as entertaining to watch as the "Tom and Jerry" cartoons at the Saturday matinees.

There were women who frequented the place, but I must not have paid much attention to them because I can't recall any special scenes involving them. I've spoken to several men who frequented Dante's in those days and they agree that women weren't the main attraction. The women who were there wore loud clothes and much makeup and preferred dimly-lit rooms. There was a woman named Lori who played the piano there, and occasionally sang a request song. Something such

Photos from Steelers Archives

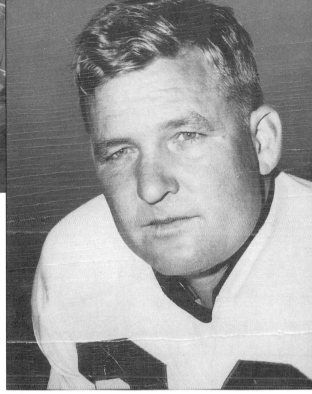

Dan Rooney and Ernie Stautner show off framed No. 70 jersey, the only Steelers' number to be officially retired.

Bobby Layne was known as "The Blond Bomber" for his combative style on the field and in Pittsburgh saloons and jazz joints.

Jim O'Brien

Steelers' lineup at one of Andy Russell's celebrity golf outings for UPMC prostate care includes, left to right, Randy Grossman, John Banaszak, Glen "Pine" Edwards, Mel Blount and Coach Chuck Noll.

as "I Left My Heart in San Francisco." Layne liked her keyboard efforts and filled her tip cup frequently. He went to other night spots on nearby Rt. 51, or in The Hill District. He liked joints that favored jazz.

Layne and Cope were among the Steelers and sports writers and broadcasters who frequented Dante's, a night spot on Brownsville Road where Whitehall says hello to Brentwood. My brother Dan, who was five years older than me, introduced me to Dante's when I was 19, and not old enough to legally drink alcoholic beverages. Everyone thought I was older and I was eager to be where the writers were, people whose stories appeared in the Pittsburgh dailies that I read religiously. Besides Cope, there was Pat Livingston, Bob Drum, Tom Finn, Tom Hritz, Doc Giffin and on occasion Roy McHugh. There were also TV types such as Ed Conway, Tom Bender and Dave Kelly keeping company after they were done working for the day. I wanted to show them my stuff, learn something from them, hoping to catch their attention. Doc Clements, a dapper physician from McKees Rocks and the father of the Clements boys who all made their mark in scholastic and collegiate sports, was usually there. His son Tommy Clements is the quarterback coach of the Green Bay Packers. Doc Clements was the one at Dante's with the silver collar bar above his dark tie. He was always the best-dressed man in the room.

Then, too, in the back room there was Layne and his sidekick, Ernie Stautner. Layne wasn't escorted by off-duty police officers or any bouncer-type entourage. That's Roethlisberger's routine. All Layne needed was Stautner, one of the fiercest competitors in pro football. Ernie had Bobby's back and that was good enough. Stautner was born in Bavararia and could put away beer like the local distributor. Some suggested he could handle 12 or 15 bottles of beer because he was from Bavaria. Like it was in his DNA. There'd be a half dozen other Steelers standing at the bar at Dante's, the likes of Lou Cordileone, Gary Ballman, Jim Bradshaw, Tom "The Bomb" Tracy, Bill Saul, Myron Pottios, Lou Michaels, John Henry Johnson and Paul Martha. There was also Jim Boston, a blustery sort who was an equipment guy with the Steelers. There were some regulars, Damon Runyon types such as Funny Sam Ballanti, who I never thought was that funny, and Doc Esky, a dentist with bad teeth who liked to get in your face when he talked.

Pottios, 73, comes from Palm Springs, Calif. every summer to participate in Andy Russell's annual golf outing. He always visits old pals back home in Charleroi when he comes to town. "We were all there at Dante's because Bobby Layne went there," he told me at dinner at Heinz Field on the eve of the golf outing. "He was the leader, in every sense of the word. Whatever he wanted we did. Nobody wanted to rub him the wrong way. He wanted guys around him. He had Ernie at his side and the rest of us out at the bar. The players back then enjoyed each other's company and we still do. That's why I'm here."

Doc Giffin was a brave bachelor because he would bring his girl friend to Dante's from time to time. A golf writer like Drum at the time, Giffin later became Arnold Palmer's right-hand-man, working out of the Latrobe Country Club, and continues to manage Palmer's golf and business affairs to this day. Giffin and his girl friend both had a serious overbite problem. Drum, who liked to ridicule people, including me, once said that the reason Giffin and his girl friend didn't get married was because "every time they try to kiss their ceramics clash!" Drum was usually as funny as Funny Sam.

Drum, a husky red-faced Irish lout from Long Island, once made a critical remark about my teeth when I took my girl friend to Dante's. I was so embarrassed by what he said to me in front of my girl friend. Within days, I went to the dentist, Dr. William McClelland, Jr., son of the Allegheny County Commissioner of the same name, to repair the dental problem. So Drum did me a big favor. I still think of him when I flash my best smile.

John Henry Johnson was one of the few black ballplayers on the Steelers of that era. He was a tough, bruising fullback—maybe the best blocking back in the NFL—and he had played with Layne and Tracy in Detroit. Johnson once took me to the Aurora Club, an after-hours club in The Hill District. I was the only white dude in the joint. John Henry refused to pay the tab—"Who's gonna make me?" he shouted—and we backed out of the Aurora Club like Butch Cassidy and the Sundance Kid when the waitress gave John Henry a hard time. His bronze bust is in the Football Hall of Fame in Canton. His loyal wife has told me from California that John Henry is suffering from dementia these days and may not recall our night at the Aurora.

I met Art Rooney for the first time that same year, standing on the sideline while the Steelers were practicing at the Fair Grounds in South Park. Mr. Rooney told me about sportswriters in New York whose work he admired. Three days later, he sent me a note at *The Pitt News* apologizing if he came off as a know-it-all. It was the beginning of a beautiful relationship and special correspondence. He would later send me postcards from Canada, California, Arizona and Ireland, which I still treasure as keepsakes. I am the only one still writing from those days at Dante's and the only journalist who goes back that far with an up-close association with the Steelers.

Imagine members of the Steelers and members of the media mixing in the same joint after hours. It will never happen again. Steelers don't go out together like that these days, and neither do sportswriters and sportscasters. Back then, the media didn't think it was their job to police the Steelers or other athletes when they were away from the playing fields and arenas.

"Plus, the sports writers were probably behaving just as badly as the ballplayers back then," offered Grossman, who works for the Wealth Management Strategies investment firm on Brilliant Avenue in Aspinwall.

Rocky Bleier's family lived over a bar his dad owned in Appleton, Wisconsin, a community that turned out the likes of Edna Ferber, Harry Houdini, Willem Defoe and Joe McCarthy. Bleier, now age 66, knows all about bars. He remembers as a rookie in 1968 going to Dante's with some veterans on the team. "It was sort of a rookie rite of acceptance by the veterans," recalled Bleier, who bounced back from leg wounds he suffered in Vietnam to star for the Steelers. Bleier makes a nice living telling his life's story as a motivational speaker. He remains the nicest guy in the world.

"It's how we perceive the character of our celebrity figures," observed Bleier, sitting this summer in a booth near the bar in the front of DeBlasio's Restaurant, not far from Bleier's home in the Virginia Manor section of Mt. Lebanon. I've been to the bar that used to belong to the Bleiers and it's not much different from Donny DeBlasio's bar and restaurant. "We don't have the Damon Runyon characters that made up the bars and saloons back then," said Bleier. "It's changed.

"Layne was long gone by the time I got here, but the stories persisted. That's how we create legends. That year of 1968 marked the end of an era of the Steelers as we knew them. It all changed in 1969 when Chuck Noll came to town and took over running the team his way. The stories were still told, true or not. They were passed on. You went to the 19th Hole hangout after practice at St. Vincent's, and the veterans talked about the good old days. Then that ceased to be, as well.

"I learned a lot growing up in the bar and restaurant business. My parents taught me how to be nice to people. You had to be good with the customers. They prepared me well for what was out there in the world. Life is about choices. I didn't always make the right choice, but I am getting better at it. I realize now, more than ever, how special it was to play for a national championship football team at Notre Dame and four Super Bowl championship teams with the Steelers. I always wanted everybody to like me; that's my hang-up."

Bobby Layne quarterbacked the Steelers from 1958 to 1962. Layne had followed his coach, Buddy Parker, from Detroit to Pittsburgh. They had won back-to-back NFL titles (1952 and 1953) with the Lions in Detroit. They came close in Pittsburgh and definitely made the Steelers more respectable. Dick LeBeau, the beloved Steelers' defensive coordinator on Mike Tomlin's staff who's been inducted this summer into the Pro Football Hall of Fame, was a teammate of Layne with the Lions. "Bobby was different, definitely his own man, and a true leader of men," allowed LeBeau. "He was fun to be around and he was one of the game's great competitors. You didn't want to get on his bad side. But I didn't keep the same hours. It was a different era."

During a recent tour of Detroit, I visited the Lindell A.C., a sports hangout near the old Briggs Stadium where the Lions and Tigers once roamed. Bobby Layne used to hold court there after practice. There are still faded and water-stained photos of Detroit's sports icons, like Layne, Hank Greenberg and Ty Cobb, Gordie Howe and Joe Louis, Rocky Colavito and Barry Sanders, displayed on the walls. Briggs Stadium has since been leveled. I saw it in its last days.

George Gojkovich

Ben Roethlisberger

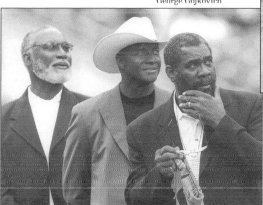

George Gojkovich

Hines Ward

Jim O'Brien

Andy Russell

L.C. Greenwood, Mel Blount and Joe Greene at reunion at Heinz Field.

Jim O'Brien

Moon Mullins

Ernie Holmes

Layne was driving from Dante's the night his car collided with a streetcar. Layne told the police it was the streetcar motorman's fault. "He swerved on my side of the road and hit me," said Layne. Noting that the streetcar was still on its tracks, the cop said, "I don't think so, Bobby." The local cops let Layne and Cope off a couple of times when they were caught driving home under the influence.

I frequented Dante's at the age of 19 and 20. I was a writing student at Pitt at the time, the sports editor of *The Pitt News*, and I wanted to be around the writers more than the Steelers. Layne could be tough on writers.

I was there one night with my dad and older brother, both named Dan. I had cautioned my dad to take it easy and pace himself that night, knowing we planned on being there a few hours. My dad usually drank in bars in Hazelwood and Homestead where everyone drank boilermakers.

My dad started off at Dante's with an Imperial and an Iron City—the proverbial shot and beer parlay—and it was downhill from there. My brother came to me later in the evening and said in a huff, "Bobby Layne and Ernie Stautner are picking on Dad and we're not going to put up with that."

"Yes, we are!" I snapped and I grabbed Dan and Dad by their collars and hustled them out of Dante's as quickly as possible. None of us was taller than 5–9. Layne and Stautner were two of the most feared combatants in pro football. What was my brother thinking? Or drinking?

There were two waitresses who were great with the crowd. Helen Kramer from Bon Air and Hilda Phillips from Dormont. Hilda died a few years back, but I still hear from Helen Kramer on occasion. She lost her husband a year ago and lives near her daughter in Wilmington, North Carolina. Her cell phone number is in my black book.

"Bobby liked Hilda more than me," recalled Mrs. Kramer in a late-night telephone conversation earlier this summer. "Layne and Stautner would be in our place about three or four nights a week. You didn't dare do anything wrong around Layne. He was wonderful with the waitresses—and tipped us well—but he could be terrible to some of the other customers. He could be on the crude side in a hurry. Ernie was his bodyguard, but Ernie was so quiet. He was so sweet. Bobby didn't want any fans swarming around him unless they were invited to do so. If he wasn't at our place, they went to the Crawford Grill up in The Hill. I'm told he would tip the waitresses better up there, giving them a $100 bill now and then. There'd be nights when Bobby would be drunk as a skunk and then have a great game the next day. Not many could do that."

Dante's was owned and operated by Dante Sartorio, who knew how to treat his customers. Any self-respecting saloon keeper should know about Dante Sartorio. He was Pittsburgh's answer to Toots Shor, the noted Manhattan bar owner and host whose gin joint attracted sports and show biz stars. When I went to New York in the '70s, I spent time with Shor to learn the lay of the land. You might see Joe DiMaggio, Joe Louis, Mickey Mantle, Jackie Gleason or Joe E. Lewis at Shor's.

"It was the best ever," claimed Cope when I asked him once to recall the scene at Dante's. "It was the 'Cheers' of Pittsburgh. Everybody knew your name. There were so many regulars, and it was the football hangout. Dante was a very congenial guy, a swell guy. He was one of my best friends. He could get along with athletes and he knew how to look after them and how to talk around them."

Cope continued to explain that when he and Dante would be discussing the latest antics of Layne, the brash blond leader of the pack, Dante would refer to Layne as "Whitey."

"That was in case some yahoo was at the bar for the first time," said Cope. "We didn't want him spreading stories about Bobby to his buddies. We protected him that way. Dante knew it was smart to do that."

In his classic book, *The Game That Was*, which still appears in great sports writing anthologies, Cope offered this reflection on Layne: "He loved to lead forth his teammates to a night on the town, and so he became a night figure, fair game for gossip columnists and hecklers. His temper complicated matters. He could not abide intruders. He experienced run-ins with fans, and although some of his best friends were cops, he occasionally clashed with the law. The combination of his good looks, his love of a good time, and his combustibility made him the most glamorous football figure of his day."

How tough was Ernie Stautner? Stautner once had his thumb completely dislocated in a football game at Forbes Field. It was hanging by the frayed and blood-stained skin. Stautner came to the sideline and got some tape from the trainer and tied his thumb to the rest of his hand, wrapping his hand like a mummy. Then he went back in the game. Andy Russell broke his little finger—"my pinkie," as he put it—and he tried to do what Stautner had done to repair the damage. "Soon after I taped my hand," recalled Russell, able to poke fun at himself, "I fainted dead away on the sideline."

As far as frequenting bars, Russell realized he was better off moon-lighting in the business world, and making more money than he was making playing for the Steelers. He came to the Steelers in 1963, my senior year at Pitt. I had an office on *The Pitt News* at the Pitt Student Union, just two blocks from Forbes Field.

"If you did go out," said Russell, "you were representing the Pittsburgh Steelers. Some guy gives you a shove to test you, but you had to walk away from it. They wanted to fight you to show how tough they were. You knew you could not do that if you were playing pro ball. If you won you'd get sued. You had to turn around and walk out. Some guys are drinking too much and they get brave."

Another linebacker, Jack Lambert, came along later and he had a different view of such things. Lambert never hid. Lambert, who turned

58 last month, was often spotted at some of the best bars in town, or whatever hotel where the Steelers were staying on the road, even though the players were told by the coaches that they were not to drink in the hotel where the team was staying.

"I'm an old-fashioned guy," Lambert once told me when I visited him at his home in Fox Chapel where he lived in his bachelor days. "I don't walk away when someone is giving me or someone with me a hard time. To me, that's part of being a man. Nobody is going to bad-mouth me.,"

When I first came back to Pittsburgh in 1979 to cover the Steelers for *The Pittsburgh Press,* I was determined to take a positive approach to my task. I was in town a few weeks when Lambert got assaulted by three really bad-news thugs at The Happy Landing, just a few blocks away from The Press. One of the thugs slammed a glass mug against Lambert's ear, causing it to tear and bleed. How bad were these guys? A few years later, one of them paid a hit man $600 to kill a guy who didn't jump into the fray with Lambert that night. He was still sore about the guy not helping him out. They also disclosed that they planned to cut Lambert's ligaments so he'd never play football again. Editors and writers at both newspapers knew what had happened to Lambert—there had been a police report—but they all sat on the story. They didn't want to upset the Steelers.

I wish now that I had followed their lead. The story didn't win a Pulitzer Prize, I didn't get a praising memo from my bosses or a bump in pay, and it caused me problems for quite a while. I called Lambert several times to talk to him but he wouldn't return my calls. I talked to Chuck Noll about the incident, and he was as upset with me as he was with Lambert. I wrote the story and it got me off on the wrong foot with Lambert. We made peace at camp. He said, "If you ever write something like that about me again I'm going to kick your ass." I nodded before he could snort fire from his nostrils at me again. Today, such an incident would be transmitted in minutes to the Internet world, with pictures and all. Today, everybody in a bar is a reporter and photographer. Everybody is a blogger or has his own website. I still believe that if you exercise wise journalistic judgment and the players trust you, in the long run you will be privy to more information, more access and write better stories.

Joe Gordon, thought to be the best public relations man in the National Football League during the glory days of the '70s, has been retired the past decade but he still visits Dan Rooney at the Steelers' complex on the South Side on occasion. He still cares about the Steelers and their image. He loves Pittsburgh, and enjoys a walk every morning across Grandview Avenue where he and his wife Babe live in a condo atop Mt. Washington. He handled publicity for the Pittsburgh Rens, the Pittsburgh Hornets and the Pittsburgh Penguins prior to joining the Steelers in 1969, the same year Chuck Noll was hired as the head coach. Talk about good timing.

"Everything is fair game these days," said Gordon, also a staunch Pirates' fan and truly a man for all seasons. "But I do believe the players' behavior is worse today. I think it's symptomatic of our society, a microcosm of what's gone wrong as regards acceptable behavior. There's been a diminishing of our values and standards. I think the guys were better behaved when Rocky and Russell and those guys were on the team. Did you see the story about the two fraternities at Indiana University of Pennsylvania and how they battled it out with baseball bats, machetes and chains? How could that happen on a college campus?"

Gordon and his good friend Roy McHugh were present at a book party at the Duquesne University Student Union in early April where a new well-researched book about Art Rooney—"Rooney: A Sporting Life"—by sports historian Rob Ruck and his wife Maggie Jones Patterson and the late Michael P. Weber was introduced. Franco Harris showed up just in time for his introduction, as is his custom. He still moves to the beat of his own drummer. It's called "Franco Time."

Here's what Harris—it's hard to believe he is now 62—had to say about his personal experience with the Steelers. "I didn't want to come to Pittsburgh," he said. "It was just down the road from Penn State. The Steelers weren't very good and I wanted to get out and see the country. What did I know? I was disappointed when I was drafted by the Steelers and I didn't get off to a good start with them. People questioned my ability and my fire. Sometimes you just observe. You see what they do. I'll never forget that scene in New Orleans after we won our first Super Bowl ... Art Rooney receiving the game ball from Andy Russell. It was so great. Pittsburgh has such a rich tradition in that way. The Steelers are good for this town. They've done so much for our city, so much for me. It was beyond my wildest dreams. I was so glad I was touched by Art Rooney. And today I think the same about Dan and his good son Art II. It's important that we are protective of the Steelers' legacy."

Grossman recalled that he went back to Temple after his first season with the Steelers and got his degree in business administration. He had signed as a free agent and, though he was confident in his ability to catch the ball and block with the best of tight ends, he always felt vulnerable. He was not eager to get into what Coach Chuck Noll referred to as "their life's work."

He says it's different for most of the high profile players today. "They're in their life's work," he said. "Anyone who gets to their second contract should have enough money to live on the rest of their life, if they never work again after they retire from football. All they need is some sound and conservative investing.

"When I was with the Steelers, we had two dailies in Pittsburgh and a few in the surrounding communities," Grossman goes on. "We had three TV stations. We had *Sports Illustrated*. Now you have radio and TV stations and newspapers devoted entirely to sports. You have so many more sports magazines. There's ESPN and Sports Center. I remember we had Steve Courson. Now there was a real ladies' man. He was like the Incredible Hulk. He was pressing girls into the bright lights above the bar at that hotel in Green Tree. 'Let me tear my shirt off and take you home with me!' That would be on TV today, thanks to instant wireless communications.

"We had compound success with the Steelers, first as players and then in the real world. There's Chuck Noll's line about getting on with your life's work. Most of us who were not big stars are still grunting along like everybody else.

"What do I know now that I didn't know then? I know what an adult knows compared to what a kid knows. You think you know everything when you're young, but you've had such a limited life experience. But, of course, my kids never wanted to hear that. Why should these Steelers?

"It's a shame today that there's a misconception that players these days don't have to get into the real world. That may be true for the high-paid superstars, but not for the regular players. The NFL life of the average player is under four years. The majority of players still have to find a job after football. They can't live off the interest and dividends from the money they make playing football. They have to live on some kind of budget, manage their money carefully, and plan for the future. He has to be reasonable. But he's 23 or 25 and he's clueless when it comes to handling money. He wants the best house and the best car and the best clothes and jewelry. And they're looking after family and friends in some cases. Some of them don't hold onto their money too long. They should talk to me. Or Andy. Or Mike. Maybe we could help them."

Andy Russell recalls how Noll and Bill Cowher used to have him and some other Steelers' alumni come in and meet the new players, to offer some advice and get them started on the right foot. I caught up with Russell in mid-May when he was hosting the 34th Annual Andy Russell Celebrity Classic. There was a dinner at Heinz Field on the eve of the golf outing that has raised $6 million for local charities to fund research at Children's Hospital and now UPMC for youngsters and adults alike. It was a good opportunity to talk with many of the Steelers, past and present.

"They used to have me come in and talk to players about post-career opportunities, preparing for their life's work, and financial matters," related Russell. "John Brown, a former Steelers' lineman who was an executive with PNC Bank, would come in and tell them how to open bank accounts and how to budget themselves. I'd talk about investments and about getting involved with the corporate community while you were playing.

"I was lecturing them, and scolding them somewhat. I told them there were too many fancy cars in the parking lot circle outside the Steelers' offices at Three Rivers Stadium. I told them they didn't need fancy cars and fancy clothes. I said, 'Don't buy any restaurants.' I told them to go back to school and do whatever they had to do to get their degrees. I told them to meet people and get another career started while they were playing. After awhile, they didn't want to hear that, or hear from me. I was going over like a pregnant pole-vaulter. So they don't call on me to do that anymore."

"In the old days you had to work, whether you were a player or an assistant coach. You weren't going to spend the off-season on vacation. I'm thankful for that opportunity I had. If you were busy it eliminates a lot of potential problems. You're not hanging out in bars. I'm big on mentors. They can be someone your own age. You have to choose who you spend time with and who your pals are.

"The Rooneys got us involved with a lot of non-profit activities around town. You met some good people. The message was clear that you were expected to be a good citizen. People ask me if it became more fun when the Steelers started winning. Actually, it was more fun before Noll came on board. We had a lot of fun back then but we were getting our butts kicked, too.

"The current Steelers have a certain attitude about what they'll do in the community. The more money they make the less willing they are to make appearances for free, or for a few thousand dollars. They don't need to do it, or at least they don't think they do. When I was playing our thinking was different. It was a good way to get out and sell yourself and to do some good in the community at the same time. We thought it was a good way to meet people. So if somebody offered us a free dinner we'd go out. You learned how to express yourself. Some guys go out and take the money but they don't think about what they're going to say. Or they're not dressed properly and they get up and say, 'I don't know what to say.' Yet they're looking for a payday."

Now the NFL is instituting a program just like the Steelers had with Russell & Co. so they can assist players in making the transition from playing careers to life after football.

I was at a Dapper Dan Dinner two years earlier where Dan Rooney was the main honoree yet only one current Steelers' player, Ike Taylor, was on the dais. "I don't understand where these players today are coming from," said Russell, a regular on the Dapper Dan dais.

L.C. Greenwood, who is 66, was a pillar at one end of the Steel Curtain. The tallest member of the team, at 6–6, Greenwood was a standout student in high school and college, and thought he was going to be a pharmacist. He has noted the change in the players' approach. He is often seen at local golf outings to raise money for different non-profit organizations. He joined John Banaszak, Rocky Bleier and Randy Grossman, for instance, at Joe Walton's annual golf outing at Robert Morris University in May. Banaszak, 60, the former head coach at Washington & Jefferson College, is the top assistant on Walton's football coaching staff at RMU.

"They have the former players come in when the rookies report right after the college draft, and they have us talk to them," said Greenwood. "They don't always want to hear what we have to say. Dwight White and I were talking to some new defensive linemen some time ago at one of these get-togethers, at least ten years ago. Dwight was talking and I was watching. One of the guys, I think it was Casey Hampton, rolled his eyes and he said, 'That was then and this is now.'

35

You've got that kind of thinking. That's what I don't understand.

"Ben McGee and Chuck Hinton took me under their wing when I first came here. I was hanging out with those guys when I first joined the team. Hinton would tell me, 'Rook, you gotta do it like this.' And I'd do it the way he showed me. Lloyd Voss helped me, too. Eventually, I found my own way. That's what I don't understand about these young players today. They don't want to get wisdom. I wanted to know what was going on.

"I got along well with those older guys. You can't lose if you do the right thing. If you treat people right it will lead to good things. If I go to a golf tournament I treat the people who are paying their way the same way I'd want to be treated. My father taught me that. The players today are different. They're always looking up into the stands to see people. I never knew what was going on up there. They're looking for family and friends. I see guys staring up there while the game's going on. I never looked up into the stands. When I came on the field I was into the game."

Joe Greene, when he was coaching the defensive linemen, had a message for his men: "Guys like me were fortunate to be playing football," said Green, 66 this September and still a member of the Steelers' player personnel department. "Football was an outlet, a release. It was a joy to be able to hit somebody in the mouth and not go to jail. I tell my guys they're living the king's life. They can get out and kick ass and not get in trouble. Hey it's football. It's not tennis. It's not golf.

"We had Chuck Noll on us all the time. Now there's a guy who created an environment for us football players to use our talent in a proper way. There are two sides to everyone's personality, a positive side and a negative side. He created an environment for us to bring out the positive side."

Greene has come a long way since his rookie season when he spit in the face of Pat Livingston, a sportswriter who covered the Steelers since their inception, who would later, like Greene, be honored at the Pro Football Hall of Fame. How would that act of defiance and derision be played by the media today?

Gerry "Moon" Mullins, 63, a businessman in Saxonburg, was a teammate for two years of O.J. Simpson at USC. So Mullins knows how players can change and become their own worst enemy. Mullins joined Greene, Bleier, Wagner, Dwayne Woodruff, Edmund Nelson, J.R. Wilburn, Larry Brown, Todd Kalis, Craig Bingham and Roy Jefferson as Steelers' alumni who attended the Andy Russell Celebrity Classic this May.

"We got away with a lot of stuff in our day," said Mullins. "We weren't under the microscope that these guys are under today, with the constant surveillance. We were wild and crazy at times. It seems like the media today is always looking for some shocking story or controversy.

"I'm envious of the kind of money they're making today. They can really retire after they're finished with football and never work again, if they don't want to. But few of them have had the experiences we had or accomplished as much as athletes. What we accomplished is unbelievable. And a lot of our guys have been successful since they left football."

J.T. Thomas, age 63, the team's No. 1 draft choice in 1973 and a starting defensive back during the '70s, has been in the restaurant business since his ball-playing days. He lives in Monroeville. He thinks the team misses Art Rooney, the team's original owner. "I think Mr. Rooney was important to the success of our team," said Thomas. "He set the tone for treating people the right way. You'd see him at practices standing in the middle of the ground crew, talking to them. He took them on road trips, even to the Super Bowl. He had time for everybody. He treated everyone the same. I learned a lot from him."

Larry Brown, age 63, has also been in the restaurant business since he retired from football. "I've had some good experiences with some of the younger players I've met at various events," he said. "Everybody is quick, including me, to say how different players are today. So it's good when I hear positive things about them. You hope they will understand their roles and make the most of their opportunities. It's a demanding life, but it's a good life. It can open the right doors."

John Banaszak, age 62, has been involved in business and college coaching since he quit playing for the Steelers. "We don't live in a perfect world," he said. "When you've got as many individuals as we did on those championship teams, things don't always go the way you wish they would."

He felt personal grief at the loss of teammates such as Steve Furness, Steve Courson, Mike Webster and Ray Mansfield, to name a few of those who have died since the Steelers won four Lombardi Trophies in six seasons in the '70s. I remember seeing him and his wife Mary holding hands to comfort each other at the funerals of those close friends. Banaszak mentioned that Sam Davis has had difficult days since suffering brain damage when he was beaten up at his home in Gibsonia by guys who wanted to teach him a lesson for not paying his bills in the cement business. Joe Gilliam gave in to drugs. Glen Edwards had a tough time financially down in his home state of Florida.

"They were such good guys," said Banaszak. "They showed the way for the rest of us. I wish we were all experiencing great things in our lives today. But that's utopia. That's not the real world."

Craig Wolfley lives in my neighborhood in Upper St. Clair. He has operated a martial arts studio and boxing gym in Bridgeville the past decade. He has done radio and TV work as an analyst and commentator on football with his buddy Tunch Ilkin. They are both 55.

"It can be difficult to find satisfaction and meaning in your life after football," said Wolfley, whose first wife walked out on him soon after his playing days were over. That's not, he once told me, uncommon among pro athletes, according to a study done by the NFL Players Association. Wolfley has since remarried and things look brighter in his life. "Few of us can step out and do it well," said Wolfley. "The rest of us have to stumble along and find our way. You have to find something to do. Your NFL pension doesn't start until you're 55, unless you opt to take a lump sum from it now. But you don't want to do that. Some guys have though. They had to.

"I see some of these young guys and I have to shake my head sometimes. I still like them and admire their ability, mind you, but I don't think there's a respect for the history of the game. Or what went down before they got here. Because of the money they're paid and the signing bonuses they receive, the rookies don't feel too humble when they arrive nowadays."

Bleier still believes today's ballplayers have merit. "It's a shame that some of them get into real difficulties," he said. "I think there is a change in young people today. They've got their head phones and they don't talk to each other like they once did. They're not as influenced by the veterans. In one sense, the players today aren't any different from the players who played back then; they're all the same. We all make money. I was happy making $50,000. That was my goal early on, to make $50,000 someday. Get a pension and some health care benefits. Athletes in general are insecure people, at least about some aspects of their life. I think everybody is insecure. Nobody is perfect. You want to be comfortable. Today, it's important how much money you make and how that compares to the other players. It's a status symbol. Then someone signs a contract for $80 million like Big Ben. What does that do to you? Now some of these young guys are playing for $5 million for a year. If I am making more money than you I am better than you because of the kind of money I make. There's a hierarchy in professional sports. There are stars, there are wannabe stars and there are average guys. It's tough to be accepted by the average guys when you get put on a pedestal. Joe Namath is an example of a super. Joe came out of here and got to New York. He became Broadway Joe. He wins the Super Bowl. You play in a different world. You become a phenom. It's tough to be a phenom. You get lost in who you are and what you want to be. People cater to you. I'd like to know Big Ben. I'd like to know what he thinks. I think he does a good job. You have to be careful. You can get too much exposure."

Hines Ward knows something about that. He got into the papers because some money had been misallocated at a bar on the South Side where he was a co-owner. Ward's words on different issues have gotten him more attention than he might have wanted on several occasions.

But Ward has been one of the most popular players in Pittsburgh Steelers history. He has demonstrated that a dedicated and determined approach to playing football and a glorious constant smile can win you a lot of fans: "I hope I have a good reputation, on and off the field," said Ward. "I watched what Jerome Bettis did. He is a true professional. He has a great attitude. He knows how to present himself to the public. He's a great people person. I see Jerome Bettis and I want to be like that. Football is not going to be forever. I have to have people skills. I'll have to have a nine-to-five job someday, and I have to be able to deal with people."

Jerome Bettis was no angel during his playing days with the Steelers. He had a well-publicized dalliance with a woman on the last night of a summer training camp session at St. Vincent College that ended up with her bringing charges against him that were later dismissed. Overall, though, Bettis had a pretty good track record and was one of the team's most popular performers.

Bettis has kept a presence in Pittsburgh through his own television show during the season and for making occasional appearances at a popular restaurant—Jerome Bettis 36—near Heinz Field. He did manage as a youngster in a difficult Detroit inner-city environment to tip toe through a veritable mine field without getting into trouble with the law.

He said Lou Holtz, his coach at Notre Dame, followed up where his parents left off discipline-wise and was a positive influence in his young life. "He was great for me," observed Bettis during a sit-down session at the Steelers' training complex on the city's South Side. "He helped me as a person and he helped me as a player. Off the field, he nurtured me. He always wanted me to be gracious and humble. He ran a tight ship."

Did Holtz ever come down hard on Bettis?

"I never crossed that line," Bettis said. "I never saw the disciplinarian side. I followed the rules. I never did anything from the start to go outside the rules. Anything you do, you have to respect rules. Rules are a part of life. It was nothing new for me. I had rules to follow as a kid. I learned quickly to follow rules.

"We had to abide by the rules in our home. You learn to make it part of your everyday behavior. With the way kids are raised today, they don't have discipline or manners. When these values are highlighted and promoted, the child understandably follows the lead. Plus, I had asthma and I had to be responsible and make sure I had my inhaler with me at all times.

"My mom was always big on manners. She made sure I opened the door for her and other adults. We always said, 'excuse me,' and 'pardon me, and 'may I' and 'please' and 'thank you,' stuff like that. She always said she wanted us to make her proud. And we tried our best to do just that. My father followed up on what she reported to him. He was the disciplinarian. I was lucky. I was blessed. We were one of the few families in our neighborhood that had two parents at home."

Kevin Colbert, is the general manager and the man most responsible for rounding up the team's playing personnel. "We try to find the best people," he said. "We look for the ultimate combination. You have to understand that as an organization we want to do it right. In doing our research about players, we sort through every aspect of that person. People with bad character make bad decisions. So much goes into the makeup of a team. Each individual is unique.

"We have to adhere to a set of rules. We want everyone to do the right thing in every circumstance. That's not always achievable. You hope you'll select people who'll do that. There's no room for selfish people who put themselves above the best interests of the team and their teammates."

Troy Polamalu may be the most popular player on the team these days. One hears good stories about him all the time from fans, reports of random acts of kindness on his part when they met him.

"The spiritual side of me is important," said Polamalu. "My own Christian beliefs are the basis for my behavior. Some people are good at sports. Like Michael Jordan or Kobe Bryant or Terry Bradshaw. I'm aware of their personal lives and they all had struggles of different sorts. They made a commitment to be great. I want to be great like that.

"But I don't want to sacrifice my personal life. I want to be able to move around and enjoy myself without attracting a crowd. I want to have my own life. It doesn't matter whether you're a baseball player, a basketball player or a football player…you lose some of your own life.

"Sometimes you lose your way, like what happened to O.J. Simpson. He went to Southern Cal before I did and he was so great, and so many people loved him. He had it all. And he lost it just as fast. What happened to O.J. Simpson? No one can make any sense of that."

The same holds true with Ben Roethlisberger, getting back to him. How did he go from having religious messages on his football shoes to wearing a shirt with an image of the devil on it when he got into trouble at a college town in Georgia?

"I got in trouble for having a religious message on my shoes," recalled Roethlisberger. "They made me get rid of that. They (NFL hierarchy) have a uniform code. That message may be somewhere else now. I probably shouldn't say that. I'll get in trouble again. But I'm not afraid to show my faith. I may be more famous now, but I don't want to forget where I came from, or what I'm all about."

Yet he did.

Terry Bradshaw has publicly blasted Roethlisberger for his behavior on several occasions.

Bradshaw says he doesn't have the best relationship with Roethlisberger. "He's made it clear he doesn't want to hear from me," said Bradshaw. "He's still upset because I told him to get rid of the bike after he had that bad accident riding it and nearly killed himself. That's okay with me. I know the Rooneys and they have to be irate about this. This is the second incident with women; that sends up some red flags.

"These guys have so much money and so much power, they feel invincible. They can do and get whatever they want in life, and they have some serious poor judgment. I like what the district attorney said, 'My advice to Mr. Roethlisberger is grow up.' I think that pretty much sums it up."

Chuck Noll, the most important individual in the history of the Steelers, and certainly the catalyst for the success the Steelers have enjoyed since he first joined them, doesn't come around to Pittsburgh much anymore. At 80, Noll has chronic back problems, and prefers to stay close to his wife Marianne at their home in Bonita Springs, Fla. Noll once offered this thought about the way he managed his team.

"You have to have faith in what you are doing," said Noll in an interview I had with him when he was still on the job. "What we've been doing is choosing people, and they have to be good people. You hope they'll end up maturing. You hope you don't have to watch them all the time. There's no way you can police them.

"When I first came here, I had to evaluate the situation. There were a lot of problems, but it wasn't ownership. It had to do with what you have to do to win. To win, you have to have the people. I wasn't competing with Art or Dan or any of the Rooneys, or them with me. We were working together. It's a team game. A lot of people can't function well as part of a team. Some people function better as individuals. If I spot a player who can't work with the group, he's got to go."

Who helped him become successful with the Steelers. "Joe Greene. Terry Bradshaw. Franco Harris. Mel Blount. L.C. Greenwood. Sam Davis. Rocky Bleier. Andy Russell. Ray Mansfield. It's a long list. Just look at our rosters through the years."

Randy Grossman is engaged as investment counselor in Aspinwall office.

Randy Grossman was on many of those rosters. Grossman is optimistic that the Steelers will do just fine in the future. So will the majority of the team's players. "There is infinite exposure," said Grossman. "That's why things seem worse these days. The players are absolutely no different at all. The media wants bad news. They couldn't get enough of the Roethlisberger stuff. It's a shame. He's done some good things in the community, too. "The guys are all the same. You could introduce 99 percent of them to your daughters. There is so much more money available today. That puts more fuel on the fire to find trouble for a young man. And there's the media and its need to fill 24 hours a day, seven days a week with stories. The guys are doing the same things they ever did. There's just so much more reporting on their activities, on and off the field. They do a lot of good things, take part in a lot of good deeds, but the media is more interested in the bad stuff. We'll get through this, just like we'll get through the recession."

Mike Wagner:
It's Critical to Keep Good Company

Mike Wagner was the safety on the Steelers' vaunted Steel Curtain the '70s, sort of the quarterback of the defensive side. He was smart and resourceful and highly respected by his teammates. Wagner didn't enjoy the high profile or the Pro Bowl status of many of his teammates but he was a tough cookie and is still taller than most of the Steelers' current defensive backs. He remains one of the most handsome, intelligent, insightful and thoughtful members of the Steelers' alumni. He thinks before he answers any questions. The first thing he said when I told him what I was looking for was that he did not want to cast any judgment or aspersion on any of the Steelers' players of today. "I'm very sensitive about it," he said.

As always, he made some good points. He works for a Pittsburgh branch of Solenture, a national firm that provides group financial and insurance protection for companies. He came to the Steelers as an 11th round draft choice in 1971 and had his degree in accounting from Western Illinois University. He later obtained a master's in business administration (MBA) from the University of Pittsburgh. He has always dealt in the high finance business. "You always have a responsibility to whomever you work for," he said, "whether it's the Steelers or some company you represent later on. You have to protect the brand name, whether it's Highmark, PNC, PPG or US Steel. That's just common sense.

"I'm not sure if there was some statement that told us what was expected of us, or something that was in the front of the team playbook as to how we should conduct ourselves, but we knew we stood for the Steelers and that meant something.

"You lead by example, not by big commands. You are working with a bunch of young people and you have to keep that in mind. You even have older people misbehave in organizations. Look at what happened on Wall Street and with some of the biggest banking firms in America. Greed and fear causes a lot of people to do the wrong thing. I don't think there are more problems," said Wagner. "There is more media. They need a new story every hour of the day, every day of the week. You have to watch yourself more than ever before. There are good and bad athletes. It's not unique to sports. In business there are people who do things they shouldn't do. Look what happened on Wall Street and in the banking industry that fueled the recession we're still in.

"The Rooney family wanted us players out in public functions representing the team and helping non-profits raise money. I had the opportunity to meet a lot of special people in the community and I realized it was important.

Mike Wagner at Atria's Restaurant & Tavern in Wexford.

"As Steelers, or even former Steelers, we are revered here in Pittsburgh. Because we enjoy that we have to respect the legacy. I think I knew we had an obligation to give something back.

"You learn to deal with fans as a retired Steeler. They're not as critical of you as they were when you were playing. I remember the first time I met you. It was at training camp at St. Vincent College. I wasn't happy with how you came on. You asked me how I fit in with the Steelers' defense, as if I wasn't as good as the rest of the guys. I think it would have helped if we had been taught how to deal with the media."

Wagner makes a good case for it being a critical choice of the kind of company you choose to keep.

"I don't want to be disrespectful to fans, or my friends or family," Wagner went on, "but when they came to town from Illinois when I was playing they were here to party. I had to back away at times. You have to make choices about who you want to be with. Some guys hang with the wrong people and they get into trouble as a result. You realize when you're a player that you have a different attitude about what you need to do before a ballgame. Hey, this is my job. Sometimes you have to push people away. You have to surround yourself with the right people. Sometimes you rely on people to help you and you have to know whether they have your best interests or not. There's always that fine line. Once in a while you might have to offend people to get them to back off.

"There's two things that the Rooneys have done. The family and the Rooney organization as such never really besmirched the Steelers. The Rooneys and McGinleys never did anything to call negative attention to the team or organization. People who work for them are held to the highest standard. You're talking about tough, young, volatile A-type personalities. You have to keep your fingers crossed. You wonder how a 22-year-old worth $5 million is going to handle that. I don't know how I'd do in that situation. There has to be a lot of temptations and you attract a lot of people who have ideas how to spend that money."

Ya gotta love it
to brave the cold

December 2008

I thought about Bubby Brister, that cerebral quarterback for the Steelers in the late '80s and early 90's, who said of conditions at Three Rivers Stadium one winter's day, "It can get tricky in here when the wind blows in off them lakes."

I thought about an NFL playoff game I covered in the early '80s on a cold and blustery day in Philadelphia between the Cowboys and the Eagles. Phyllis George, a former Miss America who was entrusted with a microphone on national television, asked Cowboys' coach Tom Landry if he'd ever coached a team under such conditions.

"Have you ever heard of the Ice Bowl?" allowed Landry in his dry manner. "We played the Packers in Green Bay for the championship one year when it was far worse than this."

That game was played on December 31, 1967 at Lambeau Field in Green Bay. The thermometer read 13 below zero and the wind chill factor was measured at minus 46 in the last game Vince Lombardi ever coached at Green Bay. Bart Starr took a quarterback sneak behind guard Jerry Kramer for the game-winning touchdown with 13 seconds showing on the clock in one of the most memorable games in history.

I thought about my friend, Sharon Pociask, out in Crystal Lake, Ill., who had attended that Ice Bowl game in Green Bay, back when she was a schoolgirl in Milwaukee. How many of your friends can say that?

I thought about having lunch with Steelers' defensive coordinator Dick LeBeau just last month at the Steelers' training complex on the city's South Side, and he introduced me to Ken Anderson, the quarterbacks' coach of the Steelers.

I remember Anderson best as a terrific quarterback for the Cincinnati Bengals. LeBeau was the coach of the defensive backs for the Bengals back in the 1981 season when they played the San Diego Chargers in the AFC championship game in Cincinnati in January of 1981. I was covering the game for *The Pittsburgh Press*.

The temperature was nine below zero and the wind chill factor reached minus 59 that afternoon in the Queen City. No one from San Diego had dressed for this event. They had played in Miami the week before in one of the wildest and highest-scoring games in NFL playoff history. I could have covered that game as well—it was played the day before the Bengals-Bills contest in Cincinnati, but passed on that to permit a fellow *Press* reporter to experience some of the action.

It was ungodly cold that day in Cincinnati. I was in a warm press box, of course. But you even felt cold in there, seeing the behavior of the frozen ballplayers on the TV monitors overhead, and their breath clouding before their noses.

The Bengals won that game and went on to play Joe Montana and the San Francisco 49ers in Super Bowl XVI in the Pontiac Silverdome. The streets of Detroit and the suburbs were ice-covered that day. It was slippery and challenging getting from the parking lot to the stadium without doing a pratfall.

So there's a history of games on cold days in pro football. Bill Hillgrove suggested on the air that it was one of the coldest days he could remember of his time with the Steelers.

I was happy to see the Steelers rally and defeat the Dallas Cowboys 20–13 on an extremely cold day this past Sunday evening. The temperature dipped as low as 19 degrees, but it felt much colder because of the wind that was blowin' in off them lakes.

The fans were freezing more than the players, that's for certain.

I watched the game in my family room, sharing a warm blanket with my wife Kathleen. I even dozed off a couple of times—especially when the Steelers' offense was on the field—and Kathie kept hitting me because I was snoring. I've been running here and there lately, doing booksignings at area malls, and it catches up to you.

I was happy that Deshea Townsend scored the winning touchdown, securing an interception and returning it 25 yards for a touch down with 1:10 left that gave the Steelers the lead. Townsend, who was born in Baitesville, Miss., and played his college ball at Alabama—that's about as Southern as you can get—is one of the most popular players in the Steelers' clubhouse.

We were told in advance of the game and most fans bought the theory that the Steelers would have an edge because this was Steelers' weather and a Southern team like the Dallas Cowboys would be uncomfortable and out of sorts in the environment. Anyone who buys that still believes they are making steel in Pittsburgh, and that workers here have a lunch pail work ethic and that this is still a blue collar community. Please…those images are all available in the archives file at the Carnegie Museum and Library.

I didn't buy that Steelers' weather theory. The Steelers practice indoors most of the time when the weather is bad. I always thought it would be a good idea to get used to playing when it rains or when it snows, so it would be best to conduct practice under all possible conditions. Mike Tomlin did have his Steelers practice outside the week before this game.

Most NFL teams are comprised of players from across the country. They all have players from the Midwest, New England the Rocky Mountain region that have played in the cold, or when it was snowing.

Let's face it; no one likes to play football when their fingers are frozen. I spent ten months in the U.S. Army at the Cold Weather Testing Center at Fort Greely. I know what extreme cold is all about. You could get a court martial if you were caught running on a day when the wind chill factor dipped below a certain number, because that increased the wind chill factor. Even so, I was chilled when I got out of the car on Sunday morning. I felt sorry for the Steelers' fans before the game even began.

Craig Wolfley, a neighbor of mine in Upper St. Clair, comes from upstate New York, in the neighborhood where the Buffalo Bills play their home games, except when they're in Toronto. Wolfley played his college ball at Syracuse. They play indoors but Wolfley walked to class on the campus on occasion when it was pretty cold out.

Even so, Wolfley was freezing his buns off Sunday as the sideline reporter for the radio broadcast of the game. He complained loud and clear about how cold it was to his buddies Bill Hillgrove and Tunch Ilkin, who were warm in the broadcast booth high above Heinz Field.

"Wolf looks a little pink-cheeked," Ilkin observed.

Wolfley went along with the theme that the Steelers had an edge because of the cold, as did the national broadcasters. "They're not used to playing in this kind of wind chillage," said Wolfley. Let it be said that Wolfley is never without a word, even if he has to make up one on the spot.

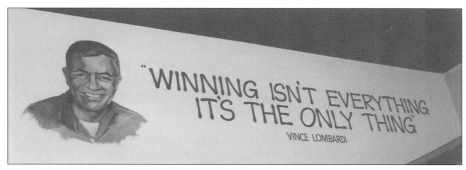

Jim O'Brien

Craig Wolfley and Tunch Ilkin are a comedy team at Steelers' headquarters and on local radio and TV shows relating to Steelers.

Recalling the Immaculate Reception
John Drugo, 66, from Johnstown:

"I know a million people must tell you they were at Three Rivers Stadium for the 'Immaculate Reception' but I really was. I came down from Johnstown with three friends of mine, and we were sitting in the end zone that Franco was running toward when he caught the deflected pass and scored the game-winning TD.

"I think we were in Section 228, Row L, seats 5,6,7,8. It looked like the game was lost and, all of a sudden, people around us are shouting "He caught the ball," or "He grabbed the ball," or "Holy hell, he's got the ball."

The next thing I know I'm hugging a state trooper. Then I'm hugging a pharmacist, a dentist and a steel worker. I hugged all of them. And, I swear I was stone sober. We celebrated at the South Fork Country Club in Johnstown that night. It's not there anymore, but our memories of that day remain with us.

"I played football at Bishop McCourt High School with Jack Ham and and Steve Smear, and I knew Pete Duranko. I was a starting guard as a senior and Ham was a sophomore on the suicide squad. He didn't even start until he was a senior.

"Ham went away to a military school for a year, and Steve Smear told Joe Paterno you ought to look out for this pal of mine. He can play. Paterno gave Ham his last scholarship that year.

"I'll tell you another unbelievable aspect of Jack Ham. He had a terrible stutter when he was in high school. When I hear him on network radio doing the Penn State and NFL games I have to really admire him and how far he's come in so many ways.

PETE DURANKO

"It's a shame what happened to Pete Duranko, him dying a year or so ago after a long siege with Lou Gehrig's Disease. I remember I suffered a concussion when I was playing high school ball, and Pete was home from Notre Dame and he came to the hospital to cheer me up. Pete was a very funny guy."

47

Art Rooney and The Cardinal
at the Allegheny Club

November 2009

I miss Art Rooney and the Allegheny Club. Mr. Rooney was the founder and owner of the Pittsburgh Steelers and one of the nicest men I have ever met in my travels through the sports world.

The Allegheny Club was the heart and soul of Three Rivers Stadium. There are fancier outposts at Heinz Field, but there's nothing quite like the Allegheny Club.

It was located at the epicenter of the stadium with spectacular views on both sides. On the interior, one had a great view of the playing field for football and baseball, and on the exterior there were the three rivers themselves. No landscape architect ever came up with a more spectacular setting. Behind the bar at one end there was a wall that was built from bricks that once were part of the outfield wall at Forbes Field. There were pictures of Pittsburgh's best ballplayers on the walls wherever one wandered. It was a mini-museum or sports hall of fame.

You needed a membership card to get in, unless you were a sportswriter, grew up in Oakland or knew someone at the door. There were some couples who came early and started a line to get on the elevator earlier than anyone else so they could command certain key standing positions above the tiered dining area so no one could possibly block their view of the playing field. First in line when the elevator opened to take up early arrivals was Jimmy Passalacqua of Canonsburg, an Italian leprechaun with white bangs on his bronze forehead. He and his wife Yolanda wanted to get to their usual positions on the terrace. They were as eager to get to the spots they always claimed as the Sooners of Oklahoma. The Passalacquas pass for Greek, too, when that gets them a good seat at the All-Saints Orthodox Church Food Festival in Canonsburg.

The Allegheny Club was a great place to wine and dine and watch the games with friends and business associates. It was a place where you could see sports and entertainment and political celebrities. Mr. Rooney liked to check out the Allegheny Club to see who was there, to shake hands and exchange warm pleasantries. He was often in the company of priests, usually his dear friend Father Bob Reardon was one of them. I think it was some kind of "fire" insurance policy for a proud Irish Catholic.

It was Mr. Rooney's custom, whenever he entered a restaurant, if he spotted priests or nuns at a nearby table, to tell the waiter to bring him their tab. Maybe it was payola for St. Peter at the Gates of Heaven.

Rooney's partner Jack McGinley would be at the Allegheny Club with his sister, Rita, their family and a priest—often Monsignor Owen Rice, the so-called "Labor Priest"—and Jack would ask me to join them

48

"for a glass of wine and a bit to eat. You're always welcome, Shamus. Stay awhile."

Fans still speak of the time they met Mr. Rooney at the Allegheny Club and how nice he was to them, like they were old friends. "We shared the same elevator once," a fan will boast as if she still had the badge of honor on the mantle at home.

I recently heard a story about Art Rooney and the Allegheny Club that tells you a lot about the man, how modesty was his greatest virtue, and why he remains such a man of the people.

This story was told to me when I attended the funeral of a dear friend Bob Milie, who had been a part-time trainer with the Steelers when they won their first four Super Bowls, in addition to being the sports information director and trainer at Duquesne University.

Milie's viewing was at the Slater Funeral Home in Green Tree. I had been there earlier for the funerals of Myron Cope, Lloyd Voss, Joe Moore, Mary Regan and the mother-in-law of my friend Mike Hagan. I was also there when Judge John Brosky's wife died and I remember a huge man in gray Bermuda shorts and sneakers offering the judge his condolences. What was that galoot thinking when he left his home that day dressed in that manner?

Cope, of course, was the color man and analyst for Steelers' football, Voss played on Chuck Noll's first team here in 1969, Moore was a beloved assistant coach at Pitt, Regan was Art Rooney's devoted secretary and Hagan had served as the business manager of the Steelers in between stints as the president of North Side Bank and Iron & Glass Bank. Mike is one of my dearest friends.

When Mary Regan was a young woman she answered the phone when you called the Steelers' offices at the Roosevelt Hotel. She'd say, "Steelers, hold on!" She stretched Steelers into three syllables somehow. She was loyal to Mr. Rooney long after he was gone and she was retired. She never volunteered stories about him. Her sister, Pat, was married to Dan Rooney, the chairman of the board. Another sister, Gerry Glenn, was the ticket manager of the Steelers for many years.

Steve "Dirt" DiNardo saw me at several of these viewings. "You're gonna run out of people to write about," he said to me with a big smile. I pointed out Rocky Bleier and Franco Harris nearby and assured DiNardo that I wasn't worried about that.

"Dirt" DiNardo is one of the colorful and omnipresent Pittsburgh sports characters. He came out of Brookline to become the head groundskeeper at Three Rivers Stadium. He considered himself a close friend of Art Rooney. Then again everyone who ever met Mr. Rooney considered themselves one of his closest friends.

DiNardo became famous when he took it upon himself to plow snow off the field to the Steelers' advantage in an AFC playoff game with the Houston Oilers back in the mid-70s. He did this during the game, on national television. DiNardo has never been a shy guy. He's 79 and long retired, but not as a story-teller. He likes to get up under your chin when he talks, and get those coal dark eyes working on you so there's no lapse in your attention.

He tells me this story about Art Rooney I had never heard before. "I'm walking through the hall at Three Rivers Stadium one Sunday when we had a home game," said DiNardo. "I see Mr. Rooney and he was with a big shot Cardinal from New York."

DiNardo did not remember the Cardinal's name, at first, but most likely it was Cardinal John Joseph O'Connor, the bishop of New York who operated out of St. Patrick's Cathedral in Manhattan.

"I genuflected and attempted to kiss the Cardinal's ring," recalled DiNardo, genuflecting like an actor on stage might, "but he pulled his hand away and said that wasn't necessary. I asked Mr. Rooney what was up with him. He said they had attempted to go up on the elevator to the Allegheny Club, but the elevator operator turned them away because he didn't know Mr. Rooney and Mr. Rooney didn't have his membership card.

"I asked him where he was going. He said he was going to his office to get his membership card. I told him to hold on. I told them to follow me. I went over to the elevator operator and I said to him, 'Are you goofy or something? What kind of 'yeg' are you? This guy owns the building. This is Art Rooney.' He still didn't know him. 'You better get him upstairs in a hurry or you'll be looking for a job on Monday.'

"So he let them on and they went up to the Allegheny Club. Dan Rooney still tells everyone that it took 'Dirt' DiNardo to get my dad and Cardinal O'Connor into the Allegheny Club."

I would hear stories about how poorly Ben Roethlisberger and Jeff Reed conducted themselves at clubs and upscale restaurants around town. Ben didn't want to pay cover charges. "You should pay me to come in," he's been reported to have said on many occasions. "I bring crowds to your place." It's said that Ben doesn't tip the valets and wait staff. Reed bares his chest, starts roaring and trying to impress the women. Anything to get attention. The cops chase him so he doesn't get into trouble.

Art Rooney never thought he was a big deal; that's the difference.

"He always made me and my guys on the ground crew feel important," declared DiNardo. "When we'd make the late-night changeover from baseball to football he'd show up at 3 a.m. just to see what was going on. He'd say, 'I came in case you needed some help.' We made him an honorary member of the ground crew.

"He used to take two members of the ground crew on the chartered airplane to all the road games. They don't do that anymore. There were 16 guys on the ground crew. He wanted to give me a Super Bowl ring once, and I told him I couldn't accept it unless he gave me 16 more rings for the rest of the guys. I told him, 'I've got to live with these guys every day.' He understood that. He always came and talked to us, and offered us cigars. He was the best kind of guy. Authentic. No phony. The real deal."

This reminded me of a story once told to me at a Super Bowl in Tampa by Bob Roesler, once the sports editor for the *New Orleans Times and Picayune*. New Orleans was going to be the site of the next

Super Bowl, and Roesler was in Tampa doing p.r. work for the Crescent City to promote the event. "New Orleans owes a lot to Art Rooney for its being in the National Football League in the first place, and for being the host city for the Super Bowl so often," reported Roesler. "It was Art Rooney who pushed the other owners to grant our city a franchise, and he also promoted the idea of having the Super Bowl there. Once upon a time, his Steelers used to play exhibition games in New Orleans.

"During Super Bowl VI week, city fathers threw a big party for the league moguls at an exclusive club in New Orleans. Mr. Rooney hadn't planned on attending, but he ran into friends as he left Mass at St. Louis Cathedral in the French Quarter.

"They urged him to show his face at the party. So he entered the club. Here's Mr. Rooney, one of the most recognizable faces in the National Football League, and when he reached the door the attendant asked for his invitation. He didn't have his invitation with him. 'No soap,' said the guy at the door. Mr. Rooney assured him he belonged, but it didn't get him anywhere.

"Mr. Rooney told me this story. He said the guy wouldn't let him in. Mr. Rooney said, 'Finally, I started to walk away and I told him that if it wasn't for me they wouldn't be having a party in there. He looked at me like I was some kind of nut.' Instead of getting someone to identify him, Mr. Rooney retreated to his hotel. He hadn't wanted to party anyhow.

"That tells you all you need to know about Art Rooney. The Chief, as they called him, was one of the most colorful and kind persons I ever knew. His word was his bond, good as gold. They don't make them like him anymore."

Jim O'Brien

Steve "Dirt" DiNardo looked after the field at Three Rivers Stadium.

Don't worry about
Dan Rooney and the Steelers

July 2008

This story was written when the Steeelers' ownership picture was in question after the league ruled that owners must divest themselves of any gambling ties.

I don't think Steelers' fans need to fret about Dan Rooney and their favorite pro football franchise. Rooney, the chairman of the board of the Steelers and one of the National Football League's most respected owners, has helped the league solve some knotty problems and issues in his distinguished career and I believe he will find a way to resolve some of the challenges that his franchise now faces.

There's been much news lately about the Steelers' ownership problems, and it will be interesting to see how it all plays out.

I think those who worry that the Steelers might be sold to outside interests and possibly move elsewhere can relax. The Steelers and Pittsburgh are one of the league's most secure franchises and they are here to stay. The Steelers and Social Security will be with us, I'd bet, for another thirty years.

The Pittsburgh Steelers are one of the NFL's best brands. The team's marketing items are among the most in demand in all of professional sports. Pittsburgh's population may continue to decline, but the demand for Steelers' tickets remains strong, and no team travels better as far as its fans are concerned. They are evident everywhere.

The Steeler Nation has no need to fear the future of this team.

All things are possible, I realize. Who'd have thought the Baltimore Colts would move to Indianapolis in the dead of the night? Who would have thought that the Cleveland Browns, packing a stadium with 80,000 plus fans regularly, would relocate to Baltimore?

How could Los Angles, the second largest city in the country, not have an NFL franchise? Steelers' Super Bowl rings are being offered for sale on E-Bay. They are owned by a former front-office staffer who has money problems. The NFL would like the Steelers to shed their association with gambling. Like that's something new. The Steelers have been involved with gambling since they came into being as the Pittsburgh Pirates back in 1933—75 years ago.

There was once a professional football team called the Houston Gamblers—Jim Kelly of East Brady was their quarterback—but the nickname would be more appropriate for the Pittsburgh team. The Pittsburgh Gamblers would make more sense these days than the Pittsburgh Steelers. There are no steel mills in Pittsburgh proper anymore. The Edgar Thomson Works in Braddock was the first such mill and now it's the only remaining mill.

BROTHERS ROONEY are, left to right, Dan, John, Art Jr., Pat and Tim.

Art Jr. at his office in The Southmark Building in Upper St. Clair

The Rooneys

Steelers' chairman emeritus Dan Rooney, the U.S. Ambassador to Ireland.

Pat and John in West Palm Beach, Florida

> *"Treat people the way you want to be treated.*
> *But never allow them to mistake your kindness*
> *for a weakness."*
> **—Advice from Art Rooney Sr. to his five sons**

It remains to be seen how the Rooney boys will work this out. Dan, the oldest son of franchise founder Art Rooney at 79, is the only one involved in the day-to-day operation of the football team. He is the chairman of the board. His oldest son, Art II, is the team president. This was before Dan became the U.S. Ambassador to Ireland.

Dan's four brothers, Art Jr., Tim, John and Pat—the twins—are involved in other family business interests. Art Jr. looks after real estate interests out of an office in Upper St. Clair, not far from his home in Mt. Lebanon. Tim looks after Yonkers Raceway in New York.

Tim is a resident of Florida, as are his twin brothers, John and Pat. The Rooneys were ready to sell Yonkers a few years back because harness racing was on the decline and a developer offered big money for the land that Yonkers Raceway occupied. Then Yonkers secured a license to have slot machines and other gambling and it became a cash cow.

Pat and John look after the Palm Beach Kennel Club in West Palm Beach, Florida. It has greyhound racing, slot machines and paramutual machines that permit betting at racetracks around the country.

Art Jr. told me that when his brothers were saying goodbye to each other after enjoying a dinner at the Kennel Club one evening in the winter of 2009—only Dan was missing—that Pat stopped him as he was about to pull out of the parking lot. He said, "Well, we all managed to make it through another winter together." To which Art Jr. added, "That did give me pause for thought. It makes you wonder."

Each of the brothers owned 16 percent of the Steelers at the time. That adds up to 80 percent. The other 20 percent was owned by the estate of the late Jack McGinley Sr. and his sister, Rita McGinley. Dan would like to buy enough of the stock he doesn't own so that he can have a majority interest and retain control of the football team.

He has offered to buy out his brothers, but his offer isn't as substantial as what Wall Street advisors have told them their share is worth.

Stanley Druckenmiller, a Wall Street investor with a Pittsburgh background who's a big fan of the team, wanted to buy the ballclub. He said he wanted Dan Rooney and Art Rooney II to continue to run the operation. Druckenmiller is one of the richest men in the country, said to be worth $3.5 billion. He says he wants to honor the team's legacy and that he's not interested in running the football team.

George Steinbrenner said something like that when he bought the New York Yankees from CBS back in 1973. Has there been an owner in sports who was more in the middle of the management of his team's affairs?

I do think that new money and new thinking could be an asset for the Steelers. Druckenmiller is no dummy. He made this money on his own. It makes me nervous that he's one of those fans who often paints his face black and gold when he attends games, but he'll get over that if he's a team owner and a more dignified posture is required from league officials. The Pirates and the Penguins could have used someone like Druckenmiller when their franchises were at risk. It's better to have one owner with deep pockets than twenty or thirty with $2 million invested apiece. It doesn't give you any financial clout. Druckenmiller is the first person with real money to step forward like this.

Mark Cuban, a Mt. Lebanon native who owns the NBA's Dallas Mavericks, had expressed interest from time to time, but never acted when there were opportunities to put his game on the line.

If you want to feel better about the Steelers I would suggest you read the books that have been written by Dan Rooney and by Art Rooney Jr. Dan's memoir is titled *My 75 Years With the Pittsburgh Steelers and the NFL.* Top writer Roy McHugh has neatly edited Art Jr's journals. It's called *Ruanaidh* (Rooney in Gaelic): *The Story of Art Rooney and his Clan.*

Roger Goodell and Paul Tagliabue, the present and past NFL commissioners, both wrote prefaces or introductions for Dan's book. It's obvious that they have the utmost regard for Dan Rooney. Tagliabue is involved in trying to resolve the Steelers' ownership issues. Goodell and Tagliabue aren't about to let Dan Rooney lose control of the Steelers.

If the Rooneys remain true to their expressed sentiments in these books, and what they are really all about, and what their father told them he wanted them to do, the Steelers will remain in the family. They can't get greedy all of a sudden.

Dan Rooney has always thought the Steelers were special, that they were different from most professional sports franchises, and that they tried to do things the right way. This current dilemma will be a good test of that posture and belief. The boys have always said they gained integrity and character from their dad.

I just missed running into Dan Rooney twice in the past week or so. I attended the Pirates; game with the Yankees last Thursday night, and the Pirates' game with the St. Louis Cardinals on Sunday afternoon. I stopped, as I usually do, at the ice ball stand of Gus Karalis at West Park, before and after the game. Gus and his wife, Estella, are two of my favorite people. I admire their work ethic and the way they interact with their customers.

Among their regular customers are Dan Rooney and his wife Pat. They live a half-mile away in the home that Art Rooney Sr. and his wife Kathleen bought on North Lincoln Avenue early in their marriage. Dan and Pat both grew up in that neighborhood and know its streets well. They met in grade school and married soon after graduating from high school. They were married at St. Peter's Church, a half-mile in the other direction from Gus's ice ball stand.

Dan likes lime-flavored ice balls. Green is his favorite color because of his Irish fervor. Pat prefers root beer syrup on her ice ball. They walk up to the ice ball stand about three evenings a week. Dan sits on a stool right next to the orange ice ball stand. He'll pose for pictures when asked, and he signs autographs.

"You got yourself in the paper a little bit this week," said Gus with a grin. Dan didn't say anything. He just grinned back. Gus knew better than to press him on the issue. They are the best of friends. Nobody else brought up the ownership controversy either.

Dan told him he'd been out earlier in the day flying his airplane out of Allegheny County Airport. The skies were dark most of the day, but Dan said he avoided the bad weather.

Linda Barnicott, an artist who resides in Green Tree, has painted some wonderful scenes of Pittsburgh. She did one showing Dan Rooney sitting on a stool at Gus Kalaris' ice ball stand, just like the scene on those two days when the Pirates were playing at PNC Park.

Barnicott has also painted scenes at Kennywood Park, of the clock at Kaufmann's, of streetcars in downtown Pittsburgh, and of Bill Mazeroski's dash around the bases when he hit the home run that won the 1960 World Series.

Kennywood Park's original family owners have sold the amusement park to a company in Spain. State officials are trying to do the same with the Pennsylvania Turnpike. Kaufmann's is gone, and so are the streetcars. It would be great to have those streetcars today.

Seven Springs Ski Resort was sold to resolve family ownership contentions. The Nutting family that owns the Pirates bought the resort in the Laurel Mountains. So the Steelers' situation is not unique. It's happened with many NFL teams such as the Miami Dolphins, the Baltimore Colts, the New York Giants, the New York Jets, to name a few, and twice to baseball's Los Angeles Dodgers.

Dan Rooney didn't go into hiding when the news hit the fan about his franchise's problems. He took a walk in the park with his wife. He mixed with the fans. He's different from most owners that way. He's not above the crowd. In fact, Dan Rooney can easily get lost in a crowd.

He and his brothers were never allowed to make a show of their wealth. They never acted like millionaires. In fact, at times they didn't seem to realize they were millionaires. Their father didn't allow any of them to drive a Cadillac. A loaded Buick was better. He never wanted them to show off. He wanted them to keep a low profile.

And they followed his lead. When they were going to dedicate a statue in honor of Art Rooney Sr. at a site just outside Three Rivers Stadium, his son Art Jr. was urged by his wife to rent a limousine so they could bring some out-of-town friends to the dedication ceremonies. Art Rooney Jr. relented after much soul-searching. He didn't think his dad would approve of hiring a limo.

As the limo neared the site of the statue, Art Jr. jumped out of the limo when it slowed down. "I didn't want my dad, or even his statue, to see me riding in a limo," Art Jr. confessed to me once at lunch at the St. Clair Country Club. Art Jr. often told self-deprecating stories about himself. "I got my job with the Steelers out of pure nepotism," he was fond of saying. "But I think I ended up doing a good job."

Now Art Jr. and his four brothers have to remember where they came from, and what they learned from their father, and to follow their heart and faith and do what's best for everybody.

Whatever happens, it won't be the end of the world. We'll still have Steelers' football and we'll still be contenders. Dan Rooney portrayed himself in his book as the last Steeler still standing.

Wellington Mara
a real Giant
in Pleasantville

November 2005

I shared some magic moments with Wellington Mara. He was the co-owner of the New York Giants football team and one of the most respected leaders in the National Football League. He brought dignity and integrity to a league that needs it more than ever because of the owners, coaches and ballplayers who bring it down with their bad behavior and bad judgment. He was a close friend and admirer of Art Rooney, the owner of the Pittsburgh Steelers. Wellington's father, Tim, was more of a contemporary of Art Rooney. Tim Mara was a licensed bookmaker. He handled some of the bets Mr. Rooney placed the day he made the big killing betting the horses at Saratoga in the late '30s.

Wellington Mara always said he was the son of an Irish bookmaker. He was nicknamed "Duke" because it went with Wellington, and the way he carried himself. I was fortunate as a young man to walk with Wellington Mara and Art Rooney. I went to Mass with them and their wives, Ann and Kathleen, on St. Patrick's Day in Maui in March, 1981. We were there for the NFL Owners' Meeting. The Maria Lanakila Church in Lahaina was a modest white-walled edifice, beautiful in its simplicity. Mr. Mara and Mr. Rooney attended mass every morning, no matter where they were. They recruited others to join them.

Mr. Mara said he was "always comfortable in the company" of Art Rooney. He said his father Tim had told him that track people were honest and you could take them at their word. One of Mr. Rooney's granddaughters married one of Wellington Mara's sons.

I always cherished the times I spent on the sideline at football fields with Mr. Rooney at the South Park Fairgrounds, when I was 19, and at Three Rivers Stadium, when I was 38 and 39 and 40. I also stood on the sideline with Mr. Mara during Giants' practices at Yankee Stadium in The Bronx, not far from Fordham, where he'd gone to school, or at Pleasantville, not far from his home in Rye. Pleasantville was the home of Pace University, where the Giants held their summer training camp, and where *Readers Digest* was produced.

It was fitting that Mr. Mara was in a place called Pleasantville. I last spoke to him when I went to Tampa to attend the Super Bowl three years ago. His Giants were playing for the championship. I talked to him for a book I was writing about Mr. Rooney called "The Chief."

His large family surrounded Wellington Mara when he succumbed to cancer at age 89 last week at this home in Rye. It caught my eye when I read that he had been battling skin cancer for over 25 years.

Mr. Mara and I both were Irish with blue eyes. We were both squinting into the sunlight one afternoon on a particularly bright day in Pleasantville. Mr. Mara always had three smiles on his face, one with his mouth and two more with his eyes. They were in a perpetual squint it seemed.

"The Irish were not meant to be out in the sun," he told me one day. "We're fair-skinned, and we're better built to be in peat bogs, caves and other dark places. That may account for why the Irish spend so much time in pubs, taverns and bars." He smiled at his own story.

Mr. Mara had a sense of fairness about him. He knew the difference between right and wrong. He knew the NFL would only be as strong as its weakest member. He had the richest franchise, but he shared the wealth with the Green Bays and Baltimores and Pittsburghs.

It's unlikely the Steelers would have been playing the Baltimore Ravens in a nationally televised game on this Monday night if there were no Wellington Maras showing the way. He helped convince Art Modell and Art Rooney and Carroll Rosenbloom to take their NFL teams into the AFC part of the merged pro football leagues back in 1970.

Modell is often cast as a villain because he later moved his Cleveland team to Baltimore, but it was the only way he could save his franchise. He, too, was a good man. And he spoke of his high regard for Wellington Mara. So did Dan Rooney.

"He was a Giant in the NFL and in life," remarked Rooney.

* * *

One day I took my father-in-law Harvey Churchman, who was visiting from McKeesport, to a New York Giants' practice at Yankee Stadium. We were standing on the sideline, watching Fran Tarkenton take the team through its paces, when I spotted Jim Trimble nearby.

I knew that Trimble, the team's player personnel director, was also from McKeesport and had once played for a semi-pro team called the McKeesport Olympians.

I called out to Trimble and asked him to come over so I could introduce him to my father-in-law. The two of them spoke for quite a long time, sharing McKeesport stories. Later, Alex Webster, the Giants' head coach, came over to the sideline as well, and said hello to Harvey Churchman and made him feel right at home.

After practice, I went into the Giants' dressing room to interview Webster, who had once been a tough running back for the Giants. "Where's your father-in-law?" asked Webster.

"He's waiting for me in the dugout," I told him.

"We can't have that," Webster said. He called out to Emlen Tunnell, the team's defensive backfield coach and once one of its best players. Tunnell, indeed, is enshrined in the Pro Football Hall of Fame. "Emlen, do me a favor and go out and get Jim's father-in-law and bring him in here where it's warm." Tunnell smiled and obliged his boss.

The next thing I knew Harvey Churchman was in the midst of the Giants. That would never happen in today's NFL.

Troy Polamalu's
'Immaculate Interception'

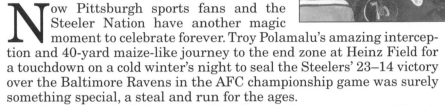

January 2009

Now Pittsburgh sports fans and the Steeler Nation have another magic moment to celebrate forever. Troy Polamalu's amazing interception and 40-yard maize-like journey to the end zone at Heinz Field for a touchdown on a cold winter's night to seal the Steelers' 23–14 victory over the Baltimore Ravens in the AFC championship game was surely something special, a steal and run for the ages.

It may come to be known as "The Immaculate Interception." Troy's theft and run rate in that kind of company. Polamalu played one of his best games ever. If he could ever learn to tackle properly, wrapping up a ball carrier's legs—a lost art these days—he'd be even better, and less likely to suffer a concussion.

Steelers' fans were getting anxious as the Ravens were moving up the field for what appeared to be a game-winning drive in the final moments of this battle of AFC North rivals. All the Ravens needed to break the hearts of the Steeler Nation was a field goal, and their kicker, veteran Matt Stover, is as reliable as any in the game. The Steelers had blown a lot of scoring opportunities throughout the contest for the second Sunday in succession, and continued to make play calls that can only be called baffling. It looked like it was going to cost them a trip to Tampa for the Super Bowl.

Joe Flacco, the rookie quarterback of the Ravens, looked like the second coming of Johnny Unitas with a Baltimore ballclub. This wasn't the Colts, but the Ravens who were once the Browns of Cleveland, and the Ravens have found a home in the Maryland port city that loves its football. Baltimore is more like Pittsburgh than Steelers' fans might believe.

Both Flacco and Unitas had been shunned by Pitt and Pittsburgh, and it looked like Flacco could lead the Ravens to a comeback triumph. I was one of many watching the game on television and pacing the floor because I thought a great season was about to go down the drain with the dirty slush of the city's streets.

That's when Troy Polamalu, the most unlikely football star ever to hit Pittsburgh, came out of nowhere, as he so often does, and reached to the heavens to pick off a pass from Flacco. I think defensive coordinator Dick LeBeau made a defensive change just before that play that put Polamalu in position to make the pick, and perhaps confused young Flacco at the same time. Most of the Steelers receivers and their defensive backs don't make the acrobatic catch that Polamalu pulled out of the gray sky. You know their names. It was the kind of grab we now associate with another former Pitt performer, Larry Fitzgerald, now the NFL's most respected receiver with the Arizona Cardinals.

Polamalu pirouetted to get his balance, did an about face, and found daylight to his right, and zigzagged here and there—it reminded me of a catch-and-run by Mike Ditka of the Chicago Bears against the Steelers at Forbes Field in late November of 1963—and ran 40 yards for a touchdown. He held the ball up with two hands—a gift to God perhaps by the spiritual free safety of the Steelers—like a priest holding a chalice or Communion host on high at a church altar. Pittsburgh went crazy. "I never heard such a loud roar in Heinz Field," recalls Bill Hillgrove, the Steelers' radio play-by-play man. "The place shook. I needed some Dramamine!"

"The Immaculate Reception" of Franco Harris has been rated the No. 1 play in the history of the National Football League, even though it wasn't really a play, more of a combination of coincidence, happenstance, hustle and good fortune than anything else. It was important because it came against the hated Oakland Raiders at Three Rivers Stadium and was the first playoff victory in the franchise's first 41 seasons. But it came in the first round of the playoffs, not for the AFC championship. So this was more of a significant feat. Franco caught the ball that had ricocheted off Frenchy Fuqua/Jack Tatum who had collided while going for a last-second Terry Bradshaw heave, and ran in a straight line—from here to there—for the game-winning touchdown in a 13–7 victory. Bill Mazeroski's home run over the wall in left at Forbes Field in the 7th game of the World Series in 1960 still rates as "the most magic moment" in Pittsburgh sports history because it was the World Series, and the opponent was the heavily-favored New York Yankees. And every one knew what had happened—unlike "the Immaculate Reception"—right away. And it was on local television, which the 1972 AFC playoff game was not.

By now, you have heard the stories about Troy Polamalu's kindness to strangers, how polite and soft-spoken he is, how spiritual and well-mannered he is, how handsome he is, and why he insists on wearing his wiry black hair hanging low on his shoulder pads. I know from personal interaction that he is different, and a great role model. I know he visits the cancer section at Children's Hospital on Fridays during the season to sing and read stories to the kids and hosts some of their parents for dinner. I knew he'd gone with Greek Orthodox priests to holy places in Greece and Turkey. He got into his share of trouble in the streets of southern California as a kid, and moved to live with strict Samoan relatives in the woods of Oregon. Most Samoans are Mormons, but Polamalu moved from Catholicism to become an Orthodox Christian in the Greek Orthodox Church a couple of years ago. He married a beautiful woman named Theodora, whose mother is Greek, and that's what sparked that conversion. Whatever faith he has embraced he has done so—the way he plays football—with great zeal.

When I first met Polamalu, at the start of his second season at St. Vincent College, I came away wondering whether he could survive, let alone thrive, in pro football. He seemed too sweet, maybe too religious, if that's possible. His favorite retreat at St. Vincent's was the campus basilica. It's quite an impressive building, with so much marble and beautiful stained glass windows. Polamalu says he spent more time there than he did on the practice fields. I would bet that most Steelers and some students have never seen the inside of that cathedral-like house of worship, or many of the other intriguing places, such as the hillside cemetery where all the Benedictine priests and brothers are buried.

Polamalu said one of his greatest thrills was being asked to carry a large cross around the exterior of his church on Good Friday in the Orthodox tradition of celebrating that holy day on the calendar.

If praying so much and making the sign of the cross continually can help one perform like Polamalu, it may catch on with the Steeler Nation. It's preferable to the chest-thumping and look-at-me gestures so many athletes perform on routine plays, even after they messed up an earlier maneuver.

This is serious stuff in a region where many have sworn to me that the actions of the Tennessee Titans in stomping on and blowing their noses into Terrible Towels, the magical cloth creation of the late Myron Cope, was an act of desecration to idols—the black and gold towel and the adored and colorful Cope—and, indeed, a sin. A mortal sin, no less, some have said.

Some regard football as a religion, though Polamalu certainly does not. He knows a miracle and a holy act when he sees one. His "Immaculate Interception" came two days after all 150 passengers on a USAirways jetliner survived a crash in New York. The chief pilot, Chesley B. Sullenberger III, age 57, successfully landed the crippled airplane in the Hudson River when it was impossible to get to an airport when the engines failed. His heroic effort was hailed as "A Miracle on the Hudson."

Polamalu's might be "A Miracle on the Three Rivers."

Take your pick. Polamalu and the Steelers' secondary would be challenged at the outset of February by Fitzgerald and Kurt Warner and the Cardinals. (I hate to see Fitzgerald finally mimicking to the Terrell Owens-Chad Johnson look-at-me gestures after a big play.) It's been 61 years since the Cardinals, and then of Chicago, won an NFL championship.

How long ago was that? Pitt's Marshall Goldberg was a defensive back with the Cardinals when they won the NFL title over the Philadelphia Eagles in 1947.

The question may be raised in Tampa about whether or not the Steelers made the right choice in hiring Mike Tomlin as the coach over two of the team's most respected assistant coaches, Ken Whisenhunt and Russ Grimm.

It now appears that the Rooneys could not have gone wrong whatever they did to replace Bill Cowher, but I truly believe they have the right man to lead the Steelers, no matter what happens in the Super Bowl. Mike Tomlin is different, too, and just as special as Troy Polamalu. I like the way Tomlin talks—he's sharp and savvy—and the way he handles himself in the public arena.

I liked it when he said he didn't care how his players evaluated him, that it was his job to evaluate them. And to the writer who posed the question, Tomlin said, "How's your editor doing?"

The Steelers should have beaten the Baltimore Ravens, but who wasn't fearful of a crushing defeat during those final moments? The same scenario could happen with the Arizona Cardinals. I don't believe God gives a hoot about the outcome of football games or any athletic activities, especially free throws in basketball, though a Catholic pal of mine insists that God cares about *all* human activities. I believed the Steelers would win their sixth Super Bowl.

I never bet on ballgames. Then I'd really be pacing the floor, perhaps praying and making the sign of the cross again and again.

TROY

Always happy to be in solitude at St. Vincent College campus.

Happy to be alive, happy to run with interception.

Don't forget Jimmy Allen came
in that famed Steelers '74 draft class

April 2009

The Steelers' 1974 college draft is regarded by many as the greatest draft class in NFL history. Stories about it surface every year at this time when the league conducts its two-day draft over the weekend.

Everybody points to the Steelers selecting four players in the first five rounds who have been inducted into the Pro Football Hall of Fame, namely Lynn Swann, Jack Lambert, John Stallworth and Mike Webster.

Some even add that you have to keep in mind that the Steelers also signed two free agents out of college that same year who became starters for them, in Donnie Shell and Randy Grossman, and valued reserves in Marv Kellum and Rick Druschel.

Most do not mention Jimmy Allen. They should. Allen was picked ahead of Webster on the fourth round—the Steelers had two fourth round choices that year. The Steelers knew they wanted Webster, but they took a chance that he'd still be available on the next round and instead they picked Allen, a defensive back out of UCLA.

They got Webster on the fifth round. Stallworth and Allen were both fourth-round choices, the first of those coming in a trade with the New England Patriots. The Steelers had no third round pick that year.

Allen also proved to be a good pick. He played on special teams and as the nickel-or-dime back on passing downs in his first two seasons. He was a member of two Super Bowl championship teams, and had the rings to prove it.

Like some other rookies in 1974, Allen took advantage of the veterans being out on strike during the early part of the summer training camp, and an opening created when the Steelers dealt away starting cornerback John Rowser. Allen never got enough playing time with the Steelers to satisfy him and he gave them a "play me or trade me" ultimatum. That ploy didn't impress Coach Chuck Noll. The Steelers traded Allen to the Detroit Lions where he became a starter and led them in interceptions during his four-year stay.

So the Steelers selected a guy who was good enough to play eight seasons in the NFL in that 1974 draft in addition to those four Hall of Fame players.

Allen was a tough cookie. Steelers from that era still talk about the time when he got into a fight with Joe Greene in the dining hall at St. Vincent College. "He earned a lot of respect with the players that day," recalled Bud Carson, the Steelers' defensive coordinator at the time. "We had Mel Blount and J.T. Thomas at the corners as starters, but Jimmy played a lot, too. He was a reliable defender."

In his book, *A Steelers' Odyssey*, Andy Russell wrote about that skirmish. Greene had grabbed some food from Allen's plate as he passed by, and Allen responded by slamming his plate against Greene's ear and nearly severed it. Greene was bleeding profusely. Later that night, Greene apologized to Allen for what he did. Greene had been upset with Allen and a few other players who had failed to attend a team beer party. Allen said he knew nothing about the party.

"I was astonished that anyone would pick a fight with Joe Greene," related Russell in his book. Jack Ham had said the same thing when I interviewed him.

Jimmy Allen had a lot of fire, but he had a lot of fun, too. He liked to sing, and he even cut a record during his Detroit days with several of his teammates that was a local hit. There was a time when Allen had so many positive things going on in his life. He was a light-hearted, spirited fellow.

In high school in Los Angeles, Jimmy Allen was a champion swimmer and even competed for a spot on the U.S. Olympic team in 1972. A fellow named Mark Spitz put an end to those Olympic dreams. During the 1972 Olympic Games held in Munich, Germany, Spitz won eight gold medals in swimming, the most by any swimmer at that point in time. Allen was an all-Pac 8 performer at UCLA. In 1973, he returned a punt 101 yards against California that is still a UCLA record.

Allen was born in Clearwater, Florida on March 6, 1952. He moved to Los Angeles to live with his uncle and aunt. He's still in the Los Angeles area. Friends and family members report Jimmy Allen sightings from time to time. In California and in Florida. He shows up at family funerals or drops by someone's house. Then he disappears. He was living in the streets, part of the large LA homeless population.

I spoke on the telephone five years ago with his wife Cora. She thought a lot of his problems stem from his feelings that he was kicked out of the NFL, just cast aside when he felt he could still play. She sounded like a good soul and she was forgiving. She still held out hope he'd come home some day.

And he did. He came home when Cora died this past year. Her mother died a day later when she was informed of her daughter's death. So it was a doubly difficult time for the family. I had sent Cora a book I'd written about the Steelers that had a story about her and her husband in it. It was called *Lambert:The Man in the Middle*. Jimmy Allen saw my telephone number in the book and called me out of the blue one day a few weeks back. He told me he'd read it and he wanted to thank me for what I'd written.

"It's a little more dramatic than my real situation," he said. "I'm fine. Things are moving along. I got some help from the league and I've got a new home. I'll be okay."

Jimmy Allen didn't sound like a guy down on his luck. His voice was strong. He could still sing, he insisted in a spirited way. He sounded upbeat, confident about his situation. It was a real surprise for me to hear from him like that. He called me about six times over a two-week spell. The conversations were short, but welcomed.

JIMMY ALLEN
*He was called
'Spider-Man'*

Jimmy Allen, who
wore No. 45 in his
Steelers' days, took a
bad fall following his
NFL playing days.

JIM ALLEN

STEELERS

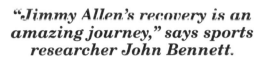

*"Jimmy Allen's recovery is an
amazing journey," says sports
researcher John Bennett.*

**Jimmy Allen enjoys reunion with
his old QB at UCLA, actor Mark
Harmon of NCIS fame.**

Jimmy Allen wasn't on the Steelers when I covered the team. I did not come back to Pittsburgh from New York until the 1979 season to write for *The Pittsburgh Press.* I'd never spoken to the man until he called one night. Yet he talked to me like we were old friends. I was just glad to hear his voice. It was like another resurrection during the Easter season. He told me he'd been close friends with Donnie Shell, John Stallworth and Mel Blount when he was on the ball club. He knew they were still interested in his wellbeing. He hoped to connect with them, let them know he was alive and well. He was now living in Victorville, a small town on the edge of the Mojave Desert, 81 miles northwest of Los Angeles. I looked up Victorville on the Internet, and learned it was a town where Sammy Davis Jr. had a bad car accident in 1954 on the way from Las Vegas to Los Angeles. Davis lost his left eye and wore a glass eye the rest of his life.

Jimmy Allen sounded like he was seeing things differently these days. He was sad about his wife Cora dying. She'd been loyal to him. She said Jimmy had resisted everyone's attempts at helping him. He was too proud; that was part of his problem, she said. She was 15 and he was 16 when they met in high school in Los Angeles. When he left his family, Cora prayed every day that he'd return. She had spoken to several Steelers and their wives whom she was friendly with when Jimmy played for the team. She was 57 when she died.

"When Jimmy was playing pro football, we lived pretty good. We were on top of the world," she told me when we spoke the first time in March of 2004. "Now we're both down on the ground. It's been difficult for me, too. I know it's been difficult for Jim to accept what happened to him. They started calling Jim 'Spider-Man' when he was at UCLA because he caught pass receivers in his web. Like my son said, 'He thought he was Spider-Man.' That was part of his problem, too.

"I remember how happy he was back then. That's the way it was in the beginning. He didn't want anyone to know how difficult his life had become. Hopefully, he can still turn his life around. I guess a lot of players have trouble dealing with their post-career situations. Jimmy is worse off than most of them, I know. I told him it was okay. We'd work things out together. I'm a religious woman and I know what's important. Jimmy always had a wonderful personality. That's why this has been such a shame. He moved here to help his aunts with her kids. That's how he got to LA in the first place."

Jimmy Allen is now 60 and he says he'll be fine. Dwight White, who died at age 58 in June last year, once said, "Most of the guys on our teams of the '70s went on to great success. Only a few have fallen through the cracks." Jimmy Allen was one of those who fell through the cracks. He is a definite dropout. He had a drug problem in the past, but he told me he was clean now. As Eric Clapton sang in one of his early songs, "Nobody Knows You When You're Down and Out."

Jimmy Allen and John Stallworth and Donnie Shell came to the Steelers that same 1974 summer and became close friends. I have spoken to Stallworth and Shell about Jimmy Allen and his situation.

They called Cora on several occasions to find out if they could help. Stallworth and Shell are both deeply religious individuals and led prayer groups and Bible study sessions when they were with the Steelers. They have become quite successful since they left the Steelers. Stallworth is now one of the minority owners in the team, a true success story. I can recall that over 25 players participated in such sessions when I covered the Steelers in 1979. Jon Kolb, Mike Webster and Mel Blount were part of those groups.

When I told Blount how good Allen had sounded when I spoke with him, Blount said, "I'm told you can talk to him one day and he might not remember he talked to you the next day. I'm happy to hear that he called you. That might be a good sign."

A Steelers' fan named John Bennett has been doing his best to aid Allen, or find the right people to do so. Bennett is a high school teacher in Shelburne, Vermont. He grew up a Steelers' fan in Wyckoff, New Jersey back in the 1970s. He was the kind of kid who memorized the Steelers' press guides. Allen came first in four of those guides—the players' biographical sketches were arranged in alphabetic order—so Allen became one of Bennett's favorites. It was Bennett, a few years back, who called Allen's situation to my attention.

For a hobby, Bennett is a member of SABR, an American baseball research organization, and the Pro Football Researchers Association. When he was tracking down some of the lesser known of the Steelers' 1974 draftees, he discovered that no one knew how to get hold of Jimmy Allen. His best friends on the Steelers and Lions had no idea how difficult Allen's life had become until Bennett told them. Bennett got in touch with Cora Allen in Los Angeles. Jimmy and Cora had been separated for ten years back in 2004, but were never divorced. Cora still cared about him and his well-being.

When I visited my younger daughter Rebecca in Los Angeles a year after that, I made some side trips in her car and tried to find Jimmy Allen. I looked for him in some places where he'd been spotted, in LA, in Long Beach and in Santa Monica. I had no luck. Those are pretty big cities and a man who wants to can get lost in them easily.

If you want to get a good idea of what life in the streets is like in LA, I suggest you read the book *The Soloist,* written by Steve Lopez, a columnist for *The Los Angeles Times.* It was made into a movie starring Jamie Foxx and Robert Downey Jr. It's about a gifted musician who becomes a street person in the dark alleys of Los Angeles and a newspaper writer who gets involved with him, and tries to help him recover his music and his life. It helped me appreciate the story of Jimmy Allen. That's' why it was so surprising to hear from him. And then he called again. And again. I'm hoping he'll call again and have some good news to share. He told me he'd sing a song for me some day.

In early 2012, Jimmy Allen was inducted into the Pearce (J.C.) College Hall of Fame. On Saturday night, September 8, 2012, he attended a reunion of his 1973 UCLA football team that included actor Mark Harmon, the Bruins' quarterback.

Dealing with stories about Big Ben
offers big challenge

July 2009

So what do you think of the Roethlisberger story? That's a question people I didn't even know posed to me wherever I went in the wake of the news development that Ben Roethlisberger, the star quarterback of the Pittsburgh Steelers, was accused by a woman who worked at a hotel in Lake Tahoe of raping her in 2008.

Most Steelers' fans, of course, want to believe that Big Ben is innocent of such a trespass. I'd like to believe that as well, but I don't know. I was not there. Right now it's one of those "he said" and "she said" stories.

The story first broke on the TV and radio news reports on the eve of Tuesday, July 21, 2009. I read the story about the allegation the next day. I went to a Pirates-Brewers ballgame at PNC Park that Wednesday with my friend Joe Gordon.

When I covered the Steelers for *The Pittsburgh Press* from 1979 to 1983, Gordon was the public relations director of the team. He was regarded as the best p.r. man in the National Football League during the glory days of the Steelers, when they won four Super Bowls in a six-year span.

When I saw Gordon that afternoon, I said, "This is one day I'm glad I am not covering the Steelers, and I'd bet that you're just as happy you're not handling their public relations."

Gordon smiled and nodded in agreement. He has been retired for about eight years but he remains close with the team's principal owner, Dan Rooney. Gordon was glad he didn't have to get mixed up with this mess. Like me, Gordon hoped Big Ben would be cleared of the accusation.

High-profile athletes often get into similar messes. Some of the stories are true, some are fabricated.

Anyone who gets excited and welcomes such a news story needs some serious help, as far as I am concerned. The Steelers were set to open their summer training camp at St. Vincent College that weekend and there would be much interest in Roethlisberger, in particular, as the team prepared to defend its National Football League title.

So far, the guys who cover the Steelers' beat on a regular basis were not the ones writing the stories regarding Roethlisberger. Regular reporters get to do the dirty work. That's so the players don't harbor any bad feelings with the beat guys in the aftermath of such messy encounters. It's so they don't get shut out of stories the rest of the season.

I recalled that I had spoken to Jim Wexell, a free-lance writer who authored a fine book called *Steeler Nation* the previous year. This was before Ben got in trouble with his well-publicized encounters with women while out of town. This was during a holiday season book fair at the Heinz History Center in December of 2008. Wexell said that someone should write a book about Ben Roethlisberger. He thought that an investigative reporter such as Bill Moushy, now on the journalism faculty at Point Park University, could write such a book. Moushy had just authored a behind-the-scenes book about James Harrison of the Steelers. "No one covering the team could tell all the stories," said Wexell, "because Ben wouldn't talk to them anymore."

I got caught in the middle of such difficult stories during my career as a sportswriter for dailies in Miami, New York and Pittsburgh. It was never any fun.

I wrote my share of tough stories, especially when I was younger and thought I knew so much, but tended to take more of a middle-of-the-road approach as I aged.

There were stories involving Terry Bradshaw, Lenny Dawson—both Steelers quarterbacks during their Hall of Fame careers—and Jack Lambert, a Hall of Fame linebacker for the Steelers. None of those stories were about sexual conduct.

I remember getting a phone call around one o'clock in the morning from the night desk at *The Press* asking me to call Bradshaw at his home. There were rumors making the rounds that he was having problems in his marriage to the former Olympian ice skating star Jo Jo Starbuck. This was in 1981 or 1982.

I said I would not call Bradshaw at his home at that hour of the day to discuss such a personal matter. Besides, I did not have Bradshaw's home number. I didn't have any of the Steelers' home phone numbers. I had ample opportunity all week long to see them before and after practice and talk to them as much as I'd like. I saw no reason or need to call them at home. That was their time.

Bradshaw survived that storm with Starbuck as it turned out and they remained married for a few years after that. Eventually, they did get a divorce. Bradshaw married again and that also ended in divorce. He has been divorced three times. His marital difficulties didn't keep him from winning four Super Bowls or being a big success as a TV football analyst.

I was writing for *The Miami News* in January of 1970 and covering Super Bowl III in New Orleans between the NFL's Minnesota Vikings and the AFL's Kansas City Chiefs. It was the last such championship games pitting the title teams of the two warring professional football leagues.

The Vikings started the week as 3-point favorites and the odds went up to 9 points by mid-week. This sparked stories in the gambling world about why the odds were changing. The Chiefs were often taken off the betting books during the '60s because there was some insider suspicion that the team's quarterback Lenny Dawson was in cahoots with known gamblers.

A Detroit gambler named Don "Dicey" Dawson, who was no relation to Lenny Dawson, often boasted to his buddies in the betting world that he was a good friend of Lenny Dawson and often spoke to him on the phone. He suggested he had solid inside information about the Chiefs and their opponents.

NFL Commissioner Pete Rozelle policed gambling allegations closely during his career. He thought it was critical that the league be above such shenanigans. It was important to maintain the league's competitive integrity. He had checked out the Dawson story several times and nothing ever materialized.

But here it was the week before the Super Bowl with the nation's sports media massed in New Orleans and such stories of Dawson being linked to gambling resurfaced.

My boss in Miami, John Crittenden, looked like and approached sports in a bulldog fashion. He wanted me to dig deep and come up with stories on Dawson. I liked Dawson. He had been a backup quarterback for the Steelers in 1957 and 1958, playing behind Bobby Layne.

It was Layne who had introduced him in the first place to Don Dawson. Layne knew Don Dawson from his days in Detroit as the quarterback of the Lions. Guys like Don Dawson are always on the scene in the pro and college sports world. They get around. They know everyone. It's their business to know everyone.

There are still stories on the Internet attesting that Bobby Layne bet on pro football games, and may have been affecting the outcomes or the final score. There are stories on the Internet accusing former Steelers' quarterback Neil O'Donnell of dumping Super Bowl XXX against the Dallas Cowboys at the outset of 1996.

That's because O'Donnell, who had the lowest interception-to-pass ratio in the league during that 1995 season, threw two interceptions into the outstretched arms of Cowboys' defensive back Larry Brown with no Steelers in the same zip code.

Such stories have been found to be without any substance by the NFL.

Lenny Dawson, by the way, directed the Chiefs to an upset victory over the Vikings in Super Bowl III and was named the game's MVP and the matter of any gambling tie-ins disappeared.

When I left New York to come to Pittsburgh in 1979 I was determined to try and take a positive approach to covering the Steelers. I sensed that the town was madly in love with the Steelers, and wasn't interested in anyone undermining that faith.

About a week after I was in Pittsburgh, I learned that Jack Lambert, the star linebacker of the team, had been attacked by thugs in a downtown nightspot called The Happy Landing. These were nasty guys and they actually threatened to slice the tendons in Lambert's scrawny legs so he could never play football again. This was serious stuff.

I also learned that my competitor on the beat for the *Post-Gazette* had wind of the incident, as did the police reporter and the editor of *The Pittsburgh Press*.

I attempted to call Lambert on the telephone to get his side of the story, but he refused to return the calls. I called him at least three times. I went to Chuck Noll, the coach of the team, to get his side of the story. I wanted his help in dealing with the difficult story, but such help was not forthcoming.

Noll was annoyed and disturbed that I was digging into this story. When I had enough information, I wrote the story. It got me off to a bad start with Noll and especially with Lambert. When the Steelers reported to training camp that summer at St. Vincent, Lambert did a lot of sneering and snorting in my direction when I joined other writers in talking to him after practice.

Lambert let it be known he was not interested in talking to me. I asked him to let me visit his room and we talked it out. Our agreement was basically that if I wrote another bad story about him he'd be kicking my butt. Enough said. Lambert and I got along famously from then on. Until he retired, and then he changed. And then he reverted to ignoring anyone connected with the media for the most part.

He wanted to separate himself from the NFL scene and he has successfully done so, often to the chagrin of most of his teammates, the Steelers' organization and, most of all, his faithful fans.

My stories about the incident involving Lambert—the thug slammed a glass mug against Lambert's ear at bar-side—were ones I later wanted to take back. No one at the office said anything about "good work" or "a job well done." I was given no prizes for my scoop. In truth, it wasn't worth it.

There were other stories—one involving a player who was cut accusing Dolphins' head coach George Wilson of racism—that did more harm than good. I thought I had both sides of the story, but the blaring headline about racism did me in. I didn't write the headline and it's the headline that usually causes the problem.

It upset and scared George Wilson's wife. I had the impression that George Wilson's mission in life was to keep his wife happy at all times. So I was the bad guy. Wilson screamed in my face the next day at the team's training camp in Boca Raton, Florida.

Some of the players stood around as he hollered at me. He suggested that it wouldn't be a bad idea for one of them to throw me in a lake nearby. I did a quick mental measure on the distance between me and the lake. Bob Griese, the team's quarterback, and Larry Csonka, the team's fullback, were behind Wilson when he shouted at me.

Griese and Csonka are both in the Football Hall of Fame now, but they were about to begin a season that would result in a 3–10–1 record and cost Wilson his job. The rap on Griese at the time was that he didn't have a strong arm. I wrote a story in the next day's newspaper about Wilson shouting at me. It was run along with a close-up photo of Wilson shouting from the sideline in a game the previous season, so readers would know what it would look like to have Wilson shouting at you.

Plus, he once considered a pro boxing career and once wiped out two would-be tacklers while playing for the Chicago Bears in a rout of the Washington Redskins in the NFL championship game. I wrote that I was hoping Griese wouldn't get an itchy trigger finger and do what his boss suggested and toss me into the nearby lake.

Noting it was 50 yards away, I wrote "surely Griese would have tossed me short of the lake and into the rocks that surrounded it." That's the way you write when you're in your 20s and think it's cool to be a wise guy.

I cringed when I saw KDKA-TV reporters on the scene with their cameramen at Lake Tahoe that week in July of 2009, and showing the window outside the 17th floor window where Big Ben stayed while playing in a celebrity golf tournament at Lake Tahoe a year earlier.

I had been watching some of that tournament on TV while visiting our younger daughter in Los Angeles two weeks earlier. I had paid close attention to how Big Ben was doing, as well as Danny Marino. Someone gave Marino a football to sign. Then he tossed it with that famous form of his to a young man racing down a nearby beach. He tossed it with ease about 40 yards and the young man caught the ball in full stride chest-high. I had to smile.

That Marino can still throw a football, I thought. It's amazing that, without any warm-up, he can fling a football like that. He's a gifted young man. When he was playing at Pitt there were rumors making the rounds that he was fooling around with illegal drugs.

It's the main reason he was such a late draft pick in the first round. More than 20 teams, including the Steelers, passed up on the chance to draft him. Marino turned out to be a model citizen in the NFL.

From the start, I thought Big Ben was trying his best to be a model citizen in the NFL. I thought he tried to do all the right things. He became so popular in Pittsburgh that it was impossible for him to go out in public anywhere without getting mobbed.

Everyone wanted a piece of Big Ben, and I think it caused him to back off a little, and retreat a bit from the public. He's a single young man, not as handsome as Marino, but not bad either. He's tall and makes more than $20 million a year playing football.

He's still up for grabs. I have no idea what happened in his hotel room in Lake Tahoe, and that's what I tell people. But I know the stories about other champion athletes such as Kobe Bryant and Mike Tyson. So anything is possible. Big Ben is Big Ben because he's not afraid to take risks. No one was going to tell him he had to wear a protective helmet when he rode his motorcycle, even after he was almost killed while riding it though the streets of Pittsburgh.

Big Ben is Big Ben because he's big and brassy. Let's just hope he didn't get stupid.

> *"Our greatest glory is not in never falling, but in rising every time we fall."*
> **—Confucius**

Big Ben begins comeback
by helping a good cause

June 2010

It was not a good day for golf. It was chilly and raining hard most of this Monday in mid-May of 2010. But Ben Roethlisberger appeared, as promised, just in time for the shotgun start at the Southpointe Golf Club in Canonsburg. He joined his foursome at the designated hole and did his part.

Roethlisberger had been a regular participant in the Hoge-Ward-Starks Celebrity Golf Classic to raise money for the Highmark Caring Place. It's a program designed to help grieving children who have suffered a loss. Maybe Ben could identify with that cause more than ever before. There were a lot of Steelers' fans angry and disgusted with Ben for bringing shame on the franchise with his selfish behavior, but there were others willing to help him get back on track.

Some of those included his teammates, and that's particularly interesting because, for whatever reasons, Ben has not been that popular with many of his teammates through the years. They know they need him at his best if they are ever to win another Super Bowl. They did that twice with Roethlisberger behind center, and performing in an MVP manner. Roethlisberger did not join in the fun before or after this celeb golf outing, leaving former Steelers' running back Merril Hoge, Hines Ward and Max Starks to host the participants in social settings. Roethlisberger tried his best to stay out of camera range. He's still not sure what he's supposed to do. He doesn't know how to act around anyone these days, ever since he was twice accused of sexual assault and all the attending media coverage. He had not yet been cleared by the NFL Commissioner's office to resume practicing with the Steelers. So he probably felt out of it.

He has been suspended for the first six games of the 2010 NFL season and that would be reduced to four games if league officials see an improvement in his behavior and demeanor.

I've attended a dozen of these golf outings sponsored by Highmark and I have seen Ben being as playful as a big kid, driving his golf cart too fast, up and down steep hills and putting it into a complete spin, but Roethlisberger was much more reserved on this outing, according to those who were there. I recall four years ago that there was a huge sign posted in the window of an office building along one of the fairways that read: BEN, WILL YOU MARRY ME? I took a picture of it and still have it in my files.

There were no marriage proposals this time around the course. There were no signs hailing his walk in the rain. He wore proper rain gear, like the other golfers, and had an umbrella in his bag. The day probably fit his mood. It was his first public appearance since he drew a suspension from the league office.

73

"Hopefully, he's putting aside his problems," said Max Starks, the left tackle whose job it is to protect Ben from being blindsided on the football field, and maybe on the golf course as well. "He's a great teammate and a great friend and he's putting aside personal issues to be out here to support us. It shows you the kind of character he has. He's out here supporting a good cause." The Steelers have always supported a great many local and national causes. This shows a more positive side of the Steelers than some of the unseemly incidents involving some individuals. There were former players also participating in a fund-raiser that day at a golf outing Joe Walton, the Robert Morris University head football coach with strong NFL ties. Sam Zacharias, a close friend and business associate of Andy Russell, says the Steelers don't get enough credit for their efforts in supporting good causes.

Starks might not convince everyone with his comments in support of Roethlisberger and his character, but he has personally shown a proper interest in supporting good causes. The late Dwight White, a member of the Steel Curtain defensive line, introduced Starks to some officials from the Pittsburgh Foundation and, several years back at the age of 24, Starks started his own program in the Pittsburgh Foundation. It focuses on children's literacy and education.

He had benefited as a young child by his membership in the Boys and Girls Club of Orlando. "It was just the right thing to do," Starks said of his efforts to establish a foundation. "So many people have helped me along the way. My Mom and Dad have always instilled that in me—service to others." Hines Ward, a stalwart Steelers' receiver, has been a big booster of the Caring Foundation and other charitable causes. He's even set up programs in South Korea, his mother's home country. Reflecting on Roethlisberger's behavior problems, Ward said, "The suspension is what it is. What's done is done. We're working on getting things back on the right track. He's been a part of this cause for years. For him to come out in the rain like this speaks volumes for him."

Roethlisberger's return was the lead story that evening on KDKA-TV news and Patrice King Brown, Ken Rice and John Shumway all weighed in on the report. That's the way it's been the past few years on Pittsburgh television stations. The Steelers have become more than just a sports story. There is too much coverage on a year-round basis. Reports on some players' every move have become par for the course.

I remember the Roethlisberger that first came to the Steelers after they drafted him on the first round in 2004. I first met him at the Mellon Mario Lemieux Celebrity Invitational golf tournament at Nevillewood. He had not yet played a game for the Steelers and already he was appearing at fund-raising events here.

I thought Ben bent over backwards in the beginning to get involved in so many worthwhile causes in the Pittsburgh area, maybe too many. He seemed eager to please, eager to get involved, and he enjoyed the attention he drew for such appearances. I remember seeing him play for the Steelers' basketball team that insurance man Tom O'Malley Jr. coordinates during the off-season. Ben can play basketball and he was a willing participant in signing autographs at halftime.

Even then, he had his personal bodyguard close at his side to assure his safety.

I can't forget that Ben Roethisberger. I don't know what went wrong with him since then. Too much money, too much free time, too much media attention, too many fawning fans. He forgot who he was when he was growing up in Findlay, Ohio.

A lot of Steelers' fans are furious with Ben Roethisberger. They think he blew a great career. They believe he betrayed the Steelers and the Steeler Nation. They believe he brought dishonor to the Rooney family and the team's much respected legacy. Many of them want the Steelers to get rid of him. He directed the team to two Super Bowl championships but many of them no longer care about his ability.

Dan Rooney knows the history of the Steelers too well, and knows that they gave away too many quarterbacks who are now enshrined in the Pro Football Hall of Fame. Roethisberger still has a shot at being in the Hall of Fame, though he has made it much more difficult to draw the voting support of sportswriters who are sick of him as well. I've had so many people come up to me when I am doing book signings lately, and tell me of their distaste for everything about Big Ben.

At this point, he has to be the leading candidate for the NFL Comeback Player of the Year award. Last year at this time, interestingly enough, I would have said that the leading candidate would have been Michael Vick. I recall that three years ago there was a summer football camp that I came across while visiting William & Mary, the alma mater of Steelers' coach Mike Tomlin, in which Roethlisberger replaced Michael Vick as the featured player at the camp.

Vick backed off because of all the bad publicity he had gotten for being involved in a dog fighting venture in Virginia. Big Ben was a big-time replacement at the time. Now this summer Big Ben had to give way as the featured attraction at his own summer camp and his place was taken by Mike Tomlin. It's interesting how these life cycles go.

I am rooting for the redemption of Ben Roethlisberger. I think he can turn things around. He may never ever enjoy the fan appeal and approval he had before he besmirched his record with his outrageous nighttime behavior, but he can gain back some of the positive aspects of being the quarterback of the Pittsburgh Steelers.

Chuck Noll's thoughts on Immaculate Reception:

"A lot of guys started believing after that. It was a gradual thing. I didn't have to sell it to them as much as it had to be sold to the fans. There was such a negative feeling about the team for so long. There was a lot of that S.O.S. stuff (same ol' Steelers) out there. If you went out in the community you were always hearing that negative stuff. It really took something like that play to sell it to the fans."

Mel is Blount about rules
for raising children

November 2009

When Mel Blount returned to his boyhood home of Vidalia, Georgia, he loved to spend time with his mother, who was 102 years old in 2009. "She's in good health, and fine physically and mentally," said Blount. "Every time I go home, she lectures me. I can count on it. I love her and respect her and, as far as she is concerned, I am still her baby."

Blount was the youngest of 11 children raised on that farm in Vidalia, which is famous for raising those "sweet onions" as well as a Pro Football Hall of Fame defensive back. "I grew up with a mother and a father," Blount continued, "and there was lots of love and just as much discipline. There were rules and expectations, and I have profited from that early experience ever since."

Blount—it's hard to believe—is now 64 years old. At 6-4, 215 pounds, Blount is still a formidable figure. He looks even taller in his signature white cowboy hat and just the way he carries himself. Everyone says he looks like he could still play for the Steelers. He smiles broadly at the thought. "That's a nice thought," he'll say, "but I don't think so. I'm happy out on the ranch, riding my horses and looking after the kids."

There are about 25 boys at any given time in residence at the Mel Blount Youth Home in Taylorstown, out in Washington County. "It's a 24/7 operation; it never shuts down," he says. "My wife TiAnda is a blessing because she makes it all work. We have about 30 employees looking after the place and the boys. These are boys who've had some behavioral problems and we're trying to turn them around and prepare them to be productive citizens.

"It's a Christian-based program. You have to study the Bible, and you have to go to church on Sunday." Blount was offering these remarks as the honored guest at the 34th Annual Willie Stargell Memorial MVP Awards Banquet presented by Champion Enterprises in conjunction with Five Starr Corporation.

He was standing tall at the podium at LeMont Restaurant atop Mt. Washington with a spectacular view of downtown Pittsburgh in the background. The lights were on at Heinz Field, where Pitt was in the process of defeating Notre Dame in a nationally televised college football game. The lights were also on at PNC Park because of the TV overhead shots and the scene resembled a Christmas display with lights twinkling everywhere.

The Penguins were beating the Boston Bruins in overtime at the Mellon Arena this same Saturday night. The weather was perfect and the outlook was positive for the next day's meeting between the Steelers and the Cincinnati Bengals. The Steelers would lose a tough one but we should all regard the weekend as a gift because the sun came out and lots of good things were going on in our town.

Bill Neal, the president of Champion Enterprises, praised Blount for remaining in Pittsburgh after his playing career when he could have gone elsewhere and been successful in business and television. "He decided to stay and help disadvantaged boys," said Neal. "He bought some land out in a rural area and opened it up to kids. When somebody takes time out of their life to do something like this you have to applaud him."

J. T. Thomas, a former teammate in the Steelers' defensive secondary and a regional restaurant operator, also praised Blount for being the best at his position—a man who actually caused rules changes in the NFL because he dominated wide receivers so much with his bump and run tactics—and the best at what he is doing to assist children to straighten out their lives.

Blount offered a serious message to his audience.

"We've got some serious problems in our communities," Blount began. "We've become immune to what's happening in our neighborhoods. Like we've been vaccinated not to let it bother us. I applaud the inner-city efforts of Champions Enterprises because they're trying to make a difference.

"The system we have now doesn't work. You can go to the Shuman Center and see a lot of men who look like us. You can go to the jail here and see a lot of people who look like us. We talk to young women who say they can't find young men who meet their standards as a possible mate. In some ways, we think we've arrived. But, in other ways, we have a lot of work to do.

"We've got to regroup. That's what we used to say at halftime when things didn't go well in the first half. We have to support organizations like Champions Enterprises. We've got to get serious about the challenges we have."

Blount has always been one of my favorite Steelers. He has been challenged in many ways in his efforts to assist young men to prosper. He's made some mistakes along the way, but his heart was always in the right place.

He was a valued member of a great team. He and many of his teammates are honored in the Pro Football Hall of Fame. They set high standards for the Steelers of today. Blount is a big man with a big smile and a big heart, and we are lucky this Louisiana stalwart came our way.

Mel Blount's mother has since passed away.

> **"We've become immune to what's happening in our neighborhoods. Like we've become vaccinated not to let it bother us."**
> **—Mel Blount**

Blount believes trust is the key

Jim O'Brien drew praise from former Steelers' star Mel Blount, the main honoree at the Champions, Inc. awards banquet.

"There aren't too many sports writers that athletes trust," Blount told the audience, "so Jim O'Brien holds a special place in our hearts. We knew we could trust him with our stories and our words. He preferred to call positive attention our way rather than write negative stories. I've always admired that in him. His books certify our accomplishments and keep us alive."

Blount and his former teammate J.T. Thomas both offered hugs when they greeted O'Brien at the MVP Awards Banquet. "That means a lot to me," said O'Brien. "I think we experienced a special time together in Pittsburgh. I believe I kept my integrity as a journalist, but I enjoyed the company of these special men at the same time. Those Steelers of the '70s were quite special and they still rate respect from the current players."

Jim O'Brien

John Stallworth and Mel Blount, both members of the Pro Football Hall of Fame and contributors to four Super Bowl titles for the Steelers, are reunited at Blount's annual celebrity dinner to raise funds for the Mel Blount Youth Home. Blount believes Stallworth is "a real success story" as an entrepreneur and a minority owner of the Steelers.

Did Steelers miss
anyone in the NFL draft?

Kevin Colbert

George Gojkovich

What did you think of the Steelers' draft? This question replaced inquiries about what I thought about Ben Roethlisberger and Santonio Holmes in my travels. I've never been a big fan of the draft madness. When I was working at *The Pittsburgh Press* and covering the Steelers I dreaded the draft stories, both in advance of the event and what followed. I always thought it was an over-rated and over-written and over-orated story. Who knows what it really means?

To me, it's another form of Fantasy Football and I don't participate in that past-time either, and I avoid all conversations on the subject. I fear you can get warts from that kind of indulgence. Fans get so caught up in Fantasy Football they think they could be a general manager for the Steelers. Then again, the Steelers never had a general manager until they decided to change Kevin Colbert's title in 2011.

I was fortunate when I was at *The Press* to have a younger side-kick on the beat named John Clayton and he couldn't get enough of the draft dialogue. He loved calling all the scouts and player personnel people throughout the NFL and finding out what they were thinking as the draft approached. He had a telephone in his ear round the clock. It was like CIA work. He must have loved it even more when he got his first cell phone. Clayton and Mel Kiper, Jr. managed to carve out careers for themselves, at ESPN, as well as national notoriety, for their zealousness and reliability in the draftnik world. I give them both credit for creating something satisfying and rewarding for themselves. They can be proud of what they have accomplished.

I just never got excited about it. I tuned into the NFL draft coverage on television every so often, just to see how it was going. As it wound down, I heard Kiper revealing his Top Ten for next year's draft class and that's when I was sure I had heard and seen enough.

I was more interested in reflecting on the Penguins' two over-time playoff contests—the disheartening defeat in three overtimes at home on Thursday and then the exciting overtime victory at Ottawa on Saturday night. The Pirates managed to make history with their worst loss in the history of the franchise by dropping a 20–0 verdict to the Milwaukee Brewers at PNC Park.

Those who stayed till the end of the Penguins' three-overtime loss or the Pirates' 20–0 massacre can always say they were there. They sat in on something special in both respects.

To me, all of that was more interesting than the NFL draft. I was also watching the NBA playoffs and some major league baseball games on television. I pay little attention to the Penguins until the playoffs. I watch all the Steelers' games from end to end. I attend about 15 of 16 games of the Pirates at PNC Park because I know there will be no playoffs.

Frankly, I never heard of Maurkice Pouncey, the center from Florida that the Steelers selected in the first round, until I read a mock draft in the newspaper the day before the three-day draft began. Ed Bouchette was right on the money with his prediction that Pouncey would be the Steelers' first pick. (*And he was a great pick.*)

I would have preferred that the Steelers selected another Florida player, quarterback Tim Tebow, with their No. 1 pick.

I will get criticized for suggesting as much, but hear me out. First off, I may be dead wrong with my opinions about the draft but they are my opinions and I offer them with that in mind. It will take a few years to see who's right and who's dead wrong.

I would never draft a center, a guard or any offensive lineman with my first pick. It is much more difficult to determine the potential of an interior lineman on either side of the ball than it is the so-called skill positions. It's easier to determine whether a guy can throw the ball, run the ball, or catch the ball than it is if he can block and tackle.

Anyone who tells you they watch the center on every play is a football snob, more interested in telling you what a smart and sophisticated fan he is.

I think Tebow is a winner, on and off the field, and one of the most versatile players available in the draft. He can play more than one position and he could be a change-up from Ben Roethlisberger. He might be a good influence on Big Ben and help convert him to being the way he was when he first joined the Steelers out of Miami of Ohio University. Big Ben was a good guy at the beginning of his Steelers' career. The scouts say Tebow doesn't throw the ball properly. He brings his throwing arm down too low at the start of this throwing motion. Coaches want to teach him how to throw the ball in a more conventional manner. Those coaches, of course, are not in the Hall of Fame, either.

Hey, for the record, Danny Marino didn't throw the ball right. Neither did Johnny Unitas. Nor Bobby Layne. George Blanda didn't throw the ball in a tight spiral. Joe Montana and Bob Griese didn't go deep too often. All of them are in the Hall of Fame and all of them were winners. I think Tebow is a winner. He beat more important teams than Jimmy Clausen of Notre Dame. I think Clausen lucked out, by the way, getting selected as Carolina's first pick in the second round. (Of course, the arrival of first round pick Cam Newton changed all that.)

I think Sean Lee of Upper St. Clair got lucky, too. He wanted to be drafted on the second round by the Steelers, but he was drafted a few picks later by the Dallas Cowboys. The Cowboys are the richest team in the NFL and have the finest facilities and Sean can still wear the same blue and white outfits he came by at Penn State. Sean Casey, another Upper St. Clair standout on and off the field, can tell Lee that playing in your hometown can be overrated. Casey was a bigger deal in Cincinnati than he was in Pittsburgh.

I think the Steelers would have been smart to draft Tim Tebow, Sean Lee and Dorin Dickerson of Pitt. They are all football players. You find a place for good football players. There's no doubt in my mind they will succeed in the NFL.

Sometimes I think the Steelers and other pro teams outsmart themselves. They overlook kids in their own backyard. The Steelers passed on Danny Marino and took Gabe Rivera. They thought they needed a strong defensive lineman. Rivera was the real deal until he was left paralyzed in an auto accident during his rookie season. But quarterbacks like Marino have a magic about them and they don't come along too often.

I watched DeJuan Blair playing ball for the San Antonio Spurs one night and the announcers were raving about then rookie front-liner from Pitt. Blair and Sam Young both proved at Pitt they could play with the best players in college basketball, yet the pro scouts didn't think they were first-round caliber choices. Blair and Young will both have long careers in the NBA.

The Steelers had someone scouting at every Pitt home game when Marino was playing for the Panthers. You had to know he had a special gift. I was in the press box one day when Curtis Martin ran for over 200 yards against Texas. There were two Steelers' scouts there that day. Yet Martin was taken in the third round by the New England Patriots. He later played for the New York Jets. Now he is in the Pro Football Hall of Fame.

Going back to Joe Schmidt, another Hall of Fame player, the Steelers have overlooked local players. I think scouts don't feel like they are working unless they come up with players from faraway places. I don't care what the Steelers' scouts say about Jason Worilds, their No. 2 pick from Virginia Tech, but I'll bet Sean Lee is a better linebacker in the NFL. I've seen Lee play since he was in high school—a standout two-way performance in Bethel Park stays in my mind—and I know he can play the game.

Didn't Jack Ham rave about Lee's ability the past few years? Certainly Ham knows a good linebacker when he sees one. The Steelers had one of the greatest groups of linebackers when they had Jack Ham, Jack Lambert and Andy Russell. You almost never see a white player on an NFL defensive unit these days. Can't white ballplayers make the grade anymore? Can't they play the game?

I honestly believe there is a bias—and I am not talking about racism here—in college and pro football regarding white prospects. If a prospect is white and he is a running back, for instance, there are doubts raised that he can't be the real thing. I know coaches who can attest to this.

One is always hearing that there are not enough black coaches or administrators in the NFL, or other pro leagues, but no one ever suggests publicly that there are not enough white players in the respective leagues. There is a concern now, for instance, that there are not enough black ballplayers in baseball. Where have you gone, Jackie Robinson?

The Steelers have not cared about the color of a ballplayer since Chuck Noll came to town. The Rooneys never cared. They were always an equal opportunity employer.

I was driving through Oakland with a young man who is a sports enthusiast and we were early for an awards luncheon at the P.A.A. So I went in a different direction, just slightly off the regular route, so I could show my young friend the boyhood home of Danny Marino. I pointed out how he lived in a humble but comfortable home in South Oakland—similar to the one in which Joe Montana grew up in Monongahela. He lived across the street from St. Regis Grade School where he started to play football. He could also walk to Central Catholic High School and Pitt. The late Art Rooney Sr. used to tell his coaches, "We've got to keep that kid in Pittsburgh."

But they didn't. I think Dan Marino was better off in Miami. He and Don Shula were the perfect team. The weather in Miami is more suitable for a quarterback than Pittsburgh.

Now Frazier Field, a sandlot venue just down Parkview Avenue from the Marino home in South Oakland, is called Dan Marino Field.

Through the years, I have thought that the Steelers missed out on a lot of great prospects at Pitt and Penn State. Once upon a time, back in the formative years of the franchise, they took too many players from Pitt and Penn State as well as Duquesne when they had a big-time football team. Then they went the other way.

You asked me what I thought of the Steelers' draft and now I have told you. I hope the Steelers get their act together in time to compete for a title again this fall. I'm rooting for Big Ben to make a big comeback in every way.

Lessons learned in sports still come into play

"The lessons I learned while playing basketball for the Citadel Bulldogs from 1963 to 1967 have proven priceless to me as both a writer and a man. I have a sense of fair play and sportsmanship. My work ethic is credible and you can count on me in the clutch.

"When given an assignment, I carry it out to completion, my five senses lit up in concentration. I believe with all my heart that athletics is one of the finest preparations for most of the intricacies and darknesses a human life can throw at you.

"Athletics provide some of the richest fields of both metaphor and cliché to measure our lives against the intrusions and aggressions of other people. Basketball forced me to deal head-on with my inadequacies and terrors with no room for tolerance or evasion.

"Though it was a long process, I learned to honor myself for what I accomplished in a sport where I was overmatched and out of my league. I never once approached greatness, but toward the end of my career, I was always in the game."
—Author Pat Conroy
from "My Losing Season" (2002)

Sports put a smile on our faces
during difficult times

February 2009

A lot of people are down in the dumps these days because of the bleak economic picture that is painted for us daily by the media. In Pittsburgh, a lot of people turn to sports to brighten their day. The success of their sports teams raises their spirits and gives them something to feel good or boast about. Some choose other forms of entertainment to help get them through the day. Some, and these include sports fans, turn to God to give them hope.

The Steelers have carried us this far, and came through in a big way when they won Super Bowl XLIII, overcoming the Arizona Cardinals at Tampa Stadium to win a record-setting sixth Super Bowl title. Now we need another savior. The Penguins have been a big disappointment to date. Pitt basketball is the best sports antidote in town right now.

The Pitt men's basketball team is now the best sports team in town to follow. The Pitt women's basketball team isn't far behind. Duquesne is doing fine in both respects, and so is Robert Morris, but nothing compares with the excitement and entertainment to be found these days at the Petersen Events Center on the Pitt campus.

Pitt has its own economic challenges right now, as does Penn State, knowing they are not going to continue to get state aid and that tuition could go up again, but everybody forgets about that for awhile when they are carrying on at The Pete during a basketball game.

The Panthers defeated West Virginia in a men's game on a winter's night in early 2009 before a raucous sellout crowd. This match-up doesn't have the same intensity it once did between these traditional rivals. Nowadays it's just another Big East battle, but such games provide a brand of basketball that is the best seen in Pittsburgh in more than 40 years, or since Connie Hawkins was flying high at the head of the Pittsburgh Pipers when they won the first American Basketball Association title in 1968.

Yes, it's that good. We don't have an ABA or an NBA team in town anymore, but we don't need one. Big East basketball is as good as it gets, whether it's the women or men who are meeting on the basketball court. (*ACC basketball will be just as good.*)

My wife Kathleen and I have bought season tickets for men's and women's basketball this winter, and enjoy them both on different levels. The atmosphere at the women's games is more relaxed than the men's, and a lot less expensive for family entertainment.

Agnus Berenato thanks everybody who comes, and embraces a great number of them as they are coming and going. She and Jamie Dixon, a disciple of Ben Howland, have done so much to make Pitt basketball relevant in every respect.

Dan Rooney, the chairman and primary owner of the Pittsburgh Steelers, and his wife, Pat, were in attendance at this Monday's night game with West Virginia. They sat just above the "PITTSBURGH" in the University of Pittsburgh sign in front of some of the best midcourt seats. They were guests of John Pelusi, a former Pitt football standout who is now a commercial real estate magnate and a member of Pitt's board of trustees, and his wife Kathy.

Across from them, sitting with the school's top boosters at courtside, was Jeff Reed, the Steelers' place-kicker and one of the heroes in their playoff drive and Super Bowl triumph. Reed's shock of dyed blond hair was a favorite with Pitt students who cheer him and offer high fives as he passes them.

Anyone associated with the Steelers is cheered wherever they appear in Pittsburgh these days, so a roar went up when Reed and the Rooneys were introduced and shown on the jumbo screen above the court. They enjoyed the attention, and were warmed by the wonderful reception.

I've seen Ben Roethlisberger and Santonio Holmes at earlier Pitt games and they both received a resounding ovation from the crowd. Former Steelers defensive back (and a West Virginia alum) Mike Logan of McKeesport was at the Pitt-WVU game. So was Steelers' personnel man Doug Whaley, a former Pitt and Upper St. Clair High star.

"Love your hair, Jeff!" hollered one student with an equally bizarre hairdo.

(This was before Reed, Roethlisberger and Holmes all got into trouble with poor judgment and boorish behavior off the field.)

Reed had become a regular at courtside but looks like he'd be more at home in the student section known as The Oakland Zoo. I'm a traditionalist, perhaps an old fogy, so I don't approve of the Pitt students' behavior at basketball games. They jump up and down on their feet the entire game, trying to distract the opposing team. They want to live up to their collective billing as Pitt's "Sixth Man." They are not watching the game; they are a part of the game.

They have a tired act of holding newspapers in front of their faces when the starters for the opposing teams are introduced. They holler out an insult to each player and the coach, and then toss their crumbled newspapers into the air. For most of them, it's the only time their hands touch a newspaper all week.

They boo the other team when it appears on the floor. This is right after the p.a. announcer has reminded us about Pitt's sportsmanship policy and how fans are to behave.

The women are much kinder to their opponents. The Pitt women's team was a Top 20 team, too, as are many of their opponents, so it was top-notch basketball. And there was singing and dancing in the aisles and it was just a lot of good-natured fun.

Anything that perks up people and raises their spirits—short of drugs, of course—is to be embraced.

I run into so many people singing the blues these days. One friend of mine was distraught because he had to give up membership in one of the two country clubs to which he belongs. I told him most people I know don't belong to one club. When someone asks you how you're doing they don't want to hear about your latest health problems or that your retirement portfolio is going into the tank.

"How ya doin'?" I overheard a man asking a woman at a coffee shop the other day.

"I can't complain," she said with a smile. "It doesn't do any good."

I smiled and complimented her on her response.

The 2009 Super Bowl brought up stories of the Card-Pitts, the woeful football team put together by the Cardinals and Steelers during the 1944 season. Many of the best players in the NFL had been drafted into military service during World War II, and the Cardinals and Steelers were in such poor shape that they couldn't go it alone. They combined forces that year and went 0–10.

Elmer Layden was the NFL commissioner at the time, and I learned something about what Layden did to overcome a dreary environment while I was doing research on the Card-Pitts in preparation for some TV and radio interviews prior to the Super Bowl.

Despite all the problems that faced his league, Layden was determined to push on. He had learned how to compete when he was a member of the famed "Four Horsemen" backfield during his playing days at Notre Dame.

He instituted an "anti-pessimism" policy for the league.

"The best thing to do in these uncertain times," declared Layden, "is to adopt a policy of 'go on living' instead of being pessimistic. We are going ahead with plans for the 1944 season."

Former Pitt basketball star and Pittsburgh businessman Curtis Aiken, Steelers' coach Mike Tomlin and Mayor Luke Ravenstahl sit at courtside for Pitt basketball game at Peterson Events Center.

"Bullet Bill" Dudley's wife
kept him humble, too

May 2009

A long-time Steelers' fan and a devoted reader of my books approached me at a book-signing at Waldenbooks at South Hills Village. He told me he remembered being at a Steelers' game as a kid at Forbes Field when Bill Dudley returned a punt for 90-some yards to score a touchdown for the Washington Redskins against his former teammates on the Steelers.

I promptly picked up my personal telephone book, a little black book, and dialed Dudley's phone number in Lynchburg, Virginia. I guess I was guilty of showing off a bit, but I wanted to knock the socks off my faithful fan.

Dudley answered the call himself. I told him what the man had told me. The game, I learned later from doing some research, had taken place on December 3, 1950. That was nearly 60 years earlier. "Sure, I remember," declared Dudley, his voice rising to suit the recall. "Joe Geri was the punter for the Steelers. He kicked the ball about 60 yards and I had to run about 30 yards to field it near the sideline. I came to a quick halt and nearly went out of bounds. When I stopped for a second, I think some of the Steelers thought I had gone out of bounds and they slowed down. I took the ball and ran it down the sidelines 96 yards for a touchdown!"

I asked Dudley, "Could you do that today?"

"I don't think so," he said. "I've lost a step since I had my knees replaced."

Then I put him on the line with my customer and they talked for a while. "Wow, that was special," said the man at the completion of their conversation. "That was Bullet Bill, huh? I never thought I'd be talking to him. Thank you."

M y wife Kathie and I visited the Virginia home of "Bullet Bill" Dudley and his wife Libba back in 2003. Dudley remained one of the Pittsburgh Steelers' most distinguished alumni, and took pride in being one of owner Art Rooney's all-time favorite players.

Dudley was an All-American halfback at the University of Virginia and the Steelers' No. 1 draft pick in 1942, the year I was born. Dudley led the league in rushing as a rookie and helped the Steelers improve their record from 1–9–1 to 7–4. Then World War II interrupted and NFL rosters were gutted with players leaving to serve our country in the military. Dudley became a fighter pilot in the Pacific for two and a half years and missed two seasons in his prime.

He was the National Football League's MVP in 1946 when he led the league in rushing, punt returns and interceptions—a Triple

Bill Dudley shows off Pro Football Hall of Fame bust and rings as well as his wife Libba in their Lynchburg, Virginia home during a visit in summer of 2003.

Photos by Jim O'Brien

Crown—that will never be duplicated these days. He led the league in 12 categories in those three departments in what might have been the finest individual season in the history of the NFL.

He was highly respected in the league for years after he retired as a ballplayer. He was elected to the Pro Football Hall of Fame in 1966. He held board positions on several levels and was a state legislator in Virginia. In short, he was a special man. It's always been an honor to be in his company.

His wife Libba is a beautiful woman, in many ways, and I learned while visiting the Dudleys that she keeps him balanced and humble. My wife Kathie has the same mission in our home.

Kathie and I were in North Carolina for a family wedding that took place on the ocean beach at Emerald Isle, but we were chased two days after the event by a hurricane that was heading toward the shore. We were told to evacuate our rental place and head inland.

So we headed for Pittsburgh. I wanted to take advantage of the extra day or two in our schedule so I suggested I call "Bullet Bill" Dudley to see if we could meet him for lunch in Lynchburg. I always liked talking to him, and recording his stories. He had played for Jock Sutherland in his Steelers' days and didn't much care for the dour Scot.

Dudley was a Virginia statesman right up there with Thomas Jefferson, and as outspoken as Patrick Henry. He told you what was on his mind. He liked me, especially after my older daughter Sarah went to the University of Virginia—"We just call it The University," he once told me—and she graduated with Phi Beta Kappa honors.

The Dudleys were gracious hosts and a winning team. I got a kick out of discovering that all of Dudley's trophies and plaques and football memorabilia—including a copy of his Hall of Fame bust—were all stored in his garage.

That's where my wife makes me keep my sports trophies and sports paraphernalia.

Or at least that's where I used to keep them. Sometimes Kathie goes overboard in her efforts to keep me humble. My trophies can't compare to Bill Dudley's, of course. He and Byron "Whizzer" White, another Steelers' No. 1 draft pick (1946) and a man who went on to serve on the U.S. Supreme Court, are two of the most decorated athletes in American sports history.

I had trophies stored somewhere in my garage (hidden safely, I thought) from my days in Little League, Pony League, CYO and the Hit & Miss Bowling League of my youth. To me, they were as precious as Dudley's Hall of Fame bust. My favorite was the one I won for making the CYO All-Star Basketball team in Pittsburgh back in 1960. That was the same year the Pirates won the World Series, which got a lot more attention in the local newspapers.

One day I came home and found a box filled with those trophies sitting at the bottom of our driveway on the day our garbage gets picked up. I was stunned by the discovery.

"How could you do this?" I asked Kathie, while trying to regain my breathing. "How could you throw out all my trophies?"

"You're living in the past," she said. "Get some new stuff."

And I did. Maybe Kathie was trying to inspire me to do something to earn some more trophies and plaques. Maybe she wanted me to work hard and gain some new honors. Maybe she didn't want to dust those trophies anymore.

I was reminded of a time when I was in the company of the great sports writer Jimmy Cannon prior to a big boxing event in Houston. A writer from England asked Jimmy why he hadn't retired by now.

"You could rest on your laurels," the Brit said in a strong accent.

"Maybe," said Cannon, sputtering because he was incensed by the man's remarks, "I don't have as many laurels as you do!"

I certainly will never have as many laurels as Bill Dudley. What I love about the man, however, is how humble and good-natured he is. It's easy to see why Art Rooney was so fond of him. Art Rooney was the same way. He was always mystified that so many people recognized him when he walked the streets of Pittsburgh. "How do they know me?" he often asked Ed Kiely, the Steelers' publicist and a frequent companion of "The Chief" in his latter days, whenever they would come away from a funeral home where folks had fussed over him.

That's the appeal of a lot of sports people in our city. Bill Mazeroski, Bob Friend, El Roy Face, Steve Blass, Mario Lemieux, Pierre Larouche, Arnold Palmer, Rocky Bleier, Andy Russell, L. C. Greenwood, Franco Harris, Mel Blount and Dwayne Woodruff, to name a few, are just regular people off the playing field. Maz and Palmer, in particular, are still baffled that so many people fuss over them when they see them.

One day I was working in the front yard of our home in Upper St. Clair. I'm not crazy about working in the yard—"or anywhere else," Kathie would add—so I was out there feeling like a man working on a chain gang, or someone trying to build a pyramid.

I was performing a chore I had promised Kathie I would do, perhaps three years earlier. I thought I was "thatching" the lawn, but then I read a landscaping guide and learned that what I was doing was "de-thatching" the lawn. Whatever I was doing, I was drawing a fancy rake back and forth through the grass and gathering dry grass and stubble. It's supposed to be good for the grass, so moisture can get to the roots more easily.

A man pulled up to the curb and got out of his car. He introduced himself and told me he was the son of Barry Foley, the last head grounds keeper at Three Rivers Stadium. "My dad died last week," the man informed me. "I wanted you to know how much he loved that chapter you wrote about him in your book *The Chief*, the one about Art Rooney. He loved it so much that we put a copy of the book open to that page in his casket when we buried him."

That's when Kathie came to the front door. She had been busy somewhere in the house, getting something in order, no doubt. She paused from her work to come to the door and to see what I was not doing. She has a sixth sense and knows when I have stopped doing a task, or when I have stopped in mid-work to chat with a neighbor. She just knows; don't ask me how.

(*I will be married to Kathie 45 years as of August 2012. We dated for eight months before we were married. So I have been trying to impress this woman for nearly 46 years. And, as I frequently tell our daughters, I haven't made a damn dent. But I will get up tomorrow and try again. I'm not giving up.*)

Sarah and Rebecca just smile knowingly when I say something like that. They know what I am talking about. They know their Mom is tough to please. She was a good role model for them and that's why they love her so much.

"What's going on?" Kathie inquired when she saw me and Barry Foley's son standing at the bottom of our front yard.

"This man told me that his father died last week," I began, trying once more to impress Kathleen Churchman. "I had written about his father in one of my books. He said his dad liked the story so much, and was so proud to be included in the book, that they put the book in his casket for the viewing and buried him with my book still in the casket." Seeking to strengthen my case for some positive feedback I went one step farther.

"That's the sixth casket I know of that has contained one of my books. That's something, don't you think?"

There, that should do it, I thought.

Kathie couldn't help herself. "I'll tell you someone else's casket your books are going to be in," Kathie came back. "Yours! When you go, all that stuff that's in the garage is going with you!"

Then she smiled. She knew that was funny. She thought my head was big enough, and didn't need to swell by someone flattering me that way.

I'm grateful to Kathie in so many ways. She gives me material for my public speaking and story-telling efforts. And, of course, she keeps me grounded and humble. My mother is smiling somewhere about all this. She always told me, "Kathie is the best thing that ever happened to you." I remembered that on Mother's Day.

"I'm not your mother," Kathie tells me ever so often when I misspeak.

"Bullet Bill" Dudley died in his native Virginia of a massive stroke at the age of 88 in early February, 2010. A sportscaster on KDKA Radio in Pittsburgh broke into the regular programming and said, "One of the Steelers' all-time greats, 'Bullet Bob' Dudley, died today...." My wife Kathie was in the car with me. "Can you believe that?" she said. "He doesn't even get his name right." And I said, "Hey, he didn't know him. He has no idea."

Still kicking after
eight Super Bowls

January 2010

L et's kick this off by setting the record straight. No, I am not the Jim O'Brien who kicked a field goal to win a Super Bowl. At least six different out-of-town visitors to our fair city over the last six weeks have asked me if I was that Jim O'Brien when they approached me at book-signings.

They seemed disappointed when I disclosed that I was an author, a writer, simply someone who has enjoyed playing sports all his life, but never did it for a living.

But I did have a story about that Jim O'Brien and his heroics in Super Bowl V, back in January of 1971. I always have a story. . .

I've covered some big-time sports events in my life—I was never a one-sport writer—and those assignments included attending and writing about eight Super Bowls. I've seen the Steelers win a Super Bowl—their fourth in six years back in 1980 at the Rose Bowl in Pasadena—and I've seen them lose a Super Bowl, their only setback in the championship game—in Tempe, Arizona in 1996.

I chose not to go to Tampa the last time to see them play the Arizona Cardinals because I decided the best way to watch the game is on television at my neighbor Ken Codeluppi's home in Upper St. Clair. Ken has a 52 inch flat-screen HDTV model. It's like going to the old Warner Theater for Cinerama. There's good food, good drink, good company, the room temperature is just right, and there's a bathroom nearby. And you can be home in five minutes after the game and sleep in your own bed. As you get older, you do get wiser about these things. Comfort is more important than being part of a crowd.

The Steelers were competing for the championship—a record sixth, if they pull it off—at Raymond James Stadium in Tampa. The last Super Bowl I attended was to see the Baltimore Ravens defeat the New York Giants there in 2001. I was in Tampa all week to interview NFL types and writers about Art Rooney for a book I wrote called *"The Chief: Art Rooney and His Pittsburgh Steelers."*

That part of my project worked perfectly. I remember telling my wife Kathie when I returned home that if I had to do it over again I would have departed Tampa on the morning of the big game and flown back to Pittsburgh and watched the game on TV. I could have seen it better than I could from an auxiliary press box high in the end zone.

I think everyone should attend one Super Bowl in their lifetime, as well as one World Series, NCAA Final Four, Indy 500 and Kentucky Derby. But being there is over-rated and watching it on TV is under-rated. I know that sports writer Bob Smizik agrees on that subject.

Now back to my Jim O'Brien story. Irish writers and speakers have a tendency to wander in their thoughts. Forgive me.

I did not actually attend Super Bowl V, but I was in Miami a few days before the title game. How I got there is a story in itself.

I was working in New York at the time for *The New York Post*. I had been nursing a bad chest cold by taking antibiotics. I had a luncheon engagement at Toots Shor's in Manhattan and my wife Kathie cautioned me not to drink any liquor. "You're not supposed to drink when you're taking medicine like that," she said, repeating what the doctor had said.

So I drank some screwdrivers that day. They're mostly orange juice, right, and orange juice has all that Vitamin C, which is good for you when you have a cold. It became Bob Prince's favorite drink when his doctor told him to cut back on the booze. He'd been a whisky and Coke man before that.

I was with the publicity man for the ABA, the American Basketball Association, whose idea of doing his job was to host a party. His name was Burt Schultz. He wasn't too big on written publicity releases. During the luncheon with two friends of his he showed off his new fur coat. Then he said, "You know, my new fur coat has never been to Bermuda."

We had all had a few drinks by then, enough so that we took his remark seriously. The next thing I knew we were in a limousine heading for Kennedy International Airport. I recall that I don't recall much about that trip to the airport. Everything we passed along the way was one big blur, like a TV picture gone bad.

When we got to the airport we learned that there were no available flights to Bermuda. But we could go to Miami. So off we went to Miami, courtesy of the ABA. It's no wonder that outlaw basketball league had financial shortcomings.

During dinner that night, everyone at the table went off to the restroom and I was left alone. I started sobbing. I didn't know where the hell I was.

When I awoke the next morning in a hotel in Miami—I don't recall which one—I immediately called Kathie back in New York. She was sobbing, too. She had wondered what had happened to me. She was worried about me.

She reminded me that she had never balked about my travels in sports—sometimes eight-day swings with the Mets or Yankees—or extended road trips with the Knicks and Nets or Rangers or Islanders. And she was right about that. "Why didn't you just call me and tell me you were going to Miami?" she pleaded.

"If I had the mind to call you and tell you I was going to Miami," I replied, "I wouldn't be in Miami. I'd be home."

She settled down. Almost instant forgiveness. Kathie was a keeper, from the start. She would, however, make me pay for that thoughtless escapade. I may still be paying.

I tried to make up for my sin of omission. While in Miami, I saw in *The Miami News*, where I had previously worked before moving to New

York, that former heavyweight boxing champion Floyd Patterson was in Miami training for a fight there with a pug named Levi Forte, who worked there as a shoe shine guy in the health spa at the Fontainebleau Hotel.

I took a taxi to the Fifth Street Gym on Miami Beach. I'd been there many times when I worked in Miami. Angelo Dundee, who trained Muhammad Ali there, would welcome me back. I did a solid one-on-one interview with Floyd Patterson and wrote the story for *The New York Post.*

We went to the Miami Airport to get back to New York. This was Friday, two days before Super Bowl V.

Burt Schultz was a member of one of those airport private clubs and we went in and caught some sports on TV. Jane Chastain, one of the first national women sportscasters, was interviewing Jim O'Brien, a rookie place-kicker for the Baltimore Colts. He was, of course, my favorite Colt since Pittsburgh born and bred quarterback Johnny Unitas.

Someone had given Jane Chastain three questions to ask O'Brien. He answered the first one, and mentioned that he'd had a dream about the Super Bowl.

Chastain dutifully and foolishly went on to her second question. I went crazy; I wanted to know what his dream was about.

When I got back to New York, I called an old friend, Ernie Accorsi, who was then the publicity director of the Colts, and later the general manager of the New York Giants. He was a Penn State man and a good friend of my friend Beano Cook. So I had connections with Ernie Accorsi. I asked Accorsi if he could get Jim O'Brien on the telephone with me. Within the hour, I had a phone call from Jim O'Brien. He was calling for Jim O'Brien.

"What was your dream about?" I asked him for openers, filling in where Jane Chastain had left off.

"I had this dream," he said, "in which someone kicks a field goal to win this Super Bowl. The problem is that I don't know if it's their guy (Mike Clark) or me."

I wrote a story for Saturday's paper about O'Brien's dream. I also noted that Jim O'Brien of the University of Maryland and Jim O'Brien of Boston College—two more of my favorite athletes at the time—had hit game-winning field goals in basketball games the previous night. That was a good omen.

As it turned out, Jim O'Brien booted a 32-yard field goal with five seconds left on the clock in a dramatic 16–13 victory for the Colts over the Dallas Cowboys in what was rated the sloppiest Super Bowl game ever. O'Brien had an earlier kick, for an extra point, blocked in that game, which was why the Colts had only 13 points after scoring two touchdowns. The Cowboys had scored a touchdown and Clark had kicked two field goals and an extra point to give them 13 points

And I had the scoop on O'Brien the day before the game, and I wasn't even covering the game.

I still believe that I often find the best stories somewhere other than the game site, or the team's headquarters. That's another way I justify not being in Tampa for the Steelers. The NFL office in New York had been kind enough to extend a press pass to me if I wanted to come.

I covered my first Super Bowl—Super Bowl IV—in New Orleans, back in 1970. I was working in Miami at the time. The Kansas City Chiefs beat the Minnesota Vikings, 23–7, and completely dominated the action. The Vikings had been 14-point favorites. It was the last game played by an AFL team. I wrote seven bylined stories on that game for the next day's newspaper in Miami. I left Miami for a job in New York a few weeks later.

I had seen the Chiefs up close during the 1965 season in Kansas City. I was serving as an editor at the U.S. Army Hometown News Center in Kansas City. We developed all those stories for hometown newspapers about what soldiers were doing during their tours of duty. I moonlighted by helping out whatever way I could in the press box at Municipal Stadium in Kansas City.

The Chiefs' publicity director, Roger Valdiserri, was from Belle Vernon and was a good friend of Beano Cook. There's that Cook connection again. Beano actually had a mischievous hand in getting me assigned to the Kansas City post after I was originally signed to go to a stenographers' school at a military fort in Indianapolis. There was a General John A. O'Brien in charge of placement, and Cook wrote to him and Attorney General Robert McNamara and told them that it would be a waste of my talent to send me to Indianapolis. It worked.

On weekends, I served as a spotter for sports broadcaster Charley Jones, who just retired in 2010, and analyst Paul Christman, the once great quarterback of the Chicago Cardinals. It was a great gig. I also worked in the press box when Charley Finley's A's were playing there in the summer. Jim Gentile and Ken Green were the A's best players, and a mule named Charley O was the biggest gate attraction.

I came home from Kansas City on one occasion, and visited Art Rooney, the owner of the Steelers, at his office at the Roosevelt Hotel. His friend, KDKA-TV newsman Bill Burns, was also visiting Rooney that afternoon. I told them tales of the Chiefs—Lenny Dawson, Bobby Bell, Johnny Robinson, Fred Arbanas, Fred Williamson, Jim Tyrer, Ed Budde, Jerry Mays, Buck Buchanan—and how good they were.

"How good could they be?" blurted Burns, a die-hard fan of the Steelers and the Rooney family. "Lenny Dawson didn't even get to play when he was with the Steelers!"

"Neither did Johnny Unitas!' I came back. "That proves nothing."

"That proves we don't know a good quarterback when we see one," said Art Rooney, always the honest handicapper. "It started when we had the draft rights to Sid Luckman, and I let George Halas have him instead."

I interviewed Dawson after that Super Bowl IV game. He was the game's MVP. He would later be inducted into the Pro Football Hall of Fame, where his bust is in the same display as the busts of Unitas, Luckman, Terry Bradshaw, Bobby Layne and Jim Finks, all former Steelers' quarterbacks. Finks found his way there for his much

Pittsburgh author Jim O'Brien enjoys a reunion with former Kansas City Chiefs linebacker Bobby Bell at Andy Russell's charity golf outing at Southpointe two years ago. O'Brien wrote a feature story on Bell for *Sport* magazine back in 1965.

admired administrative strengths with the Chicago Bears, Minnesota Vikings and New Orleans Saints.

I was back in New Orleans for Super Bowl VI in 1972. I was mainly there to cover a heavyweight championship fight on the eve of the Super Bowl. Joe Frazier of Philadelphia defended his title with an easy win over Terry Daniels of Cleveland. Ken Norton, a future heavyweight champion, was there as a sparring partner for Frazier.

I will never forget what I saw at the Hotel Monteleone, formerly a favorite haunt of famous writers such as Truman Capote, Tennessee Williams, Ernest Hemingway, Sherwood Anderson, Eudora Welty and William Faulkner. On the top floor of the hotel, I saw one of Frazier's handlers repeatedly slam a medicine ball against the stomach of Norton, who was lying flat on his back on a training table. It looked like a scene from a medieval torture chamber.

When my wife Kathie and I were at the NCAA Final Four Basketball Tournament in New Orleans in April of 2003, I took her to the top floor of the Hotel Monteleone to show her the area where Frazier and Norton had trained. It was now a health spa and workout area for hotel guests. Norton's son, Ken Norton Jr., would later be an outstanding middle linebacker for the Dallas Cowboys in the late '80s and '90s, and play in some Super Bowls.

I remember that one of my favorite ballplayers, Mike Ditka of Carnegie and Aliquippa, caught a 7-yard touchdown pass from Roger Staubach late in that Super Bowl VI. I wrote a sidebar story on Ditka in the next day's *New York Post*.

I covered a few more Super Bowls in New Orleans—still the best site to hold the big game—but the best and most thrilling game was when Joe Montana of Monongahela led the San Francisco 49ers to a comeback victory over the Cincinnati Bengals, 26–21, at Pontiac's Silverdome Stadium in Super Bowl XVI. The Detroit area was covered in ice that week.

I had covered the AFC championship in Cincinnati earlier in the playoffs, when the Bengals beat the San Diego Chargers. It was 9 degrees below zero in Cincinnati that day, and the wind chill factor reached a minus 59 degrees. It was much warmer in the press box, of course. The Chargers wanted to postpone the game, but the Bengals said no. Never has a team had more of a home field advantage in a playoff than it that game, unless it was "The Ice Bowl" in Green Bay when the Packers beat the Dallas Cowboys in the NFL title game before there was a Super Bowl.

Legendary sports columnist Jimmy Cannon and *New York Post* boxing writer Jim O'Brien interview Joe Frazier before his "Greatest Fight of the Century" with Muhammad Ali in New York.

A Great Life

When asked why he was a sports writer, Dick Young of the New York Daily News responded by saying, "I don't want to be a millionaire. I just want to live like one."

When Jim O'Brien told Red Holzman, the Knicks' head coach, what a great day he was having in New Orleans, Holzman said, "This would be a great life if it weren't for the damn games."

Bill Sharman, the Hall of Fame basketball player and coach, told O'Brien, "We were lucky to be able to spend our lives doing something we really enjoyed doing."

"It's great to do what we get to do," said ESPN's Mike Tirico at the conclusion of reporting on The Open at St. Andrew's Golf Club in Scotland in July, 2010.

"You have to know more than stats to be a sports writer," said Myron Cope upon his retirement on the Steelers' radio broadcasts. "That's not what it's all about. You have to have talent. You have to be a good writer and know how to tell a story."

"Sports is thrilling, fascinating, exhilarating and happens out of town often enough to accomplish wonderful things with an expense account."
    —From "The Joys of Sportswriting," by Vic Ziegel,
                                        New York Daily News,

"I realized that writing was a good thing to do."
                    —Sportswriter Michael Katz

Bob Uecker, a former big league catcher turned broadcaster and the star of a TV series "Mr. Belvedere," in which he played the part of a Pittsburgh sportswriter, was happy to be back in the broadcast booth of the Milwaukee Brewers after surgery during the summer of 2010.

"I'm a baseball guy and I'm doing whatever I have to do to make myself happy. Happiness is being with the team and being with our ownership. And wherever I go, I have friends I like to be with. It's a great life."

Steelers' scout gets
Hall of Fame badge

February 2010

I will always be grateful to Bill Nunn Jr. for something he did on my behalf back in the late summer of 1969. Nunn introduced me to legendary football coach Jake Gaither from Florida A&M, and made it possible for me to spend a magic evening in the company of one of the greatest coaches in college football history.

People who've read my books often tell me I was so lucky to have spent time with some of the great people in sports in my journeys with the sporting press. This was one of those times.

I thought about that evening when I read in the daily newspaper last week that Nunn was being inducted into the charter class of the Black College Football Hall of Fame. He was the only one of the 11 members who wasn't a player or a coach. He was the good scout and newspaper columnist, a man who brought proper recognition to black athletes in America back in the '50s and '60s and helped build the teams that brought glory to the Pittsburgh Steelers.

Dan Rooney hired Nunn to be a part-time scout on Bill Austin's staff in 1967, and Nunn became a full-time scout when Chuck Noll became the head coach in 1969. "Maybe it's the old newspaperman in him," Noll once noted, "but he could go into a school and get the skinny on everything. With lots of scouts, you never know, but you could really rely on Bill's information. He had every detail."

"My father, Bill Nunn Sr., was a good friend of Art Rooney," Nunn is quick to say. "My mother's cousin was once a trainer for them."

Nunn, 86, is still a part-time scout for the Steelers, the oldest man still checking out college football players for an NFL team, though he restricts his activity to analyzing game tapes these days, and doesn't travel to games any more. He is well deserving of this honor. When he was the sports editor of *The Pittsburgh Courier*—that's when I first met this impressive man—he picked a Black College All-America that NFL teams relied upon to gain awareness of outstanding players in the small black colleges.

Nunn had a hand in his early years with the Steelers in their selecting the likes of L.C. Greenwood (Arkansas AM&N), Mel Blount (Southern), Frank Lewis (Grambling), Dwight White (East Texas State), Joe Gilliam (East Tennessee State), Ernie Holmes (Texas Southern), John Stallworth (Alabama A&M), and free agents such as Donnie Shell (South Carolina State) and Sam Davis (Allen U.).

These players contributed mightily to the Steelers' success in the '70s. Nunn was one of the most respected members of the scouting staff headed by Art Rooney Jr., the second oldest son of Steelers' founder Art Rooney Sr. Rooney is quite fond of Nunn and they still get together from time to time to catch up on each other's activities.

Besides Nunn, the first class of the Black College Football Hall of Fame includes Buck Buchanan of Grambling, Willie Galimore of Florida A&M, Deacon Jones of South Carolina State, Willie Lanier of Morgan State, Walter Payton of Jackson State, Jerry Rice of Mississippi Valley State, Ben Stevenson of Tuskegee and Tank Younger of Grambling, and coaches Eddie Robinson of Grambling and Jake Gaither of Florida A&M.

I was privileged to meet and interview Robinson and Gaither, but it was to spend time with the latter that Nunn opened the door for me and made it possible. I was covering the Miami Dolphins in 1969 for *The Miami News*. The Dolphins were playing an exhibition game in Tampa against the New York Jets. Tampa was bidding for an NFL franchise and putting on a big weekend promotion to show its best face.

There was a college game on the eve of the pro contest in Tampa. It featured Gaither's Florida A&M team against Tampa University. It was the first time Florida A&M's football team was playing against a predominantly white school. In fact, the star of the Tampa team was hometown product Leon "All The Way" McQuay who had been the first black athlete awarded an athletic scholarship to the school. McQuay would go on to play six seasons in the Canadian Football League and the National Football League. I covered both games that weekend.

McQuay became a minister, I just learned, and died at the age of 45. Gaither was in his 25th year as the coach at Florida A&M. He was 66 at the time and this was his final season at the helm of the Rattlers.

I remember thinking how old and tired he looked as he lay in his bed at a hotel room near the stadium after the game that night. He was lying there, a happy man, reminiscing about his career, trying to explain what it meant to him to finally get to play against a predominantly white college team and beat that team. There was a constant smile on his face. It had been a long journey.

Nunn had spotted me in the press box that night and he took me with him to the visitors' locker room afterward and then let me tag along with him to the hotel where the Florida A&M team was staying that night. (Now that I am 70, *I don't think Gaither was really so old after all.*)

Jake Gaither looked spent. He was famous for saying he liked his players "to be agile, mobile and hostile," and he said those words with great emphasis on each element.

I was sitting in on history that night and it was Nunn who made it possible. I was the only white man in that hotel room. No one treated me like an interloper.

When Gaither retired after that 1969 season he had a career record of 204–36–4. He had graduated from Knoxville College, where he had played football, and he later completed a master's degree program at The Ohio State University. He was born in Dayton, Tennessee in 1903 and lived till he was 90 years old. I guess he bounced back from looking so tired in his hotel room that night in Tampa.

I know Nunn from two previous associations. In addition to being a Steelers' scout, he was the camp manager every summer at the team's training camp at St. Vincent College in Latrobe. He was a good storyteller and knew where all the skeletons were buried, but he was always cautious about what he actually said about the Steelers. "He knew who buttered his bread," said a dear friend and admirer. Nunn told you a lot just by nodding and saying "yeah, yeah, and yeah" when you were offering observations. He let you do the talking. He never had to deny saying anything.

I first dealt with Nunn when he was the sports editor of *The Pittsburgh Courier*, and I was a senior at Pitt back in 1963 and 1964. I had teamed up with Beano Cook to publish *Pittsburgh Weekly Sports* and I moonlighted as the public relations director for two years with the Pittsburgh Valley Ironmen football team. I wrote special features on the black members of the minor league football team for *The Courier*. In the language of that paper at the time, they were referred to as "tan stars." I'll never forget that, though I have never seen any reminder of those days or that sort of odd word usage in print in Pittsburgh.

I'll never forget the names of those Ironmen I featured in my stories for *The Courier*. They included Duke Sumpter, Gene Gatewood, Bobby Mulgado, Kenny Austin, Joe Golden, Carlos Smith, Burness Holt, Dewayne Tucker, Cal Stanley, Sam Barber and Coty Mudd. Dick Bowen and Bob Malie coached the Ironmen who played in the Atlantic Coast Football League and had their home games at Duquesne High Field.

My wife Kathie and I have socialized with Nunn and his wife, Frances, during the 80th birthday party of our friend Herb Douglas. It was held at the Duquesne Club in 2002 and we were among the 80 guests at the party. Douglas was from my hometown of Hazelwood and he won the bronze medal in the long jump in the 1948 Olympic Games in London, England.

Douglas had four men at his party who had won multiple gold medals in the Olympic Games, namely Roger Kingdom, Mal Whitfield, Charley Jenkins and Harrison Dillard. They were all class acts in their formal attire. Douglas had me seated with these Olympic stars, and he did it again five years later when he celebrated his 85th birthday at the Heinz History Center. The second time around he also had Olympians Edwin Moses and Donna de Varona at our table. Douglas knew I was into the Olympic Games, especially track & field. Nunn knew all these Olympians well. When he was talking to Douglas, he'd refer to me as "your boy O'Brien."

Nunn was a ghostwriter for Jackie Robinson for a popular first-person column in *The Courier*, when it was one of the most respected and widely-read black newspapers in the country. He was a friend and confidant of John Henry Johnson, Roberto Clemente and Connie Hawkins, all Hall of Famers in their respective sports. They trusted Nunn and knew he had their best interest at heart.

Nunn knew the Aurora Club, a popular late-night club in The Hill District, not far from where the new Consol Energy Center now stands. There used to be honest-to-goodness night clubs in downtown Pittsburgh and many after-hours clubs. Nowadays, most bars are empty by 11, unless you're in The Strip or the South Side. Nunn smiled knowingly when I told him a tale of an experience I had at the Aurora Club one night with John Henry Johnson. I was the only white man in the club. John Henry took me there. I was around 20 or 21 at the time.

John Henry was one of the toughest guys ever to play pro football. He was known for decking opposing rushers with fierce blocks. He once seized a down marker and used it like a lance to fend off someone who came after him on the sideline. That night at the Aurora he ordered us several drinks. A waitress, who must have known John Henry only too well, said to him, "John Henry, when are you going to pay for these drinks?"

John Henry stared at her and hollered out, "Who's going to make me pay?"

With that, we both got up from the table and started backing out of the dining area. We were like two cowboys—Butch Cassidy and the Sundance Kid come to mind—making their exit out of one of those western saloons. I was glad I was with John Henry. Bobby Layne, the quarterback back then, liked having John Henry or Ernie Stautner at his side in case the going got tough.

Knowing Bill Nunn was being honored at a dinner at The Four Seasons Hotel in Atlanta brought back images of those special nights. I was lucky to know Bill Nunn and his friends in the business.

Jim O'Brien

Steelers' braintrust, from left to right, Mike Tomlin, Dan Rooney, Bill Nunn Jr. and Art Rooney Jr. taking in Steelers' summer training camp at St. Vincent College. Nunn and Art Jr. delivered many key players to Steelers during the team's glory days of the '70s.

Snowstorm brings back
childhood memories

February 2010

The snow kept coming and so did so many thoughts and good memories. It was smart to stay at home last weekend. I went out several times to shovel the snow off the driveway one day and then the walkway the next day, making sure I took some measured breaks to eat some soup and sandwiches. I don't know how many passersby told me to take it easy and I was careful about the way I did what I did.

I had to make my own meals because my wife Kathie was in Columbus. She was visiting our daughter Sarah and our granddaughters Margaret and Susannah. I had convinced Kathie to depart Pittsburgh on Thursday and not her planned departure day of Friday. We were certainly warned by the weathermen that a substantial snowstorm would begin around noon on Friday. It started like clockwork and never let up.

Our telephone service and Internet service and e-mail ability were all not working. Our television was not working. It was an inconvenience at best compared to what had happened in Haiti a few weeks back, or for that matter what was happening to neighbors just a few blocks away who were without electricity and even heat in some cases.

I started out to go to the Pitt-Seton Hall basketball game on Saturday evening, but found the roads in Mt. Lebanon challenging and turned around and came back home. I listened to the game on the radio, glad that I could hear Bill Hillgrove, Dick Groat and Curtis Aiken on the air. I missed seeing Pitt playing at its best. They beat the Seton Hall Pirates handily.

My buddy Bill Priatko and I were comparing notes and memories on Sunday morning. Both of our churches were closed because they had no electricity or heat so we were at home. Thanks to our cell phones we were able to connect with one another and share stories and some news.

It was Super Bowl Sunday, of course, but hours away from the 6:25 p.m. start. Does it ever start? Does it ever end? We both thought the Indianapolis Colts would win. So what do we know about football?

We were happy to hear that our dear friend Dick LeBeau had been voted into the Pro Football Hall of Fame. Bill and I both love Dick LeBeau. He is the best kind of man you'd want to meet or know. Priatko has known LeBeau since way back in 1959 when they were in the training camp of the Cleveland Browns.

LeBeau was cut at that training camp by Paul Brown, one of the greatest coaches in the history of football. But Brown later admitted that cutting LeBeau was one of the worst mistakes of his career. LeBeau went on to a sensational career as a defensive back for those great Detroit Lions teams of the '60s. He was so deserving long ago of these Hall of Fame honors.

LeBeau is best known here, of course, as the beloved defensive coordinator of the Steelers, serving under both Bill Cowher and now Mike Tomlin. Priatko and LeBeau had been talking over the telephone in recent weeks about LeBeau's chances for getting voted into the Pro Football Hall of Fame, and LeBeau told Priatko not to get his hopes up too high because LeBeau didn't want his buddy to be too disappointed if he didn't get in this time.

Not only did LeBeau and Floyd Little, the two nominees of a special veterans' committee, get in, but so did two former Pitt players, Russ Grimm and Rickey Jackson. Grimm also served as a Steelers' assistant coach under Cowher and hails from Scottdale in Westmoreland County. Jerry Rice and Emmitt Smith were both sure-fire picks in their first year of eligibility.

I know where Priatko will be on August 7. That's the day that LeBeau and the rest of the bunch will be inducted into the Pro Football Hall of Fame in Canton, Ohio. I have gone there on at least seven or eight occasions with Priatko and his pal Rudy Celigoi to attend similar inductions and Hall of Fame games. It would have been icing on the cake if former Steelers' center Dermonti Dawson was deservedly voted in, but he came up short and will have to wait till next year. He finished in the Top Ten in the voting.

Priatko and I were both also saddened to learn on Friday that "Bullet Bill" Dudley had died at age 88 in Lynchburg, Va., following a stroke at his home. We were both admirers of Dudley, one of the late Art Rooney's all-time favorite Steelers. Dudley was a gentleman and a statesman and just a class act in every respect. I always felt honored to be in his company.

My wife Kathie and I had visited Dudley and his wife, Libba, in Lynchburg. We had lunch with them there and visited their home just a few years back, on the way home from a hurricane-shortened stay on the beach at Emerald Isle, North Carolina.

I remember being happy to see that Dudley's replica of his Hall of Fame bust was in the back of his garage. I didn't feel so bad that Kathie made me keep my Little League, Pony League and CYO trophies in a similar spot in our garage. I had visited with and interviewed Dudley a half dozen times and never tired of his stories. He was a warm fellow, a good-hearted soul, so down to earth yet so dignified.

Another former Steelers star that Priatko and I kept in touch with, Jerry Shipkey, had died in California back in November. He had been a terrific linebacker for the Steelers from 1948 to 1952. I had his bubble gum card in my collection. I liked his name. Val Jansante died last year. I liked his name, too. Jerry Shipkey. Val Jansante. Bobby Gage. He's gone now, too. There was something about the sound of their names. They sounded like football players. Like Bronko Nagurski, Bulldog Turner or Jim Thorpe.

"I've been thinking about how many of the old-timers who were such great players when we were young are now gone," said Priatko.

"Many of these fans today have no idea who these guys were, but they were great in their day."

Dudley led the league one year (1946) in rushing, interceptions and punt returns. He was the NFL's MVP that year. But he didn't care for his coach, Jock Sutherland, and he forced a trade to the Detroit Lions for the following season.

"I remember going to a Steelers' game in 1946 at Forbes Field," said Priatko. "You could walk right out on the field after the game in those days. I ended up walking alongside of Dudley, who was walking with Coach Sutherland. Dudley was shouting at Sutherland; they were arguing. I didn't know what it was all about then, but I learned later that they had disagreements. Then Dudley left for Detroit and I knew then that they had problems."

I remembered that "Bullet Bill" told me he wasn't that fast and didn't deserve his nickname. He was only 5–10, 180 pounds in his playing days. I'm 5–8½, but I was as tall as Dudley when I last stood next to him. He had knee replacements. "I've also shrunk," declared Dudley, while squinting his blue-gray eyes and laughing at his own line.

Priatko and I also shared some stories about the snowfall, and our memories of the worst snowfall ever to hit Pittsburgh. That was back in late November of 1950.

I was eight years old and Priatko had just turned 19 and was a freshman at Pitt, where he played linebacker and was the captain of the freshman football team.

"We were supposed to play Penn State's freshman team that Friday," recalled Priatko. "We were both undefeated. But the game was cancelled. The varsity was supposed to play Penn State on Saturday, but that game was postponed a week to the following Saturday. They had to play that game at Forbes Field because they couldn't get Pitt Stadium cleared of snow.

"Penn State won that game 21–20 when Nick Bolkovac of Youngstown missed the extra-point kick. And Bolkovac had been the defensive star of the game two years earlier, in 1948, when we beat Penn State, 7–0. Bolkovac had tackled my sports idol, Fran Rogel, just short of the goal line to preserve the victory and he had intercepted a pass in that game as well. Rogel was from my hometown of North Braddock, and we all looked up to him when he played at Penn State and then for the Steelers. He was another of those great Steelers' players from the past that today's fans fail to know about."

I have only a single image of that 1950 blizzard. I remember standing in the walkway in the back of our home on Sunnyside Street in Glenwood, with the snow well over my head. The official snowfall that year was 27.4"—still the greatest snowstorm in the city's history. But it was much higher because the snow had been shoveled off the walkway and was piled high alongside the walkway where I was standing.

I don't know if I did any shoveling back then, but I sure did this past weekend. It must have taken me a total of four hours, working in shifts, to clear my driveway which is about 15 yards long. It took me an hour and a half the next day to clear our walkway to the driveway.

Priatko told me some neighbors of his had a snow blower and had twice come to clear his driveway. That's what you call good neighbors.

Looking ahead to Valentine's Day this Sunday, Priatko had an appropriate snow story to suit the occasion. "This will tell you about teenage love," said Priatko. "I walked three miles in that deep snow—it was over my knees—to see my Helen who lived in Braddock back then. Her mother and brothers couldn't believe it when they saw me at their front door. She was Helen Dutka back then. I had to see my Helen. That tells you about young love."

I told Priatko that I had a girl friend when I was about 16 and didn't have a car. She lived in Greenfield, and there were many days and nights when I walked two miles or more to get to and from her house. At night, I remember I had to go past Calvary Cemetery and I always picked up my pace when I saw all those tombstones outlined by the light of the moon. I couldn't get past that cemetery soon enough.

I don't remember doing that in the snow so I must not have been in love as much as Bill Priatko was in his North Braddock days.

Dick LeBeau puts in long hours at Steelers' training center putting together game plans as the team's defensive coordinator.

It's a shame Santonio
never met 'The Chief'

April 2010

The Steelers were participating in a three-day National Football League draft of college players in April of 2010 and they would be wise to check character references more closely this time around. I have memories of two drafts that point up what the Steelers should be seeking, and what they should do their darnedest to avoid.

I remember the last line of a biographical sketch on Santonio Holmes and I remember a random act of kindness by Art Rooney Sr., the founder of the Steelers, during draft days of years gone by.

The Steelers selected Santonio Holmes, a wide receiver out of Ohio State, with their first selection in 1995. There was a listing of highlights and, I guess, lowlights in his high school and college career that appeared in the smallest print in the next day's morning newspaper. Remember how they always say to read the fine print in a contract?

Well, the Steelers were remiss in that respect that year.

After detailing how many receptions and yards gained and honors won as a wide receiver for the Buckeyes, and how he was a three-sport all-state performer in high school in Florida, there was one last line that caught my eye. It said that Santonio Holmes had three children by two different women, neither of whom he wed.

I read that line over again. And then again.

To me, that raised a red flag. I sensed there might be a real character flaw in Santonio Holmes. I recognize this is a new day and the rules seem to be more relaxed about what is acceptable behavior, but this crossed the line as far as I was concerned. The Rooneys and the Steelers organization have always boasted that they did things differently—"the right way" as Chairman Dan Rooney likes to say.

When Holmes had one of his children stay with him at his home in Florida during one off-season he spoke about it as a sign of his maturity. The newspaper story made him out to be the Father of the Year for doing what he did. Hey, being a good father means more than a month's involvement.

The Steelers sold us their mantra of operating at a higher standard than most NFL teams, that they looked for and demanded good behavior and good citizenship in their ranks. They do have a pretty good track record in this respect. But if a player is tall enough and strong enough and has talent—Plaxico Burress comes to mind—the Steelers also succumb to the temptation of adding a talented if tarnished employee to their lineup.

I also have not forgotten that Joe Greene, Mel Blount, Jack Lambert and Terry Bradshaw all had some flaws when they first came to the team. In time, they all cleaned up their act. Greene and Blount ended up setting the bar high and enforcing a code of conduct in and out of the clubhouse. Thus we enjoyed the Glory Days of the '70s.

Santonio Holmes has had more than his share of unseemly behavior during his college and pro days and admitted at the Steelers' last appearance in the Super Bowl that he had even sold drugs as a youngster. Of course, Jerome Bettis made a similar admission in his book just a few years ago. Bettis was guilty of poor nighttime conduct at the team's training camp at St. Vincent, yet he went on to win the NFL's award for being a role model. There are warts everywhere one looks if they look closely enough. No Pittsburgh sports team is without its bad boys and some of its most esteemed good boys have been bad boys on nights when there was a full moon.

Some of those incidents have been swept under the carpet, best forgotten or overlooked in the light of what has happened more recently in the lives of such stars.

I would never draft a player named Plaxico. I'd figure there was a mental cramp somewhere in the family tree. Pitt recruited a kid named Attila a decade or so ago and that turned out to be a losing proposition. Teams should avoid taking any kids named Lucifer or with nicknames like Son of Sam.

A few years back I visited an attractive restaurant in Columbus called Eddie George's 27. It is owned by the same people who gave us Jerome Bettis' 36 on the North Shore. They are similar in setup and both are popular hangouts for sports fans. Eddie George was a great running back for the Buckeyes of Ohio State and then the Baltimore Ravens.

His restaurant is on High Street just across from one of the gateway entrances to The Ohio State University. It is a great location. The walls are covered with handwritten endorsements from some well known sports figures, most of them with an Ohio State association. There is one from Santonio Holmes. One can make out an "S" and an "H" and it helps that there is a name tag at the bottom of the frame. It is displayed, ironically enough, next to one of Joey Galloway, one of the receivers the Steelers were hoping could help fill the void left by the dumping of Holmes for his chronic misbehavior.

Galloway and Ted Ginn Jr. of the 49ers have both had more than their share of behavior problems, which can be said of a lot of Ohio State's football players. Keep in mind this is the same Ohio State that backed off recruiting James Harrison because of his teen reputation and rap sheet. So Harrison ended up at Kent State instead.

Harrison has been in his share of trouble since he's been with the Steelers. Jeff Reed has been run out of more saloons by the police because they didn't want to have to arrest him for his boorish behavior.

There is also an endorsement in Eddie George's restaurant signed by Jerome Bettis and there is one signed by Charlie Batch, who has had the best job in Pittsburgh the past ten or eleven years. Batch wrote this: "I stopped by for a bite to eat with my boy Terrelle Pryor and the food is great." Below the Batch endorsement is one from—who else?—Terrelle Pryor, the pride of Jeannette and the junior quarterback of the Buckeyes that coming season.

I don't know why the Steelers have been having so many problems off-the-field of late. It's not Mike Tomlin's fault, I know that. No coach can control the off-the-field behavior of his players. There isn't a better person in all respects than Marvin Lewis, the coach of the Cincinnati Bengals, yet that ballclub has had even more problems than the Pittsburgh Steelers the past decade. Maybe the Steelers want to be the bad boys of this decade in the NFL.

The Steelers aren't going to dump Ben Roethlisberger and it has nothing to do with race. Hey, this is a team that has a black head coach, two black quarterbacks and a third they had considered adding when they were unsure of the status of Roethlisberger for this coming season. Color has never been an issue since Chuck Noll came to town. It was never an issue with Bill Cowher. And it sure isn't with Mike Tomlin.

The Steelers are as furious with the behavior or misbehavior of Roethlisberger as they were with Holmes, but they have more money tied up in Big Ben, and for a much longer period, plus he is a franchise quarterback—don't forget he has led them to two Super Bowl victories—and they are harder to find than flankers who can catch the football. The Steelers realize Holmes has star talent, but they were unwilling to live with him any longer. Ben will have a short leash from now on.

I don't know what has happened with Ben. He came from a good background. When he first joined the Steelers I thought he was actually trying too hard to be a good citizen. He initially got involved with so many non-profits, lending his presence and name to many fundraisers. He looked like a young man trying to earn his Eagle Scout badge. I think his success and the attending attention he drew changed him. I think he got carried away with who he was, or who he thought he was. "Do you know who I am?" is a question that does not play well in Pittsburgh or Peoria.

It was one Ben has been asking at restaurants and clubs across the country in recent years. He expects special attention and he does not want to pay for it. He became a pariah in Pittsburgh among the service people because of his propensity for stiffing valets and wait staff at come of the city's upscale restaurants and clubs. "I draw crowds to your place," Roethlisberger reminds maitre d's who insist he, like the rest of the patrons, come up with the cover charge. That's small and inconsiderate thinking on Ben's part.

I have often wondered why anyone who has a choice chooses to be a jerk instead of a good guy. It's all about choices. I am told Ben is better behaved since he got married and became a father.

Art Rooney Sr. recognized that. He started out as a rough and tumble guy himself, quick to battle his way out of difficulties as a kid. He could compete in any sport and boxing was one of them. But he cleaned up his act as much as any marquee figure in this town.

When he was no longer running the Steelers he still came to the office every day and did his best to be an ambassador for the team, and to offer an ear if Dan Rooney or Art Rooney Jr. sought his counsel.

The players respected him and never wanted to disappoint him. It's a shame Santonio Holmes and Ben Roethlisberger never met the man or they might behave better as well. I always say that if you spent one day in your life with Mr. Rooney you would learn enough about public relations to last a lifetime.

I was working outside his office one day during the first of one of the NFL's two-day drafts back in the early '80s. There were no cell phones in those days, something that might surprise today's teens. My mother, Mary O'Brien, was living at St. Augustine Plaza in Lawrenceville at the time. It was a senior residence. She lived there nearly 20 years.

She had suffered a painful injury in one of her calf muscles and was having some difficulty. I asked Mary Regan if I could use her phone to call my mother. Mary Regan was Mr. Rooney's private secretary and had worked with the Steelers since she was a teenager. She was so efficient and so loyal to "The Chief." She would never betray a confidence.

She said it was OK. As I was talking to my mother, and inquiring about her condition, Mr. Rooney came out of his office, moving a cigar from one end of his mouth to the other, and noting the presence of reporters in the lobby area.

When I got off the phone, Mr. Rooney asked me, "How's your mother doing?" It was a question he asked me many times, but this one I was sure was prompted by something he heard me say on the phone.

"She's got a problem, Mr. Rooney," I replied. I then detailed what was going on with my mother, and mentioned that she was over at St. Augustine. Mr. Rooney knew where every church was located in Pittsburgh. He went to more funerals and more funeral services than anyone in the city.

The next day, during the second day of the NFL draft, I was back in the same area again and I asked Mary Regan if I could borrow her phone. She said it would be OK.

No sooner did my mother answer the phone, sometime around 1 or 2 o'clock in the afternoon, than she said, "The nicest thing happened to me this morning. A man knocked on my door and delivered a basket of flowers. There was a letter with it, from Mr. Rooney. Let me read it to you."

My mother proceeded to read me Mr. Rooney's letter. It was the kind of letter that sounded like I had dictated it to him. It had the kind of positive remarks that a son would want his mother to know about. I always tried to bring home good report cards to my mother and this was the best one of all.

Years later, when I was working on a book called *The Chief: Art Rooney and His Pittsburgh Steelers*. I asked my mother if she still had that hand-written letter from Mr. Rooney. She looked for it but said she could not find it. I had personally saved some post cards he had sent to me from religious shrines in Ireland, Canada and California, but my mother was unable to locate the letter from Mr. Rooney. I would still love to have it.

Mr. Rooney was good about doing things like witing that letter to my mother, coming through in unexpected ways for people he cared about. To this day, I keep hearing good stories about random acts of kindness by Mr. Rooney. I hear good stories about Troy Polamalu, and Rock Bleier and Andy Russell. I hear mostly bad stories about Ben Roethlisberger. The reviews on Jack Lambert are mixed.

Nothing goes unreported these days. Everyone with a cell phone or wireless device is a reporter and photographer these days. Everyone is twittering, texting or blogging. Nobody knew such words when Mr. Rooney was around. The word gets out immediately on the behavior of sports personalities or celebrities of any field of entertainment. The media must follow up with reports of their own.

They say the true test of a person's character is what they do when no one is watching.

The Steelers need to exercise caution about who they draft or sign these days. Women fans, in particular, are turned off by the fact they have so many men on their team who are reckless and abusive with women. They don't expect the Rooneys to let such behavior become the norm. The Rooneys care about their reputation. They care about the Steelers' legacy. They know what their dad would say about all this. They can hear him in their sleep.

PITTSBURGH TREASURES—Pirates' broadcaster and master emcee at sports banquets Bob Prince enjoys a chuckle with Steelers' president and owner Art Rooney Sr. and sports dinner on September 25, 1975.

Steelers should learn positive messages
from Hall of Fame speakers

August 2010

The Pittsburgh Steelers should be smarter than they were before they made a pilgrimmage to Canton, Ohio in August of 2010. They had been to the mountain, so to speak, to the Mecca of their sport. They witnessed the inspirational induction of the Class of 2010 for the Pro Football Hall of Fame.

They were there to pay tribute to one of their own, the popular and respected Dick LeBeau, the defensive coordinator of the Steelers, who once starred as a durable cornerback who could pick off passes from the likes of Johnny Unitas and Bart Starr better than just about everybody at the time. His 62 interceptions were third in the league when he retired as a player and still ranks eighth in the all-time listing.

To a man, the Steelers

Steelers' defensive coordinator Dick LeBeau

love LeBeau, but now they can appreciate him even more to know what he did as a player to merit his induction into his sport's Hall of Fame.

He was going in with quite a class, one of the best in history. It included the all-time leading rusher, Emmitt Smith, and the all-time leading pass-catcher, Jerry Rice. It included two former Pitt teammates, Russ Grimm and Rickey Jackson, John Randle and Floyd Little.

Many of the past inductees were also present on the stage at Fawcettt Stadium, and it was a reminder of all the greats who have graced this game, and paved the way for the present-day players.

The great performers all became preachers when they offered their reflections at the Canton ceremonies. Those who were there or watching on television had to feel like they were attending a religious retreat. When they showed Troy Polamalu, a deeply spiritual member of the Steelers, he certainly looked like he was at such a retreat.

Sitting there, listening to those great players of the past—hearing their wisdom and philosophies about football, life, team effort, marriage, dedication, work ethic, desire and love—relates to what they are doing today in training camps and, ultimately, in their playing careers and beyond. They were listening to "the best of the best," as ESPN"s Chris Berman called the 2010 Class for the Pro Football Hall of Fame.

"Life is for the living; live it," said LeBeau. "Don't let anybody put any limits on you, or tell you you're too old to do this, or too old for that. I've had so many good things happen to me since I turned 65, which was always the normal retirement age."

They put LeBeau on first for the introductions so the Steelers could witness it and then depart Canton for the return trip to Canton. They had to watch the rest of the program on their Ipods or tapes when they got to their respective pads. They should have had Grimm go second since he had coached many of these same Steelers as an assistant

Former Pitt All-American Russ Grimm

to Bill Cowher. It's a shame they missed Grimm getting inducted.

Grimm gave one of the best speeches, but I was not surprised. He stole the show one night in Munhall when he spoke at a dinner to pay tribute to Joe Bugel, a hometown sports hero who had coached Grimm when they were with the Washington Redskins. Bugel presented Grimm for induction at Canton.

Rice, always the smooth operator, offered some words that, I hope will stick with the Steelers. He said that today's players should not be so concerned about what they can take from the game as to what they can offer the game. It had a familiar ring to it, like the famous statement once offered by President John F. Kennedy when he said that we shouldn't ask what our country can do for us but rather ask what we can do for our country.

112

I was hoping that Ben Roethlisberger, Jeff Reed and Lamar Woodley were listening carefully to these words of wisdom. Roethlisberger has brought disgrace upon the Steelers with some of his stupid night-life behavior, as has Reed, and Reed and Woodley have been complaining publicly of late about how the Steelers aren't being straight forward in their contract negotiations with them.

Reed was going to make $2.8 million for the 2010 season for kicking field goals and extra-points for the Steelers. He must realize by now they are not paying him to tackle kick-returners, judging by his poor performance in that area the previous season. Someone ought to inform Reed that he will make more money than Franco Harris and Rocky Bleier and Joe Greene and Mel Blount and Terry Bradshaw and some other Steelers' all-time performers made in their entire pro careers.

Woodley will make $550,000 on the final year of the contract he was happy to sign as a rookie. He was being paid less than others who have not performed as well, that is true. But he has no cause for complaint. He and Reed will be rewarded in kind if they play up to the team's expectations.

It's time they started thinking more about how they can help the team turn things around, and how they could hold the fort until Big Ben is able to return to action after a four or six-game suspension by the league for his boorish misbehavior. There's too much self-interest in sports these days.

I've always thought the Steelers should travel to Canton when one of their own is being honored at the Pro Football Hall of Fame. Too many coaches get caught up in a certain regimen, a routine, x's and o's, and short-change the emotional aspect of sports. Too few coaches and players read books about successful athletes or successful people in all pursuits.

I recall being at the Steelers' training camp at St. Vincent in Latrobe in July of 1989 about a week before Steelers' cornerback Mel Blount was to be inducted into the Pro Football Hall of Fame. Joe Greene, a close friend and former teammate of Blount, was then an assistant coach on Chuck Noll's staff.

Greene was grousing about his personal predicament because he would not be able to attend Blount's induction into the Pro Football Hall of Fame. The Steelers would be holding two practice sessions that same Saturday.

"I think we should all go to Canton," said Greene. "I think it would be spending our time more productively."

I could not have agreed more. I always thought it would prove inspirational for the present-day Steelers to see how players who perform in an outstanding manner will be similarly honored some day at Canton.

I have gone to the Pro Football Hall of Fame on at least a dozen occasions. I've been there with my late mother and I've been there with the best of friends. It was always rewarding to make the trip. I was always inspired by the honorees at the Hall of Fame ceremonies.

I couldn't go this time. My wife Kathie and I were in Columbus baby-sitting for our granddaughters, Margaret and Susannah. I also watched sports on TV. Tiger Woods was playing his worst golf in his pro career in nearby Akron, and Lebron James was also in Akron, his hometown, to lead a fund-raiser for kids and to help soothe some wounds caused by his decision to leave the Cleveland Cavaliers in favor of the Miami Heat.

Mike Tomlin takes his players bowling one day during training camp, and he and Bill Cowher have taken the players to a movie rather than practicing on a particular day. I think he ought to make it a tradition to take them to the Pro Football Hall of Fame when a former Steelers' star is being honored. Jerome Bettis will be eligible again next summer and if he is voted in that would be an appropriate time to take the team by

Steelers' head coach Mike Tomlin

buses back to Canton. A little history goes a long way.

Here's a story for the benefit of Jeff Reed. I remember being at a Christian-related breakfast at the St. Clair Country Club during the spring in 1995. Gary Anderson, the Steelers' place-kicker and an ardent Christian, was the main speaker.

He was involved in a contract dispute with the Steelers at that time. He wanted to be paid $1 million for the coming season. Dan Rooney didn't want to pay him quite that much. Anderson told the audience they could understand what he was going through. Some of them had asked for raises at the office.

He further told them he wasn't going to worry about it. He told them he was going to leave it in the hands of his agent, and in the hands of God.

I stopped Anderson after the breakfast session. I asked him if he trusted me. He said he did. I asked him if I could offer him a word of advice. He said sure.

I told him that most of the people in the audience could not relate to his situation because most of them weren't making a million dollars a year, or anything close to it. You had to be a top executive at one of the leading Pittsburgh companies to make that kind of money.

114

I told him I didn't think God was worrying about the contract negotiations for kickers in the NFL. I suggested he place a phone call to Dan Rooney and set up a meeting at some restaurant midway between his home in Wexford and Dan Rooney's office in Pittsburgh. I suggested he speak to his boss and get something settled.

Anderson ignored my advice. He ended up playing for the Philadelphia Eagles and then the Minnesota Vikings. With the Vikings, he had a regular season where he didn't miss a field goal or an extra point, until the playoffs that is, and it cost the Vikings a possible championship. But Anderson was good, one of the very best.

Reed is second in Steelers' history in scoring, going into the 2010 season with 733 points, behind Anderson's 1,343. Reed was that good, too.

Reed got into at least two well-publicized embarrassing incidents this past year, and there might have been more except for some kind police officers who chased him home when he was misbehaving at local bars. The Steelers could have sent Reed packing at that time, but they chose to give him another chance. They might not be as forgiving when he says his bosses have been lying to him. Someone such as Art Rooney II could take that personally even if Reed's remarks weren't aimed at him.

Reed would be smart to keep a low profile. In short, he should be quiet. Reed does a lot of dumb things, but he isn't dumb. He graduated 9th in his high school class at Mecklinburg, N.C., and he was accepted into the University of North Carolina, which isn't easy to do. He did not come in with a football scholarship but was walk-on and earned a scholarship on merit. He was an Academic All-American at UNC.

He failed in seven tryouts with NFL teams. He made the Steelers in a tryout at Heinz Field with three other kicking prospects in mid-November of 2002. He replaced the injured Todd Peterson. In other words, he's lucky to be with the Steelers and in the National Football League. He once told me he never wanted to forget where he came from. I think it's time for him to remember. Maybe his visit to the Pro Football Hall of Fame will jog his memory.

There are a few kickers in the Pro Football Hall of Fame.

(Reed was released by the Steelers after the 2010 season.)

"The Immaculate Reception"

"Last chance for the Steelers. Bradshaw trying to get away. And his pass is...broken up by Tatum. Picked off! Franco Harris has it! And he's over! Franco Harris grabbed the ball on the deflection! Five seconds to go! He grabbed it with five seconds to go and scored!
—Curt Gowdy
calling the play for NBC Television

Dick Stockton is still
fond of Pittsburgh Steelers

September 2010

Troy Polamalu and Rashard Mendenhall saved the day for the Steelers and kept Pittsburghers from falling into deep depression as the 2010 season got underway. Polamalu made the "pick" that saved the Steelers from losing the game and Mendenhall made a 50-yard run for the winning touchdown in overtime in a 15–9 opener against the Atlanta Falcons at Heinz Field. Those of us watching the game on television should have recognized a familiar face and voice telling us just what was going on in the person of Fox Sports broadcaster Dick Stockton.

This was the first serious Steelers' game of the season so it was fitting that Stockton was doing the play-by-play for national television. He did the Steelers' first and last games at Three Rivers Stadium. "No one else knows that but me," said Stockton with a laugh when last we spoke. "They don't keep records on that sort of stuff."

Stockton and the Steelers share a history, and so do Stockton and I. We're old friends, starting with his days, only a few years out of Syracuse University, when the Philadelphia-born and New York-bred Stockton came to Pittsburgh to be the sports director at KDKA-TV. He didn't talk like us and he was often critical in his commentary—though unusually soft on the Steelers—so he was an outsider and it took him awhile to catch on here.

He was special, though, a rare talent. He knew his stuff and he was cocksure he knew his stuff, and that rubbed some people the wrong way. But Art Rooney and Dan Rooney recognized that he was a cut above broadcasters they'd known and they helped him make it to the major leagues in his business.

The Rooneys recommended him through the NFL office to network TV officials and before long Stockton was doing some assignments for CBS in addition to his duties at their Pittsburgh outlet. While he was working at KDKA-TV, he went to Miami for a week in January of 1979 to cover the Super Bowl. There was a Western Pennsylvania angle.

Joe Namath of Beaver Falls was the quarterback for the AFL's New York Jets and they were playing the NFL's Baltimore Colts in Super Bowl III. The Green Bay Packers under Vince Lombardi had won the first two championships between the NFL and AFL title holders. Bart Starr, like Namath a graduate of the University of Alabama, was the MVP for the Packers in both games. Now Namath would make an "I guarantee it" boast that the AFL upstarts would win this third game and then made good on his boast. Namath was named the MVP in Super Bowl III and pro football would never be the same.

While Stockton was in Miami, I was called in to replace him in doing the local sports report on KDKA-TV for a week. I had a chance to work with the legendary Bill Burns. The TV executives tried their best to teach me how to say "downtown" so I didn't sound like a guy from Hazelwood or the North Side. It's a good thing they never got their hands on Myron Cope. I survived my first and last week as a sportscaster at KDKA-TV.

Cope and I had both been under consideration for a job as a sports commentator in the morning for WTAE Radio in 1968, and they chose Cope. It was the right decision. I didn't get kept on at KDKA-TV after that tryout week. I went to Miami a few months later to cover the Miami Dolphins for *The Miami News*. A year later, I was covering the Super Bowl in New Orleans and shortly after that left Miami for New York, where I wrote for *The New York Post* and became the founding editor in 1970 for *Street & Sports Basketball Yearbook*. I wrote three books in my first two years in New York and never looked back. I wasn't Myron Cope and I wasn't Dick Stockton, but I was doing just fine.

I'd see Dick Stockton along the way. He was one of the few national broadcasters that could do all the sports. (He is, by the way, the only sports broadcaster to have a rest area named in his honor on the New Jersey Turnpike.) He did pro and college basketball—we actually teamed up to do an Eastern Eight basketball game at The Palestra in Philadelphia the year that Norm Nixon and Duquesne University won the title—and he did major league baseball and football. I'd see him at the NBA All-Star Games.

He was teamed with Hubie Brown on those NBA telecasts. I'd had a bad experience with Hubie Brown when he was the coach of the Kentucky Colonels in the ABA. He coached the Colonels to a championship in 1975 and they beat the Indiana Pacers in the playoffs. I had written a story Brown didn't like and, worse yet, his wife didn't like.

One night I was standing outside the locker room of the Colonels at Freedom Hall in Louisville interviewing their star player Dan Issel. All of a sudden I could not see, and I didn't know why. Some one had shoved a cream pie deep into my face. I didn't see it coming. Issel handed me his white towel and earned a spot on my all-time ABA all-star team (and a chapter in my book *ABA All-Stars*). I was so embarrassed.

I felt so bad when I left Freedom Hall that night and went to room at the nearby Executive Inn. When I walked into the lobby of that hotel—my favorite on the road under normal circumstances—I was wearing a press pass on the lapel of my sport coat and it identified me as being a member of *The New York Post*. A local basketball fan, a grizzled old-timer, spotted that badge and began berating me, and swatting me with his cane.

"You New York writers caused all those problems for the Kentucky basketball team in the '50s," he hollered. He was referring, of course, to the "basketball fix" stories that caught Kentucky and Bradley and Long Island and CCNY in a real nasty story. Their players had been accepting money from gamblers in exchange for affecting the end result and scores of games in which they were playing. It really impacted the sport for quite a while. "I wasn't even in New York when that happened," I told the old fan as I hustled to the elevator.

I went to my room and wrote my stories. Dick Young of *The New York Daily News* had told me once that people don't care about your personal problems on a particular night. You have to write the story; you have to get it in before your deadline. And I did. That's all that mattered.

I didn't find out until two years later who shoved that pie in my face that night. I did not know until I had a drink in a lounge of a Las Vegas hotel with Larry Donald of *The Basketball News*. He told me it was Hubie Brown's wife. So from then on whenever I'd see Hubie Brown we'd exchange a few nasty words.

I remember once standing at a urinal in a bathroom in an arena in Atlanta and Brown coming in and standing a few urinals away and us hollering back and forth at each other. Talk about being pissed at somebody. And here you thought Ben Roethlisberger was the only one who behaved badly in bathrooms in Georgia.

Stockton saw me in a lobby of a hotel in Houston when he was in the company of Hubie Brown. Stockton could sense the tension between me and Brown. Brown later told him what was behind our rocky relationship. Stockton got after both of us and arranged a peace treaty. They should send Stockton to the Mideast to settle the dispute between Palestine and Israel. After that, Brown and I got along fine. I thank Stockton for getting us to grow up a little. But I swear some of that cream pie is still wedged somewhere in my ears.

Stockton smiles when I share stories with him. Many think of him as a New Yorker, but he was actually born in Philadelphia in 1942. So we're the same age—70—and he's one of those broadcasters who has kept his enthusiasm and his voice and is—like Vin Scully of the Dodgers and John Sterling of the Yankees—still one of the best at the mike. Stockton grew up in New York and knew both of those voices when the Dodgers were in Brooklyn and the Yankees were in The Bronx. Yeah, he makes little mistakes now and then, but it's not because he has what Art Rooney Jr. calls "old timer's disease."

Stockton has a special affection for all the Rooneys. "The Rooneys were always at my back," he says proudly.

"The thing I remember best, after I left Pittsburgh," said Stockton, "is that at some point when I would be doing the NBA finals on CBS-TV each year, I'd get a letter from Art Rooney. He'd remember my days working in Pittsburgh, at KDKA-TV, of course, and he'd write 'Dear Dick, We were in New England and I saw you on TV...,' and 'you were the best" or "you were the class" or something like that. It always made me feel great. I have eight of those letters framed and on display on the wall in my home in Boca Raton, Florida."

I have saved postcards Mr. Rooney sent me from faraway places such as Ireland, Mexico, Canada and California, and only wish I had a copy of a beautiful letter he sent to my mother when she has having a health challenge.

Stockton shared a home in Boca Raton with his wife Lesley Visser, whom I first knew as a sports writer for *The Boston Globe*, and then later as a TV sports reporter and personality. When I was working as the assistant athletic director for public relations at the University of Pittsburgh, I once ran into Ms. Visser in the Boston College gym. I told her to check with one of my assistants who was in charge of basketball publicity. "You mean you're not," she said. "That's like having Dr. J on the bench." And you wonder why I love Dick Stockton and his wife Leslie Visser? They met, I think, when they were both covering a Boston Red Sox baseball game back in the mid-70s. (*They were divorced a few years back and she has remarried.*)

I've been to Boca Raton and it's a beautiful community in South Florida. I went there in the summer of 1979 to cover the Miami Dolphins at their pre-season training camp.

"Bill Burns, who was the main guy on KDKA-TV, was a close friend of Art Rooney," recalled Stockton. "And I mean a close friend. He was with him a lot. I was 24-years-old when I began my first major television job in Pittsburgh in 1967. They thought of me as a New Yorker. I had that New York brashness about me, and I'm sure it didn't go down well with everyone there." Some fans said Stockton reminded them of Howard Cosell. And that wasn't' a compliment in The City of Champions.

Myron Cope once told Howard Cosell how well things were in his life and what a big hit he was. "In Pittsburgh," said Cosell succinctly. End of story. Cope wrote a story on Cosell for *Sports Illustrated* that is still included in many of the Best Sports Story anthologies.

I shared a story with Stockton about how I once was home on leave from the U.S. Army and I visited the Steelers' offices to see Mr. Rooney. Bill Burns was in his office. I was stationed at the Army Home Town News Center in Kansas City where I served as an editor. I moon-lighted helping out in the press box at Kansas City's Municipal Stadium, for Charley Finley's A's during the baseball season and for Lamar Hunt's Chiefs during the football season. I spotted for Charlie Jones and Paul Christman on AFL telecasts. What was really great about it was that I—who was getting about ten bucks a day in meal money from the government—was able to join the writers and broadcasters at the buffet in the media room.

"The Chiefs are a really good team," I told Rooney during the 1966 season. I mentioned Lenny Dawson, Buck Buchanan, Bobby Bell, Johnny Robinson, Otis Taylor, Willie Lanier, E.J. Holub, Mack Lee Hill, Abner Haynes, Ed Budde, Emmitt Thomas, Jan Stenerud and some other great players who were on the Chiefs. Their coach was Hank Stram. Most of these men today are enshrined in the Pro Football Hall of Fame in Canton, Ohio.

"How good could they be if Lenny Dawson is their quarterback?" blurted Burns. "We traded him away."

"Hey, the Steelers let Johnny Unitas get away," I said. "They let Sid Luckman go to the Bears. They let Bill Nelsen get away and he's terrific with the Browns. That's no barometer of how good the Chiefs could be."

Art Rooney smiled. He used to send positive post cards congratulating Lenny Dawson when he did something special. He did the same for Johnny Unitas. To Art Rooney, they were still his players.

That's the kind of guy he was. Nellie King, who passed away in 2010, once told me that we was let go by the Pirates, along with Bob Prince, that the first card he received expressing disappointment that he'd been let go came from none other than Art Rooney. "I never heard from the Pirates' owner John Galbraith," confided King. "That tells you all you need to know about the difference in the owners of Pittsburgh's two ball teams." None of this would surprise Stockton. "I got into the elevator one day at Gateway Center and Bill Burns was with some of his buddies. He kept right on talking when I got on. He didn't talk to me. He was telling them what players the Steelers were going to leave unprotected in an expansion draft to stock the New Orleans Saints. None of the sports guys in town knew who was on that list, not yet anyhow, but Bill Burns knew and he wanted me to know that he knew. He was telling these guys for my sake. He was telling me, 'You may be a hot-shot coming in here, but I still know more than you. I'm still more connected than you'll ever be.'

"They were playing a pre-season game with the Bengals at Forbes Field. I told Art Rooney my dad was coming to the game with some other family members. He said, 'Tell your father they can sit with me.' So my dad had a chance to meet the great Art Rooney.

"The Rooneys were responsible for me getting into network TV. They recommended me to the powers-that-be at CBS. They talked to Bill McPhail and Bil Pitts on my behalf. I'd only been at KDKA a short time when they did that. They had me do a post-game show on the Steelers. They helped me get my foot in the door at CBS.

"Dan Rooney was directly responsible for me getting a network connection. Bill Pitts, the executive producer of NFL football, was looking for someone to do a few post-game shows. Dan recommended me to him. Pitts saw a tape I did and he liked it. I got to do six games that first year, all Steelers games from Pitt Stadium, and that was the start of my network assignments with CBS.

"When I did my strong opinionated commentaries on KDKA, I don't know whether you noticed it or not, but I never came down too hard on the Steelers. I always seemed to miss the Steelers. That's because of Art Rooney."

I told him it wasn't much different these days.

> **"We are all individuals caught in an enormous web that consists of other people."**
> **—Tom Wolfe**

"Pittsburgh was the ideal city to get my act together."
—Dick Stockton

"Art Rooney was the No. 1 owner I've known," said Stockton. "I knew people that I respected and admired like Red Auerbach, Wellington Mara and Tom Yawkey, but no family in sports was ever kinder, friendlier, warmer and as sincere at the Rooney family.

"Now I appreciate my four years in PIttsburgh. I really became a broadcaster. It was a period in which I really gained polish on the air. From then on, I was ready for any assignment. I went from a guy who didn't know what he was doing to being a guy who knew his stuff.

"If I started out in any other city, I don't know if I'd be where I am today. Pittsburgh was the ideal city to get my act together. But I was always wondering where I was going. I wanted to get back to New York and work in my hometown."

Photo by Jim O'Brien

Dick Stockton of Fox Sports fondly recalls his days in Pittsburgh.

Photo from Steelers Archives

Howard Cosell speaks to Art Rooney during the Steelers' 50 Seasons Celebration.

Al Davis was different and he
changed the face of pro football

October 2011

A l Davis died at his home in Oakland, California last week. He was 82 and he had been challenged by ill health for several years. I last saw him on Sunday, October 2, when the TV cameras focused on him as he sat behind glass windows in the owners' box as his Oakland Raiders were defeated by the New England Patriots. He missed seeing only three games in his 49 years with the Raiders.

Al Davis didn't look good. He hasn't looked good in a long time. Some Steelers' fans felt he never looked good. His face was the face of the enemy. The silver and gold never liked the silver and black. Davis was the Darth Vader of pro football.

Chuck Noll never liked Al Davis. They were both assistant coaches under Sid Gillman with the Los Angeles and then San Diego Chargers in the early '60s. Dan Rooney didn't care much for Al Davis. He once called him "a lying creep." They later made up.

When Dan Rooney bid goodbye to his fellow owners at one of their meetings a few years ago—he was going to be spending time overseas as our ambassador to Ireland—he said, "I'll miss all of you guys, even you Al."

Al Davis came up and embraced Dan Rooney and shook his hand and wished him well on his new assignment.

Arthur J. Rooney Sr., the late owner and founder of the Steelers, liked Al Davis. He said, "He's a good football man, if he'd keep his mind on football."

Davis was always taking the league to court on one issue or another, fighting to keep his Raiders in LA or Oakland, or to relocate them wherever he wished. Davis had his own "reality TV series" before there was such a thing.

I spent time with Al Davis on at least a dozen occasions over a lifetime as a sportswriter and he was always interesting, available and quotable. I liked Al Davis.

He died the same week that another Northern California icon died. Steve Jobs, the founder and CEO of Apple, Inc., died at age 56. Both were geniuses in their own game. The Raiders won't be the Raiders without Al Davis and Apple won't be Apple without Steve Jobs. Both were innovative and inspirational and difficult to live with, and they changed their respective worlds.

Though Davis grew up in a nice home in a nice neighborhood, he liked to portray himself as a tough guy from the streets of Brooklyn. But he graduated from Syracuse University with a degree in English, so he was never able to pull it off convincingly.

I had a degree in English from Pitt, and Myron Cope accused me of playing "the poor kid from Hazelwood" role a bit much, so Davis and I had a bond. We understood each other.

Davis became the youngest coach in the NFL at age 33 in 1963 and he would later become the owner of the Oakland Raiders and one of the leaders of the American Football League. He's one of the reasons the Raiders and the AFL lived to merge with the established NFL. There was no Raider for top talent like Al Davis.

Davis was often at odds with the other owners and with NFL Commissioners whether it was Pete Rozelle, Paul Tagliabue or Roger Goodell. Davis was daring and determined. "Win, baby, win," was his slogan in running the Raiders' operation. He stressed excellence in his organization.

He liked black and silver and chose them for the team's uniforms because he thought the colors were intimidating. His Raiders won three Super Bowls and they were the chief rival of the Steelers for a long time. He and Raiders' coach John Madden never forgave Franco Harris for "The Immaculate Reception" in the 1972 playoffs.

I first met Al Davis in the office of Beano Cook, when he was the sports information director at Pitt. This was in 1961 or 1962 and I was an undergraduate at Pitt. I was the sports editor of *The Pitt News* and I helped out in Beano's office at the Pitt Field House.

This was a Friday before a football game at nearby Pitt Stadium. Davis was one of four individuals who came to Cook's office back-to-back in a 15-minute period to pick up their press box credentials for the following day.

First came Davis, then an assistant coach and scout for the Chargers. He was followed by Frank "Bucko" Kilroy, a scout for the Washington Redskins who had played for the "Steagles" in 1943; Emlen Tunnell, a scout for the New York Giants who had been a great defensive back for that club in the '50s and '60s, and then Red Smith, the outstanding sports columnist of the *New York Herald-Tribune*.

They are all in one kind of Hall of Fame or another. I was about 20 at the time and it should have been a tip-off to me that life as a sports-writer would be a good life.

I have been fortunate ever since to spend time with and interview some of the greatest names in sports. Al Davis was one of them. He was the least known of the four when I first met him.

He was wearing a black leather jacket over a black turtle neck jersey, dark sun glasses, and his hair was combed back in the "ducktail" style, a holdover from the '50s. He looked like The Fonz, a wise-cracking street corner guy from the TV Series "Happy Days" as played by Henry Winkler in a cast headed by future movie director Ron Howard. To the end, Al Davis had a "ducktail" hair style.

I ran into Davis about eight years later in a hotel swimming pool in Atlanta. I was covering a pre-season contest involving the Miami Dolphins. I was writing for *The Miami News* at the time.

We were both splish-splashing away when we came upon each other face to face. I introduced myself and he said, "I know who you are,

Jim O'Brien. I've read your stories."

I later learned that Al Davis read the sports sections of the daily newspapers in all the cities in the league. This was 1969, the last season of the AFL before the merger with the NFL in 1970.

Al Davis was a lot like Yankees' owner George Steinbrenner in that respect. They both read the sports sections from cover to cover and they were aware of what was going on in all sports, not just their sport. Art Rooney was like that, too, a man for all seasons.

I would see Al Davis at the NFL Owners' Meetings at Maui and Scottsdale and Palm Springs when I was covering the Steelers for *The Pittsburgh Press* in the '80s. Imagine getting paid to spend time in those exotic places, partying and playing tennis with the owners and coaches in pro football. I was also fortunate enough to do that in pro baseball and basketball as well. I miss those days.

Davis was always delightful company. He liked to talk to sportswriters and share his opinions on any subject. He said he didn't seek the spotlight, but other owners accused him of being a showboat.

I remember seeing Al Davis when he attended the funeral Mass of Art Rooney at St. Peter's Church on the North Side in late August, 1988.

Something ironic happened that day. The church was filled. It was SRO. There had to be sixty or seventy priests there that day. George Young, the general manager of the Giants and a long time pal of Art Rooney Jr., the team's player personnel director in the '70s, said, "No Catholic in Pittsburgh better have died that day or there'd be no priest available to give them the last rites."

Pete Rozelle came into the church to pay his respects and an usher took him down the center aisle, and seated him in the last seat available on the aisle. I was sitting in a pew directly across the aisle. Al Davis was sitting directly ahead of Rozelle on the aisle seat.

I knew what was coming. When the officiating priest told those in attendance to turn and offer a peace greeting to those in front and behind them, I smiled as Al Davis turned and, to his surprise, saw Rozelle there. They shook hands and offered thin smiles. I thought that Art Rooney Sr. was smiling overhead and that he'd had a hand in this peace offering as well. He was pulling strings as a puppeteer in heaven.

Davis was accompanied by his wife Carol at St. Peter's. Davis was always quick to introduce his wife. He called her "Caroli." She had a stroke in 1979 and nearly died. When she was deathly ill in the early '80s, Davis recalled how Art Rooney was in constant touch, sent her flowers often, sent her encouraging words, and went to visit her. Davis said he would never forget Rooney's concern and personal kindness toward him and his wife.

Carol Davis confirmed the goodness of Art Rooney. "He's one of the last of a vanishing breed," she said. "When you find somebody as special as him, you better treasure him. He's such a good man. When I was sick, he said he remembered me in his prayers."

I used to go to the Pro Football Hall of Fame Weekend activities in Canton, Ohio most summers in the '80s and '90s.

Davis would be there. Davis was often chosen by his Raiders' players to present them for the Hall of Fame induction.

I saw him present Fred Belitnikoff, Art Shell and Gene Upshaw. Davis was also inducted into the Pro Football Hall of Fame. Some of my friends feel he is undeserving, but that's mostly because they don't like him and thought him a bit of an outlaw, always opposing the league in one way or another. I talked to him inside the Hall of Fame in the summer of 1989. John Henry Johnson and Joe Greene of the Steelers got in that year, and so did Gene Upshaw. I was with my buddies Bill Priatko and Rudy Celigoi, both from North Braddock, and we were talking to a former Raider from Youngwood, Pennsylvania, the great George Blanda, and then Mike Ditka, of Aliquippa and Pitt. Davis strolled by, dressed in black. He saw us talking to Blanda and Ditka, and he thundered, "You guys from Pittsburgh are always hanging out together." He smiled and posed for some pictures.

George Blanda
From Youngwood, Pa.

Al Davis and Dan Rooney discuss football issues at Three Rivers Stadium

Among the many NFL officials who attended the funeral service of Art Rooney Sr. at St. Peter's Church on the North Side were, at left, Oakland Raiders' owner Al Davis, Philadelphia Eagles' owner Leonard Tose, forefront, and Carol Davis, at right, the wife of Al Davis.

Franco Harris endures "a week from hell"
and pays for loyalty to Joe Paterno

November 2011

Franco Harris was not at the head of the long table, where he was supposed to be, on the seventh floor of the Heinz History Center in The Strip. Franco was frequently not where he was supposed to be during his heyday with the Steelers, back in the '70s, as he often strayed from the play that was called in the huddle to search for an opening so he could run to daylight. He danced a lot.

The Steelers' offensive linemen said that Franco's running mate Rocky Bleier was reliable, always running to the hole as drawn up in the playbook, and that Rocky would be on their backside in a second, but that they had to hold their blocks longer for Franco because he might be coming back their way.

Franco has served for seven years as the chairman of the Championship Committee for the Sports Museum at the Heinz History Center. Franco has been faithful to the task. He's listed as one of the seven honorary chairmen of the committee, but he's the only one who has even been at a meeting.

The other honorary chairpersons are Mario Lemieux, Bill Mazeroski, Stan Musial, Arnold Palmer, Suzie McConnell-Serio and Chip Ganassi. Their grand names lend credibility to the sports museum, and look good on a plaque and museum promotional pieces, but Franco's real leadership has shown the way.

Franco is quite serious about his role with this group. As a player, Harris hated to be interviewed or probed about his heroics, but now he is an eloquent spokesman for the museum. He has matured and has come to appreciate the importance of the region's sports history.

He has long been an ambassador for good in this town. He has been a good example, for instance, for Homestead's Charlie Batch who's busy helping out wherever he can lend his name and presence.

Franco Harris is pictured, along with General George Washington, on a mural on the façade of the Heinz History Center, and a statue of him making "The Immaculate Reception" stands next to one of General Washington to greet visitors to the Pittsburgh International Airport.

Franco Harris has chaired every previous meeting, about every six months, and he has come prepared to discuss business. He's had an agenda. He takes notes. Josh Gibson, the great catcher and home run hitter for the Homestead Grays and Pittsburgh Crawfords, was among the topics to be discussed at this meeting. So was Franco's "Immaculate Reception."

This cried out for Franco's presence, but his absence was understandable and, indeed, forgivable.

I have served on the committee since the museum opened in 2004 and have been impressed with Franco's commitment. His presence at the meetings makes them seem more important. It's good to be in his company. He suffers my questions better these days. We have both grown up.

That's why Andy Masich, the president and CEO of the Heinz History Center, was doing his best to explain Franco's absence at last Tuesday's meeting. A light shower was falling outside and it was another gray day in Pittsburgh.

The past week had been full of dark days as the news out of Penn State University, Franco's alma mater, continued to paint a sad picture of everything that could go wrong on a college campus. Jerry Sandusky, the former defensive coordinator for Penn State's highly-respected football program, had been arrested and charged with 40 counts of criminal activity, abusing young children in his care.

Joe Paterno, the head football coach who had won more games than any coach of a major program in history, had been fired, and so was the school president, Graham Spanier. There was new fallout each passing day.

"I just got a call from Franco," began Masich, "and he's not going to be able to make it today. He apologizes for his absence, and says he is with us in spirit. You can only imagine what he must be going through at this time.

"He's back at State College to be with Coach Paterno, to be with him at this difficult time in his life. Franco's mother-in-law died last week and there was a funeral service and burial. Franco said it was a week from hell."

Bess Dokmanovich died at age 83 the previous Tuesday. Her viewing was at the Tatalovich Funeral Home in Hopewell and she was buried in a cemetery nearby on Friday. She grew up of Serbian heritage in Clairton and her daughter, Dana, has been Franco's wife since his days at Penn State.

Franco and Dana were not formally married, so Bess referred to herself as "Franco's sort-of-mother-in-law" in a wonderful article about the Steelers' star running back in a 1982 issue of *Sports Illustrated*. She lived with Franco and Dana back then in a townhouse in the Mexican War Streets of the North Side.

She helped with their son Franco "Dok" Harris and she served as Franco's secretary for his various endeavors.

That article was written by Roy Blount Jr., a terrific writer from the South, best known for writing the wonderful book about the Steelers in the '70s called *About Three Bricks Shy of a Load*.

Sometimes, when people are telling me what books of mine they've read, they often include that book, as well as Rocky Bleier's book *Fighting Back*. That was written by Terry O'Neill.

Oh well, during my New York days, there was a sportswriter named Bob Waters who always called me O'Neill. O'Neill...O'Brien... what's the difference?

I've even been told I wrote the book about Myron Cope—*Double Yoi!*—which was Myron's memoir. I just smile.

Franco, by the way, was one of the pallbearers at Myron's funeral, along with another former Steelers' star Andy Russell, and one of Myron's longtime friends, Frank Haller. I sat at a table, at Franco's invitation, with Franco, Andy and Rocky Bleier and their mates that day, and the round-table discussion was a keepsake.

These have all been major players on the Pittsburgh sports scene. Franco has done so much to make a difference in this community with his different contributions to worthy causes.

So you had to feel for Franco and other Penn Staters as they tried their best to make some sense of the sorry mess that had occurred on their Happy Valley campus. Joe Paterno had failed to do what he had to do to report the crime of his former coach, Jerry Sandusky, and to get Sandusky as far from the campus as possible.

Instead, Paterno was part of the cover-up. It was more important to protect the good name of Penn State and its football program.

Franco and Jack Ham, who both came out of the Paterno program at Penn State, to star for the Steelers and be so good that they both have been inducted into the Pro Football Hall of Fame, took different stances on the Penn State issue.

Franco felt that Penn State had done his coach wrong, by firing him. He thought his coach deserved better. Ham shared Franco's devotion to Paterno, since he has spent more time with him while serving for so many years as the game analyst on radio broadcasts of Penn State football games.

But Ham said Paterno had to be removed from his position. "They had to do a clean break," said Ham.

Ham could have been risking his position as the Penn State analyst by saying this, just as Bill Fralic felt the need to step aside from a similar role at Pitt after being critical of Pitt's athletic director Steve Pederson for firing Dave Wannstedt as the Panthers' head football coach after last season.

Talking about Joe Paterno, Ham said, "I have known him for a long time. I know all the things he has done for college football, all the players who have come through the program. He's a special man in my eyes."

Franco felt that way, too, but he wanted Paterno to prevail.

"I felt that the board made a bad decision letting Joe Paterno go," offered Franco in a public complaint. "I'm very disappointed in this decision. I thought they showed no loyalty, not to back someone who really needed it at this time. They were saying the football program and Joe were at fault."

By now, certainly you have seen the TV commercials featuring Franco Harris and Rocky Bleier as spokesmen for The Meadows Racetrack and Casino. There are several versions and Franco and Rocky are still popular players in this region, no matter the games they are endorsing. It's good to see them together again, and they look bright-eyed and enthusiastic and still make a great team.

Franco found out last Tuesday that there is a price for supporting suddenly unpopular people. He was dropped as the spokesperson, perhaps temporarily, as the casino owners decided to sever the relationship because of his public support for Paterno.

That had to be a good gig for Franco, with generous compensation still to come in the future. The body count continues.

I thought Penn State should have allowed Paterno to finish this season and retire. I felt that way at the start of the season, before any of the Sandusky sodomy stories were revealed. I thought Paterno deserved to go out with some dignity. Others disagree and take a harsher stand on the issues. Others are waiting for more disclosures before deciding how they feel about it.

Paterno's name has been removed from a Big Ten trophy that was to bear his name and that of another famous college football coach, Amos Alonzo Stagg. There was talk of removing his statue from the campus. Personally, I think they are piling it on when Paterno needs a friend. Franco felt the need to be a friend.

After all, Joe Paterno did not commit the crime. It's always the cover up, the lies, the cheating, that undermine major figures, whether you are talking about Al Capone, O.J. Simpson, Pete Rose, Barry Bonds, Roger Clemens, Mark McGwire, Sammy Sosa, and so many others. Put Richard Nixon at the head of the list.

I recall that Joe Gordon, the outstanding public relations director for the Steelers during the glory days of the '70s, often said, "Don't tell the first lie."

There was some good news to come of last week's meeting of the Championship Committee of the Sports Museum at the Heinz History Center.

It's difficult to comprehend how time flies when you're having fun.

There will be a special Negro League Baseball Exhibit coming to the former ice house on Smallman Street this summer. It will be a way to mark the 100th anniversary of Josh Gibson, who was born on December 21, 1911.

Gibson, who was called "the black Babe Ruth," played for the Homestead Grays in 1930 and 1931, sandwiched in between two stays with the Pittsburgh Crawfords, from 1927–1929 and 1932–1936.

Tony Quatrini of the marketing department of the Steelers, pointed out that 2012 will be the 40th anniversary of the "Immaculate Reception." Franco made that improbable catch and score as the Steelers gained their first playoff victory in the team's history back in the 1972 season, his rookie year with the Steelers.

Also ahead is a season-long celebration of the 80th season of the Pittsburgh Steelers. They started out as the Pittsburgh Pirates in 1933 and their nickname was changed to the Steelers in 1940.

That's real sports history. Andy Masich disclosed some other developments at the sports museum to update some of its listings and displays. He said we needed to have another meeting in a few months to outline plans.

He said he was confident that Franco Harris would be there, taking his seat at the head of the table. By then, hopefully, some of the wounds from the Penn State scandal and the grief over the death of Bess Dokmanovich will be healed. That would be a good way to start The New Year. We can be thankful if that happens.

Jim O'Brien

Sean Gibson, the grandson of Josh Gibson, the great catcher and home run hitter for the Homestead Grays, shares thoughts on plans for anniversary celebration with Franco Harris, chairman of the Heinz History Center's Championship Committee.

Jack Fleming's famous call on radio of "Immaculate Reception"

"Hang onto your hats, here come the Steelers out of the huddle. Twenty-two seconds remaining ... It's down to one big play, fourth down and 10 yards to go. Terry Bradshaw at the controls. And Bradshaw is running out of the pocket, looking for somebody to throw to, fires it down field, and there's a collision (sound volume rises). And it's caught out of the air! The ball is pulled in by Franco Harris. Harris is going for a touchdown for Pittsburgh! Harris is going in... five seconds left on the clock. Franco Harris pulled in the football. I don't even know where he came from!"

Franco Harris introduced his Penn State coach Joe Paterno when Paterno was hailed as a "History Maker" at Heinz History Center recognition dinner.

Franco Harris and Jack Ham came out of Joe Paterno's program at Penn State to star for Steelers and gain induction into the Pro Football Hall of Fame.

Jack Butler will remain the same
even in the Pro Football Hall of Fame

February 2012

Jack Butler lives in a big house at the extreme end of town where Munhall says hello to Homestead. He and his wife Bernie have been in that handsome brick mansion for about 50 of his 84 years. It's on 11th Avenue near the iconic Homestead Library.

Butler is basically a stay-at-home guy but he knows how to get to Main Street in Munhall. He doesn't know the name of the barber shop where he gets his hair cut in a conservative manner, but he knows the man holding the sharp scissors is named Carmine. He said the barber shop he favors is in a strip of shops, near the post office.

"I don't loaf there, or hang around bars there," he said when we spoke on the telephone. "I don't get out much. I don't know that many people. Some of the faces are familiar to me, but I can count on a few fingers my real friends."

He and his wife Bernie attend Mass every Sunday at St. Maximillian Kolbe in Homestead. That used to be St. Anne's. I wondered whether the priests there might be saying prayers for Butler's Hall of Fame selection. I spoke to the church secretary, but she wasn't familiar with Jack Butler, and the pastor was not present when I called. I left a message but the priest never called back to talk to me about Jack Butler.

Butler obviously likes to keep a low profile.

I asked Butler if anybody was stopping him in the street to wish him well about his Hall of Fame election. "Not really," he said. "I am getting more attention in the way of phone calls from people in the media wanting to know how I feel about it."

I spoke to Butler and two of his good buddies in the same two-hour time frame on the telephone that day. They are a lot alike: self-deprecating decent men with a gleam in their eyes, men who like to promote other men. They make you feel better.

We talked about Butler's chances of being elected to the Pro Football Hall of Fame in a voting that would take place last Saturday morning in Indianapolis, at the site of Super Bowl XLVI.

Art Rooney Jr. and Jack McGinley Jr. were both optimistic of their friend's chances. Art Jr. is the second son of Steelers' founder Art Rooney Sr., and he spoke to me from his winter home, a condominium apartment in Palm Beach, Florida. Jack McGinley is the oldest son of Jack McGinley, who owned a beer distributing company in Lawrenceville as well as a minority position with the Steelers. The McGinleys have a background in Braddock and that helps keep them humble.

Jack Jr. is a respected Pittsburgh attorney, a senior partner at Eckert Seamans Cherin & Mellot in the U.S. Steel Tower. He has a perpetual smile on his face and a gleam behind his eyeglasses and

Steelers' Hall of Fame cornerbacks Jack Butler and Mel Blount speak at Steelers' 50 Seasons Celebration at David L. Lawrence Convention Center in 1983.

Jack Butler in leather helmet days with the Steelers (1951–1959)

Jack Butler and Jack McGinley Jr. at ceremonies honoring Butler at their alma mater, St. Bonaventure University.

that makes him a popular fellow. He makes sense when he speaks, though he has to be forgiven for his excess in professing his love for Central Catholic High School, St. Bonaventure University, the Catholic Church, the Rooneys and his family. Hey, he boosts a lot of people.

Art Jr. and Jack Jr. are both minority owners of the Steelers and big boosters of Jack Butler. They both campaigned for his election to the Pro Football Hall of Fame. I have correspondence dating back to 2008 from Jack Jr. in my JACK BUTLER folder in my office files urging me to assist in the campaign

"I have dinner with Artie about once a month," said Butler, "and the McGinleys are great people, and have always been kind to me. Their dads were two of the most wonderful men I've ever met. Everyone knows what a great guy Art Rooney Sr. was, but Jack McGinley was right up there with him."

I seconded that motion. Time spent with Jack McGinley Sr. and his family, with a priest usually at the table, is treasured time. I was his guest on occasion at the Allegheny Club at Three Rivers Stadium and the P.A.A. in Oakland, where he took a daily dip in the swimming pool.

Butler, who starred as a defensive back and occasional receiver for nine seasons (1951–1959), was nominated by a special veterans committee for consideration for the honor.

"I never thought much about it," Butler said of the Pro Football Hall of Fame. "It will be nice if I get in, but it won't be the end of the world if I don't. I have other things to think about or worry about."

Jack and his wife Bernie and their daughter Maureen and her husband were in a hotel room in Indianapolis on Saturday, waiting for a phone call to tell Jack if he had been elected or not. This is the first year the NFL brought all the nominees to the site so they could be present for potential interviews.

Maureen said they had already started packing their bags to head home because they hadn't received a call by 5:45 p.m. They were supposed to make the announcement at 5:30, but it was delayed, which the Butlers didn't realize. They just assumed Jack didn't make it.

He was asked at a press conference later that day what it meant to him to be selected to the Pro Football Hall of Fame.

He caught himself saying the word "hell" and he quickly retreated to erase that in favor of "heck." He said the award would mean more to his family, and then he thought better of that and corrected that thought as well, confessing that it would mean a lot to him, too. I had stressed to him that it was a big deal and that it would sink in once he was selected and inducted.

That induction will come this summer at the sports shrine in Canton, Ohio, which bills itself as "the birthplace of pro football," even though more recent research shows that Pittsburgh was actually the first place where someone was paid to play the game. I told him they were expanding the Hall of Fame building in Canton so he could fit in.

"There has been a sentiment among the voters," said Art Rooney Jr., "that there were too many Steelers in the Hall of Fame. That hurt Butler and L.C. Greenwood, Donnie Shell and Dermontti Dawson."

They introduced the new class of 2012 before the coin flip at the Super Bowl, and they lined them up alphabetically, and Butler came first and Willie Roaf, a lineman for the Kansas City Chiefs and New Orleans Saints, stood at the other end. It would be an especially grand day for football fans from Western Pennsylvania.

Dermontti Dawson, a center for the Steelers, and two former Pitt players, running back Curtis Martin and defensive end Chris Doleman were there, along with Cortez Kennedy, a defensive tackle for the Seattle Seahawks. Martin is from my hometown of Hazelwood and went to Taylor Allderdice High. Doleman was on Foge Fazio's football team when I was the assistant athletic director for public relations at Pitt in the mid-80s. I remember Doleman was sidelined for the season with an injury in the first game of his senior year and that dearly hurt the Panthers' prospects.

Butler was the pale white guy on the left end, the one who looked like a deer caught in headlights. He looked like he had just gotten off the boat from Ireland. He wasn't sure whether to smile or cry, so he did neither.

"I think he was shell-shocked," said a friend who saw Butler on TV when the 2012 Hall of Fame class was introduced, "but I know he was happy."

Besides, his left knee was hurting. He hurt that knee making a tackle of Pete Retzlaff of the Philadelphia Eagles during the 1959 season. I met and spent time with Pete Retzlaff in Philadephia during the summer of 1963 when I was a summer intern in the sports department of *The Philadelphia Bulletin*. He taught me the proper way to catch a football.

The injury and the follow-up surgery to Butler nearly killed him, and it cut short his pro playing career. He's had a hitch in his walk ever since. He ranked as the NFL's second-leading interceptor with 52 picks when he retired. He played in four Pro Bowls. He retired a few years ago from overseeing an NFL scouting agency.

Butler still ranks second in interceptions in the Steelers' record books to Mel Blount who had 57 interceptions. Butler accomplished his mark in 103 games in nine seasons, while Blount was in 200 games over 14 years.

Butler holds the team record for interceptions in one game with four against the Washington Redskins in 1953. He still holds the team record for return yards with interceptions with 827 yards, 98 more yards than runner-up Rod Woodson.

Butler intercepted ten passes one year, and nine in another year—when there were 12 games in a season—and returned several of them for touchdowns, including a game-winner against the New York Giants. Maybe that memory came back to him as he witnessed the Giants' exciting victory over the New England Patriots last Sunday evening.

I mentioned to Butler that Ike Taylor, the cornerback of the Steelers, is regarded as a terrific pass defender these days, but that he can't intercept passes to save his life, or to turn the tide for the Steelers in close games. "He has wooden hands," said Butler.

Scouts talk that way, in short staccato sentences.

Butler returned four interceptions for touchdowns, and picked up a fumble and scored six points as well during his stay with the Steelers. Only Woodson, with five interception returns for touchdowns, topped Butler in that team category.

Mel Blount and Rod Woodson both were inducted into the Pro Football Hall of Fame in their first year of eligibility, but Butler has had to wait all this time. His situation was similar to that of Dick LeBeau, the Steelers' defensive coordinator, who got in the previous summer via a special veterans' selection committee nomination.

LeBeau was boosting Butler for induction as well.

Butler grew up in Oakland and Whitehall. He and Frank Thomas, one of the Pirates' most prodigious home run hitters, both came out of Oakland and went to Mount Carmel College, a seminary in Niagara Falls, Ontario. It's where they went to high school and it's where they both decided they didn't want to be priests.

Both went on to play pro sports. Both fathered eight children. Jack and Bernie Butler have four boys and four girls and 15 grandchildren. Jack went to St. Bonaventure College where the athletic director was Father Dan Rooney, also known as Father Silas Rooney, who was the brother of Steelers' owner Art Rooney.

Joe Bach, who would coach the Steelers in two different stints, was the head football coach at St. Bonaventure.

"We honored Jack with an honorary degree at St. Bonaventure's two years ago," said Jack McGinley Jr., a proud graduate of the Olean, N.Y., school and also the chairman of the board of trustees at his alma mater.

"So if he gets into the Pro Football Hall of Fame," said McGinley with tongue in cheek, "it will be Jack's second greatest honor."

Frank Thomas told me he used to sneak into baseball games at Forbes Field when he was a child. Butler says he remembers going to one Steelers' game at Forbes Field with his father and his uncle. "I don't remember much about the game or who they were playing," said Butler. "I was more interested in getting a hot dog and some soda pop."

That's part of the charm of Jack Butler. He's not the easiest interview. He won't toot his own horn. I recalled that he spoke several years ago at a testimonial dinner for his old teammate, the late Fran Rogel from North Braddock Scott, California (Pa.) and Penn State.

"I'm not much a speaker," Butler began his remarks that night at the Churchill Country Club. He went on to offer a brief, but to-the-point and from-the-heart tribute for an old friend. I was the emcee that evening, and I told Butler he was the best of a too long line of long-winded speakers.

"They killed it with too many speeches," Butler told Art Rooney, Jr., who was among those in attendance that evening. Even so, it was a special evening for admirers and friends of Fran Rogel, who joined the Steelers the year before Butler.

Butler came to the Steelers as an undrafted free agent in 1951 and was the last player to make the 33-man squad. He started out as a two-way end, but moved to the secondary because of an injury to a starting cornerback.

Jack Butler, Art Rooney Jr. and Jack McGinley Jr. all take pride in their Catholic faith. Art goes to Mass every morning. They are spiritual men and they are throwbacks to another era, a simpler, better era.

They speak humbly and positively and they employ expressions that have gone out of date. "Get a hot meal," Art Jr. will tell you if you have lunch with him at the St. Clair Country Club. "I owe you a steak dinner. I'm having a poor man's sandwich."

They don't use foul language. With all the heroics in his Steelers' career, Butler never would have thought of thumping his chest, or doing a specially choreographed dance in the end zone. Butler would never behave the way ballplayers do today when they make a routine tackle, or catch a pass.

Such histrionics, of course, annoy the hell—make that heck—out of people my age who remember when players didn't taunt or attempt to terrorize their opponents, or get some time on the TV highlights that night. Butler and Art Rooney Jr. were both football scouts. Butler started out helping with scouting college players for the Steelers, and then became the director of the BLESTO-V scouting organization, which was a combine that represented a half dozen NFL teams. Art Jr. was in charge of the Steelers' scouting department when they selected all those great players in the 70s when they were named the Team of the Decade, winning four Super Bowls in six seasons under Chuck Noll.

They shared some of the same press boxes, exchanged observations and notes. Butler and I spoke about scouting and he agreed that today's scouts and personnel people tend to over-analyze prospects.

"They get a big guy who is agile and can run the 40 real fast and jump real high," said Butler, "and they think he's a great prospect. But he can't play football. He doesn't know how to play the game. I only cared if they could play football. The rest of the stuff wasn't important to me.

"I wanted to know if they played well consistently. Pro football players come in all shapes and sizes. I wasn't very big or very fast, but I'm very proud of playing in the league and giving back something of myself as a personnel guy."

I've checked out the home of the Butlers whenever I have visited the Homestead Library, still a must-see landmark above where the U.S. Steel Mill once flourished, long before there was a Waterfront Complex.

The home was familiar to me because my sister-in-law, Diane Churchman, grew up in that same house. Her name was Diane Thomas back then, and her two sisters, Judy and Carole, lived in that stately home. They were Munhall marksmen, members of the championship rifle teams at Munhall High School.

"That was a long time ago," said Butler, still the good scout.

Munhall's Jack Butler knows how
to say "Thank you"

Jack Butler was the best speaker of the six former National Football League players who were inducted into the Pro Football Hall of Fame in the summer of 2012.

Butler was at the microphone in Fawcett Stadium for exactly 3 minutes and 55 seconds. That contrasts with the final speaker on the program, Curtis Martin, who spoke for 27 minutes. It took three hours to induct six players. That's overkill.

Butler said "thank you" or some form of that phrase nine times in that span. He said he was thankful, grateful, honored, humbled, happy and proud. What more is there to say?

Hey, he's 84 years old and moving as fast as he can on two bad wheels. He said he was "thankful to God." He concluded his reflections by saying, "Heck, I'm thankful to be here. I thank you all."

Butler was midway through his nine-year (1951–1959) playing career for the Steelers when Britain's Roger Bannister broke the four-minute mile for the first time—that was on May 6, 1954—and the Oxford student completed the distance in 3 minutes and 59.4 seconds.

So Butler broke Bannister's record on this balmy Saturday night by a few seconds. Martin, who came out of Hazelwood and Taylor Allderdice High School and the University of Pittsburgh, told some harrowing tales about an alcoholic father who beat his mother, giving her black eyes, burning her in hot water in a bath tub, setting her hair on fire with a lighter, and putting lit cigarettes out on her legs.

It might make for an interesting magazine story, or for a book, but not for a Hall of Fame acceptance speech. In short, rather in long, Martin told his life story, way too personally as some saw it. Martin received rave reviews in some publications for his honest account of a dysfunctional family, but drew some strong criticism in social media. Some observers said it was "the worst speech in Hall of Fame history."

Martin went into too much detail or TMI, as my daughter Rebecca says when I do the same. TMI is for Too Much Information. I felt the same way when I read "West on West," Jerry West's life story, when he revealed so many ugly details about his dad and his upbringing in backwoods West Virginia. It's a good thing Martin spoke last and not first. Butler was second on the program and he might have packed his bags and gone back home to Munhall if he had to sit through Martin's marathon talk before it was his turn to speak.

Butler thanked his wife and his eight children, but he didn't mention them all by name, thinking that he'd go over his allotted five-minute acceptance speech. That's how long Hall of Fame officials ask you to speak. I recall that Butler was the best speaker, even though he started out by saying "I'm not much of a speaker," at a dinner to honor his teammate Fran Rogel of North Braddock.

That dinner lasted from 6 o'clock to just after midnight at the Churchill Country Club and Butler told a buddy "some of those speakers killed it by talking too long."

Butler has always been a man of few words. He probably spoke longer than former Pirates' star Bill Mazeroski did the day he was inducted into the Baseball Hall of Fame, but both were well received because they are "so damn real," as Steve Blass once said of Maz. They are down to earth and uncomfortable in the spotlight, and that's part of their appeal to Pittsburgh sports fans.

I don't think the induction ceremony of the Pro Football Hall of Fame is an appropriate place to put out your family's dirty laundry.

I have been guilty of staying too long at the mike at the Sports Night Dinner at the Thompson Club in West Mifflin, and I have learned my lesson in that regard. Nowadays, I make sure I know how long I'm expected to speak and keep a close eye on my wristwatch to make sure I don't go into overtime. I remember going to a football banquet in Belle Vernon in the mid-80s when I was to be the featured speaker. I got there a half hour early, as is my custom, to meet people and pick up some items I could use in my talk to localize my remarks. The dinner started at 6 p.m. By 10 p.m. I still had not been called to the podium.

A long-time assistant soccer coach was given a surprise award upon his retirement. He said, "I don't have a script," before he went into a 24-minute ramble. Midway through his remarks, I told the head football coach who was sitting next to me, "Get him a script!"

When I got up to speak I had to remind those in attendance of why we were there. I was happy to see Butler and Martin get inducted into the Pro Football Hall of Fame. I knew Chris Doleman, one of the other inductees, from our days at Pitt. He was about to start his junior season (1983) when I was hired to be the assistant athletic director for public relations at Pitt.

I remember Doleman got hurt in the first game of his senior year (1984), a season-opener at Pitt Stadium against BYU, and missed most of the season. He was one of several players who were in the doghouse with Coach Fogo Fazio. The Panthers lost to BYU 20–14. That setback in the first game set the tone for the rest of the schedule and the Panthers finished with a 3–7–1 record. There was a lot of talent on that team. When the Panthers finished 5–5–1 the following season, Fazio was fired as the head coach. I thought he deserved another year, just as I thought Dave Wannstedt should have been given another year. Both had recruited the talent to turn out a winner.

I recall being in the press box in Martin's junior season (1993) at Pitt when he ran for over 200 yards against a tough Texas team. There were two Steelers' scouts in the press box that day. Martin did suffer some injuries at Pitt that limited his playing time. That's why he lasted till the third round in the NFL draft before the New England Patriots, coached by Bill Parcells, took him in the draft.

I ran into Martin's mother a few times when I was signing books at Ross Park Mall. She'd be wearing a New England Patriots' jacket and she'd make sure you knew she was Curtis Martin's mother. I got a kick out of her brassiness. She seemed like a strong woman, happy and proud of her son's achievements. She told me stories about her son. She never shared any stories about her husband.

I was no longer on the Steelers' beat when Dermontti Dawson came along in 1988. But he seemed like a good guy, and he was definitely a great center, following in the tradition of Mike Webster, Ray Mansfield and Bill Walsh as outstanding Steelers' centers.

This is the second time that Pitt has had two former players inducted into the Hall of Fame on the same day. Russ Grimm and Rickey Jackson were inducted in the Class of 2010.

Doleman commented in Canton that this could help Pitt in its recruiting efforts. He mentioned the problems in the Penn State program, with players abandoning ship at State College in the wake of the Jerry Sandusky Scandal and NCAA penalties. He said that Pitt should get some of its Hall of Fame football players, and other alumni, to convince some of the Penn State players that Pitt would be the perfect place for them if they are considering transferring to another school.

Doleman's idea sounds good, but it would be illegal and might draw NCAA penalties to the Pitt program. Todd Graham advanced some similar ideas when he became the head coach at Pitt. He wanted Bill Fralic and Tony Dorsett to do that. You would think a head coach in college would know the rules better than that. Former players and alumni are not permitted to talk to prospects about coming to any college. I have been asked many times in this past year what I thought about the NCAA penalties against Penn State.

Jack Butler is "the white guy in the middle" with the Pro Football Hall of Fame Class of 2012. The others, from left to right, are Curtis Martin, Dermontti Dawson, Cortez Kennedy, Willie Roaf and Chris Doleman.

At first, I wrongly thought that the NCAA should not have anything to say about this scandal since Penn State broke no rules in its conduct of its football program. But I guess Todd Graham is not the only one who doesn't know what the NCAA can and cannot do.

I think Penn State officials were so eager to not draw a four-year "death penalty" that they accepted the terms of this penalty. But I thought the NCAA went too far. I think it was ridiculous and uncalled for to strip Penn State of so many victories in recent years. They didn't want Joe Paterno to remain the winningest college football coach in Division I so they cut back on his victory total.

Hey, Joe Paterno didn't win those games. The football team did, and it's not fair to those players and those students and alumni who were part of the program to penalize them in such a manner.

I thought it was okay to ban the team from post-season bowl games for four years, and to reduce their scholarships by five each year. The new coach, Bill O'Brien, was most upset by the decision to permit present Penn State football players to transfer to another school without having to sit out a season.

Coaches always react to such things on a personal level. This was the one aspect of the penalty that was going to make O'Brien's job more challenging. I am sure he didn't buy into such a situation when he left the New England Patriots in favor of Penn State.

I think things will work out fine for Penn State. O'Brien is right to say Penn State is still an outstanding academic institution and there aren't any bowl games you can go to and have 110,000 people in the stands as they have at Beaver Stadium. I think Penn State will attract a certain kind of kid who wants to help turn things around in the program. Penn State still has one of the greatest environments any kid could ask for to play college football. Some of the great prospects will go elsewhere because they want to play in bowl games. I think Penn State will appeal to the best kind of kids.

I have to take O'Brien to task for saying that because of his prior experience as a pro football coach that he can better ready players to move to the next level. Dave Wannstedt used to say that when he was the head coach at Pitt. I don't think O'Brien's job is to prepare players for the pros. How many kids are we talking about here? Few make it to the pro level. His job, and Wannstedt's job, is to develop a clean and proud college football program, to turn out winning teams.

Joe Paterno set the bar high in that respect. Paterno made a mistake in judgment when he didn't see to it that Jerry Sandusky was fired and forced to leave the State College campus. I have friends, including Franco Harris, who ardently disagrees about this, and remain firm in their belief that Paterno did what was required of him.

Joe Paterno is dead. Taking his victories away doesn't punish him. It punishes people who had nothing to do with the Jerry Sandusky Scandal. I am a proud Pitt man, but I feel sorry for Penn State people who truly cared about the school's football team and athletic program, and have been hurt by all this.

Reunions of '71 Pirates and Steelers of '70s
rekindle great memories

May 2011

I have often been told I have a nice job. Then again, my younger daughter, Rebecca, has often reminded me, "Dad, you never had a *real* job." Many sports fans through the years have told me they wish they could have tagged along with me and met all the great sports stars I have been fortunate to meet and interview as a sportswriter and author.

I always recognized I was blessed to turn a boyhood fascination with sports and writing into a lifelong career. Yes, in my own way, I was able to make it to the major leagues in all sports. I was never a one-sport guy. I covered more sports on all levels than any other sportswriter to come out of Pittsburgh.

I was reminded of this over the past extended weekend when I spent time in the company of the Steelers of the '70s, as well as some of the great players of opposing teams in the National Football League, and the '71 Pirates.

These were the ballplayers that made the Steelers the "Team of the Decade" in the NFL in the '70s, and produced title teams—four Super Bowl champions and two World Series winners—and prompted sportscaster Howard Cosell to label Pittsburgh "The City of Champions."

It stuck and we still like to think of ourselves in that respect.

Last Thursday evening my wife Kathie and I attended a gala party at Heinz Field for the 34th Annual Andy Russell Celebrity Classic, and then I joined many of the celebrities and participants at a breakfast the following morning at the Club at Nevillewood where a golf outing was held.

From there, I hustled off to Robert Morris University, where I signed books in my "Pittsburgh Proud" series Friday through Sunday at the 33rd Pittsburgh Sports Card Show that featured the 30th anniversary reunion of the 1971 Pirates.

I worked at *The New York Post* from 1970 till 1979 and took pride in the Pittsburgh sports successes from a distance. I was covering all the sports teams in New York, but I still reveled in the accomplishments of my hometown teams, including the 1976 Pitt national college football championship team.

I returned home to work for *The Pittsburgh Press*, where I had worked while in high school and at Pitt, in April of 1979. I got back just in time to celebrate another World Series triumph by the Pirates in 1979, and to cover the Steelers when they won their fourth Super Bowl in six years.

Danny Murtaugh had managed the Pirates in 1971, and Chuck Tanner was at the helm of the ship in 1979. Chuck Noll, of course, coached the Steelers, still the only coach to claim four Super Bowl championships in as many outings.

And I wrote the first of 21 books I would write about Pittsburgh sports achievements when Marty Wolfson and I edited and published *Pittsburgh: The Story of the City of Champions.*

Andy Russell has raised over $5 million at his celebrity golf outing for local charities, most recently the UPMC prostate cancer research program. I remember covering one of his early outings with Arnold Palmer as the co-host at the Latrobe Country Club, and I have attended about 15 of these events ever since.

The former Steelers present this time were John Banaszak, Craig Bingham, Rocky Bleier, Mel Blount, Emil Boures, Robin Cole, Glen Edwards, Neil Graff, Gordon Gravelle, Jack Ham, Dick Hoak, Bill Hurley, Todd Kalis, Marv Kellum, Louis Lipps, Mike Merriweather, Edmund Nelson, Myron Pottios, Lynn Swann, Paul Uram, Mike Wagner, J.R. Wilburn and Dwayne Woodruff.

Bobby Bell and Willie Lanier, both Hall of Fame linebackers for the Kansas City Chiefs, were there, along with Isaac Curtis of the Cincinnati Bengals, Pierre Larouche and Phil Borque of the Penguins, Kent Tekulve of the Pirates, Tom Mack, a Hall of Fame center for the Los Angeles Rams, and Billy Van Heusen of the Denver Broncos.

I particularly enjoyed taking a trip down memory lane with Bobby Bell. I was stationed at the U.S. Army Home Town News Center in Kansas City for ten months in 1965 when the Chiefs were assembling one of the greatest teams in NFL history. Lenny Dawson, a former quarterback with the Steelers, was the team's offensive leader and Bell and Buck Buchanan were the leaders of the team's defensive unit.

I helped out in the press box at Municipal Stadium for home games for the Chiefs and Athletics, a real perk since I was getting about $10 a day in meal money from the Army. I spent time in the home of Bobby Bell when I interviewed him for a feature story in *Sport* magazine. He was sharing the pad with a defensive back named Fred "The Hammer" Williamson, who gained fame for his ferocious hits and went on to star in a series of black exploitation movies featuring fearsome black tough guys and gals (Richard Roundtree and Pam Greer) ala "Superfly" and "Shaft" that were popular with urban audiences in the early '70s. Williamson had once played briefly for the Steelers.

Bell and Williamson were an odd couple, and Bell had a few belly laughs over reflecting on his roommate.

Bell has been a regular at Andy Russell's Celebrity Classic for many years, and is popular with whatever foursome gets him in the draw. KDKA's Bob Pompeani, who was a student of mine once upon a time at Point Park University, is the only other member of the media at these outings. He emcees the auction and plays in the golf outing. He's got a green jacket to prove it. Those who participate in at least ten of the classics rate the same kind of blazer that is given to Masters champions at Augusta.

I was not as familiar with the '71 Bucs because I was in New York at the time as I am with the '60 Bucs and '79 Bucs. It was good to see Gene Alley, Tony Bartirome, Steve Blass, Vic Davalillo, Dave Giusti, Mudcat Grant, Richie Hebner, Jackie Hernandez, Bob Johnson, John Lamb, Don Leppert, Bill Mazeroski, Al Oliver, Bob Robertson, Charlie Sands, Manny Sanguillen, Bob Veale and Bill Virdon.

I covered the New York Yankees when Virdon managed the team during the 1974 and 1975 seasons. He is the answer to a trivia question: Who managed the Yankees for two years and never managed one game at Yankee Stadium? The Yankees played at Shea Stadium, the Mets' home field, during that span as major renovations were being done on Yankee Stadium. The venerable ballpark has since been leveled when a new stadium was constructed next door.

Terry Hanratty, a quarterback for the Steelers in the '70s, was the lone Steelers' player to be signing autographs among all the '71 Pirates at Robert Morris University. Promoter J. Paul Stogner said he wanted to have something for the Steelers' fans in attendance.

Jim Tripodi, who operates Diamond Jim's, a sports card and memorabilia shop in Beaver, is a regular at these card shows.

"I'm really getting into magazines, sports publications of all kinds and press guides," Tripodi told me. "I swear I keep seeing your name in all of them. I don't know where you found the time to have two kids."

I told him I hustled pretty good in the '70s and '80s as far as freelance writing was concerned. I loved writing about sports stars and seeing my byline in all the national publications.

Sportswriters weren't making good money in those days, so I moonlighted and took advantage of all opportunities to get my stuff published and make some money on the side.

I saved nearly all of that extra money. The fees for such stories ranged from $50 to $500 in the early years, and got better later on. I started out making $12,500 a year for editing *Street & Smith's Basketball Yearbook* in 1970, and was up to $65,000 for editing three annuals for the Conde Nast Publications by the mid-80s.

I was able to save about $100,000 for each of our daughters, Sarah and Rebecca. That included $65,000 earmarked for their college education and $35,000 for their weddings. I was right on the mark for what I needed for them to go to the University of Virginia and Ohio University, for Sarah and Rebecca, respectively. Rebecca's wedding money is still drawing dividends and interest.

I invested the rest in retirement funds for Kathie and myself. That's how you are supposed to manage your money. That's why I have little tolerance for the complaints offered by pro athletes these days during the labor contract disagreement in the NFL.

The players have this sense of entitlement, which is rampant in this country among many people. With the kind of money they are making they should be stashing away the majority of their money for future use. When NFL players compare their situation to being slaves I have to question their mentality.

They say the average NFL playing career is just over four years, yet many of them think they should be set for life and never have to work again. In truth, if they saved and invested their money wisely they would be set for life.

I worked for the *New York Post* for nine years and Street & Smiths's for 32 years, and *The Pittsburgh Press* for four-and-a-half years—the average NFL career—and draw a pension from none of them. I saved and funded my own pension.

I did what I did because I enjoyed the life. I remember Dick Young, the best baseball writer ever, when asked why he was a sportswriter, saying, "I don't want to be a millionaire, I just want to live like one." Exactly. My sentiments, indeed.

It's a great life. The Pirates, Steelers, Penguins and other pro athletes who were in Pittsburgh this past week ought to know that by now. It was good to see them again. We were lucky they came our way.

Photo by Jim O'Brien

Mark Malone, Emil Boures and Rocky Bleier are regulars at Andy Russell Celebrity Classic.

To the 2012 Pittsburgh Pirates:
Thank you for a fun ˅*and frustrating summer*

Neil Walker, Lawrence McCutcheon and Pedro Alvarez led the way with some memorable hits and fielding plays to pace the Pirates. They gave us some memories and offer hope for the future.

Photos courtesy of Dave Arrigo/Pittsburgh Pirates

Joel Hanrahan
The "Hammer"

A.J. Burnett
Ace of pitching staff

PIRATES
BASEBALL

Bill Mazeroski statue at PNC Park

Jim O'Brien

'60 World Series
sparks baseball stories

October 2009

George Coury

Jim O'Brien

I start every day searching for stories. I am always hopeful that someone will share a story about a personal experience that readers would enjoy.

People see me signing books and know that I welcome their stories so I am often approached by such story-tellers.

This happened at one of the Pirates' last games at PNC Park during the 2009 season and then again at the wall of Forbes Field where I was among the baseball fans who gathered there on October 13 to celebrate the anniversary of the Pirates' World Series triumph over the New York Yankees in the fall classic in 1960.

We still roar when we hear the broadcast call of Bill Mazeroski's home run leading off the bottom of the ninth inning to win the seventh game, 10–9, and that home run came, just to set the record straight, at 3:36 p.m., not 3:30 p.m. as recently reported in a Pittsburgh daily newspaper. The Pirates may never play in the World Series again, so we have to embrace the Bucs' history and find sources of genuine joy where we can. You can root for the Yankees or the Phillies in the World Series that got underway this week.

George A. Coury Jr., a public accountant who has to be one of the Pirates' most faithful fans, does not share my pessimism about the Pirates' future.

He actually believes management has a sound plan to build a solid contender sooner than later. (*The 2012 season did offer some hope that better days are ahead.*)

George Coury cannot be deterred from believing in the Bucs. My wife Kathie and I were sitting with friends Mary and Dan Koller. He is an executive with Allegheny Valley Bank's investment unit. Coury was sitting behind us with his daughter and some friends from Homer City. That community is located near Indiana, Pa., about 55 miles from PNC Park.

George was interested in talking to me about baseball history and to Dan about financial and tax matters. George never stopped talking the entire nine innings.

He told us that he has been a big fan of the Pirates all his life, and has missed only 16 home games in the last 40 years. Read that sentence over again. Yes, he's only missed 16 home games in the last 40 years. He said he knows he will miss one game next summer because he will be attending his daughter's wedding. Why didn't she pick a Saturday when the Bucs would be on the road?

Can you imagine being that faithful to the Pirates over that period of time, or to any team in baseball for that matter? The Pirates have set a record for major league sports teams by having 17 consecutive losing seasons. (*They have since extended to 19 consecutive seasons, the longest losing streak in American pro sports.*)

I told George it reminded me of something my friend Beano Cook once said in relation to the freeing of the 53 Americans after they were held hostage in Iran for 444 days from 1979 to 1981. Bowie Kuhn, then the Commissioner of Baseball, gave all the American hostages a lifetime pass to Major League Baseball.

When Beano Cook heard that, he said, "Haven't they suffered enough?" The quote immortalized Beano Cook, and will probably appear in his obituary some day.

Mark Ratti Sr. was easily the best-dressed individual at the gathering at the wall of Forbes Field to celebrate the 1960 World Series victory. He was wearing a gray glen plaid suit, starched white shirt and an appropriate tie. Most of the fans arrive in more casual attire.

Ratti told of an incident that related to the 1960 World Series.

"I usually come to this gathering every year since I heard about it," said Ratti, a RE/MAX realtor along with his sons, Mark Jr. and Drew in their Upper St. Clair office. "Last year, I realized too late that my wife had booked us to go to a religious retreat at the Rev. Billy Graham Center in Asheville, North Carolina and one of the days was October 13. I was going to try and get out of it, but then I realized how much my wife wanted to go and I agreed to go with her.

"We were supposed to eat dinner on the first of two shifts one evening, and we were asked if we would defer to the second seating because there were some older attendees who had asked if they could eat at the earlier dinner. We weren't that hungry so we agreed to go to the second seating.

"When we were seated I spotted a man across the table from us who was wearing a Yankees' ball cap. We started talking about the Yankees and the Pirates and I told him what was going on that day in Pittsburgh at the wall at Forbes Field. He had never heard about it, but he thought it was great that baseball fans would do something like that.

"A woman sitting next to me tapped me on the arm. She said if I was that interested in that 1960 World Series I might want to talk to her husband, who was sitting quietly next to her. She told me her husband's name was Bobby Richardson."

Yes, it was that Bobby Richardson, the second baseman for the Yankees in that 1960 World Series. He had 12 hits in those seven games and he is still the only player from a losing team to win the Most Valuable Player Award in the World Series.

Mazeroski, who hit a home run in one of the earlier Pirates' victories as well as the one that won the seventh game, should have won the award. I believe they must have picked up the ballots before that final game was completed, as often happens at such events.

So Mark Ratti Sr. did not attend the 2008 gathering at the wall in Oakland and yet he experienced a special moment that related to that event that he can boast about at all future meetings.

I thought this particular weekend was as good as it gets for local football fans. Pitt looked as good as it has ever looked over the last six years in beating South Florida on a perfect afternoon at Heinz Field on Saturday. Penn State and West Virginia were both triumphant the same day.

I have always said I liked it best when Pitt, Penn State and West Virginia are all rated in the Top 25 teams in the country.

The Steelers escaped with a wacky victory over the Minnesota Vikings. It was good theater. It was one of those games that proves that most of the pre-game analysis often bears no relation to what actually takes place in most sports events.

Who knew the Steelers were going to score touchdowns on a fumble recovery and run and an interception return?

I was rooting for Iowa to beat Michigan State because Iowa is coached by Kirk Ferentz of Upper St. Clair who was once a grad assistant at Pitt and that turned out to be one of the weekend's most exciting finishes.

I mentioned in last week's column that my oldest brother, Rich, was quite ill at Wheeling Hospital. He died, at age 81, last Tuesday, and my wife and I attended a funeral service on Friday at his church in Bridgeport, Ohio.

My brother was a big sports fan and one of the first to tell me about all the great athletes who came out of the Ohio Valley such as Bill Mazeroski, the Niekro Brothers, John Havlicek and Allan Hornyak.

That was the downside of the week. Life is like that, highs and lows. The last time I was with my brother he got me into a sports trivia contest. He was quite good at that. He took pride, for instance, in knowing the nicknames of all the major college football teams. He was always proud that I was a sports writer.

His death, my daughter Sarah pointed out to me, leaves me as the only living member of my childhood family. It makes me uneasy to know that.

It made me think about images of my mother and father, my other brother and my sister, during better days in our lives. My brother was buried in Mt. Calvary Cemetery in Wheeling. He was buried high on a hill with his family, a good distance from my family's plot.

We stopped to pay our respects at my family's plot. My mother and grandparents are buried there, along with six other members of my family, including a brother-in-law.

My mother once asked me if they should hold space for me. I must have spent too much time around Beano Cook. I told my mother, "Mom, I'm a Pitt man and there's no way I am going to be buried in West Virginia."

> *"I am the fifth of six children, raised in a home, a series of them actually, that was spotless but where I never learned what love was and am still not entirely sure I know today."*
> —**Jerry West**
> ***From West on West***

Maz and Milene
minus Muttley

September 2010

It was 11:15 a.m. on Labor Day in 2010 and Bill Mazeroski was signing his autograph, still one of the most legible and cherished signatures of all the sports figures in this neck of the woods.

This was at the Heinz History Center and Western Pennsylvania Sports Museum on Smallman Street in The Strip. Mazeroski had been honored the day before, September 5, on his 74th birthday with the unveiling of a 14½-foot statue showing him running the bases when he hit the home run that defeated the mighty New York Yankees in the seventh and deciding game of the 1960 World Series. The weather, especially for Pittsburgh, could not have been better. There'd been a record number of days with the temperature in the 90s, but this was cooler and more comfortable, easier to sit and listen to speeches.

Maz has said of his heroic home run trot that his feet never touched the ground once he realized the ball was going to clear the wall, and he's been walking on air ever since, or at least the previous weekend.

That happened at Forbes Field at 3:36 p.m. on October 13, 1960. The Pirates were celebrating the 50th anniversary of that feat, anything to distract the fans from fretting too much about the team's 18th straight losing season. The following year would be the 40th anniversary of the 1971 team's World Series triumph and that would take the contemporary Pirates off the hook once more.

There was a long line of fans waiting their turn on the first floor of the Heinz History Center, once an ice house, to say something to Mazeroski and get his signature on a children's book about him written by his daughter-in-law Kelly Mazeroski. They would also be among the first to see the history center's exhibition of *Beat 'Em Bucs—The Story of the 1960 Pittsburgh Pirates.*

I had a chance to chat with an old friend, Ray Werner, a legendary figure in the advertising business in Pittsburgh. He was telling me how a Pirates' official wasn't too keen on the idea when one of his fellow ad associates proposed the line "Beat 'Em Bucs" for an ad campaign back then. The man didn't think it was catchy enough.

But Pirates' broadcasters and fans are still saying "Beat 'em, Bucs" all these years later. It certainly caught on. Werner was one of the people present who had lent something from that 1960 season for the exhibit. He shimmied up a slippery pole in front of the Duquesne Club on October 13, 1960 and pulled down a red, white and blue banner that he kept for the next 50 years.

There was another statue of Maz up stairs, showing him swinging the bat the way he did when he launched that home run over the left field wall at Forbes Field, just to the right of the scoreboard, over the head of the Yankees' Yogi Berra, who was playing left field that fateful afternoon.

Milene Mazeroski was sitting in a black wooden rocking chair about 30 yards to the left of the stand where her husband, in his own humble way, was charming everyone.

"Everyone still remembers that day, and they love to relive it with Bill," she said. "Someone brings it up to him every day. It's unbelievable, but they're still talking about it fifty years later."

Milene was in black attire, from head to toe, and smiling proudly as she observed the activity surrounding her husband. She was dressed for a funeral, but her face was frozen in a smile, and she looked like she was having a grand time. I'd been to the Mazeroski's home in Hempfield, on the outskirts of Greensburg, on two occasions so she recognized me. She said it was okay for me to sit in the rocking chair next to her, to make myself more comfortable.

I remembered how Bill Mazeroski had sat in a similar rocking chair in the family room of their home when I interviewed him 18 years earlier. That's when I wrote the book, *Maz and the '60 Bucs*, the first adult book ever written about the 1960 Pirates. That was in 1992—the last time the Pirates posted a winning season, under manager Jim Leyland. I had also visited them back in 1970 to write a story about Bill for *Sport* magazine.

"We're in the same home," said Milene.

I mentioned that I remember there were home-made doilies dressing the tops of the couches and chairs and buffet when I visited both times. "They're still there," she said, "probably the same ones."

There is a simplicity about the Mazeroskis, an honest and humble grace, that demands respect. "He's just so damn for-real," Steve Blass has said of his one-time roommate when he broke in with the Bucs right after that World Series triumph over the Yankees.

The thing I'll never forget about that last visit to their home in Hempfield was how the Mazeroskis had sat on a bench on their front porch and waited for my arrival. It was a gray day with light rain showers. There was a chill in the air. The Mazeroski home is off the beaten path once you leave Rt. 30 near Greensburg and it would be easy to get lost on the rural road. So the Mazeroskis sat on their porch, both of them wearing colorful bulky sweaters and waited for me. "We didn't want you to miss the house," she said then and now.

"We're glad you care about our family."

I remembered that their dog was sitting on the porch with them, and that his name was Muttley, which seemed so appropriate for a dog owned by Bill Mazeroski. I mentioned to Milene that there were a lot of dogs named "Maz" in the '60s.

"Muttley's gone now," said Milene, making a face to show her sense of loss.

"What breed of dog was Muttley?" I asked.

"He was a mix, of course," said Milene. "No real breed. He was a good dog, a nice dog. But just a dog."

Maz with Dick Groat and Bob Friend

Maz and Friends

Munhall's Tom Ragan shows ticket stubs for all seven games of 1960 World Series that he used to attend the games as ElRoy Face and Maz look on.

Jim O'Brien and Maz meet at annual Homestead Lions' Club golf outing at Westwood Golf Club.

153

I remembered that her sons, Darren and David, who were both nearby with their own families at the Heinz History Center, were always good kids. They both had earned master's degrees and I never heard a bad word about them, or heard that they'd gotten into any kind of trouble. One of them told me once that he thought his dad was a Hall of Fame dad long before he was honored at Cooperstown.

I mentioned to Milene that I still run into people who boast that they were in Braddock the day that she and Bill got married at her parish church, Sacred Heart of Jesus Catholic Church, and that they had stood outside just to see the procession. That was at the corner of Talbot Avenue and 6th Street. They knew about Bill Mazeroski in Braddock before he hit that home run. That was 54 years ago. It was a church that served the Polish community of Braddock. "The church is gone, too," said Milene. "It burned down (in 1975)."

She was Milene Nicholson when she lived on Washington Avenue in Braddock. She went to Sacred Heart Catholic Grade School from first to eighth grade. Then she went to Braddock High School. I asked her if she was there when Chuck Klausing was the head football coach.

"Yes, I was there for the glory days," she said. She was there for four of the six years (1954–59) that the Braddock High football team went undefeated. They won an unprecedented six WPIAL titles while posting a record of 53–0–1. Klausing later told me Milene had been a Braddock cheerleader, just like his wife JoAn.

Her Uncle Joe owned a confectionery store a few blocks from her home. "It was the best candy in Braddock," she recalled.

Then she answered an ad in the newspaper, or maybe a friend directed her to go and be interviewed for a secretary's job in the front office of the Pirates. She landed the job assisting Rex Bowen, the team's scouting director. "The office was on the first floor at Forbes Field," Milene recalled. "It was an exciting place to go to work."

The story goes that manager Danny Murtaugh told Bill to take her out on a date. Murtaugh preferred to have his players married, so they wouldn't be wearing themselves out chasing after young women. "That's the story I heard, too," said Milene. Bill says he was scared of girls back then and afraid to ask Milene for a date.

I suggested to Milene that some of the married Pirates still pursued women on the road, that Murtaugh's theory wasn't full-proof. "But not Bill," she said with a thin smile. "I know what you're talking about."

So on a day when the Pirates were rained out, Bill, somewhat sheepishly, asked Milene if they could go out to dinner. They met under the clock at Kaufmann's. Does it get any better? Or is somebody making this up?

I asked Milene how old she was when she got that job with the Pirates. "I'm not telling you," she said, demurely. "Jim, you don't ask a lady about her age." For a second, I thought I was talking to Scarlett O'Hara in *Gone With the Wind*.

Bill remembered the impetus for the first date this way: Talking about Danny Murtaugh, his manager, he recalled, "He said, 'Take that

Bill and Milene Mazeroski at PNC Park statue unveiling

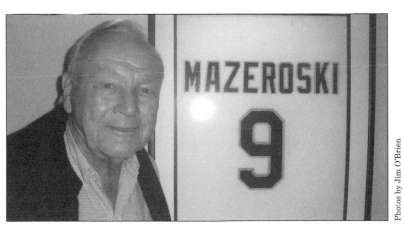

Arnold Palmer has always been a big fan of Mazeroski.

girl out!' I said, 'No.' He said, 'You're going to take her out. Ask her out.' So I did."

Bill had come from humble beginnings, growing up in a coal patch on the Ohio side of the Ohio River near Wheeling, where he was born in the local hospital in 1936. His home of two rooms was converted from an old chicken coop. Imagine the ambience. It had a dirt floor for a good while. Maz got his first baseball glove, a three-finger model, digging a deep hole for an outhouse for an uncle. His dad, a coal miner, was away from home a lot, and his mother managed to get by on $10 a week, which wasn't a lot back then or at any time in Maz's lifetime.

I've spent a good deal of time in the Ohio Valley and I've met a lot of people who remember that Maz used to do a lot of fishing, and that he even had the nickname of "Catfish." He smiled at the memory. "I caught a lot of catfish in the Ohio River because it was one of the few fish who could live in those waters that were polluted by the mills up river. There was a time when I thought I'd die from eating all those polluted catfish."

He was just 23 at the start of that 1960 season and he had turned 24 only a month before he came to bat in the bottom of the ninth inning with the scored tied at 9 runs. Ralph Terry shook off signs from catcher Johnny Blanchard, insisting on throwing a slider. He threw one for a ball. He threw a second and it didn't slide. It came up fat across the middle of the plate.

Bob Prince wasn't at the mike to say, "You can kiss it goodbye!" He was in the hallway outside the clubhouses and had no idea how the game had ended. The first Pirate pushed his way was none other than the hero of the game, Billy Mazeroski. But Prince knew Mazeroski was a shy guy, a terrible interview, and he said, "Billy, how's it feel to be part of a World Championship team." Maz said, "Great." And Prince pushed him aside, looking for another Pirate to interview.

I told Milene that her jaw had dropped the day before when the statue of her husband was unveiled by several of his former teammates, Bob Friend, Dick Groat, El Roy Face and Bill Virdon, as well as three family members. She smiled when I said that. "Did I really?" she asked.

At the program that preceded viewing the exhibition about the 1960 Bucs, Bill Mazeroski spoke briefly, as he always does, especially when he gets into the Baseball Hall of Fame, he said, "I don't like to talk. What a holiday weekend this has been. What a wonderful time. We just thanked everybody for everything."

When they unveiled the almost life-size statue of Mazeroski at the Heinz History Center, Milene stroked the hairline and said, "It's the right color hair."

When I asked her what Bill had said to her privately upon the unveiling of the other statue the day before at PNC Park, she said, "Probably something like 'geez' or 'Jiminy Christmas.' He says stuff like that. Our grandson is even saying that now."

When I asked her what she liked best about Bill, she said, "He's just a good guy, that's all. He's never going to change. He's just Bill and that's the way he's going to be the rest of his life."

Bill Mazeroski did sum up the scene quite nicely in his own succinct manner when he said, "Geez, how could anybody ever dream of something like this? All I wanted to be was a ballplayer. I didn't need all of this." I told Milene that I had seen Arnold Palmer at PNC Park the week before and that he was a big fan of Bill Mazeroski. He and Palmer were a lot alike, the best of competitors and go-getters at the game they played, yet so humble about their accomplishments. "Bill has always been a big fan of Arnie's, as well," she said. "He always wished he could play golf as good as Arnie."

I'm glad I remembered that when I first interviewed Bill Mazeroski I asked Milene to remain in the room when she said she had work to do in her kitchen. I knew that Bill was bashful and not one to talk about himself. Milene knew all of Bill's best stories—the way wives do—and she prompted him to tell this one and that one. He responded well to her cues and when he missed a beat—searching for a name—Milene filled in the blank spaces. That's why wives are more valuable than ever when you get older.

Milene and Maz check out his statue at Heinz History Center.

"Mazeroski grew up in Ohio but always will be known as a Pittsburgh guy."
—Bob Cohn
Pittsburgh Tribune-Review

Maz and Nellie King
continue to embrace us

This is another special baseball season in the life of Bill Mazeroski and the final season for his dear friend Nellie King. A statue has been erected to pay tribute to Bill Mazeroski at PNC Park. It depicts him holding his ballcap high overhead as he scoots from second base to third base when he hit one of the most famous home runs in baseball history to win the World Series for the Pirates at Forbes Field on October 13, 1960. It's an image that was captured by *Post-Gazette* photographer James T. Klingensmith.

The sculpture was done by Susan Wagner, who also did the ones of Roberto Clemente and Willie Stargell that, along with one of Honus Wagner, stand outside of PNC Park.

The Mazeroski statue is 12-feet tall, or a bit more than twice the size of the Pirates' star second baseman.

King, who gained fame as a Pirates' pitcher in the '50s and even more so as the sidekick to Bob Prince on the radio announcing team later on, died on Wedneday, August 11, at age 82 after a long courageous struggle with several health challenges, including colon cancer and pneumonia. Pittsburgh has lost one of its most endearing and enduring voices and one of the best story-tellers I've met.

Maz, of course, made it into the Baseball Hall of Fame in 2001 after a 21-year wait. I remember seeing King in Cooperstown, as excited to be there as Maz himself. He was thrilled that Maz finally made it and that he was able to be there to witness the event.

Steve Blass, another former Pirates' pitcher who became a broadcaster for the Pirates and one of its most popular figures ever, once said, "If there was a Hall of Fame for nice guys Nellie King would be a charter member." Blass and Bob Friend, Dave Giusti, Kent Tekulve, Jim Rooker and Jim Sadowski are active members of the Pirates Alumni and among King's many friends who came to see him often during his three-year stay at Friendship Village in Upper St. Clair. Whenever I visited King there, to collect more of his memorable stories, he'd tell me who'd been to see him lately, and how much he appreciated their love and loyal attention.

After his four plus seasons as a pitcher for the Pirates, King became a sports announcer at radio stations in Latrobe and Greensburg, before he was paired with Prince and Jim Woods on Pirates' broadcasts on KDKA Radio. King came to KDKA Radio in 1967 and left when he was let go a few days before Bob Prince was fired – one of he most unpopular moves in Pirates' baseball history.

King told me he interviewed many of the Pirates prior to the start of the 1960 World Series with the Yankees and asked them each who they thought would be the hero of the Series. "Only one of them mentioned Maz," recalled King. "That was Harvey Haddix, the terrific

Former Pirates at Homestead Lions' Golf Outing a few years back included, left to right, Bob Friend, Don Schwall, Ron Necciai and Bill Mazeroski.

Bob Friend and Nellie King share smiles at fund-raising luncheon in Pittsburgh.

pitcher who had such a great season. When I asked him why he thought so, he said, 'Because they'll pitch to him.' "

In other words, the opposing pitchers wouldn't get cute with Maz, and pitch around him as they might an established power hitter in that circumstance.

Remember that Maz was batting eighth in the Pirates' lineup and had hit only 11 home runs in 151 games that 1960 season. Often overlooked in reflections on that 1960 World Series is the fact that Maz also hit a two-run homer in the opening game to win that one as well.

I'm able to call up film of that famous home run that Maz hit leading off the bottom of the 9th inning – at 3:36 p.m. – on my computer any time I want to relive the most magic moment in Pittsburgh sports history. Yes, even Franco Harris of "The Immaculate Reception" fame, concedes that Maz topped his effort in that regard.

King was among those who could be counted upon to show up at the wall that remains from Forbes Field to relive that wonderful day each October 13. Even though he was in frail health, he was there with Dave Giusti the previous season and the one before that to mix with the fans.

He loved being with the fans, and was much more at ease in that role than Maz ever was. The fans love Maz, and they love that he remains such a regular guy, but he's always been a little ill at ease in crowds. He's never been comfortable in the spotlight. That's why Maz has remained so popular in these parts.

He confesses to crying when he sees a sad movie or a heartwarming commercial. He's a sap when it comes to babies and puppies.

Maz came to mind or was mentioned several times on a Sunday afternoon. My wife Kathie and I had visited our younger daughter Rebecca in Woodland Hills, just north of Los Angeles, earlier in the month. On our return home, we bumped into an old friend from my college days at Pitt.

I came to Pitt from Taylor Allderdice in late August of 1960 and two months later the Pirates were playing the Yankees in the World Series just a block and a half from the Pitt Student Union. One of the columnists on the campus newspaper and student government leaders at the time was Nate Firestone. Nate came to Pitt from Peabody High. My wife remembers him always wearing a green U.S. Army jacket in our Pitt grad school days.

He would later teach political science at Point Park and at Pitt and, I learned this particular Sunday, he enrolled in Pitt's Law School at age 44 and became an attorney and later a judge. He had to retire as a judge in 2010 when he turned 70. Nate was a sophomore when I came to Pitt and he was one of those people who stood out in the crowd.

He recalled how he often went to Forbes Field because you could get in free and sit in the bleachers from the 7th inning on in those days. Even during the World Series, imagine that.

Nate mentioned Maz and what a nice man he was. Everyone who's ever met him—with only one exception I know of—says that of Maz. (For the record, one woman has told me that Maz was not nice to

Mazeroski is mugged
by Fritz McCauley as
he races toward third
base after hitting
winning home run on
Oct. 13, 1960.

Photo from James Klingensmith/Pirates Archives

her father. I told her he must have been having an off day, or that her father mistook his mild manner and shyness for rudeness.)

Firestone said his son-in-law is Burton Morris, the Pittsburgh born and bred artist who has gained international fame with his artwork. Morris has drawn the artwork for the All-Star Game that was held in Pittsburgh a few years back, and he did a lithograph of Maz turning a double-play that is presently on sale at sports stores around town. There are 250 unframed lithographs selling at $500 apiece, and there are posters available of the same work for $10. Firestone, and his wife Debbie, a former teacher in the Woodland Hills School District, met Maz through their daughter and son-in-law.

The Firestones were visiting their children in the Los Angeles area as well, and were making a side-trip to Las Vegas for four days when we met them at the airport waiting area at LAX. "It's good that we can still recognize each other," Firestone suggested.

Our return trip to Pittsburgh was going through a stopover in Las Vegas. I lost about $30 at the slot machines at the airport in Las Vegas on the trip to California. Fortunately, our airplane was running late out of Los Angeles, and we had to hustle to make our connection to Pittsburgh on the return trip. I had no chance to lose more money. That's why I don't frequent the casinos in Pittsburgh or Wheeling or Washington, Pa. Sitting across from me on the airplane out of Las Vegas was a man who bore a strong resemblance to Bill Mazeroski. I asked the man when we deplaned in Pittsburgh if he had ever been mistaken for Bill Mazeroski. "I don't know who Bill Mazeroski is," he said. "But I'll take that as a compliment."

"You must not be from Pittsburgh," I said to the man.

"No, I'm from the West Coast," he said. "I'm from Portland."

Portland is a long way from Pittsburgh and doesn't have a major league baseball team, so the man might be forgiven. I informed him that Bill Mazeroski hit a famous home run to win the World Series for the Pirates back in 1960. "That's pretty good," he said.

When I got home, I checked my telephone messages and there was a message from Fred "Fritz" McCauley. There was a name out of my past. And it was quite a coincidence that he called when he did. When he began by addressing me as "Scoops," I knew he had to be from Hazelwood. That was my nickname when I was the sports editor of *The Hazelwood Envoy*, a bi-weekly newspaper where I was the sports editor from the age of 14 to 19.

McCauley was immortalized as much as Maz—at least in his own mind and to many of his buddies back in Hazelwood—when he was pictured chasing Maz from third base to home when Maz hit the home run to beat the Yankees.

Fritz appears in the picture as Maz is nearing third base on that famous joyous journey around the bases that day. It's almost as if McCauley had been hiding behind the third base umpire waiting to chase somebody to home plate on that momentous occasion.

Here's what McCauley said in his phone message. "Hey, Scoops. Fred McCauley here, calling you from Conneaut Lake where I've been living. I've never had a chance to meet Maz, and I'm 73 so I figure it's time I do that. Before it's too late. Maz and I might be the only ones still living from that picture. The statue is coming up and there's that gathering at the wall. I was wondering whether you could call me and let me know what's doing. I'd like to meet the man after all these years."

I remembered that two years ago I was at a Christmas party hosted by Armand Dellovade at his home in Lawrence, Pa., in Washington County. The famous wrestler Bruno Sammartino told me that while he had met Roberto Clemente and Arnold Palmer, among some of Pittsburgh's most popular sports figures, he had never met Bill Mazeroski. It was hard for me to imagine that because both men had been to so many sports awards dinners through the years. So I made it a point to introduce Sammartino to Maz at the Dapper Dan Sports Dinner later that winter. Now I will have to find a way to introduce McCauley to Maz. I know Maz would make a fuss over him and say something like, "So you're that guy!"

I checked back to my book, *MAZ and the '60 Bucs*, to a chapter where I interviewed many of the fans who had followed Maz around the bases that day. The fellow who was right behind Maz as he neared home plate was Dominic "Woo" Verrrati of Swisshelm Park.

Verrati was one of the head ushers that day and one of his responsibilities was to keep the fans off the field at the end of the game because the Steelers had a home game there in a few days, and they didn't want the field damaged. "I just lost it," Verrrati later told me. "You have to realize what a fan I was of the Pirates. Heck, I used to sell newspapers at Forbes Field and remember selling one to the great Dizzy Dean one day. So I went way back with the Pirates."

Here's what McCauley said when I interviewed him for my book: "I was 22 at the time and I was a bellman at the Hilton Hotel in Downtown Pittsburgh. I was living in Hazelwood. I got into Forbes Field at 8:30 in the morning on the day of the seventh game of the 1960 World Series. A Pinkerton guard named Riley, a short, fat guy, let me in, and told me to stay in the bathroom until the game started. I was wearing a T-shirt and jeans. I called my brother on the telephone and he brought me a dark blazer, a white shirt and a pair of gray slacks, and he slipped them through the gate to me.

"I changed and went to a runway at the end of the box seats by third base. I sat on a milk carton that had a pillow on it. I had been to 33 Pirates' games that year, and I always sat in the bleachers out in left field. That's how I knew, as soon as Maz hit the ball, that it was going out of the ballpark. I knew what a home run out there looked like. Soon as he hit it, I started running for the field. I might have been the first person out on the field. How can you say it? I was just blinded with delight.

"I caught Maz at shortstop, and had him briefly around the waist, but he threw me off. I think he took his cap off because he thought I was going to grab it. I ran after him from third to home. I'm the guy with the dark jacket flapping and my hair flying in the breeze, to Maz's right. I see myself on TV and on the scoreboard from time to time, and in commercials. I saw Maz (on TV) recently and he's put on a lot of weight. I know I can beat him to home plate now. But I've never met him in person since then.

"I'm in the picture of him heading for home that was in the Allegheny Club at Three Rivers, and at bars all over Pittsburgh. There was once a big copy of it in the J&L Steel Mill in Hazelwood. I'm opening a restaurant in Conneaut Lake called Leah Marie's Pizza Parlor and I'm going to have the picture in my place. It's nice to be a little part of history. That picture, I'm told, is on display in the Baseball Hall of Fame. Hey, I'm the only guy from Hazelwood in the Baseball Hall of Fame."

I later learned that the day after the seventh game that McCauley rode down Second Avenue, the main street in Hazelwood, sitting high on the back of a convertible automobile, waving to people as he passed them. He was holding a baseball in each hand overhead. Neither was the ball that Maz hit over Yogi Berra's head and the left field wall at Forbes Field the previous day.

No such ball has ever been identified. Several Oakland urchins came into the clubhouse after the game that day holding a baseball they boasted was the one that Maz hit. Kids in Oakland have always been enterprising if not necessarily honest.

I had a man from Bethel Park tell me one day when I was doing a booksigning at South Hills Village that his uncle had the ball. He said his uncle had been a Pittsburgh policeman and that he was stationed outside Forbes Field that day. I didn't believe his story. I asked the man for the name of his uncle. He said it was Joe Palmer.

I had to smile. Joe Palmer was the first policeman I ever knew as a kid in Hazelwood. He was a friend of my mother and he'd give me a quarter whenever I'd show him my school report card. I was hoping the story was true. It's the kind of story that Bill Mazeroski and Nellie King would both enjoy and then repeat to their friends.

I saw Mazeroski earlier in the year when he participated in the Homestead Lions' Golf Outing at the Westwood Golf Club in West Mifflin. I think it was the 15th time in 24 years, or something like that, Maz had made an appearance in that fund-raiser. And he always sticks around for dinner, sitting with his foursome and not his former teammates. That's class.

Darrell Hess, who rounds up the celebrities for that golf tournament each year, has a special fondness for Maz. "He's been very loyal," said Hess, who along with his wife Betty, has been the catalyst for so many community events and functions in their community.

"This has been a busy year for me," said Maz. "I could play golf at some event like this just about every day of the week. I've been going to some big celebrity golf outings in other cities. That's been nice. They've paid for my plane fare, had me and Milene staying in some fancy hotels, and treating us like royalty."

Milene, Maz's wife, is from Braddock and that's where they were wed. Maz remembers where he came from, in a coal patch in Ohio, close to Wheeling where he was born on September 5, 1936. So he's 75, at least for a few more weeks. I looked up that date in the *Baseball Encyclopedia*. I always have to smile when I see that Maz's stats appear right after those of Willie Mays in that big book where the players are listed alphabetically. Henry Aaron is the first name in the book. His brother Tommy Aaron is second.

Maz, by the way, hit 19 home runs in 1958, his third season with the Pirates. That's the most he ever hit in one of his 17 seasons with the Pirates. "Maz could hit with power when he first came up," offers Frank Thomas, another former Pirates' star who is a regular at the Homestead Lions' Golf Outing as well as many other charity-related outings around town. George Sisler, our hitting coach, got Maz to hit to all fields and that stole something from his power. He did the same with Clemente when he came along. He tried to get me to do that, too, but I resisted. I told him I was not that kind of hitter. I was a home run hitter."

Thomas was traded to the Cincinnati Reds on Jan. 30, 1959 with some other less famous Pirates in the deal that brought Harvey Haddix, Don Hoak and Smoky Burgess and the 1960 World Series to Pittsburgh. "I should have gotten a ring for that," says Thomas, who calls himself the "original Frank Thomas" in baseball.

He's always been a big fan of Bill Mazeroski and Nellie King.

Jim O'Brien

Steve Blass is flanked by former Steelers coach Chuck Noll and Nellie King at Pirates' Alumni Golf Outing at Churchill C.C.

Yankees still smarting
over 1960 World Series

October 2010

Pittsburgh baseball fans gathered October 13 at what remains of the outfield wall of Forbes Field to mark the 50th anniversary of the Pirates' victory over the New York Yankees in the 1960 World Series.

Several hundred of the best kind of fans will bring baseball memorabilia—autographed gloves, bats, photos, ticket stubs and their memories—and listen to a taped broadcast of the 7th game of the Series, won by the Pirates 10–9 when Bill Mazeroski hit a home run leading off the bottom of the 9th inning. It remains the most magic moment in Pittsburgh sports history.

The fun begins around 1 o'clock and continues until 3:36. Put it on your calendar. You'll swear you were at the game that day. There are at least 360,000 who say they were.

The New York Yankees are still smarting over their startling defeat by the Pittsburgh Pirates in the 1960 World Series. The Yankees were overwhelming favorites to crush the Pirates, indeed, to sweep them the way they had in the 1927 World Series when they had last met. But the Bucs prevailed in an unbelievable way to win the crown when Bill Mazeroski led off the bottom of the ninth inning in the seventh and deciding game with a home run in a 10–9 victory.

Those 1960 Pirates had staged late-inning comebacks all season. They taught us never to quit, never to give up.

The Yankees came to Pittsburgh this past summer to play the Pirates for the first time since that 1960 World Series and that prompted reflection on what occurred that October.

I was in the second month of my freshman year as a student at the University of Pittsburgh. What a way to start school! The Pirates were playing the mighty Yankees at Forbes Field on the Pitt campus, just a block and a half away from the Student Union.

Ten years later, I would move from Miami to New York to work for *The New York Post,* where I had the good fortune to cover both the New York Yankees and the New York Mets. I had opportunities to meet many of the key figures from the 1960 Yankees at Old Timers' Games and reunions.

I covered the Yankees and the Mets during the 1972 season when Yogi Berra became the manager of the Mets upon the sudden death of Gil Hodges in St. Petersburg, Fla., where the Mets were in spring training. I left camp one day early to drive to Pittsburgh where the Mets would start the season. When I pulled up in the driveway of my wife's

166

parents' home in White Oak, my mother-in-law, Barbara Churchman, came out to tell me that Gil Hodges had died, and that my editors were trying to get hold of me. There were no cell phones in those days.

One of the familiar reflections on that 1960 World Series was the sight of Berra, with his back to the infield, standing at the brick wall in left field as Mazeroski's home run cleared the barrier and sent Pittsburgh fans into a frenzy and one of the wildest celebrations the city had ever witnessed.

Johnny Blanchard was catching for the Yankees that day, a Thursday, October 13, 1960. Blanchard had signaled for a fast ball on the second pitch to Mazeroski—the first pitch was a ball—but reliever Ralph Terry shook him off, and insisted on throwing a slider instead.

He threw it high, across the chest, and Mazeroski swung and the rest is history.

When I was writing the book, *MAZ and the '60 Bucs*, I interviewed Berra, Blanchard, Terry and Whitey Ford—all pivotal players in that World Series—and, in my research, found reflections offered by Mickey Mantle and Casey Stengel. They capture the sentiments expressed by most of the Yankees and their fervent fans.

They felt clearly superior to the Pirates that season, and felt they should have won the World Series. Didn't the Yankees always win the World Series back then? Or so it seemed anyhow. That's why fans in other cities often referred to them as those damn Yankees.

The 1960 World Series was one of the strangest ever played. The Yankees set all sorts of records with ten home runs, 55 runs and a .338 team batting average. Their three victories were by 16–3, 10–0 and 12–0. The Pirates scored only 27 runs, hit only four home runs, and batted .256, yet the two teams were tied after six games.

The final game was a slugging match in which the Pirates took a 9–7 lead on catcher Hal Smith's three-run home run in the eighth inning—"a home run for the ages," said radio broadcaster Chuck Thompson—but the Yankees came back to tie it in the top of the ninth inning with a two-run shot by Yogi Berra. Then Mazeroski, leading off the bottom of the ninth inning, got hold of Terry's second pitch and drove it over the left field wall to spark a civic celebration that may not have been rivaled in sports history.

"They set all the records but we won the game," said Pirates' reserve outfielder Gino Cimoli, who made a big contribution when he came through as a replacement for the injured Bob Skinner.

* * *

There really is a Yogi Berra. There is a man in Montclair, New Jersey who looks and talks just like the fellow you have seen in the TV commercials for Aflac, driving a duck and the customers in a barber shop crazy with his strange comments. He looks funny and he talks funny, and he is the genuine article.

"The writers described me as a funny person," said Berra, "but that isn't the case at all. No one was ever more serious about baseball than me, and no one in baseball ever worked harder to succeed.

When I asked Yogi over the telephone what came to mind when he thought about the final game of the 1960 World Series, he said, "I remember the bad hop that hit Kubek's throat...when Clemente hit the ground ball to Moose at first base, and Coates didn't cover...and when that Smith fellow hit the home run...and when we tied the game in the ninth...and then Whatzisname hit the home run."

That, ladies and gentlemen, is the real Yogi Berra.

Whatzisname!

Of course, Berra remembers Bill Mazeroski, and he knows it was Mazeroski who hit the game-winning home run—he said so a few seconds later—but when asked to recall what he remembered best about the seventh game of the 1960 World Series, he said Whatzisname.

That way there would be no mistaking that it came directly from Yogi Berra.

Keep something else in mind: Lawrence Peter Berra, better known as Yogi, played on more pennant winners (14) and more world champions (10) than any player in history. He played in a record 75 World Series games. He also managed the Yankees to a pennant in 1964. He went to the plate a record 259 times, delivered a record 71 hits and banged a record ten doubles. He is second on the all-time Series records list with 41 runs scored and 39 runs-batted-in, and his 32 base-on-balls and 12 home runs rank third on the all-time list.

It should be easier to remember if you have played in two World Series ('60 and '71) like Maz. Even so, Maz has never been comfortable talking about his heroics. He was honored for "the best moment in Pittsburgh sports history" at the 2008 Dapper Dan Dinner & Sports Auction, and he said, "I wish someone else had hit that home run because they could explain it better. I still can't tell you what it meant to hit that home run. I never thought that home run would stay with me the rest of my life."

* * *

That home run has dogged Ralph Terry for the rest of his life. Many forget that two years later Terry was named the most valuable player in the 1962 World Series when the Yankees beat the San Francisco Giants for the championship.

"I should have curved him," said Terry over the telephone from his home in Larned, Kansas. "I know now I should have curved him."

Terry said this before I even asked him a question when he was told someone from Pittsburgh wanted to talk to him.

Instead, he threw a slider. In many reports it has been recalled as a fastball. But it was not a fastball. That is what the Yankees wanted Terry to throw—a fastball—but he shook off several signs by Blanchard, according to the account offered by Blanchard.

"I don't have any regrets," said Terry. "Maz isn't a hot dog. That home run couldn't have happened to a nicer guy. I just wish it would have happened to someone besides me."

No one was more upset by the home run and the 10–9 defeat by the Yankees than Terry.

"I must have warmed up five times in that game," recalled Terry, "and I was pooped by the time I got in. Both pitching staffs were shot by then. They only time we got anyone out was when they hit 400-foot fly balls or line drives at people. It was like a slow-pitch softball game.

"I can still hear Whitey Ford telling me afterward how he was going to get a Cadillac with his World Series check, but that he would have to get a Ford because of me. And I can hear Jim Coates (who gave up Hal Smith's three-run, eighth-inning home run, which gave the Pirates a 9–7 lead, and had failed to cover first base on a ground ball to first that allowed Clemente to hit safely) telling me he hated to see it happen to me, but that it better I was the goat than him.

"I didn't really feel too bad because it was my first World Series, and I loved just being there. I always knew I might get another shot at it. The guy I really felt bad for was Casey Stengel. We all knew that was his last year. It cost him his job."

* * *

Whitey Ford watched from the bullpen as Terry threw the fateful slider. Ford didn't pitch in Game 7. He is more bugged when he thinks about Game 1 of that 1960 World Series.

"I was mad that I didn't start that first game," Ford said during a visit to Three Rivers Stadium. Ford started Games 3 and 6, earning complete-game victories in 10–0 and 12–0 shutout victories. Had Ford started Game 1, many feel there would not have been a Game 7. Then, too, if there were, Ford would be on the mound in the deciding game.

He was, after all, still the ace of the staff.

From all reports, Stengel felt Ford had a tired arm and would benefit from an extra day's rest. Others say Ford was in Stengel's doghouse for keeping late nights on the road with his buddy Mickey Mantle.

"He started Art Ditmar," recalled Ford, "and Casey never said a word to me, and I never knew the reason. He was so successful most of the time so we didn't say anything about it."

Many fans of the Yankees felt the Pirates were lucky to win. Bob Friend, one of the top pitchers on the Pirates staff, said he bumped into Bob Turley, one of the Yankees' pitchers, at a celebrity golf outing a year ago, and that Turley was still saying the Yankees should have won it.

Ford hasn't forgotten how it turned out.

"They won," he said of the Pirates. "That's what counts. It's something we all think about once in a while. There's no getting around it. They played good baseball when they had to, and when the chips were down.

"Hal Smith hit the home run and, of course, Mazeroski hit the home run. When they had to perform they did. So you can't take anything away from them. They had a fine ballclub.

"Gino Cimoli said it best. He summed up the whole World Series when he said, 'The Yankees set all the records and we won the Series.' That says it in a nutshell. We did everything right except win the World Series.

"They didn't let that 16–1 setback bother them. Most clubs would have folded and said, 'Let's just get this thing over with and go fishing.' But, no, they didn't. They hung real tough every day. You can't beat that, and we didn't."

Asked whether it was the most disappointing defeat of his career, Ford replied, "Yes, that was the most disappointing thing that ever happened to me. And, you know, I played in five World Series with Mickey Mantle, and we lost three of them and won two of them. After that Pittsburgh World Series was the only time Mickey cried.

"He sat at his locker, and the big tears were coming down his cheeks. I know what he was going through. There were several of us who weren't feeling too good at that time.

"For me to see that, coming from him, a man like that, that meant a lot to me. He was hurt by that World Series there. He just shook his head. He didn't say anything derogatory at all toward the Pirates. It was just that we should have won that World Series. That's what he felt badly about. We all did. It was a downer."

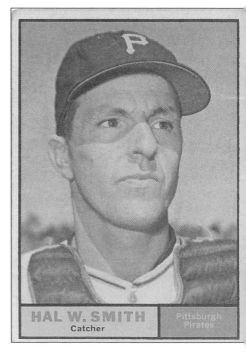

When the game was good enough
to carry the day

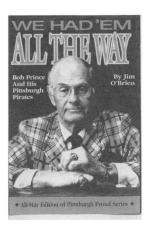

November 2010

The seventh game of the 1960 World Series did not need any window dressing. It was good enough to stand on its own merit. The 1960 World Series is still one of the wackiest in the history of Major League Baseball. The heavily-favored Yankees outscored the Pirates by 55 to 27 runs, yet the Pirates prevailed in the end, winning the deciding game 10–9 when Bill Mazeroski hit a home run over the left field wall leading off the bottom of the 9th inning.

It remains the only World Series that ended with a walk-off home run in the seventh game. There have been more than 500 World Series games played, but that seventh game was the only one in which there were no strikeouts. There were 19 runs yet the game took only two hours and 36 minutes to play.

The kinescope of the game, filmed off a black and white television set, is only two hours and ten minutes long. The commercials were eliminated, and some of the breaks between innings.

The Pirates have been celebrating the 50th anniversary of that epic event in Pittsburgh sports history this past (2010) season , anything to get fans to forget this was their 18th consecutive losing season. *(The Pirates would add to that with a 19th consecutive losing season, the longest losing streak in professional sports history.)* And unless you have been living in a cave the past few months you know that this kinescope was discovered by a curator in the wine cellar of the home of the late Bing Crosby just a few months ago.

Crosby was a celebrated singer and movie star of an earlier generation who also had a minority financial interest in the Pirates. The Pirates had a farm team in Hollywood once upon a time. Major League Baseball didn't start archiving film or tape of its games until around 1970, so until now there has not been film of the entire seventh game.

I have been among the many fans who attend a religious-like retreat every October 13 at the wall that remains from Forbes Field to listen to a tape of the radio broadcast of that seventh game but I had never seen a telecast of that game since October 13, 1960. I was a freshman at Pitt that fall and I watched the game on a television set in the Pitt Student Union, about two blocks from Forbes Field.

Sometimes I think I am the only Pittsburgher who wasn't present at Forbes Field to see the Pirates win the World Series that afternoon.

It was a thrill to be invited by Major League Baseball and, subsequently, the Pirates to attend a screening of that kinescope of the seventh game of the 1960 World Series at the Byham Theatre in downtown Pittsburgh last Saturday night.

Pitt and the Steelers and even my local high school football team at Upper St. Clair all lost games over a four-day stretch so this was a respite to see the home team win. As Ray Ratti, a realtor in the South Hills who shows up every Oct. 13 at the wall at Forbes Field, put it, "We win the World Series every year."

I attended movies at that theatre when it was the Fulton Theatre. Broadcaster Bob Costas came to town to emcee the evening's program last Saturday and he said it was great to see a full house at a theatre to see a movie about Pirates that didn't have movie star Johnny Depp as the star performer.

Costas was there and so was hometown movie star Michael Keaton, who was nine years old in 1960 and recalls the World Series as "the first major event of its kind that I experienced in my lifetime." Members of that Pirates team were present, including Dick Groat, Bob Friend, Hal Smith, Vernon Law, Joe Christopher, Bob Oldis, Elroy Face and Bill Virdon. Bill Mazeroski didn't make it—he was a late scratch to the disappointment of all—because he was hospitalized with kidney stones.

Franco Harris and Mike Wagner of the glory days of the Steelers were at the Byham Theatre as well, and so were two other former Pirates, Don Schwall and John Wehner. Nathaniel Crosby, the son of Bing Crosby, was there, along with Vera Clemente, the wife of the late Roberto Clemente. They all contributed to an exciting evening at the theatre.

The proper attire on the invitations called for "business casual" but my friend and patron Hoddy Hanna of Hanna Real Estate Services showed up in a tuxedo and lent more class to the occasion. I had three guests with me, friends Pat Santelli, Ken Codeluppi and Gene Musial and this was an early Christmas present for each of them. They were so pleased to be there. Their excitement was contagious.

Bob Prince and Mel Allen, two legendary voices of baseball, shared the mike for the NBC telecast of the game. Prince would do a few innings and then Allen would follow for a few innings. They were never on at the same time. There were no analysts explaining the significance of each pitch or pointing out strategy. Baseball fans were left to figure that out for themselves.

Prince and Allen both had rich, deep voices and spoke the King's English well. They were confident men, sure they knew enough about baseball and its history to inform and entertain the audience. They didn't have cheat sheets or ten pages of statistics to offer along the way. They were on their own and that was good enough.

I recall that Vin Scully, who has been doing the Dodgers games since they were back in Brooklyn all by himself and remains the best in the business, scolded Lanny Frattare one day at Three Rivers Stadium when he saw Frattare at his work station, surrounded by Post-It notes with stats and items he would use during the broadcast.

"C'mon, Lanny, this isn't an SAT test!" shouted Scully.

Seeing the telecast of the seventh game was enlightening. There were no instant replays, no slow-motion, few graphics. Just the game. As sportscaster John Steigerwald's dad used to scold him when he was distracted at a ballgame or begging for a hot dog and soda, "Just watch the game." When Costas asked Elroy Face if he felt any particular pressure coming in out of the bullpen to face the likes of Mantle and Maris and Berra in the seventh game of a World Series, Face reminded Costas that he had struck out Mantle earlier in the Series and added, "To me, it was just another game."

Face was fearless. I once asked a sportswriter from Baltimore named John Steadman to sum up why Johnny Unitas of Pittsburgh was such a great quarterback for the Baltimore Colts and Steadman said, "I can do it in two words: beyond intimidation."

It was that way for Face and Friend and Groat and Maz and for Bob Prince as well. They loved the big time competition.

What struck me about the telecast was the sheer simplicity of it all. There were no pierogi races, no constantly blaring music, no trivia contests, no pirate ships firing upon one another on the Jumbotron scoreboard, no fireworks, no shooting T-shirts into the stands, no Pirate Parrot, no purse searches at the turnstiles and, as Costas pointed out, the batters stayed in the batter's box and didn't back out before every pitch to adjust the straps on their batting gloves. There were no batting gloves back then. Everyone held the bat bare-fisted.

It would be difficult these days to hold the attention of fans, especially young fans, without all the extra entertainment. Kids are conditioned today to expect non-stop stimuli. I have been to some Pitt basketball games in recent weeks where everyone around me seems to be "texting" on their cell phones throughout the contest.

One young man sat next to me at one game and was either "texting" to someone out there in cyberspace or he was chewing his fingernails to the nub. His father sat next to him and they hardly spoke to one another. Some day that kid might wish he had talked to his dad. I have written over 20 books, but I have no desire to be "texting" anyone at any time of the day. I don't get it.

Costas started the program at the Byham Theatre by asking everybody to turn off their cell phones. They should do that at all sports events.

Prince was so good describing a baseball game. He mentioned that a rookie relief pitcher for the Yankees was Tom Stafford. "He wears his age—22—on his uniform," offered Prince, "but he'll soon outgrow that."

My pal Pat Santelli was critical of Prince's post-game interview of Mazeroski and team owner John Galbraith. He thought Prince came off as amateurish. I was always told that Prince did not see how the game ended and was unaware that Maz was the hero. He just knew that the 25-year-old Maz, the youngest starter on the team, was a bad interview, just shy of being on camera. He still is. Remember how he was when he was unable to deliver his acceptance speech when he entered the Baseball Hall of Fame in Cooperstown?

I loved hearing Prince's voice again. A fan once told me that "Bob Prince was the voice under the pillow for a little kid in Indiana, Pa." Another said that Bob Prince "was the sound of summer." His voice stays with us. He and Allen would describe the action, add some anecdotal material off the top of their head, and they were not afraid to be silent now and then. The silence, sometimes 10 to 15 seconds in length, added to the anticipation of what would follow. It was good theatre. An analyst wasn't jumping in on the heels of every comment to tell you what just happened.

When Hal Smith hit a three-run homer in a five-run eighth inning that put the Pirates ahead, 9–7, Allen announced that this was a home run that would be remembered forever as one of the greatest home runs in baseball history. To which Costas interjected from the stage, "Or at least for another three outs."

The film, by the way, was in excellent condition. The game was telecast in color in 1960 but this kinescope was taken off a black and white TV. It seemed more vintage in black and white. Bing Crosby, by the way, was in Paris that day rather than Pittsburgh because he didn't want to jinx the team by his presence. He asked a friend to film it for him so he could watch it when he came back home. It's fitting that, like an archaeological find, it turned up during the 50th anniversary of the most magic moment in Pittsburgh sports history.

The Pirates promoted a throwback game a few years ago in which the game was conducted the way they were back in the '60s, without all the extra hoopla, and I wish they would do it more often, perhaps at afternoon games now and then.

When the Pirates scored some runs in one flurry, the fellow in front of me at the Byham Theatre, offered a high five to his female companion. I tapped him on the shoulder and scolded him with a smile, "Hey, there were no high-fives in 1960," I pointed out.

I wanted to take my wife Kathie with me on this special evening, but she declined. She said she had some ironing to do. "Besides," she said, "I know how it ends."

There were three Pirates who hit home runs in the 1960 World Series and they were, left to right, Hal Smith, Bill Mazeroski (two) and Rocky Nelson. Mickey Mantle hit three for the Yankees, and Roger Maris and Bill Skowron both had two home runs. Yogi Berra, Elston Howard and Bobby Richardson each hit one home run for the Yankees. Richardson had 12 hits and remains the only player on a losing team to be named the World Series MVP.

Blass still beaming
over Pirates' opener

Jim O'Brien

April 2009

This was in the spring of 2009 and Steve Blass was about to turn 67. He had already celebrated his birthday. At least his birthday in baseball. The 2009 season would be his 50th season associated with the Pittsburgh Pirates in some manner, and the Pirates paid tribute to him on Opening Day.

The Pirates paid tribute to a lot of people at their Monday home opener on a rather brisk afternoon at PNC Park. The day began with solemnity, moments of silence for special people in the Pirates' past that I was fortunate to meet and spend time with, such as pitcher and coach Bruce Dal Canton, organist Vince Lascheid, promoter and special fan Guy Buzzelli. There was a tribute to the three policemen who were shot and killed in Stanton Heights a week earlier, Paul Sciullo, Eric Kelly and Stephen Mayhle.

There were honor guards from every branch of the military service. There were bagpipers and no one provides melancholy music like bagpipers. The Pirates had a PPB patch—for Pittsburgh Police Bureau—on the sleeves of their uniforms. Their hats and uniforms would be auctioned off and proceeds would go to the Fallen Heroes Fund. There were fine renditions of "America the Beautiful" and "The National Anthem" in what might have been the longest pre-game ceremony in Pirates' history. But no one complained, which is rare. There was a fly-over by four Apache helicopters. Those in attendance, especially the ones who got there early, got their money's worth and more. They saw and heard things they won't often experience at the ballpark. There was a huge turnout of 38,411, one of the biggest crowds ever for the Pirates at PNC Park, but many were late arrivals. It's not easy to find a place to park on the North Side these days, especially on a regular work day.

Blass has seen a lot of baseball games in his day, but he was acting like a kid at his first major league outing. He threw out the ceremonial first pitch, and he did so with great gusto. He came off the mound releasing the ball like he was in a World Series contest, though he was wearing a sport coat and tie, and his well-aimed pitch was caught by the best catcher in Pirates' history, Manny Sanguillen.

That's the same Sanguillen that danced to the mound and leaped onto Blass after the Pirates beat the Baltimore Orioles, 2–1, to win the seventh game of the 1971 World Series. That was the last time any pitcher went the distance in the seventh game of a World Series. Blass went the distance earlier in that World Series, again limiting the Orioles to one run. Blass remembers that Bill Mazeroski complimented him afterward on his pitching efforts, telling him it's not easy to pitch with a one-run lead, especially in a World Series.

Blass was so pumped up at the opener that he might have been able to pitch nine innings against the Houston Astros. He set the tone for the day.

Zach Duke did go the distance for the Pirates and that's another reason the day was so special. You don't see many complete games pitched in the majors any more. Bob Friend and Vernon Law—who pitched 18 innings one day—don't work here anymore; neither does Bob Gibson.

I'm glad Pirates' manager John Russell ignored the pitch count— Duke had gone over the 100 mark—and that it was a cold day in April, and only Duke's second start of the young season. Duke had dispatched the Astros on a few pitches in the eighth inning, and struck out the last batter, so he still had good stuff. The Pirates won 7–0 and Duke had a four-hit complete game shutout in his dossier. The Pirates backed him with an error-free defense. Didn't we think Zach Duke was a dandy?

A few days earlier, Paul Maholm had good stuff, too, and had a big lead on the Reds in Cincinnati. One of the Cincinnati announcers—I was watching the game on TV in Columbus during Easter weekend at my daughter Sarah's home—said something about "a quality start." He said baseball people today believed "a quality start" was when a pitcher went at least six innings and gave up no more than three runs.

That's not a quality start in my book, or in the minds of former major league pitchers from the '50s and '60s. If you give up three runs in six innings your earned run average will be 4.5. There's nothing that's quality about that number.

The Pirates had some pop in their bats, the way they did when Maholm was on the mound in Cincinnati, and they won the game easily, 7–0.

They showed highlights of Blass winning the seventh game of the 1971 World Series on the jumbo scoreboard screen and on TV monitors throughout PNC Park.

I bumped into Blass on the main concourse around the sixth or seventh inning. He had left the broadcast booth to check on family and friends who were there to celebrate his 50th season with the Pirates.

"It's especially great because they brought my high school baseball coach in from New Canaan," Blass told me. "A little school in Connecticut sent three ballplayers to the major leagues."

I shook the right hand of Blass and congratulated him on his special day. "What's really great about all this," I told Blass, "is that you have always been a good guy."

Blass beamed once more. "You're right about that," he said softly. "Thank you."

Beside his Series performances, Blass is best known in baseball circles for his sudden and inexplicable loss of control after the 1972 season. His ERA climbed to 9.8 in the 1973 season. He walked 84 batters in 88 innings, and struck out only 27. He spent most of the 1974 season in the minor leagues. He gave it one last try in spring training of 1975, and then retired.

After that, any pitcher who lost his control was said to have "Steve Blass Disease." It became a part of baseball lexicon. Some think his problems were more psychological than physical, and that the tragic death of teammate Roberto Clemente may have contributed to the loss of Blass' ability to throw a baseball across the plate. Blass never let the setback get the best of him. He never lost his sense of humor, or the gratitude he felt to have become a major league baseball player. When he became a broadcaster he often said, "I'm still living the dream."

Lanny Frattare was missing from the Pirates' broadcast booth for the first time in more than 30 years. Frattare had said that Blass was one of the most popular Pirates in team history. Blass had to count his blessings even more when he learned during the game that Harry Kalas, the main announcer for the Phillies the previous 39 years, had passed out and died in the broadcast booth in Washington D.C. where the Phillies were playing the Senators. Kalas was one of the great voices in baseball, as well as the voice of NFL Films, and was very popular with his peers. If that wasn't sobering enough, then came the news that former major league pitcher Mark "The Bird" Fidrych, famous for talking to the baseball when he was on the mound, died in an accident on his farm in Massachusetts at age 54.

I checked one of my books about the Pirates, and found an observation Blass offered in an interview I did with him several years ago.

"I'm happiest," he said, "when I'm with people who enjoy the game. Baseball has had a hold on me since I was six years old." I also remember him once saying, "There was a time when I didn't know if I was holding a baseball or if it was holding me."

He talked about how back then he used to bounce a tennis ball off a barn in Falls Village with an interesting angled roof and played a game of baseball he made up. "It's diminishing somewhat, but not a helluva lot," he said. "The thing I feel best about when I think about my days in baseball is that it was always fun. Listen to Blass on a Bucs' broadcast and count the number of times he says the word "fun" during a game. It's more telling than any pitch count.

"It's never been a tedious thing. Even in the toughest times, even when I couldn't figure out why I couldn't pitch effectively anymore, during my biggest personal tests. I always loved the atmosphere and the people I was around in baseball. Baseball's been everything to me. I love the game. I love the life. Baseball has always owned me."

I never had that kind of passion for baseball, but I traveled with the New York Yankees and the New York Mets during my days in New York, and I know how special the life can be. I've spent time at spring training in Florida. I've interviewed the likes of Joe DiMaggio, Willie Mays, Tom Seaver, Roberto Clemente, Frank Robinson, Mickey Mantle, Reggie Jackson, Phil Rizzuto, Bill Mazeroski, the wives of Babe Ruth and Lou Gehrig and so many others. I had drinks late one night at Yankee Stadium with Babe Ruth's wife Claire and vainly tried to keep up with her.

I was in the press box on Opening Day at PNC Park. I had seen what was scheduled for pre-game ceremonies and I was as curious to see how that would play out as I was to see the game itself. It was too warm in the press box. There were heaters at our feet. There was disagreement among the media as to whether the windows should be closed or open, and closed won out.

I had no idea how brisk the weather was for the fans until I left the press box to check out the crowd during the sixth inning. Temperatures were in the low 50s, but the wind made it feel colder. It was definitely more comfortable to watch the game from the press box. I have always regarded that as a privilege.

I remember being among great sportswriters at Yankee Stadium and Shea Stadium, which have given way to new stadiums in New York this season. I remember how fortunate I felt to be there, among some of my literary heroes, among men who won the Pulitzer Prize for their efforts. I thought it was the way a rookie must feel to be in the clubhouse with established stars.

I have often said that you never know what awaits you on any day at a sports venue, and the Pirates' terrific victory on Opening Day, with all the pomp and circumstance and reflections on real heroes offered a significant and special day at the ballpark.

Jim O'Brien

Steve Blass credits several sports broadcasters for helping him develop, including Penguins' play-by-play man Mike Lange, at right.. Blass also cites the help of Bob Prince, Nellie King, Lanny Frattare, Greg Brown and John Sanders.

These Pirates' pitchers
earned their keep

April 2010

Most of the former Pirates who have remained in residence in Pittsburgh were pitchers. Perhaps that's because pitchers are usually the smartest players on the team, just ahead of the catchers.

These men not only liked Pittsburgh they just thought it would be smart to stay here and pursue post-playing careers in the city that had embraced them as ballplayers. I have spent time recently in the company of Steve Blass, Kent Tekulve and Jim Sadowski, talked on the telephone with Bob Friend, and heard reports on what's going on with Dave Giusti and El Roy Face.

Blass and Friend remain two of the most popular Pirates ever to perform here. They both starred as starting pitchers, and saw World Series action. Face, Tekulve and Giusti are three of the greatest relief pitchers in the history of the game, and Sadowski was a hometown boy who had a chance to pitch relief for the Pirates during the 1974 season. Now he's pitching as a front-office executive for Hefren-Tillotson, the financial advisory company in downtown Pittsburgh founded by Bill Tillotson.

Face, Giusti and Tekulve all won Fireman of the Year Awards from *The Sporting News* as the ace relief pitcher in baseball during different seasons.

These men were all workhorses in their playing days and their strong work ethic served them well whenever they couldn't play ball any longer and had to get on with their life's work. They didn't make enough money to sit on their wallets the rest of their lives like so many of today's overpaid and over pampered players.

Starters wanted to pitch the distance, all nine innings or more, in their heyday and relief pitchers expected to pitch more than one inning. I remember reading in the newspaper during this recent spring training season that one of the Pirates' relief pitchers pronounced himself ready to pitch this season after he pitched an extended inning (four outs) in his first outing of the Grapefruit League. He was hoping to get in at least eight innings of pitching before the Pirates broke camp in Bradenton and came here to start the season.

I bumped into Steve Blass at PNC Park on that glorious Opening Day that you didn't want to end. I bumped into him after the game at Atria's Restaurant & Tavern on Federal Street. Owner Pat McDonnell and his wife Nancy stopped by to check out the crowd. And I saw Blass again this past Saturday night when we both appeared at a fund-raiser for the Myasthenia Gravis Association at PNC Park. Blass and these other former Pirates' pitchers snicker and sneer when they hear that going six innings these days is considered a "quality start," and beefs

179

up the resume of today's pitchers. Blass will turn 68 this April 18 (2010), but looks at least ten years younger.

"This is the 40th anniversary of Opening Day in 1970," offered Blass, always one to offer up interesting stories and trivia. "We started that season at Forbes Field and then moved to Three Rivers Stadium. I went ten innings in that opener and Tom Seaver went eight innings as the starter for the Mets."

I looked that one up in the record book and the Mets ended up winning that game, 5–3, in extra innings. Blass didn't mention that. Why spoil a good story? His point was that he was ready to pitch ten innings fresh out of spring training. Vernon Law once pitched 18 innings on two days rest and came back and pitched 13 innings four days later. Bob Friend relieved Law after 18 innings and pitched one inning and got the win. I don't think Law has forgiven him for that to this day.

Friend pitched more innings than any other pitcher in the team's history. He took great pride in never missing a start. He was out there every fourth or fifth day. When the team was on the road he often walked to the ballpark from the hotel where the team was staying. He thought it was important for a pitcher to have strong legs.

He was the only pitcher to lead the league in ERA while pitching for a last-place team. In 1955 he had a 2.83 earned run average and was lucky to scrape out a 14–9 record with the punchless Pirates. That was 55 years ago. Friend will be 80 this coming November. When I spoke to him on the phone at his Fox Chapel home he told me he was rehabbing from shoulder replacement surgery. I have friends who have had knee replacements and hip replacements but Bob is my only Friend to have a new right shoulder. "Can you imagine that?" he asked.

"I put a lot of wear and tear on that shoulder through the years."

Friend had a career won-loss record of 197–230. He pitched for a lot of bad Pirates' teams in those years. You had to be a good pitcher to lose over 200 games. He lost a lot of tough battles. He had more starts, more innings and more of a lot of things in the team record book. I firmly believe that if Friend had pitched for a better team, say the Dodgers or Reds or Yankees, he'd be in the Baseball Hall of Fame today. The Pirates lost over 100 games in 1952, 1953 and 1954. Friend made his debut on April 28, 1951 with the Bucs.

Friend is just as reliable these days. He is a favorite at many area golf fund-raisers. He says he wouldn't be able to resume playing golf until July. He is a long-time respected member of the Oakmont Country Club and his son, Bobby, has been a pro golfer and teaching pro for many years.

Elroy Face, who was 82 then, still resides in North Versailles. Friend said that Elroy's wife has been in a difficult struggle with cancer of late (she would die in 2012). Face lost two members of his immediate family to cancer, which prompted him to give up smoking a few years back. He loves to play golf in all the area fund-raisers. "I like to play golf," he says. "It's free, and so is the food and beer, and I always get some gifts. How can you beat that?"

Kent Tekulve, who turned 65 in May, 2012, works for the Pirates and also provides post-game analysis on Root Sports cable TV. He has been the lead sports celebrity for the local chapter of Myasthenia Gravis for more than 20 years. That's a neurological disease that has no cure, but there is treatment that can ease the difficult challenges of those who have it. One of the fans who attended that fund-raiser at PNC Park showed Tekulve a picture in which his left leg is extended high over his head as he comes off the pitching mound. "Look how high you have your leg!" the lady exclaimed.

"I can't lift my leg that high anymore," he said, always poking fun at himself. "That's one of many things I can't do anymore."

Blass and Tekulve both live near Dave Giusti in Upper St. Clair. The three of them are great about representing the Pirates' Alumni at different events in the region.

Giusti, who is 72, had been going through a rough stretch himself the previous year. First, he developed a serious case of shingles which left his eyes badly swollen like a beat-up boxer. Dave and his wife, Ginny, sent out pictures by e-mail to their friends showing how greatly Giusti was disfigured by this malady. They urged everyone to get their anti-shingles vaccine. I've done that and so has my wife Kathie. Now Giusti is challenged by other health issues. He and Ginny still plan to travel with friends to Croatia on a vacation trip this summer. It's hard to keep a good man down. (Giusti ended up not going because he just didn't feel up to it.) I always enjoy seeing these guys and hearing their stories. Sometimes I think we take their presence in Pittsburgh for granted. They not only starred as pitchers for the Pirates but they have stayed here and been contributing citizens to so many good causes. You can't beat these Bucs.

They were all pleased that the Pirates were going to erect a statue at PNC Park to honor their good friend Bill Mazeroski, and that they continue to call upon former Pirates to appear at the ballpark in various promotions.

Jim O'Brien

Bob Friend, El Roy Face and Steve Blass are were pitching mainstays for Pirates through the years.

Photos by Jim O'Brien

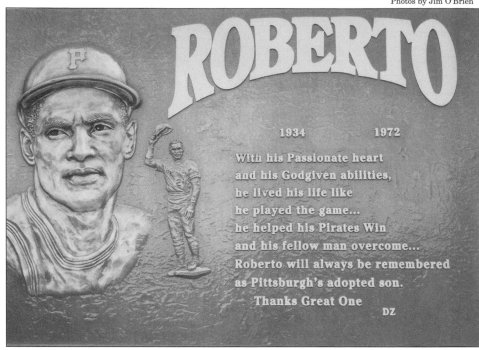

Rembering Roberto

There many reminders of Roberto Clemente on the North Shore of Pittsburgh, including a statue, a bridge in the background and a plaque, as well as other memorabilia to pay tribute to "The Great One."

Sid Bream broke the hearts
of Pirates' fans (forever)

April 2009

I sat next to Sid Bream on the dais at the 2009 Dapper Dan Sports Dinner & Auction at the Petersen Events Center on the campus of the University of Pittsburgh. We were at the far end of the front row of the two-tiered dais, to your right if you were among the thousand in attendance at the annual celebration of the Pittsburgh sports scene.

We were there to pay special honor to Steelers' coaches Mike Tomlin (Sportsman of the Year) and Dick LeBeau (Lifetime Achievement Award) and Pitt women's basketball standout Shavonte Zellous (Sportswoman of the Year).

There were 56 of us altogether on the dais, representing all aspects of sports in Pittsburgh and Western Pennsylvania. I was intrigued to be seated next to Bream. I also had a chance to chat backstage with DeJuan Blair and Sam Young, two of my favorites on the Pitt men's basketball team,

"Am I in any danger sitting next to you?" I asked Bream soon after we had introduced ourselves.

"I don't know," he said. "I do know that some people have never gotten over what I did. I'm glad Bill Hillgrove (the dinner emcee) didn't mention anything about it when he introduced me. They usually do."

Bream was referring, of course, to the most famous moment of his baseball career, when he scored the game-winning run for the Atlanta Braves to beat his former team, the Pittsburgh Pirates, in Game 7 of the 1992 National League Championship Series. It's one of the most replayed scenes in Braves' history, just behind Henry Aaron's 715th home run that broke Babe Ruth's career record.

When Bream slid across home plate with that decisive run his spikes struck the chests and hearts of Pirates' fans everywhere. I told him I had my favorite moments in Pittsburgh sports history—Maz hitting the home run to win the 1960 World Series, Pitt's Dan Marino throwing a touchdown pass to John Brown to beat Georgia in the 1992 Sugar Bowl, Pitt's Roger Kingdom winning the 110-meter high hurdles in the 1984 Olympic Games in Los Angeles, the Steelers' Super Bowl triumphs, the Penguins' Stanley Cup championships, the Pirates' World Series victories in 1971 and 1979—but that he was a key figure in one of my worst experiences as a Pittsburgh sports fans.

Sitting with Sid Bream brought something else to mind that fans shouldn't forget. He's a good guy. He continues to live in the suburbs north of Pittsburgh and is proud of his long association with the Pirates. Now 51, he looks terrific and he talks and walks the right way. His family and his faith come first in his life.

He attended Liberty University, and he has a son who's gone there, and another one headed in the same direction. "I like what the school is all about," he said of the faith-based college in Lynchburg, Va., "and the standards they set for their students."

Bream is a motivational speaker, and quick to mention his strong Christian beliefs. He was the hitting coach last season for the State College Spikes of the New York-Penn League. He said he and his wife were starting a tile cleaning business this year.

He was a lefty all the way and left his mark as a first baseman for the Pirates from 1985–1990. He was a fine fielder and a reliable hitter. In 1986 he set a Major League Baseball Record with 166 assists at first base. That's quite a record. He also played for the Los Angeles Dodgers, the Atlanta Braves and the Houston Astros.

Seated next to him on the dais were two other former Pirates, ElRoy Face and Kent Tekulve, two of the best relief pitchers, along with Dave Giusti, in the history of baseball. They were reminders of how good the Pirates were once upon a time.

Face fashioned a record-setting 18–1 record in 1959 and was the closer for the Pirates in 1960 when they beat the New York Yankees to win the World Series.

Tekulve saved three games, including the seventh and final game, when the Pirates defeated the Baltimore Orioles to win the World Series in 1979.

Face is now 71 and Tekulve just turned 52 last month. Both of them participate in many fund-raising golf tournaments in these parts. Bream asked Face why he played in so many of these events. "I like to play as much golf as I can," offered Face with a smile, "and I get nice gifts. I eat and drink for free and get to see my former teammates and meet a lot of nice people." Face said his favorite golf tournament is the one he hosts each summer at Dick Groat's Champion Lakes Golf Club near Ligonier. It's for the benefit of the School for the Deaf.

Let's get back to Bream. A picture showing him sliding across home plate to beat the Pirates in that 1992 National League Championship Series appeared in this Monday's *Pittsburgh Post-Gazette.*

"The Pirates haven't had a winning season since then," Bream reminded me at the Dapper Dan Dinner. "I don't know if I'm getting blamed for that as well."

It kept the Pirates from going to the World Series that summer, and the Pirates haven't posted a winning season in the 16 years since that happened. It appears they will be hard-pressed not to make it a record 17 straight losing seasons. Hope springs eternal in the spring, but it's difficult for Pirates' fans to believe the team will be any better this time around.

I remember watching that 1992 playoff game on the television in my family room. My wife Kathie was with me that day.

The Pirates had a 2–0 lead going into the bottom of the ninth inning. Their best pitcher, Doug Drabek, needed only three outs to put the Pirates in the World Series.

Does this sound anything like the final moments of the Pitt-Villanova game in the NCAA men's basketball tournament's Elite Eight action? The way the Pirates were playing it looked like they would beat the Braves.

Drabek gave up a lead-off double to Terry Pendleton, and then David Justice got on because Pirates' second baseman Jose Lind booted a ground ball to allow Justice to get on at first base. I remember screaming, "That's it! There goes your ballgame!"

Lind's miscue doesn't get as much air time as Bill Buckner of the Boston Red Sox letting the ball go between his legs against the New York Mets, but it should. It is equally deserving of inclusion in Hall of Shame plays.

Drabek then walked Bream to load the bases. That's when Pirates' manager Jim Leyland yanked Drabek and replaced him with reliever Stan Belinda. He managed to get two outs, despite giving up a run on a sacrifice fly by Ron Gant.

Then Francisco Cabrera, a third-string catcher for the Braves, singled to left field and Justice scored easily to tie the game. Barry Bonds fielded Cabrera's hit in left field. Bream was running all out—and he was regarded as one of the slowest base-runners in the league at the time—and surprised everyone by hustling past third base and heading for home.

Bonds' throw arrived first, but it was slightly offline towards first base. As soon as catcher Mike LaValliere caught the ball, he lunged toward the plate to tag Bream out, but Bream was able to slide under the tag and send the Braves—not the Pirates—to the World Series for the second consecutive year. Some Pirates' fans blame Bonds for that loss, and another example of how he came up short in clutch situations when he played here.

"People in Pittsburgh bring that play up to me all the time when they meet me," said Bream. "I've gotten used to it."

Rest assured Pirates' fans have yet to forgive him. Or Belinda. Or Bonds.

Sid Bream in deep thought at Dapper Dan Dinner.

Chuck Tanner had taste of real
work as teen at U.S. Steel in Homestead

February 2011

Chuck Tanner was born on the 4th of July, hit a home run on the first pitch he saw in the major leagues, and could boast that he once pinch-hit for Henry Aaron. And he hit a home run while batting for the man who would become the home run king of baseball.

Is it any wonder Tanner always had a smile on his handsome face?

Chuck Tanner had time for everyone, shared stories about baseball generously, and was one of the nicest men I've met in a lifetime of covering sports. Anyone who met him said, "He's such a nice guy."

Another manager in baseball, Leo "The Lip" Durocher, once declared that "nice guys finish last," but Tanner was proof that wasn't necessarily so.

I recall how much I enjoyed talking to Tanner as we stood in the back of the press box at Three Rivers Stadium, or sitting with him in the best seats in the house behind home plate at PNC Park. Jim Leyland felt the same way when they were both baseball scouts and sat next to each other at games at PNC Park. Leyland, now the manager of the Detroit Tigers, said he and Tanner became close friends during that spell.

"This is a life that should be celebrated," allowed Leyland.

Listening to Tanner providing insight on what he saw was a joy. It was similar to standing on the sideline at Three Rivers during a Steelers' practice with Art Rooney and listening to what he had to say. And a sportswriter gets paid to do that.

A friend of mine, Pat Santelli, went to his first Pirates' Fantasy Camp in Bradenton, Florida at the end of last month, and told me what a great experience he had.

I told him it was a shame that he didn't get to spend a week with Chuck Tanner, who served as the commissioner of the camp before his ill health prevented him from continuing in that role, and that Nellie Briles had died and wasn't there to run the camp. It had been Briles' baby from the beginning.

I told Santelli that I once told some men who were soaking up all the tips about how to improve their skills at Fantasy Camp that it was too late for them to become ballplayers. But I added, "If you learn to be as humble as Bill Mazeroski, as good-humored and resilient as Steve Blass, and greet each day with the enthusiasm and great attitude of Chuck Tanner, then you will come away from here with traits that will serve you well whatever you are doing in life."

Tanner and Briles had been standouts for the Pirates when they bounced back from a 3–1 deficit in games won in the 1979 World Series and beat the Baltimore Orioles in seven games. That was the last time the Pirates would win a World Series. It may be the last time the Pirates ever win a World Series. They were the "We Are Family" team.

Santelli said he heard at Fantasy Camp that Tanner wasn't doing well and that his friends from the Pirates were worried about him. So it was no surprise last Saturday when several people told me that Tanner had died the day before in his hometown of New Castle. He was in hospice care when he passed away.

I met Tanner for the first time in the early '70s when he was Manager of the Year with the Chicago White Sox. I wanted to interview Richie Allen, who was from Wampum, Pennsylvania, and was one of the best power hitters in baseball at the time. Allen could be difficult with writers, so I introduced myself to Tanner and asked him to pave the way for me with Allen. And Allen was as cooperative as can be for me that day in the dressing room at Chicago's Comiskey Park.

I was working at *The New York Post* at the time. When I told Tanner I was from Pittsburgh and was a good friend of Frankie Gustine, the former Pirates' infielder who owned a restaurant on the Pitt campus in Oakland, he treated me like an old pal.

Tanner never forgot where he came from because he never stayed away from his hometown of New Castle too long. No matter where he was playing, or coaching or managing in the minor leagues or major leagues, Tanner always returned to New Castle in the off-season.

"I'll always live in New Castle," Tanner told me. "I love living there. Things couldn't be better." Of course, Tanner felt that way wherever he happened to be in baseball. He loved wearing a baseball uniform and being at a baseball park. The Pirates began spring training with the pitchers and catchers reporting to Bradenton this past Monday and these Pirates will miss spending time with Tanner, and having Tanner tell them how lucky they are to be in the big leagues.

Tanner had his critics, mind you. Some cited that he was the manager of the Bucs when they became embroiled in a drug scandal involving several of his players. Some scoffed at his cheerfulness when the team was in a losing streak. What's there to be happy about? Tanner thought things were great even when they were bad at the ballpark.

His dad had worked at the New Castle Tin Mill and later for Pennsylvania Railroad. Chuck himself had worked at Homestead's U.S. Steel plant during the summers of his late high school years and came home only on weekends.

Later, following his first pro baseball season, Chuck worked at Republic Steel in Youngstown, Ohio. He had a taste of hard work, and it wasn't difficult to choose between that and baseball with the athletic ability he possessed.

He agreed with another Western Pennsylvania product, football quarterback Joe Namath of Beaver Falls, who said, "Playing sports sure beats the blast furnaces."

They weren't paying baseball players the obscene amount of money they are paying them these days—$5.5 million for a washed-up Johnny Damon down in Tampa Bay, $2 million for an indifferent and incorrigible Manny Ramirez with the same Rays, and $2 million for

Ross Ohlendorf, who posted a 1–11 record as a pitcher for the Pirates last season—but Tanner never thought twice about what he wanted to do.

"I've been fortunate that all my life has been involved in baseball," Tanner told me in an interview when I was later working at *The Pittsburgh Press*. "Not only has it been good for me, but the friendships I've made are something. I know doctors and lawyers who'd change positions tomorrow to be in sports. I wanted to do what I enjoyed doing. Money shouldn't be the No. 1 factor when you're choosing a career."

That was certainly the case when, in 1963, he went off to become a manager with the Quad Cities team in the Midwest League. Davenport, Iowa was the team's home base. "I never saw my family that season," he said. "I couldn't afford to take any of them with me. I was making about $6,000 a year. But my wife was behind me all the way. She knew that's the only way I'd be happy."

I always knew that Tanner loved baseball and his family. He was so fond of his father and mother, his wife and their children. He was away a lot and credited his wife, Barbara, with shouldering the load when it came to looking after the family. I remember when his mother, Ann Tanner, died at 70 during the 1979 World Series and I remember him caring for his wife before she died several years ago.

He talked about Barbara with the same reverence he had for the game of baseball. His love affair with baseball began when he was in grade school. "From the third grade on," he recalled, "I'd run home rather than take the school bus because it went a long way to drop everybody off, and I'd save about 15 minutes by running. I wanted to get home and listen to Rosey Rowswell broadcasting the last few innings of the Pirates' games.

"I'd have lineups written. I'd keep track of the players' batting averages and pitching records. The Pirates—they were the team. I couldn't wait to get the Sunday paper and read more about them. We couldn't afford the Sunday paper but my aunt would save it for me. There are certain guys I remember. They got this guy once named Johnny Gee, the tallest left-hander in baseball. He must've been — I thought that was really great, and I was really excited about it.

"I remember Gus Suhr. And Arky Vaughn. That sticks in my mind. Rip Sewell. Frankie Gustine. He always started out batting .400. Then he opened his own restaurant near the ballpark in Oakland. I didn't get to Forbes Field very often when I was a kid. I'd see three games a season if I was lucky."

On Tuesday, his family, friends and fans said goodbye to Chuck Tanner at his church in New Castle. I'll miss him. Any time I needed a good baseball story, or a comment on any baseball topic, I could call Chuck Tanner at his home or his restaurant in New Castle and he never let me down.

The last time I called I was looking for a story about Paul Waner when the Pirates were retiring his No. 11 uniform. It turned out that Waner was a hitting instructor with the Milwaukee Braves when Tanner was on the team, so he told me a terrific tale about Waner. At the conclusion of his story, Tanner said, "You're the only writer I ever told that story to."

Tanner knew how to charm the press corps. "Why me?" I asked him.

"Because no one ever asked me about Paul Waner before," came back Tanner. He also told me that Waner was buried in Bradenton, Florida, not far from the Pirates' training complex.

I once asked him about the guys at Fantasy Camp and Bill Mazeroski when we were in Bradenton, and Tanner said, "They're living the dream of playing with major leaguers on a major league baseball field. This is Maz's environment. He's a blue-collar kid from a poor neighborhood and he made it to the Baseball Hall of Fame. It's a great story. And he's a great guy." The same can be said of Chuck Tanner.

Chuck Tanner as he appeared at Pirates' Fantasy Camp in January of 2005.

Don Schwall still stands tall
as Pirates' ambassador on area golf courses

June 2011

Don Schwall has always been a standout performer in the annual Homestead Lions Golf Outing at the Westwood Golf Club where West Mifflin says hello to Kennywood.

At a shade less than the 6-foot-6 he was listed at in his baseball playing days for the Boston Red Sox and Pittsburgh Pirates in the '60s, and with his silver-white hair always combed in a high pompadour, he's taller than all the usual participants.

Two other popular Pirates of the past, Kent Tekulve, at 6–4, and Frank Thomas, at 6–3, also stand out in the crowd in the clubhouse.

Schwall came to the Pirates from the Red Sox along with catcher Jim Pagliaroni in a trade for Pirates first baseman Dick Stuart and pitcher Jack Lamabe and was a middle relief pitcher and an occasional starter at Forbes Field. He was always a .500 pitcher for the Pirates. He was with the Bucs from 1963 into the 1966 season when he was traded to the Atlanta Braves.

He pitched two-thirds of an inning for the Braves in 1967 and that was the end of his pitching career. That in itself is unusual.

He has lived in Pittsburgh ever since, so he was rooting for the Pirates over last weekend, that wonderful weekend when Pittsburgh was abuzz about the Pirates in particular and baseball in general.

The Pirates won two of three games with the heralded Boston Red Sox before jubilant sellout crowds at PNC Park, looking outstanding in the opening two games and something less when they committed four errors to boot away the finale. Oh well, the Pirates aren't perfect.

"I think it was great," said Schwall. "They've got some promising young players and they're playing well. They have some weak spots to shore up, but at least they are competitive and creating some excitement. You have to love that kid Neal Walker

"I liked it when they hired Clint Hurdle as manager. He's got some life in him, and he's not afraid to do things, or try things. I think he's a players' manager and he'll get the most out of them."

There was lots of talk about the Bucs at Westwood. Some of the usual Pirates alumni who usually attend the event were not there. Bill Mazeroski was playing in Mario Lemieux's celebrity golf outing, and El Roy Face and Bob Friend were unable to play.

Like those guys, Schwall mixes well with the participants and sticks around for happy hour and dinner, and shares stories with his foursome and anyone else who sits in on the conversation.

They never do a hit-and-run as some celebrities choose to do. Don Schwall has always been a class act.

Darrell Hess, who coordinates the event and lines up the celebrity sports stars, has enjoyed great success through the years fashioning

Pirates' pitchers, from left to right, Kent Tekulve, Don Schwall and Bob Friend went to Cooperstown to witness induction of Bill Mazeroski into the Baseball Hall of Fame.

DON SCHWALL pitcher

Bill Mazeroski and Don Schwall are regulars at annual Homestead Lions' Golf Outing at Westwood Golf Club.

loyal relationships with many of the most popular Pirates, Steelers, Penguins and other local athletic stars on the pro, collegiate and scholastic level. The Homestead Lions help support a lot of worthwhile local projects with money raised at this event.

Those fellows in Don Schwall's foursome at Westwood have no idea of what he accomplished before that, or just exactly who they were playing with on the 18-hole layout or at dinner in the clubhouse afterward.

Schwall is still active in the financial or investment game, teaming up with his son, Don Jr., or Dee as he is called, in his home office in Gibsonia. He does some deals in China, and helps put together some real estate deals.

He retired a few years back and then un-retired when his son suggested they work together. Don Sr. had been a vice-president with E.F. Hutton and Paine Webber, two of the biggies in the investment game. "There's no question that playing baseball helped me in my business career," said Schwall.

I've seen Schwall at this outing on many occasions, but it's only in recent years I have come to appreciate what a great athlete he was in his heyday.

I didn't realize, for instance, that Schwall was born in Wilkes-Barre, Pennsylvania. Donald Bernard Schwall was born on March 2, 1936, so he is in his mid-70s and still looks terrific. He was a handsome dude in his day, and still can smile when he checks out his silver hair in the bathroom mirror.

He was all-state as a baseball and football player in high school in Wilkes-Barre, and went to the University of Oklahoma on a basketball scholarship. He stayed two years before signing with the Red Sox, While at Oklahoma, he gained all-Big Eight honors in basketball and outscored the great Wilt Chamberlain of Kansas in a couple of conference outings.

At Oklahoma, Schwall was on an impressive pitching staff that included future major leaguers Lindy McDaniel and Ed Fisher.

He broke in with the Red Sox in an unusual manner. He started the 1961 season with Seattle in Triple A where he went 3–0 and got called up to the parent team in Boston.

He posted a 15–7 record and won Rookie of the Year honors in the American League. He was 6–0 at one point, and 13–2. He is one of the handful of players who started a season in the minor leagues and was picked to play in the Major League All-Star Game at midseason.

That was during a short span when Major League Baseball held two All-Star Games. He pitched the three middle innings. He was matched against the great Sandy Koufax of the Dodgers in those middle innings of the 1961 All-Star Game.

"The highlight of that season was when I struck out Stan Musial in the All-Star Game and, of course, winning the Rookie of the Year award. I hadn't given Rookie of the Year any thought because I wasn't even on the big league roster when the season began."

Schwall's roommate that season was another Red Sox rookie, Carl Yastrzemski. Schwall said Yaz had such a great attitude that it helped him immensely to be his roommate.

Schwall had that great season in 1961 when the Red Sox finished 33 games out of first place and 10 games below .500. The Yankees won the AL with a 109–53 record. That was the year Roger Maris and Mickey Mantle chased Babe Ruth's one-season home run (60) record. Maris had 61 to set a new record. Mantle finished with 54.

"There were so many great ballplayers during that time," said Schwall. "Willie Mays was the greatest batter I ever faced.

"The 1961 Yankees, I think, were the greatest ball team I ever saw. They had Clete Boyer at third, Tony Kubek at short, Bobby Richardson at second, Moose Skowron at first and Elston Howard behind the plate. They had Yogi Berra in left field, Mickey Mantle in center and Roger Maris in right field.

"They were the best team ever to play the game. What a lot of people don't realize is how good they were defensively. They just had incredible talent."

Keep in mind, however, that this was the same lineup the Pirates managed to beat in the 1960 World Series, which is why it was such an upset triumph, in what had to be the wackiest World Series ever. The Yankees outscored the Pirates 55 to 7 in runs, yet the Bucs won the best-of-four series with a 10–9 win in the seventh game.

In 1966, Schwall had a 2.16 ERA for the Pirates and they still traded him to the Braves where he became a teammate of Henry Aaron. "It was a different time," said Schwall. "The pitching was so good. Every team had tremendous pitching, sometimes three and four stars on the staff."

So Schwall's foursome, I'm sure, had a good time in his company and they might have picked up a good stock tip along the way at Westwood Golf Club.

Jim O'Brien

Bill Mazeroski and Don Schwall often play in charity-related golf outings.

Ralph Kiner continues
to be right up my alley

September 2009

Ralph Kiner as he appeared as the Mets' broadcaster.

I awoke to the cawing of crows one day a week ago. It was sixty degrees outside, so the windows in our bedroom were cracked open. We used to hear roosters in the morning when we first moved here 30 years ago, but those nearby farms have given way to high-end suburban housing complexes in the past decade.

It was nearly six o'clock and the sun was just coming up. I'd had a dream, really just a snippet of a dream, and I didn't know what it was all about or what prompted the image I'd seen in my pillow.

I was a young boy and I was walking up the so-called City Steps from Second Avenue, the main street in Glenwood and Hazelwood, to my home, which fronted on Sunnyside Street and reared on Gate Lodge Way. I'd seen a blueprint of our neighborhood and the grounds where my home stood was called Blair Estates. It was a humble home, for sure, the first of four row houses, but I always thought Blair Estates, Sunnyside Street and Gate Lodge Way made it sound pretty nice.

I ran into an old friend from my neighborhood last week and she jested to her luncheon companions at Armstrong's Restaurant in Whitehall that we had both lived in condos or townhouses; she wasn't sure which was more appropriate, when we were young. In any case, in my dream I turned left midway up one of the portions of the City Steps, and headed to the back door of our home on Gate Lodge Way.

And there, just ahead of me by about 30 yards, I spotted Ralph Kiner walking in the same direction. He was dressed in beige slacks and a short-sleeved pale yellow shirt, and I was pretty sure it was him. He wasn't wearing a ball cap or a hat. His biceps were larger than anybody in my neighborhood, that's for sure. Ralph Kiner was the greatest ballplayer on the Pittsburgh Pirates of my youth. I quickened my pace so I could catch up to Kiner. And that was the end of the dream. It was over before it got rolling. When I awoke, I told my wife I'll bet I was the only guy in Pittsburgh who had a dream about Ralph Kiner that morning.

Ralph Kiner was the home run king of the National League in my youth. He led the league in home runs his first six seasons with the Pirates (1946–1951) and tied with Hank Sauer of the Chicago Cubs for the home run title in 1952. That remains a record for consecutive home run titles. The Pirates traded him to the Cubs before the 1953 season. He spent two years there and finished up another season with the Cleveland Indians. His career lasted ten years and an ailing back prompted his retirement.

The Pirates were a pretty bad ball team back then, just as bad as the teams we've suffered with these past 17 seasons. When Kiner was on the ball club, the Pirates finished seventh or eighth in the eight-team National League six of those seasons. When Kiner's contract came up for negotiation after one of those dreadful seasons he pressed General Manager Branch Rickey for a raise.

Rickey refused to budge. "We finished last with you," Rickey reportedly told Kiner, "and we can finish last without you."

Billy Meyer was the manager for five of those seasons, including 1951 when the Pirates lost a record 112 games in a 154-game schedule. That's why it's still a puzzle as to how Meyer's No. 1 Pirates' uniform is among the team's retired numbers.

Kiner connected for 36 or more home runs in each of those seven seasons he spent with the Pirates. Fred Haney was his manager his final season here. Twice Kiner hit more than 50 home runs, with 51 in 1946 and 54 in 1949. He averaged 7.1 home runs per 100 at bats, trailing only Mark McGwire, Babe Ruth and Barry Bonds, among retired players, in that respect. Kiner led the NL in slugging percentage three times. He wasn't the greatest glove man, but he certainly belonged in the Baseball Hall of Fame.

If the Pirates were trailing on the scoreboard after seven or eight innings, as they usually were, the fans would stick around at Forbes Field if they knew Kiner was coming to bat one more time. They wanted to be there if there was a chance Kiner would hit another home run. Kiner was the most popular sports personality in Pittsburgh since boxing great Billy Conn, and Kiner enjoyed more popularity in this town than either Roberto Clemente or Willie Stargell when they were playing for the Pirates. And Stargell, of course, was more popular than Clemente when they were in uniform.

Clemente became more revered after his tragic death in an airplane crash into the Atlantic Ocean while delivering supplies to earthquake victims in Nicaragua from his native Puerto Rico on New Year's Eve 1972. Yes, Kiner was that big.

I used to read about him in the morning newspaper, the *Pittsburgh Post-Gazette*, when by brother Dan and I delivered the paper in the early '50s. Kiner was a favorite son and frequent topic in the columns of the paper's sports editor and lead columnist, Al Abrams. It was reading Abrams' columns as a kid that sparked my initial interest in becoming a sportswriter. His job seemed like a good gig.

Kiner was voted into the Baseball Hall of Fame in 1975 in his 15th and final season of eligibility. He garnered 273 of a possible 362 votes in the balloting, never getting the required 75 per cent of the votes until his last swing at bat in the balloting. He was a good friend of Stan Musial of the St. Louis Cardinals and the pride of Donora, Pa.

Branch Rickey once remarked that Stan Musial was the most liked player in baseball.

"He got in the first time with maybe 250 votes," recalled Kiner, reflecting on Musial. "I told him I was the greatest vote-getter in Baseball

Hall of Fame history. I probably got over 2,000 votes in the 15 years I was eligible."

I traveled to Cooperstown, N.Y., to witness Kiner's induction and lobbied for the assignment at *The New York Post.*

I first got to know Kiner up close when I came to New York in the spring of 1970. Kiner was one of the original broadcasters for the New York Mets and remained on the job forever it seems. He and Lindsay Nelson and Bob Murphy formed the Mets' broadcast team.

I had moved from Miami after a year covering the Dolphins for *The Miami News* to write for *The New York Post.* I introduced myself to Kiner, and told him I was a good friend of Frankie Gustine, a former teammate and close friend of Kiner during their Pittsburgh days. Gustine owned a popular restaurant a block from Forbes Field during my student days at the University of Pittsburgh in the early '60s.

My friends held a going-away party in my honor at Gustine's when I departed Pittsburgh in favor of Miami in 1968. We ended up that night at Pete Coyne's Bar in Oakland, where Billy Conn was not only pictured in a mural on the wall but was also sitting with his pal Joey Diven, once heralded as "The World's Greatest Street Fighter" in a magazine story. Roy McHugh, the great sports columnist for *The Press* was with us, as well as Myron Cope.

Once, in more recent years, I asked Kiner during an interview what Musial was like, and he offered a classic comment. "He's like Frankie Gustine, only with a better batting average."

If I was a friend of Frankie Gustine I had to be okay as far as Kiner was concerned. So Kiner befriended me during my days in New York, especially in 1972 and 1973 when I covered the Mets and Yankees and went to spring training with the Mets in St. Petersburg, Fla., prior to the 1972 season. Kiner opened a lot of doors for me with the media in New York. He was just always such a pleasant fellow, and he told the bartenders in the media lounge to look after me. It's great when your boyhood heroes live up to your expectations.

It was great to keep company with Kiner and all the big-time sports writers who frequented the press box at Shea Stadium and Yankee Stadium and Madison Square Garden in those days. I was fortunate to know them.

Kiner will turn 87 this coming Oct. 27. He was born that day in 1922 in Santa Rita, New Mexico, and grew up in Bakersfield, California.

I was signing copies of the books in my "Pittsburgh Proud" series this past Saturday at Hometowne Sports in Station Square when I was approached by two faithful readers of my books and my columns in *The Valley Mirror.* Jane and Bill Lebeda of West Homestead strolled by. They check out Hometowne Sports before every Steelers' game at Heinz Field, even the pre-season games. The Lebedas have two rooms of their home devoted to displaying Steelers and Pittsburgh sports-related memorabilia, including black and gold train sets. Their collection is nearly as extensive of that of Hometowne Sports.

I mentioned my dream to Bill because I knew he was old enough to recall Ralph Kiner. He told me that he and Jane had a life-size poster of Ralph Kiner somewhere in a closet or storage space in their home in West Homestead.

"The life-size cardboard likeness of Kiner was a Sealtest Dairy promotional piece we've had since the mid-50s," said Bill Lebeda. "I had a friend get Kiner to sign it when he was in town to be honored at a dinner at PNC Park about seven or eight years ago. Kiner said he was surprised to see that someone still had it.

"It's a little beat up, bent in the middle, but it shows Kiner in a batting stance," added Bill, demonstrating how Kiner appeared in the life-size display placard.

Just then, Jane joined her husband at my stand. When she caught on that our conversation was about Ralph Kiner, Jane just smiled. "That was my dreamboat," she confessed. "I just loved him when he played for the Pirates. I was living in Cresson, Pa. at the time, and this was before I knew Bill. We had a little dairy market in my neighborhood and I asked the owner if he'd give me the Kiner display when he was done with it. I've had it ever since."

She told me that she had never met Kiner. She did send him a postcard and got one in return with his signature. "I have two glasses with Kiner's likeness on them," she added. "They came with Sealtest cottage cheese in them. No one in my family liked cottage cheese, but I bought them just to get the glasses. I'll bring them to show them to you. But you better not drop them or break them, or I'll kill you."

That last line lets you know that Jane Lebeda really liked Ralph Kiner. So have I, all my life. I'll always be in Kiner's Korner, as his post-game show was called during my days in New York. And he's lived up to the role of sports hero as few do today. Any one who claims to be a Pittsburgh sports fan should know about the legendary career of Ralph Kiner.

Ralph Kiner, at left, poses at Pirates' spring training camp in 1949 with fellow outfielders, left to right, Johnny Hopp, Ted Beard and Wally Westlake.

Forbes Field memories
mark 100th anniversary

July 2009

The Pittsburgh Pirates celebrated the 100th anniversary of Forbes Field this week and it stirred up memories of the old ballpark in Oakland for many fans. My best memories go back to the mid-'50s and early '60s, as I reflect on my days in The Knot-Hole Gang, an amazing catch-and-run by Mike Ditka of the Chicago Bears against the Pittsburgh Steelers, and, strangely enough perhaps, the Police Circus.

I first went to Forbes Field with the Knot-Hole Gang in 1956, 1957 and 1958 when I was 14, 15 and 16 years old. A fellow named Frank Casne, who was the playground director at Burgwin Park in Hazelwood during the summer months, took me and other kids to Forbes Field to see the Pirates play.

Casne was a Pittsburgh school teacher and then administrator during the school year and he blew the whistle to keep us under control at our games in those glorious summer days of our youth. I attended his funeral a few years back out of gratitude for what he had given me as a kid.

We had to pay only 50 cents to go to the games, and we'd sit out in the right field stands. We were right above the great young right fielder Roberto Clemente, and we had no idea then that we were sitting in what amounted to opera seats for an up-close view of one of the greatest ballplayers to play in Pittsburgh, or any other place for that matter.

The lead-off batter in 1956 was Johnny O'Brien, the second baseman, and that was a point of pride with our family. I had an uncle with the same name.

Hank Foiles or Danny Kravitz were the catchers, Dale Long and Ted Kluszewski were at first base, O'Brien and Bill Mazeroski at second, Dick Groat at short, Gene Freese and Frank Thomas at third, Thomas, Lee Walls and Bob Skinner in left field, Bobby Del Greco, from the Hill District with his buddy Tony Bartirome, a reserve first baseman, or Bill Virdon in center field. Bob Friend or Vernon Law were the starting pitchers and El Roy Face would finish up from the bullpen.

The Pirates had losing records the first two of those three years and then posted an 84–70 record in 1958. They were two years away from winning the World Series in 1960. I was the only one in Pittsburgh, or so it seems to hear people talk about it these days, who was not at Forbes Field on Oct. 13, 1960 when Maz hit the home run to beat the New York Yankees, 10–9, in the seventh and final game of the Series.

I was watching the game on television in the Pitt Student Union two blocks from Forbes Field. The victory touched off a celebration in the city that has never been matched for its genuineness and intensity since then.

This is the façade of the entrance to Forbes Field at Bouquet and Sennott Streets.

Fans are at ease in the left field bleachers at Forbes Field

This is an overhead view of Forbes Field looking out to Schenley Park, one of the best backdrops in all of major league baseball

During my student days at Pitt, thanks to sports publicist Beano Cook, I often sat in box seats along the third base side and watched the Pirates play. Our friend "Big Bob" DePasquale was the usher in that section and took care of us. His brother "Jeep" DePasquale, the head of the ushers' union, would later serve as president of City Council.

During my senior year at Pitt, in the winter of 1963, I saw Mike Ditka make a catch and run that is still shown on NFL highlights. I was standing on the roof in right field for this memorable game.

The Pitt football team had an 8–1 record but a game that was scheduled the day before at home with Penn State had been postponed because of the assassination of President John F. Kennedy in Dallas on Nov. 22. The NFL did not postpone its games for that Sunday, and Commissioner Pete Rozelle later regretted that decision more than any other he had made in his otherwise wondrous reign as NFL czar.

Beano Cook and I were publishing a newspaper called *Pittsburgh Weekly Sports* and that's how I got a pass to be on the right field roof. I'd come up in the world from my days in the seats with the Knot-Hole Gang just below.

I had the best view of what Ditka did that day. The Bears had a terrific team that year, but they were trailing the Steelers in Pittsburgh by the score of 17–14. It was late in the game and Chicago was deep in its own territory, facing a third down and 33 yards to go.

Quarterback Bill Wade dropped back to pass under pressure and dumped the ball off to Ditka in the flat, just looking to get a few yards out of the play. In what NFL legend George Allen called "a superhuman effort," Ditka just shed at least five would-be tacklers on his way to a 63-yard ramble. Ditka, who had been an All-American end at Pitt in 1960 and the NFL's Rookie of the Year the following season, went on a zigzag run that may have covered at least 80 yards and he was drained by the effort.

The Bears would kick a field goal and salvage a tie, saving their season in the process, as they held a slim lead over the Green Bay Packers in the NFL Western Division standings. The 1963 Bears went on to win the NFL title over the New York Giants in frigid Wrigley Field, another legendary ballpark, and Ditka was one of the heroes in that game as well.

Ditka, who came out of Aliquippa to earn varsity letters in football, basketball and baseball—and was the intramural heavyweight wrestling champion—has always been my all-time favorite Pitt performer. George Halas hired Ditka in 1983 to coach his Bears and said the memory of his run in Pittsburgh, pointing up his passion and determination, factored into his decision.

After my sophomore year at Pitt, in 1962, I worked that summer as an intern on the news side of *The Pittsburgh Press*. I was assigned one day to write an advance story about the upcoming annual Police Circus. I was dispatched along with photographer Al Herrmann Jr. to go out to Forbes Field and interview some circus performers.

Herrmann and I hit it off with the circus folks that afternoon in their campground outside the centerfield wall at Forbes Field. They

200

were staying in mobile homes right by the entrance to the park I had passed through once upon a time as a member of the Knot-Hole Gang.

They told us they were going to have a party that night on the eve of the opening of the circus, and that we were invited. They told us we could bring along guests.

So we returned that night. Al brought his buddy and fellow *Press* photographer Don Stetzer and I brought my older brother, Dan O'Brien. I was 20 at the time and he was 25.

We had food and drink from every corner of the world that night. The circus performers showed us some of their stunts, and they tossed their kids into the air, and danced the night away. It was a great time.

It got dark and at one point, we all needed to take a leak but there were no port-o-johns in the area. So we walked over to the wall on the outside of the ballpark. Somehow that act seems sacrilegious now. At the time it felt like a great relief, just this side of El Roy Face. Face, by the way, later told me that the Pirates' relief pitchers often did the same thing we did in the late innings out there in the bullpen. They had no proper accommodations either.

We didn't realize that night as we stood there facing the Forbes Field wall that we were standing next to a lion cage. When those lions roared we all nearly ran through the wall onto the outfield at Forbes Field. They scared the hell out of us. I can smile about it now, but not that night.

My brother Dan was smitten with a beauty from Bulgaria who was part of the trapeze act. He asked her to go out with him the next afternoon to Kennywood Park. She obliged. When my brother showed up the next day to pick her up he learned that her father, the "catcher" in the high-flying act, would be accompanying them as her chaperone. That's the way they did it in Bulgaria, if not our Burgwin Park.

So Dan and his date and her dad, a powerfully-built man, went off to Kennywood Park together. I don't remember if they rode through the Olde Mill together or not.

But it's a good memory. My brother Dan is deceased, and so is Don Stetzer, the *Press* photographer. I call Al Herrmann on occasion to see how he's doing. We had some great times together. We later teamed up in covering the Pittsburgh Steelers together for *The Press* when the Steelers won their fourth Super Bowl in 1980. Once again I had come full cycle.

I was at PNC Park three times this week. It's prettier and shinier than Forbes Field and the ballfield itself is much better maintained, but it's too new still to provide the kind of memories many of us have of old Forbes Field.

> *"There ain't much to being a ballplayer if you're a ballplayer."*
> **—Honus Wagner**

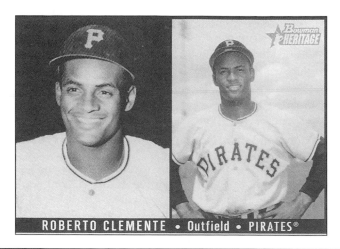

ROBERTO CLEMENTE • Outfield • PIRATES®

Mike Ditka and Bears owner and coach George Halas.

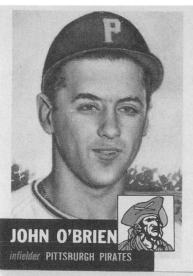

JOHN O'BRIEN
infielder PITTSBURGH PIRATES

ED O'BRIEN
infielder PITTSBURGH PIRATES

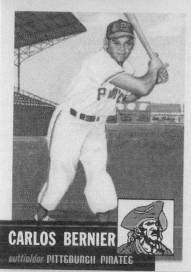

CARLOS BERNIER
outfielder PITTSBURGH PIRATES

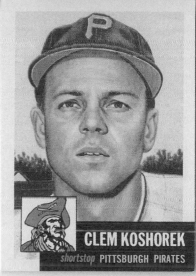

CLEM KOSHOREK
shortstop PITTSBURGH PIRATES

JOHNNY LINDELL
pitcher PITTSBURGH PIRATES

Bob Friend

PITCHER PITTSBURGH PIRATES

The Sadowski Brothers—
Lawrenceville's answer to
'The Boys of Summer'

August 2010

They still speak glowingly about the Sadowski boys back in their old neighborhood in Lawrenceville. There were 12 children, seven boys and five girls, in that row house at 3628 Mintwood Street, and three of the boys—Eddie, Ted and Bob—became major league baseball players. That's pretty good for one family, even a large family such as the Sadowski clan.

There was a time, in 1962 and 1963, when there were more Sadowskis than Joneses in the major leagues. There was another Bob Sadowski, who was playing for the Cardinals in his hometown of St. Louis, and then the Los Angeles Angels, but he was no relation to the Sadowskis from Pittsburgh. I knew about the Sadowskis then because I was a student at nearby University of Pittsburgh and Ted conducted some baseball clinics at my neighborhood playground that were sponsored by the City Parks & Recreation Department.

Eddie was a catcher for four years in Major League Baseball. He played off and on from 1960 through 1966 for the Boston Red Sox, Los Angeles Angels and Atlanta Braves. He was the last player on the Red Sox to wear No. 8 before it was turned over to eventual Hall of Fame outfielder Carl Yastrzemski. Ted was a middle-relief pitcher for three seasons with the Washington Senators and Minnesota Twins. Bob Sadowski played from 1963 through 1966 for the Milwaukee Braves and Boston Red Sox. Bob pitched the final home opener at old Milwaukee Stadium before the Braves moved to Atlanta. You had to play five years to qualify for a pension; now it's four years. So none of the Sadowskis has received a baseball pension.

Ed died from Lou Gehrig's disease at age 62 and Ted died at age 57.

That house on Mintwood Street, where it all began for the Sadowski boys, was a two-story red brick one in a row of about 40 similarly-sized homes, about 15 feet wide without a break between any of the houses. They all had basements. Each house had a long, narrow backyard, about 20 yards to Cabinet Way, an alley that separated the backyards from Sullivan Field. I visited that neighborhood on an idyllic Sunday afternoon this past May and was struck by how much the Sadowski house looked like the one in which I grew up in Glenwood. It even had the same green and white Koolvent aluminum awnings and red roses in the back of the house. Those yards are all well maintained. "It's a nice neighborhood," said Robert Grochalski, who has lived in the same row of houses for more than 60 years.

His grandfather bought the house for $13,500. One just like it had recently sold for $150,000. Prices for properties have shot up considerably since UPMC Children's Hospital replaced St. Francis Hospital in Lawrenceville a year earlier.

"I grew up in the same kind of house that you did," I told Bob Sadowski during one of our many phone conversations from his home in Sharpsburg, Georgia, about 45 miles south of Atlanta. My parents paid $2,500 for our house in Glenwood back in 1947.

"Did you have 12 kids in your house?" Sadowski shot back. "I remember us boys sleeping four across a bed. I was the youngest and I was always wearing somebody else's hand-me-downs. I saw a picture of me at my Confirmation and the sleeves on my white shirt were frayed."

Bob Sadowski must have called me every day for two weeks to offer a new story. His buddy, John Enright, a retired City police officer who lives in that row of homes on Mintwood Street, cautioned Bob one day by saying, "The man is writing a magazine story, not a book about you."

Enright even drove from the site where the wall remains from Forbes Field to Mintwood Street one day in May to determine the distance between the two places. "It's exactly 2.4 miles," said Enright. I had questioned the distance because I had read in an article about the Sadowskis that their home was two miles from Forbes Field. I thought the distance was greater.

It was easy enough if you just wanted to walk from Lawrenceville to Oakland to see the Pirates play, but the distance was a lot longer if you dreamed about playing for the Pirates or for any major league baseball team some day. When I paid my visit I saw a plaque on the cement block clubhouse that certified Sullivan Field as a "Field of Dreams," a program in which True Value and Major League Baseball renovated inner-city ball fields across the country in 1997.

Ed Rakow, another kid in the neighborhood who could walk to Sullivan Field in two minutes, also made it to the major leagues as a pitcher for Kansas City. He and the Sadowski boys all played for Jack Brick, a decorated soldier who was the manager for St. John's Lyceum and had to get to the ball field two hours before the game to line the scruffy grass field with whitewash.

Lawrenceville also boasted of the Boxing Zivics, five brothers who were all main event caliber boxers, including Fritzie, the most famous of them all, who was a world champion.

As I stood behind the Sadowski house on Cabinet Way and watched a flag football game involving men and women this particular Sunday afternoon, I noted that the batting cage and home plate at Sullivan Field were about thirty yards from the back door of the Sadowski house. I had heard stories about how all the Sadowski boys had played ball there just about every day of the week during their summer break from school. It all made so much sense when I checked out the scene. Another family lives there now, but it's still "the Sadowski house" to the old-timers in the neighborhood.

The Sadowski Brothers were, indeed, Lawrenceville's answer to "The Boys of Summer," those Brooklyn Dodgers of the '50s and '60s that Roger Kahn wrote about in his classic book. Kahn visited the former Dodgers in their homes to recount the days when they were playing and Kahn was covering the team for the *Herald-Tribune* in his hometown.

I had heard stories about how their mother, Mrs. Helen Sadowski, used to sit on a stool in that alley behind their house and watch her boys playing baseball. She would bring them buckets of lemonade when they won and just plain water when they lost. She knew something about motivating young men. She was named the "Mother of the Year" in the Greater Pittsburgh Baseball League.

Her husband, Walter, hardly ever watched the boys play baseball. He worked at Crucible Steel at 28th Street in The Strip and he thought baseball and all sports were a waste of time. The boys should be working and earning some extra money, as he saw it. He and his wife were born in different parts of Poland and had immigrated to America. He had to work hard to feed and clothe 12 children. "I knew I didn't want to work in the mill," said Bob Sadowski. "All of us worked in the mill at one time or another in our lives. It was a way of life for men in our neighborhood. I'd had a taste of it and I didn't want to go back there. My dad had a constant cough from breathing that bad air in the mill." Bob was ready to catch a steetcar to report to work one day at Crucible Steel but turned around and came home. His mother hugged him when she greeted him at the door. She didn't want him to work in the mill either. Her oldest son, Leo, was killed in military action in France during World War II. "I was only four at the time," said Bob Sadowski.

The father died when Bob, the youngest, was 12 and the boys and their mother became more closely attached than most boys and their mothers." She raised all 12 of us from then on," said Bob Sadowski. When the boys were in the major leagues they used to send their mother a piece of their paycheck on the first and 15th of the month. "So she could quit delivering newspapers," he said.

"I remember when I'd come home to Pittsburgh when I was playing for the Braves, and I'd look up in the right field stands where I used to sit as a kid, and I'd get tears in my eyes. My mother would be in the stands and see me play. That was great."

The Sadowskis lived in a mostly Polish neighborhood and it remains that way today. I met several people in their 80s who have lived in the same home all their lives in Lawrenceville. Standing alongside the 8 foot high chain-link fence that surrounds Sullivan Field, one can see The Church Brew Works, a bar/restaurant that is in part of the building that was once St. John the Baptist Church. Ballplayers once dressed and showered in the basement of St. John's and the athletic area was known as St. John's Lyceum. There were teams of that name in the Greater Pittsburgh Baseball League and in the Golden Gloves Boxing Tournament sponsored by the Dapper Dan Club of the *Pittsburgh Post-Gazette.*

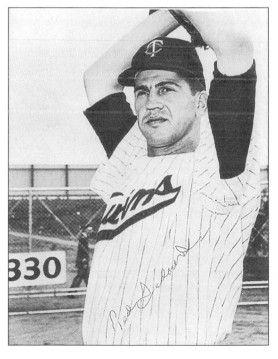

On the other side of Liberty Avenue is the Pittsburgh Brewing Company, where Iron City and IC Light were made for so many years. It closed down a year earlier, the operation shifted to Latrobe. On the hillside in the distance, one can see the Immaculate Heart of Mary Church with its patina-colored domes. That's on Polish Hill. When Pope John Paul II, the so-called-Polish Pope, was a bishop he visited that church and celebrated a Mass there. His name then was Bishop Karol Jozef Wojtyla and he was born near Krakow.

Not far away, on the other side of Sullivan Field and the Sadowski home, are the St. Augustine Church and Plaza and the Stephen Foster Community Center. The great songwriter was born in Lawrenceville on the 4th of July, 1826. A little farther away is the building alongside of the 40th Street Bridge where Washington Vocational High School was located. The boys all played basketball there and Eddie even led the team to a City League title one year. Across Butler Street from there is the Arsenal School. Johnny Unitas played on that 80-yard long oil-soaked field for $7 a game for the Bloomfield Rams before he got a call from the Baltimore Colts and became the best quarterback of his day in the National Football League. Bob Sadowski remembers seeing Unitas play at Arsenal and another short football field under the Bloomfield Bridge. So there's a lot of history to be found in Lawrenceville once you drive past The Doughboy Statue coming out of The Strip.

As one stands behind the batting cage at Sullivan Field it's possible to see the Sadowski brothers still playing baseball there. They just appear before you magically, as if they're coming out the door of their home rather than from a corn field. It helps if one has spoken to some of the surviving Sadowskis, their friends and former neighbors, or seen classic baseball movies such as Kevin Kostner in "Field of Dreams" or Robert Redford in "The Natural," or if one has a vivid imagination.

Bob Sadowski sent me some newspaper clippings and photographs and bubble gum cards. I recognized one of the stories by the typeface and the layout as one that appeared as the cover story in Pittsburgh Weekly Sports back in 1963. That was a tabloid newspaper that Beano Cook, the Pitt sports information director at the time, and I published that year and for four more years after that.

The story was written by Furman Bisher, the sports editor of The *Atlanta Journal*, and we had permission to reprint it in our paper. (Bisher was one of my early heroes among sportswriters. I read a collection of his stories in a book called *With A Southern Exposure* when I was in high school. I had spent a great part of a day with him at Super Bowl XXXV in 2001.) Bob Sadowski was pitching for the Atlanta Crackers in the International League when Bisher wrote the story. Sadowski would later make it to the big leagues with the Milwaukee Braves, where his teammates included Henry Aaron, Eddie Mathews, Del Crandall, Warren Spahn, Johnny Logan and Chuck Tanner of New Castle fame, later to be the manager of the Pirates' 1979 World Series championship team.

Bob Sadowski used to walk to Forbes Field with his brothers or some friends to watch the Pirates play. He remembers what a big deal it was to have his mother and family watch him pitch against the Pirates at Forbes Field.

"Did Bob tell you that he once struck out Roberto Clemente five consecutive at bats?" asked John Enright, the ex-City cop who stays in touch with Bob Sadowski. "He struck Clemente out three times in a row at Forbes Field, and then twice in a row when they next met in Milwaukee."

Bob Sadowski didn't tell me the Clemente story. He did tell me one about how he was a bat boy for a St. John's Lyceum team that was playing the Koller Club in a Federation League championship game at Sullivan Field. "There was a pole that was painted white that was out in right-center field," said Bob Sadowski. "We had a short right field fence—about 240 to 250 feet at best—so any ball that went over the fence to the right of that white pole was a ground-rule double. If the ball went over to the left of the pole it was a home run.

"The game was tied going into the ninth inning and it was getting dark and the umpire said it would be the last inning and then the game would be called," said Bob Sadowski. "My brother Eddie, or Edgo as we called him, hit one over the fence just to the left of that white pole for a home run. There were about 400 or 500 people at that game, and the men and women all ran out onto the field and they were mobbing my brother. It just like when Bill Mazeroski hit the home run to win the World Series for the Pirates in 1960! Only it was at Sullivan Field, right in our backyard. You do know, by the way, that Mazeroski is also Polish."

Sadowski spoke of playing ball on Pittsburgh sandlots with the likes of Frank Thomas, Bobby Del Greco, Tony Bartirome and Paul Tomasovich, and how those guys used to put on clinics for his brother Ted at ballfields around the city. "Teddy was my idol," said Bob Sadowski.

"I remember before the lights were installed at our neighborhood ballfield that guys would get their cars and line them up in the alley and turn their lights on so we could play at night."

I also had a chance to chat on the phone with John "Spike" Sadowski, who lives in St. Petersburg, Florida. He pitched for St. John's Lyceum in the Greater Pittsburgh League. He was also a standout fastball softball pitcher and, on occasion, pitched in softball and baseball games on the same day. He was offered a baseball contract with the Pirates by one of their storied scouts, Socko McCarey, whom I met many times at Frankie Gustine's Restaurant near Forbes Field.

"Spike" says some people thought he was the best athlete in the family, but he had a good job at Crucible Steel and was happy pitching on the local sandlots so he turned down McCarey's contract offer. "I don't regret it," said "Spike," a feisty sort even though he will be 84 this February. "I've enjoyed my life just the same. Lawrenceville was a tough neighborhood. You knew where to go and where not to go. Different streets were boundaries and you didn't go beyond them. You knew where you could go and where you couldn't go. We played sports at fields throughout the city. We'd play baseball against certain guys one day a week, and fight with them the rest of the week. Once we had 12 kids in our family, seven girls and five boys, and now there are just four of us, two and two. My two sisters still live in Pittsburgh. Laura lives in Oakland and Jane is in Oakmont.

"We got along great. We never had a grudge. Us boys tangled ass a few times, and then it was all over. We all played ball for Washington Vocational. I don't know if we ever all ate dinner at the same time. Our dad ate first. He was the bread-winner and we'd wait our turn.

"I remember we used to go down to the river and swim and get all sun-burned. Then we'd go play ball somewhere." He mentioned some names he remembered from those days, favorite Pirates such as Ralph Kiner and Frankie Gustine, Dino Restelli, Stan Rojek, Wally Westlake, Clyde McCullough, Gus Bell. "We'd go to Forbes Field on Boys' Day and sit out in the right field stands. We'd do that about once a month in the summer and think we'd died and gone to heaven. We loved our sports, and we knew all about Billy Conn, the great boxer from East Liberty, and Harry Greb from Garfield, and Fritzie Zivic from our own Lawrenceville neighborhood. We didn't see him much because he lived at the other end of Lawrenceville. Beyond one of those street boundaries, you know. Sandlot sports were more important in those days. It was the closest a lot of fans ever got to being around real baseball and football players like Johnny Unitas."

There was another Sadowski from Lawrenceville who made it to the major leagues and that was Jim Sadowski, now an executive with Hefren-Tillotson's financial advisory firm, and a nephew of the Sadowski Brothers. Jim remembers going to games with his dad and watching his Uncle Bob pitch for the visiting Braves.

Jim starred at Central Catholic High School and even pitched a no-hitter in an all-star game with Hall of Fame Pirates' star Pie Traynor as his manager. He remembers Traynor telling him as he came into the dugout after the game, "I'll see you in the big leagues in two years." He had another sparkling performance for the 9th Ward team against Penn Hills with Joe L. Brown and Harding Peterson of the Pirates and several scouts on the team looking on. Jim Sadowski signed with the Pirates in 1969.

"I was with them for a cup of coffee," is the way Jim Sadowski puts it. Jim pitched a total of nine innings in four games in 1974 for the Pirates and had an 0–1 record. He is a member of the Pirates Alumni and participates in many charitable functions on behalf of the team. No one knows more than he does how tough it is to make the majors and even tougher to stay, even if your name is Sadowski. So he's proud of what he and his uncles managed to do. They were good enough to wear major league uniforms, and they traveled a long way from Lawrenceville.

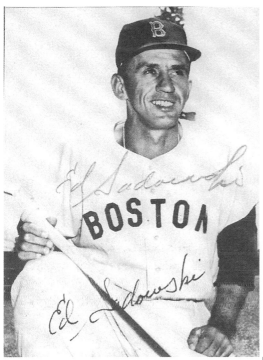

ED SADOWSKI
Catcher — Los Angeles Angels

Sadowski brothers, left to right, Bob, Ted and Ed, as they appeared on front page of *Pittsburgh Weekly Sports* back in mid-60s in a story by Furman Bisher.

MRS. HELEN SADOWSKi
"Mother of the Year"
Greater Pgh. Baseball League

Jim Sadowski of Hefren-Tillotson, a former Pirates' pitcher (1974), sees other former Pirates' pitchers, Rick Reuschel (1985-87) and Kent Tekulve (1974-1985) at Dick Groat's Champion Lakes Golf Club in Bolivar, Pennsylvania.

Donora's Musial
'Stan the Man'

February 2011

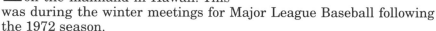

I can still see Stan Musial sitting across the aisle from me on a bus on the mainland in Hawaii. This was during the winter meetings for Major League Baseball following the 1972 season.

I was 30 years old at the time and had covered the Mets and the Yankees that summer for *The New York Post*, switching teams at midsummer during the All-Star Game break. My wife Kathie was next to me on the bus and Musial's wife, Lillian, was sitting next to him.

I kept glancing his way, taking it all in, because Musial had been one of my favorites when I was a child. I collected sports magazines and delivered the morning newspaper, and knew what a great baseball player Musial had been. He was from Donora—a Mon Valley boy— and he had to be the second best baseball player ever to come out of Western Pennsylvania, topped only by Honus Wagner who came out of Carnegie to star for the Pirates and was a charter member of the Baseball Hall of Fame.

This bus trip was the first time I was ever in the company of Stan Musial. Some one on the bus coaxed him into taking out his harmonica, which he was famous for playing, and Musial obliged and played "Take Me Out to the Ballgame." It put a smile on everyone's face. I would see Stan Musial up close on about six other occasions in my life and I never saw him that he was not smiling. In that respect, he was a lot like Chuck Tanner, the former Pirates' manager from New Castle, who died earlier this month. They always had a positive outlook on life and felt blessed to be baseball people.

As I sat across from the Musials my mind went back to my boyhood home in Hazelwood. What were the chances then that someday I'd be riding a bus with Stan Musial in Hawaii? After all, Hawaii is a long way from Hazelwood. Musial was the first player in the National League to make $100,000 a year and when you compare his production to most of the players of today and what they are making you have to shake your head in disbelief. Branch Rickey, who gained fame as the general manager of the Brooklyn Dodgers and then the Pittsburgh Pirates, once said "Stan Musial is the best liked player in baseball." That's quite a sobriquet. Al Abrams, the sports editor of the *Pittsburgh Post-Gazette*, wrote about Musial frequently as well as his friends from the Mon Valley. Bob Prince, the Pirates' broadcaster, was a close friend of Musial and talked about him a lot. So Pittsburgh baseball fans were always aware of Stan Musial.

On February 15, 2011 Musial was among those who received the Presidential Medal of Freedom from President Barack Obama at the White House. Musial's image appeared at the top of the front page of Pittsburgh's daily newspapers. He was born and grew up in Donora and we have always claimed him as one of our own.

The fans at Forbes Field in Pittsburgh and Ebbetts Field in Brooklyn loved Musial even though he enjoyed some of his greatest success at both ballparks. They called him Stan the Man."

Musial is now 90 and he has been married to his hometown sweetheart Lillian for nearly 71 years. They are both easy company. They never forgot where they came from. They put everyone at ease who came their way that afternoon on the bus in Hawaii. *(Lillian died in 2012, the day before a bridge back in Donora-Monessen was named in honor of Stan Musial.)*

In 1980, I was working at *The Pittsburgh Press* when I was asked by Boris Weinstein, a public relations and advertising magnate, to introduce and conduct an interview with Musial from trackside at The Meadows during Adios Week. Musial was a long-time close friend of Del Miller, the Hall of Fame harness racing driver who owned a horse farm in Washington, Pennsylvania as well as the neighboring Meadows Race Track. I still have a picture of me and Musial at The Meadows.

I saw him once at his restaurant in St. Louis and on a couple of occasions in Cooperstown, New York during the Hall of Fame induction ceremonies.

When I was thinking about writing this reflection on Musial, I remembered that I had a relatively new book called *Baseball: A History of America's Favorite Game* by George Vecsey, a sportswriter I had known during my New York days. I hadn't read it yet, but it was on my night stand in our bedroom. Just like when I was a kid.

I thought I should check it out to see if he Vecsey had anything to say about Musial. Sure enough, he mentioned Musial right off the bat in the book's introduction. He said when he was a kid, learning the game of baseball from his father, a newspaperman himself, that he always pretended to be either Jackie Robinson or Stan Musial. Vecsey has since written a biography of Musial that is a must read for any baseball fan from Western Pennsylvania.

Anybody who's at least 60 must have imitated Musial's unique corkscrew style of standing in the batter's box. He was 6 feet tall and 180 pounds, a left-handed hitter like few others, and he'd unwind from that curled up stance to swat hits all over the field.

In 22 seasons with the St. Louis Cardinals he had a lifetime batting average of .331, with 3,630 hits and 475 home runs. He won seven baseball hitting titles, three MVP awards and helped the Cardinals win the world championship. He was inducted into the Baseball Hall of Fame in 1969.

He made his major league debut on June 18, 1938 as a pitcher for the Cardinals and converted into a left fielder when he developed arm trouble. He had five hits in four games in his career, and once hit five home runs in a doubleheader. There were years when they had two

All-Star Games and he played in 24 in his lifetime. He and Willie Mays seemed to own the All-Star Games in the '40s and '50s.

I once spoke to Ralph Kiner, one of the greatest home run hitters in baseball when he played for the Pirates, and asked Kiner about Musial. Kiner knew I was a good friend of his former roommate from his Pirates' days, Frankie Gustine, who went on to own and operate a popular restaurant in Oakland for over 30 years. Gustine was one of the "good guys" on the Pittsburgh sports scene, popular with everyone.

"Stan was like Frankie Gustine," commented Kiner, "only with a better batting average."

Another of my favorites from my college days, former Pitt basketball coach Doc Carlson, a member of the charter class of the Basketball Hall of Fame, told me he had once tried to recruit Stan Musial to play basketball at Pitt. Doc Carlson was the director of student health services during my school days and once removed a wart from one of my fingers.

I have handwritten notes from an interview with Musial on yellow legal pads in my files. He was always a humble man. His parents had immigrated to Western Pennsylvania from Poland. Stan's original name was Stanislav Franciszek Musial and it was changed to Stanley Frank Musial when he was enrolled in school.

"If my baseball career has taught me anything," Musial once told me, "it is this: the opportunity America offers any young man who wants to get to the top of his chosen profession. I want to thank God for giving me the talents I have had and the good health so that the 22 years of baseball have been possible."

Musial also said, "I say baseball was a great game, is a great game and will be a great game. I'm extremely grateful for what it has given me—in recognition and records, thrills and the people I've met, thrills and satisfaction, money and memories. I hope I've given nearly as much as I've gotten out of it."

Musial never wanted to play anyplace but St. Louis and still makes it his home. I wonder what he thinks of the current contract negotiations between the Cardinals and their star performer, Albert Pujols, who at 31 is seeking a ten-year contract worth up to $300 million.

Maybe the Cardinals should get Musial to speak to Pujols. (*Pujols ended up leaving St. Louis in favor of the Los Angeles Angels of the American League.*)

Musial once said, "The greatest thrill in a career of happy and exciting moments was the thrill of just putting on a big league uniform, especially opening day of every season.

"Baseball has been my life. I love baseball. I like nothing better to do than play baseball. I want to my first game at Forbes Field when I was 16. A sportswriter from Donora took me to the game. I rooted for Paul Waner then. You couldn't see a game on television then.

"I enjoyed playing in Pittsburgh. They had great fans. They didn't have such good teams in those days, the '40s and the '50s, but the fans still followed them."

HANDSOME HEROES – Sidney Crosby and Mario Lemieux both saved pro hockey in Pittsburgh with their box office appeal in leading Penguins to Stanley Cup titles.

PENGUINS
HOCKEY

TWO OF THE MOST POPULAR PLAYERS in NHL history are, left to right, Eddie Westfall and Pierre Larouche. The Penguins took a 3–0 lead in games won in the 1975 Stanley Cup playoffs but the New York Islanders rallied to win the next four games, never trailing for a second in any of those final four games. It was Westfall who backhanded the game-winner in a 1–0 victory in the championship game. He was an original Islander, the club captain, and had played for two Stanley Cup winners in Boston before being drafted by the expansion team on Long Island. Larouche scored 50 goals for the Penguins during the 1976 season. Larouche lives in Scott Township and represents the Penguins in golf outings and other promotions.

A great day for hockey...
and baseball too

June 2009

The sun shines on Pittsburgh about 59 to 60 days a year, according to people who track such things for the weather service. Only Seattle, among the major cities in this country, has more overcast days, and only by a few. The scarcity of sunshine is thought to be unhealthy by medical experts.

Maybe that's why Pittsburghers and Western Pennsylvanians rely so heavily on the success of their sports teams to brighten their day. We are so fortunate in this region to have enjoyed so many championship teams. Few cities can claim as many title teams as we can.

The Penguins surprised most of their most fervent fans by defeating the Detroit Red Wings on a Friday night at the Joe Louis Arena, 2–1, in a thriller that kept most of us on the edge of our seats till the last second. The Penguins hung tough to take the seventh and deciding game of a best-of-seven series to win the third Stanley Cup in the club's history.

This championship run came on the heels of the Steelers starting 2009 by winning their sixth Super Bowl, beating the Arizona Cardinals in one of the most dramatic and entertaining NFL championship games in history.

For the first time in 30 years, since 1979, Pittsburgh could boast of having two pro teams take their league titles. We could reclaim the title of "City of Champions."

Detroit had won several Stanley Cups in recent seasons to rename a downtrodden Detroit "Hockey Town."

Dan Bylsma, the coach of the Penguins, proclaimed during the downtown parade to honor his team, "The City of Champions is much better than Hockey Town. It's a beautiful thing."

Bylsma, by the way, had to be the early favorite to be honored in Pittsburgh as the Sportsman of the Year for 2009 at the Dapper Dan Sports Dinner.

Mario Lemieux and Sidney Crosby may have saved the Penguins for Pittsburgh, and Evgeni Malkin may have been the most valuable player in the playoffs, but Bylsma saved the 2008–2009 season for the Penguins. They may not have made the playoffs if Bylsma had not been brought in from Wilkes-Barre with the thinnest of coaching resumes to rescue the club in the stretch run.

It's also nice to have a Penguins' coach you can understand, and one who thinks before he talks, unlike so many of his predecessors on the Penguins' bench.

I was on my way on a Sunday afternoon to PNC Park, chauffeuring a carload of four friends to a Pirates' game at PNC Park.

216

Photos by Dave Arrigo/Pittsburgh Pirates

Penguins' captain Sidney Crosby hoists Stanley Cup overhead at PNC Park.

Penguins are hailed at PNC Park on an idyllic day in Pittsburgh. See how clear the buildings on the horizon appear.

The real Pittsburgh sports fans still follow the Pirates. They have posted 16 consecutive losing seasons and are on schedule for a record 17th sub-.500 record. No city can claim more consecutive losing seasons by a single team than that.

Joe Gordon was riding shotgun in my car. He was a publicist for the Pittsburgh Rens, the Pittsburgh Hornets, the Pittsburgh Penguins and the Steelers of the '70s, when the team won four Super Bowls. The Hornets won the Calder Cup, the American Hockey League's championship trophy, in their final season (1966–67) at the Civic Arena before giving way to the Penguins when the NHL expanded by six teams and doubled its size the following season. Few know more about our local sports from behind the scenes than Joe Gordon. He is good company, and I have always respected his judgment. I still seek advice from him.

Gordon agreed with me that Pittsburgh has been blessed to have had so much success in sports on every level, and that fans here are spoiled. What Steelers' fan doesn't ask in July, "Do you think the Steelers can win the Super Bowl again?"

Now, of course, Penguins' fans will feel the same sense of assuredness that their team is the favorite to win the Stanley Cup again. The team is so talented and so young. There is one more season at what is now known as the Mellon Arena and then a new building, a state-of-the-art structure, will house the local hockey team.

We came so close to losing this franchise. How about them Kansas City Penguins? Or how about the Hamilton Penguins? If those don't sound right, neither do the Los Angeles Lakers or the Utah Jazz.

This particular Sunday was an idyllic day in Pittsburgh. The temperature was 75 degrees at game time at PNC Park. The sky overhead was Carolina blue with white cumulus clouds dotting the sky like so many huge cotton balls. It was so clear the city skyline over the outfield wall looked like HD (high definition) TV. The buildings appeared to be outlined by a black pen. It was surreal.

Several sternwheelers from the Gateway Clipper Fleet could be seen passing behind the outfield wall, including the mighty Majestic. There were white pleasure boats passing by in both directions, as well as a few kayaks. I'd never seen kayaks on the Allegheny River before. It was a Pittsburgh postcard. John Connelly, who had brought those sternwheeler boats to Pittsburgh to help beautify our waterways, had died in mid-May. Those beautiful boats would be his legacy.

The baseball teams of Pittsburgh and Detroit, by a strange coincidence, were playing at PNC Park. They rarely play each other. The Tigers had won on Friday night, the same night our Penguins won the Stanley Cup in Detroit, but the Pirates had bounced back to win the Saturday game.

The Sunday game was an official "Turning Back the Clock" contest as both teams were wearing throwback uniforms of the ones worn during the 1909 World Series when Pittsburgh beat Detroit in seven games for its first World Series crown. They looked terrific in their baggy uniforms, and I especially liked the cream-colored costumes of the Tigers as opposed to the ghost white uniforms of the Pirates.

The game experience at PNC Park was to replicate, as close as possible, the experience during the games played at Forbes Field in 1909.

That changed dramatically, however, after the Penguins won the Stanley Cup.

Officials of the Penguins—someone in the hierarchy was thinking the right way—contacted the Pirates' officials around midnight Saturday and asked what they thought of the idea of having captain Sidney Crosby and about 20 of the Penguins appear at PNC Park to be saluted prior to the Pirates-Tigers game. The plan wasn't confirmed until 9 a.m. on Sunday, so there was little time to get the word out that the Penguins would be appearing at PNC Park that afternoon.

I had no idea this was going to happen as I drove into one of the few parking lots that remain outside PNC Park.

It was such a special way to start the day. Max Talbot, who scored the two goals for the Penguins as they Maxed-out the Red Wings—my idea for the headline that day received one of the biggest hands, but the fans saved that for Sidney Crosby when he came out of the Pirates' dugout holding the Stanley Cup overhead.

The Stanley Cup had already made the rounds of a few bars in Pittsburgh by then. It was held out the window from the second floor at Mario's Bar & Restaurant on the South Side. And that bar has nothing to do with Mario Lemieux. The great thing about the Stanley Cup, unlike other hardware in professional sports, is that it makes the rounds, and fans get to touch and feel it, and each of the players gets a turn at taking it wherever he wants to take it.

Bill Guerin, who thinks he died and went to heaven after the last-place Islanders traded him to the Penguins late in the season, got to throw out the ceremonial first pitch for the Pirates' game. Guerin was 38 when he made his mound debut. He even came up to the press box with the Stanley Cup. He said he didn't have children the last time he played on a Stanley Cup championship team, and having his kids be part of the playoff run was special.

"Pittsburgh is a special city," gushed Guerin. "They love their sports teams here, and they love their Penguins; that's for sure. We had such great support."

I was in the press box this one Sunday and four of my friends were sitting in great seats on the third base side of the ballpark. Sportswriters were behaving like little kids, much like the young Penguins to think about it, when they had a chance to get their pictures taken with the prized silverware. I'll admit I was one of them. At a neighborhood party that night, I could boast that I touched the Stanley Cup that very day, and all the guests seemed most envious. "Why didn't you bring it to the party?" one of them asked.

It had been an idyllic day in so many ways. The Pirates beat Detroit 6–3 to take two out of three games from the Tigers. They are managed by Jim Leyland, who continues to live in Pittsburgh, and was the last man to manage a winning Pirates team (in 1992). His Tigers are in first place in their division in the American League.

Don Kelly, who lives in Wexford and grew up in Mt. Lebanon and is still the all-time leading hitter at Point Park University, made his debut for the Tigers that day. Playing left field, the 29-year-old Kelly stroked the second pitch off the outfield wall for a double as the lead-off batter for the Tigers. He had made the Pirates' roster back in 2007. He'll remember that extra-base hit for the rest of his life.

The Pirates surprise you now and then with a great outing. My personal record while attending games so far this season at PNC Park was 5–2. That's better than most of the Pirates' pitchers. It may also be the only statistic that is not displayed somewhere in the park during the game.

What I liked most about the Pirates' "Throw Back" promotion to what it was like in 1909 was the absence of the pierogi race, all the music, shooting T-shirts and such into the stands. It was baseball, pure baseball, for sure, with a little hockey thrown in.

It was a great day for hockey…and for baseball. It doesn't get any better. Now if the Pirates could only take a cue from the Penguins and finish strong and have a winning record. That would be so great for the real sports fans of this city, the ones who still go to the Pirates' games.

Joe Gordon agreed with me that it's easy to follow winners like the Steelers and Penguins and the Pitt basketball team.

My wife Kathie came home one afternoon and told me one of her friends had asked her a trivia question that morning. She wanted to know how many Pittsburgh professional teams had won championships. I said I'd have to put a pen to paper to figure that out. She told me her friend's husband had seen it in one of the Pittsburgh daily newspapers that the answer was 14.

I came up with 19.

The Steelers have won six Super Bowls. I knew the Pirates had won five World Series because I'd seen it on the façade of the press box the day before at PNC Park. The first one, of course, was against the Tigers in 1909. The others came in 1925, 1960, 1971 and 1979.

The Pittsburgh Hornets, who preceded the Penguins as the pro hockey team in town, won three. I knew they had won in their last season in town in 1967. Kathie and I were married soon after. I had been doing some of their games as an analyst to Beckley Smith Jr.'s game call on WEEP Radio that year, and during the first year of the Penguins that followed. I had to call my friend Glen Barton in Mt. Lebanon to learn that the Hornets had won the Calder Cup in 1951–52 under Coach King Clancy and in 1954–55 under Coach Howie Meeker.

"They won both championships by winning the seventh game on the road, just like the Penguins did this year," said Barton, without missing a beat. "They won their first Calder Cup in Providence, and the second in Buffalo."

I knew he knew his Hornets' history and he didn't disappoint me. We shared the news that the Buffalo Auditorium, where the pro hockey and basketball teams in Buffalo had played, was being torn down. I had covered NHL and NBA games at The Aud. It was a great old building.

The Pittsburgh Pipers won the ABA (American Basketball Association) title in 1968.

The Penguins have won three, two of them in successive seasons in 1991 and 1992 with Mario Lemieux leading the way.

The Pittsburgh Triangles, owned by Frank Fuhrer, won the World Team Tennis title in 1975. That adds up to 19.

There was a time, back in the '40s, when Pittsburgh and Western Pennsylvania boxers, claimed six of the eight division titles, not at the same time but over a year-and-a-half span. Billy Conn and Fritzi Zivic were the best known of that bunch. When the Civic Arena first opened, Fritzi and his friends referred to it as the Zivic Arena.

To me, even when our teams haven't taken titles, Pittsburgh has always been "The City of Champions."

Jack A. Wolf

Pittsburgh sports promoter Frank Fuhrer and author Jim O'Brien enjoy the scene at Oakmont Country Club. Fuhrer has promoted professional and amateur golf in Western Pennsylvania for many years. He owned the Spirits pro soccer team and the Pittsburgh Triangles of World Team Tennis. He owns one of the city's largest beer distributing companies on Pittsburgh's South Side, near the Steelers' training complex. He is a master Budweiser distributor.

Reflecting on early days
with the Penguins

March 2010

I drove past the Mellon Arena five times in early March of 2010. I checked it out closely as I went by, wanting to take it all in, so I can remember it vividly some day when it may be difficult to remember anything vividly.

I remember it when it was the Civic Arena. Some people in Pittsburgh jokingly called it the Zivic Arena, insisting it was named after world boxing champion Fritzie Zivic, a hometown favorite from Lawrenceville. I remember it when it was called the Civic Auditorium, when it first opened in 1962.

It was designed to be the home of the Civic Light Opera, summertime stage shows, mostly musicals. I can remember seeing such shows with my sister Carole when I was a little kid and they were staged on the football field at Pitt Stadium. Opening the roof of the Arena to the sky in the summer was a grand idea, but it was better in the concept than in the actual execution. There were problems and they quit opening the roof. That was too bad. I was there at least twice when it was open and it was spectacular to see the city skyline behind the stage.

It helps to know the history of these things and then you can better appreciate the Penguins and Sidney Crosby and Evgeni Malkin, if you know how this all started. I was in Duquesne Gardens a few times as a child when the Pittsburgh Hornets of the American Hockey League called it home. It had the largest ice surface in North America, according to people who keep track of those sorts of things.

My wife Kathie and I went to a Penguins' hockey game at Mellon Arena on Tuesday, March 2 to see them play the Buffalo Sabres. We hadn't been to a Penguins' hockey game together for at least ten years, and we picked the perfect night to go. It was the first game following the Winter Olympics in Vancouver, Canada and it was, in a sense, an extension of the excitement created by those games, especially the hockey tournament. That was won by Team Canada over the U.S.A. on an overtime goal by Sidney Crosby, the second Crosby to make his mark in Pittsburgh sports.

I'm also old enough to remember when Bing Crosby was a minority owner in the Pittsburgh Pirates.

More than likely, it will be the last event that Kathie and I will attend together at the Mellon Arena. The Arena was being torn down and removed from the Pittsburgh landscape in 2012 and it was something I hated to think about. We had great seats, as good as they come at the Arena. You'll never catch me complaining about the Arena just because it's the oldest building in the NHL. So what.

We saw the Hornets and Penguins play there. We saw Wilt Chamberlain and the 1967–68 Philadelphia 76ers play there—Chamberlain set an NBA record there that's still in the record books (he hit 15 of 15 shots in one game when the 76ers played a six-game schedule there when they were thought to have the best pro team in the history of the game). We saw the Pipers and the Condors play there with so many great players on opposing teams. Many of them are in the Basketball Hall of Fame. We saw Pitt and Duquesne and the Eastern Eight games there. I've seen Arena Football there, the Pittsburgh Triangles of World Team Tennis, and the Pittsburgh Spirit soccer games.

We saw Sinatra there. We caught performances by Barry Manilow, Billy Joel, Neil Diamond, Diana Ross and the Supremes, and some others. We saw the Harlem Globetrotters, the Ice Capades—they opened the Arena—a Civic Light Opera production or two, the Ringling Brothers Barnum & Bailey Circus, Disney on Parade, The Muppets.

As I sat next to Kathie at the Arena a week ago, she said, "They sure skate faster these days. Not like Andy Bathgate lumbering up and down the ice."

Kathie always catches me off guard with some of her observations these days. When we were watching the Super Bowl, she said near the end, "Bret Favre was finally too old on his last play in the Super Bowl." Art Rooney Jr., who knows a thing or two about the NFL, thought that was an insightful observation. "It was a matter of self-preservation on that last play," noted Rooney. "He didn't want to take another hit. So he threw the ball."

And, of course, everyone knows what happened then. There was a game-saving interception instead of the Minnesota Vikings setting up for a possible game-winning field goal against the New Orleans Saints. That one play probably cost the Vikings and Favre the Super Bowl, the Lombardi Trophy.

Not many women in the Arena would know who Andy Bathgate was. He had been a great player for the New York Rangers and he was playing out the string with the Penguins that first year. He had been a great one, for sure, and he beat Sidney Crosby into the Hockey Hall of Fame.

The Penguins had a lot of former Rangers that first year. The coach was George "Red" Sullivan, a tough square-jawed Irishman who had played for the Rangers. Their first draft pick was Earl Ingarfield, who had distinguished himself with the Rangers. I think Ken Schinkel had been in the Rangers' organization as well. They were all stalwarts for the Penguins that first season.

The NHL had doubled in size, going from six teams to twelve for the 1967–68 season.

Kathie and I had met in November of 1966 and started dating that winter. We went to a lot of sports events in Pittsburgh. We went to many of the games of the Pittsburgh Hornets. I was doing a morning sports commentary for WEEP Radio and I talked management into letting me do the color for some Pitt basketball games and some

Hornets hockey games. Frankie Gustine Sr. worked with me on the basketball games and Beckley Smith Jr. did the play-by-play for the Hornets games. The Hornets won the Calder Cup trophy given to the winner of the AHL playoffs.

There were hockey fans who hated to give up the champion Hornets for the often hapless Penguins, NHL or no NHL.

I remember during the Hornets' last season how I had lunch one day with Doug Harvey at Goldstein's Restaurant on Fifth Avenue in the Lower Hill or Uptown section. They had great bean soup and corned beef sandwiches. I took Doug Harvey there to interview him for *Pittsburgh Weekly Sports*, a tabloid I published and edited along with Beano Cook, who had been the sports information director at Pitt.

Harvey had been demoted to the minors by the Detroit Red Wings. He had been the best defenseman in the history of the National Hockey League. He had won the James Norris Trophy as the outstanding backliner in the league seven out of eight years, from 1955 to 1962 while playing mostly for the Montreal Canadiens and also one year with the Rangers. He had been runner-up for the award in 1954 to Red Kelly of the Detroit Red Wings, then won it for the next four years. Now Harvey was holding on to a paycheck, playing out the string in Pittsburgh, of all places.

Harvey would be in the Hockey Hall of Fame within six years of our luncheon meeting. That winter he looked lost in Pittsburgh. He seemed happy to have someone to join him for lunch, someone who knew how good he'd been. I still treasure memories like that.

Dan Koller and his wife, Mary, took us as their guests to this recent game at Mellon Arena. We had dinner beforehand at the Igloo Club. The bar area looked much like it did way back when. It reminded me of a date I had with Kathie, where her cousin Betty Jane, was with us and Beckley Smith Jr. at a table.

I thought about how many hockey games and basketball games Kathie had come to in those early years of our marriage. Kathie and I got married in 1967 so our marriage is the same age as the Penguins. That's a bond we have with the city's pro hockey team.

When we moved to New York in 1970 we got an apartment on Long Island near Hempstead, where the Hempstead Arena was located and where there was a 24-hour Western Union office. I had to drive to that Western Union office many a night to have my copy transmitted to the Manhattan office of the New York Post. Times have changed. The laptops in those days were clunky manual typewriters that required a quick and forceful strike of the fingers to type out letters.

Then they built the Nassau Coliseum about five miles from the home we bought in Baldwin, Long Island. I covered the New York Islanders and the New York Nets for two years. I can't imagine covering a pro hockey team and a pro basketball team at the same time, but I did it. The Islanders won only 12 games that first season. Some people thought their name was the Hapless New York Islanders they were referred to so often that way.

They would eventually draft the kind of players that enabled them to win four Stanley Cups. The Nets had Rick Barry and then Julius Erving as star forwards and even the New York Knicks didn't have better forwards with Dave DeBusschere and Bill Bradley. I covered the Knicks on occasion. No city ever had four forwards playing in their city that were that good. I covered the New York Rangers from time to time at Madison Square Garden and it didn't get any better as far as fans and atmosphere were concerned. The Islanders were getting great young draft choices and they were quietly assembling a team that would dominate the NHL and win four Stanley Cups.

Kathie would come to many of those games with me—especially before our girls were born—and we had to get there an hour and a half before the game started and I was usually there writing my story for another hour and a half after the game. Kathie never complained. She would bring a book or two and she occupied herself without any problem prior to and after the games. Kathie has always been much better than I am at amusing herself. She is happy in her own company.

When we first dated, she even went to see the Pittsburgh Phantoms play a soccer game at Forbes Field. The Phantoms' star player was a Dutchman named Co Prins. (He didn't prove to be as good or as popular as another Dutchman named Honus Wagner who was a Hall of Fame infielder for the Pirates.) That's when I knew she was a keeper, at least as the wife of a sportswriter. Kathie never complained when I was on the road with the basketball and hockey teams, or an eight- and nine-game road swings with the Mets and Yankees.

I knew young writers who had to give up their beats at the best of newspapers because their wives were always on their case about being on the road. I remember a young writer, fresh out of Pitt, who covered the Steelers and traveled the country with a Super Bowl team in a first-class fashion for the *Indiana Gazette*. He got married and his wife made him get off the beat. He traded in the Steelers for covering City Hall in Indiana, Pa. Talk about going from the penthouse to the outhouse.

Kathie still likes to read books. She says the best part about being retired the past two years is the time it allows her to read books.

I think if you are going to call yourself a Penguins' fan you need to learn something about Red Sullivan. His wife, Mary, used to sit at rink-side holding rosary beads in her hand and praying the Penguins would win. It's a wonder she didn't lose her faith.

You have to know about Andy Bathgate and Jean Pronovost and Syl Apps and Les Binkley. Binkley, by the way, was the very first Penguin. You have to know about Pierre Larouche, who was Mario Lemieux before Mario Lemieux. The club bought the rights to him before the dispersal draft. You have to know about Michel Briere. He was a great rookie with so much promise until he got torn up in a high-speed auto accident in Canada. That turned him into a vegetable and he would die soon after. You need to know about Brian "Spinner" Spencer and how he and his dad both died too young. You need to know about Bob Woytowich and his fan club whose members were known as "Bob Woytowich's Polish Army."

Jack Riley remembers all those guys. He was the first general manager of the Penguins. He still lives in Scott Township and he still goes to most of the games. The Penguins original colors of powder blue and dark blue and white were the same colors worn by the Toronto Argonauts of the Canadian Football League. Riley grew up in Toronto and he liked those colors. If you're a Penguins' fan you need to know that sort of stuff. Riley joins friends from his hockey days on occasion at Atria's Restaurant & Tavern in Mt. Lebanon and they share war stories.

Kathie was correct when she said the Penguins play a much faster game today. The NHL game is faster and so is the NBA game.

I can still see the Arena as it was when it seated about 9,500. It's hard to believe they have more than 17,000 seats now. Seats have been installed in every nook and cranny of the unique building. Bars have been set up in every open space.

There used to be what amounted to a quarter-mile track around the middle of the seats. The press box was originally on that level. One night, when my brother Dan and I must have had too much Iron City to drink, we had a race around that oval track. Dan fell and ripped his slacks. I can still see him running around the Arena.

There are many ghosts there. I can see Radio Rich, who helped out in the press row, and I can see Jackie Powell, wearing his hat, working behind the glass as the goalie judge. They don't have goalie judges anymore. I liked it better when there were people who put on the red light. I'm like that about a lot of things.

I would suggest to Penguins fans that you might be wise to get some good books about the Penguins history and go the games early and stay late and read those books before and after the games.

Then you'll be a knowledgeable Penguins' fan. There is a difference.

Syl Apps and Jean Pronovost were big scorers for Penguins in the '70s.

Civic Arena is missing
from city skyline but memories remain

September 2011

I had not set the alarm on my bedside clock but I awoke at 5:59 a.m. on a Monday. I had to go to the bathroom. When I returned to the bed I announced to my wife, much to her chagrin I am sure, "They just started to tear down the Civic Arena." Work was scheduled to start at 6 a.m. on September 26, 2011.

I'm not certain of what she said into her pillow, but it was a muffled acknowledgement that she had heard me. I'm familiar with that response.

Kathie and I had some of our first dates going to basketball games and hockey games at the Civic Arena in 1966, five years after it was erected. That building opened in 1961 when I was a freshman at the University of Pittsburgh. It's 50 years old.

They are celebrating that significant milestone by tearing it down. It upsets me that they are tearing it down. To the end, I was hoping some of the city's creative architects would come forth with a plan for a multi-purpose use of the Civic Arena, to save it from the wrecking ball.

I thought Governor Corbett would come through with a stay of execution order. I hoped Mayor Luke Ravenstahl, a big sports fan, would do something.

I have read where they were going to start by peeling back the steel layers of its signature domed roof. Like a Bloomin' Onion at Outback Steak House, mind you. It was that roof that made the Civic Arena so special.

It was the only indoor sports and concert arena in the world with a steel roof that opened to the skies. I was there for a stage show in its earliest years when the roof was actually opened to the skies on a clear night when you could see the skyscrapers of downtown Pittsburgh.

That idea didn't work out too well because the winds played havoc with the stage settings and curtains, and the acoustics weren't too good. The Civic Auditorium, as it was known at the time, was to be a concert hall for the Civic Light Opera and the Pittsburgh Symphony Orchestra, but they soon abandoned the building for other venues.

I'm old enough to have also seen CLO productions at Pitt Stadium when there was a Pitt Stadium. I saw the Pittsburgh Symphony Orchestra, as well as Redd Foxx and the Coasters perform at the Syria Mosque when there was a Syria Mosque in Oakland. Bette Midler said the Syria Mosque had the best acoustics of any concert hall she ever sang in, but it was leveled in favor of a parking lot behind the P.A.A. Once upon a different time, everyone played in Oakland, even the Pitt football team.

I have seen Pitt Stadium and Forbes Field and Duquesne Gardens and Three Rivers Stadium go down. I recall my wife Kathie and me watching a documentary on TV about the transition from the old Yankee Stadium to the new Yankee Stadium, and Kathie saying, "If they can tear down Yankee Stadium they can tear down the Civic Arena."

And she was right. She and many of my friends feel it's the right thing to do, that we must move on, and maybe they are right and I'm all wrong. To me, however, the Civic Arena was an important part of the Pittsburgh skyline. It reminded people that Pittsburgh was once the Steel City, that it was the capital of the industry. It was the steel-making business that put Pittsburgh on the international map.

They still make steel in Braddock, but they don't make steel anymore in Homestead or my hometown of Hazelwood, or the South Side, or in the Ohio Valley. The high school in Munhall is called Steel Valley High School, but it's merely a reminder of what this area was once all about.

The Penguins plan to build 1,200 units of housing, 600,000 square feet of office space and 200,000 feet of commercial space on the 28 acres of land.

It's supposed to re-connect The Hill District with Downtown Pittsburgh. I always thought Centre Avenue, a six-lane road, did that. And Bedford Avenue and Forbes Avenue which flank the area, did that.

The Consol Energy Center seats nearly twice as many people as the original Civic Arena, which seated about 9,500 when it opened. It would seem to me that this space is needed for parking space, more than anything else, to accommodate the sellout crowds at Consol Energy Center.

I had lots of ideas for how they could have used the Civic Arena in a multi-purpose manner, but it would have involved a consortium of city and corporate leaders, Duquesne University and the University of Pittsburgh, perhaps Carnegie-Mellon University, Point Park University and Robert Morris University, but the kind of leadership that once brought a Renaissance to this city is sadly lacking these days.

Leaders who represent the Hill District community claim that the building of the Civic Arena and the razing of the Lower Hill 55 years ago ruined the neighborhood.

That is one of the biggest lies perpetrated on the psyche of Pittsburgh. It simply isn't so. The neighborhood that gave way to the Civic Arena was a blighted area that had seen better days. It was full of ramshackle row houses, brothels and bars and deadly crime in its streets. The city police department had a special unit there, made up mostly of black police officers, to keep law and order. It was a hot spot. It was a recreation area for Duquesne and Pitt students, among others.

The news didn't get out much about what was going on there. I was a summer intern at *The Pittsburgh Press* in 1961, the year the Civic Arena opened, and I can report from experience as to why the bad news wasn't in the daily newspapers.

I took a turn with each beat reporter that summer and spent one to two weeks with each of them, from City Hall to labor to the crime beat. I was told that we didn't report black-on-black crime. "No one

View of the Civic Arena after the first layer of the roof was removed in December of 2011. This picture was taken from the offices of Merrill Lynch on the 44th floor of the U.S. Steel Tower.

cares," I was told by a grizzled veteran reporter. "We'll leave that to *The Courier.*"

The Pittsburgh Courier, at the time, was the weekly newspaper for the black community, and it was one of the most important black media publications in the U.S.A. I did some writing for *The Courier* so I know about this from a personal experience.

Carl Redwood Jr., the executive director of the Hill District Consensus Group, says his group is happy that the arena will be torn down.

"It's a symbol of the destruction of our community 55 years ago," remarked Redwood. I am sure he believes that. I know he means well and his organization is doing its best to raise public awareness about the needs of The Hill District community.

I knew his father, Carl Redwood Sr. He was a wonderful gentleman who always looked sharp. His silver hair and mustache were always just right. He was a best friend of a dear friend of mine, an Olympian medal-winner named Herb Douglas, who grew up in Hazelwood, went to Allderdice and Pitt, and won a bronze medal in the long jump in the 1948 Olympic Games. I've met Carl Jr. and his mother Dolores and have enjoyed their company and conversation.

Douglas loves Carl Jr. like a son, but refers to him as "a rebel." Carl Jr. prefers to be called "a community activist."

Douglas still owns a home at 160 Hazelwood Avenue. He stays there when he comes in from Philadelphia to attend events and meetings at Pitt, or at the Heinz History Center. Carl Redwood Sr. used to look after Herb's boyhood home for him, just to make sure no one messed with the place.

There were crack houses just across the street on Hazelwood Avenue, and crime was rampant in the neighborhood. Even so, Herb claims it's the only place where he can get a good night's sleep.

I went to the funeral service for Carl Redwood Sr. at a church in Homewood. I went there because Steelers' owner Art Rooney, who went to more funerals than any civic figure in Pittsburgh, said you should go when a good friend suffers a loss. The church was packed and I recall the singing was so much more vibrant and enthusiastic than in any suburban churches I've known.

By luck, I ended up sitting next to Nancy Bolden, the wife of Frank Bolden, who had been a columnist and editor for *The Courier*, and one of the first black American correspondents during World War II. Bolden later worked at Pitt's public relations department during my student days in the early '60s. I asked about Frank's whereabouts and Nancy said, "You aren't going to see Frank before noon these days."

I asked her to have Frank call me and he did. He gave me one of my favorite stories in my book about Art Rooney. It's called *The Chief*. Frank told me all about "nocturnal horizontal refreshment." You'll have to read the book…

I thought it was fitting that I got this story because I followed the advice of Art Rooney and went to pay my respects and offer condolence to Herb Douglas, a friend and one of my boyhood heroes.

Herb and I have discussions, sometimes heated, about what happened to Hazelwood and The Hill and the University of Pittsburgh, but we are like brothers. We do love one another.

There was a photo feature in the *Pittsburgh Post-Gazette* recently showing the stores and the business district that was once in the heart of The Hill District. It's gone.

What the story failed to mention is that the business district of The Hill disappeared when rioters who resided in the community torched those stores on the main streets of The Hill, and trashed those stores in the wake of the assassination of The Rev. Martin Luther King.

It's the same thing that happened in the Watts section of Los Angeles in a public protest and response to the assault by LA police officers on Rodney King. It's ironic that there was a King that sparked both horrific demonstrations.

I grew up in Glenwood and Hazelwood, in the heart of Pittsburgh, and I know what a neighborhood looks like that goes from good to bad. I also know that whether you are talking about Hazelwood or Homestead or The Hill, or Shadyside, Squirrel Hill, Fox Chapel or Sewickley, that the people who normally ruin a neighborhood are the people who live there.

I recall the celebrated cartoon Pogo that appeared on Earth Day when Pogo comes upon a forest that is full of refuse and Pogo proclaimed, "I have met the enemy and he is us." So true. Homicides were rampant in McKeesport, Homestead, Homewood and Wilkinsburg in 2012, most involving drugs.

When they want to reinvent a neighborhood or a shopping center there is always mention of a multi-plex cinema as part of the mix. They want to do that to revive Century III Mall and Monroeville Mall. Yet how many movie houses have disappeared from our communities over the past 20 years? There are no first-run movie theatres in downtown Pittsburgh.

My wife and I go to movies about twice a month, when there are senior discounts on Tuesday, and there's hardly anyone in the theatre units. There's a dozen or more on a good day. Movie theatres have gone the way of bookstores and Oldsmobile and Pontiac auto dealerships and Blockbuster Video stores.

Developers want to put in a mix of retail stores and residences near South Hills Village, just a mile from my home in Upper St. Clair.

I was fresh out of Pitt in 1964 and working for Marc & Co, an ad agency that is now an international player, and one of our clients was South Hills Village. So I wrote releases and ad copy relating to the early development of South Hills Village.

In any case, these developers are meeting with resistance at community meetings to discuss what can be done with this valued land site. Consol Energy's headquarters were located here for many years. They were a good neighbor. Their building was brown and long and low to the ground and blended in well with the one time farm landscape. It was unobtrusive.

Now these developers want to do with the site vacated by Consol Energy—they moved to Southpointe in Canonsburg a few years back—what the Penguins plan to do with the 28 acres that will be cleared by the leveling of the Civic Arena.

Carl Redwood Jr. believes it will rejuvenate the neighborhood. The good folks in Upper St. Clair complain that such a development will ruin their neighborhood.

When I tell my wife about this connection, she says, "Different neighborhood."

I have some great personal memories of experiences I enjoyed at the Civic Arena, but that's a column for another day. The steel domed edifice has always been the catalyst for such memories. I plan to drive down to the site every so often from now till May to take some pictures and watch it come down.

I went to the Pirates' last game of the season on Sunday at PNC Park. I had been to the game on Opening Day and a dozen or so games in between. I like to be there for firsts and lasts. That's part of being a sports historian.

Some day they will level PNC Park and Heinz Field, but I won't be here to see that.

Jim O'Brien

View from the press box high above PNC Park on Pittsburgh's North Shore.

Sidney Crosby is a class act
on and off the ice

January 2010

Somewhere on the campus of the University of New Mexico in Albuquerque this week, Jamie Stepetic is sure to catch some second glances as she makes her way to and from her classes.

I'll bet she will be wearing her Penguins' jersey—No. 87—the same as the one worn by Sidney Crosby, her favorite player on the Pittsburgh entry in the National Hockey League. She is a 22-year-old senior majoring in communications and she just loves the Pittsburgh Penguins. She watches them whenever they are on television out west.

Hockey fans across North America and Canada are encouraged to show their true colors this week in a celebration of their favorite sport. I saw a 30-second spot on television this past Sunday during the Penguins' game in Philadelphia that urged fans to wear their favorite team's jersey this week.

The Penguins defeated the Flyers, 2–1, and I knew that would be good news for Jamie Stepetic in Albuquerque.

Jamie Stepetic is the younger of two daughters of Tim Stepetic, who grew up in Duquesne, Pa., and remained in Albuquerque after he retired as an officer in the U.S. Air Force. He also taught at the local university for many years, but he's retired from that now, too. Tim Stepetic is a first cousin of my wife Kathie.

Kathie and I visited with Jamie and Tim Stepetic at the Avalon home of Tim's sister, Betty Jane Peckman, and her husband Bob, a former member of "Pure Gold," the popular singing group that offers oldies but goodies at shows throughout the area.

Jamie and her dad had been to their first Penguins' game a few nights earlier at the Mellon Arena. They had toured some of Pittsburgh's best attractions with the Peckmans, including, of course, a stop at Primanti Brothers' Restaurant in The Strip district. No visit to Pittsburgh would be complete without one of those sandwiches with French fries in the mix.

Jamie was still wearing her Sidney Crosby No. 87 shirt as we sat and watched some NFL playoff games on television, and she was still so excited about having a chance to meet Sidney Crosby and Marc-Andre Fleury outside the Mellon Arena earlier on that Thursday game day.

"Meeting the team captain and my favorite goal-tender made my day, actually probably my life at the moment," said Jamie.

The Penguins were defeated by the Philadelphia Flyers that Thursday evening, 7–4. Jamie's favorite goal-tender was pulled from the lineup two minutes into the second period. She did get to see Sidney Crosby break a scoring slump by scoring two goals.

They had great seats, right up against the glass on one of the sidelines. The seats had cost her dad $200 apiece through StubHub, an on-line ticket service. They said it was worth it, even though the Penguins got shellacked.

"We hurt ourselves with mistakes, mistakes we can't make if we are going to win," commented Crosby to the media afterward. "It was not a lack of effort, but it is not something we can accept."

Crosby can be counted upon to say the right thing in every situation, which is part of his charm. I also get lots of reports on him doing something nice as far as fans are concerned. I hear those kinds of reports frequently about Troy Polamalu of the Steelers, and I am always pleased to pass them along. I think it's important to point up proper behavior by professional and amateur athletes. We sure get enough bad news about them.

Jamie said she had been talking to a friend on Facebook who lived in Pittsburgh and is a Penguins' fan. That's how they first bonded. The friend informed Jamie that the Penguins usually had a morning skate at the Arena on the day of the game. The friend told her that she had gone to the Arena on several occasions and met a few players. "She thought that I would have a pretty good chance of running into some players as well," said Jamie.

"She said the morning skate ended around noon and told me to go to Gate Two, which was alongside the parking lot where the players parked their cars."

She said Sergei Gonchar was the first player she saw leaving the building. She said he was on his cell phone and just passed by everybody. She saw Jordan Staal and Alex Goligoski leaving as well. Imagine a young woman from as far away as Albuquerque recognizing all these Penguins in the first place.

"Sidney Crosby and his dad came walking out a few minutes later," said Jamie. "I didn't know if he was going to stop, but one of the girls standing nearby said he always did. He came through the gate and pulled his car to the side and got out to sign autographs.

"After he signed my shirt and made his way down the line that had been formed, I asked if I could get a picture with him, and he said, 'Sure.' After he left, I was still soaking in that I had just met the captain of the Penguins. Then came Marc-Andre Fleury, his usual happy self. He talked for a few minutes as he was signing autographs and then left."

He obviously had no idea he was going to be in for such a rough night. His mood and mask would be different that same evening after he got flogged by the Flyers.

"I was so excited to be at my first NHL game," reported Jamie Stepetic by e-mail after she returned home. "I knew that our seats would be right behind the glass, but it didn't click in until the usher showed us to our seats. We stood there for a few minutes soaking in the environment and talked to people standing around us.

"We were sitting on the side where the Penguins shot twice, so when all the players started warming up the Flyers were in front of us.

I recognized some of their players. The Flyers opened the scoring, with two goals only a few minutes apart. As soon as the Penguins scored everyone was on their feet cheering loudly, and we were banging on the glass to celebrate.

"Even though the Penguins lost, it was such an amazing atmosphere. The fans around us were so nice and each goal was awesome to see. I was bummed that they lost, but since it was my first NHL game it definitely wasn't a disappointment. I'm sure hoping it wasn't my last game."

I had been in a great seat behind one of the goals at a recent Penguins' game, so I knew what Jamie Stepetic was talking about, but this is obviously all new to her, while I still can see the Arena the way it was when there were less than 10,000 seats in the building when it first opened in the early '60s.

Jamie and her dad also traveled to Sewickley to check out the stately mansion that Penguins' legend Mario Lemieux calls home, and where Sidney Crosby keeps his crib. Her dad took a picture of her with the house in the background. "We didn't stay long," she said," because I didn't want to get arrested for stalking Sidney Crosby."

My wife Kathie and I were at a Pitt basketball game at the Petersen Events Center since then and we sat next to a couple that live near the Lemieux home, and frequently see Mario and his wife Nathalie, as well as Sidney Crosby, in the neighborhood streets.

"The people in Sewickley respect them, and leave them alone for the most part," said the woman in the seat next to me. "They are great neighbors. They are real down to earth people. You see Sidney once in a while on our main street, and he says hello to everyone. I think he represents the Penguins and Pittsburgh in a first-class manner."

Jamie Stepetic gets her picture taken with Sidney Crosby outside Civic Arena.

Jamie Stepetic and her dad Tim stand tall outside home of Mario Lemieux. Sidney Crosby was living there at the time.

Sidney Crosby is a Canadian sports hero forever

March 2010

Sidney Crosby can go home again. Anytime he likes. And he will never have to show any I.D. cards when he crosses the border to be with family and friends in his hometown in Canada. Sid the Kid can go home again and he will be welcomed with open arms. The local high school band might be at the airport to serenade him. He is a sports hero forever in Canada. When they talk about the Canadian-born hockey greats—Maurice Richard, Jean Beliveau, Gordie Howe, Bobby Hull, Bobby Orr, Wayne Gretzky and Mario Lemieux—Crosby will come up in the conversation.

He has become a part of hockey lore and he's only 22 years old. He won't be 23 until August. He won't fare poorly in Pittsburgh, either. This is his adopted hometown.

My wife Kathie and I were fortunate enough to be at Mellon Arena this past Tuesday night to see the Penguins play the Buffalo Sabres. Fans gave a roaring welcome back to Crosby and Marc Andre-Fleury, members of the Canadian gold medal team in the Winter Olympic Games in Vancouver, British Columbia, and to Brooks Orpik, who played for the U.S.A. team. They even gave a warm welcome to Ryan Miller, the Sabres' goalkeeper who was marvelous for the U.S.A. team and was named the MVP of the hockey tournament. They were happy to have Evgeni Malkin, who played for the Russian team, back in a Penguins' uniform.

There was a special buzz in the building because of what had transpired on Sunday. What television set in Pittsburgh wasn't tuned in to this game?

Crosby, of course, beat Miller on a clean shot from the side at the 7:40 mark of the overtime period for the game-winner in a 3–2 victory for the Canadians. It was similar to what could happen in a shoot-out. In the third period, Crosby had a breakaway one-on-one assault on Miller, but let the puck get too far ahead of him and Miller managed to thwart that goal attempt.

Miller looked like an MVP at that moment, but in the overtime—one missed shot—and he feels like the goat. Disappointment replaced his protective mask on his face during the medal ceremony.

It was quite a hockey game. "If somebody had to beat us," said Kathie, "I'm glad it was Crosby."

Just before the overtime began, I had told Kathie in the kitchen where we went to refresh our iced tea, "I have a feeling Crosby is going to beat us."

Crosby had not scored a point in the previous two games or in the 60 minutes that preceded the overtime, but somehow you felt that he would be the one that made the difference.

We had been rooting, of course, for the U.S.A.

Penguins or no Penguins, we're rooting for our country and our country's team, in every tournament, in every event of these just-completed Winter Olympic Games. They were great and so was this championship hockey team.

It was thought that the final would come down to Sidney Crosby and the Canadian team against Alex Ovechkin and Evgeni Malkin and the Russian team, but the upstart U.S.A. team surprised everyone by getting to the gold medal game. They came home with silver and that was quite an accomplishment.

The U.S.A. team was the youngest in the field, and it was felt it was put together to get ready for Russia, where the Winter Olympics will be staged in four years.

I was rooting for Ryan Malone to score the game-winning goal for the U.S.A. Malone had grown up in Upper St. Clair, where we have lived the past 31 years. Malone is 32. I had met Malone when he was 15 and playing pee wee hockey in our neighborhood. I had interviewed his dad, Greg Malone, a former Penguins' player and later a long-time head scout for the organization. The younger Malone was drafted by the Penguins in 1979. He was taken on the fourth round, the 115th player picked in the draft.

It didn't create the excitement that would occur when the Penguins picked Crosby as the first choice in the 2005 draft. That's the draft that saved NHL hockey for Pittsburgh. Malone missed out on being on the Penguins' Stanley Cup champions. I hated to see him sign as a free agent with the Tampa Bay Lightning. I thought the Penguins should have paid what they needed to keep him. He's not a star, but he makes the stars better.

I thought it would be great if Malone could come through for Team USA. His name was mentioned as often as Crosby in that final game, and he'd been playing some terrific hockey throughout the Games. It was possible.

The great ones are great because of the way they come through in such games.

"It's a dream scenario," said Crosby after the game. "Those opportunities only come along once and you have to take advantage of them. You might never get that chance again."

Author Ayn Rand wrote, "Ask yourself whether the dream of heaven and greatness should be waiting for us in our graves or whether it should be ours here and now and on this earth."

Asked to define greatness, playwright George Bernard Shaw said you had "to do what must be done."

Crosby accomplished the aims he's had since he first skated at the age of three in his hometown of Cole Harbour, Nova Scotia.

His father Troy had been a goaltender and a pretty good hockey player, but he never realized his dream of some day playing in the National Hockey League. He has lived his dream through his son Sidney and is a frequent spectator at Mellon Arena.

He remembers how Sidney used to go to the basement of their home and fire hockey pucks into the open door of a clothes dryer. He left so many black marks from misfired pucks on the face of that dryer that his dad said "it looked like a Dalmatian dog."

The first time I ever heard about Crosby was prior to that 2005 draft. I was an observer at Mario Lemieux's Celebrity Invitational Golf Tournament at Nevillewood Golf Club and I was talking to a neighbor of mine, Eddie Johnston, once a coach and front office official of the Penguins, and more recently a scout.

Johnston was the one who held onto the No. 1 draft choice to pick Lemieux when others in the organization thought they might be better off to take some of the multi-player offers that came their way from other NHL teams.

I asked Johnston if there was anyone like Lemieux on the hockey horizon. "I hear good things about a kid in Nova Scotia named Sidney Crosby," Johnston said. "He's supposed to be the next great one."

I noted that in my next column, but I don't read *The Hockey News* or follow junior hockey that much these days so the name meant nothing to me at the time.

And no one knew the Penguins were going to get the first pick in the draft at the time. They got the right pick in the NHL lottery and Pittsburgh still has a team as a result.

There are more than 70,000 reference sites to Sidney Crosby on the Internet. You can buy one of his Reebok home jerseys for $150. You can get a signed 8 x 10 photo of Sidney Crosby for $59.95, or an autographed Team Canada hockey puck with Sid's signature on it for $189.95. The price is also $189.95 for a Penguins' puck with Sid's signature on it. You can get an 8 x 10 photograph of Sid waving one of the Steelers' Terrible Towels for $59.95. Myron Cope would be proud of that, and even prouder if some of the proceeds went to his favorite charity, Allegheny Valley School.

Crosby and Ovechkin make about $9 million a year and millions more in endorsements.

Next season Crosby and the Penguins will be playing their home games in the Consol Energy Center, a $321 million showcase. If Yankee Stadium was the "House that Babe Ruth Built," then surely this building will be known as one that Sidney Crosby can call his own.

A recent story in *The Washington Post* referred to the Penguins' present home Mellon Arena as "a decrepit old arena." It may be the oldest building in the NHL, but it's not decrepit. It still has great sight lines and on Tuesday night a hockey fan couldn't have been in a more exciting place in the country.

Crosby continues to live at Lemieux's home in Sewickley. He gets kidded about that, but he knows it's a good deal.

Pierre McGuire, a hockey analyst, said, "It's appropriate that he lives at Mario Lemieux's home since he (Mario) saved the Pens at least three times. And Sidney Crosby has saved them at least once in his career."

McGuire also said, "He won't have to do it again because that's how good that team will be while he is there."

Crosby has changed his game a bit since he came to the Penguins, and he is trying to shoot more often so can score more goals. "Greatness is usually guys who aren't afraid to make changes," McGuire goes on, "and that usually makes them better."

As big as Crosby is in Canada and how popular he is in Pittsburgh, he is not a favorite of fans in some NHL arenas. In fact, in Washington, D.C., the fans call Crosby "a crybaby" and they come to the arena and put pacifiers in their mouths when Crosby comes to play. Whereas Alex Ovechkin is a villain in Pittsburgh he is the most beloved athlete in D.C. Ovechkin would be a fan favorite if he played for the Penguins. He'd be Jack Lambert on skates. Crosby would be a fan favorite if he played for the Capitals, of course.

Sidney's father prepared him for the boos he hears in D.C. and some other NHL buildings. Troy Crosby says, "I always told Sidney when he was younger that they don't boo the bums. If they're booing you, you must be doing something they don't like."

I've been in the Mellon Arena and the Civic Arena, as it was known before, when the fans booed Bobby Hull, Gordie Howe, Bobby Orr, Wayne Gretzky and Jaromir Jagr. Those are great ones. Crosby is keeping company with the likes of them now and forever more.

There was only cheering in Mellon Arena this Tuesday night.

Sidney Crosby, the captain of the Penguins, lines up at left in picture Jamie Stepetic shot from first-row seat at Civic Arena.

Eddie Johnston key
to Penguins' stay in Pittsburgh

A biographical sketch of Eddie Johnston said he is best known as the man who drafted Mario Lemieux for the Penguins. I suggested to Johnston, a long-time neighbor of mine in Upper St. Clair—his home is exactly two-tenths of a mile from mine—this information would appear in the first paragraph of his obituary some day. "It was a no-brainer," he said of his decision to draft Lemieux in 1984. The Penguins were a dreadful franchise at the time, losing more games and more money than anyone in the league, and in danger of folding.

Mario Lemieux was the savior on the ice. Eddie Johnston saved the day with this one decision. Being stubborn paid dividends this time. Both Lemieux and Johnston were born in Montreal, not far from the old Montreal Forum where Maurice "The Rocket" Richard and Jean Beliveau starred for the Canadiens. I met those two revered Montreal hockey figures once in the press room at the Montreal Forum when I was covering hockey for *The New York Post* and I remember what a thrill it was. They had been long retired, but I remembered reading about them in the sports magazines that were always at my bedside.

I first met Eddie Johnston and his lovely wife Diane—a former airline attendant who still looks the part—at a block party soon after they moved into our neighborhood in the South Hills of Pittsburgh. They were fun from the start. They urged me to get a drink for openers. They are honest to the bone, absolutely no pretension, and as Steve Blass has said of Bill Mazeroski more than once, "He's so for-real." So are the Johnstons. They have never thought they were a big deal. Eddie, in particular, remembers where he came from, and he's still thrilled by his good fortune. When the Penguins won the Stanley Cup in 2009, Diane Johnston stopped at the bottom of our driveway one day and invited us to a party at a nearby restaurant, Piccolina's in Pinebridge Mall, where the Stanley Cup would be on display. I recalled to Diane that I had a picture of her sitting atop the Stanley Cup when the team had previously won the Stanley Cup in 1992. The picture appeared in my book *Penguins Profiles: Mario and the Boys of Winter.*

"Yes, and my ass still fits," declared Diane Johnston, saucy as ever.

Eddie Johnston, who turns 77 in November of 2012, still gets out to play golf at Pittsburgh area fund-raisers as a representative of the Penguins. Former Penguins and NHL star Pierre Larouche remains an ambassador of the Penguins in the same way. Both are good golfers. Both are good friends of Lemieux and he has remained loyal to both, keeping them on the Penguins' payroll. Lemieux is loyal to those who helped him along the way.

Both have been staples in the Mario Lemieux Celebrity Invitational that was once played at The Club at Nevillewood and then was switched to the Laurel Valley Golf Club, one of the most prestigious golf layouts in western Pennsylvania, right behind the Oakmont Country Club. It went from being a wonderful event for sports fans that flocked to get a close-up look of their favorite sports celebrities from across the country to a private haven where only the rich could afford such a view. It went from public to private, and it was a loss on the local sports schedule. It continued, fortunately, to raise millions for cancer research. Lemieux has gone through a bout with leukemia that sidelined him during his storied Penguins' playing career, and he has done much to pay back for the great care he received from the Pittsburgh medical community.

Johnston did me a favor in June of 2010 by playing in the Dave Wannstedt Invitational Golf Outing at the South Hills Country Club. Wannstedt, the head football coach at Pitt, is a graduate of Baldwin High, whose football program was the beneficiary of the golf fundraiser, and I was working there as the Alumni and Community Relations Director. "I really enjoyed meeting and spending time with Eddie Johnston," said Tom Bigley of Fox Chapel, whose sons had played sports at Baldwin High years earlier. "He gave us some insights into what's happening with our hockey team."

"He was great company," said Baldwin-Whitehall Superintendent Dr. Lawrence Korchnak. "He's a fun guy and he loves to tell stories."

Johnston was the general manager of the Penguins when they picked Lemieux in the NHL's 1984 amateur draft. "I had a lot of good offers from other teams who wanted to trade for that pick," recalled Johnston," but I never considered them seriously."

Johnston said that Bobby Orr, a former teammate of his in Boston and still a close friend, and Wayne Gretzky were two other prospects that everyone recognized would be immediate impact players in the NHL. Then Johnston offered an observation that I noted at the time, but it didn't have the kind of impact it has now when I read it again.

"There's another kid right now who's regarded the same way," Johnston said. "His name is Sidney Crosby and he comes from Nova Scotia." Lemieux and Crosby are the most celebrated Penguins in the team history that goes back to 1967, but neither has been around the NHL as long as Johnston. He is a good story-teller so he is simply a more interesting subject than either of those superstar performers. He has served the Penguins in a variety of ways and the 2011–2012 season was his 27th with the organization.

He was listed as a senior advisor for hockey operations. He also previously held posts as general manager, assistant general manager, head coach and assistant coach and scout at large. Sidney Crosby is one of the most exciting athletes to put on a Pittsburgh uniform, but he hasn't been around long enough to be as interesting, say, as Eddie Johnston and Jack Riley, the team's original general manager who remains on the scene, or Pierre Larouche, one of my favorites.

Johnston was a goalie for 16 years in the NHL, minding the nets for the Boston Bruins, Toronto Maple Leafs, St. Louis Blues and Chicago Black Hawks. He won two Stanley Cup rings during his stay with the Bruins. He was the last goalie in the NHL to play in every minute of a season when he played in 70 games for the Bruins in 1963–64. That figures to be in his obituary as well. That was during my senior season at the University of Pittsburgh. That's when the Hornets of the American Hockey League were playing at the Civic Arena.

If you were around in those days you have a better appreciation for Pittsburgh's rich hockey history.

"They had a reunion of our Bruins' Stanley Cup championship team this June," said Johnston when I spoke to him in July, 2010. "We had a great time; they really treated us well. Diane and I spent six days with Bobby Orr at his place in Cape Cod right afterward. I just talked to Bobby on the phone yesterday. We have remained close. We're still good friends."

Hockey has always been in Eddie Johnston's blood. He was born in a hockey hotbed, St. Antoine Street in the West End of Montreal, a community that was just a 10-minute walk or a strong slap shot from the Montreal Forum where the Canadiens were the class of the National Hockey League. Maurice "Rocket" Richard was one of his boyhood heroes. Jean Beliveau was a big man in Montreal when Johnston was playing junior hockey on the same Montreal Royals team as Scotty Bowman, a future Hall of Fame coach. Mario Lemiuex would later grow up about ten minutes away in a section of the city called St. Henri.

Johnston's boyhood home is one of the few that remains from the block where he lived in his youth. He has pointed it out to his children when they visited his mother in Montreal and they would smile. His mother died a few years back and when Eddie mentions her the children smile again. They do the same when he tells war stories, which he loves to do. His boyhood home and his beginnings as an athlete are a far cry compared to what his kids experienced growing up in the suburbs south of Pittsburgh.

"Everybody in Canada was into hockey when I was a kid," Johnston said during a long talk we had at his home years ago. "Hockey was the No. 1 sport. It's all you heard on the radio. Everybody played baseball and boxed, but the No. 1 sport was always hockey. As a kid, I listened to 'Hockey Night in Canada' on the radio, to Foster Hewitt and Danny Gallivan and those guys.

"My dad worked at the Forum every so often, as an usher. He had a full-time job at Imperial Tobacco, where they made cigarettes. They made Players cigarettes. When they needed some extras at the Forum, he got the call. All the kids played hockey and I never saw an indoor rink until I was in high school. We'd start in October and play through March. I think I got started when I was six or seven years old.

"My older brothers got me started. I tagged after them. Tommy was three years older than me, and Billy was about a year and a half older. Everything I wore, whether it was for school, church or to play sports, was a hand-me-down. And the boys behind me wore what was handed down to me. There were three boys after me: David, Michael and Robert. Six boys altogether. We couldn't afford any girls.

"We lived in the West End, which was all Irish and Italian. It was considered the toughest section in all of Canada. It was written up in the newspapers for that. It had quite the reputation. You had to be

242

willing to fight if you wanted to survive. We had a lot of hard-working people, with very little money."

Johnston was born on November 27, 1935. "I was from three to five years old when the Depression was still going on," Johnston said. "The Depression was in Canada, too; it was all over. It was tough getting jobs and it was tough getting food. My Dad did whatever he had to, stuff like wallpapering or handyman jobs, anything he could get. I was the same way later on."

My mother often told me stories about my dad doing that same sort of thing, knocking on doors in the neighborhood, asking if there was anything he might be able to do, and she said he always came home with some money.

My mother and Eddie's mother both shared a passion for bingo. I spoke to Eddie once after he'd talked on the telephone with his mother. "She just played bingo on Tuesday," he said. "She didn't do very well. She was upset. I keep telling her she can't always win. She was on a streak for awhile. She plays about twice a week. If I visited her on a night when she was going to bingo, I'd have to wait around till she got back home. Bingo comes first. I know what nights not to call her.

"I talked to her about three or four times a week. She had a terrific attitude. I called her about every second day. She looked forward to hearing from me. She wanted to know what's going on in hockey. She was 94 when she died."

Johnston said his father died in 1972, right after the Boston Bruins won the Stanley Cup for the second time in three seasons. "He died from cancer," said Johnston. "He used to smoke four packs of cigarettes a day." I told him my Dad died at age 63, back in 1969, suffering from emphysema. He, too, was a life-long smoker.

"My dad was born in Ireland," Johnston continued, "in County Antrim. That's in Northern Ireland. We were Protestant Irish. Bobby Orr's grandfather had a shoe store over there in County Antrin in a place called Bally Mena. Belfast isn't that far from there.

"People tell me stories about my dad, and how he got to Canada in the first place. He had to get out of Ireland for his political activities over there. He came over in the late '20s; he was 20 or 21 when he came over. He was on the run when he came out of Ireland, when he got on the boat. I used to hear him discussing it with people his age, but he never really discussed it with me. I'm sure he was involved with the Irish Republic Army. He'd be on the alert for the black and tans (the British troops).

"When they had Irish dances in our community in Canada, I'd hear people telling stories. He was a tough bastard, I guess. I don't know if he did any boxing, but I knew he won some fights. I knew he was a toughie.

"People would come to him for stuff. New guys in from Ireland would come and call on my father when they came to Canada. I'd hear them in my house. A lot of the Irish that came to Canada, initially, made their way down into the states, and many of them settled in Pennsylvania. I have uncles and first cousins in the Philadelphia area.

My dad kept in touch with them. He was all-Irish. They'd bring in hurling teams from New York. I'd go to those things. They had Gaelic football and hurling. It was all part of my being brought up. Hurling was a tough game. It's something like hockey with a ball. It's big-time tough. We played it when we were kids."

Since Eddie was the third of six boys, I asked him about the sleeping arrangements in his house in St. Henri.

"There were three small bedrooms in our house. My parents had one room. The two oldest boys were in one room, and we often slept three in a bed in my bedroom. Two slept one way and the other slept the other way. I was usually in the middle. It was important to wash your feet good before you went to bed. My mother would get after you if you didn't."

I shared a big bed with my brother Dan for many years when we were in grade school. I remember Dan would pull back the sheets to check out and see that I'd washed my feet before I went to bed. If I didn't, he'd holler for our mother to see that I did so.

I remember once when our friends, Marty and Nick Wendell, stayed overnight at our house and we slept four across the bed.

"My mother would knock your head off if you had dirty feet," Johnston said. "We lived above a barber shop and a shoemaker. I remember the barber was Irish. The shoemaker's name was Nick and he was Italian. It was the only block in the district that's still there.

"We didn't have much money. We used to fight, or box, to get some money. We'd do anything to pick up a few bucks, or to help out in the house. We all boxed. I'd fight one night under one name and the next night under a different name, because the rules forbid you from fighting that often. We'd fight in the penitentiary on Saturday morning and in a small town on Sunday. We did that about once a month. The penitentiary in Montreal was called St. Vincent DePaul. I'd get $7 to fight in the pen. I was fighting at about 120 pounds. You'd win some, lose some. I did okay in most of them.

"There were a lot of guys from my neighborhood in the pen, and I always had my own cheering section. Our area turned out some pretty good pro boxers. I liked to fight. In our district, you had to like it. You'd get into it enough times. It was something to do. I still like to do roadwork. I walked five miles in Stanley Park when we were in Vancouver. I love getting out like that in the morning. Everything is so fresh. We had some beautiful days, some of the best of the year, and I took advantage of it.

"When I go to Montreal, I have taken my son Joseph and showed him my birthplace. We had a little park right next door. We played ball there. They were all dirt, no grass, just about 50 yards from our door. We had coal bins in our cellar, and we all had to help out and shovel coal and feed the furnace.

"I used to take any job I could get. Money was always short at our house. My dad got paid on Friday, and my mother would be there to get the money and make sure all the debts that we incurred that week would be taken care of."

I asked Eddie to tell me about his five brothers. "The oldest was Tommy. He was the first layman appointed to the Ecumenical Council. He had three or four audiences with the Pope John Paul. He has worked with the Catholic Church to raise money for Third World countries. There's Billy. He was in real estate. He also worked at CNR (Canadian National Railway) as a kid. David worked on the wharf and then with elevators in office buildings. Mikey worked in real estate and that stuff. Robert started off as a plumber but he ended up in real estate and that stuff, too.

"Tommy died last year after a bout with cancer."

Then Johnston switched subjects.

"I played in Johnstown. I was on a championship team there in 1955 in the International Hockey League. Mr. Frank Selke sent me there. He wanted to get me out of Quebec. I was a bad actor, getting into fights and stuff, and Mr. Selke sent me to Johnstown to teach me a lesson. I went back to Ottawa and we won a championship. Back then, I needed a little discipline. I'd fight with anybody. Didn't take much to light me up. An Irishman with a few drinks, you know.

"We had jobs during the off-season when I played hockey. You had to, in order to make ends meet. I worked in the CNR telegraph office. I also loaded and unloaded trucks at the brewery. Ninety percent of the guys on our team worked in the brewery during the summer months. This was at the Dow Brewery in Montreal, or Molson's Brewery.

"I played fast-pitch ball in a semi-pro league. I played third base. I made $105 a month, which was pretty good money for the summer. It was in the Snowdon Fastball League. Doug Harvey played in that league, and now he's in the Hockey Hall of Fame. I played for a traveling baseball team for $35 a game."

"When we won the Stanley Cup in Boston, I got Bobby Orr's gloves. I gave them to my son Joseph. He has some really nice stuff in his hockey collection. Joseph is 28 and lives in Dormont these days and most of his hockey stuff is still in our basement. He had one of Wayne Gretsky's 50-goal sticks, and he has Mario Lemieux's 50-goal stick. He's got some keepers. He's got all kind of cards. Ronnie Francis got him his first skates and got him serious about hockey. I tried to get him going, but he didn't seem to want to do it then.

"As a goalie, I always paid a lot of attention to other goalies. Jacques Plante was the best goalie I ever saw in the playoffs. He was the first goalie to wear a mask regularly. Glenn Hall was great. Lorne 'Gump' Worsley was great in the playoffs. Those were guys who won Stanley Cups. Terry Sawchuk, Ken Dryden and Gerry Cheevers all came up big in the playoffs. In our first two Stanley Cups here in Pittsburgh, Tommy Barrasso won a few of those games all by himself. He was a great goal-keeper.

"In hockey, you should never take your eye off the puck. For a goalie, it's a reflex game. You can learn the basics from anybody, but you've got to have the reflexes, you have to pick off that puck somehow, with your stick, with your glove, with your pads. Somehow, you've got to stop that puck and keep it from having people put it past you.

245

"Barrasso could handle the puck like any forward and he could make the play. He brought an extra dimension to our team. When he was hot, he could get two or three assists a night. When you're killing a penalty and you can throw it up the ice like he could it's a big edge. Barrasso was one of the premier goal-tenders. He liked playing in big games. He liked the big challenges. He was right up there with goalies like Grant Fuhr and Patrick Roy.

"It's important when you're coaching to make sure they're having some fun. You come to the rink for a purpose, but you can't take the fun out of the game or you'll lose them. If they hate to come to the building then you have a problem. The money they make today makes the financial reward of winning the Stanley Cup almost insignificant. But when you're supposed to be the best you want to prove it.

"I grew up in Montreal where they had great players like Rocket Richard and Jean Beliveau, and Bernie 'Boom Boom' Geoffrion and Doug Harvey. They were dominant almost every year. Harvey is the only defenseman I ever saw who like Orr could control a game all by himself. He determined whether it was a fast game or a slow-down game. He was that dominant on the ice.

"Harvey played for the Pittsburgh Hornets at the end of his playing career. It was in the team's last season in Pittsburgh.

"When the Penguins came into being, about 90 percent of the base of the fans had been Hornets fans. The Hornets won the AHL's Calder Cup in their last season and some fans weren't happy to have a mediocre NHL team in their place. A lot of them have died by now. A lot of them lost their interest and got away from hockey. Maybe the higher ticket prices drove some of them away.

"Hockey really grabbed hold here when Lemieux came to town. Young people got involved. Rinks started popping up in the suburbs. It was just like what happened when Bobby Orr came to Boston. Orr was as good as they come.

"I feel lucky coming to Pittsburgh. I realize how lucky I am to be doing this for a living. This is not an 8-to-5 job every day and all that stuff. It's so much easier when you're doing something you like. You would never classify what I do as a job.

"I had jobs when I was younger so I knew what a real job is all about. I worked in bowling alleys, setting pins. That's back-breaking work. Me and three of my brothers worked five nights a week setting pins at the Montreal Athletic Association. It was an exclusive club, like the Pittsburgh Athletic Association here in Oakland. The top businessmen belonged. I don't remember what we were paid a line, but it wasn't much. I delivered newspapers from 3:30 to 5 p.m. each day, and I'd go home and eat, and then I'd work in the bowling alleys from 7 to 10 or 10:30 at night. I'd work Saturday night and sometimes on Sunday at the bowling alleys.

"Somewhere in there I'd find an hour each day, usually right after school, to do my homework. My mother would make sure you did your homework before you did anything else. Somehow we found time for some hockey, too, pretending we were Richard and Beliveau and Plante.

"The French players on the Canadiens had to speak English. It was a club rule. Rocket enforced it. He'd get after those guys if he caught them speaking French in the clubhouse or on the team bus. He didn't want the English-speaking players to think the French players were talking about them."

"Chemistry is important. It was my idea to put the young players on the Penguins with a family in Pittsburgh that could look after them a little, give them the feeling of some family structure. I put Lemieux with Tom and Nancy Matthews in Mt. Lebanon. They became good friends. Mario stayed with them an extra year. Craig Simpson went there, too. I had Chris Josephs stay with Diane and George Morris in Upper St. Clair. Then, of course, Sidney Crosby started off living with Mario and his wife Nathalie out in Sewickley. What goes around comes around.

"We've been lucky in Pittsburgh. We get a great player like Lemieux, and then Jaromir Jagr. Then we get Sidney Crosby and Evgeni Malkin. We've had some of the best players in the business over a lengthy stretch."

Jim O'Brien

Two former Pittsburgh coaches, Chuck Noll of the Steelers and Eddie Johnston of the Penguins, play golf at Mario Lemieux's Celebrity Golf Outing at The Club at Nevillewood.

Recalling a strange story
in hockey history

May 2012

It was one of the strangest stories I encountered in my career as a journalist. I never knew the full story. I still don't. No one does. No one really wanted me to know the full story. It stays with me like one of those cold cases they feature on crime shows on television.

I have been watching the National Hockey League Stanley Cup playoffs and the National Basketball League playoffs on television, switching back and forth from the Pirates' games.

With the Penguins' unexpected early exit in the playoffs, I had to find other teams to root for and I found them in the New York Rangers in the East and the Los Angeles Kings in the West.

With the Los Angeles Lakers out of the NBA playoffs, I am now rooting for the San Antonio Spurs or the Oklahoma Thunder to go all the way and claim the crown.

Seeing the Rangers reminds me of time spent at Madison Square Garden, and the days in the early '70s when I covered some of their games for *The New York Post*. My main assignment back then was to cover the New York Nets of the American Basketball Association starting in 1970 and then the New York Islanders when they came into being as an expansion franchise in the National Hockey League in 1972.

I saw the Islanders put the pieces together that would win them four consecutive Stanley Cups in the early '80s. Bill Torrey, whom I first met when he was the General Manager for the Pittsburgh Hornets, was the architect of those Islanders' championship teams. He is one of seven men associated with that team who is honored in the Hockey Hall of Fame.

I benefited from that Pittsburgh bond when I covered the Islanders. I was, in fact, the first writer in New York to refer to the team as "the Islanders," before the team chose its official nickname. It seemed logical enough.

I lived on Long Island in a community called Baldwin about five miles from the Nassau Coliseum, still the home of the Islanders. The Nets have been playing in New Jersey in recent years but will move to a new arena in Brooklyn next season.

Dr. J, Julius Erving, was the star of the Nets and the ABA back then, and now they show him from time to time sitting in a special suite at the 76ers' games with the Boston Celtics. Erving was traded by the Nets to the 76ers when the ABA was absorbed into the NBA in the late '70s. He is now a Philly icon.

The other development that made me think about the strange story involving the Rangers was the death on St. Patrick's Day of this year of former Rangers' defenseman Ron Stewart. He was 79 when he died of cancer.

Stewart was one of the figures in the strange story I referred to in the first paragraph.

There's been some rough play in the NHL and the NBA playoffs, sometimes to the extreme, but none of it compares to what happened in a drunken brawl between two teammates on the Rangers back in 1970.

I was relatively new to New York in April of 1970, having just moved there after a year's stay at *The Miami News.*

On the evening of April 29, 1970, Ron Stewart and Terry Sawchuk, a Hall of Fame goalie who was winding up his storied career as a backup goalie for the Rangers, got into a fight in the backyard of the house they were renting in East Atlantic Beach on Long Island, and Sawchuk died from a blood clot at a nearby hospital.

I was told that Stewart had kicked Sawchuk in his groin with such force that he drove his plumbing deep into his stomach and injured his gallbladder and liver. Sawchuk underwent surgery three times during his short stay in the hospital.

Sawchuk took the blame for the brawl. He said, "It wasn't Ron Stewart's fault; don't blame him. I was the aggressor in the whole thing."

Sawchuk was one of the greatest goalies in the NHL and was inducted into the Hockey Hall of Fame a year after his death. He held the record for most shutouts in NHL history (103) and his final one came against the Pittsburgh Penguins in New York during that 1969–70 season.

I was sent out to do a story on the Rangers at their practice rink at New Hyde Park on Long Island. I stopped Stewart as he was coming out of the clubhouse and took him aside to interview him. I wanted to get his side of the story.

No sooner did I start talking to him, alongside one end of the ice rink, than Emile "The Cat" Francis, the general manager and coach of the Rangers, came out of the clubhouse and caught me at work.

I can still picture that moment, just a snapshot in my life as a newspaperman, of Francis moving fast in my direction. I see a lot of dark green (the color of the seats in the rink) behind Francis. He positively pounced on me. They didn't call him "The Cat" for nothing.

Francis swore at me and told Stewart to get out of there in the same sentence. Stewart seemed surprised by Francis' facial expression—his narrowed eyes even narrower than usual—and Stewart left the building, leaving me behind with an empty notebook. Francis was a little fellow, probably 150 pounds, but he looked fearsome to me that afternoon.

A week later, during a quarter-final Stanley Cup round with the Boston Bruins, I was standing at the back of a pack of reporters in the Rangers' dressing room at Madison Square Garden. We were interviewing Emile Francis.

One of the reporters, Gerald Eskenazi of *The New York Times,* turned to me and said, "I'm surprised to see you here after the way Francis treated you the other day."

And I told Eskenazi, "I'm just doing my job. The readers could care less if Francis gave me a hard time. I have to write a story and I have to hear what he has to say about this game."

Francis had created a community of sorts for his Rangers on East Atlantic Beach, near Long Beach on Long Island. That was about a 20-minute car drive to the Rangers' practice rink at a public facility in New Hyde Park.

The Rangers and the Knicks seldom had an opportunity to practice at Madison Square Garden because that building hosted so many different kinds of entertainment offerings. The Knicks often practiced at high school gyms on Long Island.

Francis felt it was safer for his players if they didn't have to drive in the demanding traffic that led in and out of Manhattan. So he told players it would be better to live on Long Island than in the city.

It didn't save Sawchuk. Precisely how the fight started and how Sawchuk incurred his injuries remains murky, but a Nassau County grand jury found the death to be accidental, absolving Stewart of blame.

None of the news media in New York really dug into this story, which still seems unbelievable. I don't think that would be the case today.

Sawchuk, who had been a star mostly with the Detroit Red Wings, was known to be a moody sort, and was disclosed to have suffered from depression at times. Playing goalie in the NHL without a face mask might do that to an individual.

He was also known to be "a bad drunk."

I visited my neighbor Eddie Johnston recently and asked him what he knew about the incident involving Stewart and Sawchuk.

Johnston, who has served in so many capacities with the Penguins, including stints as coach and general manager, said he didn't know much more than what was in the newspapers at the time.

"I knew that Sawchuk could be a nasty sort when he got into one of his moods," said Johnston, the last NHL goalie to play every game in a season and someone who once played the position without a protective face mask. "Terry was a great one. Terry had a terrible temper, I remember that. And you'd hear that he liked to drink. What goalie didn't? I recall the incident with Stewart, but no one ever really knew just what happened."

Sawchuk and Stewart shared a home on Long Island during the hockey season. They had been at a local bar that night and had gotten into an argument. Sawchuk may have owed Stewart some of the rent money for the home they shared. They started shoving one another. And it carried over when they reached their home later.

The dispute resumed and they started pushing each other on the lawn by their home. Witnesses said Sawchuk fell into a barbecue pit.

I came home to Pittsburgh in April of 1979, nine years later, and was determined to be a positive writer. I had found that in stints in Miami and then New York that it wasn't worth writing controversial stuff.

So I am in Pittsburgh about a month and I hear that Jack Lambert of the Steelers has been assaulted at a downtown night club. Someone slammed a beer mug against his ear and cut Lambert badly, causing him to bleed quite a bit. At least two guys jumped him.

I attempted to find out what happened. Lambert, after all, was the star linebacker for the Steelers, who had won their third Super Bowl the previous season. Lambert was regarded as one of the toughest players in the NFL. Who'd jump Jack Lambert?

I called Lambert on the telephone at his home three times but he never returned my calls. I went to Chuck Noll to discuss the incident, but he was not happy with me for wanting to talk about it. He offered little help or direction. He didn't want me to deal with the subject.

I would later learn that the editor of my paper was aware of what happened at The Happy Landing—that was the name of the night club, interestingly enough—and the police reporter on both newspapers knew about it. A police report had been filed on the skirmish. The beat reporter on the rival daily knew about it.

No one wanted to write the story.

I wrote the story, or what I could piece together, and I lived to regret writing the story. I didn't receive a pat on the back at the office or from any readers, and it got me off to a bad start with Lambert. He snarled at me, breathing flames I swear, when I encountered him at St. Vincent College at the team's summer training camp.

I went to his room and we worked out a peace pact. If I wrote something like that again, he warned me, I would pay the consequences.

I later learned that the guys who jumped Jack Lambert that night were bad news. They intended to hurt him. They had said they were going to cut the ligaments in his legs.

There was a third guy at the bar that night who was reluctant to take on Jack Lambert. He stayed back when his buddies jumped Lambert. He was later shot and killed by one of the combatants because of his failure to join in the fray.

I told you these guys were bad news. The killer was sent to prison and had quite a rap sheet to show for his history of misbehavior.

Martin Brodeur, the goalie for the New Jersey Devils, broke Sawchuk's record for the most shutouts (103) in an NHL career. Brodeur is still the backstop for the Devils and continues to add to his record. He's had 24 shutouts in the playoffs alone.

I saw Brodeur and the Devils play at Consol Energy Center this past season, and I asked my friend Ken Codeluppi, who has season tickets for the Penguins, if he had ever heard of Terry Sawchuk. He was not familiar with the name. Our seats were three rows behind one of the goalie nets, and I ducked at least a dozen times when a puck struck the protective glass in front of us.

I scolded him, saying that if you were going to call yourself a hockey fan, you had to know about Terry Sawchuk. He was one of the greats of the game.

Stewart bounced back from that dark night on Long Island to continue playing for the Rangers. That fight on the lawn was called "a tragic, senseless, bizarre" incident, in the words of the Nassau County district attorney, William Cahn.

Stewart would later, strangely enough, be named the coach of the Rangers. He'd enjoyed quite a career until he retired as a player in 1973. His heyday had been during his 13 seasons with the Toronto Maple Leafs. It was Emile Francis, by the way, who hired Stewart to succeed him as coach of the Rangers, the same Emile Francis who chased Stewart from the rink at New Hyde Park when I was trying to interview him. Here's another note about Emile Francis: back in 1945, when he was a professional goalie, he was the first goalie to use a first baseman's glove with a cuff added to protect his hand and wrist. Before that, goalies wore the same kind of gloves as their teammates. It had to be difficult to catch a flying puck with those regular gloves.

If you're going to call yourself a hockey fan you need to know that sort of stuff. By the way, when I was in Los Angeles this past February, we went to see the Kings play the Chicago Black Hawks at the Staples Center. The Kings were in last place in their division at the time. "They can't be very good," I said on the day of the game.

That night we watched the Kings defeat the Black Hawks, who had won the Stanley Cup themselves in recent years. Afterward, I observed, "Hey, the Kings look pretty good."

Lo and behold, the Kings won the West and are in the Stanley Cup championship round. (*They went on to win the Stanley Cup over the Devils.*) And most Pittsburgh hockey fans thought the Penguins would be playing for the Cup once again.

Comment on this story from Gerry Ezkenazi, retired sportswriter of The New York Times: "Jim did a good job of bringing back memories of this incident. I did call the Nassau County Police, but they never brought charges. Jim was always a ballsy writer."

NHL HALL OF FAME GOALIE
TERRY SAWCHUK
His death still unsolved mystery

RON STEWART
Became Rangers'
coach

Pitt's "Dream Backfield" in late '30s consisted of, left to right, Curly Stebbins, Marshall Goldberg, John Chickerneo and Dick Cassiano.

COLLEGE SPORTS
Pitt * Duquesne * Carnegie Mellon * Penn State * West Virginia

Marshall Goldberg, left to right, Mrs. Charlotte Ditka (Mike's mother) and Joe Schmidt were honored at halftime ceremony of Pitt-Miami game at Pitt Stadium in 1997. Pitt retired the jerseys of Goldberg (42), Ditka (89) and Schmidt (65). All three were All-American performers during their days at the Oakland campus.

Getting phone calls
in getaway places

July 2009

It has always been a good memory. It always makes me smile when I reflect on what happened that day outside Gate 3 at Pitt Stadium. It happened in 1983, sometime in the spring. I was walking down Cardiac Hill with my family. I was in my first of four years as the assistant athletic director for public relations in the athletic department at the University of Pittsburgh. I was accompanied by my wife, Kathie, and our daughters, Sarah, who was nine years old at the time, and Rebecca, who had just turned six.

We were approached by two men coming up the hill. Both had big smiles on their faces. The smaller of the two was Joe Panucci, and the big guy was Tony "Toodles" Magnelli. I have to smile every time I think of his name. How many guys do you know named Toodles?

They were both long-time friends of Foge Fazio, the head football coach at Pitt, getting ready for the second of his four seasons at the helm. They liked Foge because he was such a friendly guy, and they liked him even better because he was Italian.

Panucci came from a family of barbers in McKees Rocks. He was a clerk or tipstaff to some prominent judges through the years at the City-County Building. You didn't move in the courtrooms where Joe Panucci worked without being prompted by Joe Panucci. Magnelli was his neighbor and friend from The Rocks, a community with more characters per square inch than any other community in the Pittsburgh area.

Magnelli's son, also named Tony, was a solid center for the Panthers, preparing for his senior season. This was the day of the annual Spring Football Game.

These were two guys who knew how to say hello. They don't come any more garrulous than Joe Panucci. He's one of those people who always make you feel special when he greets you. This time, he was especially enthusiastic. He embraced me and kissed me on my left cheek and then he kissed me on my right cheek.

Rebecca had never seen anyone do this before. "Mom, how come that guy is kissing Daddy?" she asked.

Kathie, always quick on the comeback, especially at my expense, replied, "He either really likes your dad, or your dad is a goner."

Joe Panucci and Toddles Magnelli always laughed when I related that story to them whenever I'd bump into them for years afterward.

This story came to mind in Southern California, of all places, in the summer of 2009. Kathie and I were visiting our daughter, Rebecca, then 32, at her new apartment in Woodland Hills. Rebecca has been the general manger of a California Pizza Kitchen Restaurant in Simi Valley at that time.

One day during our stay there, I called back home to check my telephone messages. There were back-to-back calls, for instance, from my friends Dick Goetz and Joe Gordon. What struck me as strange about that is those two men and their respective home phone numbers are listed back-to-back in my personal black book of phone numbers. What are the odds of that happening?

I also received call-backs from Bill Sharman, the Hall of Fame basketball coach and player, and one of my favorites from my days of covering pro basketball, and from Jimmy Allen, a defensive back on the Steelers' first two Super Bowl teams. They both live in Southern California and I wanted to see and talk to them while I was in the neighborhood.

The call that caught my attention most of all, however, came from Joe Panucci. "I'm sorry to call you when you're so busy," he began, "but I thought you'd want to know that our dear friend Tony 'Toodles' Magnelli has died. He'd been sick for quite some time now. I need to call Foge and I want to get hold of Billy Hillgrove. 'Toodles' loved you guys."

I would later learn when I got back to Pittsburgh that Foge Fazio had come to the one-session viewing of "Toodles" Magnelli. "The place was packed," reported Panucci when I got hold of him when I came home.

He also told me that he had taken his wife Barbara to Allegheny General Hospital a few days earlier for some cardiology treatments. Joe and Barbara were both dealing with some health challenges that had left them both feeling low. My wife Kathie had seen and spoken to them a few times when they were at Allegheny General Hospital. I told Joe that Kathie had retired from AGH back in November of 2008 after 17 years as a medical social worker in the Cancer Center.

Time was moving on for all of us.

I reminded Joe Panucci that he was someone who always picked up other people's spirits. He was always such an upbeat fellow, but he was finding it more difficult to stay so spirited these days.

Panucci's call while I was in California brought back another fond memory. Once before he had caught me when I was in a warm place on a getaway mission.

That was back in 1969. I was then working as a sportswriter at *The Miami News*. Kathie and I had gone with another couple who lived in our apartment building in Southwest Miami to Key West. We were staying in a resort there and we hadn't even told our parents back in Pittsburgh where we were going. I must have told someone at the sports desk where they could reach me in an emergency.

In any case, I got a call in our Key West hideaway from none other than Joe Panucci, the pride of McKees Rocks. He was calling to tell me that a kid from his community, a quarterback named Bob Medwid, was coming to Pitt to play football for his dear friend Carl DePasqua. He liked DePasqua because he was a friendly fellow, but most of all because he was Italian.

I couldn't believe that Panucci had succeeded in getting hold of me in Key West.

There were no cell phones in those days, and we didn't have any recording device to take messages on our phones. On this trip to Los Angeles, it seemed that everyone had a cell phone in hand and was either talking on the telephone or "texting" someone. How did we ever function without these modern technological devices? Better, if you ask me.

Panucci wanted me to know about Medwid's decision to go to Pitt so I could scoop the other sports broadcasters in Pittsburgh about the story. I was living in Miami, but I was continuing to do a daily morning sports show on WEEP Radio back home in Pittsburgh.

I had been under consideration for a similar show at WTAE Radio, but they chose Myron Cope instead to do the show. They made the right choice, I know, and I accepted an offer to go to Miami and cover the Dolphins of the American Football League.

It's funny how those things work out.

It wasn't easy to stay on top of things in Pittsburgh while living and working in Miami. I remember being at a movie theater in Miami one Sunday night with Kathie and she asking me, "Why are you sweating?"

The movie theater was air-conditioned, of course, but the thought of coming up with material for a Pittsburgh audience the next morning—from my Miami outpost—was enough to make me sweat.

The movie theaters in Southern California are air-conditioned as well. More importantly, so is Rebecca's apartment. Temperatures were in the high 90s, and crept upward to 102 and 104 during our six-day stay. The heat coming up from the sidewalks seemed even hotter.

Each morning, when it was cooler, Kathie and I took Rebecca's dog Bailey for a long walk. We'd go to Starbucks for some coffee, and pick up copies of *The Los Angeles Times* and *The New York Times* to read. We'd take along a cup of ice water for the trip and give some to Bailey every so often. She did fine and we enjoyed the reunion with her. She was 11 years old then, but she appeared to be in good shape and still enjoyed her strolls.

Mark Twain once said, "You should take your dog for a walk every day…even if you don't have a dog." And we do, but it's more fun when you're in the company of Bailey. It was good to see Rebecca again, and to meet her friends at different restaurants around town. She didn't remember the incident of Joe Panucci kissing me outside Pitt Stadium. She was only six at the time. Time flies when you're having fun.

"Football simply has an iron grip was our collective psyche to the extent that America has a collective psyche anymore. We love it. God help us, we love it."
— J. R. Moehringer
From ESPN Magazine

Dan Marino and his dad
draw praise from fans

April 2011

Ican still see Dan Marino Sr. sitting in the stands at Pitt Stadium. He was the only person sitting in the stands that afternoon during spring football practice in April of 1982.

He was sitting on a metal bleacher halfway up the stadium on the 50-yard line. He had the best seat in the house to watch his son, Dan Marino, at practice with the Pitt football team. The 1982 Pitt football team was thought to be one of the best college football teams in America.

Young Marino was a pre-season All-American and high on the Heisman Trophy watch list. He had his dad's vote from the beginning.

I was working as a sportswriter at *The Pittsburgh Press* at the time and was doing a cover story for the Sunday *Roto* magazine of that daily newspaper. A year later, I would leave *The Press* to become the assistant athletic director and public relations director at the University of Pittsburgh. I would miss the Marino era with the Panthers. I missed those three consecutive years of Pitt having an 11–1 record under Jackie Sherrill.

Now Pitt Stadium is gone, *The Pittsburgh Press* is gone and Dan Marino Sr. is gone. He died last year (2010) at his home in South Florida. Only the memories remain.

He and his wife Veronica had been living in Weston, the same community where their son and his family resided. Their son had been the star quarterback of the Miami Dolphins for 17 seasons. That son, though it's hard to believe, will turn 50 this coming September. One of their neighbors and friends in Weston was Angelo Dundee, who was a trainer and cornerman for Muhammad Ali and Sugar Ray Leonard among other boxing champions, and a cherished old friend from my days in Miami.

Frazier Field, the sandlot ballfield back in their old neighborhood of South Oakland, at the end of Parkview Avenue where the family lived for so many years, was re-named the Dan Marino Field. There is also a children's hospital for kids with special needs near Fort Lauderdale named the MCH Dan Marino Center. Dan and his wife Claire have six children, and one of them has special needs. (I see Claire's mother from time to time at the Mt. Lebanon Library where she volunteers, and she gives me an update on the family.)

Dan Marino and his dad drew many laudatory remarks from the many speakers at the 25th Annual Awards and Scholarship Banquet held by the Pittsburgh chapter of the Italian-American Sports Hall of Fame at the Westin Convention Center Hotel on a memorable Saturday evening.

No one praised Dan Marino Sr. more than his son. "If I could be half the father my father was, I would feel that I accomplished something," said Dan Marino.

He was being honored as The Man of the Year and was being inducted into the local chapter's Hall of Fame. "I thought I was already in this Hall of Fame," declared Dan Marino with that wonderful smile of his. "What took you guys so long? Hey, I had 17 pretty good seasons in the NFL."

It was particularly poignant that Marino was being honored at the 25th anniversary of his recognition dinner. His dad was responsible for starting the Pittsburgh chapter of the organization that is headquartered in Chicago. His dad wanted to raise fund to help local Italian-American children with scholarships to college and to fund them if needed for young athletes to compete on an international basis.

I've always been fascinated by how many Italian-Americans have made their mark in sports and in other areas of achievement that are honored by his organization. I felt like I was back on Sunnyside Street in Hazelwood. I grew up in a neighborhood that was predominantly the descendants of families that had immigrated to America from Italy. I bowled as a child at St. Anthony's Club, an Italian-American club in our community. Nobody called it an Italian-American club in those days. It was just the Italian club.

My friends back in New York were so impressed when I was honored as a "Legend" by this chapter of the Italian-American Sports Hall of Fame back in 1999. "How'd a guy named O'Brien do that?" one of them asked.

I spoke with Dan Marino, Sr. on several occasions and enjoyed his friendship and fatherly advice.

"My dad spent a lot of time with me as a kid, teaching me how to throw a football, and how to be an athlete," said Dan Marino. "He also taught me how to be a man."

Marino was known for having a quick release, but his throwing motion was not a textbook one. Of course, Johnny Unitas and Joe Montana had their own unique throwing motions as well. Jackie Sherrill, who coached Marino during his Pitt days, once told him, "Don't let anybody change your throwing motion."

It was good to see Dan's family at the dinner this Saturday evening. His mother Veronica remembered me, and she smiled when I reminded her of the time she danced with Myron Cope at a draft party held at the home of his teammate Sal Sunseri in Greenfield back in 1982. Sunseri and Emil Boures were both late draft selections of the Steelers that year.

Marino was in the following year's draft and the Steelers had an opportunity to pick him with the 21st pick in the first round and passed on him to draft Gabe Rivera, a defensive lineman from Texas Tech. Rivera was a promising prospect but he was injured and left paralyzed by an auto accident during his rookie season. Marino went to Miami, and under the tutelage of Don Shula, became one of the outstanding quarterbacks in NFL history.

Dan Marino and his brother-in-law Larry Richert of KDKA Radio teamed up at Mario Lemieux's Celebrity Golf Outing at The Club at Nevillewood.

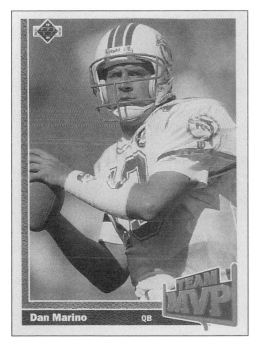

Dan Marino   QB

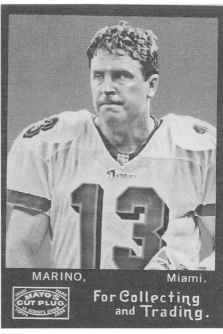

MARINO,   Miami.

For Collecting and Trading.

Dan Marino graced many bubble gum cards through the years.

People at the banquet and those I have seen since the event are still upset that the Steelers didn't draft Dan Marino. It is my personal theory that he would not have become the same Dan Marino we know and love had he stayed in Pittsburgh. Miami and Shula and the warm weather and a change of scenery were perfect for Marino.

His dad didn't regret it either. Dan Marino Sr. had worked as a truck driver for *The Post-Gazette*, delivering the paper to outposts throughout the city in the middle of the night. It wasn't a glamour job. "When people would tell me they felt bad for me that Danny didn't play for the Steelers," his dad once told me, "I said, 'Yeah, I missed all those vacations on the North Side.' Are you kidding?"

The Marinos moved to Miami after the dad retired from his job in Pittsburgh and have remained there ever since.

At the dinner this past Saturday, I also had a chance to say hello to Dan's two kid sisters, Cindi and Debbie. Cindi is married to KDKA-Radio broadcaster Larry Richert, who has emceed the dinner for more than 20 years. He was recruited by his late father-in-law to handle the task. "The price was right," allows Larry Richert. He misses Dan Marino Sr. as well, and offered kind words for his influence from the podium. "I would do whatever he told me to do," allowed Larry with a smile. "I wouldn't want to get on the wrong side of him."

One evening back in the winter of 1982, I was invited to join the Marino family at their home on Parkview Avenue for a spaghetti dinner. "Dig in," the dad ordered me. "You don't have to put on any airs at this table."

It was a great meal, I remember. The company and the conversation couldn't have been better. "Danny doesn't get treated any differently than either of the girls," the dad told me with more than a hint of pride.

Young Dan Marino was inducted into the local chapter's Hall of Fame along with an old neighbor and former boss of his, John Rosato, who has been associated with Duquesne University football for 25 years as an assistant coach and scout and recruiting director under four different head coaches.

Rosato grew up in South Oakland and his family came from the same town in Italy as the Marino family. One of their neighbors back in those days was Bruno Sammartino, who for many years reigned as the wrestling champion of the world, and sold out Madison Square Garden 187 times or more than any other individual. Bruno, now 75 and bearing a dark mustache, also spoke at the dinner. He remains a most popular figure in Pittsburgh.

Rosato told a story about how all the Marinos worked at one time or another at his family's nursery business in that South Oakland neighborhood. Danny disclosed a story I had never heard before how he almost lost a foot in his teenage years while mowing a lawn for that landscaping service.

"I was mowing grass on a hillside and the grass was wet and I was wearing tennis shoes," said Marino. "I slipped and cut off the front end of my one tennis shoe. I only bruised my toes, but I hate to think what could have happened."

He wouldn't have been honored at last Saturday night's dinner, that's for sure. John Rosato, who spoke at length about everybody in his family—and he's the oldest of 14 children—said that Danny has been after him ever since to pay for those tennis shoes he ruined that day.

"I figure I owe him some interest on that money by now," said Rosato. So he announced that he was making a donation of $1,000 to the chapter for a scholarship for a deserving student the next time around. He offered another scholarship in his father's memory.

Dan Marino was terrific at the dinner. One of the honorees was his former teammate John Brown. Remember when Marino threw Brown a touchdown pass on fourth down in the closing seconds of the 1982 Sugar Bowl to beat Georgia? It was a perfect pass over Brown's shoulder and he held onto the ball even though he was instantly hit by two defenders and was knocked head over heels in the back of the end zone. "He couldn't drop that ball," Marino said on Saturday night. "I stuck it in him."

Jim O'Brien

Dan Marino Sr. was so proud of his kids.

It was that kind of night, full of good memories. Marino has gone on to become a big hit as an analyst on CBS-TV, sitting next to former Steelers' coach Bill Cowher on the panel each Sunday.

There was never a disparaging word about Dan Marino during his entire NFL career, and he was cited on several occasions for his charitable efforts, especially with children. Fudge Browne, a community relations director with the Dolphins who grew up in Pittsburgh and was the daughter of Post-Gazette columnist Joe Browne, once told me that whatever city the Dolphins visited, Dan was always meeting a Make-A-Wish Kid or some youngster with a special need who wanted to meet a star football player.

I've always admired the Marinos. Like most popular Pittsburgh sports heroes, Dan Marino has remained humble and does whatever he can to help out. He still sends so much signed memorabilia every year to his alma mater Central Catholic and has been the prime catalyst for their fund-raising efforts.

He may not have played quarterback for the Steelers, but No. 13 is still a real Pittsburgh guy. They don't come any better.

Mike Ditka celebrates
his 70th birthday

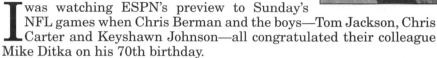

October 2009

I was watching ESPN's preview to Sunday's NFL games when Chris Berman and the boys—Tom Jackson, Chris Carter and Keyshawn Johnson—all congratulated their colleague Mike Ditka on his 70th birthday.

A cake was brought out and Ditka blew out the candles. I couldn't believe it. Mike Ditka was 70. He was born October 18, 1939 in Carnegie, Pa., and grew up in Aliquippa. I suppose I just didn't want to know that Mike Ditka had turned 70. That meant that I, age 67 at the time, would soon be there. You're old when you're 70. Everyone knows that.

I remember during my freshman year at Pitt, I was standing on the porch on the Fifth Avenue Side of the Student Union, when I spotted Mike Ditka near one of the doors. He was wearing a snug-fitting Pitt varsity letterman's jacket and a crew cut. He was the B.M.O.C.—the Big Man on Campus—and I probably stared at him for awhile.

He was a senior, already an All-American end on the football team. He played first base and the outfield for the school's baseball team, was a reserve power forward on the school's basketball team and, maybe best of all, was the intramural heavyweight wrestling champion.

He defeated a fellow football player named Ralph Conrad, who had won the PIAA wrestling title while at Altoona High School, for the title. Rex Perry, later to coach the U.S. Olympic team, wished Ditka wrestled for his varsity team. He said Ditka could have been an NCAA champion.

To me, Ditka will always be the quintessential Pitt athlete.

On October 13 of this year, I was among those out at the portion of the wall that remains of Forbes Field celebrating the Pirates' seventh game victory over the New York Yankees in the World Series on that date in 1960.

While there, we were reminiscing mostly about special days at the ballpark when the Pirates were playing. But I did mention Mike Ditka. I had seen him, from quite a unique viewpoint, make a catch and run for the Chicago Bears against the Pittsburgh Steelers that still shows up on NFL highlights.

In fact, when ESPN marked Ditka's 70th birthday on TV, they showed some highlights from his 12-year NFL career with the Bears, the Philadelphia Eagles and the Dallas Cowboys, and the first one they showed was that spectacular catch-and-run against the Steelers at Forbes Field.

That came during my senior year at Pitt. It came on a weekend I will remember as much as Bill Mazeroski's home run that won that 1960 World Series.

My four-year college career at Pitt is framed by two cataclysmic events. First, in my freshman year, there was Maz's home run leading off the bottom of the ninth to beat the Yankees 10–9 in the deciding game of that wacky World Series.

Then, on November 22, 1963, I was walking along Forbes Avenue, about a block and a half from Forbes Field, when I learned that President John F. Kennedy had been shot as he was riding in a motorcade through the streets of downtown Dallas. He would learn later that day that he died of a gunshot wound to his head.

Beano Cook and I had started an irreverent tabloid newspaper my senior year called *Pittsburgh Weekly Sports*. Beano was the sports information director at Pitt during my four years there, and one of my mentors in the business. He introduced me to the best sports writers in America and, naturally, to the best sports writing in America.

The Steelers were scheduled to play the Bears two days after the assassination of JFK. The NFL was not sure what to do. The Pitt-Penn State game that was set for that Saturday was postponed. That postponement would cost Pitt, a team that would finish with a 9–1 record—losing only to Roger Staubach and Navy on the road—an opportunity to play in a post-season bowl game. Imagine a team of Pitt's stature not getting invited to a major bowl with a 9–1 record. School officials had turned down one bowl bid, hoping to get a better one, but none came because bowl committees were reluctant to commit with Pitt having one more game to play against arch-rival Penn State.

Pete Rozelle, the commissioner of the NFL, decided to go ahead with the games. He thought at the time it was best to conduct business as usual, to get Americans back to some sense of normalcy. He later said it was a decision he would always regret. He should have cancelled the games that weekend. A nation was grieving.

The Bears were on their way to winning the NFL championship that year. There was no Super Bowl back then. There was another league, though, the American Football League. Ditka decided to sign with the Chicago Bears rather than the Houston Oilers. He was the No. 1 draft pick of the Bears, chosen by team owner and Coach George Halas. It was Halas who changed the position of tight end to be a prime receiver. Ditka was the league's Rookie of the Year in 1961, catching 56 passes for 1,076 yards and 12 touchdowns.

On November 24, 1963, two days after the JFK assassination, the Bears found themselves trailing the Steelers by the score of 17–14. It was late in the game and Chicago was deep in its own territory, facing a third down and 33 yards to go.

I was watching the game from the top of the roof in right center field. I was standing near the far end, just above the deepest part of the baseball field. It was a precarious position, to say the least. There was no guard rail. I think the Steelers let me up there rather than grant me a seat in the press box with the reporters from the daily newspapers. That was better than we fared for the Pirates' games.

Bears quarterback Billy Wade dropped back under pressure and dumped the ball off to Ditka in the flat, just looking to get a few yards out of the play. In what NFL legend George Allen called "a superhuman effort," Ditka shed at least five would-be tacklers on his way to a 63-yard rumble. One of those pursuers for the Steelers was defensive back Dick Haley, who had also played at Pitt.

The Bears would kick a field goal and salvage a tie, at 17–17, saving their season in the process, as they held a slim lead over the Green Bay Packers in the NFL Western Division standings.

The Steelers had a good team that year, too. Buddy Parker was the coach. Andy Russell was a rookie on that team. The Steelers finished with a 7–4–3 record. They lost the final game of the season in New York, by 33–17 to the Giants. If they had won that game they would have won the NFL East title and been playing the Bears again, this time for the NFL title.

The Steelers would draft Paul Martha with their No. 1 pick at the end of that season. Martha was a classmate and friend of mine during our Pitt days. You may have read the story about all the personal problems Martha has run into in recent years. He was the Golden Boy at Pitt. Art Rooney Sr. always addressed him as "Star" whenever he saw him when he was playing for six seasons with the Steelers, then one more with the Denver Broncos.

Martha is the same age I am, and it hurt to read that story. I had known about all the problems Martha was experiencing. I had spoken to him on the telephone several times while he was in San Diego and, more recently, in a senior care facility in St. Louis near his son's home there. I knew it was a good story, the rise and fall of a prominent Pittsburgh sports figure. But I passed on it. It was too personal, too close to home, and I thought I owed Paul Martha more than that. It could have been an exclusive, but there was a sense of betrayal about it.

Hearing that Ditka was 70 and Martha was having so many problems hit home with me. My wife Kathie and I called her brother, Harvey Churchman Jr., to wish him a happy birthday. He had just turned 64. I mentioned to him that he had the same birthday as Mike Ditka and he knew that.

Several of my closest friends had birthdays this month. My pal Alex Pociask turned 62. My buddy and "bodyguard" Baldo Iorio turned 93, and he was better than ever. Two friends and former Steelers associates, Bob Milie and Ernie Bonelli, both long-time residents of Mt. Lebanon, both passed away, at 82 and 90, respectively. (*Baldo Iorio would die just before his 95th birthday.*)

So my friends are growing older and some are dying. That gets your attention.

I learned over the weekend that my oldest brother, Richard, was hospitalized with a serious ailment and was not expected to live long. I was in Columbus when I heard the news. We were visiting our daughter Sarah and her family.

I remember covering a football game at Ohio State once in the mid-'70s, when I was working at *The New York Post* and that I called my brother Richard from Columbus and asked him if he wanted to come and see the game. He lived in Bridgeport, Ohio. He was in Columbus about an hour and a half later. It is at least a two-hour drive if you heed the speed limits. I recall we had a grand time in Columbus the night before the game.

The memories are rich ones. You hope you will add more to your list. Ditka was smart enough to pick winners on the ESPN show that included the Steelers, the Bears and the Saints. He owns a restaurant in Pittsburgh—it's still his hometown—and in Chicago, and he has worked for the Bears and the Saints. He is loyal, if nothing else. He knows it's not smart to offend people where you do business.

I'm still a big fan of Mike Ditka. I just have a hard time thinking he's over 70 now.

Photos by Sharon Pociask

Author Jim O'Brien paid visit to Mike Ditka's Restaurant in midtown Chicago and checked out Ditka's extensive sports memorabilia collection, with Pittsburgh and Western Pennsylvania sports figures -- Stan Musial and Arnold Palmer and Steelers and Pirates -- well represented alongside his Chicago collection.

Jimbo Covert 'Puttin' on the Blitz' at North Side brownstone

December 2011

This was in a grand French ballroom below floor level in a magnificent brownstone building on the city's North Side. There were about 150 people filling the room at a fund-raiser to sponsor disadvantaged kids to attend a summer football camp featuring the Steelers' star center Maurkice Pouncey and his pals on the team's offensive line.

It was easy to pick Pouncey out of the crowd and I also recognized his linemates Chris Kemoeatu and Marcus Gilbert, as well as linebacker LaMarr Woodley. There were a few other big men sharing the same tables but I didn't recognize them.

About a dozen waiters were strolling through the crowd to offer hors d'oeuvres—beef and chicken on a stick or cheese puffs, cheese and crackers – and there were stations for wine and beer.

The party, advertised as "Puttin' on the Blitz II," was co-hosted by Pouncey and Russell Livingston, the president of Babb, Inc., an insurance brokerage firm whose offices are in this landmark building. DeShea Townsend hosted the party the previous year.

I'd been in that building at least a dozen times over the past 30 years, twice signing my books at the firm's Christmas party, but I had not been there for a few years. Russell's father, Ron Livingston, a big Pitt booster and Steelers' fan, was running the firm back then.

I had bumped into Russell in mid-winter at The City Game, when Pitt defeated Duquesne at their annual meeting at the Consol Energy Center, and he had invited me to his party.

I knew about five people at the party and, worse yet as far as I was concerned, that's about all that knew me.

Being in the ballroom, which is mostly below street level on Ridge Avenue, brought back some good memories. I had been told once that the richest people in Pittsburgh often gathered there when William Penn Snyder resided there. He owned the Shenango Furnace Co., and had the Carnegies and Fricks at his gala parties, and the city's elite danced on that ballroom floor.

I was also reminded of days when Pitt had one of the best college football teams in the land, when Jackie Sherrill's teams went 11–1 three straight seasons in the early '80s. They were twice rated the No. 1 college football team in the country during that span.

Jimbo Covert came over to greet me and made me feel welcome and comfortable when I entered the ballroom on this Friday evening. He introduced Casey, the oldest of his three children, and a friend or two, and that was an ice-breaker.

Jimbo Covert, in case you don't recognize the name right away, was an All-American tackle on Sherrill's teams and played his last

Former Pitt offensive line coach Joe Moore is flanked by Russ Grimm, at left, and Emil Boures, two of his best protégés.

Photos by Jim O'Brien

Former Pitt teammates Russ Grimm and Jimbo Covert enjoy reunion at Italian Stag party at home of Canonsburg construction magnate and Pitt booster Armand Dellovade.

season under Foge Fazio, and was the first round draft choice of the Chicago Bears in 1983.

That was the draft class famous for producing five outstanding quarterbacks, including Dan Marino of Pitt, the last of the five picked that year. How good was Covert? He was the fifth player taken in that draft. Marino was taken 27th.

Covert played eight years for the Bears, including the 1985 season when they won the Super Bowl. He was the league's offensive player of the year in 1985 and played in two Pro Bowl games. He was named to the NFL's All-Decade Team of the '80s.

He and May were both top-notch students at Pitt, but they got pulled away from their classes after their senior football season for evaluation camps—that's when teams conducted their own tryouts and not at a combine—and for awards dinners. They came back to Pitt in later years to earn their degrees.

Covert's line coach at Pitt was Joe Moore and his head coach in Chicago was Mike Ditka. Both were legendary coaches and Covert shared good stories about both of them.

Now 51, Covert was still the best and brightest lineman in the ballroom at Babb Inc. He played at 6–4, 280 pounds. He looked success-ful in a dark blue suit, white shirt and blue tie. He is the president and chief executive officer of the Institute for Transfusion Medicine.

He told me he'd seen me a week earlier, just before Thanksgiving, signing books in the upper lobby of the U.S. Steel Building. He said he was rushing to get to a meeting with UPMC officials and didn't have time to stop.

Covert came out of Conway, Pennsylvania, a railroad town in Beaver County, and starred at Pitt. He played on an offensive line at Pitt that was better than the offensive line of this year's Steelers. You can read that sentence again. I think I got it right.

Covert was the left tackle on Pitt's imposing line. Rob Fada and Paul Dunn shared the left guard position, Russ Grimm was at center, Emil Boures at right guard, and Mark May at right tackle. All but Dunn played in the pros. Grimm is in the Pro Football Hall of Fame. Covert and May are in the College Football Hall of Fame. Boures lasted six seasons with the Steelers as a versatile lineman.

"I love Mark May and Lou Holtz together on those college football telecasts," exclaimed Covert. "They go so well together; they have such great chemistry."

He recalled Joe Moore getting after them at Pitt. "Some people think the center is the most important position on the offensive line because he has calls to make, adjustments to make, but that's just not so," said Covert. "The tackles are the key guys.

"Joe Moore used to get Grimm so upset because he'd say, 'I can get anybody off the street and teach them how to play center.' Grimm would get mad at Moore. Joe would tell him all he had to do was lean right or left, and that someone was always helping him block his man."

Covert recalled what it was like to play for Ditka in Chicago. "I liked Mike," he said. "You always knew where you stood with him.

"I remember once (early in the 1987 season) that the players wanted to go on strike to gain free agency. The Bears were one of the last teams to sign on. Ditka addressed us one day and he screamed at us, 'What the hell are you guys thinking? What the hell would you do—could you do—if you weren't playing football?'"

Covert chuckled at the memory. "Can you imagine a coach today telling his players something like that?" said Covert. "But Mike never worried about being politically correct. I see him on those game day panels with those other former players. I know he doesn't agree with much of what they say, but he just goes along playing the role of Mike Ditka."

Covert also offered the opinion that Jack Ham and Andy Russell were superior linebackers to Jack Lambert, but the Steelers' defensive scheme was set up to keep blockers off Lambert so he could make the tackle.

"Buddy Ryan's defense in Chicago was set up the same way so that our middle linebacker, Mike Singletary, could make the tackles. Don't get me wrong, though. Singletary and Lambert were both great players."

This fund-raising event was billed as a mixer, but today's players don't understand what they're supposed to do at such an event. They tend to stick together. That's their comfort level. Mike Tomlin needs to teach them how to mix.

Like most teenagers, they tend to spend too much time checking their i-Pads, Blackberrys and texting family and friends. So the patrons stood around and stared at the Steelers. Some were bold enough to approach them, shake hands and get something signed.

These Steelers had no idea, I'd bet, of the special significance or history of the neighborhood they were in. Ridge Avenue, now the center of the CCAC campus, was once referred to as "millionaires' row," when steel magnates lived in all those mansions.

Horse-drawn carriages used to come in and out of the basement of that brownstone they were in through a cut-away entry in the side and back of the building. That area has been converted into a party area for tail-gating parties hosted by Babb, Inc. before Steelers' and Pirates' games at nearby Heinz Field and PNC Park. There are murals depicting Pitt football and the Steelers on the interior walls.

If you left the back door of the building you could walk a block and a half—perhaps seven or eight minutes—and be at the front door of Steelers' owner Dan Rooney's residence.

Dan and his four brothers grew up in that home on Lincoln Avenue that was shared for years by Art and Kathleen Rooney. Art Sr. used to walk those sidewalks and talk to neighbors. Dan had a garage added to the house and cleaned it up a bit with a renovation project when he moved there from Mt. Lebanon about 20 years ago.

His wife Pat grew up in a humble row house in a large family in the Mexican War Streets about two miles near Allegheny General Hospital.

Now Pat and Dan spend most of their time in a grand home in Dublin, where Dan serves as the U.S. Ambassador to Ireland. They have attendants assisting Pat with looking after the home.

I checked out the Rooney residence when I left the party that night. There were small white light bulbs, maybe two or three strands at best, on a stark leafless tree in the front of the house, decorating the place for the Christmas season.

I spent the next day at the annual Book Fair at the Heinz History Center, where Art Rooney Jr. was one of over 50 authors signing their books. He and Roy McHugh teamed up to write a wonderful book about the Rooney clan called *Ruanaidh*, which is Gaelic for Rooney.

Someone told me at the signing session that they loved the story about how Art Rooney, on his deathbed, told Dan and Art Jr., "You should have drafted Marino."

It's a good story, but it's not true, according to Art Jr. "My dad wasn't able to talk near the end," he related. "But there were many times through the years, at family gatherings, that he'd say to us, 'You should have drafted Marino.'"

George Gojkovich

**LaMarr Woodley
Puttin' on the Ritz**

Foge Fazio was always
a Pitt man

December 2009

It was the worst week and the best week of my days in the department of athletics at the University of Pittsburgh. It was the week they fired Foge Fazio as the head football coach at Pitt. I was saddened when I received a telephone call in the kitchen of our home in Upper St. Clair from Dr. Edward Bozik, the director of athletics at Pitt.

Dr. Bozik informed me that the powers-that-be at Pitt had decided to replace Fazio as the football coach. That meant that he and Dr. Wesley Posvar, the chancellor, and Dr. Jack Freeman, the vice-chancellor, had made the decision to change coaches. I was the assistant athletic director for public relations and it was my job to inform the media of the firing. I felt sick to my stomach. I knew it would never be the same for Foge or for me. I enjoyed working with Foge. We trusted each other. I had first met Foge when I was a senior at Pitt in 1963. I was also working as the public relations director for the Pittsburgh Valley Ironmen, a minor league football team that played its home games at Duquesne High Field.

Fazio was then an assistant coach at Coraopolis High School in his hometown or at Ambridge High School. He was moonlighting as a linebacker for the Ironmen. He had graduated from Pitt in 1960, my freshman year, and had been drafted by the Boston Patriots of the old American Football League. He didn't make the cut with that pro club, but he was a standout for the Ironmen. They were coached by Dick Bowen, who had grown up in Duquesne and went on to play halfback at Pitt. He and Fazio were good friends. Bowen would later send his son, Richard, to play quarterback for Fazio at Pitt, but that didn't work out too well. Rich ended up playing tight end at Youngstown State and would one day become an outstanding high school football coach in the Mon Valley. (Rich Bowen is now the head coach at Hempfield High).

I think Fazio and I worked well together at Pitt. I calmed him down when he was upset and he was willing to listen to my counsel. I always urged him to be as positive as possible in his post-game commentary, no matter the circumstances of the day.

Fazio never pressed Pitt officials for more of this and more of that, the way the coaches who came from distant places did when they took the job. Fazio always felt that Pitt had limits on what it could do. He didn't want to break the bank. He also didn't break the rules established by the NCAA, and the same can't be said for coaches who came before and after him.

Fazio's positive outlook and his willingness to listen to me when I offered advice also helped when he was fired. This happened soon after Pitt lost by 31–0 in the final game of the 1985 season. The final season's record was 5–5–1. It could easily have been an 8–3 record except for missed field goals in the early season when the Panthers should have beaten Ohio State, Boston College and West Virginia, but they ended up losing the first two games and getting a tie in the third of those games.

Fazio had two years remaining on his contract when he was canned. I always thought Pitt pulled the string on him too fast. He had recruited quality players and they had been to two bowl games in his four years, back when it was much tougher to get invited to a bowl game than it is today.

I went to see the Fazio family the same evening I received the phone call from Dr. Bozik about his firing. Pitt leased a mansion on the campus to the head football coach in those days. It was a big house and the family room was huge and dimly-lit, I can still recall, as we sat around and discussed what had happened and what we had to do.

Norma Fazio remembered that evening, too, and talked to me about it when I spoke to her at the Copeland Funeral Home in Moon Township on a Sunday two weeks ago. I was there to pay my respects to her husband, Foge Fazio, who had died on December 2 (2009) after a three-year bout with leukemia. There were familiar faces from my Pitt days at the funeral home. The place was packed for three days. Foge Fazio had so many friends and admirers. He was wearing a mustard gold blazer, a white shirt, a blue-and-gold striped tie, and there was a Golden Panthers pin on his lapel. He was a Pitt man to the end.

"Who else could have done that?" Norma Fazio reflected.

Their son, Vince Fazio, in his eulogy the next day, said that his father was never bitter about his firing at Pitt.

I believe he was bitter, but he masked it well. He would have liked to be Pitt's answer to Joe Paterno. He would have never left Pitt for a better job. For Foge Fazio, there was no better job. His successor, Mike Gottfried, never felt that way. At the press conference to introduce Gottfried as the football coach at Pitt, Gottfried said he hoped to use it as a stepping stone to become a head coach in the National Football League some day. Imagine how that went down with Pitt authorities or the team's boosters. After he was fired, it was Fazio who first called Pitt's attention to Gottfried as a possible successor, yet when Gottfried got the job he wanted nothing to do with Fazio, his friends or anyone who remained loyal to him.

I remember best the press conference to announce the firing of Fazio. That night, in his home on the Pitt campus, I asked him to attend the press conference. He balked, at first, but then agreed to come.

I suggested what he should say. I told him he shouldn't do what his friend Carl DePasqua had done. DePasqua, who had played at Pitt and been an assistant coach and head coach just like Fazio, never wanted anything to do with Pitt after he was fired following a 1–10 season in 1972. DePasqua had been the head coach for four years and his best effort was 5–5 in 1970. He was 4–6 and 3–8 the other two seasons.

DePasqua never came around to any Pitt affairs after that.

I suggested that Fazio should say that he was proud of what he had accomplished as the Pitt coach, that he was proud of taking his team to two post-season bowl games, that he was proud of the quality of the players he recruited to Pitt. I told him to finish by saying he was always proud to be a Pitt man and that he would always be a Pitt man.

I felt like a ventriloquist at that press conference. I mouthed nearly the same words as Fazio that afternoon in a dining-meeting room at Pitt Stadium. Goose Goslin, the sports director of KDKA Radio at the time, told me after the luncheon, "I can't believe you got him to come here for this press conference."

Think about the coaches who have left their college coaching positions, such as Pete Carroll at USC or Lane Kiffin at Tennessee. Did you see any of them at press conferences to announce they were leaving those schools?

In the years after his firing at Pitt, Fazio showed up at many Pitt functions, such as awards dinners and golf outings and fund-raisers of all kinds, and he was always well received. Fazio was a popular fellow. People liked him and were happy to be in his company. There was never any tension in the room when he appeared. He was welcomed with hugs and hearty handshakes. His gleaming eyes and huge smile made everyone comfortable.

"Foge was a true Pitt man," said Pitt football coach Dave Wannstedt. "He loved this university and everyone at Pitt loved Foge. He was an outstanding football coach and an even better person. From the time I came to Pittsburgh five years ago, no one has been a better friend or supporter of what we are doing at Pitt. He will be greatly missed." Bill Hillgrove said, "Foge was always a Pitt man. He always wanted to be here."

Last year (2008), Steve Pederson, the Pitt athletic director, invited Fazio to join Hillgrove and Bill Fralic on the Pitt radio broadcast team to analyze the action. He did that again this season until his ill health forced him to give it up.

"I always liked Foge."
— Johnny Majors

Foge Fazio hosted a golf tournament for the Autistim Society the previous summer at Montour Heights Country Club near his home in Moon Township. He invited me to come and offer a reflection on our friend Myron Cope. Fazio and Cope had co-hosted this golf tournament for many years until Cope's death a few years back.

At the function, Fazio introduced me by saying I had saved him from putting his foot in his mouth when we worked together at Pitt. And he added that I had a lot to do with the fact that he had remained a member of the Pitt family. I felt so good when he made that public pronouncement. I had always thought that my advice to him was the best I had offered any coach during my four-year stay at Pitt.

Foge went elsewhere to coach after his Pitt days, but he returned frequently. When he retired as a coach, he moved back to his home area. He wanted to be closer to family and friends and, of course, the University of Pittsburgh.

I ran into Johnny Majors, another former Pitt football coach, at Armand Dellovade's annual Christmas party in Lawrence last Saturday. I mentioned that we had both lost a good friend the previous week. "I always liked Foge," said Majors. "I wanted him to be my recruiting coordinator when I first came here. He had been on Carl DePasqua's staff, and had stayed on to help us in our transition. He wanted to be an on-the-field coach and I didn't have an opening on my staff for him. So he went to Cincinnati to be an assistant coach to Tony Mason. I would have liked to have kept him as part of my team.

"Before he left, Foge took me out to meet Tony Dorsett and his family. He helped us land Dorsett at Pitt."

I suggested to Majors that Dorsett had a bigger impact on a college football program than any player in the history of the game. Majors won National Coach of the Year honors in his first year at Pitt when the Panthers went 6–5–1 in his first season with Dorsett as the star performer. Majors was Coach of the Year again in 1976 when Pitt won the National Championship with a 12–0 record and Dorsett won the Heisman Trophy. "O.J. Simpson, Herschel Walker, Tim Tebow ... none of them came up as big in that regard as Dorsett did," said Majors.

I suggested that there should be a statue of Dorsett somewhere on the Pitt campus to recognize his contribution to the school. Majors clinked his drink glass against mine. "You got that right," he said. "Merry Christmas to you and your family."

Jim O'Brien

Two former Pitt head football coaches, Foge Fazio and Johnny Majors, meet at one of Armand Dellovade's tailgate parties outside Heinz Field.

Doug Miller holds forth
in Super Bowl press box

February 2010

Iwas thinking about Doug Miller as I prepared to watch Super Bowl XLIV on television on a Sunday evening in February of 2010. Miller is one of my protégés. He grew up a block from our home in Upper St. Clair and he thought I led an interesting life. So he tagged along with me to sports functions and followed my directions on how to get from here to there.

Miller was a high school student when he came with me one evening when I pinch-hit for Bill Campbell at an awards dinner to focus positive attention on students from Steel Valley High and West Mifflin High at the Thompson Club in West Mifflin. I was speaking that night and I wanted Doug to hear what I had to say to kids his age, and how the dinner was coordinated by my friend Darrell Hess, a fellow columnist in *The Valley Mirror*.

I remember taking Miller out to Robert Morris University, when I was teaching a class in sports publicity there, and he met another young man named Miller that evening at a basketball game in the old campus gym. Sean Miller, then a grade school kid, performed a ball-handling exhibition on the court at halftime and Doug Miller helped him with the basketballs and set-ups he used to perform his tricks. Sean Miller would later star for the Pitt basketball team and today is the head basketball coach at the University of Arizona.

When Miller decided to transfer from Davis & Elkins College to Pitt after his freshman year, I told him to sign up to write sports on *The Pitt News* and to volunteer his services in the sports information department. Larry Eldridge, who had succeeded me as the assistant athletic director for public relations, was happy to have him and, in time, gave young Miller more and more responsibilities as a liaison between the football coaches and the media. Miller turned out to be a better writer than I had realized. I gave him a gold-and-blue print for success at Pitt and Miller followed it to a T and then some.

That Sunday, Miller, (now 42 years old), held forth in the press box at the Super Bowl as the senior director of news media relations for the New Orleans Saints. Anyone seeking some information about the Saints would speak to Miller or one of his assistants at Sun Life Stadium in Miami.

His story might not be movie material like "Blind Side," but it's a good story nonetheless, a real success story. It shows what a kid can accomplish if he follows his dream.

This is Miller's 22nd season in the National Football League, and his sixth with the Saints. He has worked in the press headquarters for eight conference championship games, and this was his ninth Super

Bowl assignment. The NFL front office in New York named Miller to work with the media at eight earlier Super Bowl games because of the respect they held for him.

He called me several years back for my thoughts when the league offered him a position in their Manhattan headquarters. I told him I thought he would miss the competition, the idea of caring from week to week about whether or not his team won or lost. He'd be neutral and would not have any rooting interest if he held a league position. He turned down the offer.

Miller was working for the New York Jets at the time. He worked for 16 years in the publicity office of the Jets. When Miller was a junior at Pitt, I recommended him for a summer internship with the Jets. He never came back to Pitt. Frank Ramos, the veteran public relations director of the Jets going back to their Joe Namath days, liked Miller and kept him on his staff. Miller was the third college student I had successfully recommended to Ramos. When I worked for *The New York Post* just over 33 years ago, I had recommended Ron Cohen, then a sports information director at SUNY at Stony Brook, and they liked him, and then during my Pitt days I recommended to them Brooks Thomas of Bethel Park. He took a summer internship after his junior year at Pitt and he never came back to school either.

Thomas, in time, left the Jets to become the publicity director of the New York Rangers in the National Hockey League. My prize protégé was Pat Hanlon. I had first met him when he was an intern at *The Pittsburgh Press* and then at Pitt when I went to work there in the athletic department. Hanlon was my first staff hire, and he became my valued right hand man. I later boosted him to the sports information director at the University of Oklahoma, where he worked for a few years, and then for my friend Joe Gordon with the Pittsburgh Steelers.

Hanlon later worked for the New England Patriots and in recent years has been the vice president for communications for the New York Giants, where he makes over $200,000 a year. I put Linda Venzon in charge of football media relations when Hanlon left for Oklahoma and that put her in a position to be hired as the sports information director at the University of Miami, which at the time had one of the highest profile college football programs in the country. Teresa Varley worked as a student in our office for all four years of her Pitt stay, and I talked Joe Gordon into hiring her as my assistant when I was hired to be the editor of *Steelers Digest* during the summer of 1987.

I changed my mind and didn't take the Steelers' job, but Teresa stayed and has now been there for 25 years. She grew up in the '70s when every kid in Pittsburgh wanted to play for the Pittsburgh Steelers someday, and she was small of stature and an unlikely candidate to accomplish just that, but she did. And she's still playing for the Steelers and figures to outlast any of the current club members.

One of the most satisfying and rewarding aspects of my four-year stay in the Pitt athletic department was in overseeing an ambitious internship program. Myron Cope said I had more interns than Dr. Thomas Starzl, the famed transplant surgeon in the UPMC complex.

Pittsburgh's Doug Miller, at left, is reunited with former Pitt and NFL star running back Curtis Martin at Pro Football Hall of Fame induction for Allderdice and Pitt performer at Canton, Ohio in August of 2012. Below, Miller walks with Saints' Pro Bowl quarterback Drew Brees during practice in New Orleans.

I helped steer at least 20 young men and women to college and pro public relations and media-related positions during my stay. I think I developed more pros than the football and basketball coaches combined.

All of them arrived with the right attitude and enthusiasm. I helped them sharpen their skills and taught them to be more responsible. When Miller first went to New York, he asked me if he was ready. I said, "No, you're not. But every time they ask you to do something you do it as well and as promptly as possible, and then go back and ask what they want you to do next. It's not rocket science. You keep doing that and you'll be fine." And he did. Miller has been lucky along the way, too. Like many of us, Miller will never forget 9/11/01. He was supposed to catch a flight out of Newark Airport headed for the San Francisco Bay area that day to advance a Jets' game with the Oakland Raiders. He didn't get all his work done the day before when his computer went on the fritz and he had to change his flight plans.

He missed being on the airplane that crashed into a strip-mining field in Shanksville, Pennsylvania when the passengers on board charged four al-Qaeda terrorists who had planned to force the pilots to divert the airplane to Washington, D.C. and have it crash into one of the important buildings there that fateful day. There were 40 passengers and crew on United Flight 93. All perished.

Surely, Miller would have been the only passenger on that airplane that day who knew where Shanksville was. His parents, Don and Barbara Miller, had family living in Shanksville, and Doug had gone there and to nearby Johnstown for family gatherings as a child. His parents are now retired and living in Celebration, Florida, near their daughter Becky and her family. Becky Miller worked for years at nearby Disney World coordinating fantasy weddings and receptions.

Doug Miller must think about how lucky he was from time to time. Being a big part of this Super Bowl might bring it all back. The City of New Orleans has bounced back from a disaster of a different sort and its football team has become a feel–good story that has national appeal. Doug Miller is just the man to promote such stories.

Broadway Joe Namath entertains the media on eve of Super Bowl III in Miami when he made the bold "I guarantee it" prediction that the New York Jets would beat the heavily-favored Baltimore Colts. He made good on it and the Jets became the first AFL team to rule the unified pro football ranks. Doug Miller met Namath on several occasions during his 17 seasons as a publicist with the New York Jets.

One man's opinion about Pitt abandoning
Big East to join forces with ACC

September 2011

So Pitt has decided to abandon The Big East and become a member of the Atlantic Coast Conference, more familiarly known as The ACC.

For starters, this was stunning news because I had not had a hint or heard a rumor of the possibility. If Pitt was to leave The Big East the word was that the Panthers would sign up with The Big Ten.

Frankly, I didn't think The Big Ten would be the best fit for Pitt because the football aspect would be tougher and the basketball wouldn't be as good and maybe not appealing enough for the Panthers to retain Coach Jamie Dixon.

The ACC and The Big East have long challenged for the title of the best basketball conference in the country and The Big East has usually prevailed. The decision by Pitt and Syracuse to leave The Big East in favor of The ACC tips the scales in favor of The ACC. Before there was a Big East, the ACC was definitely the finest basketball conference in the country.

Dick Groat will be happy when this happens.

Dick Vitale will be happy.

Jay Bilas will be happy.

Bill Raftery might not be so happy.

Groat, Vitale and Bilas are all analysts at courtside for the Pitt broadcast team and network coverage respectively. Groat, who grew up in Swissvale and still resides there, was an All-American at Duke in 1951 and 1952, prior to playing shortstop for the Pittsburgh Pirates.

Groat's jersey still hangs in the rafters at Duke's Cameron Indoor Stadium and his broadcast sidekick Billy Hillgrove will have a great time telling the Pitt fans back home about how Groat is a legendary figure on the Durham campus.

Then again, Groat and Hillgrove will miss visiting their favorite watering holes in Manhattan during The Big East Tournament.

Pitt used to have a close relationship with Duke back in the '50s and '60s.

Vitale has always been a big fan of ACC basketball and, at the same time, he thinks Pitt's Petersen Events Center is one of the outstanding college basketball venues in the country. Bilas is biased toward the ACC, having played basketball and coached at Duke. He will like Pitt better now. He'd always been a tad reluctant to give the Panthers their due.

Raftery coached at Seton Hall once upon a time and remains a New York kind of guy. I'm sure he'd rather Pitt and Syracuse would stay with The Big East.

I'm not sure Pitt would have gone without Syracuse leaving at the same time. It reminds me of how important it was when the NFL and AFL merged in 1970 that the Steelers, Colts and Browns all agreed to become members of the AFC to balance the size of the conferences. The Steelers got paid for that. It made the whole thing work.

I have mixed feelings about this stirring news development.

Nothing is the same in college athletics anymore. Hey, TCU, that's Texas Christian University, was about to start playing in The Big East. Does that make any sense? After Pitt and Syracuse skipped out, TCU had second thoughts about that decision and joined the Big Twelve instead.

Boston College skipped out on The Big East a few years back to join The ACC. Do you think the BC alumni liked that move? I know that Al Skinner, who was coaching the Golden Eagles at the time, didn't like the move.

Skinner, and old favorite of mine from the days when he and Dr. J played for the New York Nets, knew it was being made for financial reasons. That's what all these moves are about. That's why Nebraska is now a member of The Big Ten. That's why most of the Texas schools are now shopping in other conferences such as the Pac 10 and the Southeast Conference. That's why so many conferences now have more schools than it claims in the conference name.

Geography is no longer a consideration. Hey, we can get there by airplane easy enough. Tradition means nothing. It's the money. And no matter how much money these colleges can come by, thanks to lucrative TV contracts, you will never read that college tuition has been lowered.

Actually, I think this will be a good move for Pitt. The Panthers will be able to compete in basketball in The ACC though head-to-head competition in recruiting could get tougher for Pitt, and football won't be much different.

Pitt football fans will be better able to follow their favorite team to road games and the destinations are more attractive than in The Big East.

I think I am more familiar with The ACC than the average bear in Pittsburgh. Because of my 32 years of experience as the founding editor and editor emeritus with *Street & Smith's Basketball Yearbook,* the No. 1 annual of its kind in the country during that span, I had occasion to attend games and sit at courtside at North Carolina, North Carolina State, Duke, Wake Forest, Virginia, Georgia Tech, Boston College and Virginia Tech. I saw football and basketball games at South Carolina, when that was a member of The ACC. I saw a soccer game and some football games at the University of Virginia in the mid-90s.

I have interviewed Jimmy Valvano at N.C. State, Dean Smith and Roy Williams at North Carolina, Vic Bubas, Chuck Daly and Mike Krzyzewski at Duke, Skip Prosser at Wake Forest, John Hyder and

Bobby Cremins at Georgia Tech, Seth Greenberg at Virginia Tech and Leonard Hamilton of Florida State (when he was at Miami) and Terry Holland at Virginia. My visit with Valvano, Jimmy V, was one of the most exhilarating experiences I had in my career because he was so outgoing, engaging and so funny.

When it came time for my daughter Sarah to check out colleges we visited Virginia, Wake Forest, Duke, North Carolina and Virginia Tech. She ended up going to Virginia, where she graduated with Phi Beta Kappa honors, and North Carolina and Wake Forest were her next favorite choices. Our daughter Rebecca visited Virginia Tech, but thought the boys all looked like nerds.

My wife Kathie and I have already made plans to attend The Big East Basketball Tournament this March at Madison Square Garden and, looking down the road, we will miss our annual week in Manhattan. Madison Square Garden is still the mecca of basketball in the U.S.A.

We will definitely miss that experience.

But I have been to The ACC Tournament in Greensboro and in Charlotte and that is exciting stuff as well. They take college basketball more seriously down that way than they do in a city where Pitt is competing with the Steelers, Pirates and Penguins for attention.

Syracuse is actually a bigger loss than Pitt for The Big East because Syracuse was one of the original members and often led the nation in attendance with the Carrier Dome able to seat 33,000 or more. Jim Boeheim is a Hall of Fame coach.

Jamie Dixon had to agree to this, and I am sure Todd Graham was good to go, and probably happy the news got out on the same Saturday that his Panthers football team blew a big lead at Iowa and gave up 21 unanswered points to lose to the Hawkeyes. If Pitt improves its football program it can be an annual contender for the ACC championship.

Florida State and Clemson usually have good football teams.

It will be difficult for Pitt to out-recruit Duke and North Carolina in basketball.

Pitt has to pay a $5 million buyout to leave The Big East and is bound by contract to remain in the league for at least 27 months before moving on. Chancellor Mark Nordenberg has said he hopes to reduce that time frame for everyone's best interests. *(Pitt eventually paid $7.5 million in order to leave The Big East after the 2012–2013 school year.)*

Consider Nordenberg's comment. Nordenberg was once the Dean of the Pitt Law School and knows something about legal contracts. He also chaired some Big East committees and has been urging all the members to stay strong and united and not to depart the conference for greener pastures.

Pitt can be challenged on the moral aspect of this move. The Big East let Pitt into its club when Pitt needed such a boost to improve its floundering basketball program. These schools have worked together in tandem and, hopefully, harmony ever since.

Pitt was upset when Boston College, Virginia Tech and Miami all moved to the ACC. Now Louisville, for instance, is upset with Pitt for leaving The Big East and saying that Pitt is not a good fit for the ACC and adds nothing to the conference.

This is the same Louisville that once left the highly-regarded Missouri Valley Conference and more recently Conference USA to join The Big East. Hey, all of these schools act in self interest.

I don't like what is happening overall on the college athletic scene. I miss the storied Southwest Conference, for instance, but the times are a changing. I don't like tattoos, body piercings, and people talking on their cell phones when they are driving, or walking with their babies or children through the shopping malls, but I can't stop this degeneration of all that's good in this country.

When all is said and done I think this change will work out fine for Pitt. One can question school officials on moral grounds. Doesn't an agreement or a handshake mean anything any more?

I'm big on loyalty. I have been lucky to be married to the same woman for 44 years *(now 45)*. I have used the same printer for 20 of my books because the printer helped me get started. I don't forget that.

This sort of thing didn't happen when I was a student at Pitt in the early '60s. Back then, for instance, if Pitt gave a scholarship to a kid and learned that the kid wasn't that good they would never drive him off, or encourage him to transfer to another school.

Pitt honored its contracts back then.

There is no honor or any contracts that mean anything in college athletics these days. Show me the money, show me more television exposure, and show me the money.

Pitt has reneged on contracts it established with its own fans as far as seating for basketball and football games. This is a better deal for Pitt. That's it. I will get used to it because I have always been a big fan of The ACC.

My wife has always rooted against the teams that left The Big East in favor of The ACC. This will be a big test for her.

JAMIE DIXON
Pitt's basketball coach

MIKE KRZYZEWSKI
Duke's basketball coach

Why Priatkos pull for
Duke and Coach K

July 2010

This is a story of a beautiful relationship that has developed and endured over the past 23 years. Bill Priatko and his son Dan are devoted fans and admirers of the Duke University men's basketball program and its coach, Mike Krzyzewski.

They even know how to spell his name without having to look it up as I always do just to make sure I have it right. They share some common bonds: similar Eastern European ethnic heritage, strong spiritual devotion and Dan and Coach K. are both graduates of the United States Military Academy.

It was in July of 1989 that Bill Priatko first met Mike Krzyzewski. Coach K. was one of the marquee clinicians at the famed 5-Star Basketball Camp that was conducted annually at Robert Morris University. Priatko was employed at the time as the assistant athletic director in charge of support services for the student athletes at Robert Morris College, as it was known at the time.

They met on the sideline at the old Gus Krop Center and started chatting. Keep in mind that Priatko chats with the coin collectors at the turnpike toll booths. "Where are you from?" he says to one and all. Priatko has great personal skills and quickly developed a rapport with Coach K. And he told him about his sons, Dan and David, both graduates of the U.S. Military Academy. David, the younger of the two at 45, was then serving as a lieutenant colonel and deputy brigade commander in Iraq. It was his fourth tour there with the 3rd Infantry Division. (*David is now back in the States.*)

Priatko knew that Coach K. was a point guard and the team captain at West Point for a young coach named Bobby Knight. He showed Coach K. a copy of a media guide he had from Army that had a picture of Coach K. and Bobby Knight. "You sound like you know something about West Point," said Coach K. Bill thought he'd be interested in Dan's story.

Dan is disabled, the result of an auto accident shortly after his graduation at West Point. He was driving home to North Huntingdon when his car lost its traction on an ice-coated highway, Rt. 81 near Hazleton, Pa., and went off the road and struck the cement base of an overhead bridge. Dan didn't get the immediate medical treatment he required and suffered neurological damage that impaired his speech and his mobility. He's 50 and works part-time at a personal care center at Redstone Highlands in North Huntingdon.

I've heard him speak at sports banquets and it is inspirational stuff. You have to listen closely, but he commands that sort of attention with what he has to say.

Dan comes from a strong family. His mother, Helen, has been courageously battling cancer for more than 25 years, or the same span that the Priatkos have had this connection with Coach K. The Priatkos have spunk and staying power. They are a great family. There are two daughters, Debbie and Kathy, and they are terrific, too. Bill is 81, yet he looks like he could still play football.

He gets on his knees every morning to say prayers and to do push-ups. He also does sit-ups. I'm proud to have my family on his daily prayer list. I'm sure he prays for Mike Krzyzewski.

When Coach K. learned about Dan and his daily challenges he wanted to meet him. He was scheduled to depart Greater Pittsburgh Airport within the hour, however, and Bill told him that North Huntingdon wasn't just over the hill from the Moon Township campus. "I'll catch a later one," Coach K. said of his airplane schedule. "He's a West Pointer, isn't he?"

Bill Priatko persisted, knowing that Coach K. should catch his plane and meet Dan Priatko at a later date. Coach K. gave Bill a signed photo to Dan before he left. "To Dan, From one West Pointer to another," he wrote. They have been corresponding and meeting every year since that initial discovery of each other.

Coach K. has hosted the Priatkos each basketball season with complimentary seats for one game behind his bench at Cameron Indoor Stadium on the Durham, N.C. campus. I've seen them there when the TV cameras come Coach K.'s way during national telecasts of Duke games. The Priatkos always take a peek into the rafters at Cameron Indoor Stadium to check out the retired jersey of Dick Groat, who grew up in Swissvale and became the nation's top basketball player at Duke, and a baseball player good enough to bypass the minor leagues upon graduation from Duke and play for the Pirates.

That first year out of college, Groat was a starting guard for the Fort Wayne Pistons of the National Basketball Association—coached by Paul Birch who would later coach at Rankin High—as well as the starting shortstop for the hometown Pirates. Branch Rickey, the Pirates' GM, insisted that Groat give up pro basketball in favor of the Pirates. Groat, a great competitor, has always insisted he was a better basketball player.

Priatko knows the Groat story well and enjoys friendships and relationships with so many people in the sports world who came out of the Steel Valley and Western Pennsylvania. Priatko played football, baseball and basketball at North Braddock Scott, football at Pitt and had stays with the Steelers, Browns and Packers in the National Football League as a linebacker. He spent the entire 1957 season with the Steelers.

He went to training camp with Paul Brown's Cleveland Browns in 1959 where he became friends with Dick LeBeau. Priatko ended up playing on the team's "taxi squad," a group of reserve players who practiced with the team all year. LeBeau was among the last cuts in 1959 and LeBeau caught on with the Lions in Detroit and became one of the best defensive backs in the league. Paul Brown said it was one of his biggest mistakes in letting LeBeau get away. Priatko was among the last cuts by Cleveland the following year. I think Brown might have made a mistake there, too.

Priatko remained a strong admirer of Brown and still cherishes correspondence they exchanged through the years. Priatko has kept enough letters from famous people in sports to start a museum in his garage in North Huntingdon. He has letters he proudly shares from Bart Starr and Bob Skoronski, who starred for the Packers when Priatko competed for a roster spot at their camp in Wisconsin. The Priatkos spent a week on vacation this past year at the home of the Skoronskis in Boca Grande, Florida, not far from Sarasota. Bill called Chuck Noll, who lives in nearby Bonita Springs, during his visit to check up on the Steelers' former coach.

Priatko makes friends for the long haul. He worked at Kennywood Park as a high school student and he returns each summer to work the concession stand in the center of the amusement park. He greets and meets so many people and just loves the atmosphere. Loyalty is one of his many virtues.

Priatko planned to be in attendance with his family when LeBeau was inducted into the Pro Football Hall of Fame in ceremonies at Canton, Ohio on Saturday, Aug. 7. Priatko and LeBeau talk to each other on the telephone a few times each week, outside the Steelers' locker room after every home game, and have lunch together at the Steelers' UPMC Sports Complex at least once a month.

LeBeau is a beautiful fellow and this honor is well deserved for his credentials as a player, let alone his coaching achievements which didn't factor into his election. Russ Grimm of Scottdale, who starred as a lineman at Pitt and with the Washington Redskins and now coaches the Arizona Cardinals, was also in the 2010 HOF Class along with Jerry Rice of the 49ers and Emmitt Smith of the Cowboys.

Priatko, I knew, would be pumping all their hands over the weekend in Canton. I went to Canton many times with Priatko and his lifelong pal Rudy Celigoi, who played football at North Braddock Scott and at Rutgers, before becoming superintendent at Swissvale High and Woodland Hills High. So I know the landscape well and know what a great time Priatko would have attending all the dinners and breakfasts with the Hall of Fame class and his buddy LeBeau.

I've also been to the Duke campus on several occasions from my days as the editor of *Street & Smith's Basketball Yearbook* (1970–2003). I visited and interviewed Mike Krzyzewski and met his wife Mickie. They were an attractive couple. They treated me like an old friend. Mike even convinced one of his sneaker sponsors to take out an ad in *Street & Smith's Basketball Yearbook* after our visit.

Bill Priatko has always been an admirer of John Wooden, the basketball coach of all those national championship teams at UCLA, and mourned his passing at age 99 in June, 2010. Now the word is out that Dean Smith, the legendary basketball coach at North Carolina and a much-respected rival of Coach K., is having problems with short memory. I spent time with Coach Smith at the Chapel Hill campus, accompanied by my daughter Sarah when she was checking out college possibilities, and Coach Smith treated her like she was a gifted 7-foot center. He and Coach K. have always been class acts.

So Coach K, and Jim Boeheim of Syracuse and Jim Calhoun of Connecticut, are at the top of the heap as head basketball coaches in the college ranks.

I know how proud the Priatkos were when Coach K. directed the USA team to the gold medal with a perfect 8–0 record at the 2008 Summer Olympic Games in Beijing, China. Then he turned around and directed Duke to the NCAA men's basketball championship this past season. He was elected to the Basketball Hall of Fame in 2001.

Priatko was pleased when Coach K. turned down lucrative offers to coach in the NBA. Bill believes that Coach K. is a perfect fit for the college game where he can have a positive impact of the lives of so many young men.

Coach K. has presented the Priatkos with Duke T-shirts and golf shirts and jackets and all sorts of paraphernalia through the years. When Bill is not wearing his Steelers' Alumni attire he can often be found posing proudly in a Duke outfit of one kind or another.

Coach K. has corresponded faithfully with both of the Priatkos, and especially with Dan. He has signed such letters with this line: "From one West Pointer to another, Mike."

Coach K. tells Dan how much he admires him and his competitive spirit in dealing with his difficulties throughout his adult life. Dan was undersized for college football, but he was a running back and linebacker at Norwin High and as a place-kicker at Army and always a spirited athlete.

Both have told each other's stories in talks they have delivered at sports and church gatherings. "You inspire me," Coach K. has often told Dan. When he has presented Dan with a gift, Coach K. will salute him in a military manner. He also hugs him a lot.

If there's a break in the correspondence, Coach K. will come through and say, "Forgive me for not getting back to you sooner."

Bill Priatko has pointed out that Coach K. has often corresponded faithfully with Dan when they knew he was busy with basketball at Duke or on an international level. The Priatkos are faithful attendants at services at St. Nicholas Orthodox Church in Donora and love to talk about Father Igor Soroka, who has been the pastor there for 51 years. Krzyzewski told the Priatkos how his grandparents immigrated to America from Poland. His mother's parents started out in a coal mining town in Keisterville, Pa., not far from Uniontown. Mike's mother was born just outside of Keisterville.

Mike grew up in Chicago, but went back to Keisterville to a summer camp every year until he was 10 or 12. He suspects the purpose of such trips was to "teach you to know where you came from and to be proud of it."

He told the Priatkos, "I'm Polish and I'm proud of it. You guys are Ukrainian, so we're almost cousins. Where I grew up in Chicago, we had all ethnic groups represented. It was like a League of Nations."

Cameron Indoor Stadium, Coach K. is quick to point out, was named after Eddie Cameron, who grew up in Irwin and went to Norwin High School—the same school as David and Dan Priatko—and became the basketball coach and athletic director at Duke University. Toss in Dick Groat and you get the point that the Pittsburgh area has provided Duke with some great individuals who remain revered on the picturesque campus.

Priatko shared letters he kept from Coach K. Writing about Danny Priatko, Coach K. said, "He is an inspiration to all of us here at Duke. If all my players had his competitive spirit, we would win the national championship every year. One thing about West Pointers: we never quit."

Mike Krzyzewski added to his resume in the 2012 Olympic Games when he guided the U.S.A. to a gold medal again in men's basketball.

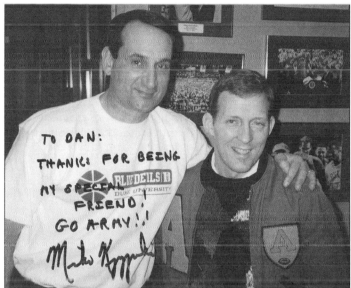

Duke Coach Mike Krzyzewski and Dan Priatko are both West Point grads.

Photos by Bill Priatko

Legendary ESPN basketball analyst Dick Vitale is a big fan of Dan Priatko and Pitt's basketball arena and fans.

When Duquesne, Pitt and Carnegie Tech
were in post-season football bowl games

There was a time when Duquesne, Carnegie Tech and Pitt all played in college football bowl games, and were among the nation's outstanding teams. Even then Pittsburgh could lay claim to the title of "City of Champions."

This was back in the late '30s, before I was on the beat, before I was even born (1942), so I had to look up most of the scant information remaining from those halcyon days. Carnegie Tech, now known as Carnegie Mellon University, was so good once upon a time that they defeated Notre Dame 19–0 at Forbes Field, Notre Dame's legendary coach Knute Rockne had so little regard for Tech that he wasn't even on the sideline that day. He instead was scouting a future opponent, thought to be a much better ballclub than the Tartans.

That occurred on November 27, 1926 and I knew about that upset because my mother, then a 19-year-old Mary Burns, was at the game and had a program to prove it. I wish I still had that program. It would be worth something. That Tech victory has been rated the fourth greatest upset in college football history by ESPN.

This column can serve as a history lesson for most Pittsburgh football fans. Some people dismiss talk of the past, saying it was before their time. But the Civil War was before my time and I still find it fascinating to read the stories of our country's deadliest war.

Tech's teams in 1938 and 1939 were nationally ranked. Following the 1938 season, the Tartans played in the Sugar Bowl where they lost to the No. 1 rated Texas Christian University or TCU team by the score of 15–7. Tech was ranked as high as No. 6 in 1938.

Their star player was quarterback Howard Harpster. I met him at a Curbstone Coaches Luncheon at the Roosevelt Hotel during my student days at Pitt in the early '60s. I know his son-in-law Dick Swanson, one of Pitt's most ardent athletic boosters.

Pitt's 1936 team went 8–1–1 and defeated Washington, 21–0, in the Rose Bowl. Pitt's 1937 team posted a 9–0–1 record, with the third consecutive scoreless tie with Fordham the only blemish on their schedule. Those were the days of Marshall Goldberg and "The Dream Backfield."

This is the 75th anniversary of Duquesne's appearance in the 1937 Orange Bowl, where they defeated Mississippi State, 13–12.

Duquesne won on a last-ditch pass from Boyd Brumbaugh to Ernie Hefferle. It was a 72-yard touchdown strike and it was reported that the pass was in the air for 69 of those yards.

That same Duquesne team defeated the Rose Bowl-bound Pitt team by 7–0 during that 1936 season. Clipper Smith was the coach of the Dukes and their center Mike Basrak was the first Duquesne player to be a first-team All-American. Basrak played for the Steelers in 1937 and 1938. I know I was introduced to Boyd Brumbaugh at a Curbstone Coaches Football Luncheon where I also met Howard Harpster. Brumbaugh's daughter bought a book from me at South Hills Village about ten or twelve years ago and told me some stories of her dad's sports exploits.

I have a personal history with Hefferle, who caught Brumbaugh's bomb for the game-winner. Brumbaugh, by the way, was a halfback on that Dukes' team. Hefferle hailed from Herminie, Pa., near Irwin. He coached the ends when I was at Pitt, and they included some great ones such as Mike Ditka of Aliquippa, Joe Walton of Beaver Falls and Mean John Paluck of Swoyersville who all went on to star in the NFL.

When I went to Miami in 1969 to cover the Miami Dolphins in their final season in the AFL, writing for *The Miami News*, I was re-united with Hefferle, who was the Dolphins' offensive line coach. He was a decent and fair fellow and had attributes I later associated with Chuck Noll when he coached the Steelers. In short, he was a class act. Hefferle helped me crack the ice with the coaching staff of the Dolphins, headed by George Wilson. Notice that Carnegie Tech played in the Sugar Bowl, Pitt in the Rose Bowl and Duquesne in the Orange Bowl. Those were elite bowls for years and especially in the late '30s when there were only five or six bowl games.

There were 35 bowl games this season. It seems like there is a bowl game on TV every day. West Virginia and Penn State have already played in bowl games, and Pitt will be playing in one this coming Saturday.

The Panthers are matched with Southern Methodist University or SMU in the Compass Bowl. It's the second straight year Pitt has played in this post-season bowl game in Birmingham, Alabama.

Somehow the Compass Bowl doesn't have the same ring as the Rose Bowl, the Cotton Bowl or the Orange Bowl.

But it could be worse. Among the 35 bowl games on this year's schedule were the Kraft Fight Hunger Bowl, the TicketCity Bowl, the Go-Daddy.Com Bowl, the Beer 'O' Brady's Bowl and Little Caesars Pizza Bowl, and the infamous Famous Idaho Potato Bowl.

Yes, there are too many bowl games these days, with whatever names money can buy, and it permits teams such as Pitt to get in with mediocre 6–6 records. When I was a senior at Pitt in 1963, the Panthers posted a 9–1 record and did not get into a bowl game.

Back in the late '30s, college football ruled in Pittsburgh. The sports pages were dominated by Duquesne, Pitt and Carnegie Tech, and the Steelers were dealt with in a few paragraphs.

The best example of the difference between the status of the collegians and the pros in those days comes in the case of Aldo "Buff" Donelli, a football and soccer star out of Morgan, Pa., in Bridgeville's backyard. In 1941, Donelli was the head coach simultaneously of Duquesne University and the Steelers. Elmer Layden was the NFL commissioner at the time. He had been a member of the Four Horsemen of Notre Dame in his playing days and had coached at Duquesne before moving on to Notre Dame as the coach.

He told Donelli he had to make a choice. He could coach at Duquesne or with the Steelers, but he couldn't do both. Donelli chose to stay with Duquesne. Of course, the Steelers were in the midst of a 1–9–1 record in 1941. I learned something else about Carnegie Tech that I didn't know before when I was doing research for this column.

In 1954, Tech went undefeated except for one tie. They were invited to play in the Sun Bowl in El Paso, Texas when bowl participation was truly for elite teams. The players on that Tech team voted to play in the post-season game, but the school administration ruled against it, saying it wanted to uphold its academic reputation. Playing in a bowl game was beneath the dignity of the Tech hierarchy.

Tech and Duquesne both gave up big-time football in the '40s because they could not afford the financial outlay necessary to compete on a national basis and, again in Tech's case, they thought it better to maintain its academic reputation. How about that, sports fans?

Duquesne Dukes in late '30s

Receiver Ernie Hefferle

Tailback Boyd Brumbaugh

Photos courtesy of Duquesne University sports publicity office

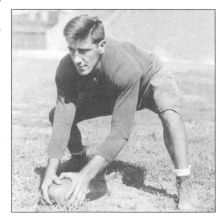

Center Mike Basrak who later played for Pittsburgh Pirates football team (1937–1938).

Not so fun times
in Happy Valley

November 2011

I picked a beautifully bound book off the shelf of a wall unit in our living room and checked the cover. A stern looking, bespectacled Joe Paterno, pictured perhaps in his heyday in the '80s, looked out at me. The title of the book was **THE PATERNO LEGACY**.

I wondered what that legacy would be now.

I knew that the Penn State football coach had signed this book for me when we shared a dais for a fund-raiser for the Foreman Foundation at the New Castle Country Club maybe a dozen years ago.

The personal message over his signature read:

"To Jim, Fun times—not so fun times. But it has been a great trip. Thanks for your enthusiasm for college sports. Joe Paterno."

I was scheduled to be the main speaker that night, a Pitt guy talking to mostly Penn State people after a golf outing to raise money for research on melanoma, the cancer that had killed one of its own, punter John Bruno. The Bruno Family lived in the same community we did, Upper St. Clair, and we'd see them around town at community gatherings.

I knew John Bruno and his parents and sister. I remember when John punted for three games for the Steelers during a players' strike. I remember that he came out of the shower room one day at Three Rivers Stadium, wearing only a white towel around his midriff, and that Art Rooney recognized him and said, "You're John Bruno, aren't you? The punter from Penn State."

John Bruno felt he had been certified as an official Pittsburgh Steeler by Rooney's gesture of recognition. Most owners of pro teams wouldn't recognize some of their own players in a police lineup. And Bruno was just a fill-in during the strike.

Art Rooney once offered the head coaching job of the Steelers to Joe Paterno, but Paterno turned it down because he felt more at home in the college game, more at home at Happy Valley. He saw himself as a college professor, not just a coach. The Steelers turned to Chuck Noll and Paterno always said the Steeler nation should have thanked him for turning down the job offer. He thought they got the right man for the Steelers.

A few days before that dinner at the New Castle Country Club, I received a phone call from the man who had invited me to speak, and he said, "We've been trying to get Joe Paterno to come to our dinner for five years, and he just called and said he could make it. But nothing's changed; you're still the main speaker."

I thought about that a moment and I came back, "No, I will defer to Joe Paterno. He's no warm-up act for Jim O'Brien."

I also knew that after a long day in the sun, and the long dinner and awards and so forth that Penn Staters would stay to hear Joe Paterno, but they might head home early after they'd heard him speak. I also knew that Joe Paterno would have no prepared message and that he would talk forever.

Still they stayed. This was Joe Paterno. They were ever faithful to Coach Paterno.

Paterno liked to rib me and needle me. He'd see me at an affair like the Dapper Dan Dinner or the Heinz History Makers dinner and he'd say, "I didn't know they let Pitt guys in here."

I picked him up at the Greater Pittsburgh Airport once in the early '80s to deliver him to the Curbstone Coaches luncheon at Three Rivers Stadium. On the way into the city, I told him about the death of my brother Dan and that I was having a difficult time dealing with it.

A year later, at the same event, he spotted me and said, "How's your sister-in-law getting along?" Paterno was like that. He never forgot a face or a name. No one has been saying that the past decade.

Last week was a terrible week for students and staff and alumni and parents of Penn State. They were stunned by the revelation of another story relating to showers in a locker room. The story broke that one of Joe Paterno's former assistant coaches, one who was thought to be next in line to succeed Paterno if he ever stepped down, Jerry Sandusky has been charged with being a serial predator of young boys—40 counts against him since 1994—someone who sodomized young boys who had been left in his care through The Second Mile foundation he had formed to help troubled youngsters.

It was a violation of everything Penn State stood for and it happened on Joe Paterno's watch, and he was guilty of looking the other way. Paterno and Penn State officials didn't report Sandusky's crime to proper authorities, to the police for starters.

They swept it under the proverbial carpet. As usual, they controlled the news. They even allowed Sandusky to stay on campus after he resigned as a coach at age 55. I remember I was puzzled at the time by his resignation because Penn State coaches stayed on the job for 35 and 40 years. Sandusky was in his prime as a coach. It didn't make much sense.

I went to one of Sandusky's fund-raisers for The Second Mile Foundation at the St. Clair Country Club a mile and a half from my home. There were lots of former Penn State football players there that day, too, and I was thinking about them last week and thinking how they must feel so betrayed.

I saw the students in the stands on Saturday at Beaver Stadium in a televised contest and I thought about them. They are the reason you have universities and colleges and schools, and they were stunned and bewildered, not knowing what to make of the week's disclosures and the ashes that were left in the wake of all that went down.

They deserved better, I thought.

I felt badly all week about this. I am a Pitt man all the way and Penn State was always the main rival, but I knew this was a stain on all schools. I worked in the Pitt athletic department for four years in the mid-80s and I know what goes on in a big-time athletic program on a college campus.

One thing I know is that they don't want to know. They are no different than most major corporations in this respect. If you tell them what's going on behind the scenes, if you tell them of any wrongdoing, of any NCAA violations in the house, you end up on the dirty end of the stick.

So I understand why the grad assistant, Mike McQueary, who witnessed what went wrong in the shower, what Coach Sandusky did to a 10-year-old boy when they were both wet and naked, didn't do the right thing and grab Sandusky and toss him against the wall and save that kid from being assaulted and abused. That happened in 2002. McQueary was 28 at the time: he was old enough to know what he should do, the proper response to what he was seeing in the shower room.

McQueary, who grew up in State College and knew the Sandusky family well, feared that he would be black-balled from college coaching for the rest of his life. Yes, he should have come to the rescue. He should have clearly detailed what went down when he spoke the next day to Joe Paterno. And Joe Paterno, who never had a boss at Penn State, should have known what he was obligated to do, by the tenets he had learned and preached during his long stay at Penn State.

Paterno came clean about that in the aftermath of the disclosure and wishes he had done more. I went to a breakfast program on Veterans Day last Friday and kept hearing how "Service above self" was the mainstay of the military.

But Paterno didn't want to make his program or Penn State at large look bad. The school president and other officials fumbled the ball as well. They didn't do what they were supposed to do. Joe Paterno has been a solid Catholic all his life. He knew the story of the Good Samaritan; he knew what one is supposed to do when they come upon someone in trouble.

After Saturday's game, when Penn State made a valiant effort but came up short against Nebraska in a Big Ten contest, a TV sports reporter interviewed the winning coach, Bo Pelini. He asked him what it was like to prepare his team for this game when all that was going on at Penn State was in the national news.

"It was a crazy week," replied Pelini, "with all those distractions."

That's it. See, to football coaches on most levels, anything outside the hundred-yard rectangle is merely a distraction. No matter how serious the incident may be it is still regarded as a distraction. Chuck Noll talked that way as well even though he, like Paterno, was smarter than most athletic coaches.

Few coaches read much more than playbooks and believe it's an x's and o's world. They would be better coaches if they read real books, such as biographies of great men and women. Joe Paterno had read some good books in his time, but that may have been too long ago.

I first met Joe Paterno in 1967, his second year as the head coach at Penn State. He had succeeded his mentor Rip Engle after the 1965 season. Engle was his head coach at Brown. It was a more civil time in the college athletic world. Pitt was playing at Penn State and you know that hasn't happened in a while. Penn State wasn't in the Big Ten at the time and Pitt wasn't in the Big East, ready to bail out for the ACC as soon as they can. There was some rhyme and reason to collegiate sports. Honor and loyalty were more important than a pay check.

Back then the host school would have a social mixer on the eve of the Saturday contest. Most college games were played on Saturday at that time. They didn't change the kick-off time to meet TV demands.

So the administrative staff, the coaches and the media would mix at a social gathering. There'd be drinks and snacks and off-the-record conversation. This particular party was held at the Nittany Lion Inn on the campus in State College.

Joe Paterno was holding court, sitting on a couch, holding a drink in one hand, and waving the other hand. He's Italian and most Italians talk with their hands as well as their mouths. It's in the DNA. The Irish know these things. They would do the same if they didn't have a drink in one hand and food in the other, or drinks in both hands.

I was there as the editor of an irreverent weekly tabloid called *Pittsburgh Weekly Sports*. Beano Cook, the sports information director at Pitt, was the co-publisher of the newspaper. I had returned from 21 months in military service in the U.S. Army, the last segment a 10-month stay in Alaska, to attend graduate school at Pitt. I was majoring in English Literature, which was Paterno's major at Brown University.

Paterno always thought of himself as a teacher. Chuck Noll saw himself in the same light. Paterno was lecturing the writers who'd come to the party. There were writers from New York City, Philadelphia, Harrisburg, Pittsburgh and State College. He wanted us to be more positive.

They don't have parties like this anymore. They've been gone from the collegiate scene for some time. The media has worn out its welcome. There's too much of an adversary relationship between the coaches and the media. That's a loss for everyone.

I see this Penn State mess in the same light. It's a loss for everyone. There are no winners.

I have shared my thoughts with my friend Franco Harris and he says that, like most of the media, I have it all wrong. Harris has his opinion and I have mine. We agree to disagree. I understand his pain about the Paterno and Penn State story. It should have been the Jerry Sandusky story.

I found another book in my collection about Joe Paterno and Penn State. It's called *For The Glory: College Football Dreams and Realities Inside Paterno's Program*.

It was written by an old friend from my college days, Ken Denlinger, a Penn State grad who went on to become a sportswriter and columnist for *The Washington Post*.

It's a positive book, detailing the experience of a recruiting class that came to Penn State in 1987 and stayed four and five years. It came out in 1994.

A paragraph on page 11 caught my attention:

"Paterno was embarking not only on what was perhaps the most critical part of the year but also of his future. Four days before Christmas, he would turn 61. Already, recruiters from the other heavyweight schools were using (his) age against him, planting in impressionable minds the thought that Paterno might not be around for their encore collegiate experience. Speculation was adrift that this might be his last class."

I had to smile, of course, when I read that paragraph. Boy, did he fool them. Then again, most of his ardent admirers think Joe didn't know when to quit. He stayed too long at the fair. He had seen Bear Bryant die soon after he retired as the head football coach at Alabama, and Paterno thought that could happen to him.

So he stayed. When TV commentator Andy Rooney died a week after he announced his retirement I thought of Joe Paterno right away. He'll hear about this, I thought, and it would reaffirm his feeling that he'd die without being the football coach at Penn State.

I thought he could serve as the ambassador of Penn State. Hey, it was called a "cow college" when he first came there in 1949 as an assistant to Rip Engle, who had been his coach at Brown. Paterno put Penn State on the map. He's the reason they have a 110,000-seat Beaver Stadium. They averaged 21,000 fans a game when Engle and Paterno first arrived from Brown in 1950. Penn State had 12,000 students and State College had 20,000 residents at the time.

Some day, I thought, they'll rename that stadium after Joe Paterno. They already had a statue of him on campus. *(It has since been removed from its site near the stadium and put in storage.)*

There was a writer who's been on campus the past year who is writing a new book about Joe Paterno. He's as stunned as any of the students on campus. He didn't see this chapter coming. Who did? He thought Penn State handled Paterno's dismissal poorly, though he thought it was something they had to do.

I think Joe Paterno has been a great coach and a good man most of his life. I think he set the standard for what a college coach and a college program should be. He became paranoid about the press and built a fort around his football program. The same thing has happened with all the Pittsburgh sports teams. There is too much security, too many ropes and barriers.

Beano Cook thinks Penn State did what they had to do though Cook believes they should have let Paterno finish this football season. I felt the same way. My wife disagrees. I'm sure a lot of people disagree.

Cook said Penn State allowed Paterno to gain too much power, the kind of power that permitted him to end the series with Pitt that went all the way back to 1893.

They say that power corrupts and absolute power corrupts absolutely. That's what happened at Penn State over the past decade.

Joe Paterno is the latest dictator in the world to be removed from his throne. He was 5-feet 8-inches tall—I had a half-inch on him—but he stood taller than anyone else in the room.

He had a little Napoleon in him.

Joe Paterno never missed an opportunity to make a point with me about something. He liked to needle me because I was a Pitt guy. Yet, when I went to work at Pitt in the mid-80s, Paterno penned a short note to my boss, Dr. Bozik, and commended him on hiring me. "This will make our job tougher," wrote Paterno.

His sports information director, and his right hand man, Jim Tarman, send me a congratulatory note. I still have both in my personal file. I just learned that Tarman suffers from dementia.

I'm familiar with dementia because my mother had it in the last four years of her 96 years. In the end, she didn't know what was going on. That might be a blessing for Tarman, a man who prided himself on his association with Penn State as much as Joe Paterno.

I believe Joe Paterno failed to do what needed to be done. He let Sandusky stay around the campus, have his own office. Paterno put the program ahead of children still to be abused by his former assistant coach. He left kids who already had been short-changed by their parents, or lack thereof, in danger.

He didn't do what needed to be done. One of my best friends feels that Paterno and everyone else at Penn State did what they had to do, and we are at odds about that now.

That will pass, I hope. As John Surma, the president and CEO of US Steel and the spokesman for the board of trustees at Penn State said, "Penn State University is more important than its football program." He said that when they fired Joe Paterno.

I felt the same way about Paterno's dismissal as I did when Dr. Bozik called me at my home one day to tell me that Foge Fazio had been fired as the football coach at Pitt. Foge had been a friend long before I went to work at Pitt. Foge was a Pitt man all the way and he would have stayed there the rest of his life if they had let him. He wanted to be Pitt's answer to his friend Joe Paterno.

They shared a bond beyond their Italian heritage.

Foge died two years ago, at age 71, much too young. I worry about Joe now. I think we all need to pray for Paterno and Penn State and hope they all survive this terrible tragedy. It's worse than what went down at Ohio State and Miami this year and probably has left Penn Staters as empty as the killings at Kent State and Virginia Tech in earlier times.

Anyone who has ever cared about college athletics has to grieve what has gone done at Penn State. Anyone who is a parent, anyone who cares about kids, and knows the difference between right and wrong has to be offended, has to feel let down.

Joe Paterno was the winningest coach in major college football history. He will turn 85 on December 21. It shouldn't have ended this way. A legendary coach has become a fallen hero; his legacy is ruined.

I'm sorry, Joe, but I guess this isn't a positive story. This is not a "fun time" in Happy Valley.

Author's tip: For more interesting reading on this subject, check out the book Game Over – Jerry Sandusky, Penn State, And The Culture of Silence – by Bill Moushey and Bob Dvorchak.

Jim O'Brien and Joe Paterno pose together in "a fun time" in 2007.

Suzie still feels
the Olympic spirit

Few Pittsburghers could appreciate the 2012 Summer Olympic Games as much as Suzie McConnell-Serio, the head coach of the women's basketball team at Duquesne University.

McConnell-Serio was a member of the gold medal-winning women's basketball team at the Olympic Games in Seoul, Korea in 1988 and the bronze medal-winning team in Barcelona, Spain in 1992. She won a gold medal in the 1991 World University Games.

"Every chance I got during an especially busy period for me (with recruiting, camps and practice for a pre-season tour of Canada), I watched the Olympic Games on TV with my family," she said with a gleam in her blue eyes. "I love the Olympic Games. When I'm in my family room I can cheer and root for them, agonize for them and feel their excitement and their pain. I know what it feels like.

"I won gold and I won the bronze; I know the disappointment of not living up to expectations."

There are many stories about athletes who overcame obstacles to succeed. Suzie's story is a good one because she is 5-feet 4-inches, and was often told she was too small.

She has modeled herself after the many coaches she has had from grade school, high school, college, international teams, Olympic teams and Women's National Basketball Association (WNBA) teams.

She is in her sixth season as the head coach of a continually improving Duquesne team and, at 46, is still as spunky and determined to win as when she was the only girl on the 4th and 5th grade teams at Brookline's Our Lady of Loreto Grade School.

Her coach then, Dan Kail, whom she still credits for her early development, predicted that someday she'd be playing for the U.S. Olympic women's basketball team.

Susie and her husband Pete Serio, who also grew up in Brookline, have four children: Peter (21), Jordan (17), Mandy (15) and Madison (14). Young Pete is in his fourth year of the pharmacy program at Duquesne, and the three girls are on the basketball team at Upper St. Clair High.

Suzie credits her parents, Tom and Sue, for her work ethic. "They always told me to stay busy," she said. "They taught me how to treat people."

Basketball is in the family DNA. Her brothers Tom and Tim have been coaches, and her sisters Kathy and Maureen played basketball, and Kathy is coaching in the WNBA. She has two other sisters, Patty and Eileen, and a brother Michael.

Tim, a successful coach at Chartiers Valley High, says of Suzie, "The one thing that sets her apart is her determination."

When Suzie went to Penn State University (1985–88) she became the school's first All-American in women's basketball. She majored in elementary education.

After her first Olympic Games experience, she was invited by Fran Mannion to be the coach of the girls' basketball team at Oakland Catholic. She took over the program in 1990–91 and won her first of three Class AAAA State Championships in 1993. In 13 years, McConnell-Serio averaged over 24 wins a season.

She blushed when asked how much money she was paid to coach at Oakland Catholic. "I was paid $4,000 a year," she said. So Suzie has paid her dues. Sometimes you have to start for little compensation.

Her husband Pete made sacrifices, too. He had to give up his job as a physical education teacher and basketball coach when his wife, after a six-year layoff from playing basketball came back to star as a player and then a coach in the WNBA.

"It's easier now because the kids are more self-sufficient," she said, "but I couldn't have done this without Pete's help. He held everything together for us. I was expecting our first child in 1990, and I had all four of my kids between 1991 and 1997, so we had a real juggling act. The kids have been great from the start."

Pete Serio said, "Her kids have been the No. 1 priority in her life."

Suzie still has the Olympic spirit. She is living proof that all things are possible if you have a positive attitude, truly believe in yourself, and are willing to work hard and make the personal sacrifices necessary to realize one's aspirations.

Wanting West Virginia
to go all the way in NCAA

April 2010

I wanted West Virginia University to win the NCAA men's basketball championship in 2010. I pride myself in being a Pittsburgh guy and a Pitt man, but I have no problem pulling for the Mountaineers to take the title at the tournament in Indianapolis.

I was rooting for Pitt and West Virginia in the Big East Tournament and then in the NCAA Tournament and that was before the Panthers bowed out in both tournaments.

"We root for them except when they're playing Pitt," proclaims my wife Kathie who has watched more of these games than I did.

Kathie roots for all the Big East teams. I remember when we went to New Orleans for the NCAA Final Four in early April of 2003 we attended a pep rally for Syracuse at our hotel and were happy the Orangemen won the title that year. You have to have a rooting interest to truly enjoy a sports contest.

Some Pitt people say they hate West Virginia and/or Penn State and they can't stand it whenever their teams have any success. They think it makes it more difficult for Pitt if those teams have success. I don't buy that. I want all the area schools to do well, and I feel the same way about our local high school teams.

We found ourselves in an unusual situation at the recent NCAA Women's Regionals at Pitt's Petersen Events Center. We wanted Ohio State to win because our daughter Sarah is on the teaching staff at The Ohio State University Medical School. But we wanted St. Francis of Loretto to make it a game and not get embarrassed by the more formidable Buckeyes. So we rooted for both teams. We saw several Pitt fans around us who were cheering for both teams in all the games. That's real sportsmanship.

I have always been a big fan of West Virginia's basketball and football teams. I know the school's sports history and tradition and I have met and interviewed many of the school's outstanding athletes and sports administrators. They are come of the classiest people I've met in my journeys as a sportswriter.

I met some of their athletic directors, Red Brown, Fred Schaus, Leland Byrd and Ed Pastilong, as well as his top aide, Tom Parsons, and they are good people. Now I like Oliver Luck

They don't come any better than Jerry West and Sam Huff, for instance, and Rod Thorn and "Hot Rod" Hundley are not far behind. I've spent time with three of West Virginia's football coaches, Gene Corum, Jim Carlen and Rich Rodriguez, and eight of their basketball coaches, George King, Schaus, Bucky Waters, Joedy Gardner, Sonny Moran, Gale Catlett, John Beilein and Bob Huggins and I liked all of them.

I got off to a bad start with Catlett—he didn't like most Pittsburgh writers—but we later made up and got along just fine.

I didn't care for Huggins when he was the coach at Cincinnati. He got into trouble there with off-the-court misbehavior and had a run-in with the school president that got him fired. He looks like a bouncer at an after-hours club and seems gruff. But I have been around him in recent years and he's good company. He has a great sense of humor, mostly self-deprecating, and he is genuine. Friends tell me of some of the kind things he does on his own without any fanfare. He likes to look tough, but he has a soft heart, as evidenced by the tears he shed soon after his Mountaineers had won the Big East title. "It means a great deal to me," he told an interviewer on the court, "because it's West Virginia."

Huggins was born in Morgantown and wears West Virginia on the sleeves of that dark warm-up suit he wears rather than a dress suit.

I have friends who are critical of Huggins and John Calipari of Kentucky because those two high-profile and well paid coaches carry some baggage from past jobs and they don't graduate many of their players. But they recruit the kind of kids who are more interested in the NBA than an MBA degree. They are paid to coach the college basketball team and in today's world when you're talking about Top 20 programs you don't have very good graduation rates. If there is hypocrisy to be scorned it's on the side of the school administrators who allow such sad academic situations to persist. The best players leave early to turn pro. It's tough to turn down that big money.

Huggins is a great recruiter and an even greater coach. He coaches to his players' strengths. We're blessed to have Jamie Dixon coaching the Pitt Panthers because he and his predecessor Ben Howland personally turned Pittsburgh into a good college basketball town. Huggins can coach with either of those men. His teams play hard at both ends of the court and they never concede anything.

Huggins knows the sports history of West Virginia University, too, and that's why it means so much for him to be the head basketball coach in his hometown. I'm pleased he hired former Duquesne coach Ron Everhart on his current staff.

Jerry West remains one of my all-time favorites. I remember when I was a student sports writer at Pitt in my freshman year of 1960–61 and I accompanied the school's cross-country team to New York City for an IC4A meet. We stayed at the Hotel Manhattan. One day I was in the lobby when the Los Angeles Lakers came through the door in their warm-up suits. They had come from a workout at the old Madison Square Garden nearby. I remember seeing West and Elgin Baylor and "Hot Rod" Hundley and how thrilled I was to see them. That was before Wilt Chamberlain joined the Lakers.

My brother Dan and I caught a bus from Pittsburgh to New York and saw the Lakers play the Knicks at the old Madison Square Garden and it was West who led a late charge, hitting one outside jump shot after another from way outside. Those field goals were worth only two points at the time, but the Lakers won that game.

I interviewed West at the Felt Forum in Los Angeles. He was so gracious and generous with his time and insights. At the conclusion of our interview, I asked him where the men's room was and he took me there. He didn't just give me the directions; he took me there. That tells you everything you need to know about Jerry West.

When I was working as the assistant athletic director for public relations at Pitt in the mid-80s, West would come to a game from time to time to scout college talent. When I asked him to go on the air with one of the broadcasters at half time he was always so willing to oblige and go on with Bill Hillgrove and Dick Groat. Or to have a picture taken. He could not have been more accommodating.

I interviewed Sam Huff at an NFL owners' meeting in Hawaii— how could I ever forget that setting?—and at the Pro Football Hall of Fame in Canton and at Three Rivers Stadium, among other places, and he was always so approachable and helpful. "I think it's important to treat the media well," he once told me. When he was finished playing pro football with the New York Giants, he became a broadcaster and also a public relations man for Marriott Hotels. He was well suited for both roles. Huff knew how to talk about the game and was a goodwill ambassador in every way. He, too, was born in Morgantown, but grew up in a primitive community in a coal patch about 30 miles away. Huff had humble beginnings and never forgot where he had come from and how far he had traveled in this world.

I had an opportunity to get to know Thorn well when I covered the New York Nets of the American Basketball Association and he was an assistant coach to Kevin Loughery. They helped me to learn how to play tennis. I helped Thorn get the head coaching job with the Spirits of St. Louis. He went on to hold a high position in the NBA league office and now he is a top executive with the New York Nets. When I was a student at Pitt, I used to travel by bus to Morgantown to see Thorn play at the old Mountaineer Field House. I also saw him play at the Pitt Field House. He and West and Hundley were all All-American performers.

I met Hundley when he was doing color for the New Orleans Jazz and then the Utah Jazz. Hundley also came from humble beginnings and liked to share funny stories about his early years. I remember Hundley holding court in the lobby of a hotel in Houston at an NBA All-Star Weekend. He was telling everyone about how his daughter had a date with the son of John Havlicek, the former star player of the Boston Celtics.

"You know how you're supposed to have a talk with your daughter before she goes out on a date?" he asked his audience. "I said to her, 'Listen if he tries anything...let him!' Can you imagine the genes at work there? What a basketball player they could produce!"

A few years back, I was traveling from North Carolina to Columbus, Ohio and we traveled through West Virginia from end to end. We entered the state at the southeastern tip. We stopped at Princeton, the hometown of Thorn. Later, as we traveled those wonderful highways that cut through the mountains of West Virginia that Sen. Robert Byrd got federal dollars to pay for, I spotted a sign for Cabin Creek. "There's a town I wanted to visit since I was 14," I told my wife Kathie. "They called Jerry West the Zeke from Cabin Creek. He hated that name, by the way." We stopped at Cabin Creek and I took some photographs. Then, we got to our destination for that night, Charleston, where we stayed at a hotel. Charleston was the hometown of "Hot Rod" Hundley.

"Do you realize," I asked Kathie, "that today we visited the hometown of the three greatest basketball players in the history of West Virginia University?"

"I know," Kathie came back, resignedly and somewhat sarcastically, I thought, "that's why I love to travel with you."

West Virginia was in the Final Four for the first time since 1959, when Jerry West was a junior. So this team, led by Da'Sean Butler, was causing the media to talk about West and Hundley and some of those early heroes.

One last West Virginia story: I traveled to Morgantown soon after I got married in August of 1967 to interview Jim Carlen, the West Virginia football coach. It was for a story for ABC-TV Sports. West Virginia was going to be featured in one of their telecasts that fall. I had planned on staying in Morgantown for two days to do the interviews. My wedding band caught Carlen's attention.

"That looks new," he said. I told him I had just gotten married the week before. "You better get home to your bride," he advised. "I'll stay with you longer today so you can get what you need. Then you get on home."

And you wonder why I'm able to root for West Virginia. I can hear John Denver singing about country roads and Blue Ridge Mountains.

WVU coach Bob Huggins directs Da'Sean Butler in Big East action.

Orlando Antigua and Ron Everhart are top basketball coaches. Antigua, a former Pitt basketball player and director of basketball operations for Jamie Dixon, is an assistant on John Calipari's staff at the University of Kentucky. Everhart has left Duquesne, where he improved the program considerably, and is now reunited with an old friend, Bob Huggins, at West Virginia.

We can learn so much
from Joe Paterno's words

Joe Paterno always liked being Joe Paterno. He played the part so well. It's like the way Mike Ditka plays the part of Mike Ditka. Once they were so serious and then, as they got older and wiser, they learned to smile and poke fun at themselves and the image they projected. Paterno had his disheveled part down to perfection.

Paterno started playing the part of Joe Paterno the way Peter Falk played the part of Colombo, the way Redd Foxx played the part of Fred Sanford in Sanford and Son. When it was his turn to speak at an awards dinner or some kind of testimonial, Paterno was never slick. He always appeared to be, like his hair, in complete disarray.

He could be real serious and still smile at what he said. There was a gleam behind those thick eyeglasses. There was a light in the attic.

Paterno liked to pontificate. I have been accused of doing the same. Maybe that's why Paterno appealed to me. I paid attention when Paterno spoke, and I always came away with a few gems, something to think about, some thing to try and do. For most of his 85 years, Paterno placed the bar high and expected us all to reach for the sky.

I saw Paterno's picture on the front page of both the Sunday daily newspapers, and read that he was growing weak, and that he wanted his family to be with him to say goodbye, that his doctors weren't optimistic. But I didn't know that he had died when I went out to Robert Morris University in the early afternoon on Sunday to see a high school basketball classic and to participate in a Hall of Fame induction ceremony conducted by the Pittsburgh Basketball Club.

I was in good company, getting honored with some outstanding coaches, former players, sportswriters and contributors to the game. It was Jerry Conboy, who had coached with distinction at South Hills Catholic High School and Point Park College, when those schools were known by those names, who told me that Joe Paterno had died that morning.

My heart ached to hear that, though I knew it was coming. I knew it was coming from the moment the Penn State hierarchy fired him as the head football coach at State College, and when they piled it on with more hasty decisions and punishments, and when the word got out that he had lung cancer, and had fallen and broken some bones at his home on the campus.

Joe Paterno never wanted to quit coaching because he feared that he would die if he didn't have something meaningful to do. His friend Bear Bryant had died soon after he retired as the football coach at Alabama. That's why Paterno wouldn't step aside, even when it was time to do so.

I recall being with Jimmy Cannon, the great New York sportswriter, when he was covering a fight in his early 60s. A writer from England approached him and asked, "Jimmy, when are you going to retire and rest on your laurels?"

Cannon was outraged. "Maybe I don't have as many laurels as you do," he responded with a snarl.

Cannon roared at me. "Who the hell is that hump?"

Joe Paterno might have died on Sunday simply because he had gotten old and frail. My father-in-law, Harvey Churchman, died when he was 85. I'd sign a warranty right now if someone could guarantee that I'd live till I was 85. But it hurt to hear the news just the same.

The crowd at the Sewall Center was asked to stand and observe a moment of silence in memory of Joe Paterno.

Then a man named Joe Tucci sang "God Bless America." Joe Paterno always enjoyed hearing that song, and singing along with it.

I believe I will always remember that setting and that solemn salute when Joe Paterno's name comes up in the conversation.

On Sunday night, after watching the National Football League's championship games, I went to my files and pulled out the Joe Paterno folder, filled with newspaper and magazine clippings, yellow legal pads with interview notes scrawled from top to bottom, and I pulled out some books I had on Joe Paterno.

The team that should have won lost in both NFL contests, and I thought about how Paterno probably would have been watching those games if he had been alive and well. Life is often about difficult losses.

I think there are at least 18 books about Paterno and others in the works at this time. There's one in the works that will deal with the Jerry Sandusky sex scandal that ripped apart the University in recent months. Joe Paterno was one of those at Penn State who did not deal with that issue properly, trying to sweep it under the carpet so the Penn State image as a school and football program would not suffer any setbacks.

The cover-up, as in so many situations, ended up worsening the situation. Joe Paterno became one of its victims.

Some of my best friends feel that Paterno did what he had to do, but I don't agree with that. Franco Harris has debated the subject with me, and I can appreciate his loyalty to his college coach, someone who helped him become a man. Joe Paterno was one of the most powerful people on the campus and I think he didn't do enough.

It points up how one can lead an exemplary life and make one wrong choice, one wrong step, and smear a lifetime of good works. It only takes one bad moment to mess up a life well lived.

When I worked as the assistant athletic director for public relations at Pitt in the mid-80s, I had a wise secretary named Bea Schwartz. She was something else. But she was smart. And funny.

"If someone steals your Cadillac," she once told me she had told one of her sons, "you can replace it. But if someone steals your reputation you can never get it back."

He was called Joe Pa and he was called St. Joseph. He was a practicing Roman Catholic and Paterno took pride in his religious bearing and upbringing. He preached that they were doing it right at Penn State.

In the book, *For The Glory: College Football Dreams and Realities Inside Paterno's Program,* written by an old friend, Ken Denlinger, I read where Paterno and his staff used to reassure parents of prospects by saying "You can trust us with your son."

When I read that, and saw references to Jerry Sandusky, the man who coached the linebackers and was regarded as a defensive genius in the college ranks, it took on a whole new meaning from the way it was written back in 1994. Who knew that Sandusky could not be trusted with anyone's sons?

There is a Penn State Hall of Fame on the campus and there is a framed letter that was sent to Paterno by President Gerald Ford, who had played football with distinction at the University of Michigan in his heyday.

Ford's letter had this line: "It thrills me to see how everyone loves and respects you."

That's the life Joe Paterno enjoyed at Penn State. When that was gone, I don't think he wanted to be around anymore.

When I was reading through all my Paterno stuff on Sunday night I came upon some quotations that had been culled from his lifetime of trying to teach us how to live.

They are worth repeating. Like Chuck Noll and so many of the coaches I've known, the best ones saw themselves as teachers.

"Success without honor is an unseasoned dish; it will satisfy your hunger but it won't taste good," Paterno once said.

Here's a sampling of some of his sayings that apply to so many situations we encounter in our daily lives:

"Publicity is like poison. It doesn't hurt you unless you swallow it."

* * *

For salesmen: "You have to perform at a consistently higher level than others. That's the mark of a true professional."

* * *

"Besides pride, loyalty, discipline, heart and mind, confidence is the key to all locks."

* * *

Talking about those bland Penn State football uniforms: "It's the name on the front of the jersey that matters most, not the one on the back." That didn't make sense because there are no names on the back of Penn State uniforms.

* * *

307

"Believe always down in your heart that you're destined to do great things."

* * *

Here's one that really strikes home in the wake of what has gone down at Penn State in recent months: "The minute you think you've got it made, disaster is just around the corner."

* * *

Here's one that explains why Paterno was lost when he was no longer held in such high esteem: "Losing a game is heart-breaking, losing your sense of excellence or worth is a tragedy."

* * *

Here's one that the Pitt basketball team should hear: "You need to play with supreme confidence, or else you'll lose, and the losing becomes a habit."

* * *

"Set your sights high, the higher the better. Expect the most wonderful things to happen, not in the future, but right now."

* * *

"I still haven't gotten that little something out of my system that I'm still not a little kid going to a football game. I'm excited."

* * *

"A mistake is always forgivable, rarely excusable and always unacceptable."

* * *

A man who met Jerry Conboy for the first time asked him if he missed coaching basketball. Conboy, who is nearly as old as Paterno, didn't hesitate in his answer. "Yes, I do. I'd go out on the court right now and show these kids how to do it, how to play basketball the right way. I don't think you ever lose the desire to coach and teach."

Keep some of Paterno's sayings in your night stand and refer to them once in a while. If you adhere to them you will sleep better.

"What you are as a person is far more important than what you are as a basketball player."
—UCLA's legendary coach John Wooden

Real sports fans are
there till the final buzzer

February 2012

I was thinking about basketball and hockey and football and how fans have been behaving in Pittsburgh the past few months. Then John Calipari came on the TV screen. I like John Calipari. He is the head basketball coach at the University of Kentucky, one of the storied programs in the history of the game.

I had the privilege of meeting and interviewing Adolph Rupp, the legendary "Baron of Basketball," on the Lexington campus back in the mid-70s, and I know a lot about what the Wildcats have accomplished through the years.

I had a chance to meet other coaches at Kentucky, such as Joe B. Hall, Rick Pitino and Tubby Smith, and they all felt privileged to coach the Wildcats.

I first met John Calipari when he was a graduate assistant coach to Roy Chipman at the University of Pittsburgh in the mid-80s. I like the way Calipari carries himself. He is a great coach and recruiter and few coaches speak as well about what they do as Calipari. He comes from Moon Township and played at Clarion University and takes pride in his Western Pennsylvania and Pittsburgh ties. There was a time when he would have been happy to be the Pitt basketball coach.

His Kentucky team was 19–1 at the time and ranked No. 1 in the country. He said he wouldn't mind if his team lost a few games because it might serve them well in the long run, when it really counts around post-season tournament time, when the NCAA championship is on the line.

Asked to explain his position, Calipari said, "When it doesn't go your way, how do you react?"

I had to smile. I have always thought it was interesting to see how teams and athletes and coaches and fans react when it doesn't go their way.

That's why I have not panicked because the Pitt basketball team has been struggling this season, why I didn't give up on the Penguins when they weren't playing that well and why I am still not stewing over the Steelers' defeat by the Denver Broncos in the AFC playoffs.

Hey, these programs have all given us more than our share of great times. I'm not going to give up on them now.

We are spoiled in Pittsburgh. We think our teams are always supposed to win, whether we are talking about pee-wee, grade school, high school, sandlot, college or pro teams. People think the Super Bowl is on the Steelers' schedule and anything less than claiming the Lombardi Trophy is a disappointing season.

Hockey fans here think the Penguins have to be a contender for the Stanley Cup for the season to be successful. It goes on and on. At least the Pirates' fans are satisfied with a win here and there, knowing their team isn't going to challenge for any kind of championship. In a sense, I think the Pirates' fans are the most fervent and faithful fans of all.

Are we only fans of our teams if they are winning?

That's a question for you to ponder today.

Pitt lost eight consecutive games this season before they beat Providence at the Petersen Events Center on Wednesday last week. I was more disappointed in the Pitt basketball fans than I was in the Pitt basketball team.

Fewer fans started showing up for the games, including the high rollers who sit at courtside in the most expensive seats, and more fans started leaving early, as soon as they figured the game was lost.

Even students who love to strut their stuff for the national TV cameras with their sometimes boorish behavior started staying in their dorm rooms rather than fill the student section at The Pete. Just for the record, I don't like it when fans insult the visiting team, and they influence the outcome of a contest by being a constant distraction. Doesn't anyone watch the game anymore?

The Penguins' fans became disenchanted when the Penguins lost six in a row, but those same fans were fast to jump back on the bandwagon when the Penguins won seven in a row.

Again, I ask, are we only fans of our teams when they are winning?

As a writer, I know that some times the story is better because a team has lost.

Art Rooney used to say, "If I weren't an owner I'd want to be a sportswriter and I would go to the losing locker room first because that's where the action is."

I have always rooted for the home teams in my heart—there's no cheering in the press box—because I know Pittsburgh is a better place to live when the teams are winning than it is when they are losing. It's good for business. It's good for the collective spirit of the city.

But some fans need to get a life.

They shouldn't rely on their sports teams to make them winners. They should rely on themselves and their own families to be winners. How are they faring in the game of life? How are they performing in their own jobs? Are they working as hard as they want their favorite teams to work so they can succeed? Are they hustling?

It isn't that difficult to understand how basketball is to be played well. As far as hockey is concerned, I think things just happen. You have to play hard and have some basic skills to succeed in either sport, but hustle will take you a long way in both.

I grew up in Hazelwood and we had a pretty outstanding coach come out of our community. His name was Pete Dimperio, and his Westinghouse High School football team ruled the City League in the '50s and '60s when I first became seriously interested in the sports pages of our daily newspapers.

Before he coached at Westinghouse, however, he coached some sports teams at Herron Hill Junior High School in the heart of The

Dave Wannstedt, defensive coordinator of Buffalo Bills, with Pitt men's basketball coach Jamie Dixon.

Dr. John Naismith, who invented the game of basketball at a YMCA gym in Springfield, Mass. in 1891, is shown explaining the game to his grandchildren.

Hill district. While there, he was asked to coach the basketball team and they even had a tennis team way back when. He admitted he knew nothing about either sport. But he knew how to coach kids. He knew how to motivate them, no matter the game.

Dimperio was a funny guy, and he poked fun at himself and the kids he coached, and was a hit on the local sports banquet circuit. Like Calipari, he could talk a good game as well as coach a good game.

Once I heard Dimperio talk about his basketball coaching prowess. "We were struggling and losing this game, and I called time out," he said. "The kids huddled around me and they looked into my eyes seeking some wisdom and what they needed to do. I looked them in the eyes and I said, 'Put the ball in the basket.' They went back out and they started to make their shots, and we went on to win. Everyone thought I was a helluva basketball coach."

Sometimes it's that simple.

One of the main reasons that Pitt wasn't winning games in The Big East was because they weren't putting the ball in the basket. Then, too, they're just not as good a team this year as they have been for so many years under Ben Howland and Jamie Dixon.

Dixon won more games faster than Adolph Rupp and a lot of other legendary coaches, but suddenly there is disenchantment with him and how he coaches, and the caliber of the ballplayers he brings to Pitt. That's ridiculous. We are so lucky to have Jamie Dixon as the basketball coach at Pitt.

I went to see some high school basketball games in a tournament sponsored by the Pittsburgh Basketball Club at Robert Morris University on a Sunday afternoon late last month.

My local team, Upper St. Clair High School, was playing the team from Aliquippa High School. The scoreboard didn't identify the teams by name, so I wasn't sure which point totals belonged to which teams when I arrived midway through the game.

I assumed Aliquippa was winning because they always have such great athletes. They looked much faster and more athletic than the kids from Upper St. Clair. It was five white kids against five black kids, five rich kids against five poor kids. Is it any wonder I thought Aliquippa was killing Upper St. Clair.

It turned out I was wrong and it was Danny Holzer's team that was winning by a good margin. They weren't as athletic as Aliquippa, but they were more team-oriented and, most important of all, they were making more of their shots.

I had a chance to chat with Mike Zmijanic, or Coach Z as he is known, during the game. Mike coaches the football team at Aliquippa and he used to coach the basketball team as well, and he was terrific at both assignments. Now he is the athletic director and coaches the football team.

He took exception to something another high school basketball coach had said about how if you have better players you will win most of your basketball games. "That won't happen if you don't let the other team get their shots," said Zmijanic. "If you swarm all over them, and deny their best shooters from getting the ball, you can beat a better team. If you hustle you can upset another team with superior talent."

Coach Z shared another story I liked. His team was losing in a basketball game and they turned it around in the second half and came away with a victory. "My wife would ask me later what I said at half-time to turn things around," said Coach Z. "I told them, 'Play better.'"

I like Coach Z because he also takes pride in being a good English teacher at Aliquippa High School.

Billy Shay played basketball at Pitt in the late '50s and he has coached at Community College of Allegheny County (CCAC) forever, or so it seems. He was among a group of local basketball coaches honored at an awards brunch held by the Pittsburgh Basketball Club last month.

There were different opinions about what it takes to win. Shay was in the company of some great basketball coaches. "No matter how good as coaches we might think we are," said Shay, "if you have better players than I do you will probably beat us."

Jerry Conboy, who coached with so much success at South Hills Catholic and Point Park College, when those schools went by those names, also said you have to have the players to win, and that was seconded by Dick Black, who coached for a long spell at Mt. Lebanon High School.

I like to talk to Black about basketball because I believe he knows his stuff. He coached for 32 years and never drew a technical foul.

He sat on the bench and didn't scold or swear at the referees or his players. He kept a rolled up program in his hand and let his players play the game the way he coached them to do in practice.

I covered the New York Knicks when they won their first NBA title in 1970 and their coach, Red Holzman, believed that "you should coach them at practice and let them play in the game."

Jamie Dixon is out on the playing floor more than he is on the bench at Pitt games. Most of the coaches these days in college ball are out on the court. They move up and down the sidelines, the way over-zealous parents do at pee-wee soccer games, telling the kids what to do. They micro-manage the game.

"I think you're supposed to coach them so they can make decisions during the game," said Black. "I don't believe coaches should be able to call time outs from the sideline. The players should have to call for time outs when the coach tells them to call time out.

"Of course, I'd like to see them make the coaches stay on the benches like they once did."

One of my pet peeves with basketball on every level these days is that there are twice as many coaches on the benches as there need to be.

I think it started when Phil Jackson was coaching the Chicago Bulls. Jackson knew he didn't know much about basketball strategy so he brought in wise college coaches to handle the x's and o's on the blackboard. He got Johnny Bach and Tex Winter to do that, and he had Frank Hamblen who'd worked with some good coaches in pro basketball and knew how to act as an assistant coach.

Before you knew it, there were five coaches on the sidelines with the Chicago Bulls, and the idea spread like wildfire. Now you see five or six business suits on the bench before a ballplayer appears. The head coach is five or six seats away from any of his players. That's absurd. He has a meeting with his assistants before he says anything to his ballplayers.

The coaches' union may like the idea because it means that twice as many basketball coaches have jobs these days. The unemployment rate in this country is high enough. The same thing happened with referees. They decided they needed three rather than two in the NBA and then it was necessary in the college ranks, and now it's needed in high school and elementary school. Now there's a fourth official in hockey.

When I was a kid, two officials worked our sandlot football games, one on each side of the ball, and no one complained. Less whistles were blown and there were fewer stoppages in play.

As an observer of basketball games, I know I have gotten smarter about the sport as I have grown older.

When I was a teenager, my favorite basketball player was Wilt Chamberlain. I was the smallest kid playing basketball on the street where I lived, yet I was fond of following the career of Chamberlain, a giant of a man at a perfectly proportioned 7-feet 2-inches. Why did I fall in love with Wilt Chamberlain when I was a kid on Sunnyside Street?

Wilt was known for his "finger tip-roll" shot. He would allow the ball to roll off his large right hand into the basket. I had that technique down pat, and liked to show my friends how it was done.

I quickly realized however that it wasn't smart to master such a shot when you were a midget. The shot, to be successful, required that you could get your hand above the rim, and just let the ball roll off your fingertips into the twine.

So I stopped practicing that shot.

Michael Jordan says you should never practice a shot you are not going to get in a game.

I met Wilt Chamberlain at Kutsher's Country Club in the Catskills where he would play in a summer exhibition game to raise funds for Maurice Stokes, a Pittsburgh born and bred basketball player who was left paralyzed by a basketball fall.

I was thrilled to talk to Wilt Chamberlain and he got a kick out of my story of my failed attempt to emulate his famous shooting form. To me, Wilt Chamberlain is still the great basketball player of all time.

It's a game where it pays to have size to go with your skills. But the most basic element of the game is that you have to put the ball in the basket.

And if you're going to be a fan, don't be a fair-weather fan. Stick around and see how your coach and his players deal with adversity, to see if they stay the course and keep competing, to see if they give it all they have to give.

You owe them that much. You owe yourself that much.

Swissvale's Dick Groat
loves March Madness

March 2008

The 2007–2008 college basketball season was a great one for Dick Groat. His Pitt Panthers posted their seventh straight 20-victory season and seemed a good bet to be invited to the NCAA men's basketball championship tournament, and Groat enjoyed several personal tributes along the way.

Groat, who grew up and still resides in Swissvale, is best known in Pittsburgh as an outstanding shortstop for the Pirates, teaming with second baseman Bill Mazeroski for one of the all-time best double play combinations in Major League Baseball. Groat led the National League in batting in 1960 with a .325 average and was named the league's MVP while leading the Pirates to a World Series championship season.

He had a fine 14-year big league career, playing for the Pirates, Cardinals, Phillies and Giants from 1952 to 1967, interrupted by a military stint. He batted .317 one summer in St. Louis. His career batting average was .286. That would make you a lot of money these days.

But Groat was a great basketball player, too. He was a first-team All-American at Duke in 1952 and was named the College Basketball Player of the Year. He is the only player ever to lead the nation in scoring and assists. He was a second team choice the year before. He was also an All-American baseball player as a shortstop for an outstanding Duke nine.

He played one season (1952–53) with the NBA's Fort Wayne Pistons, averaging nearly 12 points per game, before Branch Rickey, the Pirates' general manager, made him give it up because he feared that Groat would get worn down playing two pro sports.

Back on November 18 (2007), twelve days before his 77th birthday, Groat was inducted into the charter class of the newly created College Basketball Hall of Fame in Kansas City, Missouri. On December 20, when Pitt played Duke at Madison Square Garden, Groat was given a standing ovation by 18,000 fans when his Hall of Fame selection was announced to the crowd during a timeout. The Panthers went on to defeat Duke with a buzzer-beating 3-point shot by Levance Fields.

That night was special to Groat in so many ways. "I live and die with the Pitt basketball team," he proudly says. "Duke's my alma mater, but I'm one of Pitt's biggest fans now. I root for Duke in every other game they play."

Groat was introduced in similar fashion at one of the home games at the Petersen Events Center, and drew a long and warm applause from Pitt's fans.

Groat was also invited back to Duke on Saturday, February 9, when the Blue Devils were entertaining Boston College in an ACC

315

contest, to be recognized at halftime for his Hall of Fame induction. His jersey has long been retired at Duke, and a replica remains on display in Cameron Indoor Stadium.

He has been honored on more than one occasion at the annual Sports Night dinner at the Thompson Club in West Mifflin.

On February 23 of 2008, after Jeannette's Terrell Pryor put up some unbelievable numbers in the WPIAL's Class AA championship game against Beaver Falls—39 points, 24 rebounds, 10 blocked shots, six assists—his jubilant coach, Jim Nesser, proclaimed, "What can I say? He's the greatest athlete in the history of the state of Pennsylvania."

Maybe, coach, but not yet. Think about what Dick Groat accomplished. And he wasn't a bad golfer either. Groat continues to own and operate the Champion Lakes Golf Club in Bolivar, Pennsylvania, not far from Ligonier. Tell Terrelle Pryor about Groat and some of the guys from these parts who have had great sports careers to keep things in their proper perspective. I've seen Pryor play and he is impressive. Let's say he has great potential.

Here's a list, and it's not a complete one, to check out during study period of some of the greatest athletes ever to perform in Pennsylvania schools:

Jim Thorpe, Pistol Pete Maravich, Arnold Palmer, Joe Namath, Wilt Chamberlain, Dan Marino, Dick Allen, Christy Matthewson, Stan Musial, Arnold Galiffa, Johnny Unitas, Norm Van Lier, Reggie Jackson, Josh Gibson, Frank Thomas, Bill Tilden, George Blanda, Earl "The Pearl" Monroe, Roy Campanella, Art Rooney, Chuck Bednarik, Jack Twyman, Mark Bulger, Armon Gilliam, Jack Ham, Pete Duranko, Maurice Lucas, Maurice Stokes, Jim Kelly and Honus Wagner.

Groat gets worked up while analyzing the action alongside Bill Hillgrove on Pitt's basketball radio broadcast team. This is Hillgrove's 44th consecutive year doing this, and Groat has been with him for 34 of those years. "It's my good fortune to work with the best play-by-play announcer in the country," says a partial pal. Groat and Hillgrove both refer to each other as "roomie" and "my best friend."

Groat gets choked up every year on Senior Day (so do I), as it's difficult to see the Pitt players in their last game on campus. "Billy and I both got all teared up," Groat told Ronald Ramon, one of those seniors, during a post-game radio interview after Pitt defeated DePaul. Groat is old enough to be a grandfather to the present-day players, so it's understandable that he often addresses them as "young man" and "son" when he is talking to them.

"It's been fantastic," said Groat, when I talked to him about his experience this season. "I had no idea a lot of these tributes were coming my way. I have always told people I was a better basketball player than a baseball player. So it's nice to be recognized so many years after playing.

"I think our coach, Jamie Dixon, and the Duke coach, Mike Krzyzewski, may have teamed up long-distance to arrange the tribute at Madison Square Garden. And when Jamie came all the way to Kansas City for my Hall of Fame induction that meant a lot to me. It sure did.

"My association with Pitt all these years has been fantastic," Groat continued. "Basketball's always been my first love and I'm grateful to Pitt that they've kept me on doing the radio broadcasts. Traveling with the Pitt basketball team and Bill Hillgrove is something I truly love.

"It's kept me young. I live and die with these basketball games. The fans never seem satisfied, but these twelve years have been the golden era of Pitt basketball. Ben Howland and Jamie Dixon have done things that were never done here.

"It took me awhile to accept their basketball philosophy, I must admit. They stress defense, and I was always an offense-oriented guy. They've lost something recently from the way they usually play. They've been completely out of sync. But I liked the way they played their final home game against DePaul. That may have been their finest team effort of the season."

Groat was looking ahead to the Big East Basketball Tournament at Madison Square Garden and to the NCAA Tournament. "I'm hoping they can win four more games so the seniors will be part of 100 wins in their four-year careers," he said.

Groat has become a great ambassador for Pitt and Duke basketball. He promotes Pitt wherever he goes. I've heard Groat speak at many sports luncheons and dinners and he always speaks glowingly about the Panthers. At the same time, he says he never considered going to Pitt when he was a senior at Swissvale High.

"I played ball in the summer with some of the Pitt guys," explained Groat, "and they told me to stay away from Pitt. I liked to run and shoot. Their coach, Doc Carlson, is in the Basketball Hall of Fame, but he played a style of basketball that wouldn't have suited me. He played a highly disciplined figure-8 offense. They ran a weave and waited for the best possible shot. It was too slow for my game. It worked for them most of the time, but it wouldn't have worked for me. I went to Duke because they had a first-class baseball program under Jack Coombs, who had played for the Philadelphia Athletics, and a fine basketball coach in Jerry Jerard."

One of Groat's big fans is Armand Dellovade, a long-time Pitt booster who owns a sheet-metal construction business in Canonsburg. Groat's 1960 World Series ring had been stolen from his golf club, and when Dellovade heard about that he decided to replace it. He called Groat's youngest daughter, Allison Groat DeStefano, the general manager of the golf club, to get her dad's ring size and swore her to secrecy.

When The Fellows Club honored Groat in 1998 with the "greatest athlete" distinction at one of their luncheons at LeMont, Dellovade presented Groat with his World Series ring. Two former Pirates' pitchers, Nellie King and Nellie Briles, joined in the presentation ceremony. Briles and King have both since died.

"I think Groat belongs in the Baseball Hall of Fame," declared Dellovade that day.

"I think I know Dick pretty well," said Bill Hillgrove, who served as the master of ceremonies at that celebration, "and he was moved by this. He didn't expect this."

Sometimes I think Groat is taken for granted in his homeland, which is often the case. I interviewed him one day at the Applebee's Neighborhood Bar & Grill at Edgewood Square, not far from his home. Those places pride themselves on having pictures of local sports teams and celebrities on the walls. Babe Ruth was pictured, but not Dick Groat. So I sent them a photo of Dick Groat.

When I was covering pro basketball back in the '70s for *The New York Post* and *The Sporting News*, I met many NBA old-timers who still raved about Groat's scoring ability. He was right up there with Bob Cousy and Bob Davies and Dickie McGuire, according to the likes of Red Auerbach, Red Holzman and Marty Blake.

"I was a better basketball player than a baseball player," said Groat. "Baseball was a bigger game then. It was truly America's pastime."

* * *

My buddy Bill Priatko passed along an interesting story about Dick Groat. Bill and his son, Danny, attend a basketball game at Duke each year as guests of Coach Mike Krzyzewski. Mike and Danny are both alumni of the U.S. Military Academy. Priatko checks the Duke basketball web site from time to time and he came up with this gem:

On Senior Night, February 29, 1952, Groat scored a record 48 points in leading Duke to a 94–64 victory over North Carolina. He had set a personal high when he scored 46 points earlier in the season in a victory over George Washington.

Dick's dad, Martin, traveled to Duke to see him play his final game at Cameron Indoor Stadium. Mr. Groat stumbled over a curb and fell in the parking lot and hurt his knee. He was taken to the Duke Medical Center to be checked out. Duke held up the start of the game for ten minutes so Dick's dad could get back and see the entire game. That, of course, was before ESPN and Dick Vitale and all the games like that being on national television.

Groat was pulled from the game with 15 seconds remaining and received a standing ovation from the Duke crowd.

Dick Groat didn't mention this story, but it might be one of the reasons he gets choked up on "Senior Day." When I related this story to him, Groat corrected some numbers and said, "You might be right about that."

John Varoscak, a close pal of Priatko, played basketball at Rankin High School and at the University of Louisville where he was a teammate of All-American Charlie Tyra on an NIT championship team in 1956. Varoscak recalls as a teenager how he pressed his nose to the window of Sol's Sporting Goods to see an MVP trophy Groat had won in a basketball tournament in North Braddock. He idolized Groat and believed that he inspired him to work harder at his own game.

When Varoscak was visiting Poland a few years back, he bought a blue vase in Krakow and brought it home and gave it to Priatko to give to his friend Duke basketball coach Mike Krzyzewski the next time he went to Durham. Coach K loved the gift because he is quite proud of his Polish heritage.

Bill Priatko

Jim O'Brien

Pitt pals Bill Hillgrove and Dick Groat enjoy some golf at Groat's Champion Lakes Course in Bolivar, Pennsylvania, near Ligonier in the Laurel Highlands.

It couldn't get any better
for local basketball fans

March 2009

This is the best of times for basketball fans. This might be the best basketball season ever for Pittsburgh basketball fans. I was rooting for Duquesne to defeat Temple this past Saturday so that our city could claim three berths in the NCAA men's basketball tournament that gets underway this week. I wanted Duquesne to get to the Big Dance, as the tournament is called, joining Pitt and Robert Morris in March Madness.

West Virginia is there as well, and Penn State was one of the so-called "bubble teams" that didn't quite make it. Duquesne and Penn State will have to settle for an NIT bid, and that's a big step up for both programs. Pitt was voted a No. 1 seed and will head the East sector in the NCAA Tournament. That's a first in the history of the Panthers' program.

Pitt, Robert Morris, Duquesne, West Virginia and Penn State have all posted 20-victory seasons. The women's teams at Pitt and Duquesne both had 20-win seasons, and Pitt is going to the NCAA women's tournament.

The high school playoffs are winding down and the NBA playoffs are about to begin. And does it get any better than the six-overtime Big East quarter-final in which Syracuse outlasted Connecticut to advance to a one-overtime victory over West Virginia? I know I'm rooting for Syracuse to be successful in the South region.

I was one of those basketball junkies who stayed up till 1:25 a.m. to watch Syracuse win that marathon contest, and my wife Kathie kept me company all the way.

Pitt fans fear that the team's star performer, DeJuan Blair, might bolt for the NBA after this season. I am more concerned about our city's college coaches. I hope that all of them might consider that they already have the best basketball coaching job they could ever land.

We are fortunate to have the likes of Jamie Dixon and Agnus Berenato at Pitt, Mike Rice Jr. at Robert Morris, Ron Everhart and Susie McConnell-Serio at Duquesne, Bob Huggins at West Virginia and Ed DeChellis at Penn State. We'll be lucky not to lose at least one of them by next season.

I was a fan of Duquesne basketball before I was a fan of Pitt basketball. Fans forget that Duquesne once ruled the city in that regard.

I was 14 during the 1956–57 basketball season. I became the sports editor of *The Hazelwood Envoy* the summer of 1956. I still recall going to the Pitt Field House to see a Pitt basketball game. Dick Ricketts and Sihugo Green, who had been All-Americans at Duquesne; were both standing at one end of the floor, watching the warm-up action. Ricketts was 6–7 and Green 6–2 and they just seemed so tall to me, something of a midget in my own neighborhood. Ricketts and Green were then playing for the Rochester Royals in the NBA, and must have had a break in their schedule to come back to Pittsburgh. They were both wearing long camel-hair topcoats that made them look even taller.

I was the commissioner, sort of, for a three-man basketball league on the street outside my home in Hazelwood. My team was called the Royals because Ricketts and Green and four other players with Pittsburgh connections were on that club in Rochester. Jack Twyman of Central Catholic, Maurice Stokes and Ed Fleming of Westinghouse, and Dave Piontek of Bethel Park were all Royals. So they were my favorite NBA team. I read about them in the sports magazines I collected in my bedroom.

That's when I got hooked on basketball.

Stokes was the first black superstar in the NBA, preceding Wilt Chamberlain and Bill Russell. Chuck Cooper of Westinghouse had been the first black to be drafted into the NBA, by the Boston Celtics in 1950. So there were plenty of Pittsburgh connections in the NBA, more than there are these days.

I was also rooting for Duquesne because they hadn't qualified for the NCAA basketball tournament since 1977. That's when Norm Nixon led the Dukes to a championship in the Eastern Eight. I was working in New York at the time, but got a call to be the color/analyst for a telecast of the tournament games in Philadelphia. I was then the editor of *Street & Smith's Basketball*. So I was there the last time the Dukes gained an NCAA bid. John Cinicola was the coach. He's an NBA scout now and I see him at several Pitt games each season. Nellie King was the Dukes' sports information director. Now I was seeing him at the health center of Friendship Village in Upper St. Clair.

DeJuan Blair, by the way, reminds me of Maurice Stokes in several ways. Both were listed at 6–7, 240 pounds and both possessed great hands and were terrific rebounders and playmakers, as well as having the strength to score inside. Dick Groat, the Pitt analyst, is 76 and played with and against Stokes on Pittsburgh playgrounds when Groat was an All-American basketball star at Duke and during his one season with the Fort Wayne Pistons in the NBA. "I agree with you," Groat told me in a telephone conversation from his home in Swissvale on Sunday afternoon. "I hadn't thought about it, but they are very similar. I think Blair runs the court better than Stokes."

I suggested that everyone runs the court better today than they did in the mid-50s. It's a much faster game today than it was in the '70s.

Groat believes Blair would be better off staying at Pitt for at least one more year and developing an outside shot. "He can't play with his back to the basket in the NBA," said Groat. "I thought he'd stay until he played that great game at Connecticut. That might have convinced him and the pro scouts he could play with the big boys now."

Groat and I also agree that Blair is such a role model for young men in the city schools, a local kid who's making good, and has the greatest smile this side of Hines Ward of the Steelers. Blair is the face of Pittsburgh basketball right now. Groat thinks that Sam Young, Pitt's top scorer, is such a great athlete and will be a success in the NBA next season.

I've been watching basketball games on TV the past two weeks on a round-the-clock basis, and reading books and newspapers at the same time. I don't read during the Pitt games. But it's been a blast, and there's more to come.

I understand that some people pass on all this stuff, thinking it's silly to get so goofy anything short of "them Steelers" or the war in Iraq and Afghanistan. I pay attention to that as well, but want to have some lighter fare to balance things out. Sports-wise, I'm glad to see the Penguins have improved and have a chance at playing in the Stanley Cup championship playoffs. If they had played a year ago the way they have played this season they might not be building a new arena for them in Uptown right now.

All the local teams have had great seasons already. It's a shame, not a good thing, that Pitt didn't go farther in the Big East Tournament. Anyone who tells you that's an exhibition series or doesn't really matter that much doesn't truly understand the spirit of competition. Any athlete wants to win. They want to go all the way. Then worry about the NCAAs the next week. No one wants to go home early. Every basketball player loves to play at Madison Square Garden, and can't get enough of it.

The prognosticators all like Pitt to make it to the Final Four. I hope they're right. There are a lot of terrific teams out there among the 65 teams that were picked to play in this post-season tournament. It should be fun. That's why they call this March Madness.

Jim O'Brien

Pitt basketball coach Jamie Dixon, left, looks over shoulders of star players DeJuan Blair and Sam Young, now both playing in the National Basketball Association.

Finding treasures
at home and Ligonier

October 2009

A light rain fell on the windshield of my car as I traveled to and from Ligonier on a weekend in 2009. But in between it cleared up, and the sun broke through the low-hanging fog and the weather was perfect for the weekend getaway. Temperatures were in the low 80s. It was great walking-around weather.

My wife Kathie and I traveled to Ligonier—one of our favorite places—to participate in the next-to-the-last Country Market of the season at a field on the outskirts of downtown Ligonier. We were worried about the weather forecast calling for rain showers both days.

People were buying fresh flowers and vegetables, picking through quilts and handiwork of all sorts, sampling the food offerings. There's an eclectic assortment of stuff at the country market. It's a great scene, and Ligonier is a relaxing place. I love to see the women with "the Ligonier look," and several showed up in their riding attire. They'd taken their horses for a morning ride. For the eighth year in a row, I was signing my books under a white tent as the "feature attraction" on the program. I had my new book, *Pittsburgh Proud: Celebrating the City's Rich Sports History,* and the seven other books that are still available of the 24 I have authored altogether. I met old friends and readers.

We had a late lunch at the Ligonier Tavern. I asked for a corner table on the porch. The porch provided a New Orleans-like atmosphere. My seat also offered, by sheer luck, a window into the bar area and I could see a flat screen television from where I was sitting. Pitt was playing Syracuse in a Big East football contest. Kathie could see the screen through a window on the other side of a pillar.

I couldn't hear anything or make out the score at the bottom of the screen, so I entered the bar to get the score. "Pitt is down 24–13," a man at the bar said. "I think Wannstedt is in trouble."

He was referring to Dave Wannstedt, then head coach at Pitt, and a man whose job would be in jeopardy if he didn't soon improve Pitt's football record. "Oh, no," I responded to the news of the score. This can't be happening, I thought. I wanted Wannstedt to succeed. I like everything about the guy, except his record to date.

Soon after, Connor Lee, the Pitt kicker whom I watched play ball at Upper St. Clair High School in our community, along with his older brother Sean, sitting out the season to heal from an injury at Penn State, attempted a field goal. He kicked the ball cleanly through the uprights and Pitt was now trailing 24–17 at the 12:10 mark in the third quarter.

That's when Wannstedt and offensive coordinator Matt Cavanaugh discovered something they should have realized right at the start of the season and that is that they have more outstanding running backs than LeSean McCoy.

When Bowling Green keyed on McCoy and bottled him up in the opening game, Wanndstedt and Cavanaugh turned to an unproven quarterback in Bill Stull and had him pass 51 times in his first full game and it resulted in a stunning upset loss to the MAC visitor at Heinz Field.

Against Syracuse, they turned to LaRod Stephens-Howling and he and McCoy combined to lead the Panthers to a 34–24 victory over a sad Syracuse representative. If you wonder what happened to Pitt in recent seasons, consider the Syracuse collapse during an even longer stretch. Pitt came back to outscore Syracuse 21–7, including 18–0 in the fourth quarter.

When I took a seat at the bar, while Kathie went out and did some shopping, I reflected on how Dr. Wesley Posvar, the late Pitt chancellor, had often sat at that same bar when he retreated on weekends to his 100-acre estate in nearby Rector, where the real estate is quite costly. When Pitt was losing to Syracuse, I thought about how Dr. Posvar, my boss during my five years at Pitt in the mid-80s, would have reacted to their performance. He was a big fan, but he became unglued when things went badly for his Panthers.

I remembered some great battles with Syracuse during my student days in the early '60s.

The Pitt victory was icing on the cake for a fine day at Ligonier.

Syracuse football would come back into the picture the following day, Sunday, when I was preparing to attend a special program at the Heinz History Center in The Strip.

The event was called "Pittsburgh's Hidden Treasures, An Antiques Appraisal Show." I was looking for some of my sports stuff to see what the value of it might be. It turned out that an old friend, "Diamond Jim" Tripodi of Beaver would be appraising the value for sports memorabilia. There were about 20 appraisers there in different fields of expertise.

I took in an ABA—as in American Basketball Association—basketball that was still in the Rawling's box. It was an official league ball, signed by ABA Commissioner Jack Dolph. I was told ten years earlier that it was worth about $2,500 and now it's worth about $3,000.

I was searching for a watch that had a likeness of Muhammad Ali that was given out to the media at one of his heavyweight championship fights. Instead of numbers it had his name MUHAMMAD ALI around the dial. With the space in between, that adds up to 12 digits. I could not find it. I have since found it and it still keeps good time. I found a black notebook in one of my drawers, and opened it to discover that the first page of a spiral notebook had been signed "Best wishes, Ernie Davis."

If you have been watching any TV at this time, you'd know that there has been a lot of promotion of a movie that was coming out called "The Express," and it's the life story of Ernie Davis.

He was known as the "Elmira Express." He was born in Uniontown, but raised in Elmira, N.Y., not far from Syracuse. He was a three-time All-American running back there, and broke rushing records established at Syracuse by the great Jim Brown. He wore Brown's No. 44. He won the Heisman Trophy in 1961, the first black to be so honored.

He was the first player picked in the 1962 draft. The Washington Redskins selected him and traded him to the Cleveland Browns. Paul Brown planned to pair him with Jim Brown. But it was discovered that Davis had leukemia and, after a 16-month battle, he died in 1963. His No. 45 jersey was retired by the Browns, even though he never played a down for them. That's the respect with which he was held because of his sterling reputation off the field as well as on it.

I didn't know I had his autograph. I knew that I had taken pictures of him in the dressing room on November 4, 1961 after Syracuse had defeated Pitt, 28–9. I knew they were in a scrapbook my mother had given me when she divvied up the family photos for her children.

I pulled out that green scrapbook and found two photos. They had an orange glow about them in the dimly lit locker room, but there stood Ernie Davis and he was signing that little black notebook of mine. Sports autographs weren't as big a deal in 1961 as they are today. And I knew nothing then about having autographs authenticated. But I had picture proof that Davis had signed a black book, and it was in my possession. I also had a picture of Archbold Stadium, an old concrete stadium at Syracuse, from that dreary, dank day.

What was I doing at Archbold Stadium in the fall of 1961? I was in my sophomore year at the University of Pittsburgh, and was serving as the first non-senior sports editor of *The Pitt News* in school history. I traveled with the football and basketball team, a practice that was discontinued years ago, sadly enough. I wish I had continued to take a camera with me when I went to work after school as a sportswriter. I had so many opportunities to get photos of many of the greatest sports performers.

Since sports fans didn't ask for autographs as often as they do now, and since Davis died at age 23, there can't be many of his autographs around these days. Because of the movie, Ernie Davis has been rediscovered. Tripodi, the sports memorabilia dealer, told me Davis is in demand, and that he knows a high level Ernie Davis collector he can connect me with.

In that same black book, on the second page, is another autograph I didn't remember having. It reads "To Jim O'Brien, Best Wishes, Whitey Ford." That's the Whitey Ford who is in the Baseball Hall of Fame and had two pitching victories over the Pittsburgh Pirates in the 1960 World Series. Talk about hidden treasures...Tripodi thought it was worth about $200.00.

Kathie and I will be returning to Ligonier once more for "Fort Ligonier Days." There will be much activity in the community from Friday, October 10, through Sunday, October 12. I will be riding in a convertible car in Saturday's parade on Main Street for the second year in a row. It's always a great parade, and I'm proud to be in it. I'm told the Penn State Marching Band will be there this time.

This was going to be an especially important celebration of "Fort Ligonier Days" because it was the 250th anniversary of the battle that took place between the British and French troops at the fort there in 1758. That's the same year that a parcel of land at the point where the three rivers meet was named Pittsburgh. So Ligonier and Pittsburgh were both celebrating 250th anniversaries.

There were signs posted all along Main Street during our visit last weekend that call attention to this year's big shindig. You should make a point to go there. I get there, driving through Bethel Park, South Park, West Mifflin, McKeesport, White Oak, North Huntingdon, Irwin, Greensburg and Latrobe.

The event sponsors always hold this three-day celebration on the second weekend in October, but they got a big break this time around. The Steelers and Pitt both have byes in their schedule that weekend, and Penn State is playing at Wisconsin in a televised contest that won't begin until 8 p.m., well after all the planned activities and food and crafts booths will be shut down that day. So there will be no football conflicts to keep people away.

The schedule works for me in another way this October. That Monday, October 13, is the 48th anniversary of the Pirates' 1960 World Series victory over the New York Yankees. That's the date when Bill Mazeroski hit the home run leading off the bottom of the ninth to deliver the game winner in a 10–9 triumph. The best of baseball fans, and a few former Pirates, gather at the wall that remains from Forbes Field at 1 o'clock and listen to a tape replay of the seventh game of the Series. You have to be there to appreciate how it works, and what fun it is.

If Whitey Ford had pitched the opening game and the final game, the result might have been different. But Casey Stengel selected Art Ditmar for the first game instead. It cost Casey his job. He was fired soon after the World Series despite a distinguished career record.

Ford started Games 3 and 6 and tossed two complete-game shutouts against the Pirates, with the Yankees winning, 10–0 and 12–0. Those scores point up how crazy that World Series was, as the Yankees outscored the Pirates 55–27. "They set all the records, but we won the World Series," said Pirates' outfielder Gino Cimoli.

Yankee Stadium closed down for good last month, and will give way to a new Yankee Stadium next door next spring. In my Sunday morning search, I found a red ballcap that was given out to the media covering a heavyweight championship fight between Muhammad Ali and Ken Norton that was held at Yankee Stadium on September 28, 1976.

I'll bet that's worth something, too.

Senior Day still special
at Pitt's campus arena

March 2009

Senior Day was quite special on a Sunday afternoon in March, 2009 at Pitt's Petersen Events Center. Pitt was playing Connecticut, the No. 1 ranked college basketball team, in a nationally-televised battle of Big East giants. It was time to say goodbye to three senior starters, Sam Young, Tyrell Biggs and Levance Fields.

I had the feeling, a bad one, that we might also being saying goodbye to DeJuan Blair, a multi-talented sophomore from nearby Schenley High. The money to turn pro early might be too much to turn down, especially for someone who never had much money.

You've heard a lot of talk about Young and Blair playing in the NBA next year, but I have also come to believe that Fields has the ability to play with the big boys as well if someone is smart enough to draft him on the second round. I thought he'd be sensational with a club like the Cleveland Cavaliers, finding LeBron James and Mo Williams at the right time and at the right place to put the ball in the hoop.

I thought Fields might be more difficult to replace than Young or Blair in the Pitt lineup. He's that good at directing the offense and keeping Pitt poised in the clutch.

Plus, most of us can relate more to a guy the size of Fields, who's listed at 5–10, but looks smaller. It's harder to relate to someone like Young who can fly out of the gym, or someone like Blair who can move the building to the lower campus with a single shove.

I had been watching those guys for four wonderful years, through many thrills and spills. They've been great entertainment. Biggs got so much better, too, the way Aaron Gray got better, and the way I'm hoping Gary McGhee, the 6–10, 250-pound sophomore center can get better this off-season.

You have to have followed the Panthers when they played at the Pitt Field House, and seen them in action at New York's Madison Square Garden, to appreciate how far the program has come and where it's going this week. I have been paying attention to the Pitt basketball program since the early '50s, and I've had season tickets for men's basketball since 1984, so I know whereof I speak.

Maybe that's why I had a few tears in my eyes when they introduced Young, Biggs and Fields before the game, along with the senior reserves, the senior managers and student trainers, the senior cheerleaders, senior dance team members and senior band members. Did I leave anyone out? Did they leave anyone out? Oh, Jamie Dixon, the coach, also was kind enough to thank the crowd and the Oakland Zoo— the Pitt student section—for their outstanding support. He was also kind enough not to introduce the senior members of the Oakland Zoo.

I was glad to see North Carolina's coach Roy Williams getting wet-eyed on the sideline during similar introductions of his senior players on a day when North Carolina would defeat arch-rival Duke at the Dean Smith Center on the Chapel Hill campus. "I'm kinda corny that way," Williams would explain on television a day or so later. I guess I am, too, the older I get.

A friend who doesn't follow basketball asked me if this was the most important game in the history of Pitt basketball. I told him it was not. In fact, I said, the win over Marquette the previous Wednesday was actually a more important game because the victory sealed the Panthers getting two byes in the Big East Tournament.

I do think, however, it might have been the best scene in the history of Pitt basketball. Jamie Dixon said people who know such things told him the game tickets were as tough to come by as Super Bowl tickets when the Steelers were playing the Arizona Cardinals in Tampa the month before. I doubt the demand was quite that big, but it could have been close. It was great to hold off the Huskies for the second time that winter. It was a great tug-of-war all the way.

There was so much energy in the building. It was a record standing-room-only crowd. And I heard Bill Hillgrove say during the game broadcast that is aired in the hallways at the Petersen Events Center that Pitt doesn't sell standing-room-only space to fans, but holds it for the students. That's great to know.

My wife Kathie has kept me company in a lot of basketball arenas in our married life, but I never saw her enjoying a game as much as she did the Pitt-UConn contest. She was positively glowing the entire game and so into it the entire game. I don't think the students ever stopped jumping up and down. Jim Calhoun and his talented UConn club knew they were in Pitt's house, hostile territory. It's a shame a few bums had to swear at Calhoun. If he were our coach you'd love the guy.

He and Syracuse's Jim Boeheim and Louisville's Rick Pitino and Notre Dame's Mike Brey are the best of men and they all know their basketball. They are great competitors, and Jamie Dixon rates right up there already with all of them as far as that goes. Those guys are all quick to praise the Pitt coach.

Dixon knew his draft class of 2005 was special. He said so when he lined them up to come to Pitt. Young stayed all four years when he could have turned pro a year early, and Fields and Biggs were contributors all four seasons. They were the first class to string four consecutive 20-victory seasons, and 10-victory Big East report cards.

Dixon was the first Pitt coach to reach 100 victories, and had 132 victories after only five years going into this season. Only two coaches, Everett Case (137) of N.C. State and Mark Few (133) of Gonzaga, won more games in the same span.

Only Roy Williams of North Carolina, Few of Gonzaga and Bo Ryan of Wisconsin came into this season with a better winning percentage among active coaches than Dixon's .767.

Ben Howland turned the Pitt program around before going home to UCLA, and his disciple Dixon has done a great job in keeping things going on the same high level.

Howland was hired by Steve Pederson, now in his second tenure as the Pitt athletic director.

I thought about Beano Cook and Bill Baierl as I sat in the midst of the madding crowd at the Pitt-UConn game. Cook, the sports information director at Pitt during my student days at Pitt in the early '60s, always thought Pitt basketball could be this big if the athletic administrators paid proper attention to the program and got the right coach to lead it.

Baierl, the North Hills auto magnate, was a reserve basketball player at Pitt in his student days, and one of its biggest boosters in so many ways through the years. Baierl had died a year earlier, after following his beloved Panthers' basketball team through the Big East Tournament and the NCAA Tournament. But his spirit lives on at the Petersen Events Center. His family still enjoys great seats at The Pete.

I told Kathie at one point during the game that Steve Pederson made a brilliant move when they were planning the Petersen Events Center to have the students sitting in the bottom bowl of the building, nearly surrounding the playing floor. I mentioned this to Beano Cook when I called him at his downtown Pittsburgh apartment the following day to give him details of the scene at Pitt.

"Steve Pederson saved Pitt athletics," declared Cook. "His decision to level Pitt Stadium wasn't popular with everybody, but you couldn't impress high school prospects with that place anymore. He put them in that complex with the Steelers on the South Side and at Heinz Field. That cleared the way for the space to build the Petersen Events Center. Now it's one of the best buildings in all of college basketball. And the football program is on the way back. We'll get there."

I still believe that it would have been better to renovate Pitt Stadium, the way they did at Notre Dame, Ohio State and in Green Bay, and build the basketball arena on the hillside above it. I don't think there will ever be a college football atmosphere on the North Side. I prefer college sports on campus. But it's hard to argue with Cook's conclusion. It's hard to argue with Cook about anything.

Pederson wanted to hire Skip Prosser away from Wake Forest after Howland left, and he didn't want to hire John Calipari, the Memphis coach who was thought to carry bad baggage with him. That analysis was as questionable as our scouts who said Iraq had weapons of mass destruction.

Prosser has since died and Calipari continued to turn out great teams at Memphis and Kentucky. Either one of them might have been a solid pick for Pitt. Anybody who's not a fan of Dixon—and there are some who wear Pitt ball caps who astound me by not being fans—is nuts. He's a terrific coach and he's getting better from a public relations standpoint.

Carol Sprague, then an assistant athletic director, deserves the credit for luring Agnus Berenato from Georgia Tech to coach the women's basketball team at Pitt. Berenato has been a blessing to the program and to Pittsburgh at large. But Berenato needs to rejuvenate her program which has fallen on hard times.

I haven't followed the women's program that long. I bought season tickets for women's basketball in 2009 for the first time, and am glad I did. I felt a little weepy on Senior Night for the women as well. You just get attached to the kids and hate to see them leave. That's how I felt about Shavonte Zellous and Xenia Stewart, the two senior starters, when they said goodbye. I think the daily newspapers missed a great picture of Coach Berenato hugging both of them at mid-court ceremonies. It was definitely a Kodak moment.

Michael Dradzinski/University of Pittsburgh

Pitt's Jamie Dixon and Agnus Berenato, shown with Chancellor Mark Nordenberg, hate to say goodbye to players on Senior Night at Peterson Events Center.

Jim O'Brien

There have been some
great games at The Pete

February 2010

Wasn't that a great game? Was that the greatest game you've ever seen at Pitt? How's that rank with some of the great games you've seen? Several Pitt basketball fans peppered me with these questions as my wife Kathie and I were on our way out of the Petersen Events Center just after midnight on Friday.

A wide-eyed younger Pitt fan I haven't seen since the days when the Panthers were playing their home games at the Pitt Field House wanted to wax nostalgic about some of the great games we've witnessed in our lifetime.

This was right after Pitt had pulled out a miraculous upset of highly-ranked rival West Virginia University in triple overtime 98–95. The Panthers were down by seven points with 49.5 seconds showing on the clock in regulation time.

The Panthers had no right to win this game. It was the same way when they beat Louisville less than a month earlier at the Petersen Events Center, overcoming a five-point deficit in the last minute to win in overtime.

So the Panthers pulled off their second "Do You Believe In Miracles?"—as Al Michaels would say—so far this season.

This one may have been one of the most exciting college basketball games we saw all season. I have seen more than my share of basketball games—pro, college, high school, playground and pick-up games—in my lifetime, but this was definitely one of the Top Ten. But who's keeping score?

When my daughter Sarah was a little girl she used to rank movies we saw together, and shuffle the standings after she'd seen one that she particularly liked, such as "Pete's Dragon" or "Snow White." Maybe I should have done that with basketball games.

"You never get tired of this, do you?" one fan asked me as we exited The Pete.

No, we don't.

As Kathie and I were walking up the steps—there are 100 of them, I've been told—to the OC parking lot, I said to her, "This was like that Syracuse-Connecticut game in The Big East Tournament that went into five overtimes."

"It was six overtimes," said a big guy walking alongside of me, correcting me on the number of overtimes.

I thought I recognized the voice. I looked over and recognized it was Brian Generalovich, the president of the Pitt Alumni in recent years, but the star basketball player during my school days at Pitt. We both came to Pitt in September of 1960, just in time to see the Pirates beat the New York Yankees a month later in the World Series that was played at Forbes Field right on our campus, just a block and a half away from the Pitt Student Union.

Those '60 Pirates were big underdogs to the mighty Yankees, but they never quit and the same can be said of this season's Pitt basketball team. It was thought this would be a difficult year, but the Panthers were 8–4 in the toughest basketball conference in the country going into this Thursday's game at Marquette, with a Sunday showdown with Villanova on tap at The Pete. That should be a barn-burner as well.

When I knew it was Generalovich, I went into a spiel: "We're at Lambert Field House on the campus of Purdue University. Purdue's All-American forward Terry Dischinger is matched against Pitt's Brian Generalovich. They would both go on to become dentists. That'll never happen again in big-time college basketball."

Generalovich grinned and said hello. "You never forget that stuff, do you Jim?" he said. I smiled back. That game at Purdue was the season opener in 1961–62 and I traveled there by airplane with the Pitt basketball team during my tenure as the sports editor of the student newspaper, *The Pitt News*. In the next game, Pitt helped open the Civic Arena by playing against the vaunted Ohio State basketball team that included future Hall of Fame performers Jerry Lucas and John Havlicek, other future pros in Larry Siegfried, Gary Bradds and Mel Nowell, as well as a future Hall of Fame coach in Bobby Knight. It was a great time in my early education as a sports writer.

I reminded Generalovich of a difficult loss his team suffered at the hands of West Virginia during the 1962–63 season when we were juniors. Dave Roman of Johnstown hit an outside jumper in the last seconds of the game that should have won it for Pitt. But Pitt coach Bob Timmons had signaled to senior captain Ben Jinks to call time out just before Roman released his shot.

The referee said the shot didn't count. Timmons didn't complain. He knew he had called for a time out. So Pitt lost to West Virginia, 68–67. In those days, when Pitt played West Virginia or Duquesne half the Pitts would be rooting for the opposing team.

Pitt would bounce back and win the return game at Morgantown in the old Mountaineer Field House by a similar score, 69–68. That should have been the final score when they played the first time at the Pitt Field House.

I thought about that difficult defeat at the Field House two years ago when Ronald Ramon hit a 3-pointer from the far left corner to beat West Virginia. It's still the only buzzer-beater in the eight-year history of the Petersen Events Center.

That night, as Kathie and came away from our seats, I told her the story about that difficult last-second defeat at the Field House during my student days. No sooner had I told her about Dave Roman than Dave Roman himself walks by. He was wearing a Pitt varsity letterman's jacket—probably a leftover from his student days—and said hello.

Yeah, he said, he was thinking about his disallowed field goal when he saw Ronald Ramon become a hero for the ages with his last-second three-point shot. Roman's shot would have been a three-point field goal these days, but there was no such thing in the college game during the 1962–63 season. I hadn't thought about it until I was typing this story about the similarity in the spelling of the names of Roman and Ramon. They have the same letters in their last name, only in a different order.

Some crazy things also happened at the end of Pitt's overtime victories over both Louisville and West Virginia. There were some controversial calls and some non-calls that contributed to the madness. The crowds were crazy. The opponents and their coaches were worthy opponents. They never quit either and they had to go away feeling they should have won the game

Many fans departed the building when Pitt was down by seven points with just less than 50 seconds to play. Others, even stranger, left after the first and the second overtime periods. Someone suggested that maybe they had baby-sitters at home who needed to get to their own homes.

There were fans that left the Louisville game before it was finished, too.

I wonder sometimes that some so-called fans must come to the game just to see Pitt win. It's the same way with the Pirates, the Penguins, the Steelers, etc. As a sportswriter you are trained to be looking for the best story. Sometimes a loss or setback is the best story, depending on the circumstances.

In any case, if Pitt had lost to Louisville and lost to West Virginia the game itself still was a super show, great theater.

In a few days, Kathie and I went back to the Petersen Events Center to catch the Pitt-Louisville women's basketball game. Both teams were having disappointing seasons. Even so, over 4,000 fans showed up to "Pink the Petersen" in a special promotion to heighten breast cancer awareness. It was a heck of a ballgame. Neither team quit. They just kept coming back at one another, again and again. It was only the second Big East victory in 11 games for Pitt during the 2009–2010 season.

The NCAA women's tournament would get underway the following month at The Pete, but there's no way the Lady Panthers would be picked to play in it, not with a 13–11 record. That was too bad. Agnus Berenato, the always ebullient coach, thanked the fans over the p.a. system afterward for being loyal to her team during a difficult and challenging season. Berenato's mother died from breast cancer 25 years ago, and this has inspired her to work diligently on behalf of the Susan G. Komen Foundation for breast cancer research.

Two days before the Pitt-West Virginia game, one of the great men in sports passed away. That was Fred Schaus, who was a star player with West Virginia University and later with the NBA's Fort Wayne Pistons. One of his teammates on the Pistons during the 1952–53 season was Dick Groat, who was also playing shortstop for the Pirates at the time. Groat, now a Pitt basketball broadcast analyst, remembers Schaus fondly.

Schaus was always a class act. He coached Jerry West at West Virginia and then with the Los Angeles Lakers, and later returned to West Virginia as athletic director. The last time I saw Schaus and his wife, Barbara, was a few years back when they dedicated a highway in Morgantown in the name of Jerry West.

Bob Huggins, the current West Virginia coach, also speaks well of the influence Schaus had on him and his teammates during Huggins' playing days in Morgantown. Huggins, by the way, and Rick Pitino of Louisville, both draw a lot of heat from the Pitt fans at the Petersen Events Center, but beating their teams is satisfying and rewarding because they are both two of the best college coaches in the land.

So is Jamie Dixon. That's how he manages to beat them even when he doesn't have the most talented team.

We're lucky that Dixon and his mentor Ben Howland came our way. Pitt basketball has been great ever since.

There were rumors making the rounds in recent weeks that the Detroit Pistons might be for sale, and Pittsburgh was mentioned as one of the places where the Pistons could resettle. That's because of the new Consol Energy Center that will house the Penguins next season.

The Pittsburgh Pistons has a certain ring about it. We don't make Pistons here, of course, but we don't really make much steel around here anymore, either. We still have Pirates in Pittsburgh, that's for sure.

I don't think we need a pro basketball team in town. With Pitt and the Big East (*and soon the ACC*), we already have the best possible basketball.

Brian Generalovich is a dentist in Hermitage, Pa.

Jim O'Brien

Barbara and Fred Schaus were West Virginia favorites. They are seen as they appeared at ceremony to rename a street in Morgantown after Jerry West, who played for Schaus with the Mountaineers and the NBA Lakers.

Celebrating the city's
rich sports success

April 2009

My mother told me a long time ago that you will be judged by the company you keep. With that in mind, I know my late mother would be proud of the people I will be meeting and mixing with this Thursday and Friday.

I would be attending the 71st annual Dapper Dan Dinner and Sports Auction Thursday, April 2, and the 11th annual Mel Blount Youth Home All-Star Celebrity Roast on Friday, April 3 in the spring of 2009.

The Dapper Dan event was being held for the first time at the Petersen Events Center on the University of Pittsburgh campus, and the Blount dinner will return to the Downtown Hilton.

As a young newsboy, there were three events that used to command my attention that were promoted by the *Pittsburgh Post-Gazette*.

That was the special supplement sections on the Pirates at spring training, the Golden Gloves Boxing Tournament, and the Dapper Dan Dinner.

Each of them contained thumbnail photos and brief biographical sketches of all the sports personalities involved in each of them. I would spread the newspaper out on the floor of our front room—there was no designated family room or living room in our row house—and read those sections religiously.

So the Dapper Dan Sports Dinner & Auction has always been a big deal to me. I have been honored to sit on the dais—usually at the far end, which is just fine with me—with some of the city's most famous sports personalities the previous three years. I never won a varsity letter in sports on any level, but I found a way to make it to the majors—in all sports—as a writer.

One of my loyal book readers, Peggy Shank of Elizabethtown, Pa., often writes to me and tells me she envies me for all the people in sports I have been able to meet and interview and whom she admires and loves from a distance. "I'd love to be able to go with you," she says.

That's what I attempt to do with my articles and the chapters in my books about achievement in Pittsburgh and Western Pennsylvania sports. I try to take you with me.

They were honoring some people I truly admire at the Dapper Dan Dinner this time around. Mike Tomlin, the Steelers' head coach, was the 2009 Sportsman of the Year and Shavonte Zellous, the star of the Pitt women's basketball team, was the 2009 Sportswoman of the Year. Dick LeBeau, the Steelers defensive coordinator who has been associated with the National Football League as a player and coach for over 50 years, was receiving the Lifetime Achievement Award.

I met Tomlin for the first time at the 2007 Dapper Dan Dinner at the David L. Lawrence Convention Center. We have a mutual friend, attorney Terry Hammons, who came out of Upper St. Clair High School in my community to play wide receiver opposite Tomlin at The College of William & Mary. Hammons had told Tomlin about me and my books. Someone had given Tomlin a couple copies of some of my books about the Steelers to get him up to snuff with what his new employer was all about.

"I hope someday you'll want to write a book about me," Tomlin told me within two minutes of meeting him for the first time.

"I hope you'll merit such a book," I replied. "How about if we start with a chapter in my next book? But, Mike, I do like the way you're thinking."

He's on the cover of my book, *Pittsburgh Proud: Celebrating the City's Rich Sports History*, along with Troy Polamalu of the Steelers and Sidney Crosby of the Penguins. A few people told me when the book first came out that they thought it was premature to put Tomlin on the cover of a book about the city's top sports personalities.

Now that he is the youngest coach, 36 at the time, to win a Super Bowl I look like a prophet. Tomlin says he's now "a Western Pennsylvania guy."

I like Mike Tomlin. I like the way he conducts himself, the way he coaches, the way he handles his press conferences, the way he interacts with people, his philosophy on most subjects. We're already lucky he came our way.

Tomlin was smart to keep LeBeau on his staff as the defensive coordinator and to let him coach the system he knew and liked best, not necessarily the scheme Tomlin knew and liked best. LeBeau has been a blessing in so many ways. He's one of the most unique men I've met in sports, and one can learn so much from his manner and what makes him tick. He is truly a renaissance man.

He actually sent me a handwritten "thank you" note for including a chapter on him in one of my books. Tomlin did the same. You have no idea how rare that is in the writing world, whether it's sports, politics or the entertainment business. "This book certifies what I did in pro football," allowed LeBeau in his beautiful penmanship. "I did it, and this proves it!"

I'm excited for Shante Zellous, too. She's from Florida and can't possibly appreciate the enormity of this achievement. Maybe Agnus Berenato, her coach, can explain the significance to her. Berenato, like Tomlin and LeBeau, is a breath of fresh air on the Pittsburgh sports scene. She won the Dapper Dan's Sportswoman of the Year Award twice in the three previous years.

I met Berenato at the Hilton before she was honored the first time, and I was struck by how she held her own at a press conference with legendary Coach Joe Paterno of Penn State, saying all the proper and respectful things about keeping company with JoPa, and at the same time sharing some tongue-in-cheek humor with him. Within a minute after I introduced myself to her, Coach Berenato pulled me aside and introduced me to all of her children. I remember stuff like that.

Three of Pitt's finest all-time basketball players, left to right, DeJuan Blair, Shavonte Zellous and Sam Young as they appeared at 2009 Dapper Dan Sports Dinner. Zellous received Sportswoman of the Year award.

Ben Howland and Brandon Knight helped Panthers gain national prominence in college basketball.

I have had four season tickets for men's basketball at Pitt the past 30 years, but this year I bought a pair of season tickets for women's basketball as well. I wanted us to get on Berenato's bandwagon. I have seen my share of good basketball players in my lifetime, but none was as important to his or her team as Shante Zellous. There were games in which she put Pitt on her slender back and carried them to victory on the strength of her darting and dashing and deadly jump shot and acrobatic lay ups.

I was disappointed last week, of course, when the Pitt men and women both lost in the NCAA Tournament. The men might have won if they had protected the ball a little better in the last few minutes, but the women were definitely overmatched against Oklahoma and its strong and vocal following at Oklahoma City.

No one should forget how far the Pitt basketball programs have come under Berenato and Jamie Dixon, another former Dapper Dan award winner. The Pitt men are definitely a Top Ten program now. They gave us a great winter, a fine follow-up to the Steelers' Super Bowl triumph to start the New Year.

"So many great things have happened since I last saw you," Mel Blount was telling me over the telephone when he called to invite my wife Kathie and me to his dinner at the Hilton. "You'll never run out of material for sports books about Pittsburgh. The Steelers won the Super Bowl. Dan Rooney has become our ambassador to Ireland. John Stallworth has become part of the Steelers' ownership team. I think the world of John, and I admire Mike Tomlin and Dick LeBeau. Tomlin is a terrific coach, and I think LeBeau belongs in the Pro Football Hall of Fame as a player and a coach. He's been a lifetime contributor to the NFL. And I like the man.

"John Stallworth coming out of a small black college in Alabama and becoming not only a Hall of Fame football player, but now an owner of the Steelers is a tremendous success story. His inclusion speaks volumes about the Rooneys, too.

"I'm excited and proud of Dan Rooney being honored this way. He always let everyone know he was Irish and of his pride in his roots. He knew what he was doing when he backed Obama for President. Dan doesn't do anything without a plan. He thinks things through. I wondered what he was up to when he first came out and endorsed Obama. He told me when we met at a social event that this upset many of his friends and followers of the Steelers.

"But he did it anyhow. Right after the Steelers won the Super Bowl, when he was receiving the Lombardi Trophy from the NFL Commissioner, Dan thanked President Obama. I wondered why he was thanking President Obama. What did he do to help the Steelers win the Super Bowl? But Dan knew what he was doing. He knew there was an opening and he wanted the ambassador's position. And he got it.

"John Stallworth becoming an owner of the Steelers, on top of Obama being elected President, just shows you how far we've come in this country. I'm glad you write books about us. You keep us alive."

A mutual friend of Dan Rooney and mine told me when Rooney first endorsed Obama that he knew why he did it. He said he couldn't tell me at the time, but he would tell me when things all shook out. So I called him after Rooney was nominated to be the U.S. Ambassador to Ireland by President Obama to find out what he knew.

"That was it," said my friend. "Dan wanted to be our ambassador to Ireland. Obama says he's for change, but it's the same old same old as politics go. You take care of me and I'll take care of you. Dan will do a great job."

Ed Kiely of Highland Park, the former public relations man of the Steelers, still comes to the Steelers' complex each weekday morning for a workout. He stays abreast of things. He's been in the nation's capital when Rooney was mixing with representatives from Ireland. "He knows his way around, and they know him," confided Kiely, an Irishman himself. "I think he'll do just fine. He's no stranger over there."

Maureen Milie of Mt. Lebanon, wife of Bob Milie, who was an assistant trainer with the Steelers' first four Super Bowl winners, was born in Ireland and still returns to visit family and friends from time to time. "I'm so excited that I know our new ambassador to Ireland," she told me over the telephone. "I think this is great, coming after the Steelers won the Super Bowl again. Mr. Rooney has supported peace efforts in Ireland for a long time and merits this recognition."

When I was watching sports on TV on a Saturday, I left coverage of the NCAA women's tournament to see what else was on the tube. I caught Sidney Crosby's game-winning goal in the 4–3 win over the Rangers. I picked it up just as he received a pass on the run at mid-ice and scored the decisive goal midway through the third period.

I also came across a major college lacrosse match on ESPN2. I don't think I have ever watched a lacrosse match on TV. This one caught my interest, at first, because it featured the University of Virginia, the No. 1 ranked team in the sport in Division I competition. Our daughter, Sarah, is a graduate of UVA. I had been to Klockner Stadium in Charlottesville soon after it opened 16 years ago. I recognized the venue.

They were in the third overtime period of a stalemate with Maryland when I picked up the action. The Cavaliers won the match just one minute into the seventh overtime period of the longest lacrosse match in NCAA Div. I history. I was sitting in on history. It was like watching Syracuse win that marathon overtime game against Connecticut in the Big East tournament. You just never know when you're going to witness something special like that.

Brian Carroll scored the game-winning goal. I looked in Sunday's newspaper for something about that game. I figured there'd be a paragraph about it since it was a game for the ages. Not a word. Not even the score. Like it never happened. I've never been a one-sport guy, so I'm glad I saw it on television.

I had a great weekend in my over-the-hill gang basketball games at Upper St. Clair High School. I made my first and last shot of the Saturday-Sunday morning action. I missed two shots in between. One was a three-pointer for certain, and the last one was just inside the three-point arc to the left of the foul lane. It was the only shot I took on Sunday. It was the game-winner, in a 10–7 victory over a team I thought was much better than our team. It hit nothing but net. I had been practicing that shot for ten minutes every weekday morning for three months. I hit it, at last. It felt so good. Anyone who shoots frequently and makes most of their shots can't appreciate how I felt.

I left after one game to go to church with my wife. I had to thank God for the game-winner, in case he cared. "Enough about that shot," my wife scolded me over blueberry pancakes after church. "You talk more about your basketball games than Michael Jordan did."

That's why I love basketball. I was the oldest guy, by far, on the court. I can go weeks without making a shot. I consider every game in which I don't get hurt to be a good one. When the game was on the line, on this Sunday morning, I made the shot. I just wish it had been the game-winner for Pitt the night before. I wish Levance Fields had made the final shot one more time. They'd be showing his highlight for the next 50 years every time the NCAA Tournament was played.

The Pirates are in spring training, the Penguins have improved their team and their playoff possibilities, the flowers are coming out with April rains. It's a new season. Who knows what history-making sports event I will stumble onto with my TV channel-changer in hand? I can only hope.

Some great people always show up for the Dapper Dan Dinner and the Mel Blount Dinner. I will have my camera and notebook and pen to capture some of the activity, and consider myself a lucky man. Writing sports across America all these years makes for a great life.

Dapper Dan lineup of Steelers' leaders, left to right, president Art Rooney II, Head Coach Mike Tomlin and Defensive Coordinator Dick LeBeau.

340

That championship season
At Mt. Lebanon High

"Coach Black gave us a toolbox for life."

Andy Sharkey

March 2010

This article originally appeared in Mt. Lebanon Magazine

Dick Black did not draw a single technical foul in 37 years as a high school basketball coach. That was the most startling discovery that came out of attending a reunion of the 1960–61 Mt. Lebanon High School boys' basketball team in late September, 2010. That was Coach Black's first season as coach of the Blue Devils and that team won the WPIAL title and advanced to the semi-finals of the PIAA tournament in the school's most successful basketball season.

With that steely glare, that firm chin, that self-assuredness... surely he would have picked up a technical foul just for crossing or un crossing his legs at the end of the bench. He was quite a contrast from many of today's coaches—all five of them on some benches—who are constantly hollering at their players or the refs from end to end. Black kept his seat on the bench and seldom called timeouts.

"I didn't holler at the refs because I didn't want my players hollering at the refs," said Black, who turned 80 (on February 1, 2012) and still lives in Mt. Lebanon with his wife, Betty, a retired Mt. Lebanon elementary school teacher. "I thought I was supposed to be a role model for the kids. I didn't swear and I didn't drink, either. And I took as much pride in being the best math teacher I could be as I did being the boy's basketball coach."

Black said this while standing outside the St. Clair Country Club on a Sunday morning where he was about to join ten of his players from that championship team for brunch and the best of memories. I was with many of the returning players as well two days earlier over drinks at Atria's Restaurant & Tavern in Mt. Lebanon where I learned more about them and their once-in-a-lifetime season.

They shared omelets and hash browns and all kinds of fruit juice and coffee, but mostly stories of their past glories at the country club brunch. Dick Black was just 28 when he came to Mt. Lebanon in November of 1960, joining the staff late to fill a coaching vacancy. He had played ball at Midland High and Westminster College under some great coaches. He continued to coach at Mt. Lebanon through the 1996–97 season. He can still be seen on Tuesday and Thursday mornings working on his outside shot in the gym at the Jewish Community Center in Scott Township. He makes more than he misses and a visitor who thinks he knows a lot about basketball can pick up another nugget or two by listening to Black, who loves to talk about basketball and some of the local greats of the game.

That 1960–61 season was 50 years ago. Bill Mazeroski had hit the home run the month before Black came to Mt. Lebanon to win the World Series for the Pittsburgh Pirates over the New York Yankees, and Black, a big fan of the Bucs, said it was an exciting time in this city. Black was bringing more excitement to the suburb of Mt. Lebanon, though that was well disguised at first.

He kicked three returning players off the team soon after coming on board because they weren't heeding his rules regarding expected behavior at practices, and he took on some players no one expected him to, and did his best to change a losing culture in basketball at the school. Football, baseball, track & field and swimming all were winners at Mt. Lebanon, but basketball hadn't kept pace. Coach Black was going to insist that things were done the right way. They would be winners.

His former players still appreciate his approach, though he was a strict disciplinarian. Now in their mid-60s, most of them retired from their jobs, they realize more than ever what a powerful and positive influence Black had on their lives. They still call him Coach Black, by the way. "I could never call him anything else," said Bob Bennett, one of the stalwarts of that championship team who went on to play basketball at the University of North Carolina under Dean Smith, who is now a member of the Basketball Hall of Fame. "He was my greatest influence, right behind my father.

"Coach Black soon showed us that he was also very talented and up to date," added Bennett. "Dean Smith was known as the master of fundamentals and the x's and o's, but I saw nothing new when I arrived in Chapel Hill. I had learned it all before. Can you imagine what an advantage that was?"

Bennett, at 6–8, stood out on that team and at the reunion gathering. He was a junior on that championship team. The seniors were Lorry Hathaway, Dick Wyles, Andrew Alex, Mike Sunner and Steve Theis. The juniors besides Bennett were Drew Anthon, Charlie Cobaugh, Jim Lynch and Roth McNally. The sophomores were Jack Waltz and Rick Johnson.

Bennett practices law in the Los Angeles area and on occasion joined some special friends to have lunch with John Wooden, who won all those national basketball championships at UCLA and is one of only three men who have been inducted into the Basketball Hall of Fame as a coach and as a player. His ten NCAA championships in 12 years is unmatched by any other college basketball coach.

"No one would ever address Coach Wooden by any name but Coach," said Bennett. "It's the same way with Coach Black. They both had similar approaches to coaching basketball and leading young men. That's why I was drawn to Coach Wooden. He is my Coach Black on the west coast."

Bennett made arrangements to make it possible for the present Mt. Lebanon boys basketball coach, Joey David, to make a pilgrimage to Los Angeles to visit with Coach Wooden on several occasions. David, who's doing a great job at Mt. Lebanon, treasures those meetings with Coach Wooden.

One of Bennett's buddies from their days as athletes at Mt. Lebanon, Hal Morgans, informed him last March that Jack Waltz had died in December of 2008. Neither Bennett nor Coach Black or any of the other guys on the team were aware that Waltz had died. Lorry suggested they better get together "before something else happens."

Waltz was the surprise member of that championship team. He had just moved to Mt. Lebanon, and he was only 5–5, about 135 pounds, but so quick and so talented. Coach Black turned the ball over to his blazing fast point-guard and never looked back. "It took about five minutes to see that this guy could flat out play," recalled Bennett. "He was a blur out there and a real good ball-handler. He could also shoot and was one helluva competitor. He ate up people defensively."

His death disturbed Bennett greatly. "Aw, Jack, why did you have to be the one?" he wondered aloud.

Hathaway pointed out that Waltz won the Pennsylvania state championship in tennis in his sophomore, junior and senior years—later excelling on the tennis team at Yale. Hathaway won the WPIAL championship in the 440-yard dash in track. Dick Wyles was the starting quarterback on the football team, Andy Alex was an excellent pitcher on the baseball team and later played at Pitt, and Bob Bennett was the first baseman on the Mt. Lebanon baseball team. So these were good all-around athletes. Wyles had to give way to young Waltz as the team's playmaker but never beefed about it. Bennett and Hathaway were both all-state basketball selections.

They agreed the reunion should include some players from the 1961–62 team as well. That added Don Seymour, a junior in 1962, and Andy Sharkey, a sophomore that year. Hathaway and Wyles agreed to organize the reunion, and Seyour helped with the arrangements. They would later learn that Lee Davis, a senior varsity starter in 1961–62, had also died, as well as one of the team managers, Earl Weaver. Hertel, Johnson, Lynch and Sunner were unable to make it, but the others traveled, some of them cross-country, to be with their former teammates and their beloved coach.

"They were a great group of boys back then," said Coach Black, "and they are a great group of men now. It's an honor to have them come back and be with them. They sent me a DVD of the reunion and it was the best Christmas present I could have received."

Jason Miller, an actor and playwright, wrote an award-winning play in 1972 about a reunion of a championship high school basketball team at the eastern end of Pennsylvania. It was called "That Championship Season." I saw it on Broadway when I was living in New York. But it was a bleak look at a small town, and much had gone wrong in the lives of the players. "I saw the TV version of that show," said Bob Bennett. "Our reunion was all upbeat and positive, just the opposite. It was a great reunion."

They compared notes on their experiences, their families, their grandchildren, their careers, their retirements, and how life has treated them in general. Many of them are real success stories. Most of all they talked about their days at Mt. Lebanon High, and some of them took time to retrace the steps of their youth, and checked out backyard hoops where the asphalt was now cracked or in bad shape. "It was clearly one of the best years of my life," allowed Lorry Hathaway, "and I have been blessed with many wonderful years."

It was a special time in their lives, one they wanted to relive, as much as possible, even with some important parts missing from the puzzle that once fit together so perfectly. Because Coach Black was a late hire, the team took awhile to learn his system—he stressed defense and playing hard at both ends of the court, sharing the ball, sharing responsibilities, setting picks, boxing out on rebounds, all the fundamentals, and fairness and good sportsmanship—and it showed. Black believed you coached at practice and let them play in the games. John Wooden was the same way. Red Holzman of the Knicks coached that way.

Mt. Lebanon lost six of their first 11 games. The only way to get to the playoffs was to win the section title outright, and Washington High was usually the section champ. It's thought that Mt. Lebanon had never previously won a section title until 1961.

"We beat Little Washington to win the section title," said Bennett, who provided most of the historic data and photos about this team. "Then we beat Beaver 31–29, and the sportswriters couldn't find enough words to say how bad we were. They said Aliquippa would cream us in the next game, but we killed them. McKeesport was going to beat us, but we beat them by 9. Then Uniontown was going to kill us and we beat them by 3, somehow. They were really good and tough. Then it was Johnstown that was going to spank us, but we had no trouble with them. Then we met Hickory in the state semis, and we had a bad night all the way around, and they beat us. I have to give them a lot of credit.

"The seniors, Lorry and Dick, set a tremendous example. I never heard a four-letter word, no one ever criticized a teammate and we never spoke to an official. We knew better around Coach Black."

Drew Anthon, who lives in Lancaster, Pa., and has owned a string of major hotels and has a long career in hotel management, recalls Coach Black with reverence. "He had a great passion for teaching basketball then and right away he made a difference," said Anthon as he stood outside the St. Clair Country Club that Sunday morning in September. "He taught us how to play the game and to work hard at whatever you do. He was a great teacher for me. It was an extremely positive experience."

Charlie Cobaugh, an owner and partner with Trimaco, an international commercial paint supplies business headquartered in St. Louis, came at this from a different angle. "Sometimes you learn something from a negative experience that ends up helping you," he said. "I didn't make the team as a junior. I had to work so hard on my own to get ready for the tryouts the next season. It's hard to make the team as a senior if you didn't make it before, but he made an exception for me. Because of Coach Black, I was so determined to make it. I learned

344

what it was to overcome disappointment and it has served me well the rest of my life."

So many of the players from that team have gone on to successful careers in business. Steve Theis is an orthopedic surgeon in Pittsburgh. Andrew Alex is an attorney in Phoenix. Andy Sharkey, who lives in Great Falls, Va., was the president and CEO of the American Iron & Steel Institute before retiring in 2008.

"Coach Black taught us discipline, hard work, teamwork, respect and, most importantly, doing it right, playing by the rules and winning fair and square," said Sharkey. "While all of us were raised by good families with the right values, Coach Black reinforced those values every day and gave us a toolbox for life, not just the next game or season. We even recognized each other at the reunion, which is truly amazing."

Don Seymour, who played two seasons for Black and still lives in Mt. Lebanon, went on to Denison University and the University of Michigan Law School and practiced law for 40 years for a firm that is now K&LGates. "This is definitely a feel-good story," said Seymour. "It's about a coach and his players who after 50 years still appreciate and sense the influence he had on us during those critical developmental years of our lives. There were 15 players on those two teams and two are deceased. Ten players from places like Connecticut, Missouri, New York, Arizona and California came here to share a special time together. What more needs to be said?"

Lorry Hathaway and Bob Bennett both mentioned that Mt. Lebanon had offered the job to another coach before Dick Black got the job. Jim Daniell, the former All-America football player at Ohio State who had a brief stint with the NFL Cleveland Browns, was the major domo on the school board and led the charge to get a new coach for the basketball team.

They were going to hire Chuck Daly, who was coaching at Punxsutawney High. But Daly decided not to come in a disagreement over moving expenses. He ended up coaching at Duke and the University of Pennsylvania, and is best known for coaching the Detroit Pistons to a championship in the NBA and for coaching "The Dream Team" that won a gold medal in the 1992 Olympic Games at Barcelona.

Hathaway went from Mt. Lebanon to Bucknell University where he started each of his three varsity seasons and was the captain of the basketball team. He broke the all-time scoring record and was second in rebounds when he graduated in 1965. He was named to the All-East team along with Bill Bradley of Princeton, Dave Bing of Syracuse and Bob Weiss of Penn State. So he was pretty good. Hathaway, who has lived in Riverside, Conn., the past 35 years, was an executive with several consumer goods companies, including a stint as president and COO of International Home Foods, a $2.5 billion food company.

He went to the Wharton School of Business at the University of Pennsylvania where he had an opportunity to meet and talk to Chuck Daly, and remind him of his experience with Mt. Lebanon High. They both agreed that Mt. Lebanon ended up with the right coach. To which Don Seymour added, "The Detroit Pistons and the Community of Mt.

Lebanon were both to benefit immeasurably from Coach Daly's decision to turn down the Mt. Lebanon offer."

Coach Black rarely kept a senior who had not played varsity ball during most of his career, but he needed players that first year, and he took Dick Wyles, the quarterback of the football team. "He was mentally and physically tough, and one of the best guys I've ever known," recalled Bennett. "He had great character and leadership qualities, and Coach Black recognized that. Dick wasn't our best basketball player, but he took the big shots we had to have and he made them."

"For many of us," declared Dick Wyles, who lives in New York, after the reunion, "that 48 hours with each other in Mt. Lebanon was magical. We were cutting up so much it was like we were teenagers together again. While we were saddened by the deaths of Jack Waltz, Lee Davis and Earl Weaver, we reveled in being with each other once again. I believe the reconnection is real and lasting. We're all still in touch by e-mails. They mean the world to me. Coach Black is still the glue holding us together as a team."

Photos courtesy of Bob Bennett

The death in 2009 of the small but powerful Jack Waltz (No. 45) prompted teammate Bob Bennett (No. 33), now a prominent LA lawyer, to suggest the team "get together before something else happens." 1960-61 starters Bob Bennett, Jack Waltz, Lorry Hathaway, Dick Wyles and Andrew Alex.

John Altdorfer/Mt. Lebanon Magazine

That Championship Season of 1960-61 at Mt. Lebanon High brought together surviving players. Front, Don Seymour, Coach Dick Black, Dick Wyles, Charlie Cobaugh and Steve Theis. Back: Andrew Alex, Bob Bennett, Lorry Hathaway, Andy Sharkey, Drew Anthon and Roth McNally.

George Schoeppner
Still a class act

This article originally appeared in Mt. Lebanon Magazine

George Schoeppner was sharing stories about his athletic achievements as a student at St. Bernard's Grade School, Mt. Lebanon High School and the University of Pittsburgh. He distinguished himself in sports and in the classroom on every level. He was a respected insurance agent for many years with the John R. Couy Insurance Agencies, Inc. in the Cyclops Building on Washington Road.

Schoeppner was sitting at his favorite corner table in the main dining room of the St. Clair Country Club on a sunny afternoon in early July. Sandy Cristello, the hostess in the Terrace Room, mentioned to him that over 700 people had stood in line the previous evening at the putting green visible below the window to touch and get their picture taken with the Stanley Cup the Pittsburgh Penguins had won at the conclusion of an exciting 2008–2009 National Hockey League season. Penguins' general manager Fred Shero is a member at the St. Clair Country Club and he was responsible for bringing the Stanley Cup to the club to share with everyone there. I was invited to the club and witnessed the worshipping of hockey's Holy Grail.

Schoeppner, then 72, looked dapper in a dark blue blazer, a well-pressed white dress shirt, a pale green pattern tie, and dark green frogs on his gold cufflinks. He said his wife Barbara had bought the cufflinks as a gift. George has gray-blue eyes, so he squinted in the sun-drenched room at the St. Clair Country Club. His wife Barbara has been with us before at that same corner table. She has the most striking deep blue eyes, like the blue I'd once seen just below the surface of an Alaskan glacier.

George was gracious, gregarious and humble as he answered all my questions. He was named a Varsity Letterman of Distinction in 1995 by the University of Pittsburgh for his success in sports, his business career and his loyalty and financial support for his beloved alma mater. He's proud to be an American and had one of those miniature metal American flags as a lapel pin.

He showed me some photos he had brought along at my request. One was beautifully framed and it showed him as an All-American baseball player at Pitt back in 1959. He was in uniform standing alongside his coach, Bobby Lewis, who lived in Upper St. Clair, with the familiar scoreboard in left field at old Forbes Field in the background.

The Pirates had just celebrated the 100th anniversary of the opening of Forbes Field, and the photo of Schoeppner and his coach had been taken during the 50th year. An inning-by-inning score of a game with the Cincinnati Reds was still up from a game the night before. The Pirates scored two runs in the ninth to tie the score. It went into extra innings and the outcome of the contest is not shown in the picture. Just a tease.

There was a handwritten message on the back of the framed photo from Coach Lewis. It read: "You will always be remembered as a good student, outstanding athlete and a real gentleman. May I always be blessed with a George Schoeppner on every one of my teams that I coach and I'll always be a winner."

Schoeppner smiled when I read the letter by Lewis aloud. He also shared stories of other sports accomplishments, family, friends, his Catholic faith — "those are what I am proudest of," he said — and he was great company as usual. When we parted, I told him that my wife Kathie and I were going to the Woodland Hills Swim Club that afternoon. I mentioned that I would be seeing Harry Peterson, the swim club manager for many years, whom I knew was a student at Pitt during Schoeppner's school days. Peterson, who hailed from Dormont, was proud to say he had been the team manager for the Pitt basketball team that was led by All-American Don Hennon.

"Be sure to give him my regards," said Schoeppner.

As soon as we passed through the entryway to the Woodland Hills Swim Club we were greeted by Harry Peterson. "Our friend George Schoeppner said to give you his regards," I told Peterson.

"Ah, George Schoeppner," Peterson shot back. "Do you know he still holds the single-game scoring record in basketball at Mt. Lebanon High School? He had 55 points one night and that was before there was a 3-point basket. He was some shooter; he was known for that. He played on the freshmen basketball team for awhile with Don Hennon. George was Pitt's first All-American baseball player. And what a gentleman. He's a class act."

Now I had to smile. Harry Peterson had summarized the George Schoeppner story as well as possible. I had asked my wife what came to mind when she thought of George Schoeppner, and she said, "He's such a gentleman, and his love for his family is obvious."

There are a group of men who gather most Friday afternoons at Atria's Restaurant & Tavern in Mt. Lebanon to debate about sports and matters of international importance. They take themselves as seriously as the G20 leaders. Bob Stocker, one of the regulars, said one day, "The best baseball player I ever saw in Mt. Lebanon was George Schoeppner."

Norb Connors, a classmate of Schoeppner at St. Bernard's and Mt. Lebanon High School, offered on another afternoon, "I saw Schoeppner score the 55 points. Do you know he could throw a football 70 yards? But his mother wouldn't sign the papers to permit him to play. Football might have been his best sport."

Schoeppner said the football coaches at Mt. Lebanon High came to his home and pleaded with his mother to let him play football. "They said I could be the quarterback and they'd rest me on the bench when we were on defense," he recalled. "She wouldn't move on it. I respected her wishes, but it was one of the biggest disappointments of my life. Football was my favorite sport."

Connors and his wife, Carol, had traveled to France in May of 2008 with the Schoeppners. Dave and Sally Martz, two other high school classmates, accompanied them, as did another schoolmate, Barbara Frantz, and her husband Ted. The Schoeppners do a lot of traveling since George retired in March, 2006. They have resided since 1996 in a condo in the Woodridge complex in Mt. Lebanon, and they have a getaway condo at Hilton Head, South Carolina.

Schoeppner batted .613 his senior year at Mt. Lebanon High School to attract the attention of the new Pitt baseball coach Bobby Lewis. "Bobby told me I was his first recruit," said Schoeppner with more than a hint of pride.

Schoeppner is best known among senior sports fans in the community, however, for scoring 55 points in a game as a senior. I Googled his name on the Internet and came up with the fact that he had scored 55 points in an 89–42 victory at Waynesburg High School. He had 20 two-point field goals and 15 free throws that wondrous night. "I was taken out with a minute and a half to play because we were so far ahead," he recalled.

Schoeppner said he scored the 55 points on January 4, 1955. "As I get older," he kidded, "it helps me to remember because the point total and year were the same. This January will be the 55th anniversary of that game. That will help me even more."

Schoeppner hurt his knee playing basketball in a tournament at the Young Men's Hebrew Association gym near Pitt's Cathedral of Learning, and it eventually forced him to drop off the Pitt freshman basketball team. He never fully recovered from that knee injury, and many believe it ended any possibility of Schoeppner being a big league baseball player. He was an infielder, playing third base, second base and shortstop for the Panthers as well as on summer sandlot teams. Pitt played some of their games at Forbes Field in those days.

Schoeppner never dwells on such disappointments. It does not compare to a real loss he and his family suffered on December 4, 2004 when his nine-year-old grandson Tyler Frenzel lost his fight with cancer. Tyler was the son of George's daughter, Pam Frenzel, who lives in Carmel, Indiana. Tyler was a big fan of the Indianapolis Colts and their star quarterback Peyton Manning When Manning learned about Tyler and his illness he visited the youngster in the hospital and bestowed all sorts of gifts on him, and kept contact with Tyler throughout his illness.

Schoeppner kept me posted on Tyler's progress and setbacks. It was a sad day in Indiana when Tyler died. He had captured the attention and hearts of many Hoosiers.

George and Barbara Schoeppner have 29 grandchildren, and one great-grandchild. That's another story. This is the second marriage for both of them. Their first spouses both died. Schoeppner said his wife, Carol, died on January 4, 1995. If you are keeping score, that was also ironically enough the 40th anniversary of his 55-point game. .

They had been married 35 years. She was Carol Simpson when they were sweethearts at Mt. Lebanon High School. When she was ill and knew she was dying, she gave George a list of five women she would approve of if he ever decided to get married again. They were friends and were all free to marry.

Barbara Matthews was on that list. She was a second grade school teacher in the Baldwin-Whitehall School District. She had seven children. George and Carol had four children of their own. Their merger was bigger than that of television's "The Brady Bunch." I asked George if he checked out each of the five women before he settled on Barbara. "No, she was the only one I went out with," he said. They were married May 18, 1996, so they have been together for 16 years.

"Our kids were great friends, and I was close to her children before we were married," said George. "Some of them already called me Dad. I've been blessed to have two great gals in my life. And we've been a great family since we merged."

When he visits Carol's gravesite at Queen of Heaven Cemetery in McMurray, Barbara has often accompanied him. Carol was one of her closest friends. "I still have that list at home that Carol gave me," George told me.

I asked my wife once if she would ever give me such a list. She paused before replying. "No," she said, "I couldn't do that to my friends."

Schoeppner always smiles when I tell him that story.

Schoeppner said he has lived in Mt. Lebanon all but six years of his life. After he graduated from Pitt, he started to work at Bell Telephone of Pennsylvania and he was sent to an office in Philadelphia. He got into the insurance business at the tail end of his stay in Philadelphia. He came home to Mt. Lebanon and merged his agency with Bob Couy in 1971. They represented eight different insurance companies.

Schoeppner has learned to count his blessings. We were talking about how so many famous people had died over the previous two weeks of our meeting, including Michael Jackson, Robert McNamara, Ed McMahon, Karl Malden, Farrah Fawcett and Billy Mays.

"My heart doctor also died," said Schoeppner. "His name was Dr. George Liebler, and he was a year ahead of me at Mt. Lebanon High School and at Pitt. He and Dr. Neil Hart saved my life at Allegheny General Hospital. Today is the 10th anniversary of my quadruple-bypass surgery. They did a great job."

Jim O'Brien

George Schoeppner stands outside Mt. Lebanon High.

OLYMPIANS

Jesse Owens shows off the four gold medals he won in the 1936 Olympic Games in Berlin with Nazi commander Adolph Hitler looking on. So much for Hitler's "Aryan Supremacy" theory.

They showed
the way
for others to follow

November 2007

Sheriff John Baker shows off proud antique pistol.

Jim O'Brien

They always stood above the crowd. They were athletes with great gifts. They had size, special skills, strength, stamina and speed. They were raised by hard-working and loving parents who implanted proper values and showed them the way. They overcame adversity to succeed in sports and, most of all, in life. They suffered slings and arrows simply because they were black men. They were taunted and put down because of the color of their skin and their enormous accomplishments in competition with mostly white men. They wouldn't give in to such stupid and shortsighted thinking and they became role models for younger athletes who were paying attention.

John Woodruff and John Baker were both special men. Woodruff was known as "Long John" because of the length of his strong legs and his wondrous stride as a middle-distance runner, and Baker was known as "Big John," a large defensive lineman. Woodruff won the gold medal in the 800 meters in the 1936 Olympic Games in Berlin, Germany. One of those looking on was Adolph Hitler, the leader of Germany's Third Reich. Woodruff was the first black to win a gold medal in the track and field competition. Jesse Owens would become an international hero by winning four gold medals as a sprinter.

Their accomplishments were a setback for Hitler's Aryan supremacy theories. So much for the superiority of the white race.

Baker, a 6–7, 280 pound defensive lineman, was a star performer in the National Football League for 11 seasons, from 1958 to 1968. He played five of those seasons with the Steelers, from 1963 to 1967. I edited a newspaper during that five-year span called *Pittsburgh Weekly Sports,* and wrote about Baker and his teammates.

Baker was best known for having hit and knocked the helmet off the bald head of New York Giants' quarterback Y.A. Tittle and leaving him bowed and bloodied. The photo by Morris Berman showing Tittle on his knees in the end zone at Pitt Stadium, blood trickling down his forehead, is displayed in the Pro Football Hall of Fame. It's regarded as the most telling photo ever taken of pro football action.

Believe it or not, that photo did not appear in the next day's Pittsburgh *Post-Gazette*. Sports Editor Al Abrams said he preferred an action photo. "Nothing is happening in that picture," he's reputed to have said in the sports department that evening following the game.

Woodruff died on a Tuesday in November of 2007 at an assisted living facility in Fountain Hills, Ariz. He was 92. In his latter years, he had lost both legs to circulatory disorders. It was such tragic irony, considering that he was always known for his long legs and his long stride.

Baker died the next day at his home in Raleigh after a lengthy illness. He was 82. He had been the sheriff of Wake County for 24 years. His father, also known as "Big John," had been the first black police officer in Raleigh.

I was privileged to spend quality time on several occasions in the company of Woodruff and Baker. I visited Woodruff in Connellsville when he'd come back home for an annual community race named in his honor.

I interviewed Baker at his sheriff's office in Raleigh.

Both were so impressive and so wise. I have always been fascinated and intrigued by such athletes, such superior men who managed to remain humble despite enormous accomplishments as athletes and as community contributors.

Baker believed he might have been the only pro football player to ever have a team owner stay overnight in his home. Steelers' owner Art Rooney once gave Baker a $5,000 check toward creating a chapel in the women's jail in Raleigh. Rooney later told Baker he wanted to visit the jail to see what Baker had helped build. He stayed with the Bakers and enjoyed a home-cooked Southern meal.

Baker was one of Rooney's favorites. It was a mutual admiration society. "Some of us players used to call him Daddy Rooney," Baker told me.

Baker was one of the standout Steelers in the team's 75-year history. Black performers such as Baker and Woodruff showed the way, and made it possible for the Steelers to feel comfortable and confident in choosing Mike Tomlin as their head coach this commemorative year.

I traveled to Connellsville once again last Thursday and presented three programs for students in the afternoon and one for the general public in the high school auditorium in the evening.

I told them about John Woodruff, one of their own, and John Baker. I told them about Johnny Lujack, who also came out of Connellsville. Lujack won the Heisman Trophy as the Notre Dame quarterback in 1947.

Few communities can boast of having produced both an Olympic gold medal winner and a Heisman Trophy winner. I told them about Jimmy Joe Robinson, who came out of Connellsville and became the first black football player at Pitt. That was in 1945, two years before Jackie Robinson broke the color barrier in major league baseball.

The teachers and the kids in Connellsville need to know that. They need to know that others have come from that same community and made it big. There's a huge German black oak tree that looms over one end zone at the high school athletic field. It's sometimes referred to as "the Hitler tree."

Hitler presented German black oak saplings from the Black Forest to the 1936 Olympics gold medal winners to take home to their respective countries. Many of the American athletes tossed those saplings overboard into the ocean on the return trip. Woodruff, who grew up on a small dirt farm on the edge of Connellsville, brought his home. It still stands as a testimonial to John Woodruff and a valuable teaching tool for everyone in that community.

Pat Lanigan, a funeral director in East Pittsburgh and a loyal reader of my "Pittsburgh Proud" series of books, once told me how Turtle Creek shared a special bond with Connellsville. Both could claim a Heisman Trophy winner and an Olympic gold medal winner.

"I wanted you to know that Turtle Creek (population 6,000) produced the same tandem of champions. In fact, both of those champions graduated in the same high school class, Turtle Creek High School, Class of 1946."

Turtle Creek High School, of course, is now part of the Woodland Hills School District.

"In 1949, Leon Hart won the coveted Heisman Trophy while playing at Notre Dame. As you probably know, he was the last lineman ever to win the award. He went on to have an All-Pro career with the Detroit Lions.

"In the Rome Olympics in 1960, Lt. Col. William W. Macmillan, also a 1946 graduate of Turtle Creek High School, won the gold medal for pistol shooting."

Jim O'Brien

Proud Pitt performers in track & field are, left to right, John Woodruff, Allan Carter, Herb Douglas Jr., Arnie Sowell, Roger Kingdom and Lee McRae at Alumni Hall on Pitt campus.

McKeesport's Swin Cash
knew anything was possible at Summer Olympic Games

McKeesport's Swin Cash

I was rooting for Swin Cash to come home to McKeesport with a gold medal around her slim neck. There was so much bad news coming out of McKeesport in the summer of 2012. Young men were shooting young men over illegal drugs and petty feuds, snuffing out misspent youth.

It's happening in the public housing projects, the same environment that produced Swin Cash, one of the sweetest, kindest and most considerate young women you would ever meet. This concerns Cash and she wants to help clean up the mess—a monumental task—and steer young people to better places in their lives.

Swin Cash was in London in August playing for the U.S.A. women's basketball team that was one of the favorites in the competition. She had been to London before. She had played in Paris and Rome. She had played in Istanbul, of all places, in a warm-up to the Summer Olympic Games.

But she has never forgotten where she came from. She has played for Women's National Basketball Association (WNBA) teams in Seattle, Detroit and Chicago, but she returns often to McKeesport to see her mother and father and family. She made good on an earlier promise to found and help fund the Swin Cash Foundation—Cash for Kids— aimed at helping young people in these parts.

She is cut from the same cloth as her friend Charlie Batch, the Steelers' reserve quarterback from Homestead, who continues to do good things for young and old alike in his hometown.

Swin Cash is an attractive figure. She is tall and slim, at 6-1, 165 pounds ("Do I have to tell you that," she once asked me.) And she has done some modeling. She was the president of the student council as a senior at McKeesport High School, and was a finalist for Homecoming Queen. She has always been a great role model.

She has been in an audience at The Vatican with the Pope in Rome. She has shaken hands with former President George W. Bush at The White House, and she met Michelle Obama at these Olympic Games and is a big fan of her husband, Barack Obama. "He's an impressive man," she has said. "He's inspirational."

Swin Cash is a feel-good story from a community that needs inspiration. McKeesport has endured a bloody summer. In a two-week stretch at the end of June and the start of July, five people were shot.

Four people were shot at a party at a house in Crawford Village, and three of them died.

"Look, there's violence all around us in the whole Mon Valley and you don't know when something like this is going to happen," McKeesport Councilman Darryl Segina said last Saturday.

"I hate it. We've had vigils, we've had rallies. I don't know what more you can do."

This hits home, of course. My wife Kathleen Churchman grew up in McKeesport, first on Jenny Lind Street in the heart of the community, and most of the time in White Oak on the outskirts. Like Swin Cash, she stood tall in her class and went on to better things, except for a misstep when she married me. She's still a Tiger.

I grew up in Glenwood and Hazelwood where killings are common among the young people today. City police regard those communities as "hot spots" and do their best to keep the peace.

Charlie Batch knows the heartache in his hometown. His kid sister was shot and killed in a gang crossfire years back. She was guilty of simply being in the wrong place at the wrong time. She had done nothing to deserve an early demise. That's one of the reasons Batch does what he does today to help improve the life for young people.

Cash, at 32, was the oldest and most experienced player on an international level for the U.S.A. women's basketball team. Cash came off the bench and steadied things. Cash contributed in subtle ways to a gold medal effort in London.

Coach Geno Auriemma knew he could count on Cash in crucial stages of any Olympic contest. She was one of the mainstays of his University of Connecticut team when the Huskies won national championships in 2000 and 2002.

I have been a big fan of the Olympic Games since I was 14 and just starting out as the sports editor and columnist for *The Hazelwood Envoy*. We had an Olympic hero in Hazelwood. His name is Herb Douglas Jr. and he won a bronze medal in the long jump—then called the broad jump—in London's Wembley Stadium in 1948. There is a mural of him doing that jump on the wall of a building in the middle of Hazelwood. It's at the corner of Second Avenue and Tecumseh Street.

Douglas was also in London for the Summer Olympics, representing the University of Pittsburgh where he is an emeritus member of the board of trustees. He was also rooting for Swin Cash. I know he's met her on several occasions. They have both been honored as History Makers by the Senator John Heinz History Center.

I have seen Swin Cash mixing at the Heinz History Center with Herb Douglas and the late "Bullet Bill" Dudley, one of the greatest stars in the 80-year history of the Pittsburgh Steelers, and they both were enchanted with her smile and her grace and what she is all about.

Swin Marie Cash is a class act. Her mother is a maintenance supervisor in the McKeesport Housing Authority. Cynthia Cash was 17 and ready to start her senior year at McKeesport High School when she gave birth to Swin on September 22, 1979. Some of her family and friends had advised Cynthia to have an abortion.

Cynthia came back to McKeesport High School after she gave birth to Swin and was one of the star players on the girls' high school basketball team. She raised Swin alone in Crawford Village until she married Kevin Menifee, and they have raised three more children together.

Cynthia named her child Swintayla, which means "astounding woman" in Swahili.

"She sacrificed a lot to give birth to me," said Swin Cash. "If she didn't have me, maybe she could have gone on to college. I asked her, 'Mom, are you sad you had me when you did?' And she said, 'I wouldn't trade you for anything.' So I wouldn't do anything to hurt my mother."

I had lunch at Eat'n Park with Swin Cash several years ago and came away so impressed with her. You have to love her.

"All I want to do is live life to the fullest," she told me that day. "I want to realize all the dreams I have – going to the pros, coming back to McKeesport some day and setting up a Swin Cash Foundation. I know these things are possible."

One of the things I love about the Olympic Games is all the feel-good stories of the athletes who have overcome adversity or obstacles in their young lives to persevere and become champions. They are, indeed, inspirational stories.

I watch the Games from the comfort of a couch in my family room. My wife and I watch The Games on television and go back and forth to see what the Pirates are doing. I can jump up and clap my hands and holler, something I can't do when I am in the press box at a ballgame around town, or all the press boxes I visited as a traveling journalist for newspapers in Philadelphia, Miami, New York and Pittsburgh.

I remember jumping out of my couch and screaming when Roger Kingdom won the gold medal in the Olympic Games in Los Angeles and Seoul, Korea in 1984 and 1988, respectively. I had known and embraced Roger when he was a student at Pitt in the mid-80s and I was the assistant athletic director for public relations. He was a frequent visitor to my office in Pitt Stadium. I had met his mother and knew what she expected of her son. Now Kingdom is the head track & field coach at California (Pa.) University.

We still hug whenever we run into each other. I helped him when he needed help. I brought Herb Douglas Jr. into his life when Kingdom was competing for Pitt. Douglas helped him, introducing him to the right people, providing some guidance. Kingdom knows Swin Cash. He is rooting for her, too.

Cash came out of Harrison Village. So did Brandon Short, who led McKeesport High School to the Quad A championship in football in 1998, and went on to a successful career at Penn State and in the National Football League.

They found a way to stay out of trouble and make something of themselves. My wife wasn't an athlete—she's better at it today than she was then – but she was a good student, a good person and her parents expected her to go to college and become something.

You don't have to be a star athlete or musician to make it in this world. One of Pittsburgh's leaders recently was calling for better teachers in The Hill District. I think they need better parents in The Hill District, and every community around here.

I can still hear my mother telling me, "Stay busy and stay out of trouble."

Swin Cash credits her mother for getting her through some tough times in her life. "My Mom and I have always been so close," she said at our meeting.

Imagine what the odds were when Swin Cash was born 32 years ago that she would be competing in the Olympic Games in London someday. That she would see Queen Elizabeth and Muhammad Ali in the same venue. Swin Cash was a member of the gold medal-winning team in 2004 and missed out on making the team in 2008. She's glad to be back.

After the impressive opening ceremonies. Cash told Dejan Kovacevic of the *Pittsburgh Tribune-Review*, "Something like that, you just take it all in. It's really a special moment for all of the athletes.

"I'm so happy just to be here to help out any way I can. I want to bring home the gold."

Photos by Jim O'Brien

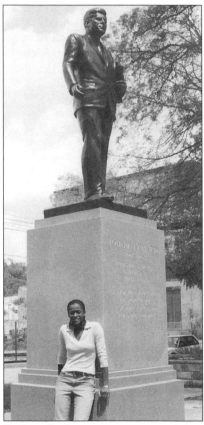

Swin Cash poses near statue of President John F. Kennedy near municipal building in her hometown of McKeesport.

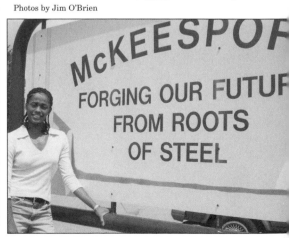

Swin Cash is a hometown treasure

Sharing a round table
with Olympians

A stack of sports magazines sat high on the end table next to my boyhood bed back home in Hazelwood, at the eastern end of Pittsburgh. I always said I lived on the sunny side of Sunnyside Street. It started with *Sport* magazine and evolved into *Sports Illustrated*, and I can still see the covers of my treasure trove. I also collected bubble gum cards of football and basketball and baseball players and memorized some of the notes and statistics on the backs of them. I sorted them out and studied them and the images remain emblazoned on my brain.

Sports news was sparse in the late '50s and early '60s. You didn't get to see all the Steelers and Pirates games, or any of the Hornets, our team in the American Hockey League, on television. Duquesne had the best basketball team in Pittsburgh in those days, but there was no March Madness. There were no round-the-clock sports talk shows on radio and TV. I recall that Joe "The Screamer" Tucker had a 15-minute report around dinnertime on WWSW Radio. He was also the voice of most of the sports broadcasts in the city. Rosey Rowswell and Bob Prince did the Pirates. Sun-Telegraph sportswriter Jack Henry and Pirates' Hall of Fame third baseman Pie Traynor had a sports show each evening.

I lived about five miles from Oakland where all the teams played in those days, yet it might as well have been 500 miles away. We didn't have a car and my dad didn't even know how to drive one. Less sports news was better. It left more to the imagination. Sports figures were magic figures that lived in some Wonderland far away.

There were national highlights on newsreels screened between the movies and the cartoons on Saturday at the local movie theater.

Track & field was one of my first loves. I knew all the ace athletes from around the world and knew their stories. I even had my own track & field team when I was 12 and 13, consisting of kids who were nine to 11 from the neighborhood. I conducted track meets on Sunnyside Street where I lived, and had T-shirts with SUNNYSIDE A.C. across the chest. I started writing about our athletic activities and that's how I landed a job as the sportswriter of our local weekly at age 14.

If you know this you can appreciate how I felt on a Saturday evening at the outset of the month. I was the co-emcee, along with WQED's Chis Moore, of a dinner at the Heinz History Center and Western Pennsylvania Sports Museum in the Strip.

We were there to celebrate the 85th birthday of Herb Douglas Jr., one of my first sports heroes in Hazelwood, who won a bronze medal in the long jump in the 1948 Olympic Games at Wembley Stadium in London. He calls me at least once a month from his residence in Philadelphia. He still maintains his boyhood home in Hazelwood. He stays there when he comes to Pittsburgh. He still insists it's the only place where he can get a good night's sleep. Soon after our arrival at the Heinz History Center, Kathie asked Herb if anyone in his family was present for his special honor. He pointed to his wife Minerva, who was standing nearby, and then he hesitated as he searched the crowd in the lobby and, finally, nodded in my direction and said, "And Jim's here."

I felt like someone had just put an Olympic medal around my neck. My wife Kathie and I were seated at a round table with a galaxy of Olympians. We were surrounded by greatness. Best of all they were good company.

To my left at the table, clockwise, sat Roger Kingdom, Harrison Dillard, Donna de Varona, Edwin Moses and Dr. Charles Jenkins. All were gold medalists in Olympic Games competition. You have to be a fan of the Olympic Games to get a real appreciation for this assembly. The lone woman in that group of gold medalists, de Varona, was a great swimmer and ABC Sports analyst.

Then, too, there was Rev. Jimmy Joe Robinson at our round table. He was once a civil rights leader in Pittsburgh and marched in The South with the Rev. Martin Luther King Jr.

Rev. Robinson was the first black football player to perform at Pitt in 1945, two years before Jackie Robinson broke the color barrier in major league baseball. Robinson was joined a few weeks later by Herb Douglas and Alan Carter on the Panthers' eleven. Arnie Sowell sat nearby. He was the favorite in the 800 meters in the 1956 Olympic Games and one of the greatest track stars in Pitt history, but he finished fourth in the Games.

Josephine Guercio Brennan, a real fireball who lived in West Mifflin, paid tribute to her childhood neighbor and friend. Douglas credits her for pushing him to study hard and successfully run for class president as a senior at Taylor Allderdice High School. Wes King, who grew up with Douglas in Hazelwood, also spoke of his early years.

All of them paid tribute to Douglas as a friend, mentor and counselor. He has been all of those to me as well through the years. He's been an inspiration to many. He was not only a success in sports, but he was one of the first black athletes to make the transition to the corporate world as a prized executive. He's been a great ambassador for all he represents and he's moved among giants in every respect.

When I've complained about a problem here and there in my business, Herb Douglas scolds me and boosts me at the same time. "You can't hope it will happen," he says, "you've got to make it happen."

My sports magazines came to life when I sat at this round table at the Heinz History Center. King Arthur never kept better company at his round table. These men and women had achieved great things. This was a black tie affair so they looked so attractive and dignified.

They still walk tall and proud, yet they are humble and so down to earth, and easy to be with. They let their records speak for themselves, and they remain grateful for those like Herb Douglas who helped them achieve greatness in their Games.

Heinz History
Center President
Andy Masich,
left to right, with
Olympian Herb
Douglas Jr. and
Franco Harris.

Two of the greatest
hurdlers of all time
are Harrison Dillard
and Edwin Moses.

Photos by Jim O'Brien

Author's wife Kathleen Churchman O'Brien is flanked by two-time Olympic
gold medalist hurdler Roger Kingdom and Olympic swimming medalist
Donna deVarona at 85th birthday party for Herb Douglas Jr.

Photos by Jim O'Brien

Herb Douglas Jr., third from left, is joined by Olympic gold medalists Harrison Dillard, Mal Whitfield and Dr. Charlie Jenkins at the Duquesne Club.

Herb Douglas Jr., enjoys company of Tony Dorsett and Rev. Jimmy Joe Robinson at Pitt reunion at Alumni Hall. Dorsett led Pitt's football team to a national championship when he won the Heisman Trophy in 1976, and Robinson and Douglas were the first African-American athletes on the school's football team in 1945, two years before Jackie Robinson broke the color line in Major League Baseball in 1947.

The Olympic Games have always been a personal favorite

August 2008

I have been a life-long fan of the Summer Olympic Games. The Olympic Games in Helsinki in 1952 and Melbourne in 1956 were the first to gain my attention. I read about them in the newspapers and magazines, poring over the pages and committing the names and feats to memory.

I really got hooked with the Olympic Games in Rome in 1960. They were the first Olympic Games to be shown on television. Whatever happened in Rome during the day would be shown at night in America.

The satellite technology was in its infancy so there was no live television of the Olympic Games in 1960. Film was flown to the U.S. and there was a five-hour time difference in our favor so the coverage was fairly current. The 1960 Games were the first on commercial TV.

Jim McKay, who recently died, was the studio host, stationed in New York. He helped edit the film and wrote the script himself. He would become the face and voice of future Olympics coverage.

Sometime after the Olympics in Melbourne in 1956—when I was 14-years-old—and the Olympics in Rome in 1960—when I had just graduated from Taylor Allderdice High School—I formed my own track & field team on the street where I lived.

The team was called the Sunnyside A.C. I lived on the shady side of Sunnyside Street. We had black jerseys with white trim and our mothers ironed the lettering and numbers on our jerseys. My team members ranged in age from nine to 13. I passed out miniature trophies from the local Murphy's 5 & 10 Store that had gold medal plates with the inscription "World's Greatest Athlete."

I laid out a quarter-mile track on the street. I urged my father to run it one day—he had some City Parks track medals in a drawer in his bedroom—and then worried that might have a heart attack. He was 42 at the time and trim as can be, but I thought he might be too old to run a quarter-mile. I built a broad jump pit—now the event is called the long jump—across the street from our row house. I fashioned a discus from some wood scraps I found at the local lumberyard and I secured a black duckpin bowling ball at the local lanes for the shot put. Dick Caliguiri, later the mayor of Pittsburgh, looked after those bowling lanes for his father. He gave me a ball that was pretty nicked up, but suitable as a shot put.

One of my favorite Olympians was Parry O'Brien of USC. He had won the gold medal in the shot put at Helsinki and Melbourne and was the favorite in Rome. But he was beaten out by Bill Nieder of Kansas and had to settle for the silver medal.

Many of the names of our Olympians from 1960 remain familiar to me. Rafer Johnson of UCLA won the gold medal in the decathlon when that feat also gained one the title of "the world's greatest athlete." He beat out C.K. Yang, a friend and teammate at UCLA, who represented Taiwan in those games. Johnson was a handsome and articulate athlete and was the captain of the 1960 Olympics team. He was the first black to carry the American flag at the Olympic Games.

Taiwan wanted to compete under the banner of The People's Republic of China, but was refused permission by the International Olympic Committee. China did not compete in the 1960 Games.

Dave Simes of Duke—pronounced Sims—was the favorite in the 100 meters dash, but finished second. He and Bobby Morrow of Abilene Christian were America's two best sprinters in the late '50s. I remember them both being pictured on the cover of *Sports Illustrated*. They were both white. The top three medallists in the 100 meters in Rome were white. That points up how long ago that was.

We also had an outstanding sprinter in Ray Norton, later an NFL performer, but he finished last in the 100 and 200 meters in Rome. John Thomas of Boston U. was the clear favorite to win the high jump, but finished fourth—the worst place to finish—and didn't medal.

Wilma Rudolph of Tennessee State was the star sprinter on the women's team in Rome. She had worn braces as a child, one of 17 children in her family, because she suffered from polio. Hers was an amazing comeback story.

I loved to read inspirational stories such as Wilma Rudolph's remarkable tale of courage. There was a red hardbound book that didn't have a dust jacket on it that was in the library at Allderdice High School. It could not be checked out. I went to the library often to read the stories of the Olympians who had overcome hardships to triumph in athletic competition. Now I write books like that one.

Muhammad Ali was Cassius Clay in 1960, a brash 18-year-old light heavyweight boxer from Louisville. Clay was one of the favorites in the Olympic Village, but not nearly as big a figure as recently-penned history would have you believe. Boxing wasn't one of the big sports in the Olympics. Cassius Clay, by the way, was smitten by the charms of the beautiful Wilma Rudolph and made a play for her, but she was dating Ray Norton.

Neither was basketball that big a sport in the Olympics then, but we certainly sent a great team to Rome. It was led by Oscar Robertson of Cincinnati, Jerry West of West Virginia, Jerry Lucas of Ohio State, Walt Bellamy of Indiana, Bob Boozer of Kansas State and Adrian Smith of Kentucky. Talk about a Dream Team. Our big foe back then was Russia. There were strong political overtones to our competition with Russia in every sport. The Cold War was going on, and it was important to gain an edge in every area of competition and comparison.

Our team was so strong that year that two players who were cut at the training camp—John Havlicek of Ohio State and Lenny Wilkens of Providence—would later be inducted into the Basketball Hall of Fame. We won the gold medal in basketball and won our games by an average of 30 points.

Robertson and West formed a great guard combination. "One black and one white, with all that was going on in the country at the time," said West, "for us to stand there (on the podium) with our gold medals, it meant a lot."

I learned what West said and about Clay trying to charm Wilma Rudolph, and about Taiwan's team while reading a wonderful new book by David Maraniss. It's called *Rome 1960: The Olympics That Changed the World.* I was half way through it when I wrote this column, but should have finished it by now.

I had read two other books by Maraniss, a Pulitzer Prize-winning journalist who formerly wrote for *The New York Times.* One was *Clemente: The Passion and Grace of Baseball's Last Hero*, and *When Pride Still Mattered: A Life of Vince Lombardi.*

A telling line in the Maraniss book on the 1960 Olympics goes like this: "Usually you lose because some one else is better that day."

I also learned that Parry O'Brien revolutionized the shot put by starting out with his back to the area where he'd be tossing the shot. He'd do a 180-degree spin, getting more behind his heave, and it was referred to as "the O'Brien glide."

I attended the Baldwin Invitational Track & Field Meet this spring and was surprised to note that only a few threw the shot in the same manner as Parry O'Brien. I also noticed that the winner did use what I now know is called "the O'Brien glide."

These books by Maraniss bring back special memories, none more so than this latest epic. I know the track & field performers and the basketball players and some of the gymnast from those 1960 Olympic Games.

That was a big summer in Pittsburgh, too. The Pirates were in a torrid pennant race in the National League for the first time in a long time.

I would enter Pitt in September of 1960. One month later, the Pirates were playing the New York Yankees in the World Series right on our campus, just a block away from the Pitt Student Union where I worked on the student newspaper. What a great start for a school year!

One learns a lot in the Marannis book. It fleshes out the background stories of those favorite athletes from my teen years. He deals in details with the star athletes from other countries, especially Russia. This, like his other books, is a story that goes well beyond the world of fun and games.

When I was growing up in Hazelwood I was excited to learn that a young man from our community had won a bronze medal in the 1948 Olympic Games in London. His name was Herb Douglas. Like me, he had gone to Allderdice and Pitt.

When I was in eighth grade at St. Stephen's Grade School, I used to pass his home at 160 Hazelwood Avenue on the way to take a metal shop or wood shop class—it was called a "released time class"— on Friday afternoon at Gladstone Junior High School. The school was near his home. I'd often stop and stare at his home, hoping he might be visiting, or that he'd come out on the porch so I could see him.

I had a chance to meet him after I had graduated from Pitt and we became good friends. I hear from him at least once a month now. He calls from Philadelphia, where he now lives. He became a big success as an executive with Schieffelin & Somerset, an international wine & spirits company now known as Hennessy & Moet. He's still a wonderful role model. I've helped him celebrate his 80th and 85th birthdays at parties in Pittsburgh. His boyhood heroes were Jessie Owens and John Woodruff, who won gold medals at the Olympics as track & field performers. He was also a big fan of Joe Louis.

Douglas says the 1936 Olympic Games were a renaissance for black athletes as Owens won four gold medals in the 100 and 200 meters, in the long jump and as a member of the 4x100 relay team and Woodruff won a gold medal in the 800 meters.

Hitler and his Nazi regime were espousing propaganda about the Aryan Supremacy, and America's black athletes shot down that theory and then some with their achievements and medal-winning efforts in those Games in Berlin.

"Up until then we didn't have our own heroes in sports," declared Douglas. "After that, we did, and they served us well."

HOMETOWN HERO—There is a mural of Herb Douglas Jr. depicting him as he won the bronze medal in the long jump in the 1948 Summer Olympic Games in London. This mural is on the wall of a building at the corner of Second Avenue and Tecumseh Street in Herb's hometown of Hazelwood.

BASKETBALL

Robert Pavuchak/ABA All-Stars

Mike Lewis and John Brisker of the Pittsburgh Pipers flank Tom Bowens of New Orleans Bucaneers in ABA action at Civic Arena in late January of 1970. Lewis had played at Duke and Brisker at Toledo. Brisker disappeared while engaged as a mercenary in Uganda in later years and was never found. He was a terrific scorer and rebounder and a physical force on and off the floor, especially in the Pipers' locker room. He and Art Heyman got into it in one of the infamous feuds. Brisker was ejected from so many games for fighting that he was called "the heavyweight champion of the ABA." He was legally declared dead in 1985.

Going one on one
with Bill Sharman

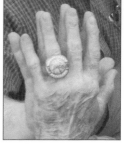

August 2009

I was in basketball heaven. On a memorable Tuesday evening in 2009, I spent three hours in the company of Bill Sharman, one of the all-time greats in the game of basketball. Sharman is one of three men who have been honored by the Basketball Hall of Fame as both a player and a coach. John Wooden and Lenny Wilkens are the others similarly enshrined at the Springfield, Massachusetts mecca.

Sharman and I sat on the deck of his son Tom's home in Peters Township, about six miles from my home in Upper St. Clair and 16 miles south of downtown Pittsburgh. It was a balmy evening with the temperature in the 70s, and Sharman put on a light jacket because it seemed a little cool for him, having just come from Southern California where it was at the hundred degree mark most days of late.

I know that firsthand because I had been visiting our daughter Rebecca in Los Angeles a week earlier. While there, I had attempted to meet with Sharman, who lives in El Segundo Beach, but our schedules were such that we couldn't find a mutually acceptable time.

We spoke on the phone while I was in Los Angeles, but it's not easy to understand Sharman on the telephone these days because he strained and ruined his voice a dozen or so years ago, and speaks in a screeching voice now, like he's hollering at you from the bottom of a well. There's still a joy in his voice, however, and he's happy with how things have turned out for him.

I was surprised when he called me on the telephone at my home last Tuesday, July 29, and told me he was staying at his son's home in nearby Peters Township. Tom Sharman got on the phone and asked me if I could come and see his dad that night. I didn't hesitate a moment to reply that I would.

"You're leaving too early," my wife Kathie cautioned me as I hurried from our home. Like a little kid looking for an autograph.

Here I had hoped to see him in Los Angeles where we had gotten together for lunch at the Marriott near the LA Airport two-and-a-half years ago, and now he was almost in my backyard. That Hyatt stands on Century Boulevard, where I passed on this recent trip to LA. I remember catching a bus at that same site with members of the New York media to cover the Knicks in the NBA championship series back in the spring of 1970.

That's the series where Jerry West made the 55-foot shot, and where Willis Reed of the Knicks limped out of the locker room to challenge Chamberlain in the playoff finale, won by the Knicks. Reed had missed the sixth game with a leg injury and the Knicks had lost the game. The series was even at three victories apiece. I was sitting in the first seat at the mid-court break in the press row at Madison Square

Garden for the seventh game, and Reed pressed on my right shoulder as he stepped up onto the wooden playing floor for the pre-game warm-up. It was one of the most dramatic moments in NBA playoff history.

Reed made his first two jump shots in the lane, and Chamberlain and the Lakers never recovered from the shock of seeing him out there when he wasn't supposed to be able to play. Reed never scored any more points, but it was enough to get the Knicks off and running.

Tom Sharman said he was happy to hear some things about his dad that he didn't know. His parents were divorced when Tom was seven. His dad had remarried. Tom, who was nearing his 50th birthday, is a health and physical education teacher at Mellon Middle School in the Mt. Lebanon School District. He's been there for ten years and previously taught for five years in the Keystone Oaks School District.

Tom's wife Susan had made a peach pie for dessert and served it with a healthy dollop of vanilla ice cream on the dish. Peach pie ala mode and Bill Sharman...it doesn't get any better. There was a basketball hoop in the driveway of this sylvan setting, a basketball sitting at the bottom of the pole, so it was just perfect. Their daughter Katy, ready to start her senior year at Peters Township High where she is a member of the volleyball and track and field teams, was not home during my visit. Neither was Joyce Sharman, Bill's wife, who has family in Indiana, Pa.

I said I'd need an hour with him, and ended up staying three hours on that deck. If I had a pup tent I might have camped out on the deck till dawn.

"Did you see our team play this year?" Sharman had asked me when we first spoke in Los Angeles the week before. "We were pretty good."

Sharman, then 83 and maybe a little thinner than when I last saw him, still served as a paid "special consultant" for the Los Angeles Lakers. He once coached the team to an NBA championship, and later served as president and general manager and then as a consultant.

Lakers' owner Jerry Buss has kept him on the payroll because Bill Sharman is such a standup guy, with great knowledge about basketball and the people who play the game, and he's someone you'd want to keep on your side, or at your side. He's good company.

He remembers how he had to beg former Lakers' owner Jack Kent Cooke to let him hire one assistant coach, K.C. Jones, and how most NBA and college teams now have four and five assistants. It's even crazier to have that kind of staff on a high school level. A coach is separated by four men in business suits from his players. And some of them have huddles at timeouts to talk among themselves instead of instructing their players.

"There's a coach for every player," said Sharman, and I could tell he agrees with me that's it a bit foolish to have so many coaches on the bench. It's also costly for the colleges, in particular.

Sharman teamed with Bob Cousy in the '50s to form one of the greatest backcourt combinations in NBA history. Cousy was a slick ball-handler and the best passer of his era, and Sharman was the best shooter of his day. He played ten seasons with the Celtics, averaging 17.8 points a game.

Sharman was coached by the legendary Arnold "Red" Auerbach. He played alongside Cousy, Bill Russell, K.C. and Sam Jones, Tom Heinsohn, and Frank Ramsey. He coached Chamberlain, West, Elgin Baylor, Rick Barry, Zelmo Beatty, Willie Wise, James Jones and Kareem Abdul-Jabbar, just to name a few of his superstar performers.

When he was coaching the Warriors he remembers Barry telling him he was going to break his free throw percentage record. "I figured there was no way he was going to do that shooting under-handed shots," recalled Sharman. "But he did." Barry is still the all-time leading free throw shooter with a .960 career average at the foul line. Sharman ranks third behind Calvin Murphy.

Bill Sharman is a sweet man, and one of the best people I've met in basketball. I introduced him to my mother once and from then after he always asked, "How's your Mom?" What delighted me when we first spoke on the telephone this time around was that he sounded so excited to hear from me again, wanted to get together, and gave me a big hug when we said hello and goodbye at his son's home.

We had shared something special together, like many of the Steelers from the '70s who showed up for the annual Ray Mansfield Memorial Golf Tournament that same day at the Diamond Run Golf Club out near Wexford. When some of those Steelers give me a hug when we see each other it makes me feel that we enjoyed something special together when they had the best football team in the National Football League.

That happened the last time I bumped into Julius Erving, who was Dr. J in the ABA and the NBA.

I first met Bill Sharman when I was covering the ABA as well as the NBA during my nine years in New York, from 1970 to 1979.

In 1970–71, Sharman coached the Utah Stars to an ABA title and was a co-recipient of the ABA Coach of the Year honors. The following year he guided the Wilt Chamberlain and Jerry West-led Los Angeles Lakers to an NBA record 33-game win streak, a then-record 69–13 win-loss mark, the first Lakers' championship in more than a decade, and was named NBA Coach of the year.

Sharman helped me a lot in those days. He was one of four pro coaches who sent me extensive scouting reports on all the pro teams that I used to write *The Complete Handbook of Pro Basketball* for three seasons. I can't imagine any coaches doing that today. At the time, I was also the editor of *Street and Smith's Basketball Yearbook* and wrote a column on pro basketball for *The Sporting News* and *Basketball Weekly,* so I devoted a great deal of attention to pro and college basketball.

Sharman is one of two men to win NBA and ABA championships as a coach. The other was Alex Hannum, who also coached a Chamberlain-led team (the Philadelphia 76ers) as well as the Bob Pettit and Cliff Hagan-led St. Louis Hawks to an NBA title, and won an ABA title in Denver. Sharman is the only coach to claim championships in three different pro leagues as he also coached the Cleveland Pipers

Bill Sharman shows off some sports memorabilia at a hotel in Los Angeles in winter of 2007. Sharman coached the Lakers to an NBA title and he was once a star player for the Boston Celtics and was in the Dodgers' organization at the same time.

to a championship in the first and only full season of the old American Basketball League. That was in 1961–62.

Pittsburgh had a team in that league, the Pittsburgh Rens (short for Renaissance), led by 19-year-old Connie Hawkins. The Cleveland Pipers were owned by Cleveland shipbuilder George Steinbrenner, more famous now as the owner of the New York Yankees. Steinbrenner initially hired John McClendon, who had been the first black head coach in pro basketball, and brought in Sharman at mid-season. The ABL folded midway through its second season.

Steinbrenner also once boasted that he'd trade one of his ships in exchange for Connie Hawkins. I conducted a successful campaign to get Connie Hawkins into the Basketball Hall of Fame when I was on the nominating committee for that Hall of Fame. Hawkins later played for the Phoenix Suns, the Los Angeles Lakers and the Atlanta Hawks.

Sharman has been associated, as a player, coach or front-office administrator and consultant, with 15 championship teams in pro basketball, including the Lakers' success in 2008–2009. Sharman is a big fan of Phil Jackson then the team's coach, and Kobe Bryant, the team's star player.

He says Bryant is one of the hardest working players in the league, and believes he has matured to be more of a leader and team player the past few seasons.

To fully appreciate why it was such a splendid occasion for me to be sitting on a deck with Bill Sharman, sharing stories about our days with the ABA and NBA, you need to know a little background.

When I was growing up in my boyhood home in Glenwood, in the inner-city of Pittsburgh, I had quite a collection of sports magazines on the nightstand by my bed. I still have one of them, even though the cover is missing. It is from 1952. Sharman is pictured in the same section as Dick Groat, who had just played his rookie season with the Pittsburgh Pirates as well as his first season with the NBA's Fort Wayne Pistons.

"I played against Groat in baseball and basketball," said Sharman. "He was quite the competitor. He had a great outside shot, he could really score, and he played tough on defense. He'd have been one of the great guards in our league if he had stayed with it. But he had to make a choice, and he stayed with the Pirates. We've seen each other and spoken about those days."

Sharman was a star backcourtman, teamed with Bob Cousy, with four NBA championship teams with the Boston Celtics. Cousy could dribble the ball behind his back when nobody else was doing that. In that 1952 magazine I have, Cousy was chosen as the best player in the NBA, and a 5-foot-9 guard at Seattle University named Johnny O'Brien was picked as the best college player.

Is it any wonder I got hooked on basketball so much as a ten-year-old fan? That Johnny O'Brien, as well as his twin brother Eddie, later played with Groat as infielders for the Pirates after their basketball playing days at Seattle. They were from Perth Amboy, N.J., as I recall.

The Pirates had a better basketball team than a baseball team in those days. They had two great running backs in football as well, with Heisman Trophy winner Vic Janowicz (1960) and Paul Giel, runner-up to Notre Dame's Johnny Lattner in 1953 for the Heisman Trophy.

Sharman played professional baseball in the Brooklyn Dodgers minor league system from 1950 to 1955. He was called up to the Dodgers late in the 1951 season, but did not appear in a game. As a result of a September 27 game in which the entire Brooklyn bench was ejected from the game for arguing with the umpire, Sharman holds the distinction of being the only player to have ever been ejected from a major league baseball game without ever appearing in one.

"I get more attention about that, it seems, than anything I did in basketball," said Sharman with a smile. "I still get asked about that."

He also was in the Brooklyn dugout later in that 1951 season when Bobby Thomson of the New York Giants hit a walk-off home run—the so-called "shot heard round the world"—to win the playoff for the National League title that year. Ralph Branca, of course, gave up the home run to gain lifetime notoriety as well.

So Sharman had a front row seat in baseball history. (It's a little known fact that Bob Prince, the "Voice of the Pirates," was in the broadcast booth to witness Thomson's home run.)

That cherished magazine from 1952 has thumbnail photos and brief bio sketches of all the star performers in all sports. I still love to flip through its well-worn pages. It brings back so many good memories.

"We were lucky," said Sharman, "to be able to spend our lives doing something we really enjoyed doing."

When I last sat with Sharman at a restaurant off the lobby of the Marriott Hotel in Los Angeles, he was wearing one of the championship rings he'd been given by the Lakers. Our waiter was enchanted by the sight of this large ring, and asked about it.

Sharman removed it from his ring finger and let the young waiter hold it, and slip it onto his own finger. Then Sharman gave it to me. I couldn't get it on my finger. This surprised me because I have small hands. "So do I," said Sharman.

With that we pressed our extended right hands against each other, and discovered that we both have the same sized hand, but Sharman's fingers are a tad slimmer.

We did this again on the deck of the Sharman home in Peters Township, and smiled at the memory. "I know you can't palm a basketball," said Sharman in almost a shriek. "I'll be darned, but I never could either, and everyone wants to be able to do that."

Small hands might have helped Sharman more than it did me because he was one of the most accurate shooters of his day. He had a hand in bringing the 3-point field goal to the ABL and he promoted the idea of using it when he got involved with the ABA. Sharman should also be in the Basketball Hall of Fame as a contributor.

The three-point field goal had been experimented with in college basketball back in 1933 and again in 1945, but was never officially adopted into the game at those times. It was first used on a regular basis when the ABL came into being in 1961.

Abe Saperstein, a Chicago-based basketball promoter who founded and owned the Harlem Globetrotters, wanted to have "a home run shot" when he started the ABL.

Saperstein knew Sharman because Sharman was a member of an All-Star College team that toured the country with the Globetrotters after Sharman had starred at Southern Cal as a collegian. Saperstein spoke to Sharman about his ideas. Sharman's first coaching job was with the Los Angeles Jets in the American Basketball League, but he was let go at midseason and ended up suing the team in a famous sports legal case (Sharman vs. Longo) in 1967. But it was in the ABL that he got reacquainted with Saperstein.

"He wanted to have the 3-point field goal from 25 feet out," recalled Sharman. "He had me shoot some shots from that far out, and I told him it was too difficult of a shot and it wouldn't be much of a factor. So I told him to measure the shot to the back of the rim instead of the front of the rim. That made a big difference."

The distance has been altered since then, and it's shorter for the women and college basketball, but it has been a popular aspect of the game.

The ABA's red, white and blue ball originated with the Harlem Globetrotters, who put on quite a show with their ball-handling wizardry.

In addition to bringing the three-point field goal to the ABA (NBA officials called it a "gimmick" but adopted the 3-point field goal in 1979), Sharman was the first coach to conduct day-of-the-game shoot arounds. He had done that on his own when he played for the Boston Celtics. He was always anxious on the day of the game, so he'd go out and burn off some energy by shooting baskets in the morning or afternoon at any gym he could find.

He thought it would be a good idea when he took over the Lakers. He had to convince Chamberlain that it was a good idea to do that. Chamberlain wasn't convinced until the Lakers went on that 33-game winning streak that season.

There was an apocryphal story making the rounds in those days that Chamberlain, who could be a tough cookie, balked at the idea, and told Sharman he was willing to come out to the arena once each day. "I'll come out in the morning, or I'll come out in the evening," Chamberlain was reputed to have said. "You take your pick."

Sharman insists that never happened. "Wilt wasn't always easy to deal with," said Sharman, "but he was a great player, and I got along fine with him. We won the league championship, so my ideas must have been sound."

Sharman served during World War II from 1944 to 1946 in the U.S. Navy. The gymnasium at Porterville High School in a rural community in California is named in his honor.

As a player, Sharman was one of the first guards to shoot better than .400 from the field. He led the NBA in free throw percentage seven times, and his mark of 93.2 per cent in the 1958–59 season remained the NBA record until Ernie DiGregorio topped it in 1976–77. Sharman still holds the record for consecutive free throws in the playoffs with 56. He made over 50 straight free throws on three occasions in his career. He was born in Abilene, Texas a town that turned out a lot of great shooters in the early days of the wild, wild West.

Sharman was named to the All-NBA First Team from 1956 through 1959, and was an All-NBA Second Team member in 1953, 1955 and 1960. Sharman played in eight NBA All-Star games, and was named the 1955 NBA All-Star Game MVP. Sharman ended his career after 11 seasons with the Celtics in 1961.

His best days were during my high school days. As I drove home that night from seeing Sharman at his son's home, I couldn't help think back to those days when I read stories about him and Bob Cousy in my boyhood bedroom. I started a three-man basketball league on the street outside my home, and kept stats and everything. My team was called the Royals because the Rochester Royals, who had five or six players with Pittsburgh connections, were my favorite NBA team. About ten to twelve NBA games were shown on black-and-white television in those days.

What were the chances then that someday I'd be sitting on someone's deck going one-on-one with Bill Sharman?

"It's been great to see you and spend time with you," said Sharman as I went down a steep set of steps from the deck to the driveway where my car was parked. "I'd come down, but my legs don't work so well on steps like that."

Bill Sharman and Jim O'Brien meet for breakfast in surburban Los Angeles in spring of 2012. Inset, Sharman and O'Brien have the same size hands, on the small side, but Bill was one of the best shooters in NBA and O'Brien can't buy a basket these days. Sharman shows off his NBA championship ring.

Learning from Dr. King
and Doug Smith

January 2010

I was listening to a wonderful sermon last Sunday on the topic of courage as characterized by Dr. Martin Luther King Jr. It was delivered by Rev. Jim Gilchrist, the pastor of Westminster Presbyterian Church in Upper St. Clair. It was the day before we celebrated the birthday of Dr. King.

I was inspired to pick up a copy of a book on leadership and Dr. King at the church library on the way out and to reflect on an old friend and fellow sportswriter, Doug Smith.

I'm forever grateful to Doug Smith because he taught me how to play tennis, a game for life, and how we taught each other something about human relations, another game for life. We're the same age, in our late 60s (now 70 in my case), and we can relate to the same stories.

Smith and I both covered the New York Nets in the American Basketball Association in the mid-70s. Those were the Nets of Julius Erving, known simply as Dr. J, when the Nets twice won championships in the ABA. Smith wrote for *Newsday,* a Long Island daily, and I wrote for *The New York Post.*

I think we learned a lot from each other.

One night in 1974 or 1975 we shared a hotel room in Memphis, just two blocks from the Lorraine Motel where Dr. King was shot and killed on April 4, 1968. He was shot as he stood on the balcony outside his hotel room.

Dr. King had delivered his famous "I've Been to the Mountain" speech only the night before he was assassinated in Memphis. When we traveled with the Nets, normally we had our own hotel rooms. But there was a shortage of rooms at the hotel where we were staying this night in Memphis, and Doug Smith and I were asked to share a room.

There seemed to be a certain irony to that. It was the only time it ever happened in the three or four years we both covered the club, and it happened in Memphis, of all places. There was a time when this would not have been permitted. Doug Smith is black and I am white. We had twin beds and we talked away the night.

Smith and I got along well. I was usually so competitive about my newspaper work that I seldom became chummy with the competition, but it was different with Smith. He tested me from time to time about race relations, one time almost cruelly when my wife Kathie and I were visitors at his home on Long Island. He startled us by playing a tape of Malcolm X, the controversial Muslim minister, assailing "whites as devils" in one of his famous speeches. Smith later apologized for doing that. Malcolm X and Dr. King were concerned about the same civil rights issues, but Dr. King chose to take a non-violent approach.

When Smith visited our home on another occasion, he pointed out that a neighbor of mine across the cul-de-sac had one of those black lawn jockeys in front of his house. Most blacks, understandably, found those comic-looking statues offensive and insensitive.

Smith would smile at me a lot when we were having a conversation about such stuff, like he knew something I didn't.

We both were fond of Dr. J. Smith was also a big fan of Arthur Ashe, the great tennis player. They had played in the same tennis circles back in Hampton, Virginia. Smith had been a member of the Hampton University championship tennis team in his schooldays. Ashe was the first black man to win a U. S. Open singles title. Smith and Ashe remained friends through the years, a connection that helped Smith considerably in the tennis world.

When we were covering the Nets, Smith would often play tennis on the road with the Nets' coaches, Kevin Loughery and Rod Thorn. Somebody associated with the opposing team in that town would be the fourth in their doubles pairings. Then they'd drink a few beers afterward and talk about basketball for another hour or so.

I thought Smith enjoyed a tremendous edge on me in covering the club because of this extra time and conversation he enjoyed with the coaches.

I wanted us to be competing on a level playing field, so to speak, so I asked Smith if he'd teach me how to play tennis. I wanted to play tennis so I could do my job better. I had an old wooden frame tennis racquet at home that I think I used once as a teenager. I think it was a Fred Perry model. There wasn't even a net on the tennis court where I'd used it in my hometown of Hazelwood, back in Pittsburgh.

The next road trip took us to Greensboro, North Carolina, for a game with the Carolina Cougars. I brought along my tennis racquet. I called Doug Smith in his room and asked him if we could go out and hit some tennis balls that afternoon. He said, "Sure, I've got us a match today. "

I was stunned. I had not played any tennis and I was certainly not ready for a match. He had us paired against Loughery and Thorn. Loughery was 6–3 and Thorn was 6–4 and both had played guard in the National Basketball Association only five years earlier. You talk about learning a sport under fire.

We played on beautiful red clay courts that afternoon and somehow I managed not to embarrass myself too much. From then on, I got to join Smith and the coaches in their tennis outings. Most basketball players pick up tennis in a hurry and can really cover the court.

I got interested in tennis and started covering it for *The New York Post,* and covered the U. S. Open at the West Side Tennis Club. I played in some media tournaments there against some pretty famous folk, like the great photographer Gordon Parks. My wife took up the sport and is still at it today. She also plays platform tennis and pickleball. So Smith changed our lives in regard to recreation and exercise activities.

One day I called my wife from the West Side Tennis Club to tell her I was on the winning team in a mixed-doubles match against a woman who had won 18 Grand Slam titles, the legendary Sarah Palfrey Danzig. Most of her titles came in doubles, but she won the U. S. Open singles title twice, and was runner-up twice.

"How old is she?" Kathie came back, always wanting to spoil things.

Mrs. Danzig was 62 at the time and I was 32.

A few years later the U. S. Open was moved from the West Side Tennis Club to a new tennis complex at Flushing Meadows. I was on the winning team there in the first tennis tournament ever conducted on those now hallowed grounds. I'm always lucky in these tournaments to draw an outstanding partner. Mine was a young writer for *The Wall Street Journal*, but I don't recall his name.

We beat a team in the semi-finals that included Bud Collins of *The Boston Globe*, one of the most famous sports writers of all time. He was a tennis analyst for NBC and then ESPN. He always wore colorful getups and he was more interested in entertaining the onlookers this day than competing seriously, so we took advantage of that and beat his team. I'm always hoping John McEnroe will mention that bit of trivia when he's telling stories during the national telecasts of the U.S. Open.

In the finals, the other team was led by Will Grimsley, the syndicated columnist for The Associated Press. He was the president of the U.S. Tennis Writers Association. Grimsley usually was on the winning team in this tournament. Not this time. Smith was standing on the sideline wondering, no doubt, how the hell I was still out on the court and he was on the sideline. He was much the superior tennis player. But he encouraged me.

Our team won. I was 36 at the time and Grimsley was 64. He and Collins are enshrined in the Tennis Hall of Fame. I am not.

I did cover World Team Tennis as well, and had an opportunity to meet some of the greatest tennis players in the world such as Billie Jean King, Chris Evert and Virginia Wade, Pancho Gonzalez, John McEnroe, Rod Laver, Ken Rosewall, Vitas Gerulaitis and Bobby Riggs. I handled public relations for the Baldwin Tennis Club where we lived on Long Island and had many of those star tennis players conduct free clinics at the club.

Smith went on to take my place at *The New York Post* when I left and returned home to write for *The Pittsburgh Press,* where I covered the Steelers. Later on, Smith began a 15-year run as the tennis columnist for *USA Today*. He traveled to places such as Paris, London and Melbourne to cover tennis on an international basis. "It's hard to believe," Smith said recently. "Me coming from a community where it was unlikely I'd ever get to play tennis. And then doing what I was doing for a living. It was a great run. "

It was Smith who broke the story that Ashe had contracted AIDS. He became one of the most prominent and influential tennis writers in the country. He covered all the majors. When he retired he became a visiting professor in the Scripps-Howard School of Journalism & Communications at Hampton University.

He edited and wrote an updated version of Arthur Ashe's three-volume book "Hard Road to Glory: A History of the Black Athlete in America. "He has written some other books about tennis. I'm proud to call him a friend.

I ran into Smith several years ago at a hotel in Tampa that served as headquarters for Super Bowl XXXV in January of 2001. We enjoyed our reunion. I was there to interview NFL people and the media about Art Rooney for my book *The Chief*. I remember I introduced Smith to "Deacon Dan" Towler, once a bruising running back for the Los Angeles Rams who hailed from Donora, Pennsylvania.

I received a late Christmas card from Smith at outset of 2008 and it brought back a lot of memories. I wrote him a letter and let him know that I had won an MVP Award from Champions, Inc., an African-American organization in Pittsburgh that promotes positive activities for black youth in the community.

I wanted Smith to know I was staying the course. He had been a good influence on me.

Doug Smith and the late great Deacon Dan Tower from Donora had a chance to meet at Super Bowl XXXV headquarters in Tampa, Florida in January of 2001.

Munhall's Jim Bukata introduced
me to Wilt Chamberlain and ESPN

March 2012

I was thinking about Wilt Chamberlain and Jim Bukata. Bukata loved basketball and most sports so he'd be proud to see his name in the same sentence as Wilt Chamberlain.

Chamberlain was back in the sports pages because Friday, March 2, 2012, was the 50th anniversary of his 100-point game for the Philadelphia Warriors against the New York Knicks in Hershey, Pa., of all places. It is by far the most points ever scored by an individual in a game in the National Basketball Association.

There were about 4,000 people in the Hershey Arena that night, but many had been drawn by a match-up of a basketball game featuring football players from the Philadelphia Eagles and Baltimore Colts that opened the doubleheader. Many fans left the building after that first game and didn't stick around to see Chamberlain's record outing.

Chamberlain had been one of my boyhood heroes. I was the smallest kid on Sunnyside Street in Glenwood where I was the commissioner of my own basketball league when I was a teenager. We had three-man teams and the hoop was just below my parents' bedroom window.

Bukata knew about my infatuation with Wilt Chamberlain. Bukata and I both worked in New York through most of the '70s. We were at Kutsher's Country Club in the Catskills one summer for the annual fund-raising exhibition game featuring top NBA players.

Wilt was always there. They were raising money to assist in the care of former NBA All-Star Maurice Stokes, who suffered a crippling brain injury while playing in an NBA game. He hit his head in a hard fall, later had a stroke, and was restricted to a hospital bed and wheel chair.

Stokes had first starred at Westinghouse High School in Pittsburgh and then St. Francis of Loretto College near Altoona. He gained national attention for his play in the NIT in New York.

Jack Twyman, who had played at Central Catholic High in Pittsburgh, and was a teammate of Stokes with the Cincinnati Royals, became his legal guardian and prime fund-raiser for his care.

I was in my room at Kutsher's Country Club the afternoon of the game, relaxing and reading the sports pages when there was a loud knock at the door. I opened the door and there, much to my amazement, was Wilt Chamberlain. He was 7-foot-1 and he had to lower his head to get through the door. He was wearing a purple basketball jersey and matching purple shorts. To me, he's still the most dominant basketball player in history. Bukata had asked Chamberlain to visit me.

Chamberlain stayed and talked to me for awhile. I took some photos of him that I still have in my photo album. I had a chance to talk to him later that night when he held court at the bar at Kutsher's after the basketball game. Wilt was an entertaining story-teller. He had stuttered as a kid, but he overcame that handicap to become downright eloquent. It was a day I will never forget.

Most sports fans in Pittsburgh are unaware that Wilt Chamberlain also set another record that still stands when he was playing for the Philadelphia 76ers at the Civic Arena in Pittsburgh.

He made all 18 shots he took against the Baltimore Bullets. That same month Chamberlain canned all 15 shots he attempted against the Lakers, and then all 16 shots against the Bullets in Baltimore.

I was there so I remember it well. This was during the 1967–68 season. The 76ers of that season have been voted the greatest NBA team ever. They posted a record of 68–13, the best in the league history up until that time.

That record was later broken by the Los Angeles Lakers during the 1971–72 season when they won a record 33 straight games and posted a 69–12 record. I had breakfast with Bill Sharman, the coach of the Lakers that season, in El Segundo Beach, Calif., late last month. Sharman remains one of my all-time NBA favorites, one of only three men to be in the Basketball Hall of Fame as both a coach and a player.

Chamberlain led the league in scoring seven seasons, was the league MVP four times. He once had 55 rebounds in a game and averaged better than 20 rebounds a game. He even led the league in assists once. Chamberlain could do whatever he wanted to do on a basketball court and often tried to attain certain goals just to amuse himself.

The night he made all 15 of his shots, usually dunk shots, he was in the midst of making 34 straight shots, also a league record. I had a speaking engagement last month at the Cambria Suites across from the Civic Arena. I could see the building, now with a maroon roof on it instead of the gleaming steel surface, and I thought about Chamberlain and what he did that night.

That great 76ers team played six of its home games that memorable season at the Civic Arena. Two Pittsburgh entertainment moguls, Jason Shapiro, the owner of the National Record Mart, and Gabe Rubin, who operated the Nixon Theater, paid the 76ers $50,000 in advance to get those six games for Pittsburgh.

The following season, Rubin and Shapiro teamed up to buy a franchise in the new American Basketball Association. Their team, the Pittsburgh Pipers, would win the first championship in the ABA, then move to Minnesota for the second season. In the ABA's third year, Pittsburgh had a team once again, aptly named the Pittsburgh Condors. They went the way of their endangered namesake a year later.

Jim Bukata came to mind for a few other reasons. Bukata died at age 69 of pancreatic cancer a couple of months ago. That hit home.

We were the same age. I first met him when I was the sports editor of *The Pitt News* during my student days at the University of Pittsburgh. Bukata was a member of the sports staff of *The Daily Collegian*, the newspaper at Penn State University.

The newspaper staffs of the two rival schools would play a touchtag football game on the morning of the game played between Pitt and

Penn State. I remember we played that game in 1963 on the lawn of the Cathedral of Learning.

Both football games had to be postponed because of the assassination of President John F. Kennedy in Dallas a few days earlier, Nov. 23, 1963.

Jim Bukata and I shared some other bonds. He was handling public relations for an upstart professional soccer league when the Pittsburgh Phantoms played at Forbes Field in 1966–67. He was later associated with Joey Goldstein in New York. Goldstein was one of the great sports public relations guys of that era.

When I became the founding editor for *Street & Smith's Basketball Yearbook* in 1970, Bukata asked if he could help in some way. He was such a great source of information about high school and college basketball players.

Bukata authored a feature called "15 Freshmen of Influence" for our magazine for nearly 30 years.

I was working for *The New York Post* for a nine-year stretch from 1970 to 1979, and I'd see Bukata often at sports press conferences and events. Some time in the mid-70s, I was offered the job as director of public relations and marketing for the ABA, but I was happy doing what I was doing.

I recommended Bukata to the ABA administrators and they hired him. He was well respected by the media throughout the league. Bukata is credited with coming up with the slam-dunk contest that is now a major part of the program for the NBA All-Star Game.

It was part of the weekend activity in Orlando at last month's mid-season extravaganza. That started back in January of 1976 when the ABA conducted its All-Star Game in Denver. League officials were looking for a way to put "some buzz" in the All-Star Game, one that would be nationally-televised.

It was Bukata who suggested the slam dunk contest. It featured five players, four of whom would become inductees into the Basketball Hall of Fame, and it was won in spectacular fashion by Julius "Dr. J" Erving.

When the ABA was assimilated into the NBA after that season Bukata went to work for the New York Nets and New York Islanders, two teams that I covered for *The New York Post*. Bukata assisted those teams' established public relations director Barney Kremenko. Kremenko had been a baseball writer in New York once upon a time and was credited with giving Willie Mays his nickname as "The Say-Hey Kid."

I left *The New York Post* in the summer of 1979 and returned home to Pittsburgh to write for *The Pittsburgh Press*. It was good timing as both the Pirates and Steelers would win championships that season.

I continued to serve as editor of *Street & Smith's Basketball Yearbook,* which required me to travel to New York now and then to work on the magazine layouts.

It was during one of those visits, in September of 1979, that I took a bus from midtown Manhattan to go to Bukata's home in New Milford, N.J. He had invited me to dinner at this home and an overnight stay.

I can still remember taking a bus from the Port Authority Bus Terminal on 8th Avenue and 42nd Street, just a block from Times Square. It's the largest bus terminal in the United States and the busiest bus terminal in the world, with 7,200 buses and 200,000 passengers going through it on an average day. It services more than 60 million people in an average year. It's funny what you remember…There are times anymore when I can't remember somebody's first name, somebody I should know well, yet I can remember that bus ride to New Milford like it happened yesterday.

I sat in the middle of the bench seat in the back of the bus that day. There was a crease in the seat padding. Hot air was blowing from the engine directly into the small of my back. It was not a comfortable ride. That night, Bukata was so excited about a new venture that had just come into being, ESPN, a sports cable station. We stayed up till about 2 a.m. in a den in the basement of his home watching kick-boxing on his television set. Bukata told me ESPN was going to be a big deal. I wasn't convinced, not with kick-boxing and rodeo as featured sports in the beginning.

Bukata would work for IMG, a global sports media outfit. He went all over the world to help promote televised sports events. Bukata got his start in the business while a student at Munhall High. He contributed stories to *The Homestead Messenger,* one of the predecessors of *The Valley Mirror*. I will always be thankful to him for introducing me to Wilt Chamberlain and ESPN.

Jim O'Brien

Chamberlain as he appeared while visiting Jim O'Brien's room at Kutsher's Country Club in Catskills back in the mid-70s.

A little boy who loved
a giant named Wilt the Stilt

October 1999

Istill can't believe that Wilt Chamberlain has died. He was a giant, seemingly indestructible, the most physically impressive person I've ever met in the sports world. So I was stunned when I heard he had been found dead in his home in Bel-Air, outside Los Angeles. I agree with those who say that while Michael Jordan was the best basketball player ever, Wilt Chamberlain was the most dominant.

As a teenager, I kept a close watch on Wilt Chamberlain. I read every story about him in *Sport* magazine, the daily newspapers and looked forward to when he would appear on the Sunday NBA telecast on ABC-TV, with Chris Schenkel and Pittsburgh's own Jack Twyman calling the shots in the late '60s.

As great as Chamberlain was, you didn't get to see much of him on TV in the late '50s and early '60s. There were no round-the-clock sports shows on TV or radio back then. No ESPN, no sports talk shows. So every game on TV, no matter the sport, was special.

In Pittsburgh, we got to see the Steelers and the Baltimore Colts on TV, which meant I had a chance to see another boyhood hero, Pittsburgh-born Johnny Unitas in action on the black and silver screen.

Chamberlain, at 7–2, 275 pounds, was the biggest of sports stars. When I would be fooling around with a basketball at the hoop in front of my house, I would mimic my favorite pros and attempt to shoot shots the way they did. Wilt had this finger tip-roll shot in which he would extend his right arm and let the ball roll off his finger tips down into the hoop. It helped to do that shot effectively if your hand was extended higher than the hoop.

I'm not sure why I was so enamored with Wilt Chamberlain. Maybe it was because I was the smallest kid my age in my neighborhood and in my class at school. I was a little boy who loved a giant.

Chamberlain came to Pittsburgh in the mid-60s to play in a series of games for the Philadelphia 76ers that had been farmed out to the Civic Arena. Here was a team that had the greatest attraction in the game and they had to go elsewhere to chase money. Jason Shapiro of National Record Mart here had to shell out a mere $50,000 in advance money to land a six-game package for Pittsburgh pro basketball fans. So Wilt did his thing at the Civic Arena, too. Another game was farmed out to Hershey, Pa., and that's where Wilt scored a record 100 points in a game against the New York Knicks in 1962.

When I went to New York in 1970, I was immediately assigned by *The New York Post* to cover the New York Knicks in the NBA playoffs. I was part of a four-man team of reporters who covered the Knicks in the Eastern finals against the Baltimore Bullets and then in the NBA finals against the Los Angeles Lakers.

The Lakers included Chamberlain, Jerry West and Elgin Baylor, three of the best who ever played the game. Yet the Knicks prevailed, winning the first NBA title in the team's history. I remember Bill Bradley, one of the Knicks standouts who has since campaigned for President of the U.S.A., telling me that his mother had uncovered an album Bradley kept as a child that was devoted exclusively to newspaper and magazine clippings of Chamberlain. A special time comes to mind. It occurred a year or so later at Kutsher's Country Club in the Catskill Mountains north of New York City. NBA players gathered there each summer to play a benefit basketball game to raise funds for Maurice Stokes. He had been a great player at Westinghouse High School here in Pittsburgh, and at St. Francis of Loretto and in the NBA. He was stricken with a crippling brain disease, and teammate Twyman looked after him. He died in 1970 at age 36, but the game continued in his honor.

Chamberlain always came to the Stokes game at Kutsher's. A friend of mine who knew how I had idolized Chamberlain as a kid urged him to go to my room at Kutsher's. That friend, by the way, was Jim Bukata, who grew up in Munhall and got his start in the sports business as a stringer for *The Homestead Messenger*. I was in my room when there was a knock at the door. Imagine my amazement when I opened the door and Wilt Chamberlain was standing there. He ducked under the doorway and filled the room. That night, Chamberlain came to the hotel bar and entertained everyone with his stories. He had a rich baritone voice, an easy smile and hardy laugh. He wore a white blouse, with a turned-up collar

JACK TWYMAN
Stokes' guardian

and puffed-out sleeves, looking like a swashbuckling Errol Flynn in one of those pirate movies.

I thought about times like that when I heard Chamberlain had died. I was driving home at night from Latrobe High School, where I saw a portrait of Arnold Palmer in the hallway of his old school. If Palmer was the most popular athlete ever to come out of Pennsylvania, certainly Chamberlain was the most intriguing.

The news of his death shook me more than when I first learned that Pirates great Roberto Clemente had died. Maybe it was because I was older. It struck me that Wilt was 63 when he died of congestive heart failure. My dad was 63 when he died. Those of us who love basketball miss The Big Dipper.

Armon and Sean succeeded in
sports with strong work ethic

September 2011

I had never considered Armon Gilliam and Sean Casey in the same sentence or the same breath. They were two of Pittsburgh's highest-paid professional athletes in history and they played at neighboring high schools in Bethel Park and Upper St. Clair, respectively, and I followed their careers from their teen years till their retirement years.

Oh, Arnold Palmer has made more money because of his endorsements, commercials, car dealerships, golf design, et al., but Gilliam and Casey made more money strictly for playing sports than anyone else who called Western Pennsylvania home.

It wasn't until a chance meeting with Sean Casey's parents, Jim and Joan, on a Sunday morning in early May of 2011 at breakfast at the Eat 'n Park Restaurant at South Hills Village that I learned of the link that Casey and Gilliam shared.

"They were both unheralded as high school athletes and no one was after them to offer them scholarships," said Jim Casey. "They both surprised everyone by their success in sports."

"I thought Sean had a partial scholarship at Richmond," I told his parents.

"Yes, for $1,000 a year," Joan Casey came back. And Richmond is a pricey school. Tuition, room and board came to about $20,000 a year at the time. Sean Casey picked up a full scholarship for his junior and senior years.

"But he was rich even then," I said. "He has always had that great personality. And he and Armon were both nice guys," I added. "They were two of my favorite ballplayers. They were always eager to talk with me whenever we met. You and Armon's parents both did a great job raising your boys."

Armon Gilliam, who changed the spelling of his name to Armen when he was playing in the NBA, played a little football and wrestled when he was in middle school in Bethel Park. He did not make the basketball team until his junior year in high school.

He was not offered a single scholarship upon graduation. So he went to junior college in Independence, Kansas, and from there to the University of Las Vegas, where he developed into an All-American performer for Jerry Tarkanian's nationally-ranked Rebels. He was the second player picked in the 1987 draft by the Phoenix Suns right after the San Antonio Spurs selected David Robinson of the U.S. Naval Academy.

Tim Grgurich, who grew up in Lawrenceville and played and coached basketball at Pitt, was an assistant to Tarkanian at the time and worked closely with Gilliam and had a big hand in his development on the court. Grgurich has been an assistant coach in the NBA for several teams ever since.

Alma and James T. Gilliam at their home on Elm Street in Bethel Park during interview for story about their son Armon.

rmon Gilliam stands outside Eat 'n ark Restaurant at South Hills Village.

Myron Brown and Armon Gilliam were good friends and among the few Pittsburghers ever to play in the National Basketball Association. Gilliam grew up in Bethel Park and Brown grew up in McKees Rocks and now resides in Kennedy Township. They both played in many fund-raising basketball games in the Greater Pittsburgh area through the years.

Gilliam, a 6–9, 235-pound power forward played 13 seasons in the NBA and averaged 13.7 points and 6.9 rebounds in his career. He was always respected for his work ethic and the way he carried himself. He was popular in every clubhouse.

He was such a big man, yet I was always amazed by how he could walk into a restaurant or a library in his hometown and nobody would notice him. He could stroll the aisle at Giant Eagle in Bethel Park and go unrecognized. He was one of the least known big-time athletes in town. He may have been in a dead heat with two-time Olympic gold medal winner Roger Kingdom in that category.

I met Arman a few times at the St. Clair Library over the past two years to go over some writing he was doing. He had expressed a desire to do some writing, and wanted me to help him. He was always easy company.

In early May, 2011, he collapsed after playing in a pickup basketball game at LA Fitness near Bridgeville, and was pronounced dead that evening at St. Clair Hospital in Mt. Lebanon. He was only 47 years old.

I remember seeing Armon play in pickup games through the years, most recently against the Pittsburgh Steelers in a fund-raiser at Bethel Park High School. I remember when his father, James T. Gilliam, worked as a front counter clerk at the post office just across the street from the hospital where his son was taken.

I had written about his father when I was 14 and the sports editor of *The Hazelwood Envoy*. James T. Gilliam won the heavyweight title of the Pittsburgh and New York Golden Gloves Tournaments back in the mid-50s. He fought for the Glen-Hazel Boys Club during a span when they won the Golden Gloves team title 11 of 12 years. They also had a champion bantamweight called Jimmy Gilliam. Eugene Tippett of Homestead was a star boxer on that team.

The Rev. James T. Gilliam, now 80, is the pastor of the Shiloh Baptist Church in Library, and has been long retired from the post office. Armon provided funding for many projects at his father's church through the years. Armon got his size and strength from his father, and his determination and spirit from his mother Alma. They are great people.

"I didn't know that," said Jim Casey when I told him about Armon's father. "I've read where Andrew McCutchen of the Pirates is the son of a minister in Florida. I think kids whose dads are ministers have their heads screwed on straight."

Some do, and some don't. Joe Gilliam, the gifted quarterback of the Steelers in the early 70s, would be an example of a minister's son who walked on the wrong side of the street, ruining his career with illegal drug usage. Surely, Armon Gilliam walked the talk offered by his dad in his Sunday sermons. Armon Gilliam is no relation to Joe Gilliam.

I got to know Armon over the past dozen years. I had interviewed him for a book called *Hometown Heroes* in the same seating area at that Eat 'n Park Restaurant in South Hills Village back in 1998. I had met with him in that restaurant and at the Upper St. Clair library over the last five years to critique his writing.

Armon Gilliam was ambitious, but in subtle ways. He moved to the beat of his own drummer, and it was a relaxed beat. He went back to school and got his business degree, something too few professional athletes ever do. He coached for a few seasons at the McKeesport campus of Penn State University. He conducted clinics at Ringgold High School. He was a bit of a Renaissance man. He played the bass guitar, the saxophone and sang at his father's church. He spoke with a soft voice and there was a smile in his bright eyes.

No athletes from this area ever made as much money as Sean Casey and Armon Gilliam. In 11 seasons in the major leagues, Casey's salaries totaled $41,295,000 and surely he made a few dollars on the side. That's over forty million! His best one season salary came in 2006 when he was playing first base for the Pittsburgh Pirates and making $8.5 million. That's pretty good, huh?

Then think about this: in 13 seasons in the NBA, playing for six different teams, Gilliam's total earnings were $83,000,000. That's 83 million dollars! My daughter Sarah is the same age, 37, as Sean Casey. They were classmates at Upper St. Clair High School. Sarah graduated Phi Beta Kappa from the University of Virginia when Sean was an hour's drive away at the University of Richmond. She graduated four years later from the University of Pittsburgh School of Medicine.

She is a pediatric oncologist/hematologist at Nationwide Children's Hospital in Columbus, Ohio where she treats children with cancer and does research on blood disorders. She makes good money, but she has yet to earn a million dollars in eleven years as a doctor. She doesn't complain about that. She leaves that up to her father. There were over 20 future physicians who graduated in the same 1992 class at Sean Casey— that's quite a story in itself—and Casey probably made as much money as all of those doctors combined over the same decade.

Every time I see Sean Casey, he is quick to ask, "How's Sarah?"

"Sean always liked Sarah," said Jim Casey on two occasions during our breakfast meeting. We met completely by chance.

We were seated at a table near the rear of the Eat 'n Park Restaurant on a Sunday morning after we'd come from church, and the Caseys were seated next to us. They had their granddaughter, Carli, who is 6, with them.

Carli is one of four children of Mandi and Sean Casey.

I remarked that there is a photo of Carli's dad, when he was 8 years old and wearing a baseball uniform, that is in my book, *Glory Years*, a sequel to *Hometown Heroes,* in which they strongly resemble one another. "She looks just like him," agreed Joan Casey.

They said Sean had caught an airplane out of Pittsburgh International Airport at 7 a.m. that day to fly to Phoenix for the Major League Baseball All-Star Game. He would be returning this Thursday to Pittsburgh where he makes his home. The Caseys are happy to live so close to their son and grandchildren.

Sean works for the Major League Baseball Network as a studio analyst. He also does a show called "The Mayor's Office."

When Sean was playing for the Cincinnati Reds he was the most popular player on the team and came by the nickname "The Mayor." He was voted "the most popular player in baseball" in a poll of players by *Sports Illustrated*.

I mentioned to the Caseys that Branch Rickey, the GM of the Brooklyn Dodgers and Pittsburgh Pirates in the '50s, once remarked that Donora's Stan Musial was "the most liked player in baseball."

"And they're both from this area," Jim Casey said of Sean Casey and Stan Musial.

When Armon Gilliam was an All-American at UNLV he came by the nickname of "The Hammer" because of his physical play under the boards. His coach, Jerry "Tark the Shark" Tarkanian, was shocked to hear the news of Armon's premature death. "He was such a great person," said Tarkanian. "Everybody loved him and he loved everybody. He was such a people person and such a caring guy. He would give you the shirt off his back. I am all shook up over this."

Early medical reports indicate Gilliam died with an extremely enlarged heart.

Several of the New York Yankees, Derek Jeter, Alex Rodriguez and Mariano Rivera called in sick for this year's All-Star Game, saying they wanted to heal their hurts for the second half of the season. Sean Casey played in three All-Star Games and thought he was the luckiest man on earth to be so honored.

I remember seeing Sean Casey carrying a portable TV camera with him in the dugout, clubhouse and on the field when he participated in the 1999 All-Star Game at Fenway Park in Boston. "He was so excited to see Ted Williams," recalled his father.

I checked out the chapter I wrote on Sean Casey to see what he had said about that All-Star Game experience. When I was working for big city dailies, I always loved going to All-Star Games because, simply enough, the game's greatest players, past and present, would be there. Everybody who was anybody in the sport was there. I wanted to be in their company; I wanted to interview them and write stories about them. You could fill up a notebook with stories.

"I felt like I had just won a contest," Sean Casey commented about playing in the 1999 All-Star Game. "It's a time I'll never forget. Being ten feet away from Mark McGwire, when he was smashing the ball out of the park in the home run derby... It was the end of the century, and it was the greatest experience I'd ever had in my life. I couldn't stop smiling. It was just so amazing.

"My dad is big on history so I learned a lot about baseball at an early age. I always thought to appreciate the game today you had to know about the game before. I know there were a lot of guys who got this going, who paid their dues and set the standards for the rest of us to live and play by. I always thought I had an obligation to learn the history of the game.

"So I knew about Stan Musial and Warren Spahn and Pete Rose, and was special to see them all up close like that. I saw Rollie Fingers, Nolan Ryan and Johnny Bench. All those legends. I got chills. When Ted Williams came out in the golf cart I got the ultimate chill. The history of the sport was right there on the field. It was one of the most amazing experiences." I wish Gene Collier could feel that way.

There weren't many observers who saw Sean Casey as a future major league baseball player when he was in his teens.

"I know I have a special gift," Sean Casey confided to me. "I thank God for that every day. I read a statistic that only six to seven percent of professional baseball players ever make it to the big leagues, and only four percent make a career of it. I realized my goal of making it a career. I'm still involved in major league baseball."

Sean is giving back to his community as well. This year he provided the seed money and the leadership to build a Miracle Field in Upper St. Clair for mentally and physically challenged youngsters to play baseball.

He said his parents were always positive. They were always behind him. His dad didn't feel so hot this particular Sunday morning. He told us he had been in St. Clair Hospital for three days during the week with a bout with pneumonia. He was there, though he didn't know it, when they brought Armon Gilliam to the emergency room.

Jim Casey had collapsed and passed out on the kitchen floor of their home. He pointed to a small divot in his forehead where he had struck the floor. "That's what he has to show for it," said Joan Casey.

"I still feel a little tired," said Jim Casey.

The previous time I had seen Jim Casey he was checking out the newspapers and magazines at the Upper St. Clair Library. "I'm retired now and I have time to do this," he told me that day. "I didn't realize they had so much at this library. It's really great."

He was as excited as his son at an All-Star Game.

That's also the last place where I saw and spoke to Armon Gilliam. "I'm still working at my writing," he told me that day, just a few months ago. "I've gotten some of my writing published. I'd like to do more."

Sean Casey was all smiles when All-Star Game was played in Pittsburgh in 2000.

Previs appreciates Pittsburgh
from his view in London

Steve Previs probably set some kind of record in transforming himself from a professional athlete to working in the real world. One Friday in the fall of 1973, Previs was playing for the Carolina Cougars in Greensboro, preparing for his second season as a hardnosed guard in the American Basketball Association. The following Monday morning he was working on a cattle ranch in Georgia.

"I became a cowboy," said Previs. "It's the only 'job' I have ever had. And it was tough. Delivering calves at 3 a.m. in January in the freezing rain is not exactly fun. Rounding up strays and branding ornery Charolais steers is not as romantic as Hollywood would have you believe."

Previs reflected on those days recently in the lobby of a hotel in the South Hills, ten minutes from his boyhood home in Bethel Park where his mother Eleanor lives. He starred in basketball at Bethel Park High in the mid-60s and then the University of North Carolina.

The Carolina Cougars signed Previs and UNC teammate Denny Wuycik, from Ambridge, to play in the ABA. The team's owner was Tedd Munchak, later the ABA commissioner.

Munchak embraced Previs like a son, thinking Steve's future was in business, not pro basketball. "I think he was testing me with that job on the ranch," said Previs. "He wanted to see if I had the guts to stick it out.

"After that, he put me to work on a hog farm, then a beef packing business, then as a route truck distributor for his snack food operation. He had me learn the real estate business and the financial side of business.

"Tedd was a tough entrepreneur. 'Pay attention' was one of his favorite sayings. Most of the time the problem and the solution are right before your eyes."

Today, Previs, at age 62, is working as a sales trader with Knight Capital Europe Ltd. in London. He has been living in London the last 21 years.

"It's a big sprawling, complicated place, full of history," he said. "I travel to work by the tube (subway) and am usually there in about 15 minutes. I start to work at 5 a.m."

Previs may have been late to work a few times the past week because the Summer Olympic Games are going on in London, and there are three million more people in the city.

He believes our basketball team should prevail. "If they don't walk over everyone else and win the gold," he said, "they should collectively crawl into a hole."

Previs says he hasn't owned a car since he's been living in London. He still remembers how to drive one when he comes back to Chapel Hill, N. C. and Pittsburgh, two of his favorite places.

He still loves his coaches at Carolina, Dean Smith and Bill Guthridge, and returns for team reunions. "I learned so much from them," he said. "Suffice to say that mental toughness and taking personal responsibility for one's actions are two of the more important things.

"Those were four of the most unbelievable years ever. If I could give the ultimate gift to anybody, I'd give them four years of Carolina basketball. I wouldn't trade that experience for a billion dollars and that's the gospel truth.

"My father, also Steve Previs, was a natural-born salesman. He passed away in 2008. I miss him a lot. He taught me the value of hard work and P.M.A.—Positive Mental Attitude. I always try to be upbeat about the market and the economy. I guess I'm a natural born bull.

"I left Pittsburgh when I was 18, and I have lived and worked all over the world. Pittsburgh is a great town with wonderful people. I am proud of the way the city has changed. Before we moved to Bethel Park, my older brother John and I spent a lot of time as kids with our aunts and uncles on the South Side, just down the street from those massive steel mills. Now they are gone and parks, recreation areas and shops have replaced them. The football and baseball structures are world class. The rivers are clean. The architecture is fantastic. And the attitude and pride of the people is something to behold. What a change from the dreary place I left in 1968."

Jim O'Brien

Steve Previs reflects on career in interview at Crowne Plaza in Upper St. Clair.

Jerry West and Aaron Smith
overcame childhood challenges

November 2011

I was listening to Jerry West and I was thinking about Aaron Smith. I doubt that Jerry West and Aaron Smith have ever appeared in the same sentence in the sports pages, but they share a strong bond, and not just because they both played basketball in high school.

Both suffered severe beatings at the hands of their fathers and often feared for their lives and those of their family members when they were children. They have startling stories to share.

West has been the symbol of the NBA for most of his adult life, as a star with the Los Angeles Lakers, indeed, one of the greatest basketball players of all time, and as a coach and front-office executive with several franchises. The image on the NBA logo is a silhouette of Jerry West.

Smith is regarded as one of the greatest defensive ends in the history of the Pittsburgh Steelers. He retired after the 2012 season, his 14th year in the National Football League.

Smith was on the sideline Sunday night at Heinz Field, wishing he could be out on the field to fend off the game-winning drive by the Baltimore Ravens in the final four minutes of a critical AFC North match-up that was seen on national television. But he was on the injured reserve list and not eligible to play.

The Steelers gave away the game the way Pitt did the night before at the same site against Cincinnati. It was a difficult weekend for Pittsburgh football fans. Penn State was dealing with a sexual abuse scandal involving one of its former assistant coaches, with some administrators accused of being complicit in a cover-up.

In short, it was not a good weekend for our favorite teams and schools.

Smith felt as helpless as he often did as a child growing up in a trailer park in Colorado Springs. When he was eight, nine and ten years old, he told me he slept with a baseball bat under his pillow in case his father came after him when he was sleeping.

He used to tell his father he loved him, hoping that would keep him safe from the verbal and physical assaults his father committed on Aaron's mother and siblings.

West said he was so angry with his father he wanted to kill him. West now discloses that he slept with a rifle in his bed to defend himself from any assaults.

West was being interviewed by Scott Simon on his Saturday morning talk show on NPR this past weekend. The former West Virginia University All-American and NBA icon has a new tell-all memoir out called *West by West: My Charmed, Tormented Life.*

In his book, West tells a dark side of his life I had never heard disclosed. He has suffered from depression and said he didn't know what love was really all about because his father was always swearing and hitting whoever was nearby in a humble home in Chelyan, West Virginia. His mother withheld affection, and was a cold sort. West's first marriage ended in divorce.

The family mail came to a Cabin Creek post office address, and hence West was heralded in a national magazine article I read as a teen in *Sport* magazine called "The Zeke from Cabin Creek."

I did know that West hated that nickname the way his giant teammate Wilt Chamberlain hated being called "Wilt the Stilt." West still speaks with a West Virginia twang, but he never thought of himself as a hillbilly. He was proud to call West Virginia home.

I interviewed and spoke with West on at least a dozen occasions in my career as a sports journalist, but he never mentioned the madness of his upbringing.

He always seemed like the epitome of athletic success, a true Horatio Alger story. He seemed so confident, one of the greatest clutch performers I'd seen in any sport or athletic endeavor.

I have interviewed Aaron Smith once, and he let it all hang out. "How big is your book?" he asked me when I approached him about doing an interview for: *Steeler Stuff: Stories About A Championship Season and a Remarkable Journey.* "I have lots of stories to tell you."

The hair went up on the back of my neck as he shared his stories, and talked about the terrible tirades of his father, Harold Smith, a 6–4, 250-pound hard-drinking unhappy man who wreaked havoc on his family. I felt like I was in a confessional box hearing Smith's disturbing story, or that Smith was supine on a psychiatrist's couch.

"I can't remember when my father wasn't swearing at us," said Smith. "I thought it was the American way.

"When I was a young kid I often told my father how much I loved him, hoping he'd spare me the next time he went on a tirade."

So many kids are ruined by being raised in this kind of environment. They never recover from it, or find happiness in their own lives. Often they repeat the sins of the father.

That's not the case with Jerry West and Aaron Smith. They are two of the best people I've met in my 55 years as a professional sports writer. They have always been popular in the clubhouse, team leaders. In that sense, they are like Bill Mazeroski, Arnold Palmer, Roberto Clemente, Willie Stargell and Mario Lemieux.

West and Smith had great reputations with the media because they made themselves available, and they were generous with their comments and reflections. They set the best example. They were model citizens.

I wasn't planning on including Smith in my book about the Steelers because I hadn't read anything interesting about him at the time, about five or six years ago. But when I was in the Steelers' locker room one day he smiled and said hello, and made me feel comfortable in his company.

His story ended up being the first chapter in the book because his story was so compelling. To this day, I have yet to read the story of his difficult upbringing in any newspaper or magazine.

He and his wife Jaimie have five children, and much has been written about their child Elijah who has a rare form of leukemia, but appears to be faring well with proper medical treatment. The Steelers, to a man, have rallied around Smith and his family in that regard.

Aaron Smith has gotten involved in many fund-raising events for local agencies involved with looking after challenged children, kids who have suffered from neglect and abuse, children looking for foster or adoptive parents. Smith stands up for kids because he can understand their plight.

I recall seeing him and some of his teammates at a fundraiser organized by Charlie Batch, the Steelers' reserve quarterback from Homestead. It was a night of games to benefit Every Child, an East Liberty based agency that looks after hard-to-place children to find foster and adoptive parents. The event was held at Dave & Buster's on The Waterfront in Homestead.

Smith has also worked with Auberle Foundation in McKeesport and the Holy Family Institute in Pittsburgh. The latter organization, supported by the Rooney Family, has honored him as their Man of the Year on one occasion at a luncheon I attended at Heinz Field.

Jerry West was always one of my favorite professional athletes. We go back a long way.

I recall traveling through West Virginia about 12 years ago when I saw a sign on the highway that heralded Cabin Creek as the home town of Hall of Fame (1979) star Jerry West. I told my wife Kathie that I had wondered where Cabin Creek was since I was a teenager. I got off the highway and visited the community. It made me realize just how humble were the beginnings of Jerry West.

We stopped that same day in Princeton—the hometown of Rod Thorn—and stayed over night at a hotel in Charleston—the hometown of "Hot Rod" Hundley. I told my wife, "Do you realize that today we were in the hometowns of three of the greatest players in the history of West Virginia." To which she replied, "I know. That's why I love to travel with you." I saw West playing against the Knicks at the current Madison Square Garden over Penn Station in the NBA championship playoff series in 1970.

I saw West hit a 60-foot shot in The Forum in Los Angeles during that same series that sent the game into overtime. "I wanted the ball when the game was on the line," he said. That's why they called him "Mr. Clutch."

West starred for the Olympic basketball team that won a gold medal in 1960 and he played 14 seasons in the NBA and he was in the All-Star Game every season. He was one of the league's greatest scorers and he was a terrific playmaker and rebounder as well. He and Oscar Robertson, Michael Jordan and Kobe Bryant are the best guards I've seen. I visited West in his office in the same building when he was the Lakers' general manager. When I was leaving, I asked him if he could direct me to the men's room. He took me there. It was a small gesture, but to me it told me so much about Jerry West.

He has always been so down-to-earth. When I worked as the public relations director for the athletic department in the mid-80s, West would come to the Pitt Field House to scout college talent for the Lakers. Whenever I asked him to do a pre-game or half-time interview on Pitt's radio broadcast, West was always willing to oblige.

The last time I saw him was on August 14, 2000 when I traveled to Morgantown, the community where West Virginia University is located, to attend a ceremony where they named a street after Jerry West. His coach at WVU and with the Lakers, Fred Schaus, was present for the ceremony. Schaus was also a class act. West Virginia Governor Cecil H. Underwood was there as well. West was kind and obliging to everybody that day.

Jim O'Brien

Steelers' Aaron Smith takes a break at St. Vincent College in Latrobe.

West Virginia Gov. Cecil Underwood helps Jerry West display new sign designating a former stretch of Beechurst Avenue as "Jerry West Boulevard."

397

BOXING

Light heavyweight champion Billy "The Pittsburgh Kid" Conn from East Liberty trains at boxing camp near Millvale that was owned by boxing trainer Nate Liff, at left. Is that a bird in Liff's left hand? For sure, it's not a stop-watch.

We're never going
to be an ambassador to Ireland

October 2009

Here's a tough question for the day: What do Art Rooney Sr., Jim O'Brien and Billy Conn have in common? Well, for one thing, we are never going to be confused with the Blessed Trinity.

But the answer is that we all blew our chances to become America's ambassador to Ireland. In each case it's because of something we said. That's often the source of difficulty for anyone who's Irish.

Billy Conn, of course, was the most famous fighter ever to come out of Pittsburgh, born and bred in the city's East End.

He fought Joe Louis for the heavyweight boxing title twice. In their first fight, back on July 18, 1941, there were 54,486 fans on hand at the Polo Grounds in New York, and that included an estimated 6,000 Conn supporters who traveled from Pittsburgh to New York, most by train, to root for their favorite fighter.

Conn had campaigned as a light heavyweight fighter and had won the title in that division. But he surrendered the title to move up and fight Louis. Louis had been on top for four years. He was 27 and Conn was 24. Conn weighed in at 169 pounds and Louis at 199 pounds, but those weights were not the ones that appeared in that day's late editions of the afternoon newspapers. They didn't want the boxing fans to know how much bigger Louis was than Conn.

Conn was so popular in Pittsburgh in those days, that a Pirates' game at Forbes Field was interrupted the evening of their first fight as they broadcast the fight over the public address system and play resumed after the fight was concluded. Imagine that.

Conn was a clever boxer, savvy and quick on his feet. Conn was beating Louis going into the unlucky 13th round. He was advised to stay away from Louis, who packed a lethal punch, and tie up the heavier fighter through the 15th round. But Conn's huge ego got the best of him. He was determined to knock out the great Joe Louis. That would impress his buddies back in East Liberty.

Conn went after Louis in that 13th round, pressing him with a flurry of punches. Louis knocked out Conn with a right to the jaw. Afterward, when Conn was questioned about his strategy, he responded, "What's the sense of being Irish if you can't be stupid?"

That didn't boost his popularity in Ireland or with the Irish in New York or even Pittsburgh, for that matter.

Years later, Conn told Louis, "You should have let me win that fight. We'd have made so much money with a rematch."

And Louis told Conn, "I let you have the title for 12 rounds and you didn't know what to do with it."

That was the fight where reporters prodded Louis beforehand about how he could handle the swifter Conn, and he responded with one of the most remarkable lines of all time: "He can run but he can't hide." Conn and Louis met again, after they both had been in the military service, and it was no contest this time. Conn looked out of condition. Louis knocked out Conn in the 8th round on July 19, 1946.

Conn and Louis were both popular pugilists and became "America's Guests" when their fighting days were over. Both worked as greeters in Las Vegas hotels. Both were often paid to attend big fights to lend their presence to the event. I had an opportunity to talk to both of them on different occasions when there was a big fight in Las Vegas.

Promoters paid to get Conn to come to Ireland in the summer of 1972 to help boost the gate for a fight in Dublin between Muhammad Ali and an opponent named Alvin Lewis. That fight took place on July 19, 1972. Conn was the toast of the town in Dublin, treated like a king wherever he went. As he was about to return home to America, he was interviewed at the airport in Dublin. "So what did you think of the old homeland?" one Irish newspaperman asked Conn.

Without thinking twice, which was his nature, Conn came back with this: "I'm just glad my mother didn't miss the boat."

And that's how Conn blew any chance he might have had of becoming America's ambassador to Ireland.

Art Rooney Sr. had been a top-notch boxer in his heyday, even qualifying for the Olympic Games in Antwerp, Belgium. He declined to go. Sammy Mossberg went instead and won the gold medal. Upon his return to America, Mossberg fought Art Rooney in Pittsburgh and Rooney beat him again.

Art Rooney and Barney McGinley promoted fights in Pittsburgh. Their biggest promotion was the fight at Forbes Field in which Archie Moore won the heavyweight championship against Ezzard Charles. That was on a 10-round decision on May 20, 1946.

Rooney was quite proud of his Irish heritage, mind you, but Tunch Ilkin, the former Steelers' standout tackle who remains on the scene as an analyst to Bill Hillgrove's play-by-play call of the Steelers' games on radio here, recalls how Mr. Rooney often greeted him.

Ilkin was born in Turkey. In fact, his beautiful mother once held the crown of Miss Turkey. Ilkin grew up in Chicago, but often boasted that he was born in Turkey. So whenever Mr. Rooney spotted Ilkin, his favorite player of the 70s, according to his son, Art Rooney Jr., he would always say:

"Tunch, my boy, how are the Turks doing? Are they still killing each other like the Irish?" I can still get a chuckle out of Ilkin when I remind him of that exchange.

That's how Art Rooney blew his chances of ever being named an ambassador to Ireland.

Then there's my story. As Billy Conn said, "What's the sense of being Irish if you can't be stupid?"

I was offered two positions by Dan Rooney through his right-hand man Joe Gordon, the team's publicist during their first four Super Bowl triumphs, and into the '80s.

It was in the mid-80s that Gordon offered me the job as editor of a weekly newspaper the Steelers planned to publish called *Steelers Digest*. I was offered $35,000 and told I could continue to write books about Pittsburgh sports and do free-lance writing on my own.

I accepted the job and kept it about as long as Conn had the heavyweight championship crown in his hands, and then turned it down. I just didn't want to go back on the road with the Steelers, or any sports team for that matter. I recommended two beat writers for the assignment, both working on Westmoreland County newspapers at the time. One was Bob Labriola and the other was Vic Ketchman. Labriola took the job and still has it. Ketchman, by coincidence, ended up editing a similar weekly for the Jacksonville Jaguars. When that paper folded, Ketchman became the keeper of the Jaguars' website.

Gordon didn't think either of them would be interested since they were writing for daily newspapers, but I thought they would jump at the chance. It was a better job than the ones they had, that's why.

Gordon later came back with another offer. He said that Dan Rooney wanted me to serve on the board for the American-Ireland Fund. Rooney and Tony O'Reilly, the former Irish rugby hero who ran the Heinz Co. on the North Side, were the movers and shakers behind the American-Ireland Fund.

The organization raised money for peace-keeping efforts in Ireland. I never felt the same way about Ireland as the Rooneys. My grandparents on both sides were born in America. Then, too, we lived on a street in Hazelwood where most of the residents were of Italian heritage. I'm not into genealogy. I know there's no money or royalty in the bloodlines and I fear what research might turn up in the way of knaves and thieves.

As a kid, it never made much sense to me to pound my chest and proclaim that I was Irish. All it would get me was to have some Italian kids pounding on my chest in response. So I kept a low profile on St. Patrick's Day. Columbus Day was a bigger deal in my neighborhood.

So when Gordon asked me to be on the board for the American-Ireland fund I declined. Worse yet, like Conn I was a bit of a smart-ass. I said, "I'm not from Ireland. I'm from Hazelwood."

There went my chances of ever being America's ambassador to Ireland. I realize now that was a big mistake on my part. I don't think Dan Rooney has ever forgiven me for that retort. He always looks like he's wearing shoes a size too small when he sees me coming. I'd be willing to tote his suitcases if I could accompany him to Ireland these days.

I remember that whenever I visited the Steelers' offices and was wearing a suit or a nice sports coat. Art Rooney would see me coming and holler out, "Hey, Dan, come out here and see this dude from Hazelwood!" I might have been living in Upper St. Clair at the time, but to Mr. Rooney, I was from Hazelwood. To him, that was a better address. He also told me "you're a real Pittsburgh guy." To him, there was no greater compliment.

I'm happy for Dan Rooney. He wanted to be the ambassador to Ireland. He knew the job was open. He campaigned for it when he campaigned for Barack Obama for President.

Dan Rooney had to love being named the American ambassador to Ireland. And I'm happy for him. I am sure that his dad and Billy Conn would second the motion.

Art Rooney and Billy Conn in their heyday.

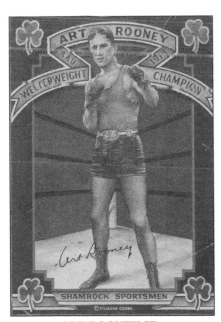

Artwork by Merv Korning as commissioned by Art Rooney, Jr.

ART ROONEY SR.
Steelers' Hall of Fame Owner

BILLY CONN
"The Pittsburgh Kid"

Fight champ Fritzie Zivic
still flailing away in Lawrenceville

January 2011

A friendly brown-uniformed UPS courier told me I could find photographs of Fritzie Zivic on the wall at Hambone's in the heart of Lawrenceville. "It's 4207 Butler Street," he said authoritatively, "just across from the parking lot." I had lunch at Hambone's once about ten years ago with local luminaries Tom Samuels and Larry Werner, so I knew where to go.

Once inside the indistinctive door of Hambone's, I spotted two photographs in the first booth of Fritzie Zivic, flailing away at Beau Jack, Henry Armstrong or Lou Ambers, I'm not sure which, then a Terrible Towel was draped over a bar above the second booth, and then two photographs of Billy Conn over the third booth.

The first booth at Hambone's isn't as warm or inviting as the first booth in Bill Mazeroski's Bar and Restaurant in Yorkville, Ohio—Bills' Ribs, owned by Maz and his late friend Bill DelVecchio—where a galaxy of photos of Marilyn Monroe frame the booth, but it's a hallowed dining spot just the same.

There were Terrible Towels everywhere in Hambone's. The Terrible Towel was my mentor Myron Cope's creation. Cope boxed a little as a young man and he loved the fight game. We first met at the Dapper Dan Golden Gloves Tournament at the Pitt Field House in February, 1977 when I was 14 and he was a young sports writer for the *Pittsburgh Post-Gazette*. Cope would be proud to be represented between Billy Conn and Fritzie Zivic. He knew them both and wrote about them many times.

Conn and Zivic were both world champion boxers back in the early '40s. Conn came out of East Liberty and Zivic from Lawrenceville. Before them, there was Harry Greb of Garfield, which is in between East Liberty and Lawrenceville, and Greb is still considered one of the greatest fighters of all time.

Conn, who was much bigger than Zivic, won a split decision over his friend Fritzie when they fought in December of 1936 at Duquesne Gardens in Oakland. They were both bloodied by the tenth round of what was reported to be an exciting fight. It was a fight that drew much interest in Pittsburgh because both were popular sports figures.

Their framed photographs can still be found on the walls at Connolly's Pub & Restaurant at 129 West 45th St., near the Allegheny Cemetery, the bar with the neon sign for Killian's Irish Red in the window, and probably a few other saloons along Butler Street.

I drove past the Wilson-McGinley Beer Distributing warehouse at the bottom of 36th Street in Lawrenceville as I had to pay a visit in that neighborhood. I remembered visiting one of the owners, the late Jack McGinley Sr., in his office there one afternoon. He also had

A Dapper Group

The Monroeville Dapper Dan Club honored, from left to right, Fritzie Zivic, Ted Kwalick, Dick Hoak, Zeke Shumaker, Paul Martha and Joe L. Brown at November, 1968 sports banquet.

Drawing of Fritzie Zivic by Marty Wolfson, "Greater Pittsburgh History of Sports"

FRITZIE ZIVIC
(of Lawrenceville)
WELTERWEIGHT

photos of Pittsburgh great fighters on the walls, as well as the black silk trunks worn by Ezzard Charles when he fought Jersey Joe Walcott for the heavyweight before a big crowd at Forbes Field on July 18, 1951. Walcott knocked out Charles in the seventh round of one of Pittsburgh's most famous fights.

McGinley's father, Barney McGinley, was a co-owner of the Steelers and he and Art Rooney Sr. used to promote fights in Pittsburgh. Jack even showed me correspondence from a mutual friend, Angelo Dundee, the cornerman for the great Muhammad Ali. Jack and I were lucky to receive post cards and short letters from Angelo Dundee during his world travels with prize fighters.

From there, I could see the nearby St. Augustine Plaza where my late mother lived for more than 20 years in the '80s and '90s. The mother of broadcaster Bill Hillgrove, who grew up in Garfield, was also in residence there during that same period.

Zivic died in 1984 after a long battle with Alzheimer's disease and an 18-month stay at Veterans Hospital in Aspinwall. He was inducted into the Boxing Hall of Fame in 1993.

His wife Helen told me he heard from many boxing people during his stay at the Veterans Hospital, but none were more loyal in calling, she said, than Sugar Ray Robinson. That was good to hear. Robinson, considered by many to be "the greatest fighter pound for pound," scored a ten-round decision over Zivic at Madison Square Garden in 1941. There are pictures with Zivic and Robinson together at some saloons around town.

Zivic fought seven future Hall of Fame fighters and nine world champions. He defeated such men as Henry Armstrong, Charley Burley (once in three fights), Sammy Angott, Jake LaMotta and Red Cochrane.

Hambone's didn't look any different from my previous visit, like it's frozen in another time, so Conn and Zivic figure to be there for awhile.

Roy McHugh, a former columnist and sports editor at *The Pittsburgh Press*, wrote a farewell column to Zivic in which he reflected on the city's three greatest fighters, Greb, Conn and Zivic. The column contained this memorable line: "If you owned a saloon in Pittsburgh, photographs of the three were every bit as essential as a liquor license."

There was lots of Steelers' stuff and black and gold decorations at Hambone's, and about six men at the bar just before noon in late January. The Steelers would be hosting the New York Jets in the AFC Championship in four days and the town was abuzz with talk of the Steelers going to the Super Bowl once again. It was 25 degrees, with a cold breeze blowing in off the Allegheny River, and no day for a leisurely stroll on Butler Street to check out all the bars in search of more Fritzie Zivic relics.

Four to five inches of snow would fall that afternoon, and the TV and radio weather reports were panicking Pittsburghers into leaving work early, but the usual rush hour still extended into two hours or more.

Jack McGinley Sr. shows the black boxing trunks worn by Ezzard Charles in his famous fight with Jersey Joe Walcott in the summer of 1951 at Forbes Field. Walcott, at 37½, was the oldest fighter ever to win a title in any weight class. He KO'd Charles at 55 seconds of the seventh round.

Pittsburgh boxing lineup includes, left to right, Sammy Angott, Pete Aaron, Fritzie Zivic, unidentified boxing official, Charley Burley, Ted Yarosz and Al Gainer.

Just before it started o snow, I went to the Heinz History Center on Smallman Street in The Strip that afternoon and checked out the boxing display on the fourth floor of the old ice house in the Western Pennsylvania Sports Museum.

There are distinct black and white photographs of Greb, Conn and Zivic there, too, on a wall with other boxing champions who came out of the Pittsburgh area. There was a 16-month period, spanning 1939 to 1941, when six of the eight recognized boxing divisions were championed by boxers from Pittsburgh and Western Pennsylvania. That's when Pittsburgh first became known as "The City of Champions." The photographs are familiar to anyone who cares about the city's boxing history.

Pittsburghers had the Pirates and local boxers to root for before the Steelers started producing champions in the National Football League in the '70s.

The boxers included Conn and Zivic, light heavyweight and welterweight champion respectively, and lightweight champion Sammy Angott of Washington, Pa., and featherweight champion Jackie Wilson of Homewood, middleweight champion Billy Soose of Farrell (who looks like a choir boy in his picture).

There's also a photo of Greb, a middleweight and light-heavy champion in the '20s and billed as "The Pittsburgh Windmill," and one of Charley Burley of The Hill District, regarded as one of the city's best boxers who never got the chance to compete for a championship because he was black and more so because his style made opposing boxers look bad.

I wondered why Teddy Yarosz of Monaca, a middleweight champion, was not included in the display, but no one on the Heinz staff could answer that question. Yarosz belongs there.

Yarosz is pictured, by the way, along with Conn, Greb and Zivic with Andy "Kid" DePaul of Green Tree, the Pennsylvania boxing chairman, Don Alderson and a host of other lesser-known Pittsburgh prize fighters, in the back room of Atria's Restaurant & Tavern on Rt. 19 as Dormont gives way to Mt. Lebanon traveling south.

I was taking a photograph with my digital camera of a near life-size framed photo of Zivic at Atria's one afternoon in January, when a waitress, Deanna Hilligoss, spotted me doing so. She wanted to know what my interest was in Fritzie Zivic. When I told her I was doing a magazine piece on Zivic, she smiled and asked me if I had seen the green scrapbook high on a shelf over the doorway leading to the long bar at Atria's.

I had not. She summoned a tall waiter and had him take it down for me to see. It was professionally put together with photos of some of America's greatest fighters, and it included Greb, Conn and Zivic, along with Jess Willard, Jack Dempsey, Gene Tunney and Rocky Marciano. It was like being on a successful archaeological dig.

These are magic monikers in the fight game. *Monikers* is a word Al Abrams would use in his column when he mentioned Phil Mangieri,

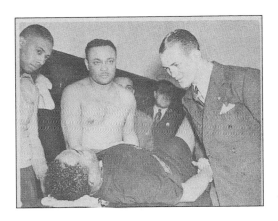

FRITZIE ZIVIC and Beau Jack, throw a couple of rights and end up looking like a model for a pretzel, March 1943.

The famous fighting Zivic brothers. Left to right standing: Joe, Fritzie and Eddie. Seated: Pete and Jack.

the Japanese Ambassador, or Pittsburgh Phil in his notes at the bottom of his column under "Sportspourri;".

Billy Conn and Fritzie Zivic were two of the first Pittsburgh sports personalities I learned about as a child. When I was eight years old, I helped my older brother Dan to deliver the *Post-Gazette* in the morning before we went off to school. I'd devour the sports page of the *Post-Gazette* when we'd get home, starting with sports editor Al Abram's column, always on the far left side of the front page of the sports section.

His "Sidelights on Sports" column was must reading. He often mentioned Zivic and Conn in his column, along with other Pittsburgh sports personalities such as Ralph Kiner, "Bullet Bill" Dudley, Art Rooney and a host of characters he came by in his bar-hopping routine. Conn was the first Pittsburgh Sportsman of the Year at the Dapper Dan Sports Dinner founded by Abrams and his associates. That was in 1939. Zivic was the award-winner the following year of 1940. If you fancy yourself a real Pittsburgh sports fan you must familiarize yourself with the story of Fritzie Zivic. There was a time when some referred to the Civic Arena as the Zivic Arena.

There really was a Zivic Arena, a fight camp in Hickey Park in the Millvale area that Fritzie bought to train fighters and to promote fights there.

All told, Zivic had 230 fights that are in the record books and several more that didn't make it. His official record was 158–64–9, winning 80 fights by knockouts. Most of his losses came late in his career. Like most boxers, he didn't know when to quit. When he was ill toward the end of his life, doctors said he had suffered brain damage from all the blows he absorbed. His nose was broken so many times it was like putty, and he's get a rise out of fans by pushing his rubbery nose from side to side.

He had more than a few fights in his day in the streets of Lawrenceville.

There were five Zivic brothers who grew up in the 9th Ward, the "Irishtown" section of Lawrenceville, and they all became boxers. They all had some main event fights on local cards. Pete and Jack Zivic were members of the 1920 Olympic team. Joe and Eddie were also boxers. The family was known as "The Fighting Zivics."

Talking about his tough boyhood neighborhood in Lawrenceville, Zivic once said, "You either had to fight or stay in the house. We went out."

Fritzie's birth name was Ferdinand Henry John Zivcich. His father was Croatian and his mother Mary Kepele was Slovenian and they settled in the mill town of Lawrenceville as did many ethnic groups who immigrated to this country from Europe.

Lawrenceville would later boast of the Sadowski Brothers, three of whom played major league baseball and others who starred on local sandlots in baseball and softball.

Fritzie's biggest fight was when he won a 12-round TKO over the great Henry Armstrong to win the welterweight championship of the world before a record crowd at the old Madison Square Garden on October 4, 1040.

One of his champion opponents, Lew Jenkins, said of him, "Fritzie was the only guy I know who could start a fight in an empty room."

They called him "the Croat Comet" and they called him "the dirtiest fighter" in boxing. He succeeded Greb in that regard. "If you're doing to fight you better fight dirty," said Zivic.

He was known to stick his thumb into an opponent's eye, scrape the laces on his gloves across the face of a foe, hit below the belt and on the break. He used his head, his elbows, his forearms and his knees, anything to hurt you. Yet he was proud to say he was never disqualified in 230 pro fights. Like the other fighters of his day, he trained at the Pittsburgh Lyceum, just across the street from Epiphany Church in the Lower Hill, or where Chatham Center is now located, across from the Consol Energy Center where the Penguins play.

One of the people who looked after him at the Pittsburgh Lyceum was Joe Luvara, who was a masseur, a cut man and a corner man in local boxing circles. His name often appeared in Al Abrams' column. Luvara's daughter, Denise Luvara Robinson, who is the catering director at Atria's, and her son, Devlin, brought me some scrapbooks their family had kept about Joe Luvara and it included many newspaper clippings with stories about Fritzie Zivic, Billy Conn and the Pittsburgh Golden Gloves. Denise handed me boxing gloves that Zivic had worn. They were soft and thin, I thought there wasn't much padding and you'd feel knuckles if someone hit you wearing those gloves. It felt strange to hold those gloves.

It was like a trip down memory lane, seeing all those stories written by Al Abrams, Myron Cope and Roy McHugh and Jimmy Jordan and Jimmy Miller. I'd met all those men in my teen years and they were all helpful to a young writer.

When I was 14, I was the sports editor of *The Hazelwood Envoy*, and covered the Glen-Hazel Boys Club in the Golden Gloves. The Glen-Hazel team, coached by Cy Obremski, won the team title 11 times in a 12-year stretch during those days. That's how I met Myron Cope and the Pittsburgh fight people in the first place. Billy Conn and Fritzie Zivic were often introduced over the P.A. system and took a bow in the ring at the South Side Market House or the Pitt Field House.

I first met Fritzie Zivic when I was about ten years old. My mother, Mary O'Brien, worked as a sales clerk at the State Store on Second Avenue in Hazelwood. Fritzie Zivic used to come there as a sales rep for a wine company. He was also a beer salesman, a boilermaker and a road worker for Allegheny County in his post-boxing career. Years later, I remember visiting his wife Helen at their home in Scott Township after Fritzie had died. Helen died about two years ago in the San Francisco area where she lived with one of her children.

You always wish you had visited these folks a few more times to get more of their stories.

My favorite Fritzie Zivic story

A fight fan told me this story years ago. I don't know if it's true or not. I like it just the same. One of the younger Zivic brothers was scheduled for a fight in Youngstown, Ohio in early 1949, soon after Fritzie Zivic had officially retired from the ring. A few days before the fight, the Zivic boy broke his hand in training.

The Zivic family traveled to Youngstown any way, not wanting to miss out on a payday. Fritzie offered to take his brother's place. The manager of the other fighter objected to this. "I've got a good young fighter on the rise," he protested. "He's undefeated but he's only had a few pro fights. I'm not going to put him in against Fritzie Zivic, even an old Fritzie Zivic."

Fritzie turned on the charm and told the manager he would make sure his fighter would go at least four of the scheduled six rounds. "I won't hurt him," Fritzie promised.

So the fight went on. Fritzie fouled the young fighter to and fro. It was the only way Fritzie knew how to fight. When he hurt the young fighter, however, he'd hold him up, to make sure the fight went the promised four rounds.

When the bell rang to start the fourth round, Fritzie went to mid-ring and extended both of his gloves. He caught the young fighter off guard. Instinctively, the young fighter put forth his gloves as well and bumped them against Fritzie's gloves, usually a way to signify that this was the final round. It was a way to acknowledge respect, that it had been a good fight.

Suddenly, the young fighter realized what he'd done. "Hey, this isn't the last round!" he yelled at Zivic.

"Yes, it is," came back Zivic, who then proceeded to put away the young fighter in the fourth round. "I kept my promise."

From Bill Mellon collection

GOLF

AT OAKMONT

Jack Nicklaus and Arnold Palmer were paired in many memorable matches through the years.

50th anniversary
of U.S. Open at Oakmont

June 2012

Arnold Palmer was honored by Steelers at Heinz Field.

The 1962 U.S. Open Golf Tournament at Oakmont was won by first-year pro Jack Nicklaus in a playoff with Arnold Palmer in one of the greatest upsets in golf history.

I have never thought of this event when I was considering the greatest sports events I have ever witnessed, not until I received a telephone call from New York earlier this year.

George Roy, who was working on a documentary to mark the 50th anniversary of that event for the USGA, called me to see if I had possibly been at Oakmont way back then, perhaps in my high school days, as he put it.

I told him I was at Oakmont all week for the 1962 U.S. Open, working as a summer intern at *The Pittsburgh Press*, and writing photo captions for the staff photographers. With my media badge, I was often inside the ropes and even sitting on the fringe of the greens. In short, I had the best seat in the house.

I have always considered having a first-row seat in the middle of one of the four sides of the ring for "The Fight of the Century" in 1972 between Muhammad Ali and Joe Frazier as my favorite sports event that I covered as a sports writer.

Right behind was having a front-row seat at mid-court for the NBA playoffs in 1970 when I was in my first few months as a staff writer for *The New York Post* and reporting as part of a four-man team on the Knicks' first NBA championship as a close second.

I was 28 at the time which added to my excitement, and I was 37 when I covered the Steelers winning their fourth Super Bowl in six seasons in January of 1980, beating the Los Angeles Rams at the Rose Bowl in Pasadena. That's also high on my list.

I suppose it was because I wasn't actually writing about the event that caused me to overlook the 1962 U.S. Open Golf Tournament. Never again. The call from George Roy prompted me to reflect on that special experience and realize how lucky I had been as a young man to be at Oakmont to see the upstart Nicklaus knock off Palmer, then called "The King" because he ruled the game of golf.

I was 19 years old when I was rooting, like so many Western Pennsylvanians, for Arnold Palmer to win the U.S. Open at Oakmont June 14–17, 1962. He was the biggest man in golf at the time, and looked like a natural to win. He would be playing in front of people who knew him, rooted openly for him, and worshipped him. He knew the course; he had played it many times as an amateur, and had opportunities to practice on it as a pro.

It was just 40 miles far from his home in Latrobe.

414

Palmer had been the British Open champion the previous July, and had won the Masters in April for the third time in five years. He was at the top of his game.

It was the first time I was ever at a country club in my life, and I was a bit nervous about my status on those hallowed grounds. I am still nervous whenever I am invited to attend some special event at the St. Clair Country Club, Valley Brook Country Club or the South Hills Country Club. When you grow up in Glenwood, next to Hazelwood in the inner-city of Pittsburgh you are not that familiar with country clubs.

One of the waitresses at the Oakmont Country Club was a sister of one of my aunts, whose maiden name was Mary Ponzini. That was almost the only way anyone in my family was going to get into a country club back then. I was on my best behavior, but I kept thinking that at any moment someone was going to unmask me and tell me I'd have to leave the grounds.

It was as if I had the words **RUFFIAN** or **RIFFRAFF** spelled out in block letters on my forehead.

It all came back to me after I heard from George Roy of Flagstaff Films in New York City.

"When you were in high school," he began, "did you by chance get out to the U.S. Open at Oakmont in 1962?"

I said that was the summer after my sophomore year at the University of Pittsburgh and that I had a position as a summer intern on the city-side news staff at *The Press*. I explained exactly what my assignment was that day and how rowdy the crowd had been while cheering for Palmer, the hometown favorite, against the young brash upstart from Ohio, a first-year pro named Jack Nicklaus.

I said the crowd cheered for Arnie and insulted Jack regularly, calling him "Ohio Fats" and "Fat Boy," and actually stomping on the ground when Nicklaus was attempting a putt. Even Steelers' fans didn't behave that badly back in those days.

Palmer apologized to Nicklaus at one point for the way his fans were behaving. Woody Hayes, the feisty football coach at The Ohio State University, where Nicklaus had first gained attention on the golf course, was following Nicklaus in the company of Charlie Nicklaus, the father of the young blond golfer. Charlie Nicklaus owned and operated a drug store in Columbus that Hayes had frequented on a regular basis.

Woody and Charlie got into a few verbal confrontations with the crowd over the way they were trying to distract Jack Nicklaus. Hayes was known for having a fiery temper and eventually lost his job at Ohio State for assaulting an opposing player in a sideline skirmish. You wouldn't want to mess with Woody Hayes, or Charlie Nicklaus.

Some reports on that event, particularly one by an old friend on the sports beat, Jerry Izenberg of *The Newark Star-Ledger*, indicated that one could actually feel the ground around the green quake when the members of Arnie's Army started marching in step, stomping on the ground when Nicklaus was putting.

I don't know about that, but Nicklaus insisted afterward that he was not aware that the crowd was a bit unruly. He was too focused on his golf game to notice.

Then, too, the men's U.S. Open is being held this June 14–17 at The Olympic Club in San Franciso, and they will be marking the 50th anniversary of the storied event that was played at Oakmont. It is still regarded as one of the greatest upsets in golf history.

Once George Roy realized I had been a witness to what went on that week at Oakmont, he scheduled a visit to our home in Upper St. Clair. That's why there were two television trucks in our driveway the morning of February 28, 2012.

Roy had told me I was a good story-teller. His company Flagstaff Films produced sports documentaries for network and cable television stations. He was working on such a documentary about the 1962 U.S. Open that will be shown on NBC before the final round on June 17, at 2 or 3 p.m.

Roy used to run a similar TV documentary filming company called Black Canyon and I was interviewed and appeared in a documentary called "Pistol Pete" The Life and Times of Pete Maravich," and another one about Roberto Clemente. The Maravich piece won an Emmy Award. Roy's company has won six Emmy Awards and several other distinctions through the years. I got ample air time on both of the documentaries about Maravich and Clemente, I am proud to report.

I recalled how author Shelby Foote was featured so often in a documentary about the Civil War that was done by award-winning Ken Burns. "I want to be your Shelby Foote," I told Roy and did my homework on the 1962 U.S. Open prior to his visit to my home in Upper St. Clair.

I will explain how I was able to have one of the most up-close views possible at the 1962 U.S. Open. I was working that summer as an intern at *The Pittsburgh Press*. I had been awarded a *Wall Street Journal* Scholarship of $500 in addition to the pay I drew working on the city-side or news side of Pittsburgh's leading daily at the time.

It was a wonderful internship and that summer proved to be very important in shaping my career. Each week I would shadow a different established reporter on his or her beat. One week I'd be at City Hall, the next week in the local judicial courts or police station, the labor beat, the real estate beat, you name it. At the city morgue, I even witnessed an autopsy of a woman who'd been found murdered in the streets. Her body was badly bruised with purple splotches everywhere. I had a front-page story all week when I was assigned to keep watch on a protest at Western Penitentiary where several prisoners climbed a water tower to complain about conditions at the prison. I was given an opportunity to write columns and they appeared above and below some nationally syndicated columnists such as Robert Ruark, Bishop Fulton J. Sheehan and Jim Bishop and local writers such as Gilbert Love and Barbara Cloud.

I hit it off well with the editor, John Troan, and the managing editor, Leo Koeberlein, and they invited me to return the following

WTAE's Ed Conway interviews
Arnold Palmer at '62 Open.

Reporter Frank Christopher and
photographer Al Herrmann Jr. led the
way for summer intern Jim O'Brien
that memorable week at Oakmont.

Arnold Palmer as he appeared
at 1962 U.S. Open

Jack Nicklaus was in his first season as a
pro at Open in 1962.

Photos by Jim O'Brien

summer. I chose to go to Philadelphia instead to have a summer intern-ship at *The Philadelphia Bulletin*. I wanted to be with the sportswrit-ers in Philadelphia, among the best in the country. It turned out to be a big mistake. I worked the overnight shift and I seldom got to write any stories. I came home early that summer. I was wasting my time in Philly.

That summer I worked at *The Press* was also when I started fre-quenting Dante's, a saloon/restaurant on the border of Brentwood and Whitehall where all the top sports writers and broadcasters as well as some of the outstanding Steelers, future Hall of Fame players such as Bobby Layne and Ernie Stautner, were among the regulars. I wanted to be around the writers. I wanted to hear their stories, learn from them, show them my stuff, and seek their advice and approval. Myron Cope, Bob Drum, Ed Conway, Tom Bender, Pat Livingston, Dave Kelly, Doc Giffin were among the media who frequented the joint.

That 1962 summer was a great summer. I knew, for sure, I wanted to be a sportswriter. I was just 19, too young to be in any bars, but I was eager to make my mark.

One day at *The Press,* I overheard some of the bosses discussing plans for coverage of the upcoming U.S. Open. They were talking about who was going to do what, and they were going to send some reporters from city-side as well as the usual sportswriters to cover the event. When they stated talking about the photographers, I stepped forward and volunteered to go out to Oakmont and write photo captions.

I was assigned to tag along with Al Hermann Jr. When I came back to *The Press* in 1979, after working a year in Miami and nine years in New York, I teamed up with that same Al Hermann Jr. in covering the Pittsburgh Steelers. John Troan and Leo Koeberlein were still in charge of the paper and they were the ones who brought me back to town. They forgave me for not returning for a second summer as an intern in 1963.

They told me that I was going to be the next sports editor of *The Press,* and succeed Pat Livingston in that post. They didn't tell me they were going to retire before that would happen. So it didn't happen and I left to take a position as assistant athletic director for public relations at the University of Pittsburgh.

I can still remember that special week at Oakmont in the sum-mer of 1962 even though it's been 50 years since the U.S. Open was played on its hallowed grounds.

I had no idea I was about to witness one of the greatest upsets in golf history, when a pro rookie from Columbus, Jack Nicklaus, would knock off the great Arnold Palmer, then playing at the peak of his game, in a head-to-head playoff round.

Nicklaus had just joined the pro tour after many successes as an amateur at The Ohio State University. I have watched Nicklaus on TV when he has hosted his annual golf tour outing at Muirfield in Dublin, Ohio. It turns out he liked the layout at Oakmont so much that he has included some of its features in his own course, including those famous furrowed sand traps known as Oakmont when he designed and later reconfigured some of the holes on his own course.

He used the same rakes with the four-inch tines widely separated that he'd seen in the maintenance shacks at Oakmont. Only now they were called "Jack's Rakes."

I thought about the first time I saw him at Oakmont. All the top golf writers and some of the leading sports columnists in the country were at Oakmont that summer of 1962 and they hung out in a media room in the basement of the club house. Several of them told stories. One of the ones who held court the most often was Oscar Fraley. He had authored the book *The Untouchables*, which was turned into a popular TV series that I watched religiously (from 1959 to 1963). So I introduced myself to Oscar Fraley and shadowed him in the clubhouse that week. Bob Drum, the golf writer of *The Press* who lived in Bethel Park, was a close friend of Palmer and a favorite among the golf writers because he was quite the character.

Oakmont was regarded as a monster of a course, a true test for veterans and downright unfair and unforgiving for rookies. It still has the same status today among the world's greatest and most challenging golf courses. That's why they play so many U.S. Opens there.

Its greens were glossy, and it had those infamous furrowed sand bunkers—"the church pews"—that made it different from every other golf course in the country. They have since been eliminated from the course, along with many of its signature trees.

"Go get 'em, Arnie!" fans were yelling from the outset. There was no question as to who was the hometown favorite. The gathering loved Palmer's bold, attacking style, his humble low-key manner of responding to questions in the press tent. The way he waved to the gallery, grinning back at them when they shouted his name. Plus, he was from nearby Latrobe. He was a hometown hero, one of their own.

Arnie's Army marched across the course like troops in field movements during the Civil War.

They played 36 holes on the last day of the tournament in those days. Palmer had 70 in the morning and 71 in the afternoon, and finished in a tie with Nicklaus. I got to see this by taking a position around the fringe of the greens, writing down the names of whomever Al Hermann Jr. captured with his camera. A reporter named Frank Christopher accompanied us on our tour of the course.

Palmer and Nicklaus had an 18-hole playoff on Sunday and Nicklaus carded a 71 and Palmer a 74, and the outcome never seemed to be in question.

Palmer should have won. He was the better golfer at the time, but he did not. He had 11 3-putt greens and Nicklaus carded just one 3-putt green. That was the difference. I still have color photos I took that weekend of some of the top pros, including Palmer, Nickaus, Billy Casper, Gene Littler and Gary Player.

Palmer lost a playoff the following year to Julius Boros in the U.S. Open, and never won an Open again.

419

Palmer won often enough, however, to retain his position as the premier player in golf. He became a multi-millionaire, the first to fly an airplane of his own, and he showed the way for others to follow.

He won seven Grand Slam titles and the U.S. Amateur title when that was something special. I had an opportunity to visit with him at his workshop at the Latrobe Country Club, to dine with him in the men's grill at that same club, to interview him at Oakmont a few times. I wasn't one of the golf writers, but Palmer was always pleasant and generous with his time and thoughts. It helped that I knew Doc Giffin, who came out of Crafton and succeeded Bob Drum as the golf writer at *The Press*, and then became Palmer's press agent and right-hand man in 1962.

I always thought that every time I talked to Palmer it was a special occasion, a real treat. I always thought of how much my golfer friends would have liked to have been in our company on those occasions. I always wanted my father-in-law, Harvey Churchman, to be there because he loved to play golf and he was a big fan of Arnie Palmer.

In his terrific book, *A Good Walk Spoiled*, John Feinstein wrote, "No one has ever been loved and revered and *worshipped* like Arnie. Palmer has been the single most important player in the history of golf."

Palmer also played during a safer period than Tiger Woods when the players weren't under the same scrutiny as they are today.

Arnie has always been one of the guys, but he's never stopped wanting to win. When he tees it up with Nicklaus and Player in a special fund-raiser, he will want to win. So will Nicklaus. So will Player. That never ends.

"That's why we still tee it up," Palmer has often said.

Palmer could tell the young players about the times he played a round with President Dwight D. Eisenhower, and how he and Ike popularized the game of golf in America as well as around the world.

There are things that have changed that Palmer doesn't appreciate much. "Anyone who would charge for an autograph ought to be ashamed of themselves," he has said. "It's an honor and a privilege to be asked for an autograph. I just don't know what's wrong with these people.

"A lot of players just don't understand how lucky we all are to be doing what we do. I look at my life and all I can do is be thankful for everything I've been given by so many people over so many years. It's just too much damn fun to ever stop."

But, in time, he had to give up competitive golf. It got too frustrating; his standards are still so high. "Well," he said," I guess everything has to come to an end somewhere."

Talking to some special people in Pittsburgh on a recent Sunday at Oakmont made me feel as privileged as Palmer to have kept the company I've kept all these years.

And so far, I've never been chased from a country club.

NEW YORK,
NEW YORK
AND WRITERS

Pulitzer Prize-winning author Norman Mailer and Beverly Bentley, a former model and the fourth of his six wives, enjoy courtside seats at Madison Square Garden to see the Knicks play in the early '70s. Knicks were the hottest ticket in town, even hotter than the tickets at nearby Broadway shows. Woody Allen, Dustin Hoffman and Elliott Gould were frequent court-side fans in those days.

Authors and athletes are
main attractions on vacation tours

August 2009

I like to mix business with pleasure when I am on vacation. I can only take so much of pure vacation or relaxation. Then I get antsy. I have this thing about athletes and authors and I like to take advantage of where I am to visit people and places en route that are of special interest to me.

My wife Kathie and I have visited some distant places in recent years where I take detours to do things I want to do, and she is usually agreeable to my side trips.

Once back in April of 2003 we were walking around the French Quarter in New Orleans when I suggested we should seek out the Hotel Monteleone. It's a famous hotel there that was once frequented by famous writers such as Tennessee Williams, Eudora Welty, William Faulkner and Truman Capote. I had visited it once to check out Joe Frazier when he was training on the top floor for a heavyweight championship fight with Terry Daniels in the Crescent City in January of 1972.

Frazier's sparring partner was future heavyweight champion Ken Norton. I will never forget the sight of one of their handlers holding a humongous medicine ball high over Norton's supine form on a training table and slamming the ball down onto his stomach. It seemed like a medieval torture chamber.

Cockfights and dogfights are frowned upon and outlawed in most locales but it's okay to abuse human beings in boxing, extreme fighting, football, rugby and a few other combative activities. The difference, I suppose, is that humans can make a choice about whether or not they want to subject themselves to such punishment.

The Super Bowl was played in New Orleans that same weekend as the Frazier-Daniels bout and I wrote a sidebar about Mike Ditka catching a 7-yard touchdown pass from Roger Staubach as the Dallas Cowboys beat the Dolphins 20–3.

Once, when we were driving from North Carolina to Ohio, departing from the seashore home of Kathie's relatives to go see our younger daughter, Rebecca, when she was a student at Ohio University, we motored from one end of West Virginia to the other.

We entered the state at the southeastern tip and we stopped at Princeton so I could take some pictures. Princeton is the hometown of Rod Thorn, an All-American basketball player at West Virginia back in the 60s. Then we got off the highway when I spotted a sign hailing Cabin Creek as the hometown of the great Jerry West, also an All-American and one of the greatest players in the history of the NBA. Then we stopped overnight in Charleston, the hometown of "Hot Rod"

Hundley, who preceded West as an All-American at West Virginia back in the '50s.

"Do you realize," I asked Kathie as we unpacked our bags at the hotel in Charleston, "that today we have been in the hometowns of the three greatest basketball players in the history of West Virginia University?"

"I do now," Kathie came back. "That's why I love to travel with you." I suspect she said that with more than a hint of sarcasm.

On the way back from Chicago last year we stopped at the Indiana Basketball Hall of Fame and the Clark Gable Museum in Cadiz, Ohio. I just like to do those things.

I remember when I was on a boys-only get-away with my pal Alex Pociask that we passed by an estate in Flat Rock, North Carolina where the poet Carl Sandberg had lived from 1945 until his death in 1967. When we were in Asheville, we saw a home where the writer Thomas Wolfe had lived. We visited the Vanderbilt family's Biltmore estate, once known as the largest private home in America.

On a later trip, when we visited Alex's alma mater at Michigan Tech in Houghton, Michigan, I talked him into a side trip to nearby Laurium where there is a memorial park dedicated to George Gipp, the first All-American football player at Notre Dame. On the way to the Pociask family farm in Wausaukee, Wisconsin we stopped in Appleton to visit a bar and restaurant once owned by the parents of Rocky Bleier. Rocky lived upstairs of the bar before he went off to Notre Dame where he captained a national championship team in his senior season. Appleton is also the hometown of writer Edna Ferber, movie actor Willem Defoe and Senator Joseph McCarthy, who chased after Communists in America, and Harry Houdini, the famous magician.

We stopped in Green Bay to visit the Packers' Hall of Fame and a restaurant named Lombardi's that had pictures of the great coach and his Packers all over the place.

That's my idea of a real vacation.

Once, when I was in Baltimore on the Yankees' baseball beat, I had a great doubleheader. I went to a cemetery where Edgar Allan Poe was buried and checked out his tombstone. On the same day, I visited a museum dedicated to Babe Ruth. I believe the building was once a boys' home where the Bambino resided as a teenager.

When Kathie and I were in Los Angeles three years ago, visiting our daughter Rebecca once again, I had lunch with Bill Sharman, a Hall of Fame player and coach in the NBA, as well as a big success as a coach in the ABL and the ABA. I tried to do that again this spring, but could not find a good time when both of us were free.

A week or so later, Sharman called me from his son Tom's home in Peters Township, and we got together for an evening about 12 miles from my home in Upper St. Clair.

A week after that, Kathie and I traveled to North Carolina once again, and made a side trip to South Carolina to see our friends, Cecil and Rich Corson. Rich drove me 25 miles to Beaufort (Bue-fort) one day. That's the home of one of my favorite writers, Pat Conroy. We stopped at a local bookstore where Conroy was scheduled to appear later in the same month for a signing of his newest book, *South of Broad*, about the city of Charleston.

I checked out the pier in Beaufort, and some of Conroy's favorite hangouts. I just liked being in Conroy's home community. I have read about ten of his books, including *My Losing Season, Lords of Discipline, Prince of Tides, The Great Santini, Beach Music* and *The Water is Wide*. Yes, I'm a big fan of Pat Conroy. So is my friend Andy Russell, the former Pittsburgh Steelers Pro Bowl linebacker. "I'm three-fourths of the way through his newest book," Russell reported to me when we returned, "and it's just great."

The Corsons set up a surprise visit to our dinner table by Dave Sauer, a Pitt athlete and classmate of mine during my days at Pitt in the early '60s. Sauer starred at Avonworth High and was a member of a great freshman five that became the base of a great varsity team while I was at Pitt. The Corsons and Sauer reside at Del Webb's Sun City at Hilton Head, a beautiful 55-and-over community.

The other four freshmen at Pitt in 1960 were Brian Generalovich of Farrell, Paul Krieger of Uniontown, Cal Sheffield of New Brighton and Paul Martha of Wilkins Township. Martha and Rick Leeson of Scott Township were the two star running backs on the freshman football team that went 6–0 that year. That's when there was a separate freshman team for basketball and football. As seniors, that team would go 9–1 and not go to a bowl game in 1963.

I became the sports editor of *The Pitt News* as a sophomore and traveled to West Lafayette, Indiana by airplane to see Pitt play Purdue in the season opener. Generalovich, the star forward for Pitt, was matched against All-American Terry Dischinger of Purdue. Both of those outstanding basketball players became dentists. That doesn't happen these days.

"I was fortunate to come to Pitt with so many great players," recalled Sauer. The basketball team went 19–6 in Sauer's junior year and qualified for the NCAA Tournament, a much tougher feat in a smaller tournament field in that era. I was at the NCAA first-round game at the Palestra in Philadelphia when Pitt lost to NYU, 93–82. NYU was led by All-American Barry Kramer and Happy Hairston.

The Pitt basketball team went to the NIT in New York after their senior season. They were 17–8 that year. Bob Timmons was the coach of the Panthers in that period.

Sauer was a physical education teacher and basketball coach at Canon-McMillan and at Churchill and later the Woodland Hills School District. He also coached briefly at Bethany College, outside of Wheeling, West Virginia.

While we were staying on Emerald Isle, North Carolina with Kathie's brother Harvey Churchman and his wife, Diane, I was also able to visit Tom Kerwin, who lives nearby on what is called the Crystal Coast.

Kerwin was the backup center to the great Connie Hawkins on the Pittsburgh Pipers' team that won the first championship in the

Former Pitt basketball star Dave Sauer keeps in great shape

Tom Kerwin shows off game programs from his Pipers' days in Pittsburgh.

American Basketball Association (ABA) after the 1967–68 season. Kerwin had gained some All-American mention as a 6–9 frontliner at Centenary College, setting rebound records that were later broken by Robert Parrish.

Kerwin was playing ball for an AAU team called the Phillips 76ers when he was approached to play for the Pipers. Top players made good money, some better than NBA players, when they played for corporate-sponsored teams in AAU competition back then.

So Kerwin had some bargaining power. He had a full-time job and got to play in a highly-competitive amateur league. Kerwin signed a two-year contract calling for $15,000 a year to play for the Pipers. "Connie was definitely better and the best player in the league," recalled Kerwin, "and he kidded me about making more money than he was making."

Joe Gordon, who was the public relations man and later the general manger of the Pittsburgh Rens of the American Basketball League, had a copy of a contract that Hawkins had signed to play for the Rens for $6,000 a year back in the early '60s. Hawkins was 19 at the time, and had been bounced out of the University of Iowa during his freshman year because of allegations that he'd been involved with gamblers who were seeking to fix games. The ABL and the Rens folded midway through their second season. Hawkins was later cleared of those charges and permitted to play in the NBA.

The Pipers left Pittsburgh after they won the first ABA title in favor of Minneapolis. Kerwin chose to stay in Pittsburgh. He married Gwynn Grant, a nurse from Mt. Lebanon whose father Bill Grant coached the swimming teams at Pitt and for a longer span at Mt. Lebanon High School.

I used to catch Kerwin at Atria's Restaurant & Tavern in Mt. Lebanon. "I like it here," Kerwin said of his town home near the Atlantic Ocean, "but I miss Atria's and all my friends in Pittsburgh."

It was a great vacation. I brought back some seashells I picked up along the beach, but I was even happier to see some special places and people and to pick up some stories along the way.

Two of ABA's finest centers, Spencer Haywood and Connie Hawkins, meet at ABA reunion in Indianapolis.

It was a great time
to be in New York

March 2010

It was hard to believe 40 years had gone by. The New York Knicks celebrated the 40th anniversary of their remarkable 1970 NBA championship season in late February, 2010 at ceremonies in Madison Square Garden.

It's one of the most memorable championship series in sports history, and the highlights are still shown often on ESPN Classics and other sports shows.

That's the one where Willis Reed, the captain and center of the Knicks, returned to action after missing a game with a thigh injury, and sparked his team to a thrilling victory in the seventh and final game with the Los Angeles Lakers. Whenever I see the signs for Captain Willis Fish Markets in North Carolina, I can't help but think of Willis Reed. He's still the Captain in the mind of many Knicks' fans who long for those glory years in the NBA.

I had one of the best seats in the house for that series and certainly for the final game at the Garden. My seat on the press row was front row at midcourt, just at the break, where the players from both teams entered and exited the court on the way to and from their respective locker rooms.

No one on the team, or in the press row, knew if Reed would be able to play in that final game. He had gone down hard in the fifth game and was unable to continue in that contest, or to play in the next game. The Lakers' lineup included Wilt Chamberlain, Jerry West and Elgin Baylor and it was thought the Knicks could not win without Willis Reed in the middle.

Reed showed up late in the warm-up session, walking with a noticeable limp when he came out of the locker room, and the capacity crowd of nearly 19,000 went crazy at the sight of the team's big man. If you watch closely, as I always do, when a video of his entrance is shown on television highlights you may be able to see that when Willis steps up on the court—it was about two inches off the surrounding surface—he pushed off the shoulder of a sportswriter at the end of the break in the press row. You got it. That right shoulder belonged to yours truly. Willis pushed off it as he stepped gingerly onto the playing floor. Marv Albert, the Knicks' radio broadcaster, couldn't contain himself. "The crowd is going crazy," Albert bellowed.

Reed hobbled onto the court. He scored the team's first four points, hitting two short jump shots, and then had to sit down. He'd given his team the lift it needed. The Lakers looked like they had seen a ghost. "Willis provided the inspiration, and I provided the devastation," says Walt "Clyde" Frazier, the flamboyant and gifted guard of the Knicks.

Overlooked sometimes in the review of that championship contest is the fact that Frazier put up some unreal figures: 36 points, 19 assists and five steals. He played his usual strong defensive game. He beamed as he drove away from the Garden that night in his brown-and-beige Rolls Royce and has admitted he partied long into the night.

Frazier endorses a men's hair darkener so his hair is darker these days than it was when he was playing for the Knicks. Reed has a gray frosting on his hair. They were among the Knicks from that storied team who returned to the Garden to be honored at a game late last month. Bill Bradley, who became a U. S. Senator, was there as well. Frazier, Reed and Bradley are all in the Basketball Hall of Fame, as is their teammate Dave DeBusschere, who died several years back.

Phil Jackson was unable to be there. He was one of Reed's back-ups, along with the late Nate Bowman. Jackson was busy coaching the Lakers. He has replaced Red Auerbach as the NBA coach with the most championships under his belt. Cazzie Russell and Dick Barnett , who both were starters, came back for the ceremonies, as did Donnie May, Bill Hosket, Dave Stallworth, Johnny Warren and Mike Riordan, all valued reserves.

I wish I had been there to see them and talk to them and reminisce about those days.

That was 40 years ago. I was 27 when I moved from Miami to New York. I had covered the Super Bowl in New Orleans that January—the Chiefs' victory over the Vikings in which ex-Steelers quarterback Lenny Dawson was the game's MVP—and now I was in New York in March of 1970.

My first assignment by sports editor Ike Gellis of *The New York Post* was to be part of a four-man team that covered the Knicks in the NBA semi-finals against the Baltimore Bullets. The Bullets' lineup included Gus Johnson, Earl "The Pearl" Monroe and Wes Unseld. They are all in the Basketball Hall of Fame. Then the Knicks defeated the Milwaukee Bucks and Lew Alcindor (later to be Kareem Abdul-Jabbar) in five games in the Eastern Finals.

The lineup for *The New York Post* was pretty good, too. It included veteran Knicks' beat man Leonard Lewin, and nationally-syndicated columnists Milton Gross and Larry Merchant. I was the fourth man in the lineup. It was an easy assignment. I could write features and sidebars and didn't have to worry about getting all the details. (If we would have had another former Pittsburgh sportswriter on our staff at *The New York Post*, namely George Kiseda of *The Philadelphia Daily News*, we would have had a lineup that could match that of the Knicks and the Lakers.)

I felt honored to be included. There were nearly 19,000 at Madison Square Garden for every game that season, and the buzz in the building was unbelievable. It was different in those days. No one showed up in a Halloween costume. They showed up to see a great basketball game, to be spectators of a super game between the best the pro game had to offer. They were there to watch and cheer.

428

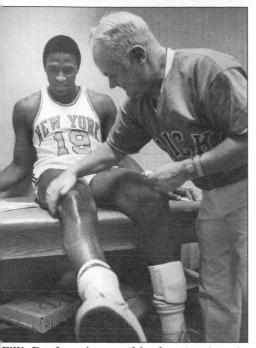

Willis Reed receives soothing heat treatment salve to sore right knee from Knicks' trainer Danny Whalen during title series with Los Angeles Lakers in 1970. Whalen was also the humorous and popular trainer for Danny Murtaugh's 1960 Pittsburgh Pirates.

Opposing centers Wilt Chamberlain and Willis Reed shake hands before playoff game between Los Angeles Lakers and New York Knicks at New York's Madison Square Garden.

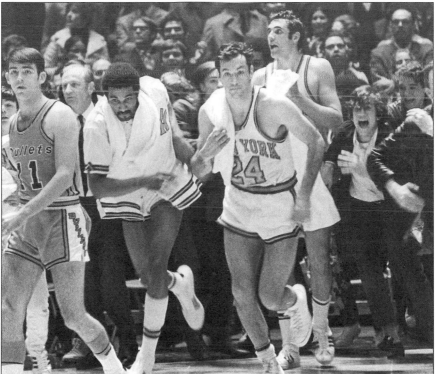

Red Holzman, Nate Bowman, Bill Bradley and Dave DeBusschere race onto court after Knicks' playoff victory in spring of 1970.

It was such an electrifying environment. I knew I was in the big leagues. The *New York Post* was one of the first daily newspapers in America to take the NBA seriously and cover road games regularly.

We had four guys on the sports-writing staff named Leonard. Dolly Schiff, the owner of the newspaper, and most of the staff were Jewish. I was one of the few not from New York and not Jewish.

It was a great place to be. There were writers on *The New York Times* who would later win Pulitzer Prizes, and there were knowledgeable veteran writers on the *New York Daily News*, then the No. 1 circulation daily in the country. So the competition was keen. I was keeping great company. I should have felt some fear going into that environment, but perhaps I was too young to consider the nature and strength of the competition I would find there.

I traveled with the Knicks to Baltimore and then to Los Angeles. I covered the first game in the semi-final series at the Garden and the Knicks beat the Bullets, 120–117 in double-overtime. I thought it couldn't get any more exciting than that, but it did.

I was at the Los Angeles Forum the night Jerry West hit a 60-foot shot—and it was a shot and not a desperate heave—at the buzzer to tie the game on a two-pointer. There were no three point field goals in those days. The Knicks won that one in overtime, 111–108, on one of those patented kick-back jump shots by Dick Barnett. The Lakers won the next game at the Felt Forum, also in overtime, by 121–115.

Reed fell down hard while trying to make a driving shot in the fifth game, and he was forced to leave the game. The Knicks trailed by 16 points late in the game, but they rallied and won the game for their beloved Captain.

"I can't believe it's been 40 years," said Reed, who won regular season and post-season MVP honors that year. The Knicks won the first title in the team's history, and I just happened to come to town at the right time.

The Jets and Joe Namath had upset the Baltimore Colts in 1969 and the Mets pulled off the Miracle of 1969 in winning the World Series, so I came to New York at a great time.

I ended up covering the New York Nets of the ABA when they had Hall of Fame forwards such as Rick Barry and then Julius Erving. They were forwards who could not only score but make the play, just like Bradley and DeBusschere. And they were all in the same city. There was twice as much of everything in sports in The Big Apple.

I covered the New York Rangers and the New York Islanders. I covered the latter club in its first season when they won only 12 games, one of the worst records in NHL history. They went on to draft the right players each year and ended up winning four straight Stanley Cups. There were times when I covered the Jets and the New York Giants. And in March of 1971, I had a ringside seat, one of the four best in the Garden, to cover the Fight of the Century between Muhammad Ali and Joe Frazier. Sometimes we get lucky in life.

My timing could not have been better. In 1970, I moonlighted as the founding editor for *Street & Smith's Basketball Yearbook* and kept

430

Willis Reed, Wilt Chamberlain and Walt "Clyde" Frazier were key figures in 1970 NBA championship round. The Knicks won their first league title in history that spring.

George Kalinsky

that position for 23 years, and continued to write as a contributing editor for that magazine for another ten years. I wrote a column for the next nine years on pro basketball for *The Sporting News*. I wrote three editions of *The Complete Handbook of Pro Basketball* and a soft-cover book called *ABA All-Stars*.

I used that extra money to save for the college education and wedding receptions for my daughters, Sarah and Rebecca. I still have Rebecca's wedding money in the bank. Those extra jobs enhanced the quality of my family's life.

I thought about all of this when my wife Kathie and I traveled to New York earlier this month to attend the Big East Men's Basketball Tournament. We stayed at The Roosevelt Hotel. That's where I stayed when I came from Miami to New York to be interviewed for the job as editor of *Street & Smith's Basketball Yearbook*. I remembered having lunch at the Crawdaddy Restaurant at the hotel three straight summers with Nancy Lieberman of Old Dominion, the greatest women's basketball player in the college ranks at the time. She and her mother Renee would come in from Far Rockaway to see me.

Kathie and I walked to and from Madison Square Garden each day for a week. The walk was about a half-hour in each direction. We also rode the subway to the southern tip of Manhattan for lunch with a niece. We walked some familiar paths. We spent a lot of time in the bowels of Grand Central Station and Penn Station.

There are sights and sounds in New York one never sees or hears in Pittsburgh. It's constant theater. The lights on Broadway are brighter than ever, and certainly more plentiful than they were when we lived on Long Island. Some things have remained the same; some are different. Downtown New York is cleaner, I swear, than downtown Pittsburgh.

We traveled to and from New York by train for the first time. There had been problems because of the weather with airplane and automobile transportation for most of February. I thought this was a safe and reliable way to do it. But nothing is foolproof. It took nine hours to get there and we did plenty of reading and relaxing. The train ride home was delayed by four hours because of severe storm damage in New York area over the weekend.

Two days later there was a train wreck, a head-on collision, on rails we had traveled past the Edgar Thomson Works in Braddock. I had recognized the place traveling past it during daylight on the way to New York and at night—all those twinkling lights—on the way home. One of the engineers was killed in the train wreck. So I guess there is no safe way to travel long distance. Being in New York brought back the best of memories. I left in 1979 to come back home to Pittsburgh, and the timing couldn't have been better. The Pirates won the World Series that fall and the Steelers won their fourth Super Bowl in six seasons at the end of that 1979 season. I've been fortunate and I do count my blessings.

Budd Schulberg wrote books
about ambition and the boxing world

August 2009

One of my literary lions died in the summer of 2009. Budd Schulberg was one of the authors who got me excited about books and writing when I was a student at Taylor Allderdice High School in the early '60s. I picked up a paperback book by Schulberg called *What Makes Sammy Run*, and I was engrossed with his stories about the sordid side of Hollywood. I was 16 or 17 at the time. I had not read many novels then. Our grade school did not have a library and we had a few books at home, but none that interested me. My brother Dan had the complete collection of "Classics Illustrated," and I read them repeatedly. I still think those comic book versions of the classics were superior to the original books. They were beautifully illustrated.

I found books in the library at Allderdice by Ernest Hemingway and William Saroyan, and books about heroes of the Olympic Games, and I couldn't get enough of them.

Sammy Glick, the protagonist in *What Makes Sammy Run*, grew up on the Lower East Side of New York and worked as a copy boy for a newspaper there. He was ambitious and he worked hard—and never stopped running—and became a big success as a ruthless movie magnate in Hollywood. The story was set in the 1930s.

Schulberg grew up in New York but moved as a young man to Hollywood, where his father was the boss at Paramount Studios. Schulberg learned all about the movie business in Hollywood. His father begged him not to publish *What Makes Sammy Run* because he thought it would ruin his relationships with the people who ran the business. Some thought the portrayal of an ambitious Jewish young man was anti-Semitic.

The book became a best-seller and Sammy Glick became synonymous with someone who was wildly ambitious and would stab people in their back to get to the top. Schulberg once described the character he had created by saying "He was like Horatio Alger gone mad." That book was originally published in 1941, a year before I was born.

I was working as a copy boy on weekends in the classified ad department of *The Pittsburgh Press* so the book had a lot of appeal to me. I was ambitious, but I was never into backstabbing and have never understood anyone who took that approach to their career. I've known a few only too well.

I still have that copy of *What Makes Sammy Run*. I had to shore up the front and back covers long ago with tape and cardboard to hold it together.

I still have copies of *The Harder They Fall*, and *The Disenchanted*, which Schulberg also wrote. The first one was about the dark side of

433

boxing and the second about the dark side of Hollywood, a favorite subject for Schulberg.

Schulberg is best known for writing the screenplay for *On The Waterfront*, a movie that revealed the dark side of boxing and labor unions on the docks in New York. It came out in 1954. That movie won eight Oscars, including best screenplay by Schulberg.

There was a memorable line in that movie. It came from the mouth of Marlon Brando, who played the part of a washed-up boxer named Terry Malloy who raised pigeons on the rooftop of the tenement where he lived and raised hell on the docks with longshoremen and union bosses. Malloy had become a longshoreman and was struggling to stand up to his corrupt labor union.

Malloy is sitting in the back of a car with his older brother Charley, played by Rod Steiger. Charley is an attorney for the mob. "I coulda been a contender," says Terry Malloy. "I coulda been somebody. Instead of a bum, which I am." Terry's girl friend in the movie was played by Eva Marie Saint, who won an Oscar for best supporting actress. Brando won an Oscar for best actor. Lee J. Cobb was terrific as the boss of the labor union.

Terry Malloy was befriended by a priest, Father Barry, who was played by actor Karl Malden, who died at age 97 in July of 2009.

Schulberg was always a big boxing fan. He published a collection of his stories on boxing called *Sparring With Hemingway*.

I covered boxing for *The New York Post* in the mid-70s, including "The Fight of the Century," pitting Muhammad Ali against Joe Frazier at Madison Square Garden. It was held on March 8, 1971, and it was a fight that more than lived up to the hype.

Schulberg was captivated by Ali and wrote several magazine pieces defending Ali for refusing to enter the military service.

Schulberg often showed up for press luncheons and workouts before big fights in New York, and I was one of the writers who loved to sit and listen to him and some other older writers swapping stories about their experiences in the fight game. I remember one that was held before the first Ali-Frazier match-up where Schulberg, Norman Mailer and William Saroyan were all in attendance. This was at Gallagher's Steak House. Usually such press gatherings were held at Toots Shor's.

Former boxing great Joe Louis was at that same luncheon, but I was more enthralled with the presence of the great writers. For a writer, it was like being present at "The Last Supper," or with Hamilton, Jefferson and Adams at the signing of the Declaration of Independence.

There were some great sports writers there that day, no doubt, the likes of Red Smith, Arthur Daley, Milton Gross, Dave Anderson, Larry Merchant, Vic Zeigel, Stan Isaacs, Jerry Izenberg, Robert Lipsyte and top newspaper columnists such as Pete Hamill, Jimmy Breslin and Murray Kempton. That trio would turn out some top-notch books as well. Horace McMahon, who played the part of one of the detectives, Lt. Mike Parker, in the TV series "Naked City," was usually there.

I remember once going to one of the Ali-Frazier press conferences at Shor's. It was held in a second floor banquet room. On the way up

Norman Mailer

Pete Hamill

Horace McMahon

Budd Schulberg

William Saroyan

Jimmy Breslin

54th Street, I saw Joe E. Lewis, the nightclub singer and comedian being helped out of Jilly's, owned by a friend of Frank Sinatra. It wasn't noon yet, and Lewis was obviously drunk. He was being assisted to a cab at curbside. It was winter and it had snowed in New York City a few days earlier and the streets were still wet and sloppy in the aftermath. About ten minutes later, when I went up the stairs at Shor's, I saw the actor Horace McMahon sitting in a chair at the top of the stairway. McMahon had played the part of the tough-talking Lt. Mike Parker in "The Naked City," a police drama series on ABC-TV in the late '50s and early '60s. Inside, shaking hands with all comers was the great boxer Joe Louis. He was paid to help promote big fights like this.

He and his pal, Pittsburgh boxing great Billy Conn, both were paid to be greeters at Las Vegas casino hotels. Conn had been to Shor's saloon on several occasions. I remember telling my wife Kathie when I came home that day that New York was the only city in the world where you could run into Joe E. Lewis and Joe Louis on the same street on the same day.

Schulberg had a bad stutter, and often squeezed his pale blue eyes shut when trying to express himself. His words were worth the wait. Despite his speech problems, Schulberg loved to tell his stories. He had a stage presence about him, an interesting face, bearded and with bushy eyebrows, salt and pepper in both.

As a young writer, I always took advantage of opportunities to keep company with great writers. I thought I could learn something from them, and was honored just to be in their presence.

When I took my first job as a sportswriter with a daily newspaper, *The Miami News,* I would frequently visit an after-hours club called Julie's Pad to be able to sit at the bar with the likes of Edwin Pope and Jack Mann, two little guys who were giants in the sports-writing field. Pope is still at it with an occasional column in *The Miami Herald.* Mann died in 2000 at the age of 74.

When I was listening to their stories, or those of Jimmy Cannon, a columnist in New York I got to know when I moved there in 1970, I felt like I was sitting at a table at a café on The Left Bank in Paris with Hemingway. Cannon claimed to have done that when he was a WWII correspondent

I was driving with my wife Kathie through West Virginia in the summer of 2009, returning from a vacation in North Carolina and South Carolina, when Kathie saw an item on the first page of *USA Today* that Schulberg had died. We passed under an overhead span called Longevity Drive as she read the story about Schulberg's passing.

It brought back some great memories of days spent in New York, when I was fortunate to keep company with some special people.

I went into some bookstores and our local library when I got back home hoping to find some of Schulberg's books. There were none to be found on any of the shelves. That's too bad. I kept looking and I finally found a copy of *What Makes Sammy Run* in pristine condition at Half-Price Books and bought it for $2. What a bargain. Budd Schulberg's book held up. It is still a good read.

Toots Shor's
in the Naked City

Mention of "Toots" Shor's Restaurant & Saloon brings other memories of how magical doors were opened to me by going to New York to be a sportswriter.

I could have gone earlier than 1970. I had been offered a job when I was a senior at Pitt to come to New York and write sports for Newspaper Enterprise Association, a wire service that supplied stories for newspapers all over the world, right behind the Associated Press and United Press International. It had been my goal to get to New York. Murray Olderman, a multi-talented newspaperman, illustrated his own sports columns. He had succeeded Harry Grayson as the sports editor at NEA.

I remember flying to New York for an interview with Olderman. I took advantage of being in New York and attended three stage shows in the Broadway district that weekend. I saw "Luther" on Friday night, "A Funny Thing Happened on the Way to the Forum" starring Dick Shawn who had replaced Zero Mostel in the lead role, and, finally, "Oliver," which I absolutely loved. I mimicked Fagin in singing "You've Got To Pick A Pocket Or Two, Mon," for a good while after that. I still do on occasion.

Olderman offered me a job, but the pay was lousy and I told him so. "You're trying to sell me on romance and eating beans out of a can in a one-bedroom apartment," I was brazen enough to give Olderman a piece of my mind. "I can make more money in Pittsburgh where it costs a lot less to live."

He smiled. We would later run into each other at Super Bowls or big events and he was always gracious and friendly. He forgave me the brashness of my youth.

I talked to some people at *Sports Illustrated* and hit if off with several of the executives, but nothing ever materialized. One of the top guys, John Tuite, was a Pitt grad and someone that my colleague Beano Cook knew well. Andrew Crichton was another editor I spoke with at *SI*. They hired a fellow from Princeton instead of me. His name was Frank Deford. He turned out to be maybe the best sportswriter in America. They made the right draft pick.

Back in Pittsburgh, I was picking up a payday here and there doing free-lance pieces, and editing *Pittsburgh Weekly Sports,* but making chump change. I was doing a morning sports commentary on WEEP Radio and producing and doing on-the-air work with Pitt basketball games and some Hornets hockey games. I was under strong consideration to do a sports commentary each morning for WTAE Radio.

One day I was at a social gathering and Myron Cope came over to talk to me. "Hey, Jim, I just want you to know I've talked to some people at WTAE and they may want me to do a radio show for them," Cope said. "I know they've been talking to you, too. I hope there'll be no hard feelings if I get the job. I've got a family now and I can use that job. I'm not trying to take anything away from you."

I said there'd be no hard feelings. There never were. Once again, WTAE made the right choice in Myron Cope. That's when I was offered a job to write sports for *The Miami News*. When John Crittenden, the sports editor told me I'd be covering the Miami Dolphins in their final season in the American Football League I jumped at the chance. Crittenden hadn't told me he had already offered that beat to two other guys on his staff. But that's another story.

I spent a year in Miami. That's where I made great connections in boxing with Angelo Dundee and Chris Dundee, the famous trainer and boxing promoter brother combination originally from Philadelphia, and that's where I first got to meet Cassius Clay. He wasn't Muhammad Ali yet. The Dundees knew the Rooneys and McGinleys from earlier boxing promotions in Pittsburgh. They remembered staying at the Pittsburgher Hotel in midtown. If I knew the Rooneys and McGinleys I was all right with the Dundees. It was the beginning of a beautiful relationship. What times I had in the company of the Dundees and what characters I met in the Fifth Street Gym on Miami Beach and at other outposts about the country.

The Dundees always provided me with an entrée to Ali. Angelo used to send me and other writers hand-written post cards on his world travels. Art Rooney Sr. had the same custom

I came to New York when Toots Shor and his saloon were in their waning days. He was still America's most famous saloonkeeper, but he was now in his third location—at 5 East 54th Street—and his place simply wasn't as popular as it had been. It had once been one of those places to see and be seen, right up there with the Stork Club, the El Morocco and 21 Club. Bernard "Toots" Shor was 67 when I met him in 1970.

Joe DiMaggio and then Mickey Mantle used to hang out at Shor's. DiMaggio helped make the place popular even though he wasn't a sociable sort. Jackie Gleason ate there for free. Jimmy Cannon, one of America's most celebrated sports columnists, came there often. Cannon especially liked to be there when DiMaggio was at the same table. Cannon once characterized DiMaggio "as the loneliest man I've ever met." In time, Cannon became a recluse himself. I visited him once in a Manhattan hospital when he was sick and dying, and I heard him telling a nurse something that Wilt Chamberlain once said, "Nobody loves Goliath." Shor introduced me to Joe E. Lewis in his place one night. I met a woman who had been a secretary for Walter Winchell, once one of the most powerful newspaper columnists in the country. Winchell invented the Broadway dashes and dots notes celebrity column. Shor's wife, "Baby," had been a Ziegfield Follies showgirl. I met them all. I thought I had gone to the land of Oz.

Joe E. Lewis liked to drink and he poked fun at himself about this in his comic routine. Whenever he'd pick up a cocktail, he'd cry out like he was at the race track, "It's post time!"

Some of his famous lines were "I distrust camels and anyone else that can go a week without a drink." And, "You're not drunk enough when you can still lie on the floor without hanging on."

When I was growing up in Pittsburgh, I had seen Joe E. Lewis several times on "The Ed Sullivan Show," and as a mystery guest on "What's My Line?" His biography was called *The Joker's Wild*. A movie was made about his life. When I met him, however, he was just a drunk. My mother worked at a State Store where they sold wine and spirits, and later at a beer distributor so I got to know a lot of drunks in my youth. I knew one when I saw one.

The actor Horace McMahon frequented Shor's, especially when there was a boxing press conference. McMahon and Paul Burke had been the lead detectives in a police drama series, "The Naked City," that was a Sunday night staple on ABC from 1958 to 1963. That's when I was in high school and college and I watched it regularly.

It was well done. It was the "Law and Order" of its day. It was in black and white back then, of course. The detectives worked out of the NYPD's 65th Precinct in New York. The show was shot in New York, especially around Greenwich Village and it was my introduction to the greatest city in America.

The theme song was by Pittsburgh-born composer Billy May "Somewhere In The Night," and a voice-over at the conclusion said, "There are eight million stories in the Naked City and this has been one of them." It was done in a documentary-like manner and it was must watching on Sunday night.

It featured some great established actors such as Luther Adler. I once saw Adler play the part of Tevye in "Fiddler On The Roof" in a stage show in Seattle the weekend I was discharged from the U. S. Army after ten months in Alaska. Other great actors seen in "Naked City" included Walter Matthau, Jack Warden, Eli Wallach, Burgess Meredith, Mickey Rooney and Aldo Ray.

Better yet, and this is unreal, some research turns up information that many actors were on the show at the start of their careers, including Rip Torn, Jack Klugman, Tuesday Weld, Peter Falk, Robert Duvall, Carroll O'Connor, Jean Stapleton, George Segal, Martin Sheen, Robert Redford, Sylvia Miles, Jon Voight, Sandy Dennis, William Shatner, Christopher Walken and Dustin Hoffman. How about that lineup?

I had a chance to meet and talk to Robert Redford and Dustin Hoffman during my days in New York. They'd show up at some events. Hoffman often sat at courtside at Knicks' games, as did Norman Mailer and Woody Allen. I remember talking to Hoffman one day at a tennis club in Long Island City. He was fond of Dave DeBusschere, the power forward for the Knicks and they'd play tennis from time to time.

I'm only 5–8½, but I am pleased to report that I am taller than Woody Allen, Dustin Hoffman and Robert Redford, but much smaller and slower than Dave DeBusschere.

I was new in town in 1970 and Shor embraced me. Some of the better known sportswriters had stopped coming to his place. So he was eager to help fashion a new fella in town. If he liked you, he called you one of his "crumb bums." It was like Art Rooney referring to you as "a real Pittsburgh guy." Something had changed and sportswriters weren't staying out so late at night anymore. Shor saw me as a new ally in the newspaper business. I got the same treatment, in the beginning, from Howard Cosell. Then Cosell changed and he got mean with everybody. He didn't spare me toward the end.

Toots Shor was a big burly guy with a rough voice, originally from Philadelphia. He commanded everyone's attention. He had once been a bouncer in an after hours' club in Manhattan and you'd better behave in his company. He was a wise guy and liked to crack jokes and get a rise out of his customers. He had a lot of Howard Cosell in him.

I had heard about Toots Shor so I welcomed the attention and the chance to meet so many famous people. I had lunch there one day and interviewed Ethel Kennedy. The attorney general's wife was promoting a Special Olympics project embraced by her sister-in-law Eunice Kennedy Shriver.

I was so overwhelmed, frankly, by keeping company at Shor's with Ethel Kennedy that I stayed at the bar after she departed, drank too much, and showed up under the weather that night to help cover a Knicks-Celtics game at Madison Square Garden.

You know how when you have had too much to drink and you try to cover up by walking ramrod straight and speaking slowly and distinctly? That's what I did. But it didn't fool Milton Gross. Our paper's lead columnist was sitting next to me at the courtside press table. "Have you been drinking?" he asked me at one point.

I knew better than to lie to Milton Gross. I remember I couldn't read any of my notes in the first half that night. My notes were more legible after intermission. Leonard Lewin was the main beat writer on the Knicks. My job that night was to do the Celtics' clubhouse. The Knicks crushed the Celtics. I think I asked some pretty tough questions of Dave Cowens and John Havlicek. Cowens didn't suffer me too well. Havlicek couldn't get upset with anybody.

Somehow I survived that day, that evening, and turned in my copy on time. That never happened again during my nine years in New York, not when I was working a game. That's how I stayed nine years in New York. I returned to Shor's from time to time, and Toots would take me around and introduce me to people. There was a story that Yogi Berra met Ernest Hemingway one day at Shor's, but Berra didn't recognize the name of the famous author. Sinatra would stop there on occasion. Judy Garland and Marilyn Monroe and Orson Welles had all been seen at Toots Shor's at its earlier locations.

Federal agents padlocked Shor's place in 1971. He owed nearly $300,000 in back taxes. Shor died in 1977 and he was said to be broke.

I remember one time that my wife Kathie and I had lunch with Howard Cosell at the Warwick Hotel, just across the street from ABC's headquarters in Manhattan. This was on August 18, 1971.

Cosell noted in the morning newspaper that Horace McMahon had died at age 65 the day before in Norwalk, Connecticut. It was six months since I had seen McMahon at Toots Shor's. Cosell talked to us about McMahon, whom he knew from the boxing scene. Kathie and I were driving to Pittsburgh after our luncheon meeting, and we tuned in to ABC Radio Sports to catch Cosell's show. He was talking about McMahon. "He's saying just what he told us," said Kathie. "It's the same script." I told her there was no script; Cosell was speaking off the top of his head.

Roberto Clemente met the Yankee Clipper, Joe DiMaggio, when Joe D was playing in an Old Timers' Baseball Game at Shea Stadium in New York as part of a doubleheader attraction with the Pirates playing the Mets.

George Steinbrenner was a big fan
of Art Rooney and Connie Hawkins

July 2010

George Steinbrenner was an admirer of two of Pittsburgh's most popular sports figures. He promoted Art Rooney, the owner of the Pittsburgh Steelers, as a model for what the owner of a professional sports team should be, and he once made a novel offer to get Connie Hawkins for his Cleveland basketball team.

When Steinbrenner died at age 80 a week ago most of the stories were about his year with the New York Yankees, and what a demanding and controversial owner he had been with that great baseball team.

But Steinbrenner, much like Art Rooney, was a big fan of all sports. Al Davis, another owner with a controversial reputation, is like that, too. These guys read the sports section from start to finish and know what's going on in every sport. They take great pride in going toe-to-toe with sportswriters to show such knowledge. These guys could host their own sports talk shows.

Like me, Steinbrenner was the sports editor of his college newspaper. He was a top-notch track and field performer as a hurdler and oversaw the student newspaper's sports section at Williams College in Massachusetts. How could I not like a guy like that?

I got to know George Steinbrenner during the nine years I worked as a sportswriter for *The New York Post.* I was in my second year of covering the Yankees and the Mets when Steinbrenner bought the Yankees from CBS for $17 million in 1973. In New York, you had a wonderful situation in that you covered the National League for half the season, and then switched to the American League after the All-Star break, or vice versa.

Steinbrenner once suggested I come to work for him, but I declined the offer. I told him I wanted to remain his friend and I didn't think that would be possible if I worked for him. He already had a reputation for being a tough, demanding guy who would become known simply as "The Boss." I wouldn't have lasted long. I'm not good with in-your-face leaders.

Frank Fuhrer, who has promoted golf, tennis and soccer in Pittsburgh, is like that. I always admired Frank Fuhrer and he's accomplished so much good in this region. If you perform at the highest level Fuhrer will reward you, but he is ever demanding. He became a big success in the business world with his approach, and he has been a loyal supporter of golf, in particular, and tennis and soccer. His Pittsburgh Triangles won a World Team Tennis title, a championship in "The City of Champions" that is often left out of the lineup of championship teams.

Steinbrenner bought 40 some copies of my book *The Chief: Art Rooney and His Pittsburgh Steelers,* and had them delivered to his home in Tampa about nine years ago. He sent a copy to each of the owners in Major League Baseball and enclosed a personal hand-written note. "I urge you to read this book about Art Rooney," he advised. "This is what a sports owner should be." He sent me a highly complimentary letter about the book.

I attended a birthday party for my friend and boyhood hero Herb Douglas at the Duquesne Club about a year after Steinbrenner had bought my book. It was an 80th birthday party for Douglas, and my wife Kathie and I were among the 80 guests. We sat at a table with three former Olympic gold medal winners and their wives that evening.

Douglas knew I knew a lot about track & field, so he seated me at a table with Harrison Dillard, Dr. Charles Jenkins and Mal Whitfield. Roger Kingdom was at a table nearby. All had won gold medals in two different Olympic Games. Douglas had won a bronze medal in the long jump in the Olympic Games in London in 1948.

In talking to Dillard, one of the all-time great hurdlers, he mentioned George Steinbrenner. They had competed against each other in high school in Cleveland. Dillard said Steinbrenner was a pretty good competitor in track.

A few days later, I wrote a letter to Steinbrenner, as I did on occasion, and I told him about my conversation with Harrison Dillard, and how complimentary he had been in regard to him, and shared his positive memories of their scholastic days.

That same week I received a two-page typewritten letter from Steinbrenner with his reaction to my letter. You would have thought I had presented him with the Nobel Peace Prize, the Pulitzer Prize and an Academy Award all in one swoop. That's how pleased Steinbrenner was to hear that Harrison Dillard still remembered running hurdles against him in their high school days.

The Yankees had won 11 pennants and seven World Series during his tenure since 1973, yet Steinbrenner positively bubbled about hearing what Harrison Dillard had to say about him. I still have Steinbrenner's letter in my office files.

Steinbrenner's father, Henry George Steinbrenner II, had been a track & field star, a world-class hurdler, while at Massachusetts Institute of Technology. He graduated with a degree in engineering in 1927 and later became a wealthy shipping magnate. He ran the family firm, Kinsman Shipping, operating freight ships hauling ore and grain on the Great Lakes. When young George took over the business he made it even more successful, after taking it through a tough stretch, and the Cleveland-based firm became known as the American Shipbuilding Company.

In between college and taking over the shipping business, young Steinbrenner thought about becoming a college football coach. He had joined the U.S. Air Force following college, and was commissioned a second lieutenant and was posted in Lockbourne Air Force Base in Columbus.

He stayed on in Columbus when he was discharged and did postgraduate study at The Ohio State University (1954–55), earning his master's degree in physical education. He served a graduate assistant to the legendary Woody Hayes—their leadership styles are similar—and the Buckeyes were national champions that year and won the Rose Bowl. Steinbrenner later served as an assistant football coach from 1955 to 1956 at Northwestern and from 1956 to 1957 at Purdue. Steinbrenner was with the Boilermakers when Lenny Dawson was their senior quarterback in 1956.

In 1960, against his father's wishes, Steinbrenner entered the pro basketball business, gaining a franchise with the Cleveland Pipers of the American Basketball League. That league was the brainchild of Abe Saperstein, who had founded the Harlem Globetrotters and introduced the red, white and blue basketball to the game.

That's when I first heard about George Steinbrenner. I had just graduated from Taylor Allderdice High School and was a freshman at Pitt in 1960. In my second month on the campus, the Pirates beat the New York Yankees in the World Series thanks to a home run in the bottom of the ninth inning of the seventh game by Bill Mazeroski. I would become the sports editor of *The Pitt News* the following year. I paid attention to the ABL because Pittsburgh had a team in the league.

Steinbrenner hired John McClendon, the coach at Tennessee State, to be his first head coach. Thus McClendon became the first black head coach in pro basketball. They had a disagreement and parted company at mid-season. Steinbrenner replaced McClendon with Bill Sharman, the former great guard of the Boston Celtics.

Steinbrenner showed he knew something about coaches and sports when he hired McClendon and Sharman. Both are in the Basketball Hall of Fame. Steinbrenner was ahead of his time when it came to running a pro sports franchise, even then.

The Pipers went on to win the first and only ABL title. The league was disbanded during its second season of operation. Even though his team won the title, Steinbrenner thought the Pipers could be better. He looked with envy at the Pittsburgh Renaissance team, known as the Pittsburgh Rens.

The Rens had the league's star player in 19-year-old Connie Hawkins, who would later play for the Pittsburgh Pipers in the American Basketball Association when they won that league's first title in the 1967–68 season, and with several teams in the National Basketball Association in a Hall of Fame career.

Steinbrenner once approached Archie "Tex" Litman, the owner of the Rens, with unusual trade bait. "I'll trade you one of my ships for Connie Hawkins," said Steinbrenner. Litman's son, Joe Litman, was a classmate of Lenny Dawson during Steinbrenner's stint at Purdue. Hank Stram, later Dawson's coach with the Kansas City Chiefs, also served an apprenticeship at Purdue.

Pittsburgh's Joe Gordon, who was the public relations man and then general manager of Litman's Rens team, went to work for Steinbrenner in Cleveland for three weeks, but decided that wasn't for him. "I had room service in my hotel all three weeks," recalled Gordon. "But I never got paid for my work. It was a good experience, though, and I don't regret it." Gordon would go on to become the publicist for the Pittsburgh Hornets, the Pittsburgh Penguins and the Pittsburgh Steelers.

See, even then, George Steinbrenner had big ideas and wanted the league's best players on his team. He accomplished in one season what LeBron James failed to do in seven seasons—bring a pro basketball championship to Cleveland. *(James more than made up for that in Miami with the Heat and with the U.S. team in the 2012 Summer Olympic Games.)*

George Steinbrenner may have lacked Art Rooney's warm manner, sense of humor, compassion and smile in his approach, but he was every bit as tough as Rooney as a competitor. Art Rooney had advised his five sons to treat people the way they wanted to be treated. "But never let them mistake kindness for a weakness," he often reminded them.

Some of his critics have complained that many of the stories are making George Steinbrenner out to be a saint when he was, indeed, a difficult person. Art Rooney could have told them that's what happens if you hang around long enough.

George Steinbrenner "The Boss" of New York Yankees

Paying tribute to Furman Bisher, one of the best in sports writing business

April 2012

I spent four fine days mostly on a couch in our family room, from Thursday to Sunday, watching The Masters on television. My wife Kathie kept me company most of the time, reading a book and catching the best golf shots on replay, the way she watches most sports events on TV these days.

Neither one of us was feeling so hot. We were nursing head colds we had caught in Columbus the week before when we were looking after our granddaughters. We were content to cool our heels for the extended weekend.

On Sunday, they showed an empty seat and working space in the press tent at the Augusta Country Club, with one of those soft crumpled summer hats displayed on some sort of post. It was there to mark the spot where Furman Bisher would have been. Bisher covered his bald spot with one of those crumpled summer hats, the sort I remember the Pirates' Chuck Tanner wearing at the ballpark.

That's when I learned for the first time that Furman Bisher, someone I truly admired in the sports writing profession, had passed away on March 18. I was in Phoenix that weekend and I missed that item in the local newspapers. Maybe it wasn't big news in Phoenix. I forgot about my head cold.

Furman Bisher was known as "the dean of sports writers at The Masters." It only seemed like he'd been there from the beginning, but he'd been covering sports on a big league basis for nearly 70 years.

He had been a sportswriter and columnist for the *Atlanta Journal-Constitution*, and was one of the most beloved and respected men in the business. When I was a student at the University of Pittsburgh in 1962, I came across a book by Bisher called *With a Southern Exposure*. It was a collection of some of his best columns. I was smitten with his writing, his topics, his approach and style, smooth as syrup.

One of his first hires when he was the sports editor in Atlanta was a young writer named Edwin Pope. I got to know Pope when I worked in Miami. He still provides a column on occasion for *The Miami Herald* and is one of the true gentlemen in the profession. I used to stay out late in Miami just to spend time with Pope and another great sportswriter, Jack Mann, at an after-hours joint called Julie's Pad. Pope and Mann liked to talk and I was a better listener in those days.

I reflected on Furman Bisher as I watched The Masters. I had learned earlier on Sunday that Mike Wallace, the stormy news reporter and commentator at CBS TV, one of the mainstays of "60 Minutes," had died. But I didn't know Wallace and had never spent any time in his company so it wasn't as personal a loss.

I wish they had mentioned Jim Huber, who had covered golf on TV for three decades for Turner Broadcasting and did wonderful well-thought-out interviews and offered essays about his favorite game, and knew his way around the Augusta course, a slice of golfers' heaven.

One of Huber's colleagues called him "the golf poet." Huber and I had worked on the same sports staff at *The Miami News* back in 1969. He was interested in the human aspect of sports, so we were on the same page. I liked his work. He won an Emmy Award for his efforts. I'd smile when I'd see him on TV and I'd wish we'd run into each other again. So we could share tales about our old boss, John Crittenden, the rival columnist of Edwin Pope in Miami.

Huber had died at age 67 of acute leukemia back in January. I'd bet that Huber was fond of Furman Bisher during his long stay in Atlanta.

I last saw Furman Bisher when I traveled to Tampa, Florida in late January of 2001 to be at the Super Bowl when the Baltimore Ravens defeated the New York Giants. I was there all week to interview owners, management types, former players and sports media about Art Rooney, the late owner of the Pittsburgh Steelers.

I was researching my book *The Chief: Art Rooney and His Pittsburgh Steelers,* and I simply sat in the lobby of the hotel that served as the NFL's Super Bowl headquarters and picked off people I recognized as they passed by, and interviewed them to get their take on Art Rooney. It worked beautifully.

The writers had some personal experiences with Rooney they remembered fondly, and I don't know why I was so taken with that. Hey, writers know how to tell stories. That's why they're writers.

Whenever I have covered a major sports event such as the Super Bowl, The World Series, any kind of All-Star Game, I always sought out the company of the best sports writers in the business.

I was not in their league, but I wanted to be with them. I wanted to hear their stories. I was always more impressed and intrigued with being around great writers, and not just great sportswriters, than I was of being around outstanding athletes and sports personalities. I thought something good would rub off on me.

When it came to sports personalities, I was always more impressed by those who had been great when I was a kid, and reading about them in newspapers and sports magazines. So I loved interviewing Joe Louis or Joe DiMaggio, Jack Dempsey and Red Grange, even more than Muhammad Ali and Mickey Mantle.

The best sportswriters tended to keep company with their peers, and they were attracted to each other like magnets. I'd join them and was never made to feel like an intruder or an upstart. I respected and admired them and I think they liked that. I wanted to hear from them, to learn from them.

So I spent time with Red Smith, Dave Anderson, Dick Young, Larry Merchant, Milton Gross, Stan Isaacs, Joe Gergen, Steve Jacobson, Tim Moriarty, Gene Ward, Bob Waters and Arthur Daley from New York, Furman Bisher from Atlanta, Edwin Pope from Miami,

Joe Gilmartin from Phoenix, Stan Hochman, Ray Kelly and Sandy Grady from Philadelphia, Blacky Sherrod and Edwin Shrake from Dallas, Bud Jenkins from Fort Worth, Jim Murray and Melvin Durslag from Los Angeles, Bob Broeg from St. Louis, Bud Collins from Boston, Brent Musburger, Bill Gleason and John Carmichael from Chicago, Jerry Izenberg from Newark, Dave Brady from Washington, D.C., Jack Murphy and Jerry Magee from San Diego, Joe Falls and Jerry Greene from Detroit. They were among the best in the business.

When I was in Tampa working on my Art Rooney book I made a special effort to spend time with Furman Bisher. He was always such a nice man, a courtly figure, with a soothing southern voice. I even took him to lunch in Tampa. I listened and lapped up his stories.

When I was first starting out in the business, back in 1969, I used to spend time in the company of Jimmy Cannon, the great sports columnist from New York, to hear him sharing stories about spending time with Ernest Hemingway on the Left Bank in Paris during World War II. It didn't get any better. I had read Hemingway's *A Moveable Feast*, about his days in Paris, when I was stationed at Fort Greely, the Army's Cold Weather Testing Center near Fairbanks, Alaska. Cannon brought that book to life with his personal stories of time spent with Hemingway.

Bisher was 82 at the time we met in Tampa. He lived till he was 93 and he didn't retire from his position at the newspaper until 2009. Asked what he planned to do after he retired, he said, "I'm going to get up in the morning and think of something to write."

This was the man who had the only published interview with Shoeless Joe Jackson in 1949, the first time Jackson had spoken to a newspaper reporter since he was involved in the Black Sox Scandal in 1919.

Bisher drank tea with Ty Cobb—"the Georgia Peach." He had seen Cy Young pitch. He saw Joe Louis box. He played golf with Bobby Jones. Even so, he wondered why people seemed so interested in talking to him. "People look at me like I'm a museum or something," he once exclaimed.

The great Grantland Rice had led that kind of life. I wanted to lead that kind of life. I had a great run for about 15 years, but I wanted to get off the road, I wanted to grow up with my family. I thought that was important, too. I regret some of my career decisions, but I don't regret the time spent with my family.

I don't play golf, but I love to watch it on TV. The pro golfers are so good and only remind me of why I don't play golf. It takes a lot of time – too much time, I thought – to be good at golf. And, if you're not any good, it's a frustrating exercise, one that seems to provoke a lot of swearing. Mark Twain called golf "a good walk spoiled."

Of course, even Tiger Woods indulges in swearing these days, and behaving poorly on the golf course. I started off on Thursday wanting to see Tiger Woods win this Masters. I want to see him bounce back and be the best again.

A day later, I switched favorites and wanted to see Phil Mickelson win it. I read a story by Gerry Dulac in the *Post-Gazette* that prompted me to change my mind.

Mickelson had gotten up at 7 a.m. on Thursday to go watch Arnold Palmer, Jack Nicklaus and Gary Player hit ceremonial tee shots to start The Masters. Most of the pros slept in. Mickelson was about eight hours from his tee time, yet he got up out of respect for the greats of the game, the men who made this sport the money machine it is today, and paid proper tribute to them just by his presence.

This was also duly noted by the TV announcers. Mickelson gets it. He understands how to respond to the golf fans and how to deal with setbacks and triumphs. You have to like a guy like that.

Mickelson was the sort of professional athlete that was attractive to Furman Bisher as a column subject. Bisher wrote about the best in all sports and was one of the first national columnists to write about motor sports—NASCAR racing—once regarded strictly as a redneck diversion.

We ended up on Sunday rooting for Bubba Watson, who won the title and the green jacket in a playoff. He had competed at the University of Georgia so Bisher would have loved writing about Bubba Watson.

I talked to Bisher about Art Rooney and the Steelers. I found my notes from that interview in my files over the weekend.

"The Steelers used to stop by to play an exhibition game in Atlanta in days gone by," said Bisher, "and that's how I first met Art Rooney. He'd make a point to get to know you. He made you feel more comfortable than any other owner. He always had that cigar in his hand or in his mouth. He seemed to welcome you. He seemed to sense your discomfort.

"I've known his son, Dan, for a long time, too, and Dan has always been easy to deal with. I appreciate that.

"I have very little contact with athletes in this day and age, so I spend more time talking with the owners and administrators. More and more, I rely on my relationships with old-timers. I heard Paul Harvey say on the radio that 20 percent of all the players in the NFL have a criminal record. So I'm not thrilled with most of them these days.

"Guys like Art Rooney appealed to me. He was a good citizen. Pittsburgh should have been proud to have an Art Rooney living there, even if he didn't own the Pittsburgh Steelers. He suffered through some of the worst periods. One year it got so bad they had to split the year with the Eagles. It was a different world then. The owners were compatriots, and relied on one another.

"They leaned on one another. They counted on one another. Nowadays, I don't even know some of these owners. Back in the days of Art Rooney, these guys were in this together. It was a fraternity. Wellington Mara and Art Modell would appreciate what I'm talking about.

"Wellington Mara is a fellow who kept the league together when they decided to go into revenue sharing. He had the best market in the league in New York. He wanted what was best for the league. Rooney came from one of the smaller markets, but he was always for what was good for the league, or so I've heard anyhow.

"I think I helped Wellington Mara get into the Pro Football Hall of Fame. I got up at one of the voting meetings and I said simply, 'What kind of Hall of Fame is this that Al Davis can get into it and Wellington Mara can't?' That's all I said. He got in that year. I think they ought to put Art Modell in, too. Speaking of Al Davis, I think it's a disgrace that he got in. He's a guy who tried to destroy the league.

"I didn't vote for Ralph Wilson of Buffalo, either. Show me what he did. Art Rooney did something. Wellington Mara did something. I guess I'm getting a little callous."

I think I talked Furman Bisher into voting for Lynn Swann for the Hall of Fame. Bisher wanted to vote for John Stallworth over Swann. He thought Stallworth was more deserving. Bisher ended up, in time, voting for both of them.

Bisher was born in Denton, North Carolina and he was named after a Baptist minister named James Furman. Young Bisher, James Furman Bisher that is, even attended Furman University for a year before transferring to the University of North Carolina at Chapel Hill.

He started out at age 20 as the editor of a newspaper in Lumberton. I've been to Lumberton. There's never been much going on in Lumberton. A Pitt sprinter named Lee McCrae came from Lumberton, and I visited his home before the 1988 Olympic Games. But Bisher managed to move on, first to Charlotte, and then to Atlanta.

He certainly left his mark and he and his knowing smile will be missed by many who were lucky enough to know him and read him.

Photos by Jim O'Brien

Furman Bisher was the celebrated sports columnist of the *Atlanta Journal-Constitution*.

Edwin Pope is the sports columnist of *The Miami News*.

Being a journalist
is a worthy profession

August 2010

GRANTLAND RICE

To be a journalist is an honor. I heard some-one say that last Thursday as I passed one of the screen presentations at the Newseum in Washington, D.C. I didn't know who said it and the attribution was missing by the time I checked the screen. It was a voice from on high, one of those God-like voices, and it struck home with this passerby.

It made me smile. I agreed, of course, and I never felt more pride in affirming that comment as I did after touring the Newseum. I couldn't get enough of it and I came back the next day. Admission tickets are good for visits on consecutive days.

I had never heard anything about or read anything about the Newseum until Anne and Doug Smith suggested we check it out when my wife Kathie and I were staying with them in their townhouse near the waterfront in the nation's capital.

It's a six-story building on Pennsylvania Avenue, not far from the Capitol Building, where five centuries of news history meets up-to-the-second technology, There are 14 major galleries and 15 theaters and it captures the world's greatest news stories. It covers so many facets of the media, especially the printed word. I saw so many magazine covers I recognized from having read them in my youth.

I had my mother buy me a toy printing press when I was eight years old and I have been employed in the newspaper business, or something associated with the media, since I became the sports editor of *The Hazelwood Envoy* in my hometown at age 14.

This was a great way to wind up a week's vacation that started with us visiting my wife's brother and sister-in-law she was Diane Thomas while growing up in Munhall—at their home on Emerald Isle, North Carolina. My brother-in-law is Harvey Churchman of White Oak. Their home sits on Bogue Sound in a spectacular setting that is always exciting to the eye. And you can walk to the beach on the Atlantic Ocean in ten minutes.

I read two books while there that also made me feel good about being a journalist. One is called *Sportswriter: The Life and Times of Grantland Rice* by Charles Fountain and the other is called *The Longest Trip Home,* a memoir by John Grogan. He is better known for writing *Marley and Me*, which once topped *The New York Times* best-seller list. Grogan is a columnist for *The Philadelphia Inquirer*.

Rice was the most famous and most respected sports colum-nist of his day, from the 20s through the 50s, best known perhaps for writing the line about "it's not whether you win or lose, but how you play the game," and for dubbing the Notre Dame backfield "The Four

Horsemen" in the mid-20s. I would have loved to have led the life that Grantland Rice enjoyed. He kept company with the likes of Babe Ruth, Jack Dempsey, Bobby Jones, Babe Didrikson and Ty Cobb. He played golf and cards with them all.

I laughed out loud while reading Grogan's personal tales of growing up in an ultra-Catholic home, and felt so sad at the end when I read of his parents' problems as they got old, and when his father died and his mother had to go to an assisted-care home. We learned, upon arriving in Emerald Isle two weeks ago, that Kaye Cowher, the 54-year-old wife of former Steelers' coach Bill Cowher had died from skin cancer in nearby Raleigh.

I remember talking to Kaye in the press box on several occasions when Bill was coaching the Steelers. I had met their three daughters, all of whom followed in their mother's footsteps by playing Division I basketball, two of them at Princeton and one at Wofford. Kaye had played at N.C. State and later in professional basketball. I thought about the Cowher family and wondered how they were dealing with this setback.

The Newseum provided the same sort of extreme emotions. Watching Elvis Presley on TV at the height of his popularity and seeing the way newspaper reporters were portrayed in many movies brought a smile. Seeing a report on "The Attack on America" on 9/11 still brings tears to one's eyes and cheeks.

One of the displays points up the problems many major newspapers are experiencing these days. It showed some of the newspapers that have folded such as *The Christian Science Monitor,* the *Ann Arbor News, Rocky Mountain News* and the *Seattle Post-Intelligencer.* It also offered hope for small town papers and weeklies and monthlies that fill a special niche, or provide hometown news that can't be found elsewhere. It cited how important it is to maintain vital newspapers and why we should support them as readers and advertisers.

On the first floor of the Newseum each day the front page of at least one daily newspaper in each state is on display. They are faxed daily from the different newspapers to the Newseum.

The admission for adults is $20, and seniors get in for $18. You can use the tickets on two consecutive days.

There is a display of Pulitzer Prize-winning photos. There is also a display of dramatic sports photos by Walter Ioos of *Sports Illustrated.* He was the photographer who came to the Steelers' training camp at St. Vincent College in the early '70s and shot pictures for the book by Roy Blount Jr. titled *About Three Bricks Shy of a Load.*

He has stunning portraits of Muhammad Ali and Joe Frazier. I covered their "Fight of the Century" in March of 1971 at Madison Square Garden. There are dramatic photos of Wilt Chamberlain, Michael Jordan, Magic Johnson and Kobe Bryant, some of the greatest basketball players of all time, and of Pele, the great soccer player. My boyhood hero, Johnny Unitas of the Baltimore Colts, is shown in one of the large murals. I interviewed all of those sports greats during my days of working in New York.

There is a terrace atop the building that affords a spectacular view of many of the famous monuments in D.C.

I forgot to bring my camera the first day and that prompted a return the following day. I want to go back to the Newseum because there is still so much we didn't see, plus there are other museums nearby that merit a visit.

I was impressed with what I saw in D.C. The Metro is a clean and efficient subway system. The downtown area is kept clean. People seem better dressed than one finds in downtown New York, or Pittsburgh, for that matter. Many people nodded and smiled as they passed, and some even said "good morning" or "good afternoon."

I worked with Doug Smith when I was in New York. He covered Dr. J and the Nets for *Newsday* on Long Island, and I covered them for *The New York Post*. He got me into tennis in the 70s, and that in time got my wife into the sport as well. Tennis is a sport for a lifetime, so his gift to us was like a variable annuity.

Doug went on to become the tennis writer for a 15-year span for *USA Today*.

He covered major tournaments in New York, London, Paris and Melbourne. It was a great gig. A few days before I arrived in D.C., Doug told me that Tony Kornheiser wanted to join us for dinner. I was excited about the prospect because I had not seen Doug or Tony since I was in Tampa for a week prior to the Super Bowl back in January of 2001 to conduct interviews with NFL people and sportswriters regarding Art Rooney for a book I was doing called *The Chief*.

Kornheiser covered the Nets from time to time, and other sports on Long Island when he was at *Newsday*. He went on to write a column for *The Washington Post*. Then he was the star of a nationally-syndicated radio sports talk show on ESPN, and was an analyst on Monday Night Football, and is still teaming up with Mike Wilbon on "Pardon the Interruption," the top-rated sports talk show on television. He's made millions of dollars for doing all this—annually.

Kornheiser is an entertaining fellow with strong opinions about all topics and it made for an interesting dinner meeting at McCormick & Schmicks in Washington D.C.

At dinner, he invited Doug Smith and me to join him afterward at a book signing party at a book store in northern Virginia called Politics and Prose. Dave Kindred, a former columnist for *The Washington Post*, has written a book called *Morning Miracle* about that newspaper's struggle to survive.

Kindred and Kornheiser were both among the early contributing writers to *Street & Smith's Basketball Yearbook*. I was the founding editor of that national publication from 1970 to 1992, and continued after that as a contributing writer for another ten years. Kindred and Kornheiser both told me it was the first magazine they were ever invited to write for on the national scene. Kornheiser thought he was paid $100, but I corrected him on that. He and Kindred were both paid $300 for the articles they contributed. "I know it was more than I was making in a week back then," commented Kindred, who was a columnist for the *Louisville Courier-Journal* at the time.

"And you were paid promptly," I reminded them. "I believed in big bylines and fast pay."

Smith and I both bought a copy of Kindred's new book. We helped him sell a dozen copies at his first outing. I was reminded that it's difficult to sell books no matter where you work.

Two other retired writers were on hand for Kindred's signing session. They were George Solomon, the former sports editor of *The Washington Post*, and Ken Denlinger, a former sportswriter for that newspaper. He's written a fine book about Penn State coach Joe Paterno called *For The Glory*. I had a history with both men.

Solomon was a sports writer with the *Sun-Sentinel* in Fort Lauderdale, Florida in 1969 when we both covered the Miami Dolphins. I was working at the time for *The Miami News*. Denlinger had graduated from Penn State University. We recalled how we had played in a touch-tag football game on the lawn of the Cathedral of Learning when I was the sports editor of *The Pitt News* and he was on the staff of the *Daily Collegian*. He said they beat us that morning of the Pitt-Penn State game that was played at Pitt Stadium.

It was good to see them all. We had enjoyed some great times together. Solomon remembered that when we were covering the Super Bowl in 1970 we drove one day from New Orleans to Baton Rouge to see "Pistol Pete" Maravich of LSU, the nation's leading scorer, in an SEC basketball contest with Auburn. We ran out of gas in our rented automobile by some bayous on the way back to New Orleans that night. Such days were special, I realize that more than ever now.

I had no idea when I set off on this vacation trip that I would be seeing these guys. It was a great way to wrap up a get-away trip.

The total experience brought back memories of having had the opportunity to write for newspapers in Pittsburgh, Philadelphia, Miami, New York, Kansas City and even Fort Greely, Alaska. Doug Smith had been stationed in Fairbanks at the same time. He graduated from Hampton Institute in 1964 and that was the year I graduated from Pitt.

He did military service in Vietnam while I was one of the lucky ones who stayed in the U.S.A. I'm hoping we can all get together again sooner rather than later.

Upon returning home, Kathie and I attended a Mass at St. Bede's Church in Point Breeze to celebrate the life of Dan Hudak, a journalist who died at age 43 from cancer. I didn't know him, but he must have been a special guy. The church was packed and the tributes in the local newspapers spoke of a life well lived. My wife is a friend of his wife, Julie. He left behind three little kids, Ben, Lilly and Sarah, ages 9 to 4. Julie and Kathie have been partners off and on in platform tennis league competition for 18 years. Kathie knew about Dan's illness and how difficult his life had become.

But he was always the competitor and showed great courage in the face of trying times.

I recognized many in the church. Mrs. Elsie Hillman was among them. Dan Hudak helped her with keeping her archives in order and writing speeches for her for almost 20 years. At one point, he wrote some sports stories for *The Pittsburgh Press*. Mrs. Hillman has helped me as a patron with my writing and publishing efforts. For her, his passing was like losing a son. She acknowledged as much when I spoke to her in the church narthex or vestibule following the service.

Dan Hudak took pride in being a journalist.

Once more, I felt great pride in being a fellow writer and historian.

Jim O'Brien holds a copy of "Morning Miracle" by Dave Kindred at a book signing in suburban Washington D.C. attended by, left to right, ESPN's Tony Kornhiser, Dave Kindred, George Solomon, Doug Smith and Ken Denlinger, all sports writers out of D.C. Kindred's book is about life at *The Washington Post*.

Pat Conroy on going to games

"What a good thing it is to go to games. What strange joy is felt as you leave the flatness of your daily life, the fatigue of routine, and the killing sameness of jobs to move among thousands toward a brightly lit field house at night."
—From *"My Losing Season"*

PITTSBURGH

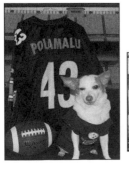

GUYS
AND
GALS

Yvonne Zanos and Phil Musick
are missed by many

January 2010

Pittsburgh has lost two of its most beloved members of the media. Phil Musick and Yvonne Zanos were two proud Pittsburghers who became members of our own families, or at least it felt that way. They both touched our hearts and minds on many occasions.

We let them into our homes and they took a seat on a couch in the corner and never left. Whatever we offered them was just great and they were glad to be welcomed.

Musick grew up in Garfield, and reminded us of that often in his heartfelt columns in *The Pittsburgh Press* and the *Pittsburgh Post-Gazette,* as well as in his talk show on WTAE Radio. He told us about family and friends. And about brown-eyed girls who stole his heart.

Zanos grew up in Bethel Park, a beautiful girl who became a model and then a TV personality at WTAE-TV and for a longer spell at KDKA-TV and remained a model for us the rest of her life.

Musick was 71 when he died from congestive heart failure and Zanos had turned 60 two days before she died from complications from ovarian cancer. She passed away last Friday with family and friends at her side at the Family Hospice and Palliative Care Center in Mt. Lebanon. I had been there a few months earlier for my friend Bob Milie of Mt. Lebanon, the former sports trainer at Duquesne University and with the Steelers of the '70s, so I know Zanos was in a good place at the end. Those hospice people are great.

We all knew Zanos was ill; she shared that with us to help us deal with our own challenges. Like the '60 Pirates, she never quit, she never gave up.

Musick graduated from Peabody High School and Duquesne University, and had the kind of inner-city experience I could relate to when I read his columns. I thought he and Roy McHugh of *The Press* and free-lance magazine writer Myron Cope were the best writers in town. They were good models for anyone interested in the writing game. So was George Kiseda, who grew up on the South Side and started out on the sports staff at the *Sun-Telegraph*, and was one of the few local talents to move elsewhere. He was a star basketball writer for *The Philadelphia Bulletin* and *Philadelphia Daily News* and later a desk man at *The Los Angeles Times*. He might have been the best basketball writer ever.

One of Musick's friends, sportscaster Bill Hillgrove, grew up in Garfield as well and they both wore their hometown tag like a badge of courage. Hey, boxing great Harry Greb came out of Garfield, too. They were tough guys with soft hearts. That's why people have embraced them here. They are "real Pittsburgh guys." Steelers' owner Art Rooney thought that was the greatest compliment a guy or gal could come by in this town. When Phil's father died, Mr. Rooney attended the funeral and that meant a great deal to Phil, according to a story shared with me by Art Rooney Jr..

Zanos graduated from Bethel Park High School and Bethany College in Bethany, West Virginia. She finished first runner-up in 1971's Miss Pennsylvania USA Pageant.

Her husband, Jim Zanos of Munhall, told people that when he first laid eyes on her when she was a model he knew he was going to marry her.

I knew Jim better than Yvonne. He was a top-notch end on the Pitt football team, and earned varsity letters in 1957 and 1958. He was a teammate at Pitt of Bill Kaliden, who came out of neighboring Homestead at the same time, and earned varsity letters at Pitt the same years. Kaliden was a quarterback and Zanos was one of his reliable receivers.

After he graduated from Pitt, Zanos was an owner and host at the Den of the Golden Panther, where the Pitt Pott Restaurant & Bar had previously held forth on Centre Avenue, near the intersection of Craig Street, just a few blocks from Pitt Stadium. It was always packed on game days. Zanos or one of his buddies on the Pitt football team were always in the doorway to check I.D. cards—not always that closely—and to maintain law and order in the joint. I went there once or twice in my school days at Pitt, but Frankie Gustine's Restaurant was my favorite haunt.

The Den of the Golden Panther was the sort of place I am sure Musick frequented. He liked being any place there were interesting and amusing people. He was always looking for somebody to write about. Zanos counted Mike Ditka of Aliqippa and Ron Delfine of Canonsburg among his teammates at Pitt. Mike Lucci of Ambridge used to serve as a bouncer at the door on occasion. They were a great bunch. I went to Pitt a few years later, and learned all about them. It was great to see them then and it's still the same way today.

Musick and Zanos never forgot where they came from. They were proud of their roots, and they were always down-to-earth individuals. They were celebrities in this city, no doubt about that, familiar faces that would get a second look wherever they traveled. But they were always approachable, always had the smile for anyone who said hello to them or recognized them. They didn't think they were above the crowd.

They enjoyed their audience. My wife Kathie and I would run into Yvonne and Jim Zanos at South Hills Village or at the Giant Eagle in Bethel Park, and she always had the quick smile and the easy exchange. Jim always looked like he'd just come away from a nap. He was so laidback. She was natural and so friendly and for real. It has been my experience that most of the KDKA-TV personalities are like that.

My wife told me she saw Yvonne just a week before she died and thought she looked great. I had the same feeling when I saw Foge Fazio a few weeks before he died in late November from leukemia. He, too, was always bright-eyed and bushy-tailed.

It's always easy to be in the company of Patrice King Brown, Jennifer Antkowiak, Jon Burnett, Bob Pompeani, Mary Robb Jackson, Lynne Hayes-Freeland, Harold Hayes, Brenda Waters, Bob Kudzma and Dennis Bowman. It was that way with Patty Burns and her dad Bill Burns, and Ray Tannehill and Fred Honsberger. Jack Bogut has always been easy company.

Yvonne Zanos began reporting at KDKA-TV in the late 1970s on "Evening Magazine." Jon Burnett and Liz Miles were the co-hosts of that show in the early '80s. Our daughter Sarah loved that show. She watched it nearly every evening around dinner time. I had a chance once to introduce her to Liz Miles and, for Sarah, it was like me meeting Elizabeth Taylor or Marilyn Monroe.

These people become part of our lives. We see them so often. They come into our homes on a regular basis. They speak to us in many ways. If we like them, we embrace them like family.

We trusted them. If Yvonne Zanos, the ultimate consumer reporter, told us that a new product lived up to its billing we knew we could buy it and it would work. If she advised us otherwise there was no way we would buy it. She was a consumer advocate who was looking out for us. Only Oprah had more of an influence on what women would and would not buy when they went shopping.

Zanos was always upbeat, even during the last few years when her prognosis with ovarian cancer was not that optimistic. She remained optimistic even if her doctors didn't. They were being honest. She was being Yvonne Zanos. She had bright eyes. Musick often mentioned bright-eyed girls or significant others he referred to as "the brown-eyed girl."

He wrote to us about "Some Things I Think I Think," which was a form that worked well for a nationally-syndicated columnist named Jimmy Cannon I came to know in my New York days. Phil borrowed from the best, but he was original in the way he wrote. He'd read something the great Red Smith had written and then he'd put a Pittsburgh slant on it. I liked him because he was willing to cut his wrists and bleed in public about something personal in his life.

He had two daughters of his own and adopted five kids who came over from Cambodia. How many guys do you know who would do something like that? I thought he was the genuine article. When you read his column you thought he had written it just for you. Bob Prince had that quality on the air during Pirates' broadcasts. He always said he was watching a baseball game and telling a guy on the other side of the fence what was going on.

When people like this pass away it is, indeed, like a death in the family.

Musick's death, in particular, was a bit eerie for me. Only the day before he died I thought about him, and two of his fellow workers and colleagues, Bruce Keidan and Dave Ailes. They were all sports editors of Pittsburgh newspapers in their day. That was my dream job when I was coming along in the business, but I never got that opportunity. In that respect, I fell short of my goal.

I had spent time in the same press boxes at Pittsburgh sports venues with them. Joe Gordon, the Steelers' publicity director during the glory days of the '70s, used to take members of the media out to dinner the night before the games when we were on the road. So I spent some good times in their company.

Musick was always a good story-teller and he was funny. Gordon recalls him being like a Damon Runyon character. I have some of Musick's books on the Steelers and Roberto Clemente in my personal library. I had him contribute to some of my own sports books. I respected his work.

Musick, Keidan and Ailes all have disappeared from the Pittsburgh sports scene in recent years. I'm not around as often as I used to be myself. But I haven't heard much about them. I do get reports via the grapevine from time to time that they are all having one kind of health challenge or another. That's what happens when you're in your mid-60s. I wondered about how they were doing. I wondered when I'd be hearing about one of them next, and thought that, no doubt, it will be when one of them dies.

The next morning I received an e-mail from my best friend Alex Pociask, who is working in Rio de Janiero that Phil Musick had died. Alex's wife, Sharon, who is residing near Chicago, had e-mailed him that news tidbit. It took somebody in Brazil to tell me that Phil Musick had died.

Yvonne Zanos

Phil Musick

"God was having a good day when he created sundresses."
—**Phil Musick**

Aldo taught his family
to be thankful every day

November 2009

Aldo Bartolotta always boasted that he never had a bad day. You would greet him and say, "How are you doing, Aldo?" And he would always respond by cocking his head sideway like he was sharing the Divinci Code and proclaiming, "I'm fine, thank you. I never had a bad day."

He told me once that he told his wife Joan that he wanted his tombstone to have an inscription on it that read: HE NEVER HAD A BAD DAY.

Joan—whose friends call her Jo-Ann—later told me, "I'm going to have this message on my tombstone: HE PASSED THEM ALL ONTO ME.

I thought about their humorous remarks as I approached them at the Marshall Marra Funeral Home in Monongahela on a Thursday afternoon in November of 2009. I figured there had to be some bad days the previous three years, especially the previous Monday when their son, Bruce, just 55, finally succumbed to the lymphoma form of cancer that he had battled bravely during that period.

Bruce Bartolotta was the CEO of Mon Valley Foods and the owner of three Giant Eagle stores in Finleyville, Fisher Heights and Uniontown. His dad and uncle had founded the stores and worked hard, often seven days a week in the early years, to make them successful. Theirs was a Horatio Alger rags-to-riches story, indeed.

Leo Bartolotta was the tough-minded businessman in the back room, handling things in the office, and Aldo was the face of the business, better at mixing and schmoozing with customers. Aldo knew how to talk to people. He has a warm smile and a glint in his blue-gray eyes. You're comfortable in his company. He has one of those soothing voices, like the late Fred Rogers, and it's always a beautiful, or at least a good, day in his neighborhood.

At the funeral home, Joan and Aldo were comforting their family and friends, rather than the other way around. I had not seen such long lines in a funeral home, or so many flowers, since I attended the viewings of Art Rooney, the Steelers' owner and founder, and that of his wife Kathleen at Devlin's Funeral Home on Pittsburgh's North Side years ago. Someone observed at Kathleen's funeral that the place looked like Phipps Conservatory, the botanical showcase in Oakland.

The floral displays at the Bartolotta viewing spilled over into adjoining rooms at the Marra Funeral Home. So did the line of friends who'd come to pay their respects.

"I cried my eyes out the past few days," Aldo said, as he held my hand firmly. "I don't have any tears left. He was such a good son. I always taught my children to be generous and to give back to the

MON VALLEY'S FINEST— Monongahela is fortunate to have business leaders like Ken Codeluppi of Wall Firma on Main Street and Aldo Bartolotta, owner of Giant Eagle in Fisher Heights.

Stan "The Man" Musial Bridge Re-naming Ceremony May 4, 2012

Bruce Bartolotta and his father Aldo Bartolotta were a great team at Giant Eagle in Monongahela for so many years.

community. But I didn't realize until I was here last night and talked to so many people he had helped some way or another. I had no idea he had done some of the things he had done. He never said anything to me about it."

When you go to a funeral home do you ever wonder what it will be like when you die?

I have often heard that it depends on the weather as to how many cars will be in the funeral procession. I don't know about that. It was a perfect day for a funeral this Thursday. It was overcast and there was a light rain most of the day. It was not easy to find a parking space near the Marra Funeral Home, but they had lots of men in black on the sidewalks outside to direct drivers to a place to park. As it turned out, I later learned that there were 72 cars in the funeral procession.

I went to the funeral home with a friend and neighbor, Ken Codeluppi. He owns a business on Main Street in Monongahela, and knows its backstreets. I had introduced him to Aldo Bartolotta a few years earlier and invited him to join us for lunch on several occasions at the Back Porch Restaurant. Ken had called me the day before and left me a message that he wanted me to know about the death of Bruce Bartolotta. But I had already seen it in the obituary section that morning. At first, I thought it might be Aldo's brother who had died, but I would learn that it was his son. Aldo told me later he was the only one left in his original family. I know how that feels.

Aldo took Ken's right hand in his right hand and he grasped my right hand with his left hand and held on to our hands the entire time he was talking to us. He was still sharing insights and words of wisdom—that's what he does—and he spoke clearly and calmly, showing no outward evidence that his heart was heavy with grief.

Aldo always told me I could invite any of my friends who could appreciate the gathering to the Back Porch Restaurant. Aldo always picked up the tab. I always encouraged Aldo to talk at the table and to share his upbeat philosophy on life and business. It was better than any MBA course at Carnegie Mellon University or the University of Pittsburgh's Katz Business School.

Bartolotta had come up the hard way and worked his way to success. He shared his success. I remember him telling me that a friend who was moving out of Monongahela had this big, impressive house and how he approached Bartolotta about buying it. Aldo went home and asked his wife Joan what she thought of the idea, and she said, "We don't need a house like that. Our friends are comfortable with where we live now. We don't need a showy place like that."

He loves to talk about Pitt. He has season tickets to Pitt football games, and I see him often at tailgate parties and other parties hosted by our friend Armand Dellovade, who owns a sheet metal business in Canonsburg. Dellovade is an equally big Pitt fan and a generous man as well. Neither has ever forgotten where they came from, and how fortunate they have been. Frank Sarris of Sarris Chocolates in Canonsburg was the same way, and was often in their company.

Mel Bassi, an attorney and banking executive in neighboring Charleroi, would join us at Bartolotta's table at the Back Porch Restaurant. He was a good man and we all mourned his death a few years back. Rudy Andabaker, Bill Priatko and Lou "Bimbo" Cecconi, who had all played football at Pitt in the late '40s and early '50s, would be there. Priatko's pal, Rudy Celigoi, who had played football at Rutgers, would come with him. Those men all became coaches and educators and now they were going to grad school again as they listened to Aldo Bartolotta tell his stories.

I have been fortunate in my lifetime to know men like these, and the likes of Art Rooney, Doc Carlson and Frankie Gustine, going back to my student days at the University of Pittsburgh. My pals Bill Priatko, Alex Pociask, Mike Hagan, Ron Temple, Gene Musial, Pat Santelli, Baldo Iorio and Jerry Morrow pass along good advice these days. I have listened to and learned from all of them.

I passed Park Avenue. That's a famous two-mile stretch in Monongahela. There's been a TV documentary done about it called "An Extraordinary Street."

Joe Montana grew up in a home on the high side of Park Avenue. I always thought it was quite a coincidence that Joe Montana lived on Park Avenue and Dan Marino lived on Parkview Avenue in South Oakland. Both came from good Italian families and their humble homes were similar. Fred Cox lived on Park Avenue. He not only had a long career in the NFL but he was also the inventor of the Nerf football. That made him more millions than pro football ever did.

Carl E. Vuono, a four-star general and chief of staff of the U.S. Army, grew up on Park Avenue. So did Jim Jimirro, the founder of the Disney Channel. So did Dr. Ronald V. Pellegrini, a world renowned cardiothoracic surgeon in Pittsburgh. Scott Zolak, another NFL quarterback, grew up in Monongahela. His dad, Paul Zolak, was regarded as the best athletic director in the WPIAL when he was at Ringgold High School and then Bethel Park High School.

I was lucky to meet most of the Mon Valley's finest athletes through the years and talk to them and share their stories to inspire others to follow their lead. I look forward to my next luncheon meeting with Aldo Bartolotta at the Back Porch. I am confident it will be a good day. There is a bridge on the Mon Valley Expressway named in honor of Joe Montana (*and now one named for Stan Musial*). I think they should name a bridge after Aldo Bartolotta.

Jim O'Brien

Aldo Bartolotta, Joe Chiodo and Joe Natoli meet at Armand Dellovade's annual "Italian Stag" fete at Dellovade's estate in Lawrence, Pa.

Visiting G-20 venues
a week later

October 2009

Here's a G-20 story you will not get anywhere else. My good friend Gus Kalaris played a role in helping keep Pittsburgh safe and secure for all the international giants who visited our fair city for a few days last month.

Kalaris is "The Ice Ball Man," a gentleman in his 70s whose family has sold ice balls, popcorn and peanuts from a bright orange stand in West Park on the city's North Side for over 70 years.

We can all learn a lot from Gus Kalaris. He is one of the city's most successful and long-standing entrepreneurs. His task might appear humble to some, but this is a man who has a great work ethic, one that could be emulated by the ballplayers who ply their trade just a few blocks away at PNC Park and Heinz Field.

One day Gus dropped a 75-pound block of ice on his foot to start the day. His toes started to swell and they hurt like hell. Gus got a pair of large scissors and cut a piece of leather from the toe of his shoe so the swollen toe wouldn't rub against the inside of the shoe. It didn't hurt as much that way. And he continued to make ice balls the rest of the day.

Gus's work is seasonal, naturally. He's out there about three-fourths of the year when the weather is good. He is a North Side landmark. Customers come from everywhere because they believe he has the best ice balls in the city. He makes his own syrups with a family recipe, he cleans and polishes his stand routinely, and he shaves the ice himself. He'd never resort to crushing the ice with a machine.

When someone asks him if his forearms get sore, he smiles and reaches into his pocket and pulls out two $20 bills and rubs them on his forearms. It's one of his routines. "That makes my forearms feel better," he says with the timing of a vaudevillian.

I go to see Gus when I want to find out what's going on in Pittsburgh. He gets along with everybody and he talks to everybody. One of his dearest friends is Dan Rooney, the owner of the Steelers, whose home is just a few blocks away.

Before Dan and his wife Pat moved to Ireland, where he now serves as the American ambassador to Ireland, the Rooneys were frequent visitors to Gus's ice ball stand. They even invite Gus and his wife, Estelle, to their holiday season parties.

"Dan's the richest guy on the North Side, and I'm the poorest," Gus likes to say, even if it's stretching his syrup a little bit. Gus owns some properties on the North Side and he manages his money in a thrifty manner.

He told me a story just before G-20 got underway that stays with me. Gus told me he wasn't going to be open on the Thursday and Friday the event would be held in downtown Pittsburgh. He feared the worst.

The police and National Guard had set up a fortress of sorts nearby on the edge of West Park, and Gus was among those thinking some bad things might happen during G-20.

One day one of the city's political leaders stopped by to see Gus and get an ice ball, and Gus gave him some advice.

"See that train running behind me," began Gus. "A lot of trains come by here all day long. See what's on those trains? See how many tankards are going by? They all contain some kind of flammable liquids. Some of them are explosive. You know where those trains go from here? They go on an elevated track across the Allegheny River and they run directly behind the Convention Center."

Gus said the guy he was talking to slapped his forehead as if he'd just discovered the electric light bulb.

The guy also saw to it that trains that traveled on those tracks were halted somewhere in Ohio for three days during the G-20 Summit.

So maybe Gus saved the day for the delegates to the G-20 Summit. He smiles at the thought.

I traveled to Ligonier to do a book signing at the Country Market there on the Friday of the G-20 Summit. A week later, I spent Thursday at the Omni William Penn Hotel and Friday and Saturday at the David L. Lawrence Convention Center.

A week after the G-20 Summit, I was in two of the main venues that hosted the world leaders. Several of the delegations, including China's, stayed at the William Penn, and they all spent time at meetings at the David L. Lawrence Convention Center that's named in honor of the former mayor of Pittsburgh, governor of Pennsylvania, and close friend of the late Arthur J. Rooney, Dan's dad and the founder of the Steelers.

My assignment at the William Penn was as the featured speaker at a luncheon for commercial realtors and building managers in the city. They'd just come off a tension-packed period in their lives, wondering what could go wrong during the G-20 Summit and if, indeed, their buildings would still be standing when the world leaders left town.

The city, if anything, over-prepared for the event, but better safe than sorry. Some mistakes were made, there were some overzealous police efforts apparently in Oakland and Shadyside, but overall we got through it okay.

There is still much hand-wringing over what transpired, and whether or not Pittsburgh benefited by hosting the event. I am of the belief that it was great for the city.

I thought the protestors got way too much space in the newspapers and air time on the radio and TV. I've never been into protesting. I'm into promoting. I'm not sure if many of the protestors knew what they were protesting about.

What they proved most of all was that they are not interested in promoting Pittsburgh and the U.S.A. in a positive way to the world.

I think there will be long-term benefits for Pittsburgh. It put us on the international map for a few months, and there will be long-term gains from it.

We may have made a mistake in closing down the city for a few days, and turning it into a ghost town, or like one of those Will Smith sci-fi movies, but the intentions were well-grounded.

Some businesses had to close for a couple of days. That's not really a crisis. Most businesses are open too many days anyway these days.

Is another two-day holiday going to hurt that much in the long run? It was not a crisis. How does it compare to what the people in the South Seas are still enduring after two major earthquakes devastated that region? That's a crisis. Ours was an inconvenience at best.

When I was a student at Pitt I never protested anything, except maybe losing a few too many football games. I've learned through the years not to do that anymore, either. It's not that important in the general scheme of things.

A week ago I wrote about all my favorite football teams losing their games over an extended weekend. This past week all my favorite football teams won their games. Life is like that. You win some and you lose some.

I think Pittsburgh came out a winner in the G-20 sweepstakes. I wish Chicago had landed the 2016 Olympic Games, but they are going to be in Rio de Janeiro instead. City officials there might want to consult with Pittsburgh leaders on how to secure a city for such an international gathering.

They might also want to get together with Gus Kalaris to see what he thinks.

Artwork by Linda Barnicott

Steelers' owner Dan Rooney sits on stool while visiting his food friend Gus Kalaris at his iconic ice ball stand at West Park in Rooney's neighborhood on the North Side.

'Only in America' phrase
rekindled at funeral home viewing

February 2012

I turn to the obituary pages of the two Pittsburgh dailies each morning to check to see if anyone I know has died, and when the funeral services will be held.

My late friend Tom "Maniac" McDonough referred to the obituary pages as "the Irish sports section."

He thought there was something about death that appealed to the Irish. They loved going to wakes. "It's the only way you see old friends," said McDonough.

When I was a kid, I used to deliver a newspaper to Leo Sullivan, a nattily-dressed funeral director on Second Avenue in Hazelwood. In the summer, he wore a straw hat and wide suspenders which set him apart from the pack.

We had a standup routine. I'd see him standing on the porch of his funeral home, and I'd say, "How's business, Mr. Sullivan?"

He'd smile and say, "It's dead."

The names of six remarkable men I have known appeared in the obituary notices over the past two weeks.

One day, I knew three people in a row in the paid listings, a personal record I think. Their names were George Esper, Fred Fetterolf and Thomas "Red" Garvey (as in E, F,G). The other three names I recognized on other days were Fred Yee, Bernie Powers and Tunch Ilkin.

In Ilkin's case, his wife Sharon, age 55, had died after a difficult six-year battle with breast cancer. Tunch remains one of the most popular Pittsburgh Steelers, first as an offensive lineman and now as a sidekick providing analysis to the play by-play call by sports broadcaster Bill Hillgrove.

Among the pictures on display at the Beinhauer Funeral Home in McMurray was a framed cover of *Sports Illustrated* that had two cheerleaders at Indiana State University flanking the great Larry Bird. One of the beauties was the future Sharon Ilkin.

The Ilkin children often kidded their dad that their mom made the *SI* cover, but their dad never did. Tunch told them his black Steelers' helmet was visible at the bottom of one of the covers in the '80s.

"We'll miss her dearly," Tunch told me. "But she was in such pain. She was a woman of great faith, so she'll be fine."

Let me tell you a little about each of these men I mentioned earlier.

Fred Yee's daughter Michelle is my next-door neighbor in Upper St. Clair. Her father, who lived in Bethel Park, has been ill the past year. He died of cancer at age 76 at St. Clair Hospital. I'd see him in the driveway or yard for the past five years. He loved to play golf each morning at South Park. We'd talk sports.

He is the only person of Chinese descent who has been inducted into the Western Chapter of the Pennsylvania Sports Hall of Fame. He played basketball at Pitt in the mid-50s and he won five City League championships and a state title while coaching the boys' basketball team at Schenley High School and then won five City League championships coaching girls' softball at Carrick High School. He must have been some motivator.

Our friend Bernard "Baldy" Regan, a Pittsburgh politician and sports promoter, used to praise Fred Yee by saying, "Only in America can a Chinese guy coach an all-black basketball team to a state title."

Baldy borrowed that phrase from Harry Golden, an editor and publisher of the *Carolina Israelite*, who wrote a popular book called *Only In America* in 1958. I read it when I was a student at Taylor Allderdice High School.

The "Only in America" tag is applicable to most of the men I have mentioned.

Tunch Ilkin came to America as a child from Istanbul, Turkey and marries a cheerleader from Indiana State. He returned after being cut from the squad at his first Steelers' training camp to play 13 seasons with the Steelers and one year with the Green Bay Packers. He was one of Art Rooney's all-time favorite players.

Fred Yee grew up in Little Allentown, a stretch near Beltzhoover and Arlington on the backside of the South Side Slopes, unfamiliar to most Pittsburghers. His family ran a laundry business.

When Yee's team won the state title in 1978, students at Schenley High created a banner they hung in the hallway renaming the school "Schen-Yee High."

There were two sports personalities I recognized at Yee's viewing, Lou "Bimbo" Cecconi, who starred in several sports at Clairton High and the University of Pittsburgh, and whose last job was in administration at Steel Valley High School. "Look at how many people are here," Cecconi observed. "That's a real tribute."

Paul Tomasovich, a tall, husky fellow best known as "the Babe Ruth of Pittsburgh softball," and more recently a sports official, was present as well. Tomasovich was a close friend of Baldy Regan. I have been fortunate to know such fascinating fellows.

"I was refereeing a basketball game between Schenley and Farrell at Farrell," recalled Tomasovich. "Fred was on the sideline coaching Schenley, and he called out, 'Paul, Paul' and signaled for a time-out with 14 seconds showing on the clock. His team was down by a point.

"I stood by his huddle to hear what he was saying to his team. He told them to get the ball to his star player, Sonny Lewis, who was a really good player. He told Sonny to hold onto the ball and that Farrell would foul him. He told Sonny he'd make both free shots and Schenley would win.

"Schenley inbounds the ball to Sonny Lewis and he immediately unleashes a long shot and misses. That's the ballgame, folks. As I am running off the court, Fred calls out to me again, 'Paul, Paul, tell me, was I speaking to those guys in Chinese?'"

There are always such stories shared at funerals. There are laughs to go with the tears, and the solemnity of the occasion. You are never quite sure what to say. I used to admonish my mother as we were entering a funeral home not to say, 'He looks good.' Now I frequently find that's my thought exactly.

I saw Tunch Ilkin's mother near the head of the receiving line and I remembered that she was once "Miss Turkey." As I held her hand, I said, "You are still Miss Turkey." She smiled and said, "That was a long time ago."

What do you say to a man who has lost the love of his life much too early?

Here's what I said:

"Tunch, me boy, how are the Turks doing? Are they still killing each other...like the Irish."

Tunch smiled and hugged me. It was something Art Rooney Sr. used to say to him whenever he saw him in the lobby or locker room at Three Rivers Stadium. Tunch told me that when I was interviewing him in my family room for one of my books about the Steelers. Tunch has always been a favorite topic. He's a good man, a good story.

Tunch told me how much Sharon had suffered and that she was in a better place. When Tunch first came to the Steelers he was a Muslim. But his teammate and still loyal sidekick, Craig Wolfley, influenced him spiritually and Tunch converted to Christianity.

Wolfley's father was ill during training camp and Ilkin was impressed with the strength Wolfley gained from his Christian faith. I know Wolfley well because he lives on the next street in my neighborhood of Upper St. Clair. In time, Ilkin preached at churches and youth gatherings. He even tried, but failed, to convert Myron Cope. Cope married a Presbyterian, but he was proud to be a Jew.

Try to imagine that conversation between Cope and Ilkin.

There were lines out to the parking lot at the Ilkin viewing for one of the afternoon sessions. I saw several former Steelers such as Edmund Nelson, Dwayne Woodruff, Bill Hurley, Craig Wolfley. Members of the media present were Gene Collier, Jerry Dulac, Ed Bouchette, Paul Alexander, Bob Pompeani and Dan Potash.

It was the same room where I had attended funerals for former Steelers Ray Mansfield, Steve Furness and Lloyd Voss.

I had not seen or heard of George Esper in a long time, but I met him in the summer of 1963. I had an internship at *The Philadelphia Evening Bulletin,* when George was writing at the Philadelphia branch of the Associated Press.

He was a friend of George Kiseda, then a sportswriter for *The Bulletin*. Kiseda was a Pitt grad from Pittsburgh's South Side and he got his start as a sportswriter with the *Pittsburgh Sun-Telegraph*.

He was a great writer, one of the best ever to cover basketball at The Palestra or city hall in Philadelphia..

Esper and I each had rooms in the upper level of a home owned by the mother of Ralph Bernstein, the sports editor of The Associated

Press. Esper hailed from Uniontown. His parents had immigrated to America from Lebanon. His voice positively crackled when he spoke.

He went on to become an AP correspondent covering the war in Vietnam and he won several major awards for his coverage. How fortunate I was to share a summer with him when I was a student, and learn from him and Kiseda. Philadelphia had some of the best sportswriters in the business at the time, such as Larry Merchant, Stan Hochman, Jack McKinney, Ray Kelly, Jack Kiser, Hugh Brown and Sandy Grady and I hung around them as much as possible. They were great mentors.

Esper and Fred Fetterolf both qualify in the "Only in America" category as success stories.

Fetterolf was a mild-mannered but enterprising young man as a student at Grove City College in the early '50s. He stood five feet, five inches tall, yet he won varsity letters in three sports for the Grovers. He played on the football, basketball and golf teams. Yes, basketball. At 5–5! He may have given a half inch to Myron Cope.

Fetterolf went on to become a giant in the corporate world. I met him when he was the President and COO of the company in 1979, his second year in that position. Vince Scorsone, who had come out of McKeesport High to star as a lineman at Pitt, was a vice-president at Alcoa at the time. Fetterolf was proud to show his spiritual side and lent his presence to many good causes.

Fetterolf and Scorsone ordered 1,000 copies of each of the first two books I wrote and edited with Marty Wolfson, namely *Pittsburgh: The Story of the City of Champions* and *Hail to Pitt: A Sports History of the University of Pittsburgh*

I never would have been able to write and publish 20 books about Pittsburgh sports achievement if I had not had that kind of support at the start. So I will always be indebted to those great gentlemen.

I remember Scorsone telling me a story about running into Duke Weigle, his football coach at McKeesport, prior to entering Pitt as a freshman. Weigle wanted to know what Scorsone planned to major in at Pitt.

"I'm going into phys ed, Coach," said Scorsone. "I want to be a coach like you someday."

"No, you don't," said Weigle. "You should major in business. You'll be better off."

Scorsone did just that and look what it led him to at Alcoa. "Those were the days when you did whatever your coaches told you to do," said Scorsone.

Fetterolf was one of many patrons I have lost in recent years. Some of the other special people who made these books possible included Bill Baierl, Bill Tillotson. Eugene Barone, Steve Previs Sr. and Mel Bassi. They are all deceased.

Red Garvey and Bernie Powers were both coaches and they had Mt. Lebanon ties, starting with St. Bernard's and then South Hills Catholic. Garvey coached for a couple of years with the football program at Pitt in the late '60s. I'd see him on the Pitt campus and, in more recent years, bump into him at Atria's Bar & Tavern in Mt.

Lebanon. Powers became the director of the City Catholic League sports programs.

I saw Jerry Conboy at Garvey's viewing at the Laughlin Funeral Home in Mt. Lebanon. Conboy was a terrific basketball coach at South Hills Catholic and Point Park College.

We agreed that we were going to too many funerals lately.

I blame it on Art Rooney. He's the one who told me why you have to go to the funerals. What he told me made more sense than what Yogi Berra said, "If you don't go to your friends' funerals they won't come to yours."

Bill Hillgrove and Fred Yee pose at halftime of a basketball game at the Civic Arena.

Photo from the Yee Family

Jim O'Brien

Sports official Paul Tomasovich was once hailed as softball's "Babe Ruth" on Pittsburgh sandlots for his home run hitting prowess.

Jim O'Brien

Tunch Ilkin, Craig Wolfley and Edmund Nelson survey the scene at Steelers' training camp at St. Vincent College.

WAMO of my youth
has been long gone

June 2009

W AMO is no mo. The city's only black radio station has been sold. WAMO has been with us for over 60 years, and I remember it well from my teenage years. It was one of the first stations to play rock 'n roll when some serious thinkers thought that it was a sin to listen to such maddening music. It was even worse, perhaps a mortal sin, to dance to that music. Elvis Presley was shaking his hips and we did our best to mimic his pulsating moves.

If we got too close when we were dancing a slow song the nuns who chaperoned the dances would move in and pull us apart, admonishing us to "leave room for the Holy Ghost."

Since WAMO went even further than most of the mainstream stations, and played some way out stuff for the times, and was, indeed, a black station, it was considered reckless or seriously rebellious behavior for a white kid to be a fan of that format.

Through the years, the station went from Doo Wop to Hip Hop. Now it's going to Do What? The Sheridan Broadcasting Corporation, a minority owned enterprise, has sold it for $9 million and it will now be a Catholic-related station (106.7 FM) with a religious format. The station's 35 employees have been let go. The announcement of the sale caused a lot of commotion and outcries in the city.

Some long-time listeners of the station, however, have expressed the opinion since the sale that the station has been in decline for some time, selling out in another way by playing so much rap music, appealing to the worst element of ghetto youth. I'm sure there were many who expressed similar opinions when I was listening to WAMO back in the '60s.

The city schools have sold out as well, approving and encouraging the writing of rap songs as if they were serious literature. That's another story.

The station has an interesting history. It started out in Homestead as WHOD in 1948, and it became WAMO in 1956. My father and both of his brothers all worked at Mesta Machine Company back then, so we made streetcar trips from Glenwood to Homestead on occasion, and were aware of WHOD's location. I can remember seeing a sign for WHOD on the side of the building at the corner of 8th Avenue and the Hi-Level Bridge. It was directly across the bridge entrance from Chiodo's Bar & Restaurant. Now the same span has been renamed the Homestead Grays Bridge and Chiodo's landmark establishment has given way to a Walgreen's. That's called progress in some places.

Things change. Former Steelers' coach Chuck Noll liked to say that the only constant in life was change. I always wondered how Pitt loyalists allowed someone from Nebraska to come here and level

Pitt Stadium, and now I wonder how the black leaders of Pittsburgh allowed WAMO to get away from serving the city's African-American community.

But the black leadership has been absorbed into the mainstream elite of the city. That's good in some ways, bad in some other ways. It's a loss for the black community. The same holds true with regard to the sale of WAMO.

WAMO moved to The Bluff, near the Duquesne University campus, in 1960, my senior year at Taylor Allderdice. It relocated to downtown Pittsburgh in more recent years.

When I was in high school I used to listen frequently to Porky Chedwick and John "Sir Walter" Christian, two of WAMO's legendary deejays. Before that, they had a deejay named Mary Dee, and she was one of the first female personalities to serve in that capacity. Mal Goode, who grew up in Homestead, got his start at WHOD and went on to become the first black newscaster on national television.

Porky Chedwick had grown up in Munhall and bugged WAMO management to put him on the air, and they finally did. There was no one quite like him.

He talked the jive talk, and there were people who heard him on the air who assumed he was black. He played the music at many high school dances in the region, and that's when people found out he was definitely a white guy. He was known as "Pork the Tork." He even talked dirty on the air, mumbling obscenities sometimes that only his most loyal listeners could understand, like they were secret code words or something.

He'd say stuff like, "This is your daddio of the radd-io, your platter pushin' poppa. The bossman of WAMO! I'm spinnin' all these dusty discs for those cats out in East Liberty. The girls there are really hot. They won't even talk to those guys from Homewood and Hazelwood. They're headed for Hollywood!"

I remember seeing him tooling around town in a white convertible, with teenagers in his company, hollering out to us as he passed our gang on Second Avenue in Hazelwood. I think he lived for awhile in the Glen-Hazel projects. So did Darrell Hess, our fellow *Valley Mirror* columnist, and he's known Porky Chedwick longer than I have.

During a ten-month stint in the military service in Alaska in 1966, I used to sit in occasionally for the deejays on the radio station at Fort Greely, the Army's Cold Weather Testing Center, and I'd mimic my man, Pork the Tork. I'd do the same patter on the air at the Alaska outpost—"This is your platter pushin' papa"—and it made me popular at the P.X. and NCO Club. I'd never heard of payola, but I know the guys in the kitchen at the mess hall would give me some treats if I'd play some of their music requests. Those steaks were terrific when cooked right one at a time, which we could do in our kitchen at the TV/Radio station where we bunked down at night.

I'd gotten to know Porky Chedwick during my student days at Pitt. In my senior year, I started a weekly tabloid with Pitt sports publicist Beano Cook called *Pittsburgh Weekly Sports*. Porky would interview me during his show and we'd talk about Pitt and the Steelers and Pirates. He called me "Professor" and "Dictionary," because he thought I had a voluminous vocabulary.

He'd say, "Throw a big word at us, Professor Jim." And I'd respond with an offering of "ubiquitous" or "omnipresent," something I'd picked up by reading *30 Days to a More Powerful Vocabulary*. He even addressed me as "Dr. J," and that was long before Dr. J—Julius Erving—came along to thrill the basketball world.

That's why I have such warm memories of WAMO.

It had a powerful signal when it was 600 on the AM dial.

I remember attending a Rock & Roll Revival Show at New York's Madison Square Garden in 1970. It was the first of 25 sellout shows at the Garden through the years. I remember hearing the promoter, Richard Nader, saying at the beginning of the show that he first fell in love with the music listening to Porky Chedwick on WAMO when he was a kid.

The Five Satins sang "In the Still of the Night" as headliners on that Garden show. Nader also brought back Little Richard, Chuck Berry, Jerry Lee Lewis, Carl Perkins, Bill Haley & His Comets and Bo Diddley. The Beatles and the British Invasion had knocked them out of the limelight for years, but the revival shows brought them back to center stage once more.

Now Porky Chedwick is 93, and he and his wife Jeanne are living in Tarpon Springs, Fla. They moved there from Brookline about five years ago. Porky comes back to town on occasion for a birthday celebration or for a special event. He's still fun to talk to, and he hasn't lost his passion for the music game. Nowadays, they both have hugs for me when we bump into each other at Century III Mall or South Hills Village.

I remember as a teenager going to a rock & roll stage show at the Leona Theater in Homestead. There was a big white luxury car parked on 8th Avenue in front of the theater and it had dark black exhaust fumes soiling a spot on the back of its trunk. The car belonged to Bo Diddley. He headlined the show along with the Del Vikings from Canonsburg. The Del Vikings were all in the military service at the time and they wore their dress uniforms. Now the Leona Theater is no mo.

Porky would introduce some of the acts at such shows. I remember seeing the Drifters and Red Foxx featured in a show at the Syria Mosque in Oakland during my Pitt days. Bette Midler said the Syria Mosque had the best acoustics of any theatre she'd played, and now it's a parking lot behind the P.A.A. in Oakland. Things change. I didn't realize until last week that WAMO was derived from W—the lead letter on many radio stations at the time, as in WWSW—and A-M-O for Allegheny, Monongahela and Ohio, the city's three rivers. Later on, the motto for the station was WAMO, as in We Are Moving On. That's an ironic message now.

It was a station that broadcast civil rights meetings live and provided a voice for the African-American community as the *Pittsburgh Courier* newspaper continues to do these days. It's where I first heard about Tiger Rose and Silver Satin champagne, which sold for 99 cents.

They'd play music such as "Great Moogly Moo" by The Spaniels, and "Glory of Love" by the Silvertones. And there was the wonderful patter of Porky Chedwick and Sir Walter. It was part of our education. You came home from school and turned the TV on to "Dick Clark and the American Bandstand," and then listened to Porky and Sir Walter.

I haven't listened to WAMO in fifty some years. Things have changed. The kids have all these high-tech gizmos and they get their music from different sources, downloading what they want to hear. Traditional media is on the decline. I subscribe to Sirius Satellite Radio and I listen to oldies but goodies whenever I take a long trip.

There are no commercials. I can change from stations that carry music from the '40s, the '50s, the '60s, the '70s and the '80s. I can listen to Cousin Brucie, who was big when I lived in New York in the '70s. He is a soul brother of Porky Chedwick. They talk the same way.

It always amazes me that all you need to hear is two or three notes and you know the song and the performer. My wife Kathie and I play a game —I must admit I prod her to play along—about guessing the name of the song and the performer. I'm pretty good at it, and she's even better, just like in Scrabble and crossword puzzles.

She did not listen to WAMO when she was a teenager growing up in McKeesport. Her parents would not have permitted her to do so. We both admit now that going to those teenage dances was stressful stuff, worrying about how you'd be received, whether anyone would dance with you. Those oldies but goodies bring back good and bad memories, just like the passing of WAMO.

Porky Chedwick at work at WAMO Radio Station.

A gentleman of Verona
visits South Hills Village

June 2000

A gentleman from Bethel Park boards a bus nearly every day and goes to South Hills Village. The shopping mall is his main street. He goes there to walk and to be with people, even though he is critical of many of those people.

"It's a circus," he says. "It's full of half-naked girls and gypsies. I have little in common with most of them."

His name is Philip Monti—that's Italian for mountain, he tells me—and he traces his family's roots to Italy, more specifically to Verona. He says he speaks fluent Italian, the cultured Italian idiom, that is, the Florentine Italian. He says his prayers in Latin. He spouts Shakespeare, his favorite author and playwright. Philip Monti, in a sense, is a gentleman of Verona. He's also a bit of a snob. I love that in him.

He is a true Damon Runyon character. I have talked to him, from time to time, over a five or six year period. He stops by to chat and expound on world matters whenever I am signing books at South Hills Village, as I did the day before Father's Day.

Monti is one of my mall people. I have my regulars at South Hills Village, Ross Park Mall and at Century III Mall in West Mifflin. At Century III, for instance, I can always count on a visit from Mavis Trasp, known as "my Christmas angel" and as "the Cookie Lady." She and her daughter, Sherry, always stop by to see me at Waldenbooks and help me out, getting me soft drinks. They are cheerful and kind to every passerby.

Philip Monti is cut from the same cloth, only an older cloth.

To say Philip Monti is old-fashioned is to shortchange him. He's from another age, a more refined period of history. It's as if he was just unearthed from a time capsule that was buried in Bethel Park 40 to 50 years ago. His clothes are all that old. "It cost me more to get them cleaned now than what I paid for them," he complains.

Philip Monti complains a lot. He does so, though, in a charming way. He's pedantic, to say the least, and likes to come off as a cultured figure. He is 5–4, 135 pounds, but is much taller when he stands on his Thesaurus. Or Bible. He takes great pride in his Italian heritage and his Catholic faith. His picture should be next to the word "curmudgeon" in the dictionary. He boasts that he walks every day and doesn't eat out. "You can't watch your weight when you eat out all the time," he explains. "I know how to cook." Olive oil is the secret to his culinary success and his svelte figure.

He is a dapper fellow, even if his clothes date him. He turned 86 last month. His wardrobe turned 50, at least. He's dressed for "Guys and Dolls" every day he comes to South Hills Village. I love the guy.

Jim O'Brien

A Gentleman of Verona: Philip Monti models his '50s finest.

"I haven't bought a thing in 20 years, but good manners have never been outdated."
—Philip Monti

Here's what he was wearing on Saturday: you can start at the bottom with bright black and white wing-tipped shoes or at the top with a straw hat with a colorful band around it. Who wears straw hats in the summer these days? He said the shoes cost him $49.50 and that he priced them the day before at Johnson & Murphy for $169.

"I keep wooden shoehorns in them from the country club where I once worked," he said, with more than a hint of pride, "and I pull socks over them to keep them clean and unscratched."

His outfit was pale yellow and gold, for the most part. His striped sport coat was made of silk. He had me feel the lapels. "It cost me $5 to get it cleaned the other day," he said. "That's highway robbery. They want $300 for a coat like this today." He had a pocket handkerchief puffed up just so. He wore pale yellow slacks, a light blue dress shirt, a yellow and gold paisley tie, held in place with a tie clasp. Who has silk sport coats or wears tie clasps anymore? "I know what class is," he says. "I haven't bought a thing in 20 years, but good manners have never been outdated."

He confesses, with a smile and glint behind his glasses, that his costume is a bit dated. "Even my dreams are used," he said. He files and buffs his fingernails and brushes his shoes regularly. "You're never fully dressed without a shine and a smile," he says.

He's full of lines like that and other stuff as well.

He was born in Russelton, near New Kensington, but was raised in Bethel Park where he remains. He was married, divorced, and his ex-wife is deceased. He has no interest in the women where he resides. "We have nothing in common," he complains. "Most of them are intellectually bankrupt."

He is self-educated. He says Shakespeare, Voltaire and Dante are his favorites. "I know my wines, too," he says. Don't you just love him?

He worked as a bartender, greeter and clubhouse attendant at the Oakmont Country Club, Shannopin Country Club, Pittsburgher Hotel, the Union Grill and sundry nightclubs. He met Red Skelton, Jackie Gleason, Danny Kaye, Gene Kelly and Perry Como there. "Como was a shy guy from Canonsburg," recalled Monti. "He was afraid to come out and sing."

He remembers Art Rooney coming around the Pittsburgher Hotel and paying off money he owed other sportsmen. "He had a reputation for always paying what he owed people," recalled Monti. "He had a horse room on the North Side and people could bet on races at the big tracks."

Monti first went to work in 1929, at age 15. "I worked from 7 a.m. to 7 p.m. for $1," he says. "It was during the Depression and I had to go to work to help out at home." So he is tight-fisted with his dollars these days.

For the record, he has never bought one of my books. "For $26.95," he howls, "I could buy a new sport coat!"

FAMILY AND FRIENDS/

OLD NEIGHBORHOODS

Celebrating Father's Day
and then Grandfather's Day

June 2009

Susannah and big sister Margaret get set for sliding board descent.

Father's Day was a full day. There was much activity, much reflection and it went from being Father's Day to Grandfather's Day. I felt good about both roles.

Any day that includes playing basketball, going to church, brunch, family and friends, a miniature butterscotch sundae, two fresh homemade oatmeal raisin cookies, talking to my daughters Sarah and Rebecca, spending much of the day with my wife Kathie, sitting on my porch reading the Sunday newspaper from front to back, a bit of a book, and hush puppies is a good day, a day well spent.

I reflected on my father a good deal, something I don't do that often, and thought about some funny incidents I recall in his life. I wasn't sure I should laugh or cry. He died at the age of 63 in 1968, when I was 26 and in the second year of my marriage. He drank too much and smoked too much, but he was a good worker and faithful to his family and, I believe, he did his best.

The older I get the more I respect and miss my father, Dan O'Brien. What I realize now and what I appreciate the most is that he was never in my face. He loved me and I always felt comfortable and secure in his company. He was popular at work and in the local watering holes, and my friends liked him. He looked after my friends, and offered them food and soda pop when they'd come to our home, and that was not something I recall my friends' fathers doing when I was at their homes.

He smiled easily and there was a pleasantness about him.

I do some things that my dad did and I don't do some of the things he did, so he was a good role model in that I learned from his example, good and bad. My mother always boosted him to us kids, and she never complained about his imperfections.

"He always loved you kids," she'd say. "We didn't have a car, but we took you kids to a lot of places."

If my mother was giving him a hard time about something, hollering at him from a different floor in our home, he'd smile and tell us, "I still love her." Then he might sing a little song such as "Let's all sing like the birdies sing" or "Peg o' my heart." He usually had spent much of the day drinking to loosen his vocal chords.

Maybe I was thinking too much about him early in the day. My wife spotted a tear or two on my cheek as we were driving to Ohio in the afternoon. She asked me why I was so maudlin. Funny thing, the first thing I thought of when she said that was that I was happy to be married to a woman who knew the meaning of the word maudlin.

I think Father's Day is a good day to reflect on your father and your own family.

That can make you feel sad and glad. The latter won out by far.

Kathie brought me a greeting card and a gaily wrapped gift from Rebecca, our younger daughter, for starters on Father's Day. Rebecca, who lives near Los Angeles, always picks her cards carefully. She had one with a drawing of a dog with a bright red heart in its mouth. That was her dog Bailey, a mixed Chow and a family favorite.

The printed words hit home and, even more so, the handwritten ones from Rebecca touched my heart. She had also called and left a message on the telephone. She was at work early, as the senior general manager of a California Pizza Kitchen Restaurant in Simi Valley, California. I called her and spoke to her.

I told her I had spent the previous few days at book-signings prior to Father's Day and that I'd seen some real sights among the passersby. I told her that it made me feel so proud that she and her older sister, Sarah, had turned out the way they have. They've always been good kids. They had great attitudes and respected their parents and did their best to make us proud of them. "Right, Dad," Rebecca came back. "No tattoos, no body piercings, no drugs, and we didn't get pregnant out of wedlock!" My girls, indeed, had the formula to keep their father happy. One time both Rebecca and Sarah complained to me on the telephone that they had to work on a weekend. They do so frequently. "Hey," I told Rebecca, "I always had to work on weekends." To which she replied, "Yeah, Dad, but you never had a real job."

We had planned to drive to Cambridge, Ohio to meet Sarah and her children, Margaret, age 5, and Susannah, 13 months old at the time. Sarah said Cambridge was half way between Pittsburgh and Columbus. Not really. It is 90 miles from Pittsburgh and 70 miles from Columbus. We left Pittsburgh a bit early, in case there was any road construction going on, so we had time to stop in Wheeling and visit the cemetery next to Wheeling Park where most of my family is buried. The grass was cut and things are pretty well maintained, which was reassuring. I stood and stared at the tombstones, noting the birth dates of everyone. The biggest marker had BURNS on it. That was my mother's maiden name. This was her family's gravesite. My dad's tombstone had SON-IN-LAW on the rear side of it. Some distinction, huh? My mother is there next to her mother. Her father and mother both died before I was born so I never knew them. My sister and brother, niece and two nephews are there, too. We were there for only ten minutes. That was enough. I'm glad we stopped.

Kathie and I arrived at the Cracker Barrel Restaurant in Cambridge at exactly 5 o'clock. Just before we turned into the parking lot we received a telephone call on Kathie's cell phone from Sarah. She said they were about 15 minutes away. They arrived at 5:20 p.m. We expect them to be late.

Sarah brought me a greeting card. She picks her cards carefully, too, and drew a mustache on the father on the front of the card. It read: "Happy Father's Day to someone very special who also makes me feel very special, too!" There were gift cards enclosed for TGI Friday's and Olive Garden. Rebecca had sent me three pairs of undershorts from the Gap, and a gift card for The Cheesecake Factory. My girls know my basic needs. I couldn't have been happier with my gifts.

We had a nice lunch in Cambridge, with a big table in a corner, so we were out of the buzz of the rest of the restaurant. It was easier to talk. I get a kick out of watching Susannah sitting at a dinner table these days. She seems older than her age the way she comports herself. She is a serious eater and stays focused on her food much better than her older sister Margaret ever did. Or their mother, for that matter. Margaret is more into talking than eating.

Margaret talks a lot. And she knows it.

After dinner we went to a nearby DQ, or Dairy Queen, for some dessert. That's where I had the miniature butterscotch sundae. I used to enjoy them on occasion when I was a kid and having lunch with my mother at a drug store in our home town.

Susannah was high stepping around the table on the outdoor patio. We went there so she could do that without being a pain to people at nearby tables inside the restaurant. We have never confused restaurants with playgrounds. We kissed Susannah goodbye, and hugged her mother, and took off for home with Margaret secured in the backseat of our car.

It was a two-hour drive and Margaret talked for an hour and a half before drifting off into a deep sleep. She reminds me so much of her mother except for the talking part.

We were bringing her to our home for a week's stay. We had planned all sorts of activities. She told us she wanted to see the dinosaurs at our museum in Pittsburgh. I told her I'd take her to our playground and to our library, which she loves from previous visits. I told her we were going to see the movie "Up," and that her grandmother was taking her to a children's stage show at the Little Lake Theater in Canonsburg. We'd go to our swim club and see some relatives.

We had enrolled her for the five-day week at the Barefoot Bible School at Westminster Presbyterian Church. Margaret and her sister attend Day Care at the Jewish Community Center in Bexley, Ohio, just a few miles from their home. So she has a different slant on some of the Bible stories, which I knew she'd be eager to share with her classmates and anyone else who'd listen.

Rev. Jim Gilchrist, the pastor at Westminster, had delivered a thoughtful sermon that morning about Father's Day. He mentioned that a woman had once told him that grandchildren were a gift from God to parents for not killing their teenage children.

Spending time with Margaret and Susannah is like reliving the early days as parents of Sarah and Rebecca. You worry more about their well being because you don't want anything to go wrong on your watch.

Being a father is a wonderful role and so is being a grandfather. I never felt that more deeply than last Sunday. It was the best of times, even if I was a little maudlin at times.

Christmas season
was always busy with my mother

This was written in 2002.

I can't believe my mother will be 96 this Christmas Eve. But she was born on Dec. 24, 1906, so it must be true. I am still interviewing her all the time, trying to find out information about family and friends, but her mind is quite selective in what it is willing to release. My dad drank too much and smoked too much, and that contributed to his death at age 63. Mom remembers that, but all she'll say now is, "I always loved him. He always loved you kids. He never left us."

Some years back, I wasn't impressed with that. But the more mothers I meet at book-signings whose husbands no longer are a part of the family I realize that my Dad not leaving us was a plus in my life. I knew that my mother and my father loved me. They had their moles, but they never thought I had any.

"He didn't drive, but he took you kids to a lot of places," she'd say.

"He always went to work," she'd continue. "During the Depression, he didn't have a job for about six or seven years. But he went out every day and knocked on doors, and asked for work. He'd do whatever he could do to make some money. He always brought home some money."

That story has become my personal mantra. I've never been afraid to knock on doors, and ask for work. And I still smile, and think of Mom's story, when I come home with some money.

I also subscribe to Rocky Bleier's boast that "every payday is a good payday."

The Christmas season was always a busy time of the year for both of my parents. My dad went to a lot of parties at this time of year. Most of those parties were held in neighborhood bars and speakeasies. There were 36 bars in a mile-long stretch between Hazelwood Avenue and the Glenwood Bridge in my hometown of Hazelwood. My Dad was familiar with most of them, and ran a tab in a half dozen of them. I delivered newspapers to most of them, from the time I was eight or nine, helping my brother in the beginning, to the time I was 13, so the bar owners knew me, too. I was Dan O'Brien's boy. They treated me well.

When my dad cashed his paycheck from Mesta Machine Company in West Homestead at the Hazelwood Bank at one end of town, he walked, not always steadily, a veritable minefield on his way home. He had to leave a lot of that money at many of those bars to clear his accounts. My mother never knew how much he'd be turning over to her by the time he reached our door. Sometimes, she acted as if she'd hit the numbers, sometimes she was saddened by the shortfall.

This was a busy time of year for my mother as well. She worked as a sales clerk at the State Store on Second Avenue. My dad and mother were both good workers. This was the busiest time at the State Store. Everybody was buying liquor and wine to celebrate the yule season.

I met many interesting characters whenever I'd go to the State Store to see my mother. She worked a swing shift, and I'd join her for lunch on the days she worked the early shift. Sometimes I'd have to wait in the back, between the tall rows of whiskey and wine, and I'd read the labels. Many were quite attractive. They were in special decorative boxes during the holiday season.

Some customers came regularly and were well known. There was "Duffy the Drunk" and "Duffy the Boxer," and a woman with scraggly dishwater gray hair known as "Swing and Sway" for her walking motion. The unkind critics would say she was staggering. The winos would bum money outside the State Store till they had enough money to buy some Tiger Rose or Corby's. I met one of my first pro football players, Chuck Cherundolo, who had been a center at Penn State and with the Steelers. He was a wine salesman. So were two local boxing heroes, Fritzie Zivic of Lawrenceville, and Charlie Afif from The Hill. Zivic had been a storied world champion.

Mom and I went to lunch in local restaurants. To me, Isaly's was The Colony or LeMont of Hazelwood. The waitresses all knew us. It started a lifetime of me and my mother going to lunch together. "I don't think you and your mother ever see each other that you're not eating," my wife Kathie would say, sarcastically, of course. It was at this time of year, when I was eight years old, that I asked my mother to buy me a toy printing press, an Ace model, when we were Christmas shopping at the Hazelwood Variety Store. That's how I got started in this business. My mother never turned me down. She always believed in me even when she shouldn't have. She was always my biggest fan.

Jim O'Brien

Author's grandpuppy "Bailey" joins his mother Mary O'Brien at Asbury Heights, a senior care complex in Mt. Lebanon.

You can't go home again...
that's certain now

Thomas Wolfe warned us. The prodigious and wonderful writer from North Carolina is well remembered for the line: "You can't go home again." There were times I thought he was wrong about that, but not anymore. I'm certain now that Wolfe was right.

I was scheduled on July 1 to attend the Homestead Lions' Annual Golf Outing at the Westwood Golf Club in West Mifflin. I had a stop to make at The Waterfront in Homestead on the way. There are several routes I can take to get to Homestead from my home in Upper St. Clair.

Somehow I always find myself choosing the one that goes through Hazelwood and Glenwood, where I grew up. I lived for nearly 26 years on Sunnyside Street in Glenwood. Then I got married, a week before I turned 26. I will mark my 42nd wedding anniversary on Aug. 12 and my 67th birthday on Aug. 20.

When I say that Hazelwood is my hometown, as I often have, I am guilty of social-climbing. I actually grew up in neighboring Glenwood.

I lived the first five years at 5413 Sunnyside Street, the first of three row houses. My father, I was told, was born on a couch in that house. His family moved to the adjoining Almeda Street later on. The O'Briens lived on one side of a duplex house on Almeda, and the Burns family lived next door. My mother, Mary Burns, lived in that house as a young woman. That's where my father and mother met and courted one another. A story like something out of "Ozzie and Harriet."

That duplex house is still standing. Many homes nearby as well as Burgwin Elementary School, where I went to kindergarten, are closed and shuttered. But the duplex looks fine, and people still reside there.

When I was five we made a big move from 5413 Sunnyside Street to 5410 Sunnyside Street. It was a three-bedroom roughhouse, one of four. I still have a photo of me at age 5 sitting on a hassock on the sidewalk in front of 5413 on moving day. Two families moved out of it before we moved in. There were "flats" nearby where as many as six and seven kids lived in one-bedroom apartments.

There was a two-story wooden mansion across the street from 5410 Sunnyside Street that was cut up into six different apartments. There was a big basement with one of those level-to-the-ground doors—like the one where Dorothy's family fled to during the storm in "The Wizard of Oz"—and it was said that it had once been a part of "The Underground Railroad" that helped slaves get from the South to Canada way back when. It resembled the house above the motels in the Alfred Hitchcock classic movie "Psycho."

I had a lot of fun growing up on Sunnyside Street. I was 14 when I started writing stories about the games our gang was playing in that neighborhood. I started slipping them under the door of the local bi-weekly newspaper, *The Hazelwood Envoy*, and that's how I got started in this business.

I shared a bedroom with my older brother Dan as well as an interest in sports. I put up a backboard and a hoop on a telegraph pole outside my home. I laid out a running track and built a basic broad-jump pit on Sunnyside Street, and laid out a ballfield on an empty lot nearby known as "The Horseshoe Lot." I formed the Sunnyside A.C., raised money somehow and got all the guys T-shirts with SUNNYSIDE A.C. across the front, and bought little trophies at Murphy's 5 & 10 Store that had gold plates on them that read: World's Greatest Athlete. They were prizes for track & field events I staged on Sunnyside Street. I don't know what the neighbors thought about all this. My mother thought I was enterprising.

Most of our neighbors were Italians. There were some others who were Irish, some Hungarians and Germans. There were boundaries as you grew up. You were allowed to go so many streets from the house as you got older. In the summer, you were expected to be home when the street lights went on.

Being able to fight was important. You always knew just where you rated on the fight scale, as if *Ring Magazine* had included you and your boyhood buddies in their monthly rankings. You knew who you could beat, who could beat you and who would be a draw. A fellow named Rege Bain, a milk delivery man, put some old mattresses down on the floor of his garage, and we boxed and wrestled there, so you always knew where you stood in the tough-guy category.

If you had a beef with somebody you duked it out in the street. That's how you settled feuds. No one brought a gun to settle a feud. If I heard that someone was bringing a baseball bat or a chain I thought it was a good idea to just stay home that day.

My mother's mantra was "Stay busy…and stay out of trouble."

It still works.

You knew everyone on the street because no one ever moved away, or at least it seemed that way. Nearly everybody's dad came home drunk on pay day so you didn't think it was anything strange or out of the ordinary that your dad spent a lot of time in nearby bars.

One father who didn't drink, a mail carrier, used to listen to the Pirates' games on the radio on his porch, and we were welcome to join him. We thought that was a big deal, listening to Bob Prince broadcasting the Pirates' games on the radio. Homer Metro, that mailman, knew a lot about sports. I later learned that he bet on many of those games. I guess everyone had one vice or another in the neighborhood.

We played street games, and were inventive about what ideas for games we came up with. As we got older, we invited the girls to join us in our street games. I was warned early that I was not allowed on any motorcycles or motorbikes, or to shoot anyone's B-B gun. I did shoot someone's air rifle one day and the pellet bounced off a sidewalk and into the window of a neighbor's storm door. My parents had to pay to replace that window pane and that was the end of my days as Davy Crockett.

We played hop-scotch near the house of Marge and George Young. It was at the corner of Sunnyside and Almeda Street. We called their home "Marge's Menagerie." She and George didn't have any children. A niece used to spend time with them in the summer. The Youngs had dogs and cats and birds and turtles and hamsters in their home. They let us see them on occasion.

More importantly, the Youngs had the first television set in the neighborhood, sometime in the early '50s. In the summer they'd let us stand out on their porch and peer though a glass storm door and watch their television. There house is shuttered now. Marge always kept a nice yard, but it's overgrown now.

I saw that shuttered house when I drove by the old neighborhood on the way to Homestead on July 1. Someone had been shot and killed in the doorway of an apartment house that was two doors away from the Young residence on Almeda Street. I had read about the killing in the daily newspaper. A 30-year-old man was shot twice by someone who fired through the door at him. The victim's name was misspelled and mispronounced in the first reports on television. First, they said the crime occurred in Hazelwood and then they changed it to Glen-Hazel. I knew better. I knew the Virginia Apartments well.

It was five doors from my home on Sunnyside Street. It was one of the stops on my morning newspaper route. I delivered papers to several doors in that apartment. There was no security door at the front entrance in those days. Now there's one with a sign at the top of it that reads "NO LOAFING."

I sold magazine subscriptions and Christmas seals at several of the apartments in the Virginia Apartments. I thought rich people lived there, richer than most of us in the neighborhood anyhow. I know better now. A woman named Mary Dietz was always nice to me at the Virginia Apartments.

We used to play a form of football in the yard behind the Virginia Apartments. There were steel drum garbage containers lined up against the back wall of the apartment house. We played football in a 15-yard patch by the garbage cans in the dead of the night. It was hard to see anyone. We'd line up three or four to a side, and just hit whoever had the ball. It was great fun until someone in the apartment would invariably ruin it by hollering out, telling us to get the hell outta there.

About six months ago, one of my childhood girlfriends called me to tell me they had leveled my home on Sunnyside Street. I drove over to check it out and found that my home was still standing, but that the houses on both sides of it had been removed from the landscape. I had never seen the sides of my house before. I took some pictures of it while it was still there. The childhood friend has since died, like too many of my boyhood friends.

The street looked so different. The row homes where my dad had been born had given way to a newer strip of homes. They looked nice. My broad jump pit was gone. So was an outcropping of rock on one of the strips of grass and dust where I had played as a child.

I used to draw roads in the dust that surrounded that outcropping. To me, it was a mountain and I pushed my toy automobiles around the base of it, pretending I was driving those cars somewhere out West.

Back in 1994, a 19-year-old woman was executed where my boyhood mountain once stood. She had reported on some neighborhood drug activity, and three men surrounded her there and shot her twice in the head.

Old neighbors told me there has been lots of drug activity in that area in the last 20 years, some of it at the Virginia Apartments.

Out of curiosity, I wanted to check out the Virginia Apartments at the outset of this month. I wanted to see where that man had been shot and killed. Maybe I watch so many "Law and Order" and "CSI: Miami" shows I think like a detective anymore.

So I drove through Hazelwood and saw where the Hazelwood Bank was missing, where The State Store where my mother worked as a clerk was an empty lot as well. Isaly's, where we often had lunch together, was long gone, as were the other restaurants where we had shared so many wonderful times.

The main street, Second Ave, was missing many storefronts. The two movie theaters and three bowling establishments were missing. Dimperio's Market, one of the few that stayed so long, had a chain fence enclosing the front of it at 1 o'clock on a Wednesday. The owners said they got tired of being robbed and cheated by customers. And there are people in Hazelwood worried about the Mon Valley Expressway coming through there and killing the community.

Gladstone High School, St. Stephen's Grade School and Burgwin Grade School are all closed down for good. There are no schools in Hazelwood. There are no doctors or professional physicians of any kind there anymore. There's no one to tell the kids about colleges they might attend some day. The corner candy stores have all been gone a long time, as well as the family-owned markets. The swimming pool at Burgwin Park was not open, and the landscape around it, once the pride of "Chief" Bennett, the groundskeeper, was overgrown, weeds galore.

I saw no one I knew on the streets of Hazelwood or Glenwood.

I pulled up to the curb on Almeda Street. It's a one-way street now; it didn't used to be. I was parked at the corner by Sunnyside Street. I got out of my car and looked up Sunnyside Street. Something was out of whack. I felt disoriented. I saw a house I recognized, but it was coming up too soon on my sightline. There was a huge gap between Marge Young's home and Homer Metro's home.

My house was gone. There was nothing on the sidewalk to help me identify the exact spot where it once stood at 5410 Sunnyside Street. I had swept that sidewalk many times, at my mother's urging, yet I didn't recognize the pattern. It had been dark red bricks when I was a boy. Someone had put a cement cover on it.

I counted in my mind and there were nine homes missing, nine families I remembered. Yet it did not look as if there was room for two or three homes. How had nine homes fit in that empty space? Then I remembered that our row homes were exactly 15 feet wide.

I couldn't comprehend what had happened. I felt like the air had gone out of me. What had happened to our green and white awnings? I remembered that all four families had agreed to get Koolvent aluminum awnings at the same time, but three of us got green-and-white awnings, and the unit at the end got burgundy and white awnings. How that made any sense always eluded me.

When my home was standing it was easier to remember so much activity in our home. I knew where all our furniture fit, the faces of my childhood, different incidents. Everyone who lived with me at 5410 Sunnyside Street is gone now. I'm the only one still alive. Sunnyside Street has a No Outlet sign across the street from my home. But I never thought of it as being a dead-end street until now.

Street signs point the way home in Glenwood.

Jim O'Brien's boyhood home was in the middle of that gap between the home of the Metros, at left, and the Youngs. The house at right was known as "Marge's Menagerie."

Photos by Jim O'Brien

The Virginia Apartments on Almeda Street was scene of homicide in June 2009.

The windows have been replaced in the doorway where shooting took place.

There are missing
pieces in my hometown

I never really heard Hazelwood until I returned to my hometown after ten months in Alaska. I had served the final ten months of a 21-month stay in the military at the U.S. Army's Cold Weather Testing Center at Fort Greely, Alaska. It was somewhere out there between Fairbanks and Anchorage. That was in 1966. I was 24 at the time.

There was no noise outside the white building where we lived in Alaska, about a mile's walk from headquarters and the barracks where most of the soldiers slept at night. When you walked through the snowy paths going from one end of the military post to the other you would listen to make sure some wolverine didn't sneak up on you. Sometimes you wish one would, so you could be like Ernest Hemingway and show off your outdoor fighting skills.

Sometimes you'd see buffalo sorting through the garbage they knocked over in the waste cans outside your building. Those buffalo were big and slow moving and you didn't believe Buffalo Bill was such a big deal after all. If you couldn't hit a buffalo with a rifle shot you would have to be blind or have a serious case of the shakes.

I never knew how noisy Hazelwood could be. There were street cars clanging, the trains were hooting like night owls—is there any sound more lonesome than a passing train at night when the engineer sounds the horn? Dogs were barking in all the backyards behind our house. Even some boats sent up a horn blast as they went by, making sure other boats knew they were nearby.

There were also discernible smells that gave it character. There were no such smells in Alaska, just clean, crisp air. Sometimes you forgot how cold it was in Alaska. You'd make that long walk from one end of the post to another, from the mess hall or the library or the NCO Club, and you didn't realize how cold it was until you sat on the toilet and saw that your inner thighs had turned blue.

That didn't happen in Hazelwood. Our row house sat on the side of a hill. On the upside, which was the sunnyside of Sunnyside Street, it was two stories high. On the backside, which was called Gate Lodge Way, it was three stories high. That row house sat on a plot of ground called Blair Estates on a street map I remember seeing once. I wondered how the hell such a humble home, 15 feet wide at best, could sit on Blair Estates between Sunnyside Street and Gate Lodge Way. They sounded rich. There was a blue-gray wooden mansion across the street from our house that was said to have been involved in the Underground Railroad once upon a time, a hiding place for slaves who were escaping from the South and headed to Canada, but how could you prove something like that?

There were six different families living in that mansion. The place was divided up this way and that way to accommodate all those families. Some of the residents were real characters, and that was the charm of the streets. There were "flats" nearby, those "railroad car" flats where there was a small porch, a small kitchen, a half-bath, a sitting room, a bedroom, and as many as five or six children kept close company with their parents in some of those places.

A woman lived in the "flat" closest to our home and her name was The Rev. Edith Frazier, and she conducted séances in her place. She was listed as "a spiritual advisor." We had a clubhouse under her back porch, and we sat in there with girls in the neighborhood and thought it was a helluva place to hang out. If we heard anything going on in Rev. Frazier's flat we also figured it was ghosts talking out loud. Being scared added to all experiences as a kid.

We were always out on Sunnyside Street doing something. We played street games and we made up games if we got tired of the games we knew best. We didn't come home until we had to on summer nights. The rule was to get home when the street lights went on. We played all kinds of games and we were never bored.

The girls were great, if still somewhat of a mystery, until we discovered a new game called "You show me yours and I'll show you mine."

The only time I was in my bedroom was to read and sleep, or to play on the floor with my Fort Apache set. I was way ahead of my times. I played with my miniature cowboys and Indians and sometimes the Indians won. There were times when my brother Dan, who was five years older than me, shared a large black bed that once belonged to our parents and there was another time when we slept in bunkbeds. He had the upper berth because he was bigger and I had the lower berth because I was smaller.

We had a little gas stove in our room and it's a wonder we didn't die from leaking fumes or some other failure, when I think back on it now. Nobody worried about it then. You just accepted the way things were then. There were three bedrooms at best in that rowhouse, yet two families moved out when we moved in. Our parents slept in the room opposite ours on that top floor. That's the one where one of the families that had lived there had a kitchen in the room, with a stove and all. Those families had to share a bathroom facility in the basement.

The basement was a half-level higher than the kitchen in our house. Talk about split-levels. We had a bathroom put in soon after we moved in, I mean a real bathroom. Up until then, I remember we had a garden hose hanging up in the rafters and that provided us with a shower. There was a plastic curtain hanging from the rafters and it would stick to your knees and shoulders and, of course, your ass when you were taking a shower. And there was a stand-alone toilet and a stand-along sink next to it. That was it until we had a real bathroom installed with a real bath tub.

The walls must have been real thin because we could hear the next-door neighbors when they were taking a bath on the other side of the wall. There was an old woman and her daughter who lived there for a long time—Suzie and Rose Marie—and the daughter was always cursing the mother about something while she was taking a bath. That was a great source of amusement and wonderment to me and my brother. We'd be quiet so we could hear them raising hell with each other.

They were gone by the time I came home from Alaska and now there were other neighbors. None of them took good care of their backyard, so my mother had me mow their lawns and prune their hedges and praised my efforts to the hilt so I would do it again in two or more weeks. I remember sweeping the sidewalk in front of the house and the backporch behind it.

I remember as a child sitting on a glider on that back porch with my mom, waiting for my dad to come home from some bar. She'd be holding supper until he got home. On payday, we often ate late. I remember sitting on that porch with my mom and listening to the rain playing a tune on the aluminum awnings overhead. I always felt safe sitting on the porch in the rain with my mother. We talked and we never lacked for something to talk about.

That was when I was ten or twelve. Now I was 24 and I was back from the Army in Alaska and it was like I had come home to a new country. I could hear and smell Hazelwood this time around. I could hear my parents as well. They both snored and one of them had a short snore and a long whistle, and the other had a long snore and a short whistle. I don't remember now which was which.

I think my dad must have had sleep apnea. No one knew about that back then. He'd holler out every now and then, like he'd been jolted from his sleep. He'd holler, "Mary! Mary!" Or, "Mary, Mary, oh hell!" And then he'd go back to sleep again. Mary was my mother's name. Sometimes I'd hear them whispering about this or that, and I didn't remember hearing them talking to each other before I left for the Army.

Hearing them talking, I think, bothered me some, and I felt like an intruder in the house. I thought it time to be moving on, to getting a place of my own, and I think that prompted me to get married as much as anything else. It's a good thing I found a young woman who wanted to marry me, and thought I had promise, because it was time to move on. She's still with me and I am a lucky fellow.

There was so much noise at night it was hard to stay asleep. I could hear the street cars on Second Avenue, just a half block away. The Glenwood Car Barns were nearby where my Grandfather O'Brien had been a street car conductor. I could hear the trains at night. The Glenwood Yard of the Baltimore & Ohio Railroad were just behind the street car barn. My Grandfather Burns, my mother's dad, was the yardmaster there after he moved his family from Bridgeport, Ohio.

My mother was never crazy about Hazelwood. I think she moved out of there a week after my dad died. That happened in 1969, about a year and a half after I got married. My dad died at age 63 from emphysema. He smoked too much and drank too much. I don't smoke and I don't drink hard liquor and I know how much beer I can handle before it's time to head home. So I learned a lot from my dad.

My dad was a pleasant drunk. There were some mean drunks on Sunnyside Street. Everybody's dad was a drunk, it seemed, so it was no big deal. The only guy who didn't get drunk, I learned later on, was a serious gambler. He blew most of his money on sports. When I think back, my dad was never in my face about anything, and I appreciate that more than ever these days. The older I get the more I like my dad.

I remember when I was 11 and was slated to be the ring bearer at my sister Carole's wedding. Her friends from work filled our kitchen on the eve of her wedding as we were about to depart the house to go to St. Stephen's Church for the wedding rehearsal. Only my dad was missing and was slated to be the father of the bride.

I spotted him coming up the walk that led to our back door. He was swaying like a suspension bridge in a bad storm. I noticed he had the loop from a half gallon jug of wine wrapped around his ring finger, a glass ring, and the finger and his hand, for that matter, were drenched in blood.

I went out to intercept him. He told me he'd been in a fight with his favorite foe and had smacked the guy over the head with an empty wine bottle. Better that, I thought, than a filled wine bottle, especially one that big.

I escorted my dad into our kitchen, leading him past the wedding party, most of them standing there with their jaws agape. I guess they'd never met my dad before. I took him up the steps—turning to tell my mother to put some coffee on—and led him into that bathroom I was boasting about earlier.

I got him cleaned up pretty good. The wedding party had departed for church by the time I finished cleaning him up. Then someone drove us to the church. I was only 11, but somehow I felt responsible for my dad.

About a dozen years later, when my brother Dan got married, I made my dad stay home from the wedding reception. My dad had gotten drunk at the breakfast for the wedding party that morning. I know this sounds sort of awful and everything, but it was just my dad being my dad. I didn't hold it against him and he didn't hold it against me.

There weren't many role models for dads in our neighborhood so my dad suited me just fine. Who knew any better?

One time my brother Dan told us about one of his friends who was getting married, a Jimmy O'Connor, and we all whispered about it and didn't want my dad to know about it. When I walked into the wedding reception at a union hall on the South Side the first person who greeted me as I walked across the dance floor was dear ol' Dad. He must not have wanted us to know about it, either.

I could hear boats blowing their horns as they passed by on the Monongahela River, just a half-mile from my home. There were two junkyards flanking the Glenwood Bridge on the other side of the river, and a slaughterhouse nearby on that side of the river.

When the wind was blowing our way it was wicked stuff. In the summer, you had to keep the windows open otherwise you'd suffer the heat in the silence of your bedroom. If you opened the window it was a little cooler even if the smell might make your eyes water.

There was a distinctive smell at the other end of the town. There was a sulfur plant where Hazelwood gave way to Greenfield, where Second Avenue touched Greenfield Avenue. When you'd pass by that plant while riding on the streetcar you'd smell that smell—like rotten eggs, they'd say—and you knew you were in Greenfield. When kids in our neighborhood passed gas of their own, ruining the room for their buddies, somebody inevitably would holler out "Greenfield!" It signaled that someone had, as they say, cut the cheese.

I had stacks of sports magazines on the night stand next to my bed. I read *SPORT* magazine, *The Police Gazette, True* and, eventually, *Sports Illustrated*. I couldn't get enough of them. My cowboys and Indians and metal soldiers gave way to black and white trading cards with pictures of the Steelers and the Pirates and great American Indian Chiefs.

I loved sports. I organized games on Sunnyside Street every day during the summer. I kept stats on our baseball, softball and basketball games. I had a ball for every sport in my house. I put up a basketball court on Sunnyside Street, just in front of my house, and put spotlights outside my parents' bedroom to light up the hoop and the surrounding area. When I was 14, I formed my own track & field team. I loved what I read about the Olympic Games. Those were the 1960 Olympic Games in Rome, and I still remember our best athletes in those Games.

I bought little trophies that said WORLD'S GREATEST ATHLETE on them at the Murphy's 5 & 10 on Second Avenue in Hazelwood. My team was called the Royals and we were all part of the Sunnyside A.C. I made up the rules for our basketball league and didn't let anyone play man-to-man defense because I didn't want anyone guarding me too closely.

Damn, we had fun, playing football in our neighbor's yards at night, banging into garbage cans and raising all kinds of hell, making noise, annoying the cranky old people. Now my boyhood home is gone, and so is most of the neighborhood. The storefronts on Second Avenue are missing. Most of the homes on my boyhood newspaper routé are gone. It's like a ghost town. The memories remain.

My boyhood home is gone. It was torn down about two years ago. When I first saw that hole in the lineup of homes that remain on Sunnyside Street it took the wind out of me. Nothing remains. Nothing I touched is there. Everything remains intact in my mind, for now anyhow.

I can still see everything and everyone in my mind's eye. I can still hear the noises at night. And the Monongahela River is still moving, its current going north when it goes by my old neighborhood, then south on its way to Uniontown and Morgantown. Not many rivers can say that.

Some things stay the same. The Pirates were a pretty bad ballclub back in the '50s when I was a child. They lost over 100 games in 1952, 1953 and 1954 when I was 10, 11 and 12. In 1956, the first name in the Pirates lineup on Opening Day was O'Brien, J. That was Johnny O'Brien, a second baseman. His twin brother Eddie O'Brien was on that team, too. Just like family.

The Pirates were pretty good on Opening Day. From 1937 to 1954, the Pirates won their home opener at Forbes Field 16 of 18 times. That always gave you hope that the season would be a good one. It was mostly misleading.

I didn't get to go to the home openers back then. The only time I was able to go to a game at Forbes Field as a child was with the Knot-Hole Gang. You needed only 50 cents and you could go to the game with other kids from the Burgwin Recreation Center.

We sat out in right field, just above Roberto Clemente. That's a pretty good seat. Now I sit in the press box on occasion at PNC Park. That's a pretty good seat, too.

Jim O'Brien's boyhood home at 5410 Sunnyside Street as it looked in early '60s. Jim took pride in the way he cut the grass and the hedges. Just before the home was leveled in 2010 the yard was overgrown with weeds.

Photos by Jim O'Brien

Jim O'Brien's boyhood home at 5410 Sunnyside Street, at left, is now missing from landscape.

Cemetery comes alive
for visitors on
Memorial Day

June 2005

A neighbor called with a strange inquiry on a recent Sunday evening. She wanted me to recommend a good cemetery. Celia Christman wasn't ill or feeling pain. She was feeling patriotic. "I want to do something with my daughter Julie to mark Memorial Day," she explained. "Could you recommend a cemetery where there'd be a lot of soldiers buried? I figured you'd know."

My first recommendation was Allegheny Cemetery, with Calvary Cemetery and Homewood Cemetery right behind. There's also a small church plot across from the Duquesne Club on Sixth Avenue downtown that has the graves of soldiers from the Revolutionary War.

I gave her directions on how to get to Allegheny Cemetery in Lawrenceville, but I wasn't convinced Celia could find it. That same night I was watching television, and a soldier just back from Iraq was admonishing all of us for missing the true meaning of Memorial Day. He said it was more than a holiday, a picnic day. It was a time to pause and properly reflect on those who served our country.

Bright and early on Memorial Day of 2005, I called Celia Christman on the telephone and said I would be willing to drive her and her daughter, Julie, a 14-year-old eighth-grader at Fort Couch Elementary School in Upper St. Clair, to the Allegheny Cemetery.

I talked my wife Kathie into accompanying us on the trip. Celia Christman formed a thriving book club in our neighborhood that Kathie enjoyed a great deal. This would be a return favor. I later realized I had done myself a favor. Kathie reminded me that I had some brochures about Allegheny Cemetery somewhere in my office, and we found those tour guides, and they were helpful.

Allegheny Cemetery is a Pittsburgh treasure. Composer Stephen Foster and actress Lillian Russell are buried there. So is Josh Gibson, a Hall of Fame baseball player, Rosey Rosewell, the original "Voice of the Pirates," jazz musician Stanley Turrentine, and Pittsburgh TV talent Don Brockett. There are marvelous mausoleums of a different era to behold. There are large sections where soldiers are buried, including one just for soldiers from the Union and Confederate armies in the Civil War. Some of the gravestones read simply "Unknown." One Union soldier was identified as James Cry. There are fields where small American flags are posted at each gravesite, and the overall effect is overwhelming, as in Flander's Fields or the Cliffs of Dover. We found the graves of soldiers from the Spanish-American War, World War I and II, Korea and Vietnam.

498

A family of 12 arrived in three cars, from Indiana, Pa., I learned by talking to them. They planted artificial white flowers on the grave of Frank Day who'd been a cook in World War I. He grew up in Houston, Tex., but came to Pittsburgh and settled in the South Hills, a granddaughter told me. He didn't die in the war. "He just got old," she said.

While we were there, much to our surprise, a small parade made its way through the cemetery paths. Two men in doughboy uniforms from World War I led the parade. There were about 20 men and boys wearing the Union blue marching behind them, and women in costumes of that period trailing them. About 50 or 60 Vietnam veterans rode motorcycles. The bands of Langley High School and Westinghouse High School also paraded. Pete Flaherty, the prototype of the professional Pittsburgh politician, was there, smiling and shaking hands and saying hello.

The city of Pittsburgh is full of such surprises. Julie Christman told me she had never been to Lawrenceville, or Garfield or Polish Hill, places I mentioned to her. She had been to the zoo in Highland Park.

There are special places to visit in the city, whether it's Carnegie Museum or Phipps Conservatory or Allegheny Cemetery. There's the Children's Museum, the Aviary and my friend Gus Kalaris' ice ball stand in West Park. Whether you attend a Pirates' game at PNC Park or the Three Rivers Arts Festival, you will gain a greater appreciation for Pittsburgh. The suburbs may be safer, but the inner city is more interesting.

Jim O'Brien

Civil War period re-enacters parade through Allegheny Cemetery in Lawrenceville to mark Memorial Day.

Pennies from heaven
are daily gifts from my father

June 2003

I had a 26-day streak going. I was keeping pace with the Pirates' Kenny Lofton and we were both chasing Joe DiMaggio. For 26 straight days, I had found at least one coin when I went for a walk, or at some point in my daily activity. Most of them were pennies, of course, but there was a quarter, two nickels and a dime. My pursuit of pennies became a mini-obsession.

The streak started in southern California, when my wife Kathie and I were visiting our younger daughter, Rebecca, during her birthday week in early May. We went for long walks twice daily with Rebecca's dog, Bailey, and I started finding coins wherever we went. Talk about the California gold rush. No wonder Rebecca came here, I thought, there's money in the streets.

Once I got started, I had my nose to the pavement as much as Bailey. I turned it into a game. I picked up where I had left off when we got back home, and was earnest each day in my search for coins as I got in my daily exercise. I even found four pennies on one of the outdoor basketball courts in Upper St. Clair. There were 12 fellows there that Easter morning, but none of them saw those copper coins. Or maybe no one wanted to bother to stoop to pick them up. I always feel a little richer when I find coins, and I'm never too proud to stoop and pick them up. There's satisfaction in finding money. It's a good way to start the day. They are pennies from heaven, a gift from my father.

My father, Dan O'Brien, used to come home and boast about finding money, mostly along the curb, when he walked from one end of town to the other. He didn't have a car, so he walked a lot. My mother used to boast that my Dad always came home with money during the Depression. He was out of work, like a lot of men in those dark days, but he knocked on doors and did tasks to earn some money.

That was a story that served me well. I had to knock on a lot of doors to get paid as a newspaper delivery boy, and sometimes I had to knock several times to get someone to answer the door. I was never timid about knocking on doors to get money.

So I thought about my father when I found all those coins. It was our link. I had been thinking about my mother every day since she died in March, and now, for a change, or because of some change, I was thinking about my father.

Recently, I found a framed photograph of my father in a box in the cupboard in my home office. It was taken in 1922. He was 17 at the time. He is shown looking dapper in a dark suit, his hair parted distinctly, lying on his side on a picnic blanket on the grass by Gladstone School on Hazelwood Avenue in our hometown. I wonder what he was thinking. I have put that picture on permanent display on one of my desks He was working at the Baltimore & Ohio Rail Road in Glenwood at that time, and soon after he took a job as a drill press operator at Mesta Machine Company in West Homestead and remained there over 35 years. I got his picture out on Sunday to show my daughter Sarah when she came to see us on Father's Day. I shared it with friends as well. None of them ever met my dad. They didn't know much about him. I didn't know him for long as an adult. I was 27 when he died at age 63. He died in the old Homestead Hospital.

I remember Dr. Dee, the Mesta company physician, intercepting me in the parking lot and telling me that my father had died a half hour earlier. It's a scene framed in my mind.

Kathie asked me what I wanted for dinner on Father's Day. I said I'd like flank steak. That was one of my father's favorite dishes. I grilled it on the side-porch, and everybody said they enjoyed it.

Sarah gave me two short-sleeved shirts, one blue and one gray, my colors, and a card that had a hand-written note referring to me as "our biggest fan." I felt good about that. Rebecca called from California, and it seemed farther away than ever as we spoke.

She had sent me two cards for Father's Day. One was from Bailey—"someone who looks up to you"—who referred to herself as my "Grandpuppy." The other was from Rebecca. It showed a fellow typing at a computer. She had drawn in a mustache and a "J" on the breast pocket. It read: "You could write a book..." and when you opened it the message continued, "about having perfect children." She also had some hand-written notes, like I always do when I send out cards.

I'm the only father in our family now. My dad and Kathie's dad are gone, but not forgotten. They left me with a legacy, some good memories, things to try and emulate, and a heavy responsibility.

Being a father is a full-time job and a serious task. Looking for pennies won't make me as rich as having children of my own.

Author's parents, Mary and Dan O'Brien, are dressed for Easter Sunday in late '50s.

Many coincidental meetings
can leave one puzzled

March 3, 2005

I am often astounded by coincidences that occur in our daily lives. A recent Saturday morning comes to mind. I was scheduled to do a book-signing at Ross Park Mall, and had planned to meet some ardent baseball fans beforehand for coffee and conversation. Prior to meeting them I was going to have breakfast at Eat'n Park Restaurant at South Hills Village.

Before I left the house, I picked up a scrapbook and a textbook. The scrapbook had been given to me in early January by Joe Thomas of Upper St. Clair. Thomas, 83, is a lifelong baseball fan who grew up in New Brighton. As a 12-year-old, he went to a Pirates game with his father on Saturday, May 25, 1935 and witnessed Babe Ruth of the Boston Braves hitting three home runs at Forbes Field, including his last one—No. 714. The scrapbook he gave me had newspaper pictures and clippings from the '30s.

I thought the guys I was seeing at Ross Park Mall would enjoy checking it out.

The Pirates had opened their spring training camp in Bradenton, Florida that same week.

I took the textbook with me because I like to read it before I start writing a new book. It's called *The Literary Journalists*, and it contains stories by the likes of Gay Talese, Joan Didion, Hunter Thompson and Tom Wolfe. It was the textbook for an evening master's level literature class in reading non-fiction that I took at the University of Pittsburgh in the mid-80s. I was working there at the time, as the assistant athletic director for public relations, and I could take such classes free of charge.

It was a useful class taught by Dr. Bruce Dobler. I have often given him and that class credit for turning me loose on writing books about my sports experiences as a daily newspaperman in Philadelphia, Miami, New York and Pittsburgh. I had highlighted many paragraphs in the opening chapter of that textbook and wanted to review it. I hadn't bumped into Dr. Dobler in five or six years.

Here's where it got weird. At Eat'n Park, I was seated in a booth next to a gentleman who was by himself. It was Joe Thomas. I invited him to join me. He ate poached eggs and hash—a combination I've never had—and told me more baseball stories. He was at Forbes Field on October 13, 1960 when Bill Mazeroski hit the home run to defeat the Yankees and win the World Series, and had other interesting stories to share.

Thomas had cut class one day at Carnegie Tech to see Frankie Gustine's debut playing for the Pirates, and years later he saw Roberto Clemente make a great throw in his first game at Forbes Field.

His scrapbook proved to be a big hit at Ross Park Mall. When I was finishing up at the book-signing session, a gentleman with silver hair and a broad smile in the middle of a silver beard stood by my table. It was Dr. Bruce Dobler. I couldn't believe it. I reached into my blue bag and pulled out the textbook from his class. Dr. Dobler couldn't believe that.

"You did it!" he said. "Damn, I saw your display of books inside, and I said to myself, 'Damn, he did it!' You did what you told us you were going to do in that class."

I thanked him again for what I felt I had gained from that class. We had a bit of a history. One night in class, Dr. Dobler declared, "If you want to be a big-time writer you can't concern yourself with the impact or effect your story might have on your subject."

I took him to task for that one, saying you were, indeed, responsible for what you wrote, and that you had to ask yourself whether it was worth it or not when you were writing a critical piece or a story that might prove damaging to an individual. You had to exercise some journalistic judgment. You had to have some compassion for people. I said that there were documented cases of men and women committing suicide over unfavorable stories about them.

I remember saying, "Mother Teresa isn't the only one who should have any compassion in this world." The pen can be mightier than the sword and should be used wisely and with some concern for others. I've made mistakes in that regard, especially in my early years as a journalist.

Dr. Dobler and I had an exchange of phone calls and letters—his was a bit heated, I thought, and had an expletive in it none of my previous teachers had ever invoked. But he did invite me to stay with the class. At the next meeting, Dr. Dobler did a 180-degree turn on that issue, and he apologized to the class for making such a statement.

I worked hard and came on strong in the stretch and got an "A" for the class. On the final night, Dr. Dobler singled me out and gave me credit for contributing much to the class. It made me feel good.

At Ross Park, we ran into each other again, 15 minutes later, in the parking lot. He made some additional nice statements about what I'd done since that class about 20 years ago. He smiled. I smiled. It's never too late to get a good grade from one of your teachers. My parents would have been pleased.

* * *

Dr. Bruce Dobler died at age 71 in his apartment in El Paso, Texas. Friends said he had been suffering from depression and physical ailments. His death was suspicious. He had taught non-fiction writing courses in Pitt's Department of English for 28 years.

A kid at Kennywood Park
once again

I was invited to ride in a trolley at Kennywood Park for the Fall Festival Parade at the tailend of the 2008 season and 2009 season. I was in good company, riding along with three former members of the Pittsburgh Steelers: Dick Hoak, Randy Grossman and Bill Priatko, the pride of North Braddock. We were joined by a familiar Pittsburgh figure, Mr. McFeely, or "Speedy Delivery" from Mister Rogers Neighborhood, during our evening at Kennywood Park.

People lined the trail we took through the park. They clapped their hands, or waved at us, or shouted out a greeting of recognition. I recognized some of the faces and some of the faces recognized me. Those that knew me shouted out my name, and I felt like a king being hailed by my people. Then the faces changed, as I was taken—almost by magic—back to my childhood. I was a kid at Kennywood once again. That's the beauty of Kennywood Park. You're young again.

I recognized rides I had taken as a kid, and I could still envision rides that are no longer there. I remembered the Danceland. It's gone from the scene, but not my memories of it. That's where we'd go to meet up with our parents from time to time, to let them know we were still alive, to bum some more money, to see if they still had any more tickets for the rides. You needed tickets for the rides back then; it was different. I remembered riding ponies where the Log Jammer now jammed. I remember a pony that kept trying to nip me in the ankles as I rode alongside a girl named Nancy McCann from our grade school. It took me a long time to get comfortable around horses after that, but now I love to visit a horse farm in the South Hills and feed and pet the horses there.

The three roller coasters at Kennywood Park were all terrific and terrifying at the same time. I always liked The Turtle and The Old Mill and The Rocket. My mother didn't ride too many of the rides, but she liked The Rocket, too. It was a smooth ride, and you could see the whole park from up there above the lagoon. I remembered my brother Dan—he's gone now, too—rocking the seat when we were in the top seat on the Ferris Wheel. He enjoyed scaring me. I can remember Dan and wearing identical shirts during one visit to Kennywood. Remember when couples did that?

Did you ever steal a kiss from a girl friend in the Olde Mill?

The music from the merry-go-round goes with you wherever you may go in life. I was always stumbling through Noah's Ark, and I still do. I remember the cartons of chocolate milk they passed out at the Mesta Machine Company picnic. That is gone, too.

So much has changed. Except my recall. I remember being abandoned by my sister Carole—that's exactly what I told our mother had happened that day—and walking around the swimming pool for hours hunting for my sister. She was busy with boys, showing off in her new swimsuit. I was burned so bad that I couldn't turn over in bed that night without suffering great agony. I can still see the sepia-toned post-cards that you could get for a penny in the Penny Arcade. There were cowboys and movie stars and sports celebrities. We kept those cards for a long time. I wish I still had them. They'd be worth something.

What I remember best is the joy I had every time I went to Kennywood as a kid. I ran in races for prizes there. I always played a round of miniature golf with my Uncle Rich O'Brien. He usually let me win. No wonder I loved my Uncle Rich. He was my favorite relative. I try to be like him as I take my grandchildren through the park these days. My dad didn't drive a car, but we could always get on streetcars or trolleys and get to the Highland Park Zoo and Kennywood Park. We never went on vacations when I was a kid, so Kennywood was as good as I knew for getaway fun. The streetcar barn, where they kept the cars and trolleys at night, was only a block from my home in Hazelwood. But riding one to Kennywood Park was pretty special.

In a way, the trolley was the first ride of the day. When you made that big bend by the Rankin Bridge you knew you were getting closer to Kennywood, closer to heaven, huh? You could see the dam there on the Monongahela River. It was quite a view. I thought about things like that as I was paraded past the people last fall.

Two weeks from now, my wife Kathie and I are taking our older granddaughter, Margaret, who just turned 6, to Kennywood Park. She's never been there before, so we will be introducing her to the amuse-ment park of our childhood. We'll be spending the day in Kiddieland. I hope we will ride the racing cars. That was one of my favorite rides.

I expect we'll also take the train ride. That doesn't bump around so much and I will probably appreciate that aspect of the ride more these days. I am sure that some of the rides I liked might be missing.

Jeff Flicko/Kennywood Park

KENNYWOOD PARK is the place to be for Mr. McFeely ("Speedy Delivery") from Mister Rogers' Neighborhood, in the forefront, with Jim O'Brien, left to right, and former Steelers Randy Grossman, Dick Hoak and Bill Priatko who rode a trolley around the West Mifflin amusement park in a fall parade.

It's better to take your grandchild when you're going to Kennywood Park

July 2012

I asked my 8-year-old granddaughter Margaret what I should write about Kennywood Park. "That you got all wet," she responded with a bright smile. At least she didn't laugh like that crazy woman who's in a glass case at the entrance to the Olde Kennywood RR.

I do think that seeing her grandpap getting soaked was the highlight of the day at Kennywood Park for Margaret.

It happened on the three or four times that we rode the Log Jammer together. She sat in the front of the log-shaped shell the first time around and then she invited me to sit up front for the ensuing trips in what is essentially a roller coaster on water. She knew the splashes had their greatest impact on whoever was riding up front.

The more I complained or the more I was in distress, exaggerating in most cases for effect, the more Margaret laughed. She was having a great time.

As we came away from our umpteenth ride on The Racer, she proclaimed to one and all, or at least her grandpap and grandma, "This is the greatest park in the world!"

I have been to Kennywood Park in recent years, but mostly to ride along with Steelers' Alumni, in one of those Fantasy Parades they have near the end of the season.

My buddy Bill Priatko pulls in some of his friends to ride around the park and wave at the people along the way. Priatko, who grew up in nearby North Braddock, just across the Monongahela River, and now lives in North Huntington, worked at Kennywood Park as a teenager.

Now he comes back as a Kennywood Park alumnus and works one of the refreshment stands until the students are out of school. Then he goes back at the end of the season when the students are back in school. It helps keep him feeling young.

"I just love the atmosphere and the people you meet," opines Priatko, in his 70s and happily retired.

"Everybody is smiling at Kennywood Park. I complimented a woman on having such a nice smile and she said, 'How could you not smile at Kennywood Park?' I feel the same way."

I rode the rides this time at Kennywood Park, rides I didn't think I'd be riding when we left our home to go to the amusement park that day.

My wife Kathleen lived for the first two or three years of her life in the community of Kennywood, that slice of land that frames the park, yet she was never a big fan of the amusement park. So I was so pleased to see her get into the spirit of the occasion when we went there, and joined Margaret and me on so many of the rides.

She, too, was having a great time. Neither Kathie nor I expected to ride the roller coasters, and especially as many times as we did. I guess the secret to having a great time at Kennywood Park is to take a kid along with you.

Our ribs are still aching a bit. We blame it on having our sides rattled so much on the sharp curves on the roller coasters, but maybe our ribs hurt because we were laughing so much, and so hard. I've been taking pain killers for Kennywood Park.

We came to Kennywood Park a day after they held Media Day to officially introduce a new sensational ride called the Sky Rocket. It's a state-of-the-art roller coaster that goes from zero to 50 mph in under three seconds. It defies gravity as you go over the top. It plummets 90 degrees. It's only going to enhance Kennywood Park's reputation for having the greatest collection of roller coasters of any amusement park in the country.

Jeff Filicko, the public relations director at Kennywood, was our host and he told us right off the bat, "There's a 45-minute wait for the Sky Rocket, but it's worth it," he promised. I smiled and said, "No, thanks." It's not that I hate long lines. I hate being frightened.

I headed for Ye Olde Mill. Only it's now called Garfield's Nightmare. It was the place where you could sneak a kiss from your girlfriend in the dark passageways as you floated through in a boat. Margaret didn't like my description of the place and she passed on it. "Too scary," she said.

So we headed for the merry-go-round. She wanted to make sure she got on a horse that went up and down and was sure she didn't want to ride the tiger that was stationary. I love the merry-go-round because the Kennywood Park of my youth comes back to life as I ride around in circles.

When people buy one of my books about Pittsburgh sports I always tell them there are two books. Mine and yours. You read my stories and look at the pictures I have selected and you think of your stories and see your own images.

I can still see the Dance Land and the swimming pool even though they are both long gone from the scene at Kennywood Park. And I realized The Rocket wasn't there any longer, either. My mother loved to ride on The Rocket. It was a smooth ride over the lagoon and you could see the boaters below and survey the entire amusement park as you went in circles. It was a relaxing ride.

It has been replaced by the Sky Coaster. I can't believe this ride. It's like going to the top of the Eiffel Tower and swinging across a lake on a vine. I remember as a kid that they always had these high-wire acts or clowns getting shot out of cannons on the stage in the center of the lagoon. Kennywood Park had to pay these circus acts to come and perform at the park.

Now people pay the park to provide amusement for one and all. Three people chip in over $60 to take a swing over the lagoon. No matter where you are in the park you pay attention to the Sky Coaster. You watch two or three people take a deep drop on this long cord and then they swing back and forth a few times before coming to a stop. Those tied down to what looks like a raft or a super-sized stretcher for someone who has suffered a back injury are always screaming as they soar across the lagoon.

I bumped into a young blonde woman who was volunteering at the Homestead Lions' Golf Outing the next day at nearby Westwood Golf Club and she said she had taken that ride at Kennywood Park. Her name was Emma and she seemed quite sane. "They put you in something like a straight jacket so you're safely attached to that flat surface," she said. "It scared the heck outta me."

I suggested that straight jackets are usually used to restrain crazy people and Emma just smiled.

I could still see my mom and dad, my brother Dan and sister Carol, my Uncle Rich. My Uncle Rich always played miniature golf with me and Dan. They're all gone, and so is the miniature golf layout. The Turnpike has given way to the Sky Rocket.

The Whip wasn't where it used to be and someone told me the next day where it was now located. It's in Lost Kennywood.

We did ride The Turtle and that is still a fun ride. The attendant didn't fill up the units with a full load of patrons, though, letting some go with one or two people per Turtle. That makes the lines longer and slower, and the fun of that ride is bumping into each other on the hairpin curves.

I took Margaret through Noah's Ark, but it's completely different than it was when I last took that ride. I didn't like it as much. It was pretty barren.

Kathie and I took Margaret to Kiddieland after we rode the merry-go-round. Margaret seemed to enjoy all the rides there, and said that maybe next year we can bring her little sister, Susannah, now four years old. We filed that idea.

I rode some of the rides with Margaret in Kiddieland and was quite comfortable with that. Then we rode The Race Car. That is still one of my favorite rides at Kennywood Park. Those steel cars still look brand new. Kathie rode with Margaret at the wheel, and I was right behind them by myself.

I noticed that not as many people play the games that are still all around the amusement park. They're probably too tame compared to the blood and guts games the kids play on their video games at home and in the car.

Not as many people pack picnic baskets to bring to the park. I think Kennywood Park can get by with fewer picnic pavilions. I remember them being full at the Mesta Machine Co. and Westinghouse picnics. I think they could make room for more rides.

We rode the Olde Kennywood RR. When the Edgar Thomson Works at U.S. Steel came into view, I wanted to tell everyone on the train that they were looking at the only place where steel is still produced in the Pittsburgh area. But I didn't want anyone putting me in a straight jacket so I remained silent and enjoyed the view.

Once we left Kiddieland we rode the Jack Rabbit and then The Racer, and then the Jack Rabbit and then The Racer. There was no turning back. Margaret loved them both. We did save the Thunderbolt for a return visit. Margaret can't wait to go back. I am scheduled to ride around the park in the parade again this fall so maybe she can visit us that day from her home in Columbus, Ohio.

I can't remember being with Margaret where she laughed as much. I was surprised, frankly, by how many high-flying rides Kathie came on, more than I ever remembered her doing. We had pizza and cold drinks, funnel cake and ice cream and even had chicken tender dinners at the Parkside Café. I remembered that when I was a kid I thought that only the rich people ate there. All the refreshments were first-rate, I thought. When I suggested we take one last ride on the merry-go-round, Margaret wasn't interested. "That's boring," she said. I must admit I can't wait to bring Margaret back to Kennywood Park.

Photos by Jim O'Brien

Author's granddaughter Margaret Zirwas on Kiddyland roller coaster in 2012 and on Elephant Ride in 2010. Margaret meets a new friend, Kenny Wood.

Traveling from one field of dreams to another is fun

June 2002

Mike Ditka and Pat McDonnell were hosts at Ditka's Restaurant in Chicago.

A woman was offering a eulogy to her friend at a funeral service at Westminster Presbyterian Church in Upper St. Clair. She was sharing stories about their experiences together, and most of the stories centered on shopping trips they had made to New York and other cities. Our deceased friend and neighbor had grown up in Clairton. My wife Kathie was at work that day, back in 1999, so I went to the memorial service alone. I remember thinking that Kathie never did anything like that, going with her girl friends to faraway places without me. I think I said a prayer thanking God that she didn't.

About three weeks later, Kathie asked me a question. "What do you think," she began, somewhat slowly, "if Sharon and I went on a vacation with some other girls? Just the girls…on a getaway vacation."

What could I say? Of course, I replied, "I think that would be OK."

She and Sharon Pociask were the best of friends, and so were Sharon's husband, Alex, and I. About a few weeks before the girls were to depart for Scottsdale, Ariz., Alex Pociask and I panicked simultaneously. I have become such a co-dependent as I've gotten older. Alex and I decided we didn't want to stay home alone, so we planned a trip to Virginia, North Carolina and South Carolina. We had a great time and we learned that we traveled well together.

He wanted to see some golf communities and I stopped to see some retired football coaches and baseball players I wanted to interview for my books. Our plans meshed nicely.

Then in the summer of 2002 the girls went on their third "girls only" vacation and Alex and I went on our second such trip. We weren't able to do it the previous year because he had just taken a new job. "You have no idea how good these vacations are," Kathie told me. "For us, it's great not to have to look after you guys for a full week."

Well, Alex and I are fast learners. We now think the "girls only" vacations are a great idea. Now we get to go places and do things that wouldn't particularly appeal to our wives, or their friends.

This year Sharon invited one of her neighbors and friends to tag along, so Karen Saracco went with them to Williamsburg, Va. Kathie and Sharon had gone to Palm Springs, Calif. the previous year.

Alex planned our trip this year, and I added to it as we went along. He was taking me back to his boyhood farm in Wausaukee, Wisc., and his alma mater, Michigan Tech on Michigan's Upper Peninsula. We were going by way of Chicago, where we visited his daughter, Dr. Kara Nance, and her husband Colin, and their two-year-old daughter

Karina. Then we went to Milwaukee and visited his in-laws, Jacob and Lori Stearle.

Now here are some of the things we did, and you'll see what sports enthusiasts left to their own schedule might do on an eight-day trip while traveling 2,131 miles. We stopped in South Bend, Ind., and visited the College Football Hall of Fame and checked out the campus at Notre Dame University. We checked out the refurbished football stadium, Touchdown Jesus and the Golden Dome.

In Chicago, we went to the sold-out Cubs-White Sox baseball game at Wrigley Field. Alex was able to get us seats seven rows directly behind home plate. It was like being in the batter's box. It was a 3-D blast. He even managed to get us a parking pass right at the main gate of Wrigley Field. We had dinner at Mike Ditka's Restaurant and Mike stopped by our table and talked to us for awhile. His place is now managed by Pat McDonnell, who grew up in Lincoln Place and now lives in Upper St. Clair. McDonnell owns and operates three Atria's Restaurant and Tavern outlets around Pittsburgh. Two of our daughters' friends from Upper St. Clair, Dr. Jenny Jackson and Kara Spak, joined us for dinner. They are working in Chicago.

We toured Milwaukee and had lunch at Miller Park, site of this summer's All-Star Game. We visited the bar and restaurant once owned by Rocky Bleier's parents in Appleton, Wisc. There are still pictures on the walls of Rocky from his days at Notre Dame and with the Steelers. Bleier now lives in Mt. Lebanon, a suburb just south of Pittsburgh. We visited a memorial park for George Gipp, Notre Dame's first All-American, in Laurium, Mich.

We stopped in Green Bay and visited Lambeau Field and the Packers Hall of Fame, and restaurants that are shrines to Packers' coach Vince Lombardi. We toured Alex's alma mater with three football coaches. We stopped to see some of his former teammates. We took four boat rides, one on a canal off Lake Superior and one on Lake St. Clair. The other two took us to and from Mackinac Island, a real tourist treat.

On the way home, we stopped at Comerica Park and the abandoned Tiger Stadium in Detroit, and saw the stadium the Ford family is building for the Lions. We did that and so much more. We can't wait for the girls-only next vacation trip.

When I got home I attended the Pirates-Expos game at PNC Park. It really is the best baseball park in America. It's not the biggest or the most expensive, but it's the right size and it looks like a baseball park and it shows off the city skyline so well.

I liked Comerica Park in Detroit, and thought Miller Park in Milwaukee was an engineering marvel and prettier on the outside than PNC Park, but not as good a setting when you are in your seats. Wrigley Field still holds its own with any baseball park in America.

Seeing how they have refurbished Notre Dame Stadium and Lambeau Field only reinforces my feelings that they should have done the same with Pitt Stadium and Three Rivers Stadium for the Steelers. I think the fans would have been happier, too. But it's too late now.

Hank Greenberg was big in Detroit before he played for the Pirates.

George Gipp, Notre Dame's first All-American football player is honored in his hometown of Laurium, Michigan.

Alex Pociask and Jim O'Brien visit Comerica Park in Detroit during "boys only" excursion in Midwest.